Mind in Everyday Life and Cognitive Science

Mind in Everyday Life and Cognitive Science

Sunny Y. Auyang

A Bradford Book
The MIT Press
Cambridge, Massachusetts
London, England

This book was set in Bembo by Best-set Typesetter Ltd., Hong Kong

Printed and bound in the United States of America.

Library of Congress Cataloging-in-Publication Data

Auyang, Sunny Y.
  Mind in everyday life and cognitive science / Sunny Y. Auyang.
    p. cm.
  "A Bradford book."
  Includes bibliographical references and index.
  ISBN 0-262-01181-6 (alk. paper)
    1. Cognitive science. 2. Intellect. 3. Thought and thinking. I. Title.
BF311 .A797   2001
153—dc21   00-064591

上獻我父

To my father

Contents

Mind in Everyday Life and Cognitive Science

1

Introduction

1 The Emergence of Mind

"Space, the final frontier." This opening line in a popular television series irritates many cognitive scientists, who protest that the final scientific frontier is not space but mind. Many people would agree; with the science of mind we attempt to study and understand ourselves, as we distinguish ourselves foremost by our mental abilities. Some, however, would ask the scientists: Are you really confronting the final frontier? Is it *mind* that you are studying? You have produced remarkable results on neural excitations and brain anatomy, computer and robot designs. But what is the relevance of these results to our everyday experiences? Can they tell us who we are, how we understand and feel, why we care for others, what are the meanings of life? How many of your claims on knowledge about mind have scientific basis, how many are hype?

The frontier of mind shares a similar predicament with the frontier of space. Scientific explorers of both have made tremendous progress. Most of what we know about the universe was discovered in the last few decades, and so was most of what we know about the processes underlying mental phenomena. However, both frontiers face immense unknown territories, and the headwinds are strong.

Based on the law of gravity and the observed dynamics of galaxies, physicists infer that as much as 90 percent of the universe is dark and hence escapes detection of our telescopes and antennae. Almost all dark matter resides in immense interstellar and intergalactic space, which precludes practical contemplation of on-site investigation. Earth-bound experiments also face a dim prospect, as high costs discourage public funding for them. Physicists have produced many speculations about the identities and properties of the dark matter. However, the only consensus seems to be that it is nothing like any ordinary matter familiar in the luminous part of the universe. This means that dark matter is mostly beyond the ken of the current standard model of elementary particle physics.[1]

Mind is no less perplexing than space. We know that we have rich and multifarious mental processes because we consciously engage in those processes all our waking hours. Yet to cognitive science, most of our conscious experiences are like dark matter to the standard model in particle physics. Many mental phenomena are marginalized not because they are too remote and strange but because they are too close and familiar, so that they are easily taken for granted and stepped over in the initial scientific advancement. Our ethical restraint from all-out experimentation on humans and other animals rightly regards knowledge as one value among many. For research, however, it poses an obstacle not unlike the vast distance of space. Philosophical doctrines that are concerned exclusively with marketable information and esoteric techniques steer the research agenda from our conscious mentality, similar to political decisions that ground costly physical experiments.

Take vision for instance. To see is not merely to detect light, which a simple camera can do. Seeing implies recognition and finding the environment meaningful, which no supercomputer can yet achieve. We open our eyes in the morning and automatically see a coherent and intelligible world. Young children effortlessly see mountains that protrude partly from behind clouds and flowers from behind leaves. What are the nature and structure of our visual experiences? How do we get the experiences? As our most important sense whose underlying processes engage almost half of our cerebral cortex to provide roughly 40 percent of our sensual input, vision is intensively researched. With advanced brain imaging technologies and experiments on cats and monkeys, whose visual systems are similar to ours, neuroscientists traced optical pathways from photoreceptors in the retina deep into the cortex. Microscopically, they found individual neurons sensitive to special features such as contrast or motion and discovered their operating mechanisms. Macroscopically, they identified many distinct but interconnected areas in the cortex, each concentrating on certain special functions such as differentiating faces or words. The amount of knowledge we have on the neural mechanisms and brain anatomy for optical signal processing is staggering. Scientific ignorance on visual experiences, alas, is equally great. In a book detailing the advances in vision research, cognitive scientist and molecular biologist Francis Crick (1994:24) wrote:

"We do not yet know, even in outline, how our brains produce the vivid visual awareness that we take so much for granted. We can glimpse fragments of the processes involved, but we lack both the detailed information and the ideas to answer the most simple questions: How do I see color? What is happening when I recall the image of a familiar face?"

Cognitive scientists in other areas face the same predicament. Surveying the science of memory, Endel Tulving (1995) remarked: "Research in cognitive psychology and neuropsychology of memory has produced a wealth of data. . . . However, our success has been somewhat less remarkable in interpreting and making sense of this abundance of data. There is less agreement among practitioners as to what the findings and facts tell us about the larger picture of memory." The problem Tulving identified, "the imbalance between what the facts about memory are and what they mean," is not confined to memory or vision research. The disparity between scientific facts and their interpretations is far worse for cognitive science as a whole, where controversies rage as to what the torrent of results tell us about big pictures of mind.

What goes on in vision, in which I am simultaneously conscious of my own experiences and making sense of events in the world? How do I recall the past and anticipate the future, one of which is no more and the other not yet? Who am I, what is my sense of self? What are the meanings of my existence, autonomy, and freedom of action? How is it possible that a chunk of physical matter like me raises such questions at all? Why is it that among all matters in the universe, only a few chunks are capable of experiencing, thinking, feeling, sympathizing, knowing, doubting, hoping, choosing, speaking, and understanding each other? What are the peculiar characteristics of these capacities? These are some of the big questions about mind. I think science will eventually give some answers, but it will take a long time. In the present cognitive science, not only the answers but the questions themselves are like the dark matter of the universe. Unlike the dark matter, which has little influence on us except gravity, experiences, meanings, and deliberate actions concern us most intimately and are regarded by many as the essence of mind. By putting them aside, cognitive science has incurred the criticism of having lost sight of mind.

This book is concerned with big pictures of mind, especially the human mind, and their relationship to the results of cognitive science. What are the arching structures of human experiences and understanding?

How are they illuminated by scientific findings? How does our intuition about them help scientific research? To answer these questions, I propose a model—*the open mind emerging from intricate infrastructures*. I believe that it accounts for both scientific results and our everyday experiences better than the model that dominates current interpretations of cognitive science, which I call *the closed mind controlled by mind designers*. A comparison of the two models brings out the general structures of everyday experiences and serves as a critique of the interpretations of cognitive science.

My model of the open mind emerging from infrastructures consists of two theses that are introduced in this and the following sections. First, the locus of cognitive science is not mind but mind's infrastructures or mechanisms underlying mental phenomena. Properly interpreted, results on infrastructural processes enhance our understanding of mind. Mistaking infrastructural processes for mental phenomena, however, leads to confusion and obscurity. Second, we cannot hope to explain how mind emerges from the self-organization of infrastructural processes without clarifying what it is that emerges. Thus we must analyze the structure of our mental abilities, which I call mind's openness to the world. For this we return to common sense and everyday life, for they are the primary and most important arenas of our mental activities. Explorers of space have to boldly go where no one has gone before. Explorers of mind have to deftly delve into where everyone dwells every day and see the familiar anew.

The Closed Mind Controlled by Mind Designers

Cognitive science is a consortium consisting of psychology, neuroscience, linguistics, anthropology, philosophy, artificial intelligence (AI), and more. Coming separately from schools of science, humanities, and engineering, these disciplines have different aims, presuppositions, concepts, and methods. Such diversity increases the difficulty in interpreting results, not only because the results are fragmentary, but also because aims and presuppositions subtly color meanings. For example, as an engineering discipline, AI mainly aims to design and build artifacts that perform certain tasks efficiently in serving certain preconceived purposes. Some philosophers turn it into an ideology that puts manufactured efficiency before natural mentality and artifacts above human beings as the paradigm of the mental. When cognitive science falls under the shadow of such ideologies, the relevance of its results to human understanding becomes ever more obscure.

By mental phenomena, I mean the activities described by common-sense mental and psychological terms such as experience, feel, care, concern, recognize, err, believe, desire, think, know, doubt, choose, remember, anticipate, hope, fear, speak, listen, understand, and intend. Faced with such broad and variegated phenomena, science usually adopts the strategy of divide and conquer. Thus a discipline in cognitive science approximately cuts out a manageable range of phenomena, neglects other factors, and scrutinizes the selected phenomena in detail, effectively putting them under an intellectual microscope. Microscopes are powerful tools that enable us to see many things otherwise invisible to us. Once we look into a microscope, however, we lose the big picture. This poses little problem if microscopists are keenly aware of the limitations of their view. Unfortunately, some people are intoxicated by the power of and the patterns revealed by the microscope and fancy that the instrument has provided all there is to see. They are like the proverbial blind men who claim that an elephant is nothing but a pillar or a hose, or whatever part they happen to have touched.

Technique worship is the bane of interpretations of cognitive science, as it encourages wanton extrapolations of results obtained by a limited technique. Thus some people maintain that because a technique of behavioral conditioning works for pigeons, it not only applies to humans but delimits human psychology. Others maintain that because computers can perform some clever tasks, all mentation is computation. Each new research technique—digital computation, artificial neural network, dynamical theory—becomes an *-ism* claiming that it exhausts all there is to mind. Vaunting the techniques of laboratory psychological experiments, neuroscience, or AI, the most influential interpretations see mind as nothing but behavior, nothing but brain, nothing but computation.

Most disciplines in cognitive science share a characteristic: they pay little attention to conscious experiences but concentrate on unconscious processes. They study not thinking processes but neural and brain processes. You are aware of your thinking but not the neural processes that occur inside your skull; however, neuroscientists can monitor those processes with tools such as imagers and electrodes. One reason for the emphasis on unconscious processes is the constraint of finely controlled techniques of scientific research. These techniques are powerful in investigating unconscious processes, which are relatively rigid and simple. They are less adapted to investigating everyday experiences that, being far broader and more complex, burst the narrow focus of laboratory experiments.

So far, cognitive science has focused on unconscious processes that a person is unaware of and cannot voluntarily command. Limitations of current knowledge are acknowledged by Crick, Tulving, and many other scientists. However, some technique-worshipping interpreters maintain that unconscious processes have exhausted mental phenomena. Consequently, they regard mind as nothing but a closed entity without consciousness, experience, understanding, and freedom of action. The closed mind is the star in prevailing interpretations. It underlies the doctrines that mind is nothing but behavior, brain, or computer. Behaviors are conditioned; computers are programmed; the brain is an organ dissected and monitored. Thus mind is ripped from autonomous persons and given to alien control.

Like a computer program running inside a black box or a brain severed from the animal's body, the closed mind is a solipsist and is mostly disembodied. Models of it draw a chasm between an inner mental realm and the outside world as depicted in figure 1.1a. Imprisoned inside, the closed mind has access only to mental representations, also called symbols, stimuli, sense impressions, and other names. I must emphasize that mental representations are radically different from ordinary representations that we use every day, such as the little black marks on paper that you are looking at now. Ordinary representations such as letters and words are physical entities and they are meaningful to the autonomous person who knows that they represent something else. In contrast, mental representations are mysterious entities inside the head that are meaningless to the closed mind just as 0s and 1s are meaningless to digital computers that operate on them. The closed mind sees only mental representations and has no way of knowing that they represent or are caused by things in the world. When our physical bodies are counted as parts of the physical world, mind becomes not only closed from the world but also disembodied.

To account for meanings and knowledge, most models rely on godlike agents that are external to the closed mind. In view of the vogue of talking about designing mind, I call these external agents *mind designers*. Like computer programmers who endow strings of 0s and 1s with meanings, mind designers control meanings by establishing correspondence between mental representations and physical objects. The bulk of philosophies of mind and cognitive science is a war among various schools of mind designers. Some mind designers project their own thoughts into the minds of their subjects, just as some people attribute their own thinking

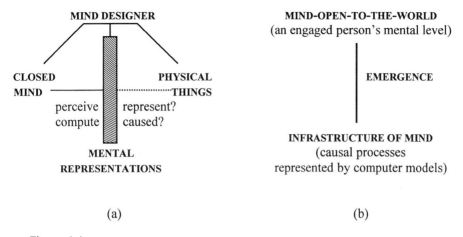

MIND DESIGNER

CLOSED MIND —— PHYSICAL ·················THINGS
perceive represent?
compute caused?

MENTAL
REPRESENTATIONS

(a)

MIND-OPEN-TO-THE-WORLD
(an engaged person's mental level)

EMERGENCE

INFRASTRUCTURE OF MIND
(causal processes
represented by computer models)

(b)

Figure 1.1
(a) Models of the closed mind controlled by mind designers posit mind existing independent of the world and closed off from it. The closed mind perceives or computes with meaningless mental representations. Mind designers match the representations to things in the world, thereby assign meanings that are known only to themselves and not to the closed mind. (b) My model of the open mind emerging from infrastructures posits mind as a high-level emergent property of a person engaged in and open to the natural and social world. As a complex physical entity, a person has at least two organization levels connected by the relation of emergence. The infrastructural level consists of many unconscious processes, which cognitive scientists study and represent by computer models. The infrastructural processes self organize into conscious processes on the mental level, also called the engaged-personal level. On the mental level, mind opens directly to the intelligible world without the intermediary of mental representations.

to their digital computers. Others deny the inner realm altogether and judge subjects by the efficiencies of their overt behaviors and interactions with the environment. To evade the criticism that genuine thinking resides in mind designers and not in the closed mind, many models keep mind designers in the closet or deliberately confuse their functions with the closed mind. In such models consciousness degenerates into an ephiphenomenal inner feeling, intelligence into the efficiency of performing externally assigned tasks, intentionality into an instrument for behavioral control, and autonomous persons into automata.

I reject models of the closed mind controlled by mind designers because they violate our most basic experiences. We need no mind designers. We do depend on other people in our community, but our mental lives have significant autonomy. I do not see mental representations or other entities inside my head. I see, directly and immediately, trees and buildings, things and people in the great wide world. I understand, without the intervention of Big Brother, your speech. Consequently, my most immediate experiences are meaningful to me. The spontaneous meaning-fulness of experiences is an essential characteristic of mind that everyone counts on in their daily life.

The Open Mind Emerging from Infrastructures

The findings of cognitive science about unconscious processes cannot be ignored by anyone interested in mind. But neither can our conscious expe-riences be ignored. In an attempt to account for both ordinary experi-ences and scientific data, I offer a model of *an open mind emerging from the self-organization of intricate infrastructural processes* (figure 1.1b). The model is analyzed into three parts: *a mind open to the world*, which is what we are familiar with in our everyday life; *mind's infrastructure*, which consists of the unconscious processes studied by cognitive science; and *emergence*, the rela-tion between the open mind and its infrastructure.

Cognitive science is difficult to interpret because it professes to study mind, but the unconscious processes it focuses on are drastically different from the mental processes that we are aware of. It is partly to account for this difference that prevailing models resort to the dichotomy between the closed mind and mind designers. In lieu of this dichotomy, my model explicitly posits at least two interrelated organizational levels of a person and explains how they are connected. I call them the *mental* and *infra-structural levels*. They exhibit different properties. Properties describable by commonsense mental terms such as experience, think, and see occur only on the mental level and not on the infrastructural level. They constitute the open mind by which we understand ourselves and each other. They are eclipsed in cognitive science, which concentrates not on the mental but on the infrastructural level.

Mental experiences and infrastructural processes all belong to a person, but they operate on two organizational levels of the person. This does not imply that experiences involve some mysterious, nonphysical sub-stance or spiritual force; there is no such thing. A mindful person is a phys-ical entity and a highly complex one. Complex entities typically have internal structures that exhibit features at many scales and levels of orga-nization. Water, for example, is on the macroscopic level a continuous fluid with various flow patterns, and on the microscopic level many discrete colliding molecules. Similarly, a person harbors many organizational levels with drastically different characteristics. The mental and infrastructural levels are at the top of the hierarchy. There are other levels, for instance, the neural level featuring excitations of single neurons or small groups of neurons.

Levels are familiar fixtures in cognitive science. To understand their full significance, one must both identify the primary level for the phenomena at issue and its relations to other levels. Taking organizational levels seriously enables me to offer an alternative to the prevailing interpretation of the focus of cognitive science. Instead of regarding unconscious processes as belonging to a closed mind operating like a digital computer inside its case, I interpret them as causal processes, which scientists often represent by computer models. These causal processes, which are the underlying "mechanisms" of mental experiences, constitute the infrastructure of mind. Infrastructural processes are mechanical not in the narrow sense of belonging to mechanics but in the broad sense of being automatic and lacking experience, intention, and other mental attributes. Like other causal processes, infrastructural processes are governed by rules in the same sense that planetary motions are governed by Newton's laws, although in their case the rules are tedious and lack the generality of laws of physics. Many causal processes are susceptible to computer modeling; physicists use computers no less than cognitive scientists. When cognitive scientists talk about computation or the computational mind, they usually refer to causal processes in the mental infrastructure. Computer modeling is a powerful tool in cognitive science, but it belongs to the scientists, not to the processes that they study.

Take speech comprehension for example. On the mental level, you hear and understand your colleague saying: "Let's go for lunch." Your experience is open and meaningful; it connects you not only to the speaker but to your physical and social world, food and its availability. Your linguistic ability depends on many processes in the infrastructural level: some parsing sounds into words, others assessing word meaning, still others discerning grammatical structure. These infrastructural processes do not understand what they process. They are merely caused by the acoustic stimuli and unfold automatically. They go so fast we are unaware of them. As conscious speakers, we take their operations for granted. Cognitive scientists, however, pour tremendous efforts into identifying them experimentally and characterizing them theoretically. They also show us how the malfunctions of various infrastructural processes, such as those caused by focal brain injuries, impair speech production or comprehension in various ways.

Infrastructures presuppose what they support; they are integral parts of a larger system where they play certain roles. Thus the mental infrastructure presupposes the mental level. Cognitive scientists delineate infrastructural processes according to their *functions* in mental life, such as their contributions to vision, memory, or speech comprehension. Brain imaging technologies make big impacts on cognitive neuroscience because they reveal the patterns of brain excitation when subjects deliberately engage in certain mental tasks. Thus when scientists zoom in on particular brain regions, they presuppose not only the context of a conscious subject but also the relevance of the brain regions to the mental task that they understand intuitively. The importance of the mental context, dismissed by proponents of the closed mind, is expressed clearly by cognitive psychologist James McCelland in summarizing the themes of a recent scientific conference. Referring to neurologist Alexander Luria, McCelland (1996) remarked: "He used the findings of localizationists to show that each part [of the brain] has its own special role. But he noted the poverty of considering these parts in isolation and insisted that they must be seen as working in concert to achieve system-level functions such as perception, communication, and action."

Perception, communication, and action are activities on the mental level. The contexts they provide imply that the mental infrastructure occupies center stage of cognitive science, but not the whole stage. Even as the scientific spotlight shines on the mental infrastructure in center stage, it leaves the whole stage—an engaged person's mental life—dimly visible as the presupposed context that confers significance on the infrastructure. The dim light illuminates mind from an angle that has hitherto remained in total darkness. The functions of an infrastructure constrain the characteristics of both the infrastructure and what it serves. Because of the symbiosis of infrastructures and superstructures, knowledge about one sheds light on the other. Infrastructural ruins preserve information about ancient civilizations, which archaeologists read eagerly. To those who ask the right questions, infrastructures speak legions about what they serve. The remain of a Roman aqueduct is eloquent about the magnificence of the culture whose sustenance it once carried. Similarly, the complexity of the mental infrastructure leaves its students awe-strick by the sophistication of the mind that it supports. It dispels forever the picture of a simple and passive mind infinitely susceptible to external control and conditioning.

For instance, many people regard vision as a purely receptive process in which mind is like a photographic film being exposed to light, and memory as a simple retrieval process in which mind is like a computer fetching a file from its hard disk. Thus visual and mnemonic experiences have minimal structures, and mind is like a blank slate. This picture is refuted by scientific findings about the highly elaborate mental infrastructure. So much construction is going on in the visual infrastructure and reconstruction in the mnemonic infrastructure that even our most immediate visual experiences and casual remembrances have complicated structures. Mind is always active. Contrary to models of the closed mind controlled by mind designers, the spontaneous structures in our ordinary experiences ensure our sense of personal identity and mental autonomy.

Although knowledge about the mental infrastructure illuminates the structure of mind, its light is indirect. Infrastructural processes lack understanding and feeling. Therefore they are qualitatively different from mental processes. To explain mind directly, we have to show how the two kinds of process are causally connected, how a process on the mental level *emerges* from the self-organization of many processes on the infrastructural level. Cognitive scientists call this the *binding problem*, which demands an account of how myriad unconscious processes combine into the unity of consciousness. Many regard its solution as the Holy Grail, as it will answer the question of how our mental and physiological properties are related. Unfortunately, the knights are still out and it is unlikely that they will return soon with the Grail.

I am mainly concerned with structures of our experiences on the mental level and how they are illuminated by scientific knowledge of the mental infrastructure. A substantive explanation can be given only by the solution of the binding problem. Since science is only beginning to tackle the problem, we have to be content with a general account of the connection between the mental and infrastructural levels. Fortunately, we need not speculate in the vacuum. Multiple organizational levels are commonplaces in complex systems, therefore to explain the connection between levels and the emergence of high-level properties is a task shared by many sciences. Many scientific theories exist for less complex systems. We can learn from them and borrow some productive ideas in relating mind and its infrastructure. In a previous study (Auyang 1998), I found examples from various sciences showing that emergent properties are never easy to explain, and the connection between levels is a bridge that requires firm anchors on both levels. Thus philosophers are deluding themselves when they think they can give easy answers for mind by considering only the neural or infrastructural level.

Take a familiar example. Fluids are made up of particles. Their flow and turbulent motions are emergent properties that cannot be understood by summing particle motions, for they pertain to the large-scale structures that span the whole fluid. Physicists had long known the laws governing particle motions; however, they did not directly deduce fluid motions from the particle laws. They could not; such brute force deduction would go nowhere. They first developed fluid dynamics that clearly describe macroscopic flow characteristics. Only then did they develop statistical mechanics to connect fluid dynamics to particle motions. Why did they need fluid dynamics first? Didn't they know what fluids are?

From time immemorial people have poured water, fought floods, irrigated crops, and negotiated currents. We all have some intuitive and practical ideas about the properties of fluids but they are too vague and crude to guide scientific analysis. Even as we deal with river rapids and pounding waves, we cannot describe fluid motions clearly. Thus we cannot say exactly what fluid properties we want explained in terms of particle motions. To characterize fluidity systematically requires a theory of its own. Fluid dynamics enables physicists to delineate macroscopic properties clearly and to pinpoint the characteristics most favorable for building the bridge to particle motions. This example shows that the bridge between two organizational levels must be anchored at both ends. It collapses if we lack clear understanding of one level.

Our present knowledge of the mental level is similar to knowledge of fluids before fluid dynamics. Everyone has an intuitive understanding of mental phenomena; we depend on this understanding in our dealing with each other. Our commonsense mental concepts serve us well in daily intercourse. They also work in framing the tacit context for the mental infrastructure in research. However, they are too vague and crude for the scientific bridge between the mental and infrastructural levels. Everyone knows in his gut what it is to see or to believe. To explain more precisely the meaning of having a visual experience or entertaining a belief that may be false, however, has taxed philosophers for millennia. Now scientists inherit the headache. What is it to have a visual experience? As Crick remarked, we lack not only detailed information and but also the scientific concepts to address such questions. In tackling the binding problem, we come to the problem of spelling out the basic peculiarities of the mental level. What properties emerge from the binding of infrastructural processes? What are the phenomena that we expect the science of mind to explain? To answer these questions we must turn to our everyday experiences. Just as an unexamined life is not worth living, unexamined experiences are not up to scientific explanations.

2 The Openness of Mind

Mind is the frontier of science; it is also the foundation of science. Without mind, science does not exist, although the universe that science studies does. Empirical science is based on experience and observation; scientific theories are products of our intellect; scientific research is a purposive human enterprise, an expression of our capacity to wonder, our aspiration to know, our urge to control. One cannot properly analyze the structure of science without examining the nature of the human mind. Conversely, systematic investigation of mind must include an account for the presuppositions of science. Thus the science of mind is also an inquiry into its own foundations and conditions of possibility.

Self-criticism is crucial for the interpretations of cognitive science. More than in other sciences, here philosophers are prone to confuse science with scientism, the technique worship that reaps it profit by abusing the name of science. To see the significance of cognitive science properly, we must recognize a fact tacitly denied by most models of the closed mind controlled by mind designers: Science is a human enterprise without divine power. Scientists are not gods or godlike mind designers but ordinary men and women. Research is not a miracle but a mundane activity not qualitatively different from any other profession. Scientists and folks in the street think about different things, but they think in the same general ways, and their thinking shares the general characteristics and structures of the human mind. These characteristics, which I summarily call *mind's openness to the world*, are the topics of my analysis, because they provide a big picture of mind.

Science and Common Sense
You see clouds gathering. You believe that it is going to rain. You hope that it will not, but realize that it is not up to you. You decide to take an

umbrella when you leave home. Seeing, believing, hoping, and deciding
are some of the most common mental activities that everyone engages in
every day. They are equally fundamental to empirical scientific research,
where they are generally called observing, hypothesizing, and predicting.
All cases share the common characteristic that our observations and beliefs
are mostly about events and states of affairs in the world that is physically
outside us. It is common sense that reality goes in its own way independent of our thinking, so that hopes can shatter and predictions fail. We are
aware of our own fallibility, so that we often doubt our eyes and judge
our beliefs false. Scientists, too, make falsifiability an essential criterion of
their hypotheses and theories.

People see; cameras do not see but merely register light. See, believe,
doubt, hope, and act are parts of the mental vocabulary that expresses what
most people mean by mind and embodies commonsense psychology or
folk psychology. Commonsense psychology is indispensable to understanding of ourselves and each other; everyone knows and uses it
intuitively. It is ordinary and not glamorous.

Once some visitors found Heraclitus warming himself at the hearth.
They turned back scornfully, because they deemed the activity too ordinary for a great thinker, who should be doing extraordinary things such
as contemplating the heavens. But Heraclitus said, "Come in, there are
gods here too." Telling the story in *Parts of Animal* (654), Aristotle exhorted
his students to overcome the "childish aversion" of the humble and ordinary. Aristotle poured great effort in examining everyday thinking and
practice, and he was far from alone. Immanuel Kant labored to analyze the
general structures of ordinary objective experience, value judgment,
and aesthetic appreciation. Martin Heidegger went farther in putting everyday life in the center stage and argued that human existence is essentially
being-in-the-world. I follow their paths. In doing so I buck the fashion in
current philosophy of mind and interpretations of cognitive science.

Obsession with esoteric techniques bolsters aversion to the ordinary.
Some philosophers promoting the closed mind controlled by mind designers dismiss commonsense psychology as radically false and deserving elimination in favor of something more glamorous, such as computation or
vector activation in the brain. Ordinary experience is like bird's flight, they
say; if we are concerned with it, we can never build airplanes. We want
something high-tech, something analogous to aerodynamics. Yes, we need
aerodynamics to understand flight, but aerodynamics is not obvious. If we

were too arrogant to examine flying birds and other natural phenomena, if we were tempted by technique worship into mistakenly identifying flight with projectile because we have made slingshots that can kill birds, we may never discover the principles of aerodynamics. Similar arrogant disregard of ordinary experiences underlies doctrines of the closed mind; the claim that the brain or the computer exhausts mind is like the claim that the slingshot exhausts flight.

Albert Einstein knew better than those philosophers who, having learned some technical jargon, use "ideal science" as a bludgeon to beat up everyday thinking. He explained (1954:290, 324): "The scientific way of forming concepts differs from that which we use in our daily life, not basically, but merely in the more precise definition of concepts and conclusions; more painstaking and systematic choice of experimental material; and greater logical economy." Reflecting on the foundations of physics, he remarked: "The whole of science is nothing more than a refinement of everyday thinking. It is for this reason that the critical thinking of the physicist cannot possibly be restricted to the examination of the concept of his own specific field. He cannot proceed without considering critically a much more difficult problem, the problem of analyzing the nature of everyday thinking." If analysis of everyday thinking helps physical research, how much more can it contribute to research on mind.

Theoretical thinking is important in this book, because for big pictures of mind we must introduce theoretical concepts. Some people confuse theoretical thinking with either the view from God's position or idle speculation in contrast to practice. As I will explain, it is neither. Theoretical thinking is not the exclusive property of professional nerds but a common mode of human mental ability that everyone exercises as they cope with the world. Not all of our activities are theoretical; most are not. For instance, you are not thinking theoretically when you enjoy a drive and your car's perfect handling. Suppose, however, that suddenly you hear a clanking noise under the hood. At once your car ceases to be a handy equipment and becomes an object that grabs your attention and tears you from myriad other factors in the rich context of your living experience. You slow down and accelerate, listen to the frequency of the clanks, speculate about their cause. You forget the scenery and look for a place to pull over, preferably a service station. You disengage your attention from many experiences and focus it on a single piece of equipment; disconnect the equipment from its context of use, regard it as a mere thing, try to figure out how it works and what is wrong with it. Your thoughts become explicit and perhaps even verbal. You have adopted a *theoretical attitude* by which you try to cope with a specific problem.[2]

Life is full of glitches that call for the theoretical attitude, which is a mode of our usual thinking. In systematically refining the theoretical attitude, science has developed many powerful techniques. Do not be fooled by scientism into believing that these techniques have divine power. As Einstein reminded us, they are based on the common human mental ability that underlies ordinary thinking. At a time when scientism trashes common sense and provokes a backlash against science and reason, perhaps the best approach to mind is Kant's motto of the Enlightenment: Dare to use your own mind.

The Intelligibility of the World as the Basic Structure of Mind

What are the major characteristics of our usual thinking that are so difficult to analyze? "The eternal mystery of the world is its comprehensibility," wrote Einstein (1954:292). "It is one of the great realizations of Immanuel Kant that the postulation of a real external world would be senseless without this comprehensibility." Comprehensibility, Einstein hastened to explain, modestly means producing some order and making some sense of ordinary experiences by appropriate general concepts; in other words, intelligibility. Its mystery is expressed by another physicist, Erwin Schrödinger (1961:10): "It is precisely the *common* features of all experiences, such as characterize everything we encounter, which are the primary and most profound occasion for astonishment; indeed, one might almost say that it is the *fact that anything is experienced and encountered at all.*"

The founders of relativistic and quantum physics marveled not at their esoteric theories but at the most ordinary mental ability, for that is what separates us from other things. It is our mind that makes things encounterable and the world intelligible. How it achieves that is still a mystery. Scientists of mind may reply to Einstein: "Sorry, we do not believe that the mystery is eternal." Nevertheless, they would do well to heed his insight: The basic structures of our mind lie not in qualia or intelligence hiding inside the head. It lies in the intelligibility of the world and the encounterability of objects.

Consider the visual experience of seeing a tree. What are its peculiarities? It is not the vivid colors and the detail of leaves; cameras, both conventional and digital, can achieve comparable resolution. Unlike the camera's registration, my visual experience is meaningful. I can make some sense of it, if the sense is no more than awareness that the tree is an external object that persists independent of my seeing it. In this primitive sense, I separate the *object* from my experience of it, and hence am aware of myself as a *subject*. This subjective apprehension of objects marks the consciousness that distinguishes visual experiences from light detection. When I see the tree, I have a visual experience of it and it is intelligible to me; its intelligibility is an essential aspect of my experience. Experiences belong to mental subjects, but they are *of* objects in the world. Intelligibility is descriptive of the objective world, but only in relation to knowing subjects. Einstein wondered at comprehensibility, Schrödinger at experience. Their remarks respectively emphasize the objective and subjective sides of mentality, but simultaneously stress that the two sides are inalienable. This double-sided structure encompassing experiences and intelligibility, subjectivity and objectivity, I call mind-open-to-the-world. It is what the closed mind lacks.

Openness is the mental capacity by which we experience things, care for other people, and turn the blind and indifferent environment into an intelligible and meaningful world. Mind can be open to the world only because it belongs to persons who are physically part of the world. People with open mind are neither pure thinkers nor mere brains; they are fully bodied, manipulating things purposively and communicating with other people through various physical media. Therefore I maintain that the open mind belongs not to the brain, not even to a person in isolation, but to a person radically engaged in the natural and social world. The mental level where mental phenomena occur is the *engaged-personal level*.

The open mind of people engaged in the world accentuates meaning and understanding. Therefore it is much more than the "situated cognition" in AI, which, like other AI projects, stresses only behavioral performances as evaluated by mind designers. So far, robots with situated cognition are like insects. They are situated in the environment in the sense of being interactive parts of it, behaving intelligently in the eyes of external observers, and processing information informative not to themselves but to mind designers. Their situation does not imply openness because they do not understand. People are not only parts of the world but are also open to it in the sense of finding its objects intelligible and events informative for themselves. The difference between people and insects or robots is the essence of the open mind. To sketch a theory for it is an aim of this book.

Subjective Perspectives and Objective Invariance

Of course we see things in the world—need it be said at all? Openness
is so fundamental to our mental activities and so prevalent in our experience it is usually taken for granted. Only in rare cases where it fails do
we take notice, so that by "you must be seeing things" we mean not
normal vision but illusion. Our ordinary experience of seeing real things
is so obvious and intuitive many people cannot see any problem with it.
To Einstein, Schrödinger, and others who seriously ponder the relation
between mind and world, between beliefs and reality, however, this ability
is precisely what is most wonderful. The closed mind, for instance, is unable
to see or form beliefs about things and events in the real world. A computer has no inkling about the weather when it runs a program that its
human designers interpret as a model for weather prediction; it simply
operates on meaningless symbols. Similarly, the closed mind playing with
mental representations has no inkling about the real world and hence
cannot believe in anything about it. That is why models of the closed mind
are so counterintuitive and why their promoters are so eager to trounce
common sense.

A major aim of the science of mind is to analyze human understanding, to explain how we manage to find events in the world intelligible. Therefore it cannot tacitly appeal to our intuitive notions of
mind but must articulate the intuition explicitly. This turns out to be more
difficult than many people think. In seeing or knowing the world,
our mind is not like a mirror that simply reflects external happenings.
It spontaneously injects certain structures so that even our most immediate sensual experiences are meaningful. But then how can we say
that reality is independent of our observation and thinking? What does
reality mean? How can we ever know anything about it? How is it
possible that we simultaneously claim objective knowledge and are
aware of our own fallibility? These are big questions that demand explanations from the science of mind. Their answers have many ramifications
because mind and reality touch all our concerns. Inadequate answers fuel
current controversies in science studies where, to the dismay of scientists,
it is fashionable to deny the objectivity of scientific knowledge (Koertge
1998).

Most cognitive scientists need not tackle these questions because they
are mainly concerned with details of particular mental phenomena, for
instance, how to perform a particular mental task or how to diagnose a

particular mental disorder. Those satisfied with tinkering with small aspects of mind can tacitly rely on our commonsense understanding of mind and its objective knowledge. Those striving for a clear big picture of mind and a comprehensive interpretation of the great variety of scientific results and everyday experiences, however, find themselves facing the difficulty of accounting for mind's relation to the world.

Models of the closed mind do contain an insight. Our experience and knowledge of the world are partial and not isomorphic to the world itself. To account for the fallibility of experience, a theoretical model of mind needs at least two variables, one of which accounts for objects in the world. What is the second variable? Models of the closed mind take it to be mental representation; we make mistakes when our mental representations mismatch with objects. Unfortunately, mental representations are so overpowering they become a screen that completely shuts mind from the world, thus creating the necessity of appealing to mysterious mind designers.

My model of mind-open-to-the-world jettisons mental representations and mind designers. Instead of the variable of mental representation, I posit the variable of *subjective perspective*, which covers both physical and intellectual viewpoints. Mental representations are something inside the head private to the mental subject. Perspectives or viewpoints put the subject squarely in the world; I see an object from my perspective, which is a position in the world relative to the object.

An open mind coping with the world's vicissitudes is much more sophisticated than a cooped-up mind playing with meaningless mental representations. Consequently models of the open mind are conceptually more complicated than models of the closed mind. They must account for the relation between subjective experiences and the objects of the experiences. This relation is the fruitful problem for the science of mind. It is also a hard problem; models of the closed mind can only relegate it to the godlike mind designers, whose ability they never explain. My model accounts for the relationship by stressing that the subjective perspective is not a constant but a *variable* with many possible values. A person adopts a particular perspective in a particular experience, but he is simultaneously aware of the possibility of many other related perspectives, some of which he may adopt in other experiences. Thus his open mind must have enough structures to accommodate many possible perspectives; to synthesize experiences from these perspectives, transform among them, compare them, and extract certain invariant features that he attributes to the objects of his experiences.

The synthetic structures of the open mind are presuppositions and preconditions of all our encounters with of objects, everyday and scientific. Because of them we can acknowledge many perspectives without degenerating into relativism or social constructionism where reality evaporates and caprice reigns. Our acknowledgment of subjective perspectives is accompanied by our ability to transform among the perspectives, which explains the *objectivity of our knowledge*. This objectivity issues not from God's position but from the human position, hence it contains awareness of its own vulnerability. It holds equally in our everyday lives and in empirical science. Science is a human endeavor. It does not, cannot, claim to put us in God's position. However, neither does it concede the objectivity of its results. This is possible because the human mind is intrinsically open to the world.

An Outline of the Book

This book not only presents a conceptual framework covering the open mind and its infrastructure but substantiates it with examples from everyday life and cognitive science. Because of the bulk and diversity of ordinary activities and scientific results, the conceptual analysis is spread out. To bring out the thread of my argument, I list the major points and their locations in the book.

Chapter 2 surveys major theories of mind and explains how most fall under the rubric of the closed mind controlled by mind designers (figures 1.1a and 2.1). These models sharply distinguish an inner realm for the closed mind and an outer realm accessible only to mind designers. Most theories emphasize either the inside or the outside, sometimes to the extent of rejecting the other side. Computationalism and connectionism are examples of inside theories; behaviorism and dynamicalism outside theories. In discussing them, I introduce and explain many traditional and technical concepts that will become useful later in the book. The final section of the chapter presents several theories that abolish inner–outer dichotomy. Chief among them is existential phenomenology, from which I borrow major ideas but not terminologies, because I think they are obscure to most of my intended readers.

The conceptual structures for my model of the open mind emerging from infrastructures (figures 1.1b and 3.1) are mainly presented in chapters 3 and 8, the former addresses mainly with emergence, the latter openness. These two theoretical chapters are separated by case studies that substantiate the model with factual results from cognitive science and explanations of how the results are relevant to ordinary experience.

As mentioned in the preceding section, my model consists of three parts: the mental level, the infrastructural level, and the relation of emergence connecting the two. The mental level is the arena of common sense and our everyday life. I leave the analysis of it with its structure of mind-open-to-the-world to chapter 8. The other two parts of the model are addressed in chapter 3. They provide the conceptual framework for interpreting the experimental results from diverse areas in cognitive science.

Section 7 of chapter 3 introduces a self-consistency criterion for theories of mind and explains why it is violated by models of the closed mind. Then it introduces my model of the open mind emerging from infrastructures and its underlying hypothesis: *mind is an emergent property of certain complex physical entities*. This hypothesis is different from crass materialism that reduces mental phenomena to neural and other phenomena. A nonreductive conception of physical mind obtains because many organizational and descriptive levels are necessary for the understanding of complex entities in general and mental beings in particular. Disparate levels and their interconnections must be taken seriously, and that is always a difficult task. Lip service merely covers up their importance. Sections 8 and 9 introduce the infrastructural level for mindful persons, describe the characteristics of infrastructural processes, place them between the neural level below and the engaged-personal level above, distinguish computation from causality, and reveal that most talks about the computational mind actually refer to causal infrastructural processes. Sections 10 and 11 survey various attitudes toward the relation between two descriptive levels and explain why the usual scientific approach is not dualism or reductionism but synthetic analysis. Synthetic analysis introduces a theoretical framework that encompasses both levels, analyzes the whole to find productive parts, and explains how the parts self-organize into salient structures of the whole. *Emergent* properties of the whole produced by self-organization are defined in contradistinction to *resultant* properties produced by aggregation. Many general ideas of synthetic analysis and emergence are illustrated with examples from fluid dynamics and chaotic dynamics. Using these ideas, section 12 explains why mental processes are emergent and not resultant and why mental causation is nothing mysterious. It refutes doctrines of the disunity of consciousness by revealing hidden assumptions that rule out emergent properties beforehand. Synthetic analysis allows different scopes of generalization for different levels and gives precedence to the level for the phenomena at issue. Therefore, although infrastructural processes are contained within a person's skin, mental concepts can account for factors outside the skin to describe the person's mental states. *Situated properties* of individual entities that include external factors are common in the sciences, as illustrated by examples from physics. Section 13 explains how mind is a situated property of an individual person, thus paving the way for the analysis of mind-open-to-the-word in chapter 8.

The open mind is so intuitive I am comfortable relying on our everyday mental vocabulary to describe it in chapters 4 to 7. Everyone understands "Tom sees a tree" or "Tom loves Mary" and knows that Tom is concerned about a thing or a person in the world, not a mental representation in his head. To articulate the understanding explicitly and frame an adequate theory for it, however, is not simple. Chapter 8 is my attempt.

Section 22 of chapter 8 presents the central feature of mind-open-to-the-world: the mental subject does not exist independent of the intelligible world. I come to know myself as a subject only by differentiating my experiences from the objects of the experiences. Thus subjectivity, objectivity, and intersubjectivity rise and fall together. Section 23 surveys various meanings of intelligence, consciousness, and intentionality. I explain why some concepts are not fruitful in scientific investigations of mind and how my analysis of the open mind differs from them. In section 24 I note the logical affinity among intentionality, time, and possibility, and take these concepts to be the keys to mind. I contend that the most basic mental ability is to break free from the actual and immediate present and to imagine possibilities. As the presupposition of generalization, possibilities underlie all concepts, including temporal and objective concepts. In section 25 I model the structure of the open mind by a framework with two interrelated general concepts: *mental perspective* and *object*. The gist of the model is that mind depends on many perspectives and the possibility of transforming among them, thus holding the object as that which is invariant under the transformations. Contrary to relativism, the multiplicity of perspectives engenders *objectivity* of mind, the precondition of science. Analysis of mental perspectives in section 26 reveals that a full sense of the *subject* depends on one's ability to conceive oneself from both the first-person and third-person views. Generalizing perspectives leads to the notion of *intersubjectivity* as a three-way relation among two persons and the objective world that they share. Thus subjectivity and intersubjectivity are both open to the world; neither implies an inner self accessible only by introspection. Section 27 analyzes the intelligibility of the objective world, both in everyday routines and as described by the sciences. It teases out characteristics of knowing-how and knowing-that, or skills and theories, and holds that both are practiced in mundane activities, as both are essential to the intelligibility of the world. Finally, section 28 explains how language constitutes much of our mental activity, not only by making explicit our tacit understanding but by being an essential medium of thinking. Only with language can we explicitly think about past and future, narrate our autobiographies, and exercise freedom of action.

Chapters 3 and 8 emphasize the theoretical framework. They contain many scattered examples that mainly illustrate the particular concepts at issue. To substantiate the conceptual framework further, chapters 4 to 7 examine four major areas in cognitive science and explain how various mental faculties are subserved by their respective infrastructures: the language organ, perceptual pathways in the brain, memory systems, and emotive circuits. These chapters emphasize factual discoveries but do not neglect their conceptual interpretations. Each chapter contains two sections. One explores phenomena and theories for the mental faculty at issue; the other brings discoveries on the mental infrastructure to bear.

Each mental faculty is complex. Therefore I do not attempt to provide a comprehensive picture. Instead, I try to focus on one important conceptual issue: the modularity of mind in the context of language; the concept of objects in perception; causality in memory; reason in emotion. In many places the issue is framed as a three-way debate among defenders of the open mind, the closed mind, and mind designers. I argue that the complexity of the mental infrastructures upholds the emergence of the open mind. For instance, the heavy two-way traffic in the visual infrastructure discredits the theory of a closed mind passively registering optical stimuli. The spontaneous constructive nature of memory militates against the dictate of mind designers. Many conclusions drawn from these case studies are used in chapter 8 for the general model of the open mind.

2

The Prevailing Theory of Mind and Its Discontents

3 How Mind Loses Its Body and World

We exercise our mental abilities all the time. *Exercising* mind, however, is different from *thinking about* mind; we use mind to think about a lot of things besides mind. Everyone exercises mind, but not everyone reflects on or thinks about the nature and characteristics of mind. Such reflections are mostly for scientists and philosophers. They are also the purpose of this book, which tries to frame some concepts and theoretical models to describe and explain mental phenomena as they occur in everyday life and in scientific laboratories.

The closed mind is so counterintuitive one wonders how it comes to dominate theoretical models. These models vary on a Cartesian theme in which an inner mental realm is closed off from the outer physical realm. They share some important concepts, the meanings of which have become muddled by overuse. Therefore I start by clarifying concepts and tracing their roots.

"Cartesian" is not a good word today. Descartes bashers are legion, but many are also avid vendors of Cartesian concepts dressed in high-tech jargon. The superficial bashing presents a frivolous or dogmatic Cartesianism, but this is unfair. The Cartesian theme is an earnest effort to find a theoretical representation for a complex phenomenon, providing simplifications to make the problem tractable. I reject it because I think its simplifications are on the wrong track, not because it addresses the wrong problem. Descartes identified important questions about mind that face us today. To see them more clearly, let us get a historical perspective.

Ancient Conceptions of Mind

We are naturally mindful and automatically wield mental abilities. Anthropological research has found no culture that is purely behaviorist in its conception; mental notions such as belief and false belief are universal. With subtle variations in meaning, psychological terms such as thinking, feeling, acting, perceiving, speaking, understanding, caring, craving, remembering, anticipating, willing, and dreaming are used in the daily conversations of people everywhere on Earth, from antiquity to now. They are phenomena to be observed and explained by sciences of mind. Nevertheless, they are practical and not theoretical. Although people understand and deal with each other by these concepts, they are hard put if asked to elaborate.

Theoretical concepts of mind, by which we do not merely use everyday mental notions but treat them and mental capacities themselves as objects of discourse or investigation, are less widespread and evolved haltingly. Some cultures do not have a concept analogous to our "mind," others have concepts that differ widely from those of modern Europeans and Americans. For instance, Illongots of the Philippines hold a concept of mind that fuses what we now know as mentality and vitality (Lillard 1997). This cross-cultural variation is not surprising when we realize that the theoretical concept of mind familiar in the Western world is itself a late introduction. Aristotle, for example, would be more in tune with Illongots than with modern Greeks.

Homer did not have a unitary notion of mind or soul. *Psyche*, the word for soul in later Greek that is the stem for psychology, is in Homer the breath of life that leaves the mouth or escapes from wounds when a person dies. *Nous*, the word for mind or intellect in later Greek, is in Homer the capacity to realize and understand a situation, to imagine and plan, to penetrate appearances for deeper insight, as to recognize Aphrodite in the guise of an old woman. These are all practical intelligence, and realization and recognition dawn as immediately as vision. *Noein*, to know or to think, never means discursive reasoning in Homer.

Homer did not describe the functions of psyche in life. By the sixth century B.C.E., psyche became the body's vital principle present in all living organisms, holding together, controlling, and strengthening individuals. Besides thinking in humans and locomotion and perception in higher animals, activities of the soul also included digestion, growth, and reproduction, which we now classify not as psychological but as physiological.

Mind for the ancients always intimately tied to the world. Pre-Socratic philosophers, materialists one and all, regarded the soul as some stuff such as air that suffused the body and its surrounding, thus making the organism a part of the cosmic whole. They explained thoughts in terms of some peculiar mixtures of bodily constituents. Parmenides, for example, held that mind is inseparable from being. The pre-Socratics contrasted nous with *aisthēsis*, sense perception. Sense perception has access only to the changing and partial surfaces of things that form the basis of beliefs in most people. Mind can penetrate into the constant real world as a whole that is the basis of truth. By making explicit the possibility of mind to be deceived and to err, these philosophers brought out the role of logical reasoning and discursive argument in attaining truth. *Logos*, which for Heraclitus was mainly the noun for "to say," became increasingly central to reason (Fritz 1974; Wright 1990).

Aristotle clarified the thoughts of his predecessors. Furthermore, he put the notion of the soul as the principle of living organisms with mind as its intellectual component into his own theoretical framework of form and matter, actuality and potentiality. As the form of organisms as wholes, the soul is the actuality for the potentiality of organic bodies. It is natural, because form and matter are both present in all things. Aristotle analyzed the soul in terms of its various functions: practical intelligence, technical know-how, reason, and theoretical knowledge. His definition of nous was rather narrow, confined to reason, the base for knowledge and belief. He sharply distinguished reason from perception and intelligence, denying the former but not the latter to animals. Like Aristotle, Thomas Aquinas did not include in mind passive sensory images, which we follow the British empiricists in regarding as quintessentially mental.

Continuing the Aristotelian practice of locating the study of soul within biological investigation, the Stoics and Epicureans took advantage of scientific and medical advancements in the Hellenic age and developed even a stronger materialist view of mind. Thus from the pre-Socratics onward, Western thinking has had a strong tradition for the monistic and naturalistic conceptions of mind. In this tradition mind is a part of the natural order and susceptible to study by natural science. Detailed formulations of it change as our scientific knowledge changes (Annas 1992).

Whereas the monistic conception has its roots reaching back to pre-Socratic thinkers, the dualistic conception also has a long root that traces back to Plato. Plato believed that the relationship between soul and body was deeply problematic and defied our understanding. In several of his dialogues, especially *Phaedo*, the soul appears as a substance separate from but on a par with body, it is immortal and, for it, the body with its desires and pleasures is a nuisance. This dualist view was revived by Neoplatonists in the third century. Plotinus proposed a clear distinction between body and soul and used it as an approach to the Platonic distinction between the physical world and the immaterial world of forms. As something incorporeal and noncomposite, the soul is not subject to destruction. The idea of the immortal soul was seized enthusiastically by Christians, among whom was Augustine of Hippo, an avid reader of Plotinus. Augustine's writings were very much a part of the intellectual milieu of educated Christians in the seventeenth century, when mind-body dualism received its definitive formulation from René Descartes (Robinson 1970; O'meara 1993).

Modern Conceptions of Mind

Discussions in the philosophy of mind tend to focus on Descartes's theory of soul substance and consequent mind-body dualism. However, Descartes changed the notion of mind in two ways that are at least as important as dualism. First, he acknowledged the importance of inner awareness and first-person experience, which supplement the mainly third-person view of mindful beings in ancient writings. Second, by defining a person as a thinking thing, "a thing that doubts, understands, affirms, denies, is willing, is unwilling, and also imagines and has sensory perceptions," Descartes expanded the mental realm by absorbing into mind many functions of psyche that were not part of nous. His ideas were clarified and consolidated by British empiricists who made unconceptualized sense impressions into the foundation of mind. Enriched by romanticism, the resultant conception of mind covers the whole fabric of conscious life: perception, sensation, imagination, understanding, memory, anticipation, feeling, thinking, doubt, resolve, mood, and skill. It developed concomitantly with the rise of modern science and the assertion of personal individuality. They have become the pillars of the contemporary view in which we understand the universe and ourselves as autonomous subjects in the natural and social worlds.[1]

Since Descartes, epistemology has replaced metaphysics at the center of philosophy. Philosophers scramble to analyze the mind that distinguishes us from other animals; to investigate the nature of knowledge, which we acquire by way of our mental activities; to criticize or justify our knowledge and reasoning. John Locke systematically analyzed the nature of human understanding, which Gottfried Wilhelm Leibniz disputed point by point. David Hume studied human nature, especially properties of mind that enable us to think, feel, and evaluate. Immanuel Kant elucidated the structures and limits of theoretical and practical reasons and aesthetic judgment. Although traditional philosophical views often emphasize rationality, they cover most if not all our mental activities, not the least the assessment and choice of ends. This broad view contrasts sharply with the narrow view in which mind is nothing but the computation of means to achieve given ends.

Mind-Body Dualism and Mind-World Dichotomy

"I think, therefore I am." What kind of being is this I who exists in pure thinking? This question is important, because this I, disembodied and closed off from the world, is currently influential in the interpretations of cognitive science.

Wrapped in a thick dressing gown, Descartes sat meditating by the fire that kept out the winter cold in north Holland. It was the end of the 1630s, more than a decade after Galileo Galilei published his major works in physics. New ideas were boiling everywhere. Descartes, himself a philosophical leader in the intellectual revolution, realized that he and his tradition had many false and dubious opinions. Determined to retain only true ideas, he embarked on a project to doubt everything he could, establish a ground of certainty, and build knowledge on this impeccable first principle.

He started by scrutinizing sensual experiences. Could anything be more certain than that he was sitting by the fire in a dressing gown, a piece of paper in his hand? Could anyone but the insane deny that that hand was his? Yet, he could be dreaming, and in dreams he experienced illusions of corporal bodies. No, he decided he could not unquestioningly believe in the existence of physical bodies. Thus in his radical doubt Descartes assumed that the sky, the earth, all sounds and sights, all external things, all physical matter, indeed his own body, were delusions or dreams conjured by an omnipotent demon bent on deceiving him. What then was left that was not delusory? He observed: "I noticed that while I was trying thus to think everything false, it was necessary that I, who was thinking this, was something. And observing that this truth '*I am thinking, therefore I exist'* was so firm and incapable of shaking it, I decided that I could accept it without scruple as the first principle of the philosophy I was seeking."[2]

Descartes claimed that his mind—his thoughts and ideas—can be secured on their own in isolation from his physical body and the physical world. The I who confidently said *"cogito ergo sum* (I think therefore I am)" was not the I who sat by the fire doubting; the latter was embodied and engaged in the physical world, the former was not. By upholding the certainty of the disembodied and disworlded mind, Descartes gave a clear formulation to dualism, actually to two forms of dualism.

The Cartesian doctrine can be analyzed as two major aspects. The first, *mind-body dualism*, asserts that the structure of mind is totally distinct and decoupled from the structure of physical matter. For Descartes, this is possible because mind is the property of soul substance. Soul substance, however, is not necessary for dualism. One can reject it and still hold on to a mind-body dualism in which mind is totally abstract and disembodied; and that is the crux. The second aspect of Cartesianism is *mind-world dichotomy*, which introduces an inner mental realm that is totally isolated from the outside physical universe. Trapped in the inside, mind becomes a solipsist.

These two aspects of Cartesianism are distinct. For instance, the doctrine that identifies mind with the brain in a vat rejects mind-body dualism but retains mind-world dichotomy, as the brain's activities are decoupled from events in the world. The mind-world problem is as deeply entrenched as the mind-body problem. Most theories of mind still cannot escape the chasm that cuts mind off from the physical world. Consequently, they fail to account for meaning, which resides in the intelligibility of the world.

Today the soul substance is mostly discredited and dualism is out of fashion, but only in name. Cartesian ideas of a disembodied and solipsist mind whose characteristics are totally independent of the physical universe continue to be influential under many guises, as we will see. But first let us examine the Cartesian ideas more closely so that we will recognize them in new clothes.

Mental Representations and the Veil of Perception

Sensual perceptions are the most immediate and prevalent human mental activities. Thus theories of perceptual experience determine to a significant extent theories of mind and, by inference, theories of knowledge and science.

Is seeing believing? No, Descartes answered, because one can hallucinate. The possibility of illusion led him to decouple mind from both the body and the outside world.

It is undeniable that we have illusions occasionally, seeing things or hearing voices that are not there. Therefore the Cartesian position sounds reasonable. Under its influence, Locke and other empiricists maintained that illusions are possible because what we see immediately are not things outside us but sense impressions inside us, which may not correspond to things outside. Thus they split perception, the primary relation between mind and the world, into two parts by introducing screening entities that are internal to us. Locke (1690:563) wrote: "'Tis evident, the Mind knows not Things immediately, but only by the intervention of the *Ideas* it has of them."

Thus began the downhill journey in which mind slid from not knowing things immediately to not knowing things at all. Ideas are given to us and our perception of them is certain. We make no mistake about them; mistakes occur only when we try to infer things from them or try to match them to things outside. Thus ideas become a *veil of perception* that drops between mind and things, creating an inner and an outer realm. Hume (1739:253) described this empiricist doctrine with an apt metaphor: "The mind is a kind of theater, where several perceptions successively make their appearance."

Ideas, what the old empiricists called the internal entities that allegedly separate mind from external things and events, have acquired many other names: sense impressions, sense data, stimuli, surface irritation, transducer input, activation vectors, mentalese, symbols, most generally, mental representations. Some mental representations, for example symbols, are discrete; others, such as activation vectors, are distributed. Some, such as sense impressions, occur in perception; others, such as mentalese, occur in thinking. Whatever their shapes, functions, or names, they share a fundamental characteristic. They constitute a veil that screens mind from the world. Mind coils safely behind the veil and has access only to mental representations. It organizes mental representations on their own, independent of any requirement that they somehow relate to physical things in the world.

"Representation" is one of the most confusing words in the literature of mind because it has several meanings. Unfortunately, I cannot think of an appropriate word to replace it in mental representation. I emphasize that "mental representation" is a technical term in an influential class of theories about the fundamental structures of mind. These theories assert that mind is a solipsist that not only exists but has all its structures independent of the world, for it sees and knows and manipulates not things that are publicly accessible but only mental representations that are private to it. Mental representations are peculiar to the *world-independent* mind, or the *closed* mind as I call it. They should not be confused with other notions of representations that are frequently used in cognitive science and our daily discourse. Since a theme of this book is to reject mental representations while preserving other representations, let me digress from my historical account to distinguish them.

We deliberately use physical sounds and patterns for representation. Signs, symbols, and other representations occur everywhere. They come in all forms and at all levels of technology. Words are representations, so are traffic signals, mathematical equations, pictures, movies, video games, flight simulators, and computer-generated virtual reality. These representations are physical entities, sounds, and lights in the world and are publicly accessible. Their general meaning of standing for something else is clear; so is the fact that what a specific symbol purportedly represents need not be realized in actuality. In most cases we have access to what the representations stand for; we can see both the word "tree" and the plant that it represents. Nevertheless, we are not dismayed if we find that there is no entity in the world that answers to the word "centaur." As explained in chapter 8, such errors and mismatches bring to relief the intuitive idea that representation is a much weaker relationship than isomorphism.

Mental representations are totally different from ordinary and legitimate representations. Without ordinary representations, we can still lead a mental life, albeit a diminished one; we would have no language, but we can still see and manipulate things. However, according to Cartesian models, without mental representations we would not have any mental ability at all, as they occur at the most primitive level of mental processes. They are not publicly accessible entities in the world but are private entities in the head accessible only to the mental subject. They absolutely and eternally screen us from entities in the world, unlike movies and other "virtual realities" that deceive us only occasionally. You can never see trees, all you can ever see are mental representations inside your head. How you know that mental representations stand for real trees is not only obscure but, as we will see shortly, untenable. Mental representations create the private show in the controversial Humean theater in your head. Do not let their advocates confuse you by invoking uncontroversial theaters that we routinely go to for entertainment.

Physicists use the symbol F to represent force, the equation $F = ma$ to represent a law of motion, and the function $\mathbf{x}(t)$ to represent the motion of a planet. Theoretical representations are the staple of science. Like other scientists, cognitive scientists try to frame theoretical representations whenever they can. Noam Chomsky's universal grammar, for example, is a theoretical representation of our syntactic ability (see section 15). Theoretical representations come in many forms, including computer modeling, and have clear meanings in the activity of scientific research. The computer models and other theoretical representations in cognitive science no more suggest mental representation than $F = ma$.

In most scientific theories, representations are *intellectual tools* used by theoreticians and do not enter into the *objective contents* of the theories. Although F represents force, it is a theoretical tool and not a part of the physical reality represented. In some cases, however, representation occurs in the contents of a theory, usually as a technical term for a relation between two entities that the theory describes. Group theory, for example, includes group representations that are structures more concrete than abstract groups. Two technical notions of representation with objective meanings occur in cognitive science. The first is mental representation, which I maintain is a false concept. The second is legitimate and productive.

It is common sense that we see things; even most Cartesians agree to that. Seeing involves a lot of processes, of which we as seeing subjects are not aware, but that cognitive scientists are trying to probe experimentally and explain theoretically. Intuitively, the structures of these processes must be correlated somehow with the objects seen. Cognitive scientists often call this correlation "representation," some structures "represent" or are "representations of" some objective features. For instance, when they discover neural processes that discriminate colors, they say colors are represented in the brain by these processes. Thus representation here signifies an objective correlation between a kind of neural activity and a kind of optical feature. This legitimate technical meaning should not be confused with mental representation. First, it explicitly signifies a relation between events in the world and processes associated with mind, a relation that is dubious for the world-independent mind with its mental representations. Second, it is always important to ask in the science of mind, who sees the representations, who makes sense of them? Mental representations are seen by mental subject. Representations in cognitive models are seen and interpreted only by cognitive scientists; the subject is unaware of them. I maintain in chapter 3 that the two technical senses of representations apply to two organization levels. Mental representations allegedly occur in the mental level in which we are conscious. Representations in cognitive models apply to the infrastructural level, of which we are not aware as mental subjects. The distinction is important, for at issue is the most basic structure of mind and hence the very notion of a mental subject.

Two-Part Theories of Mind and the Evaporation of the External World

Having distinguished various meanings of representation in cognitive science, let us return to mental representations and the models of the closed mind that they imply. Mental representations and the veil of perception were introduced as devices to simplify theories of perception and mind. The veil creates an inner and an outer realm, and the inner–outer dichotomy enables us to divide a theory of mind into two parts. The first part, which portrays a closed mind trapped behind the veil of perception having access only to mental representations, is addressed by *methodological solipsism*; the closed mind is a solipsist. The second part of the theory tries to connect the closed mind to the outside world by claiming that it can somehow infer the properties of physical objects from the perception of mental representations. A successful inference would allow the mind to realize that mental representations represent things in the outside world. Consequently, the second part of the theory is now called the *representational theory of mind or perception*. At the bottom of the two-part theory is the Cartesian assumption that mind can stand on its own independent of the physical world. Thus one can study inner awareness first and worry about its optional relation to the outer world later. This is the broad theoretical framework for most philosophical and cognitive scientific discourses on mind.

At first blush, the veil of perception and the two-part theory it creates solve many problems, including hallucination, illusion, dream, and falsehood. In perception, we experience the show of mental representations inside the veil. A perception is illusory if the show does not correspond to the reality outside. A second look, however, raises the mind-world problem that threatens the distinction between illusion and reality. How does mind, trapped behind the veil and with access only to the show, get ideas of reality, correspondence, truth, or falsity in the first place? Aware of the problem, Locke asked (1690:563): "But what shall be here the Criterion? How shall the Mind, when it perceives nothing but its own *Ideas*, know that they agree with Things themselves?"

The closed mind is justified to regard the ideas that it sees as representations of external things only if it succeeds to infer from ideas to things. Can the inference succeed? Locke tried to base the inference on the assumption that some simple ideas, such as whiteness and bitterness, are caused by external things. How does the solipsist mind ever get the notion of causation, not to mention what cause its simple ideas? Locke (1690:564) answered that the simple ideas are "the product of Things operating on the Mind in a natural way, and producing therein those Perceptions which by the Wisdom and Will of our Maker they are ordained and adapted to." Notice that he appealed to the Deity at the crucial point of his causal account.

Can the closed mind manage without divine intervention? Remember, we are considering the basic nature of mind itself, including the limits of its power of inference. The closed mind can infer from one idea to another and construct complex ideas from simple ones. But still everything remains inside. To suspect that ideas or mental representations are caused by external objects, mind must be able to sneak out from behind the veil of perception and study causal effects in the world directly. But this is impossible for a mind that is aware only of mental representations. Despite much effort, empiricists fail to account for mind's ability to infer causes of mental representations. Once the veil of perception descends, it is unbreachable. *Thus the two parts of the theory of mind are incompatible.* One part must go. Empiricists forego the outer part for being less relevant to mind. Since there is no justification for the mind inside to assume that mental representations are caused by anything outside, the external world may as well be nonexistent. Consequently, mind is closed off from everything except mental representations, and "representation" becomes an empty word, a mere name. This possibility, dreaded by Descartes, became a conclusion in George Berkeley's idealism: To be is to be perceived.

God Comes to the Rescue

Keeping only the inner realm and letting the external world evaporate have at least two chronic and fatal flaws. First is the question of who

watches the show in the Humean theater and understands mental representations. Hume went in to look but could find no one. But then how
does the show make sense? We will leave this question of the self and subjectivity to section 26. Here we consider the second question: how do
mental representations acquire meaning for the closed mind? Meaning
resides in the world. When we are not solipsists but people living in the
natural and social world, our thoughts are meaningful to ourselves. We
explain coherence of our experiences by referring to the world that,
despite its chaos and complexity, is crudely stable and coherent on our
level of cognizance. How does the closed mind achieve this? What
accounts for coherence among its impressions? Who confers meaning on
its mental representations?

The old philosophers had a guarantor of last resort, God, whom they
called on to bring back the external world, hence to confer meaning and
explain the coherence of ideas and mental representations. Locke was
neither the first nor the last to invoke the Deity in his causal explanation
of perception. After doubting the physical world away, Descartes promptly
got it back by first arguing for the existence of God, then justifying the
existence of the world by God's perfection. God is good; therefore he
would not allow that evil demon to deceive me completely. A way to
salvage the world from Berkeley's doctrine of "to be is to be perceived"
is most vividly expressed by Ronald Knox's limerick:

There was a young man who said, "God
Must think it exceedingly odd
If he finds this tree
Continues to be
When there's no one about in the Quad."

"Dear Sir:
Your astonishment's odd.
I am always about in the Quad
And that's why the tree
Will continue to be,
Since observed by
Yours faithfully,
God"

Rationalists appealed to God no less than empiricists. For Leibniz,
minds are windowless monads. Nevertheless, the thoughts of these closed
monads are coherent and accord with each other because they all conform
to the preestablished harmony ordained by God.

The Rise of Hubris

God quit the business of bailing out troubled explanations; however, proponents of the Cartesian models found substitutes. The crucial idea in the two-part theory is the appeal to a third party to account for the connection between the closed mind and the external world. This third party may as well be some special class of people: scientists, engineers, programmers, experts, philosophers, culturalists, social constructionists; most often it is tacitly assumed to be proponents of the closed-mind model. I call these substitutes of God mind designers. Mind designers all share the peculiarity of having some ability that is categorically beyond the closed mind.

Many models identify the ordinary human mind with the closed mind behind the veil of perception or its modern variant, the veil of formality. Furthermore, they assume that the closed mind can be supervised and controlled by mind designers, someone who somehow has access to both sides of the veil and hence can interpret its configurations as representations of the external world. How mind designers accomplish the feat is never explained or accounted by these doctrines, but neither was God's omnipotence explained by old philosophies. These doctrines become more popular with the computer model of mind; as creators and users of computers, engineers assume a godlike status with respect to their products and tools. Thus these models make scientists and engineers into some kind of superhuman and happily talk about designing mind.

A mutation occurs when God is replaced by certain classes of human beings. God transcends all humans. We are equally before God who endows us with mental abilities. Thus the idea that each human being can understand the words of God directly without mediation of high priests was liberating and democratizing. The effect is reversed with the notion that some humans can usurp God's throne. As we will see, it spawns hubris, *theospectivism*, with insidious effects in many areas.

Modern versions of the closed mind controlled by mind designers divide people into two classes: ordinary people with closed minds and an elite group of mind designers with superhuman abilities. This division destroys the humanistic and egalitarian inclination in our commonsense conception of mind. Ordinary people are no longer treated as autonomous beings. Instrumentalism and behaviorism explicitly put them on the same footing as artifacts, as mere efficient means to satisfy the ends of mind designers, subject to control and engineering (see section 5).

The Cartesian Trojan Horse: The Closed Mind Controlled by Mind Designers

The two-part theory of mind has now become a model of the closed mind controlled by mind designers. I call the model a *Cartesian Trojan horse* for short; the closed mind hides inside the horse like Greeks, mind designers push the horse from outside like Trojans. As for the autonomous and conscious person who knows his own mind and finds the world intelligible for himself, he is as lifeless as a wooden horse in mind-designing philosophies (figure 2.1).

Scratch the surface of any major theory of mind in contemporary cognitive science and philosophy of mind, and chances are that you find a Cartesian Trojan horse underneath. Computer users play Trojans and Intel chips inside computers play Greeks; electrode-wielding neuroscientists play Trojans and neural excitations play Greeks. Some philosophers side with the Greeks, others with the Trojans, still others try desperately to make the two join hands. The shadow of the Cartesian Trojan horse spreads to all areas related to mental abilities, as many aspire to be mind

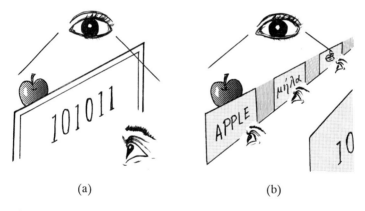

(a)   (b)

Figure 2.1
(a) The Cartesian Trojan horse is a model featuring mental representations that create an inner mental realm and an outer physical realm. Trapped inside like the Greeks in the Trojan horse, the closed mind, depicted by the eye on the right, sees only the mental representation 101011 and not the apple. A mind designer, depicted by the eye above, assigns meaning to 101011 as the representation of the apple. Through meanings, it controls the closed mind, like the Trojans who control the fate of the Greeks hiding inside the Trojan horse. The model fails to account for the mental life of an autonomous person. (b) A variation fragments the closed mind into a pandemonium of homunculi. It destroys the unity of consciousness without alleviating the problems of the Cartesian Trojan Horse.

designers. Those in scientism wave the banner of "science" whereas those
in cultural studies attack science. Retrospective mind designers style themselves as evolutionary high priests who speak the mind of Mother Nature.
Prospective mind designers are eager to rewire the brains of future children. Much of the philosophy of cognitive science is an imperial war
among various mind designers who fight for hegemony to impose their
own brand of design on the closed mind.

The Cartesian Trojan horse can camouflage itself by ostensibly attack-
ing Cartesianism. Some philosophers replace the big screen of the Humean
theater by televisions and fragment the closed mind into a pandemonium
of homunculi. Daniel Dennett (1991) accompanies his pandemonium
model by an fierce attack on what he calls the Cartesian theater, which
is a place in the head where the big screen allegedly sits. Descartes did
speculate the pineal gland to be the site of conscious experience, but the
speculation on spatial or centralized location is a trivial point to which
few people subscribe. Hume explicitly rejected it in his comparison of
mind to a theater and cautioned readers not to be misled by it.[3] The big
fuzz over the Cartesian theater is a smoke screen that distracts attention
from the real problems of Cartesianism symbolized by the Humean
theater. Dennett's attack on the Cartesian theater retains the crux of the
Humean theater. His model of mind as a pandemonium of homunculi
leaves the Cartesian Trojan horse intact, for the homunculi are all closed
inside. It only replaces the Humean theater by Humean televisions,
destroys the unity of consciousness, and adds what Plato ridiculed in his
original comparison of mind with the Trojan horse: several senses are
hiding inside us like warriors in the Trojan horse (*Theaetetus* 184). The
Platonic Trojan horse posits the disunity of the mind inside. The Cartesian Trojan horse adds mind designers outside and emphasizes the inner-
outer dichotomy. I discuss the problems of the Platonic version in section
12. Meanwhile, I concentrate on the Cartesian version.

4 The Closed Mind as Brain or Computer

The three most influential models of mind in the twentieth century are
mind as nothing but behavior, nothing but computer, and nothing
but brain. They are all models of the closed mind controlled by mind
designers, but differ in their relative emphasis on closedness or control.
Behaviorism and its variants, which emphasize the Trojans controlling the

Cartesian Trojan horse, are discussed in following section. This section surveys several philosophies that emphasize the Greeks inside the horse. Chief among them are computationalism and the mind-brain identity thesis, also known as reductionism. These two theses cast long shadows. Even those who try to break away from them sometimes fall under their spell. We will look at one such case, the philosophical debate between internalism and externalism.

The closed mind knows no meaning; meanings are assigned by and known only to mind designers. Such ignorance is common to computers inside black boxes and brains inside skulls. Instead of treating the brain as an inalienable part of a person who thinks, the mind-brain identity thesis disregards the person and treats the brain by itself, disembodied and dis-worlded, as portrayed by a brain in a vat. The person with a brain is open to the world and knowledgeable of meanings; the brain in a vat is not. To confer meanings on the closed mind as a brain in a vat, the mind-brain identity thesis calls in neuroscientists to administer electrode stimulations. However, it keeps neuroscientists in the background and attributes their thinking to the brain. A computer operating on meaningless symbols is like the brain in a vat. Responsible versions of computationalism try to address the problem of meanings and acknowledge that a satisfactory answer is yet to be found. Sleazy versions claim the problem solved by surreptitiously projecting the thinking of computer programmers and users into the computer. Neuroscientists and computer programmers are mind designers in the Cartesian Trojan horse. Although they are necessary for the closed mind to be meaningful, they are deemphasized in computationalism and the mind-brain identity thesis, which focus on the closed mind.

Computer Worship

Earthlings fall to their knees before the altar of bomb in the movie *Return to the Planet of Apes*. Less graphic but more pervasive, the bomb's shrine is taken over by its sibling one year its junior, the computer. The bomb is barbarous; the computer gives an enlightened and rational image. Not for the first time, man creates a god and tries to cast himself in its image. This time, though, the god shares the bomb's characteristic of being a tool. Does the tool-using animal submit himself to the powerful tools he has created? Or are those who control the tools trying to impose their power on their fellow beings?

Computer worship sets the philosophical tone of cognitive science, which is dominated not by human psychology but by artificial intelligence. In four decades AI has gone through three major waves: symbolism, connectionism, and dynamicalism. Each generates great excitement as philosophers argue whether mind is symbolic computation, vector coding in connectionist networks, or dynamic motion. Partisans fight bitterly, but they tacitly agree on one point: the paradigm of mental beings is not natural but artificial, after which the human mind should be patterned and reengineered. They disagree only on which artifact should be the paradigm, digital computer, connectionist network, or dynamicalist robot. Their polemics reveal their attitudes toward not only computers but also humans.

To gauge their attitudes, let us first look at an example. MYCIN is a successful AI expert system for diagnosing certain kinds of bacterial infections and recommending drug therapies. In building it, human knowledge engineers studied the appropriate medical area; debriefed physicians, pathologists, and other relevant experts to gather a vast amount of medical knowledge and know-how; developed a precise vocabulary to express the know-how; encoded the knowledge in a set of rules; and repeatedly tested the rules in experiments and improved them. Their effort was well rewarded. Operating on the rules they wrote, MYCIN diagnoses more accurately than most interns and junior doctors. However, this does not imply that MYCIN knows bacteria or disease; it would try to find an antibacterial drug even for a victim bleeding profusely from a gunshot wound. It depends on humans to consult it and interpret its output in the appropriate real-life situations (Buchanan and Shortliffe 1984).

What do we make of MYCIN and computing machines like it? Social scientists find that the computer has two popular images, as a beneficial tool and as an awesome thinking machine.[4] Philosophers of mind add a third, as the paradigm thinking being. Most people treat computers as versatile tools for a great diversity of jobs, ranging from calculation, simulation, data management, word processing, to surfing the Internet. In this view, MYCIN is a valuable and high-performing diagnostic tool; knowing and thinking belong not to it but to the experts and engineers who designed it and the medical workers who use it. Many AI workers agree to this. For example, the engineers who designed DEEP BLUE, the chess machine that beat world champion Gary Kasparov, detested the popular description of the contest as "man versus machine." Instead, they preferred to see it as "man the performer versus man the tool builder." Many AI workers who once disagreed and held computers to be awesome thinking machines learned from experience. Burned by the bust of their earlier hype, AI firms switched to the beneficial tool image. They now market their goods and services not as autonomous decision makers but as "knowledge-management tools" or "reengineering software"—corporate reengineering, not mind reengineering.[5]

It appears that the free market is more efficient in challenging dogmas than tenured academia. The image of computers as awesome thinking machines has had the philosophy of mind under its palm more completely and for a much longer time. Alan Turing, a pioneer of computer science, first suggested that computers have the potential to think. Such pronouncements are eagerly picked up by the news media, now as then. Early in 1950, the cover of *Time* magazine featured a computer dressed up as a military brass with the caption: "Can man build a superman?" Thus was born the myth that computers think like humans and are potentially far more intelligent and powerful. In this picture, MYCIN not only understands bacteria and disease but exhausts what it is to understand. It and DEEP BLUE are examples of computers thinking better than humans. Marvin Minsky, a founder of AI, said that the second generation of computers would be so intelligent we humans will "be lucky if they are willing to keep us around the house as household pets." With their penchant to generalize, philosophers go farther and claim that computers not only think like humans but assimilate humans. Exaggerating the superiority of computers, some philosophies call for reengineering not only corporations but mind itself. It becomes fashionable to talk about designing mind (Edwards 1996; Haugeland 1997; Dennett 1998).

Starting 1960, philosopher Hilary Putnam (1975) published a series of influential papers stating "that (1) a whole human being is a Turing machine, and (2) that the psychological states of a human being are Turing machine states or disjunctions of Turing machine states." Along similar lines, Allen Newell and Herbert Simon (1976), founders of AI, proposed the physical symbol system hypothesis, which asserts: "A physical symbol system has the necessary and sufficient means for general intelligent action." Turing machines are universal digital computers. The paradigm of physical symbol systems is the digital computer, especially one running on a symbol-manipulating language such as LISP. These doctrines, often claiming to be the foundations of cognitive science, have dominated the philosophy of mind for a long time. According to them, if humans are mental, they are necessarily symbol systems or Turing machines. David Johnson, who edited the proceeding of a recent conference assessing the cognitive revolution, summed it up: the central doctrine of good old-fashioned cognitive science is "A living, thinking, intelligent human being is a digital computer made of flesh and blood" (Johnson and Erneling 1997; Posner 1989).

Flesh and blood belong to the body, which can equally well be made of silicon. Mind resides in computation, the essential feature of which is pure formality and abstraction. Because it is easy to compare mind and body with computer software and hardware, Cartesian dualism enjoys a revival. Computationalism, with variations known as functionalism, machine functionalism, or strong AI, asserts that all that is necessary to have mind is to have software, notably an algorithm or a computer program. Software is abstract, immaterial, and hence immortal. So is mind. The AI worker Ray Kurzweil (1999:128) declared "*We will be software, not hardware.*" As software, we will be immortal, for "our mortality, the essence of our identity, will switch to the permanence of our software." The disembodied *cogito* and the immortal soul return with a vengeance.

Computational Representational Theory of Mind

Computationalism has many versions in philosophies of mind and cognitive science. Some are what computer scientists call technobabble. With the proliferation of computers, computer terms find their ways into every corner of our daily speech. Many of them are useful and some metaphors do enrich our vocabulary. When abused, however, they become technobabble that confuses and misleads. Computer scientist John Barry (1991:4–5) discerned several circumstances in which this occurs: when technical terminology is used as filler or decoration; when it is employed intentionally for obfuscatory purposes; and when it is used by those unfamiliar with its meaning to pretend that they know what they are talking about. Technobabble thrives in the philosophy of mind: mind is a set of activation vectors in a connectionist network; a syntactic engine driving a semantic engine; a serial computer implemented on parallel hardware. These technical terms cloak obscure philosophies with "scientific" cosmetics. However, their real effects are to snow readers and confuse the issues, for philosophers seldom explain in what sense the human mind can be regarded as a virtual machine or connectionist network. Technobabble

generates catchy sound bytes. These may sell, but they are too impoverished in contents to sustain reasoning and argument. Thus I will ignore
them.

Fortunately, not all versions of computationalism are technobabble, so
rational discussion is possible. The most clearly articulated and carefully
presented version is the computational representational theory of mind
(CRTM) developed by Jerry Fodor (1975; 1981; 1998), Zenon Pylyshyn
(1982), and other. Here as in other varieties of computationalism, the focus
is on computation identified with thinking. The computational level, also
called the level of symbols or level of mental representations, functions as
a *veil of formality* that, like the Cartesian veil of perception, creates the
inside and outside of the Cartesian Trojan horse. Around the veil of formality, CRTM divides into three parts: the *representational theory of mind*,
accounting for the symbol–meaning interface; *implementationalism*, accounting for the symbol–matter interface; and the *computational theory of mind*,
accounting for the operation of symbols as the middle wheel that turns
the interfaces on two sides. Both interfaces are viewed from the symbolic
side. Because symbolic transformation is in the controlling position, cognitive theories can ignore both meanings and physical processes, which
will follow automatically if they get the algorithms right. So we arrive at
the computationalist conclusion: cognition is computation and computation is algorithmic symbol manipulation. I will leave implementationalism
to section 10 and concentrate here on the computational and representational aspects of the theory.

We must carefully distinguish symbols in computer models of mind
from ordinary symbols that we use. Ordinary symbols such as words are
meaningful; symbols in computationalism are not. Their essential features,
which underlie the precision of computers, are discreteness, formality, and
absence of meaning. Symbols are discrete entities recognized only for their
forms or shapes, not meanings, as meanings are always inexact and thus
always a big problem for the computational mind. For CRTM, if symbols
transform according to proper algorithms, coherent meanings automatically follow. Furthermore, although the algorithms are formal, they are
guaranteed to be susceptible to mechanical implementations. Properly
implemented, the succession of symbols becomes causally efficacious in
driving the mind. This is an important criterion, because our mental activity must be able to motivate our action. Thus symbols constitute a middle
wheel that turns the causal gear inside the head and the meaning gear
outside.

Figuratively, CRTM posits various "boxes" in the head corresponding to various psychological modes, for instance, the believe box or desire box. Suppose you are entertaining the belief that it rains. Then there appears in your head's belief box a succession of symbols that transform according to certain algorithmic rules. Your mind is computing. Because the symbols are physical, their transformations causally drive you to act in certain ways, for instance, to look for an umbrella. Your belief, of course, is meaningful. How is it so? Mathematical logic guarantees that if the computational algorithm is correct, the succession of symbols can have a coherent interpretation. My account here is figurative, but CRTM does not merely give metaphors in technobabble. It spells out the operation of the symbolic wheel clearly by using two major ideas in mathematical logic.[6]

CRTM is valuable for presenting a rigorous account of a two-part theory of mind. Whether that account is nearly adequate for an explanation of mind, especially the human mind, however, is another story. A major problem is the meanings of symbols. Suppose we accept that coherent interpretations can be found for the sequences of symbols with the right algorithms. Those interpretations, however, are still formal, for they are all that mathematical logic can guarantee. To be really meaningful, at least some of the symbols that appear in your belief box must acquire *physical* interpretations by systematic correlation with physical objects, for instance the weather. How can you achieve that if you are a computational mind?

The Problem of Representation and Mind Designers

Fodor (1981:26) mused that the computational representational theory of mind predates the computer by 300 years: "It is, in fact, a Good Old Theory—one to which both Locke and Descartes (among many others) would certainly have subscribed." In the terminologies introduced in the preceding section, computationalism shifts emphasis from perception to reasoning, and replaces ideas by symbols and the old veil perception by a veil of formality. All the same, the veil closes mind from the world. Whereas ideas are picture-like images in the old theory, symbols and mental representations in the new theory can take on any shape, anything that need not resemble what they allegedly represent. Whatever their shapes, they are items behind the veil of formality, and nothing except the nuance in the names "symbol" and "representation" suggests that they stand for anything. The closed mind inside can construct complicated structures by

Figure 2.2
Trapped behind the veil of formality, the closed mind sees only mental representations. It can relate mental representations that it sees at different times and construct complex representations from simple ones. However, it can never know that
the mental representations represent physical objects. To it, the physical world
does not exist. Consequently, the closed mind ends in empiricism, idealism, solipsism, or phenomenalism.

combining symbols, but it cannot link the structures to anything outside
(figure 2.2).

Consider what some people cite as a good example of mental representations. Imagine a robot that moves around on top of a table and
sounds an alarm whenever it is about to fall off. It does so because it contains a piece of sandpaper in the shape of the table. As its main wheels
turns on the table, a tiny wheel moves on the paper proportionally and
closes a circuit to trigger the alarm whenever it reaches the edge of the
paper. Some theorists say the robot has a rudimentary mental representation that represents its position on the table top (Johnson-Laird 1993:xii).
The fatal flaw of this notion of "representation" is apparent in the example.
The robot has absolutely no idea of the table top or its position. It will
sound the alarm all the same if it moves on the floor, or if there is nothing
that matches the shape of its sandpaper. As far as the robot is concerned,
its tiny wheel is geared to its main wheels, and it sounds an alarm if its
tiny wheel brushes the edge of its sandpaper, full stop. It has no notion
that any part of it represents anything else. Representation is meaningful
only to outsiders, especially those who design the robot specifically to
move on the table.

Consider another example that reveals both the solipsism and disembodiment of the computational mind. SHRDLU is an AI program we

humans interpret as playing with blocks and answering questions about them. It sounds real, but it is all virtual reality, for the blocks do not exist. SHRDLU plays only with symbols that are totally meaningless to it. It cannot care less if it is so rigged that a certain combination of the symbols triggers a nuclear bomb that incinerates a city. Being disembodied and insulated from the world, nothing matters to it. SHRDLU has been hailed as a good simulation of mind. It shows how virtual reality in the Humean theater, much older than the current computer-generated craze, has become an enchanted hole for mind as a mole. Its real nature is frankly exposed by Fodor (1981:231–2): "The device is in precisely the situation that Descartes dreads; it's a mere computer which dreams that it's a robot." SHRDLU's predicament is endemic to the computational mind: "As long as we are thinking of mental processes as purely computational, . . . they have no access to the *semantic* properties of such representations, including the property of being true, of having referents, or, indeed, the property of being representations *of the environment*."

The computational mind is as closed as the digital computer that churns inside a black box heedless of what happens outside. Thus computationalism is plagued by the same question that stymied Locke: how can the closed mind possibly know that its mental representations are meaningful? Fodor (1981:203), who adopts methodological solipsism, acknowledges: "We must now face what has always been *the* problem for representational theories to solve: what relates internal representations to the world? What is it for a system of internal representations to be semantically interpreted?" *The* problem remains outstanding. As long as it finds no satisfactory solution, the computational mind is doomed to be a Greek inside the Cartesian Trojan horse with the trap door locked from outside.

Not all philosophers are as forthright as Fodor. Some talk as if the problem of meanings has been solved by the so-called cryptographic constraint. Computer programs have coherent interpretations; therefore the existence of computers proves that coherent meanings will follow automatically with the right programs. Critics immediately counter that coherent interpretations obtain in computers only because they have been built into computers by programmers in the first place. Programmers have certain meanings in mind and write programs to embody those meanings. Thus the cryptographic answer to the problem of meanings is not different from those of Leibniz or Locke. In Leibniz's words, meanings depend on a preestablished harmony ordained by some superior being. Or to prarphrase Locke, the syntactic sequence of symbols in a computer has coherent meaning because by the wisdom and will of its maker they are ordained and adapted to.

The intervention of a third party is frankly acknowledged by some computationalists. Pylyshyn (1984:63) admitted: "the interpretation typically is effected by the user, not the machine." Thus enter mind designers who control the closed computational mind. The computational mind does not know that mental representations represent anything, but computer programmers and other mind designers do. Mind designers interpret some mental representations as input and output, but to the computational mind itself, input is just "oracles" that appear miraculously. In short, meanings are controlled by mind designers, and as far as they are essential to mind, so is mind.

Connectionism and Distributed Representation

Arguments for CRTM are developed for digital computation and symbolism, the oldest and most famous paradigm of AI. However, its central ideas of mental representations whose interpretations are controlled by mind designers apply equally to other forms of computation, such as connectionism. The major difference is that connectionist mental representations have a form that is different from symbols.

A *connectionist network* is a web of interconnected units called nodes, each with many possible degrees of excitation. The nodes are causally coupled by connections. Each connection has its weight, which determines its relative coupling strength and hence its importance in the network. The influence of node 1 on node 2 is the excitation level of 1 times the weight of the connection from 1 to 2. Depending on the sign of the weight, the influence can be excitatory or inhibiting. A node is an elementary computing unit as illustrated in figure 2.3a. It sums the excitation values it receives through the input connections from all other nodes, determines its own degree of excitation according to a simple rule, and exports excitation through its output connections to other nodes. Excitation levels and connection weights are all continuous quantities like ordinary physical quantities (Rumelhart et al. 1986).

Nodes in a connectionist network are usually arranged in layers, as illustrated in figure 2.3b. There are the input layer, the output layer, and any number of hidden layers whose nodes are not exposed to the external environment. Programmers selectively excite nodes in a network's

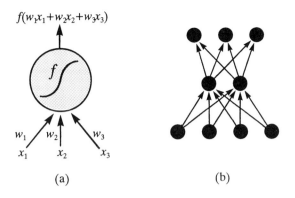

$f(w_1x_1+w_2x_2+w_3x_3)$

w_1 w_2 w_3

x_1 x_2 x_3

(a)   (b)

Figure 2.3
(a) A node, depicted by the circle, is a simple computing unit with many input and output connections. Here w_1 is the weight of the connection between the depicted node and node 1 (not drawn). When node 1 is excited at the level x_1, its input to the node is w_1x_1. The node sums the contributions from all its input nodes, transforms the sum according to a simple rule f to determine its own excitation value $y = f(w_1x_1 + w_2x_2 + w_3x_3)$. Its excitation value becomes the input to the nodes it connects to. (b) A connectionist network contains many nodes arranged in layers. The programmer sets the nodes in the input layer (bottom) at certain excitation levels. Excitation spreads across the network, and equilibrium excitations of the output layer (top) provide the answer the programmer wants.

input layer and interpret it as a problem that they pose to the network. The nodes spread the excitation to other nodes through their weighted interconnections, until the whole network settles into a stable state. Programmers than interpret the steady-state excitation pattern of the output layer as the solution to their problem.

Each node is rather trivial. The power of networks resides in the interconnections among nodes. The pattern of weights of connections determines the characteristics of a connectionist network. How are connection weights set? Engineers can design a network by fixing the weights according to preconceived criteria. They can also train a network by exposing it to examples and adjusting its connection weights in light of its performance. There are many training procedures. The most successful is supervised by a teacher who knows the desired solutions to sample problems. For each sample input, the teacher modifies the network's connection weights by minimizing, according to some statistical criteria, the difference between network's output and desired solution. The sample presentation and weight modification are repeated until the teacher is satisfied with the agreement between outputs and desired solutions. Once the network is trained on the sample set, it can be used to solve new problems in the same domain.

Connectionist networks are also called artificial neural networks or simply neural nets, and their nodes are sometimes called neurons. These are metaphorical names. Although the networks are inspired by the brain and have some neural flavor, they lack neural realism. Natural neural organizations in the brain are much more complicated than that in connectionist networks, and they operate with different principles. Unlike connectionist nodes, output synapses of a natural neuron are either excitatory or inhibitory, not both. More important, the teacher who controls learning and adjusts the connection weights does a tremendous amount of work. There is no hint that such teachers exist in the brain, or that the mechanisms necessary for their operations are compatible with the structures of real brains. The general connectionist techniques are applicable to neurobiology, as they are to many other fields. However, a connectionist network is generally *not* a neural model, and it is rash to suggest that the brain or its web of neurons operates like one (Crick 1989).

Connectionist networks constitute a general computational modeling technique that is applicable in physics and areas that are not remotely biological. Because the technique is abstract and general, scientists can use it to represent real neurons if they choose. However, most connectionist networks that make the news, for example, the text-reading NETalk or car-driving ALVINN, are not neural at all. They are theoretical or practical models that scientists or engineers build to represent or emulate the infrastructures of various mental abilities. Your pen-based computer or palm-held organizer uses connectionist networks to translate your handwriting into printable letters and numerals (Yaeger et al. 1998). Judge for yourself how neural it is.

Connectionism was as old as symbolism, but for two decades was banished by symbolism for being inept. When it returned with new techniques in the 1980s, it vowed to replace symbolism as the sole model for cognition. Symbolists countered that connectionism offers not cognitive explanations but only implementations of symbolic models, which alone are genuinely cognitive. Both sides are attended by armies of philosophers (Clark and Lutz 1992; MacDonald and MacDonald 1995). As the fervor starts to subside, however, the two approaches become mutually complementary. symbolism is superior in emulating calculation and logical deduction, parts of reason. Connectionism is better in emulating pattern recognition and associative memory, parts of intuition. Despite the continuing conflict of ideologies, many scientists are working on interactive models that use both symbolic and connectionist ideas.

James McClelland, a leading connectionist, remarked: "Representationalism is essential in connectionism" (Baumgartner and Payr 1995:133). As a model of mind, connectionism still depends on mental representations, but its mental representations lack both the discreteness and perspicuity of symbols. Connectionist representations are distributed and often called activation vectors. Each idea or entity is represented not by a single node but by a pattern of excitation distributed over many nodes, and each node contributes to the encoding of many ideas. Such distributed and superposed representations are the strong suit of connectionist networks, for which they are also called parallel distributed processing (PDP).

Although connectionism and symbolism have different forms of mental representations, they share the problem of interpreting their respective representations. Here, connectionism fares no better than symbolism. It too depends on outside mind designers to interpret the activation vectors of the connectionist networks. Teachers who train many networks are the most obvious mind designers.

Consider, for instance, NETalk, a star connectionist network. It contains three layers of nodes. Its input layer successively encodes a seven-letter moving window of the consecutive letters of a text; its output layer encodes the corresponding phonemes. It was trained through the repeated input of a corpus of 1,024 words, whose desired output was the phonetic transcription of a child's reading. For each seven-letter input, a teacher adjusted all the weights in the network to minimize the difference between its output and the child's speech. After 50,000 sessions, in which each word was presented approximately 50 times, NETalk was 95 percent accurate on the sample text. It was then tested on a new text and achieved 78 percent accuracy. Hooked to a voice synthesizer, its output produces recognizable, although not error-free, speech (Sejnowski and Rosenberg 1987).

Some connectionists talk as if NETalk involves no programming. Their critics counter that it is free only from symbolic programming, but it needs a considerable amount of preprocessing and programming in a different style. Its input and output are predigested by humans who know not only the structures of texts and the phonemes but also the correct correlation between the two. These structures they program in a peculiar way into the network. Even after NETalk graduates from school it depends on people to interpret its input and output. Without their interpretation, NETalk does not read any text. Thus connectionism is a version of Cartesian Trojan horse, where the network plays the Greeks inside and its teachers and users the Trojan outside.

Mind as Brain

Of the three major models of mind, good old-fashioned behaviorism is out of fashion now, although the ideology persists in philosophies such as instrumental behavioralism. Computationalism has perhaps passed its zenith. The mind-brain identity thesis, which holds that mental states are supervenient on if not identical to brain states, has bottomed out and is now on the ascent, riding the tide of neuroscience. It is common to find scholars writing that the brain, not the person, sees or thinks.

The reduction of mind to brain is most apparent in the expression "mind/brain," which many authors prefer to "mind." Cognitive neuroscientist Antonio Damasio (1994:xvi, 118) complained that many of his colleagues commit the Cartesian error of regarding mind as "just embrained," not "embodied in the full sense of the term." He wrote: "Surprising as it may sound, the mind exists in and for an integrated organism; our minds would not be the way they are if it were not for the interplay of body and brain during evolution, during individual development, and at the current moment." For many nonacademicians, what is most surprising is Damasio's surprise at finding mind the property of the whole organism, which reveals how deeply entrenched is the idea of a disembodied mind.

No one doubts that the human brain, where *brain* is shorthand for the central nervous system, is the most important part of the human body responsible for mental processes. To understand mind completely, we must understand the brain's operations. The brain is necessary for mind, hence brain death is a widely accepted criterion for the death of a person. Mind-brain identity is contentious for going a step farther and maintaining that the brain is not only necessary but also *sufficient* for mind; the rest of the human body, not to mention the natural and social world, is superfluous except as life support; mind will be intact if brain is detached from the remaining body and kept in operation by artificial nutrient and stimulation. In short, mind is the property not of a whole person or a whole organism but of its brain alone. When scientists have unraveled the neural mechanisms of your brain, they will have understood your mind exhaustively. For you are nothing but a pack of neurons, a chunk of gray and white matter.

The most extreme form of mind-brain identity is eliminativism, which advocates eliminating those mental states that cannot be identified with brain states. Lifting the idea of vector coding from connectionism, eliminativist philosopher Paul Churchland claims that brain states code vectors in n-dimensional vector spaces. Seeing red, then, is identical to a brain state with a certain vector. As we are now, we see things in the world but not our own brain states, which is why people in many cultures discovered the functions of the brain much later than the functions of other organs. Churchland (1989:106) assumed, without justification, that people can be somehow reengineered so that they can see their own brain states by direct introspection: "[W]e learn to recognize, introspectively, n-dimensional constitution of our subjective sensory qualia, after having internalized the general theory of their internal structure." In his ideal future, commonsense psychological notions will be eliminated and children will be trained from birth to look into their brains. Instead of seeing the pink or smelling the fragrance of a newly opened rose, they will perceive and talk of only the activation vectors in their visual cortex or olfactory bulb. Notice how eliminativism closes the mind. In seeing the rose's color and smelling its sweetness, our mind is open to the physical world in which we live. In introspecting their brain states, reengineered children are aware of only mental representations in the form of vectors inside their skulls. Nothing outside matters; the door is slammed on the mind. How would the children know what if anything the inner vectors mean? Ask the trainers, mind reengineers, and mind designers who control meanings. Welcome to Aldous Huxley's Brave New World.

Mind as the disembodied and closed brain is even more vividly illustrated by the brain in a vat. Imagine unlucky you being drafted in the Brave New World for a project in which your brain is surgically excised from the rest of your body, kept alive in a vat filled with the necessary nutrients, and stimulated with electrodes controlled by mind designers aided by powerful computers capable of mimicking your sensual stimuli. Let us grant for argument's sake that because your brain in the vat is undamaged and operating, its states are mental and conscious, whatever that means. Do its experiences resemble, at least in essential ways, your experiences such as you have now? Does it possess all vital dimensions of mind embodied in a whole person active in the world? Is it possible that we are brains in vats without knowing it? Of course, answer proponents of mind-brain identity.

Dennett, an advocate of AI and designing mind, agreed in principle. His only reservation was the computing power of mind designers who control the electrodes. Mortals, unlike demons with infinite computational capacity, may not emulate successfully all your actual sensory input and motor output. However, for what the computer can manage, the experiences of your brain in a vat will not differ from those of you the person, albeit a partially disabled one. Dennett (1991) described how your brain can experience itself as a paralyzed person lying on the beach listening to music, enjoying the warm sensation of sun on its belly, and worrying about the possibility of a sunburn.

The problem with the brain in a vat is not as superficial as Dennett depicts, maintain other philosophers, including born-again Putnam (1981) who repudiated his former computationalism. No matter how powerful the controlling computer is and how cleverly it administers stimuli, the brain in a vat still lacks abilities crucial to the embodied human mind. In particular, it lacks the ability to refer to things in the physical world. As nothing but brain, mind is as detached from the world as mere computation.

An organism's body, including limbs, sense organs, viscera, and circulatory, hormonal, and immune systems, causally connects the brain with the external physical world. By discarding the body, the brain in a vat brings out two tenets of Cartesianism: never mind about causality, because mental structures are immune to a complete and radical change in the causal relations between mind and world; and do not bother with body, as mental contents can be completely purged of the awareness of the body itself without gross distortion. Both tenets imply that the structure of mind is independent of the causal activity of the organism of which mind is a property; mind depends only on mental representations, which take the form of electrode stimuli here. Both tenets are untenable.

When you in your flesh and blood body kick a beach ball or stand on the beach thinking, "I'll lie down there for a sun bath," you not only interact physically with the ball or the beach but know about the interaction. Knowledge of causality and awareness of things, even when vague and tacit, are crucial elements of your mental life. If you realize that causal relations fail, then you decide you are not seeing but hallucinating about the beach and the sun. You know there is a close relationship between the contents of your thought and the etiology of the thought; your seeing the beach is partly caused by the presence of the beach. The relationship and knowledge are important for your successful coping in the world. Without them, the notion of thoughts *about* objective states of affairs becomes meaningless. This is precisely what happens to the disembodied brain, where body, the base for causal interaction, has been eliminated in favor of mind designers' control.

When your brain in the vat, properly stimulated by mind designers, imagines a sun-drenched beach and thinks, "I'm lying on the beach," it does not and cannot have any causal interaction with any beach. Its "lying" is a mere illusion. Besides absorbing nutrition, all the physical connections it has are with the stimulating electrodes. Nevertheless, it does not have the slightest idea about the electrodes and never thinks, "Here comes that darn electric stimulation." It continues to believe that it is having an embodied perception complete with the causal implications familiar to embodied experiences.

We do dream, hallucinate, and deceive ourselves. However, such delusions are *partial*, *local*, and *occasional*, occurring in an experiential framework in which we are mostly awake and lucid. Our sober state, in which we more or less assess correctly our causal relations to the world, is the mainstay of our conscious life. Only against this sober background can we recognize occasional delusions as such, distinguish their contents from reality, and say that in dreams and hallucinations we experience as if we see and hear things. In contrast, the delusions of the brain in a vat are *absolute*, *global*, and *eternal*, relentlessly affecting all its states.

The absoluteness of delusion distinguishes mental representations from ordinary misrepresentations such "centaur." It is also what makes mental representations and brains in a vat untenable. For if we were forever completely illusory without any possible contrast with reality, it would be otiose to distinguish between illusion and reality. If all were illusory, calling it "reality" instead of "illusion" would be merely a matter of naming. Also, it would be senseless to say illusions are experienced *as if* they are perceptions, for we would never have a perception in the first place. Everlasting complete delusion is the fate of the brain in the vat. The main point of the experiment is similar to Descartes's evil demon. It hinges on the brain's being fooled into believing it is lying on a beach instead of being stimulated by an electrode; into believing in false causal origins of its experiences, not for some situations some of the times, but for all situations all the times. The brain in a vat not only has thoughts whose contents and etiology are totally dissociated, it is also completely ignorant of the dissociation and has no possibility of discovering the dissociation. It is in the same boat as the Cartesian *cogito*, who is certain because he has lost the capacity to doubt. One can doubt only if it is possible to err and to know that he can err; for his thoughts and reality to agree on some occasions and disagree on others. This possibility vanishes with body and world, because there is no reality beyond thoughts. Descartes in flesh and blood can doubt; his disembodied *cogito* cannot. The incapacity is inherited by the brain in a vat.

In sum, the difference between the embodied and disembodied brain is much more fundamental than the computational power of its mind designers. It cuts so deep it easily topples the claim about the disembodied brain's experiences. Do thoughts of beach and sunshine belong to the brain in a vat or to the mind designers who control the stimulating electrodes and interpret the responses of the brain? The brain in a vat and its controller bring out the Cartesian Trojan horse in mind-brain identity.

Internalism and Externalism

How do meanings occur to the brain in a vat or to the mind identified with the brain underneath the skull? The problem of meanings is most apparent in the philosophical debate on internalism and externalism, which are theories of meaning. Externalism was first proposed by Putnam, and it prompted him to abandon his former theory of mind, computationalism.

To explicate the meaning of meanings, Putnam staged a thought experiment. Imagine a twin Earth where everything is identical to Earth, except that the molecular constitution of the colorless fluid that people drink and call water is not H_2O but XYZ. Suppose you know nothing about molecules and you think: "I'd like some water." Your twin on twin Earth, who is molecule for molecule identical to you, also thinks: "I'd like some water." The mental states of you and your twin are identical because your brain states are identical. But you refer to H_2O and your twin refers to XYZ, as chemists and other experts can testify. Because a term's referential range is determined by its meaning, it follows that you two have different meanings for "water." Thus Putnam (1975:227) concluded: "Cut the pie anyway you like, 'meanings' just ain't in the *head*!" This doctrine has come to be called externalism in contrast to internalism. Internalists such as John Searle insist that meanings are in the head; where else can they be? (Pessin and Goldberg 1996).

If you are a philosopher, probably you would groan at the mention of twin Earth: not again! If you hear the story for the first time, probably your reaction would be incredulous: our body is mostly water. How can one and his twin be molecule for molecule identical if water is XYZ on twin Earth? Philosophical thought experiments are often inconsistent because they abstract too much and too carelessly. However, this time the trouble is not fatal. Its point remains in force if, instead of water, twin Earth is different only in that the metal that airplanes are made of is called aluminum as it is on Earth but is actually molybdenum. You and your twin mean different stuff when you both think "aluminum." Therefore meaning is external to the individual person, because it is dependent on the environment. This is the crux of externalism.

Suppose I ask you: "May I borrow your car?" We both know that the word "car" refers to a thing in the world outside of you and me. In common sense as in traditional philosophy, meaning has always been closely related to reference, which has always been regarded as a relation between words and things. Why then has externalism created such a philosophical commotion?

Tyler Burge (1979), who developed similar theses for the social determination of meanings, called externalism *antiindividualism*. The name is suggestive, as the doctrine takes meanings not only out of the head but also out of mind, and hence endangers the minds of individual persons. Internalists argue that knowing the meaning of a word is a mental activity and mind is the property of individual persons. Each of us knows his own mind as he cannot know another's, and the contents of our thoughts are often causal factors of our actions. By alienating meanings from a person's mental activities, antiindividualism and externalism imply that a third person may know what you are thinking better than you do. If you are not a chemist or a molecular physicist, you do not know what you mean when you think: "Water! I'm so thirsty." The meaning of "water" is known only to those experts. Furthermore, when meanings are determined by factors beyond the ken of individual persons, as externalism asserts, how they function in individuals' thoughts to affect their decisions and actions becomes a mystery.

Externalism is a theory of meaning. It rests on a theory of mind, which is a theory of the closed mind that is akin to Putnam's computationalism. Externalists and internalists agree that mind is inside the head and quarrel about where to locate meaning, outside or inside. Crucial to the externalist position is the solipsist mind dear to many internalists. The externalist twin Earth thought experiment is framed to accentuate the identity of mind with brain: you and your twin have the same mental state because you have the same brain state. The brain is inside the head, and that implies that mental states do not presuppose the existence of anything outside. Putnam (1975:220) acknowledged mental states such as jealousy and perception, which obviously presuppose external objects. To account for them, he simply adopted a methodological solipsism that reinterprets them so that one is jealous of his own hallucinations or perceives figments of his imagination. In my terminology, mind is concerned only with its mental representations. Under this methodological solipsism, the twin Earth example shows that knowing the meaning of a term cannot be a matter of being in a certain mental state. Therefore, externalists conclude, meaning must be determined by external factors, such as the judgment of experts.

Once the nature of mind is clear, it becomes obvious that mental states enclosed underneath the skull fail to fix meanings. The big mystery is how experts can know any meaning if their mind is similarly closed. As far as mind is concerned, Putnam still clung to the crux of computationalism, but he came to realize that this closed mind is incapable of knowing meanings. To account for meanings, his externalism specifically introduces experts who have superior power not available to ordinary minds. The experts, who are merely appealed to but never explained, are another form of mind designers.

The basic problems of externalism have been identified by many philosophers. Donald Davidson (1987) pointed out one that is similar to the skeptic who doubts the existence of the outside world. It shares the same faulty picture of mind as those it attacks, the old Cartesian picture where the closed mind inside the head knows nothing of objects in the outside world but their alleged representatives: sense data, qualia, symbols, mental representations. And it inherits the old problem of how it is possible to beat a track from the inside to the outside. Putnam's solution, division of linguistic labor between experts and the closed mind, is another variation of the old Cartesian theme. The experts play the role of godlike mind designers who bestow meaning, and their introduction completes the Cartesian Trojan horse.

5   The Control Power of Mind Designers

The Trojans play God, controlling the fate of Greeks inside the original Cartesian Trojan horse. Mind designers in modern variants are godlike, possessing abilities that are categorically different from the closed mind and mysterious to it. However, their specific abilities vary. Some, such as the programmers in computationalism or the scientists stimulating the brain in a vat, claim access to both inside and outside of the veil of perception or formality. Others do not care about what goes on inside. They are like Trojans who seal the trap door in the horse and let the Greeks perish inside. Despite the difference, the two classes are equally domineering. This section concentrates on various forms of behaviorism that are mostly concerned with predicting and conditioning behaviors.

Theospectivism
Most mind designers retain remnants of divinity. When the human mind is identified with brain or computation and closed off from the world, those that assign meanings to mental representations must have capacities that transcend the human mind. They must be able to access the world without experience or thinking, otherwise they would be trapped like the ordinary human mind. Consequently the world accessed by mind designers is naked reality, whose furniture is given and totally uncontaminated by any conception. Knowing naked reality, mind designers are in possession of absolute truth. Extending these ideas, we arrive at the philosophical position whose "favorite point of view is God's Eye point of view," as Putnam put it. This view is not contaminated by ordinary mental process, so the world it accesses is absolute naked reality. Thus, Putnam (1981:49) wrote: "On this perspective, the world consists of some fixed totality of mind-independent objects. There is exactly one true and complete description of 'the way the world is.' Truth involves some sort of correspondence relation between words or thought-signs and external things and sets of things." He called this position, which he criticized, "metaphysical realism," others call it "objectivism."[7] I prefer to call it

theospectivism for clarity. As noted in chapter 8, realism and objectivity have useful commonsense meanings for humans and should not be confused with any God's-eye point of view.

Some people think that science can be theoretical only if it attains God's-eye point of view that is free from all human perspectives; it can be objective only if it attains "the view from nowhere," in Thomas Nagel's (1986) words. They mistake objectivism for objectivity and theospectivism for the theoretical attitude, as if science can be objective and theoretical only if scientists become God. Science and theory have nothing to do with theospectivism. Theory derives from *theōría*, the Greek word for viewing and contemplation. Theospectivism issues from the perspective of *theós*, God. The two are distinct.

The aspiration of theospectivism is illusory. Those who claim that they have achieved divine neutrality devoid of all human perspectives are merely blind to their own inherent biases. They are more deeply prejudiced than those who lay on the table their own peculiar perspectives and try to compensate for them somehow. Scientists are not gods but human beings who have learned to view and contemplate critically and systematically. Theoretical reason is basically common sense. It is not created but developed, refined, and applied in larger scales in scientific research. Science is never omniscient. No matter how much it develops, it remains a human endeavor and shares the finitude of the human mind. To explain how we humans can view and contemplate without pretending to be God is a major task for the science of mind. It is also an analysis and critique of the foundations of science, including the science of mind itself. One of its tasks is to discredit the Cartesian Trojan horse, which leads to theospectivism.

Interactive Behaviorism

It appears that one way to escape the Cartesian Trojan horse is to deny that anything is inside and consider only an entity's external behaviors and interactions. This is the approach of behaviorism, which generally regards mental entities as black boxes that behave in complicated ways and interact adeptly with their environment. All one needs to have mind, behaviorists maintain, is to behave and interact appropriately, to respond to stimuli and be susceptible to behavioral conditioning. Therefore they prohibit scientists to use mental and psychological concepts in describing people.

Behaviorism dominated the study of mind in the first half of the twentieth century, but became the target of attack in the cognitive revolution of the 1950s. Although explicit behaviorist doctrines are discredited in cognitive science, behaviorist ideas survive quietly in various guises. For instance, critics of computationalism often complain that it is a form of behaviorism, as it leaves out experience and understanding and is concerned only with behavioral intelligence, which is essentially behavioral efficiency. The behavioral tendency becomes more pronounced with the recent rise of dynamicalism in AI, which builds robots.

Unlike good old-fashioned behaviorism, which concentrates on a system in isolation, recent models emphasize systems that interact with the environment. Variously called the *ecological approach* and *situated cognition* in AI, they are united by their rejection of the mental entity's first-person view. Consequently they have little if any use of psychological concepts. Presently, these models apply best to insects and insect-like robots, the meanings of whose interactive behaviors are assigned by ecologists, AI engineers, or other mind designers. They belong to a variant of behaviorism, *interactive behaviorism* (figure 2.4).

All entities, animate or not, have behaviors and interactions. Why are some mindful and others not? Can criteria of mindfulness be articulated without referring to processes internal to the system or using mental and psychological concepts, as behaviorism claims? What is the status of behav-

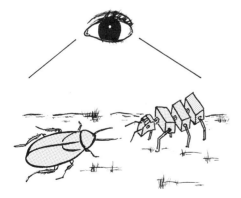

Figure 2.4
Various brands of behaviorism deny mental processes and treat entities like black boxes that behave and interact with their environment in complicated ways. They may be appropriate in characterizing insects and insect-like robots, whose behaviors they evaluate and control as mind designers.

iorists who are capable of prediction, a mental ability behaviorism denies to ordinary people?

Ecological Approach

James Gibson's (1979) ecological approach deprives perception of mental processes and holds that it can be explained by appropriate responses to what ecologists call environmental "information." The theory, based on Gibson's lifelong research on vision, is a big improvement over old-fashioned behaviorism. It makes at least three innovations. First, it replaces fixed-eye vision by mobile-eye vision. Electrodes on the brain in a vat may simulate sense stimuli, but they cannot simulate the brain's motion. Animals are mobile, and their motion contributes essentially to their perception of their surroundings. Second, it brings out the rich complexity of environment factors. The motion of the perceiver greatly enhances the complexity of the optical patterns that strikes the perceiver's retina, the analysis of which is Gibson's greatest contribution to vision research. Third, it replaces responses to arbitrary retinal features by responses only to some invariant features that can be correlated with specific properties in the environment. Thus perceivers attune to environmental properties directly without mediation of sense impressions or other mental representations.

When an animal moves, the optical stimulus on its retina is no longer fixed even if the environment is constant. It is an ever-changing optic array, an optic flow, as Gibson called it. Gibson emphasized the brimming richness of the flow's structural complexity and maintained that it contains *all* necessary information about the environment and distal objects. The chief information he called affordance, which depends on the features of both the environment and the animal, so that the animal directly resonates with specific environmental features and responds accordingly. Examples of affordances for the frog are small moving shapes and large looming shapes; the frog responds to the perception of the former by lashing out its tongue, to the latter by leaping away. No one doubts the complexity of optic flow. However, many dispute Gibson's assertion that structures of optic flow are already in the form of information that can be "picked up" by the perceiver with minimal process on its part (Fodor and Pylyshyn 1981).

Gibson rejected all mental processes and all conceptual involvements in perception. Memory, too, he deemed superfluous. In his ecological approach, an animal picks up and responds to certain features in the complex optic flow. Its motion contributes to the subsequent optic flow, establishing an automatic feedback between optics and responses. Thus a string of immediate responses constitute intelligent behaviors with little mental contribution. As the animal adapts to the environment, feedback becomes more fluent and resonates more to affordance. Thus perception involves no mental structure and is mostly unconscious. A heat-seeking missile is a good ecological perceiver; heat is the affordance it perceives, or the information it picks up, and its motion resonates with the heat source.

This approach regards an ecological perceiver as a part of the environment reacting appropriately to certain specific features in the optic flow that ecologists recognize as information on distal objects. It allows minimal structures for the mental subject, puts all complexity in the environment, and places so much emphasis on the interface between the subject and its environment that the two become fused together. Gibson insisted that affordance, what the perceiver perceives, is "both" and "neither" subjective and objective. That is because ecological perception has no means to distinguish subjectivity and objectivity. Perceivers are moving-sensing systems tied into their environment. No surprise, a persisting criticism is that the ecological approach leaves out the mental subject.

Many features of ecological perceivers described by Gibson have been proved by subsequent research on insects. Vision plays crucial roles in insect behaviors and is closely coordinated with self-motion. The compound eyes of insects have high temporal resolution, which makes them most sensitive to the flow of optical stimuli and adapt to detecting motion. The fly's deft flight, evasive maneuver, and precision landing make robot designers green with envy. To find out how the fly achieves these feats, scientists insert microelectrodes in the fly's brain, monitor the excitations of individual neurons, and correlate them with the optical input to the fly's eyes and its motor output in flying performance. They find specialized neurons that are finely tuned to the optic flow resulting from a specific type of flying motion, say, pitching or rolling, thus establishing a direct causal link between vision and motion. Thus the fly's complex abilities are managed by relatively simple nervous systems that coordinate visual and motor systems with minimal intermediate steps. This closed sensor-motor control loop serves the survival of insects admirably (Krapp and Hengstenberg 1996; Giurfa and Menzel 1997).

It is unclear how the ecological approach distinguishes insect perception from human perception. Humans do have perceptual experiences that fall within the ecological model; for instance, subjects stumble when optical flows on their retina generate the illusion that they are walking in a "moving room." However, we can do much more. We can recognize objects in perception, as things separate from us, as different kinds of things. Recognition seems to have no place in the ecological approach to perception.

Engineering Considerations for Building Robots

Many of Gibson's ideas anticipated dynamicalism, the third wave in AI that rose in the 1990s after the reign of symbolism and rebellion of connectionism. Like the other two paradigms, the concern in AI dynamicalism is mainly to design and build artifacts to serve certain human purposes. Engineers try various design methods and debate their relative merits. All three paradigms are ingenious. Unfortunately, in all three cases engineering methodologies are confused with engineered products, which are enthroned by computer worshippers as models of mind, including the human mind. In considering AI, we should carefully separate the performance of the engineered products, the fruitful debate on engineering methodology, and the dubious extrapolation to the philosophy of mind. We will start by looking at how engineers think.

Dynamicalist engineers build dynamical systems, situated agents, alife (artificial life), animats (artificial animals), and mobots (mobile robots). You probably know some of their products. DANTE II, which explored the crater of an active volcano in 1994, was a mobot. So was SOJOURNER, the rover that roamed the surface of Mars during the summer of 1997. What is the best way to build robots and rovers? No surprise, engineers discovered the importance of the physical body and its interaction with the environment, which builders of chess machines hardly have to consider (Webb 1996; Brooks 1999).

A ball flies in a baseball game. How do you regard the ball mentally? It depends on whether you are a baseball player or a physicist. Physicists can theoretically calculate the ball's trajectory and predict where it lands, provided they know the ball's initial velocity and spin, wind speed and direction, and other relevant conditions. Good baseball fielders need not be good theoreticians, as they do not have to answer where the ball will land, they just have to be there to catch it. How do they do it? Films of competent fielders performing under controlled conditions suggest that they keep their eyes on the ball and run with a speed that maintains zero acceleration for the tangent of the gaze's elevation angle (McLeod and Dienes 1996). Although fielders have a large conscious goal in mind, in operation they coordinate what they see and how they run based on instantaneous local information. At each moment they adjust their running by their sight of the ball, thus letting minute variations be guided by the ball. To achieve this, they rely on their bodies in the baseball field, which physicists forsake in their theoretical representations. In many situations the fielder's embodied mind outperforms theoretical computation, especially when realistic factors cannot be determined precisely.

Physicists represent the ball's motion theoretically. In a similar vein, engineers of symbolic systems try to develop comprehensive theoretical representations for various tasks and encode the representations in the systems. Their method works for simple or closed domains where they can delimit a body of knowledge, but becomes ineffective in perceptual and motor control tasks, where a system must operate in the open and changing world. It is unfeasible to develop comprehensive representations for the world with all its surprises. Even if by brute force engineers produce some approximate models, the results are complicated and cumbersome, requiring much longer processing times than humans or even insects need to accomplish similar tasks. In such cases, it is better to emulate the baseball fielder. This is the approach of dynamicalism.

Consider the task of reaching out and grasping a cup of coffee. In symbolism, engineers develop a theoretical representation of the whole scene, including the cup's shape, the hand's joints, the distance between the cup and the hand, and the movement of the fingers targeted for a firm grip. They then encode the theoretical representation into a computer program. The machine that runs the program operates on abstract representations and lacks the benefit of concrete bodily responses. For it to work, its program must anticipate all possible situations and the exact response to each. The program and its underlying theoretical representation oversees the whole operation from an external point of view, and the enormously complicated supervision requires Olympian capability. In contrast, you reach out and grasp the cup without much thinking. Bound to your body, you see the cup not from outside perspective but from yours, taking into account only the few features relevant to the task. You move your hand to the cup's proximity and let your fingers comply with its shape. You let the feel of the touch halt your finger's movement instead of obeying cumbersome rules such as "if the distance between the cup and the index finger is zero, stop the finger."

From such examples, AI dynamicalism contends that to build robots that can move and find their ways in the real world, we need not develop a theoretical representation of the world. Such cumbersome representations just get into the way. All we have to do is build systems that can participate in the world, adapt to its nooks and crannies, and let it provide the structure and continuity necessary for successful navigation. Of course, to be part of an environment and interact with it, the systems must have genuine physical bodies.

Dynamicalists aim to design robots that can operate in a rather complicated environment. The robots may occupy only a small niche in the environment, but within the niche they should be flexible and robust enough to deal with vagaries and contingencies. This they would accomplish by their general ability to adapt, not by storing abstract representations developed by human engineers. Generally, dynamicalist robots do not receive input in the form of symbols predigested by humans. Instead, they have physical sensors that directly gather raw physical signals from their environment. Like a real cockroach, an artificial cockroach's legs and sensors interact physically with its environment. Thus it can be attuned to the particular physical conditions in each step and use the direct feedback from the environment to drive its next move. It deals only with factors relevant for the particular case, hence its design avoids the intellectual overhead for generalization.

A dynamicalist robot is a system with many parts engaging in several adaptive processes, but it usually lacks the central processor typical in symbol systems. For each adaptive process, the perceptual sensors and motor controls are connected rather directly, and together they extract just enough factors from the environment to operate. To design such input-output circuits, engineers learn from the well-studied neural mechanisms of insects and amphibians, for instance, the mechanisms by which frogs avoid large moving objects and snap their tongues at small moving objects. Various adaptive processes are layered on top of each other with minimal interconnection. A higher layer may intervene with the operation of a lower layer. However, there is no central controller that surveys all the sensory input and orchestrates coherent responses of the system as a whole. Instead, coordination is established by simple interconnections among the parts and constraints imposed by the physical body. For example, Beer and Chiel's (1993) artificial cockroach lumbers through the noise and clutter of the ordinary laboratory. Each of its six legs has its own sensory input and a connectionist network that controls it to swing and raise rhythmically in frequencies that vary with the level of excitation and other inputs. The legs learn to coordinate with each other by simple inhibitory links between neighboring networks.

So far, dynamicalist robots have succeeded in emulating some reflexive behaviors such as crawling and swimming (Taubes 2000). This is an important achievement, because many of our movements are reflexive. However, we can also think and feel. You drive your car with little attention, putting your mind on automatic pilot that dynamicalist robots can emulate. However, you can at any time regain control and deliberately make a turn because you've just decided to go shopping. This mental capacity is totally beyond robots. Dynamicalism has difficulty incorporating manipulable data structures with which symbolism emulates higher cognitive functions such as reasoning. Consequently, the intelligence of its robots is not much above those of insects.

Some dynamicalists argue that higher cognitive capacity will emerge when more simple systems are layered. For almost a decade, Rodney Brooks (1999) and his group have been working on an ambitious project, COG, a robot shaped like a human from the waist up. COG is equipped with pliable spine and neck, gyroscopes for stabilization, flexible arms, touch-sensitive hands, ears capable of locating the source of sound, and eyes capable of turning and focusing on specific objects. Despite its human-like physical attributes, its operating principles and behavioral achievements are not radically different from those of robotic insects. Brooks pursues a bottom-up approach and claims that intelligent behaviors can be achieved by accumulating layers of stupid behaviors. COG has caught the popular imagination and appeared in many popular magazines and television shows. Some philosophers brag that when it is finished in a few years, it will solve all mysteries of consciousness (Dennett 1998). Journalists who are tracking its progress, however, find their enthusiasm dropping fast; it can do very little but seems be nearing the wall of learning, which Brooks laments to be the fate of all artifacts (Horgan 1999). Much of the AI community is skeptical from the start (Kirsch 1991). When asked to comment on Brooks's bottom-up approach, Minsky replied, it is "bottom only" (Stipp 1995).

Situated Cognition and Mind as Motion

To AI workers, an artificial cockroach is a "situated agent" with "situated cognition." In both dynamicalism and the ecological approach, a *situated* system is one that is an interactive part of the environment, full stop. A dynamicalist robot is a system situated in its environment, where *in* has the same sense as a cockroach moves in its ecosystem or the earth moves in the solar system. I differ from them in demanding more. For my engaged-personal level, subjects are not merely situated but *are aware* that they are situated. Thus they are also open to the world in the sense of finding objects intelligible and events informative, caring about them, and forming meaningful beliefs about them. Imagine yourself a tourist taking movies of crowds in a foreign city. Your camera automatically chooses the best focus and exposure, indicating that it is picking up affordance. You and your camera intercept similar optical flows, both change as the result of perception, and both are situated in the environment in the AI sense. However, I insist only you are a mental subject. Your camera is a technological marvel for information processing, information informative to you, not to it. It performs superbly in serving your purposes, not its; it has none. It is merely situated in the environment. You are not only situated in but also open to the world.

Since the behaviors of merely situated agents and other dynamicalist robots are directly driven by interactions with the environment, many people find it natural to treat them simply as dynamical systems. Beer (1995) wrote: "In order to understand the behavior of autonomous agents, we must generalize our organizational notions from computational systems to *dynamical systems*." The dynamical view of cognition traces back to Nobert Wiener's cybernetics in the 1940s, which has an affinity to control theory. A connectionist network, too, is generally a dynamical system subjected to a large number of weak constraints. It evolves and finally settles into an equilibrium state where as many constraints as possible are satisfied, with priority given to the stronger ones. Rumelhart et al. (1986) wrote: "The primary mode of computation in the brain is best understood as a kind of relaxation system in which the computation proceeds by iteratively seeking to satisfy a large number of weak constraints." Dynamicalism differs from the more general dynamic view of cognition in at least two ways. It considers *interactive* dynamical systems, and it uses the mathematics of dynamic system theories, which solve differential or difference equations (Port and van Gelder 1995).

Generally, a dynamicalist robot is a subsystem in a larger dynamical system. Engineers treat the large system as a whole and focus their attention on the continuing interaction between the subsystem and its environment. It is important to note that the subsystem itself consists of several parts. Situated cognition includes coordination of the parts with each other as the subsystem interacts with its environment, for instance, coordination of robotic arms as they manipulate things.

To design situated systems, engineers find the mathematics of modern dynamics handy. Dynamics, including nonlinear and chaotic dynamics, is not only a hot research topic in many areas but has also become popular. In the current euphoria, it is advertised almost as a panacea to difficult problems in all sciences. Soon dynamicalism turned from an engineering technique for building robots to a doctrine in the philosophy of mind that sees mind as motion (Clark 1997).

The mathematics of dynamics is powerful. It has proved itself in many theoretical models for processes such as the separation of odors in olfaction and the development of reflexive walking movements. However, how much has dynamicalism told us about *mind*? All physical systems are dynamical systems. Many are interactive, many are chaotic, and many exhibit emergent properties. The atmosphere is a chaotic dynamical system in which air molecules organize themselves into hurricanes, jet steams, and other weather features. Saturn's ring is a system well suited for interactive dynamical theories. It is a subsystem within a larger system that includes not only Saturn but also the adjacent planets, and its evolution is closely coupled to their gravitational fields. It is made up of many parts, numerous small particles herded by a few large satellites. As the result of interacting with its environment and its internal coordination, the ring has intricate structures. Thus it fits the criteria of situated cognition. It is nevertheless not mental. What are the peculiarities of those systems that we call *mental*? Dynamicalism provides no answer.

Dynamicalist robots lack a sense of self. Dynamicalists focus their attention on the interaction between the robot and its environment so much they sometimes describe mind as the diffused property of the large system containing both the robot and the environment. Robots interact with their environment and change their internal structures because of the interaction, but they do not find their environment meaningful and intelligible. Engineers regard robots as intelligent for behaving appropriately in interaction, but they are mind designers who define the criteria of appropriateness. As William Clancey (1997:180) remarked in his deep analysis, "situated roboticists have rigged environments and imaginatively interpreted robot interactions." Yes, robots can move in the environment by themselves and are more independent than symbolic and connection-ist systems; however, when it comes to mental capacities, they are not autonomous. They still depend on their interpreters for meaning. They are still controlled by mind designers.

Scientists of Mind and Their Subjects

The preceding paragraphs presented two debates. The first is the engi-neers' debate on whether theoretical representations of the tasks, which work for many symbolic expert systems, are efficient in building mobile robots. The second is the philosophers' debate on whether mind is a sym-bolic or a dynamical system. The topics are distinct, but are often con-fused. It is a common mistake in the discussion of mind to confuse the thinking of scientists of mind with the thinking of subjects that the sci-entists investigate.

The engineers' debate expresses how engineers think. As a piece of data in cognitive science it has the same status as physical theories or polit-ical bargaining, which expresses how physicists or politicians think. To eval-uate its contribution to the study of mind, let us distinguish the *science of mind* from the *methodology of efficiency*. A science of mind asks what it is to think and how we are capable of thinking at all. A methodology of effi-ciency takes thinking for granted and looks for ways to think more effec-tively, solve problems more efficiently, or encode our reasoning in artifacts to make them perform difficult tasks to serve our needs. These method-ological questions are addressed ostensibly by AI and quietly by all trades. Education imparts not only knowledge of facts but methods of reason, training students to discern, judge, and think. Scientists, engineers, execu-tives, and other professionals are constantly improving their intellectual techniques for their jobs. The methodology of efficiency is practically para-mount, but it is only marginal to the scientific understanding of mind, as it asks only how to think better, not how we are able to think in the first place. Because it presupposes the basic capacity to think, it has jumped over the central problems of the science of mind.

Whenever we talk, understand each other, build tools, or probe the unknown, we engage in deliberate mental activities. Often we use symbols and representations, including natural, mathematical, and computer languages. Scientists and engineers are not exceptional. Theories and engineering designs embody our systematic and refined thoughts about the world. They contain two typical aspects. The first is the *objective contents* ascribed to the objects the theories are about. Second, theories contain *instrumental elements* that do not describe the objects at issue but are intellectual tools by which we handle objective contents. An example of objective content is the relative motion of planets; examples of instrumental elements are various coordinate systems physicists choose to represent planetary motion.

Instrumental elements in scientific theories engender relatively little confusion when the theories are about inanimate things with no mental properties. Scientists treat them as theoretical elements and claim them to be their own thinking. Physicists use the symbol F to represent physical forces, knowing that they, not the forces, are the ones who use the representation. When theories are about mind and mental systems, however, serious confusion can occur. Now scientists are thinking about potential thinkers, theorizing about potential theoreticians, and using symbols to represent potential representation users. Therefore they must be triply careful to make clear to whom the mental concepts in their theories refer. Who use representations, who hypothesize, who compute, who think?—scientists or the entities they investigate; engineers or the computers that they build? Much confusion arises from carelessly mixing up what scientists think with the subjects they investigate think, or attributing the thinking of engineers to the computers or robots that they build.

To build thinking machines is an ambitious engineering goal, but it is a difficult goal. Wishful thinking sometimes misguides AI engineers to project their own purposes and understanding into their products. Knowing this danger, most computer scientists make deliberate efforts to distinguish their own thinking from computers or computer programs. Terry Winograd explained to reporters: "I claim that *I* have insights, but I do not claim that these insights are embodied in the programs" (Baumgartner and Payr 1995:286). Harold Abelson and Gerald Sussman (1996:xvii) ask students of their introductory text in computer science to separate three foci: the human mind, computer programs, and the computer. They emphasize that computer science embodies a powerful method for humans to think about complex phenomena: "A computer language is not just a way of getting a computer to perform operations but rather it is a novel formal medium for expressing ideas about methodology."

Philip Agre (1997) and William Clancey (1997) patiently explained why it is paramount to distinguish between what AI engineers think and what their products think; between an ethnography of AI research and an account of AI products.

Computer programmers customarily give meaningful names to their programs, data structures, or subroutines that are fragments of a program. The practice is usually innocuous; meaningful names are easy to remember and make the programs more intelligible to programmers. Troubles come when some people attribute the meanings of the names to the programs as their properties, for instance, assume that a program named UNDERSTAND actually understands, as if a good name can make up for what a program lacks. Such practice has drawn criticism from within the AI community. Drew McDermott (1976) criticized his colleagues for "wishful mnemonics," stating that those who engage in the practice "may mislead a lot of people, most prominently himself." Citing examples from AI writing, Winograd (1990) showed how they "slipped from a technically feasible but limited notion of agents as subroutines, to an impressionistic description of a society of *homunculi*, conversing with each other in ordinary language."

Unfortunately, AI's soul searching has made no impression on philosophers who promote AI products as paradigms of mental beings. What McDermott castigated as "sloppy thinking" and Winograd as "sleight of hand" has been turned into the basis of the philosophical doctrine of homuncular functionalism. What homuncular functionalists claim as support is none other than the careless talk that computers "understand English" and "recognize questions." This position, which deliberately confuses the thinking of scientists or engineers with the thinking of their objects, has created much muddle in the philosophy of mind.[8]

Cognitive Modeling and Pure Design in AI

The AI ideology has so dominated cognitive science that authors of a textbook found it necessary to emphasize: "The term *computational* should not be taken to mean that artificial intelligence ought to be the central or dominant discipline in cognitive science rather than an equal partner" (Stillings et al. 1995). Undoubtedly AI contributed many techniques and computational tools that prove invaluable in studying mind. Over the years, however, the nature of AI changed. In many areas, including game playing and theorem proving, it pursued two distinct approaches that researchers call *cognitive modeling* and *pure design*. Cognitive modeling tries to simulate the human ways of performing a given task. Pure design aims for systems that perform the task in whatever way is most efficient. A common strategy in pure design is massive search, which takes full advantage of the computer's ability to perform millions of computations in split seconds to search through all possibilities to find the solution.

Given the difference between humans and computers, it comes as no surprise that the pure design approach produces better results. Consequently, the number of papers on cognitive modeling dropped steadily and vanished in the annual conferences of the American Association of Artificial Intelligence. This is the case with chess. Early versions of CHESS adopted the cognitive modeling approach that imitated the strategies of human players. Their results were mediocre. Then in 1973, CHESS 3.0 switched to pure design and adopted the brute force search method. Its rating jumped. Today's top chess machines, including DEEP BLUE, rely on custom-designed chips and pruning rules to search through billions of positions to find the best move. Human players also search, but to a much lesser extent. They rely on their extensive knowledge of the game and ability to recognize patterns and reason intuitively to form strategies. Thus Campbell and Tan, who designed DEEP BLUE, denied that it thinks or can shed light on how human chess players think. Instead, they insisted that its performance has no bearing on the question of whether computers can think (Horgan 1999:207).

With the trend toward pure design, AI becomes more and more pure engineering with less and less relevance to understanding the human mind. Simon, a founder of AI, explains it best: "Most of us now make a fairly consistent distinction between Artificial Intelligence and cognitive science, in terms of the purpose of the research and the way the research is tested. Either the purpose is to make computers do intelligent things—that is Artificial Intelligence. Or else one might be interested in how human beings think, and one would use the computer as a model of human thinking, which is to be tested against real instances of human thinking" (Baumgartner and Payr 1995:242). Today's AI is mostly the methodology of efficiency, whereas cognitive science aims at the basic structure of mind.

Natural Science of Mind versus Mind Engineering

Cognitive science includes disciplines from science, humanities, and engineering. Inquiries in all disciplines are creative human activities, but their major purposes are different. Science attempts to understand phenomena as they naturally are. Scientists try to discover principles for phenomena that exist independent of their purposes, desires, and investigations. Engineers aim to design and build artifacts that serve preconceived human purposes by performing specified functions. Thus they want to make sure that the artifacts conform to their purposes, behave according to their requirements, and are under their control. Whereas social science studies society and tries to understand it as it is, social engineering tries to redesign society according to certain preconceived ideologies and reshape it to fit preconceived policies. Social history shows that attempts to engineer without proper understanding can only lead to disaster.

As Simon's distinction between AI and cognitive science indicates, most cognitive scientists adopt the natural scientific approach to the study of mind that respects our natural mental abilities. Fodor, for instance, maintains that cognitive science aims to understand thought and is distinct from attempts to build intelligent machines, "which is an engineering problem and has no intrinsic scientific interest as such" (Baumgartner and Payr 1995:86)

Mind engineering too has its advocates. Dennett (1987:29) emphasized that mind is a "*designed* object," disparaged the natural scientific approach as either "Crystal" or "Chaos," and extolled the "control power" of AI engineering as the only proper approach to mind. These claims bolster ideologies that put computers, robots, and other artifacts above humans in matters concerning mind.

Designed objects are not merely objects that exhibit designs. We can loosely call exquisite structures or features serving certain functions "designs," such as the designs of snowflakes or eyes. In this sense, it is legitimate to say that an object with intricate design has no designer and no one who made it with the purpose of performing certain tasks. To say a designed object has no designer, however, is doublespeak. Designers have control over what they design, and mind designers are not exceptional. Engineers are somewhat like gods to the artifacts they design, a position natural scientists never have to their topics. Therefore Dennett's instrumental behaviorism logically associates the control power of AI and mind as a designed object.

Instrumental behaviorism is a philosophy of mind that promotes mind engineering. It maintains that people do *not* believe and desire. Our ordinary concepts of believing and desiring are false fictions whose *only* function is for mind designers to predict behaviors, regardless of whether or not they are behaviors of thermostats, chess machines, or people. Notice the implied godlike superiority of mind designers. Prediction is belief. To predict, mind designers must be able to believe, an ability that instrumental behaviorism explicitly denies to ordinary people, who belong to the same category as thermostats. Furthermore, because beliefs and desires are fictitious, mind designers can attribute any belief or desire to any entity, as long as they think that it is what the entity ought to believe rationally under the circumstance, and that it helps them to predict the entity's behaviors.[9] Without using the name of instrumental behaviorism, this philosophy of mind has been put into practice. The twentieth century has seen many lives lost and families destroyed when totalitarian governments ascribed fictitious "corruptive" beliefs or "counterrevolutionary" desires to people, insisting that these were what the people ought to have, based on their blood, history, or social class.

Our general conception and treatment of people are partly cultural, partly sociopolitical, partly biological, and partly objective. They depend heavily on our general conception of mind, because we consider mental properties to be our defining characteristics. If we regard as crucial to mental properties the capacity to be aware of one's own experience, to understand one's situation, care about the meaning of one's life, feel sorrow and happiness, think freely and rationally, choose one's goals, and act intentionally, then we would agree that a person should be treated only as an end in itself and never as a means. On this basis we acknowledge certain basic rights of other people, such as their rights to life, liberty, and the pursuit of happiness. In contrast, we would be tempted to treat people as mere instruments if we regarded mind as nothing but the capacity to perform assigned tasks efficiently, consciousness as a property shared by hand calculators, and intentionality as one shared by thermostats. If people and things are separated only by the degree of behavioral intelligence, it is reasonable to consider "smart" things ahead of "stupid" people. If mind is nothing but computation, there is reason to treat people as we treat computers, like computer designers who do their best to make consumers get rid of smart computers as quickly as possible so that they will buy ever smarter ones.

Newell (1990:85) rightly observed: "Computers are, in effect, *kept systems*." Other artifacts, be they connectionist networks or dynamicalist robots, are similarly kept systems, because their functions and significance

depend on their designers and users. Artifacts are designed to be controlled, to serve the whims of their masters. A kept mind is a closed mind;
once opened to the world, mind would balk at being kept. Instrumental
behaviorism and other philosophies that pattern human beings after artifacts and kept systems are strongly dehumanizing. They dismiss autonomy
and the freedom of action as myths; condemn respect for living organisms
as vitalism; attribute fictitious thoughts for the expediency of control;
regard human beings not as machines of flesh and blood but as machines
of meat, as in meat grinder, which is what the trenches of the First World
War are called. Dennett (1998:286) is frank about it: "There is something
about the prospect of an engineering approach to the mind that is deeply
repugnant to a certain sort of humanist."[10]

Reverse Engineering and Evolutionary Psychology

Antihumanist philosophies have spread the control power of engineering
to many other areas. Some extreme doctrines in evolutionary psychology
are cases in point. Creationists believe that our mind was created by God.
Scientists usually believe that many general mental structures evolved in
millions of years. Evolution and common descent are fruitful assumptions
in the science of mind. Scientists presuppose them when they compare
the behaviors of different species of animals and use nonhuman animal
models to study cognition. However, one must be careful about evolutionary arguments, for the market has dangerous ideas that turn evolution
biology into another form of creationism, retroactive creationism under
the control not of God but of reverse engineers.

Evolution is simply change. Thus it is more general than evolution
by natural selection, which specifies a particular mechanism of change.
If an organismic trait or behavioral process evolved by natural selection,
it can be said to be an adaptation that is fittest for survival in a specific
environment. As an evolutionary mechanism, however, natural selection
has many competitors: migration, genetic drift, genetic linkage, self-
organization, developmental constraint, and historical accident, to name a
few. It is usually extremely difficult to determine which mechanism was
responsible for the evolution of a specific trait. To decide scientifically
whether a trait is an adaptation requires laborious research in paleontol-
ogy, geology, population genetics, comparative genetics, and comparative
morphology. Often the best of efforts fails to yield the data required for
a decision. For evolutionary scientists have a deadly enemy, time, that
destroys much data required for deciding whether a trait is an adaptation.

It is especially difficult to decide whether "soft traits" such as social behaviors are selected because they leave scant fossil records. Cognition, intelligence, and mental abilities fare even worse. Here another source of evolutionary data, comparative study of existent species, only trickles. The human species has very few relatives. The two closest, the chimpanzee and gorilla, differ from us precisely where mental abilities are concerned. Evolutionary biologist Richard Lewontin (1998) assessed the situation soberly: "Despite the existence of a vast and highly developed mathematical theory of evolutionary processes in general, despite the abundance of knowledge about living and fossil primates, despite the intimate knowledge we have of our own species' physiology, morphology, psychology, and social organization, we know essentially nothing about the evolution of our cognitive capabilities, and there is a strong possibility that we will never know much about it."

Take language, for example. We noncreationists believe it evolved, but how, we do not know. Gathering evidence from comparative neural organization, development, and many other areas, Terrance Deacon (1997) argued cogently that it is unlikely that natural selection can account for the evolution of our language faculty. To assert, as Chomsky and Fodor do, that our language faculty is innate but refuse to spin adaptation stories for how it has evolved is not a surrender to mysticism. It is simply intellectual honesty.

Not everyone is so cautious. Sociobiology, the controversial theory asserting the optimality of existing social behaviors on the assumption that they are naturally selected in biological evolution, transformed into evolutionary psychology during the past fifteen years. Several philosophers and cognitive scientists cite natural selection to explain intentionality, morality, mental representation, and all kinds of psychological traits. Combining natural selection with AI, Dennett (1995) treats Mother Nature as a design engineer whose handiworks are to be deciphered by reverse engineering.

The notion of reverse engineering originated in the analysis of computer hardware and is now mostly used for software. Engineers often want to decipher the specific design principles of a finished product without benefit of its original drawings, as Soviet engineers tried to discover the principles of an American computer obtained by the KGB. The power of reverse engineering has been much hyped. In her book detailing the history, meanings, and methods of reverse engineering, Kathryn Ingle emphasized that it is far from a panacea; it is a specific method for solving some system-specific problems. She wrote (1994:4) that after researching all relevant areas: "I felt that I had read as much 'technobabble' as I could stand." I wonder what she would feel to read that reverse engineering is "the right way to do cognitive science" or "biology is not just like engineering, it *is* engineering. . . . the task of reverse engineering in biology is an exercise in figuring out 'what Mother Nature had in Mind'" (Dennett 1998:254; 1995:185). Why should mind and organic evolution be studied not by natural scientific methods but by reverse engineering? What has one presupposed in advocating the reverse engineering approach for cognition and evolution?

Reverse engineers and natural scientists both assume that some regularities can be found in the phenomena that they study, and both try to discover general principles by examining specimens. Their presuppositions and approaches, however, are different. Natural scientists proceed without assuming that the regularities they seek are designed to serve some rational purposes. Reverse engineers proceed on the knowledge that theirs are. The purpose and general design principles of "forward engineering," in which reverse engineers are versed, help tremendously in their backward reasoning. The claim that cognitive science or evolutionary biology is reverse engineering has strong metaphysical implications. It implies that Mother Nature had some forward engineering principle, some designing rationality in the creation of natural minds and organisms. There is no evidence for the alleged principle.

Given the dearth of evidence, most talks about how particular traits are "designed" by natural selection are what paleontologist Stephen Jay Gould called "just-so stories," groundless speculations decorated with the technobabble of reverse engineering. They degrade evolutionary science into retroactive creationism, which merely replaces the creationist's God by Mother Nature. Like God, Mother Nature is reticent and needs mouthpieces. Retroactive creationists style themselves as her high priests and make up stories about what she had in mind in designing this or that trait. Evolutionary biologist Allen Orr (1996) aptly concluded his review of Dennett's book promoting evolutionary design by quoting Friedrich Nietzsche (1886:9): "[W]hile you pretend rapturously to read the canon of your law in nature, you want something opposite, you strange actors and self-deceivers! Your pride wants to impose your morality, your ideal on nature—even on nature—and incorporate them in her; you demand that she should be nature 'according to the Stoa,' and you would like all existence to exist only after your own image—as an immense eternal glorification and generalization of Stoicism." Replace the Stoa with evolutionary reverse engineers and Stoicism with retroactive creationism, and you get the picture. Evolutionary reverse engineers are ambitious mind designers who try to extend their control power everywhere.

6 Mind Engaged in and Open to the World

Cartesianism has been under attack for centuries. Its notion of the closed mind controlled by mind designers persists partly because it is the easiest mental model. It can dominate cognitive science also because here artifacts—computers, connectionist networks, dynamical systems—become the paradigms of mind, so that computation displaces meaning and understanding. Artificial mind can do without body or world because it is a kept system. Its flesh and blood human designers and users, working in the physical and social world, take care of meanings.

Whenever people are the paradigms of mental beings, embodiment and engagement become essential, although their theoretical representations pose great difficulty. Embodiment and engagement are different issues, as an embodied mind is not necessarily incompatible with solipsism. Philosopher Charles Taylor (1985) provided a clear analysis of *engaged agents*, emphasizing their autonomy, understanding, and concern with significance. Therefore engagement is different from AI's situated cognition with its emphasis on interactive behaviors evaluated by mind designers.

Decades before the cognitive revolution, continental phenomenologists developed sophisticated analyses of the embodied and engaged human existence. Many psychologists also emphasized environmental influences. Now, discontent is noticeable within cognitive science, as some scientists contend that computationalism and behaviorism alike have no place in the truly mental. More and more, embodiment and engagement become key words in the literature (Kirshner and Whitson 1997; Hurley 1998). The literature is diverse and multicultural. Researchers with different agendas opt for different forms of embodiment and engagement. Here I review several approaches. They are far from exhaustive. For instance, they leave out sociologists and socially oriented philosophers, who have always rejected solipsism. As I adopt many concepts that they variously developed, I also take this opportunity to clarify the meanings of the concepts as I use them in this book.

Developmental Theories

Several scientists with biological orientations maintain that an organism's mental abilities depend on their history of acquisition. This history is embodied because organisms must cope physically in their living environments in both growth and organic evolution. Among these theories is the "genetic epistemology" of developmental psychologist Jean Piaget.

Drawing on his extensive empirical work with infants and children, Piaget proposed that newborns come equipped with sensorimotor organs and limbs but no cognitive ability. They have the notion neither of objects nor of self; they fuse their environment with their own motions and are unable to conceive a world distinct from and independent of themselves. "It is precisely when the subject is most self-centered that he knows himself the least, and it is to the extent that he discovers himself that he places himself in the universe and constructs it by virtue of that fact." The process of self-discovery occurs as infantile subjects continually interact with their environment through perception and action. They gradually develop concepts, assimilate the environment to the most suitable ones, and accommodate the concepts to events and effects of their actions. Through several stages of sensorimotor development in the first two years of life babies construct increasingly elaborate notions of objects, causes, space, and time; in short, notions of a permanent world existing independent of their perception and action. Simultaneously, as they discover the external world, they discover themselves as distinct from other objects. "Acquiring possession of the object as such is on a par with the acquisition of self-perception," Piaget (1954:x) wrote. "This organization of reality occurs, as we shall see, to the extent that the self is freed from itself by finding itself and so assigns itself a place as a thing among things, an event among events."

Piaget contributed to not only psychology but philosophy. His influence peaked in the 1970s but remains strong among developmental psychologists, although some of his doctrines have been challenged. Recent experiments showed that infants a few months old already have some appreciation of rigidity and continuity of motion. They are a long way from grasping the full concepts of objects, but by noticing some differences, they are not as cognitively impoverished as Piaget described. Despite disagreement regarding the age when infants form satisfactory concepts of self and object and the possible contribution of innate mental structures, two of Piaget's points are widely accepted. For infants to acquire a sense of self, they must be able to differentiate themselves clearly from their environment and recognize their independence. And to develop the mental differentiation, sensorimotor exercises are indispensable. Development occurs as the babies open themselves to the world (Meltzoff and Moore 1995; Bertenthal 1996).

Existential Phenomenology

Phenomenology was founded by Edmund Husserl at the beginning of the twentieth century. Developed and modified by many philosophers, it flourished for several decades and is still influential in continental Europe. Husserl's (1913) phenomenology has a strong idealistic strand. To study the fundamental structures of mind and intentionality, he maintained, we must abandon the cultural world permeated with scientific notions and return to examine the *lived world*, the world of immediate experiences. By systematically comparing variations of experiences, we can discard arbitrary changes and extract invariant features as the objects that we experience. This much most people agree.

Husserl also prescribed a phenomenological reduction that abandons our "natural attitude" and adopts the equivalent of what cognitive scientists call methodological solipsism (see section 4). In our natural attitude, our perception and thinking are mostly directed at things in the world. Phenomenological reduction "brackets" the things and the world so that its attention can focus on pure mental acts and analyze their structures. Husserl found consciousness where cognitive scientists find computation. Nevertheless, their minds share the fate of being deprived of the world. It is no surprise that Husserl's best students refused to agree.

Existential phenomenologists, notably Martin Heidegger (1926) and Maurice Merleau-Ponty (1945), adopted many of Husserl's ideas but rejected his phenomenological reduction. Contrary to Husserl, who still engaged in Cartesian meditation, Heidegger abolished the whole Cartesian scheme with its worldless subject inside and unintelligible things outside. He scorned the notion of a mind inside the "cabinet of consciousness" and refused even to talk about consciousness, which he took to be something hiding inside.

When Kant, critical of the Cartesian framework but not totally extricated from it, presented a proof for the existence of the external world as a refutation of idealism, he wrote (1781:34): "It still remains a scandal to philosophy and to human reason in general . . . that the existence of things outside us must be accepted merely on *faith*, and that if anyone thinks good to doubt their existence, we are unable to counter his doubts by any satisfactory proof." Heidegger (1926:205) retorted: "The 'scandal of philosophy' is not that this proof has yet to be given, but that *such proofs are expected and attempted again and again.*"

Those who gladly accept Dr. Johnson's kicking a stone as a satisfactory refutation of idealism would agree with Heidegger. Why would anyone in his right mind need philosophical proofs to believe that external things exist? Being open to the world is the essential and most obvious characteristic of our mentality. It is impossible to characterize mental properties adequately without invoking the world with which our mind is inextricably concerned. This is Heidegger's point.

The scandal of philosophy is far from over, as we saw in the representation theory of mind and the debate between internalism and externalism (see section 4). The big problem in cognitive science is the meaning of representation in mental representations, which signify the relation between closed mind and the world. Kant's proof for the existence of the external world is a heroic attempt to answer a similar question. The question persists, as do efforts to answer it. Heidegger argued that the scandal lies in the question itself; it is precisely the formulation of the question in such ways that makes it insolvable. The two-part formulation assumes that mind can exist as a closed entity on its own; that it can think meaningfully without regard for things outside; that only as a second thought does it worry about the existence of things. Under this assumption, philosophers first posit mind and universe as two entities independent of each other and ask how they can be related. It is perhaps the most insidious form of dualism. What it puts asunder, no power can unite. Heidegger held that this dualist picture, which is the source of skepticism and solipsism, grossly distorts our being, *Dasein* (being-there), as Dasein is radically and essentially being-in-the-world. Merleau-Ponty (1945:xi) illustrated: "There is no inner man, man is in the world, and only in the world does he know himself." Mind does not and cannot exist without its world, for the intelligibility of the world *is* its essential feature. Thus it requires neither proof of nor bridge to the outer world because it has no inner-outer dichotomy to start with.

Human being is essentially being-in-the-world, which is different from situated cognition discussed in the preceding section. The *in* in being-in-the-world is not merely the *in* as a tree grows in its ecosystem, and the world is not merely an environment as the warm ocean was the environment for the first life on Earth. Any thing, animate or not, has its environment with which it interacts causally. Human beings too have their environment in this sense, but their world goes beyond it. Our world is not merely a blind causal force but is intelligible and meaningful to us. Things in it *exist* in the original Greek sense, which means "to stand out from." Because things are significant and useful for us, our *being-in* the world is not merely physical occupancy but also care, involvement, and understanding with certain states of mind. Only because we are *in* the universe in this peculiar sense can we turn the blind *environment* into a meaningful *world* that we can choose to trash or preserve. Heidegger set himself the task of analyzing the meaning of our being-in-the-world.

The primary meaning of our being, he argued, resides not in theoretical and scientific thinking but in our everyday handing of things and being with other people. Imagine yourself driving a car, negotiating the sharp turns, enjoying the scenery, listening to music on the radio, musing about the friend you are going to visit. The car handles so well you are almost oblivious of it; it is so integrated into your activity it has become a part of you, so to speak. All things—your friend, the car, the music, the road, the scenery—are interrelated and constitute your world with its primary meaning, a living meaning. Everything is significant and contributes to your purposive activity, but the significance is tacit and not explicitly articulated. The car is something you maneuver to keep on the road that leads to your friend. The car, the road, and your friend are handy. They relate to each other, and together they constitute the world of primary significance.

If the car breaks down, however, it ceases to be *handy equipment* and becomes a mere *thing present* to you[11]. Then you switch to the theoretical attitude and try to figure out what is wrong with the thing and what to do with it. In doing so, your world acquires a secondary significance. According to Heidegger, the theoretical attitude is a common mode of being human, albeit a secondary and derived mode. When you switch to the theoretical attitude, you abstract from many cares and concerns that you are normally involved in, focus your attention on a few things, and make them stand out by themselves as things in space and time. You trade the richness of wider experience for the clear and refined vision of a few objects. The world to which your mind is open is thereby narrowed and impoverished, but it is not closed off. It is still meaningful to you. You still stand firmly in the world, your judgment is still objective or about objects, your understanding is still influenced by your background knowledge and cultural heritage, although the influence is correspondingly weakened by your abstraction from other concerns and your striving for intersubjective agreement. In this sense, theoretical reason is a general aspect of mind whose functions pervade our daily activity: perceiving, cognizing, understanding, and thinking. We exercise our theoretical reason whenever we devise a tool, explain an event, classify an object, or report a perceptual experience as simple as "there's a chair in the corner."

Usually, the functions of theoretical reason are small in scope and so embedded in our daily routines they are hardly noticeable. When something goes wrong to disrupt a smooth routine, however, they come to the fore to deal with the problem. Science refines, develops, systematizes, and applies in large scale this theoretical attitude that everyone is capable of on smaller scales. It sees a simplified world more clearly from a vantage point, not an alien world from God's position.

Illiterate street vendors can make change correctly without knowing formal arithmetic. This is an example of know-how. Heidegger maintained that such know-how and practice, by which we deal with things concernfully in our everyday life, constitute the primary intelligibility of our being-in-the-world. One can make this tacit intelligibility more explicit by interpretation and articulate it by verbalization, such as specifically recognizing the thing one is using to be a hammer or describing it in words. We achieve supreme explicitness in scientific reasoning. However, no matter how far scientific articulation is developed, it can never exhaust all the primary significance of our everyday world. It always takes for granted something that is tacitly understood in the primary intelligibility of the world that continues to function as the indispensable background to all our scientific knowledge.

I basically agree with Heidegger; my model of mind as the intelligibility of objects follows from his meaning of beings. Heidegger's phenomenological analysis, although profound, is famous for its obscurity. His word-twisting terminology alone would alienate most English readers. Therefore I critically borrow only major ideas from him. For explication I keep to the theoretical approach familiar to scientists and illustrate mental phenomena in the general framework of complexity theories.

Phenomenology made an impact on cognitive science when Hubert Dreyfus (1972) used it to launch a scathing criticism of AI. This earned him the eternal wrath of much of the AI community, but it produced some positive results. Some AI researchers, such as Winograd and Flores (1986), examined their professional practice from an existential phenomenological viewpoint. Reading their book, Clancey (1994) said he was struck by the idea that "I realized that I don't have any patterns, associations, or preferences stored in my mind." When recently AI turn to dynamical systems and situated cognition, some engineers found themselves repeating what they hated Dreyfus for saying, even when they had little sympathy with phenomenology. In explaining his approach of "intelligence without representation," Brooks (1999:97) wrote: "In some circles much credence is given to Heidegger as one who understood the dynamics of existence. Our approach has certain similarities to work inspired by this German philosopher (e.g. [1]), but our work was not so inspired. It is based purely on engineering consideration." It is encouraging that phenomenology and the engineering of intelligent robots, whose concerns and styles of reasoning cannot be more different from each other, converge on a similar conclusion. The Cartesian Trojan horse with its intermediary mental representations is untenable. Outside AI, other cognitive scientists are trying to bring phenomenology to bear on their respective areas of investigation (Petitot et al. 1999).

Mind's Eastern Embodiment

Heidegger's analysis addressed all general aspects of Dasein. Merleau-Ponty's argument for the primacy of perception offered a detailed phenomenological analysis of how the structures of perception depend on our body and the perceived world. As concrete as their descriptions of living experiences are, they are theoretical and involve general concepts such as spatiality and sexuality. They are philosophical theories whose topics are pragmatic and life experiences. This is a fatal flaw, according to Francisco Varela, Evan Thompson, and Eleanor Rosch.

Varela et al. (1991) insisted that phenomenology breaks down because Husserl, Heidegger, and Meleau-Ponty reflected on pragmatic matters theoretically, and the theories themselves lacked a pragmatic dimension. Theoretical reason cannot overcome the rift between science and experience. Varela and company asked: "But if we turn away from reason, if reason is no longer taken as the method for knowing the mind, what can be used instead?" They found nothing useful in Western philosophy and science. Consequently they turned to the East, to the mindfulness meditation of Madhyamika Buddhism.

Mindfulness meditation is a practice in which the meditator's mind comes into the presence of itself so that it gains insight into its own nature and functioning. According to Buddhism, one finds no self in meditation but only five aggregates: forms, feelings, perceptions, dispositions, and consciousness. This selfless state of being is the technical meaning of *mindfulness*. Meditators find that our ordinary state, in which we pursue our selfish goals, are not mindful. Varela et al. (1991) identified human experience and embodiment with mindfulness, as the meditation brings one's mind and body together. Western theoretical reflection, including phenomenology, is disembodied, because it is not mindful and leaves out the presence of mind itself.

I wholeheartedly support the effort to expand the intellectual horizon beyond Western philosophy and thinking, and I hope that meditation can become a useful method in cognitive science. However, I am skeptical that the peculiar sense of embodiment attained in mindfulness meditation is compatible with openness to the world. As Varela and Jonathan Shear (1999) point out, mediation is similar to Husserl's phenomenological reduction and the introspective method used in early experimental psychology and abandoned later. All three strive to gain "the view from within." All three have problems relating to the world.

Varela, Thompson, and Rosch rightly emphasized the importance of practice, but they were too restrictive in their range of practices. Meditation is a practice. So are all our mundane activities, from taking a bath to writing computer programs. They are not as conspicuous as meditation because they are not as esoteric, but their mundane nature makes them more, not less, illuminating about mind. Mindfulness is a special state in which one achieves tranquility by detaching oneself from selfish yearnings and the buzzing events in the world. It may be superior to ordinary mental states where one is confounded and exhausted by chasing after desires and happenings. Even so, it cannot displace everyday mentality as the basic topic for the science of mind, because everyday mentality is what most of us *are* most of the time. Most activities of meditators, and all activities of nonmeditators, are not mindful. Our everyday state of being does not have to be the best. Heidegger called it fallen and inauthentic, but nevertheless maintained that it is the most important for understanding mind. I agree. At issue is scientific investigation of natural mental states, not value legislation or conversion of people. Therefore I stick to a more ordinary sense of embodiment, in which all our mundane mental activities, unmindful as they are, are embodied. It is the embodiment that Merleau-Ponty described most concretely.

Explanations and Experiences of Mind

Unlike Varela, Thompson, and Rosch, I refuse to turn away from reason and theorizing. Reasoning is both an essential mental ability that an adequate science of mind must account for and an indispensable process for the practice of scientific research. For neither is it sufficient; there is much more to mind than rationality, and science also needs circumspection and intuitive judgment. However, it is necessary for both, including gaining knowledge about mind.

I think that Varela et al.'s abandonment of reason is based on a confusion between the practice of theorizing and the topic of theories, between experiences and explanations of mind. The five aggregates are theoretical descriptions of what meditators experience in practice. Their general status is not different from theoretical descriptions of structures of our ordinary experiences offered by phenomenologists.

Human abstract thinking or theorizing is a fully embodied practice, complete with the sense of frustration, feeling of headache, and other factors that Heidegger called "mood." These pragmatic factors are usually not included in topics that scientists or philosophers think about, but this does not imply that the topics are necessarily disembodied. Suppose you are writing a paper on backache and your back aches while you work. It suffices that your paper includes adequate descriptions of the general causes or characteristics of backache; descriptions of your own discomfort while producing the paper would be beside the point. Heidegger gave extended descriptions of the embodied pragmatics of theoretical thinking. Varela and company wrongly dismissed it as disembodied and merely theoretical.

There is a difference between *existential knowledge* and *theoretical knowledge* of mental states. Consider philosopher Frank Jackson's (1982) story about Mary who is confined to a black and white room and sees the world only through a black and white television. Being a brilliant scientist, Mary has learned everything there is to know about color vision, from light to reflectance spectra to retinal excitation to the working of the visual cortex. Now suppose she is released from the room and sees the colorful world for the first time in her life. Does she learn anything new? Jackson answered obviously yes. Behavioral and eliminativist philosophers answer obviously no. They are talking about two kinds of knowledge. Mary does not acquire any more theoretical knowledge by her visual experience. If her theoretical knowledge is adequate, she should have known all along, by measuring the light in her room, that she was not seeing color. Nevertheless, she does gain existential knowledge of color vision. I think more than a few people would gladly trade the knowledge on paper for the knowledge in life. Mary's existential knowledge will make her a better painter and a better scientist of vision, because science is theoretical but not merely theoretical.

By the very conscious nature of mind, a person in a mental state is spontaneously aware of its contents. The awareness can be regarded as a kind of knowledge, as people say they know they are in pain or they know their own minds. This is existential knowledge of mental states that we acquire by being in the states and possess as subjects of experiences. Embodied, immediate, prevalent, intelligible, but often poorly articulated, existential knowledge is distinct from the theoretical knowledge in which mental states occur as objects. It is rather data for theoretical explanations of mind. Mindfulness meditators gain existential knowledge for a special kind of experience by disciplining their states of mind. Meditation provides data in addition to our ordinary experiences but cannot supplant them.

I understand *theoretical* in the modest sense of the theoretical attitude described by Heidegger. Much if not all of epistemology is concerned with theoretical knowledge, also known as objective knowledge, as it is about the objects that we know through perception and inference. Science develops the theoretical attitude and produces highly systematic theoretical knowledge. Scientists exercise their refined theoretical reason, partially detach themselves from most value judgments, inspect systematically certain classes of phenomena, carefully assess information gathered in perception and experiment, and think in highly conceptualized and symbolized forms. Theorizing is a mental practice. In investigating mind, however, scientists regard mental beings and states as objects, thus they seldom if at all consider explicitly the existential knowledge that they themselves are immediately conscious of as theorizing subjects. Such considerations of themselves would be at best superfluous in a scientific theory. Suffice that a theory of mind describes mental beings capable of existential knowledge generally.

Following custom, by *knowledge* of mind without qualification I refer to theoretical knowledge. Therefore *to know about* a mental state is different from *to be in* that mental state. Theoretical knowing is a peculiar mental state that is distinct from the mental state that happens to be the object of theoretical knowledge. Having theoretical knowledge about a mental state does not imply that we are in that mental state or that we can transport ourselves into it. One can learn the causes and symptoms of pain without ever being in pain. The science of mind provides general knowledge about mental states, but it does not put us into the states to experience their phenomenal fullness.

To be in a certain mental state is always a concrete and particular event. A state of a complex being typically has a staggering number of facets, all of which are relevant to its particularity. When I am in a particular mental state, I experience the full richness of its facets, although perhaps hazily. The concrete details constitute the *phenomenal consciousness* of my state of being. Phenomenal consciousness has low degree of conceptualization, because conceptualization usually abstracts from particularity and fullness of details. Therefore phenomenal consciousness is inarticulate and difficult to communicate. Imagine yourself standing at the rim of the Grand Canyon and seeing the colorful landscape. Now try to describe your phenomenal visual experience. Even if you are good with words you will find your account falling short of your experience. Verbal description is perhaps the least abstract operation of theoretical reason. More particular details will be discarded when science seeks general principles in higher abstraction.

You are in a different mental state when you are enjoying the sight of the Grand Canyon than when you are wracking your brain to find the words for it. Thinking is a specific mental process complete with its own phenomenal feelings such as frustration. In communicating our thoughts linguistically, we abstract from most aspects of our phenomenal consciousness and articulate only certain salient aspects in the propositional form. Thus the propositional content, although important as knowledge, does not exhaust all the features of a mental state.

I agree with Varela et al. that theoretical knowledge invariably leaves out many details of phenomenal consciousness. Theoretical representations of complex phenomena invariably abstract, generalize, universalize, idealize, and approximate. In extracting the salient regularities of wide classes of complex states, representing them in words and symbols, and seeking general principles, we blur or discard many particular details, regarding them as irrelevant to theoretical understanding. When we apply

generalizing and idealizing theoretical reason to our own states of being, the difference between concrete and abstract, between particular and
general, becomes glaring.

Theoretical reason is much broader and more versatile than logical
inference because it is inalienable from objective experience, whereas logic
abstracts further from the relation to the physical world. Nevertheless, it
is only one mode of our mental capacity. Therefore we must be realistic
about what science using theoretical reason can tell us about mind with
its great variety of modes. With its penchant for abstraction and its emphasis on general principles, science would probably never capture the full
richness of particular living experiences. In this respect it may be inferior
to the arts and literature. Despite the limitation, however, I am more san-
guine about theoretical reason than Varela et al. I think that to a certain
degree of abstraction science can give embodied activities a proper place
in its theoretical representations and explanations, even if it cannot fill in
all their details.

A Rigid Notion of Embodiment

Adopting some arguments of Varela et al. but not following them into
Buddhism, George Lakoff and Mark Johnson (1999:20,77) advocated a
specifically rigid notion of embodiment: "An embodied concept is a neural
structure that is actually part of, or makes use of, the sensorimotor system
of our brain. Much of conceptual inference is, therefore, sensorimotor
inference." They claimed that our thoughts are mostly based on a few
hundred "primary metaphors," examples of which are important is big,
bad is stinky, and control is up. These metaphors are embodied in the specific sense of being determined by the peculiarities of our sensorimotor
organs and hard-wired in our brains. "Our brains are structured so as to
project activation patterns from sensorimotor areas to higher cortical areas.
These constitute what we have called 'primary metaphors.' Projections of
this kind allow us to conceptualize abstract concepts on the basis of inferential patterns used in the sensorimotor processes that are directly tied
to the body."

This is a highly specific notion of embodiment in which the peculiarities of our limbs and sensory organs determine most of our thoughts.
Our sensorimotor equipment does contribute to our thinking. The case
of color is a case in point; the systems of color words in various languages
share a general pattern that conforms to the characteristics of the pho-

toreceptors in our eyes. However, this is the best case; apart from it Lakoff and Johnson offered few other examples. I reject their narrow notion of embodiment, because I doubt that scientific evidence exists for the general brain structures that they allege; they give no reference. Sensorimotor areas in the brain do project to areas for higher cognitive functions. However, I know of no evidence that the projections preserve entire activation patterns that are recognizable as sensorimotor inferences or metaphors such as "control is up."

Lakoff and Johnson demand a lot from the embodiment of mind. They stipulate strong and rigid sensorimotor restrictions and contributions, where sensorimotor inference dominates abstract inference. Our sensory and motor organs are highly specific and thus impose very narrow constraints on the range of inference. The neural structures in our brain are far more complex and hence far more versatile. Our eyes are sensitive only to visible lights, but we can think of the entire electromagnetic spectrum from gamma ray through ultraviolet and infrared to radio wave. Such thinking is not metaphorical but theoretical. We can develop science because our minds can transcend the specific limitations of our sensorimotor organs.

Lakoff and Johnson base much of their theory on the strength of metaphors. Metaphors are important to our thinking, both in enrichment and heuristic, but their roles should not be overstated. Lakoff and Johnson present several basic schema onto which a great variety of phenomena can be mapped and take this to be the evidence for metaphorical thinking. Because the schemata are couched in sensorimotor terms, they conclude that all mapped phenomena are conceived as sensorimotor metaphors. I contend that the same mapping can be interpreted in a different, non-metaphoric way that undermines their thesis.

Sciences have many examples in which a certain mathematical structure is applicable to many phenomena that are widely disparate. Riemanian geometry, for example, can describe anything ranging from space time to colors. Such application is possible because all phenomena involved share a certain structure that is captured by the mathematics. They are isomorphic as far as that particular structure is concerned, and therefore can be mapped from one to the other. To recognize isomorphism is a powerful cognitive capacity. Once we see that two phenomena are isomorphic, we can transfer our knowledge about one to the other. Unfortunately, isomorphism is usually not apparent and escapes most people. Metaphors are helpful because they bring together two isomorphic or partly isomorphic phenomena, so that people can pattern a strange phenomenon after a familiar one. However, metaphors usually fail to bring to relief the isomorphic structure, therefore they are often misleading and not susceptible to further generalization.

Theories supersede metaphors by bringing out isomorphic structures explicitly. Using theoretical reason, we discern and clearly articulate the structure hidden in a familiar phenomenon, which enables us to see the structure more readily in strange phenomena. This power of generalization is the secret of the success of science. In theoretical sciences, the discerned structure is often articulated in mathematical terms that are applicable to other areas. Mathematics is not necessary, however. General concepts such as space, time, and causality express general structures that are hidden in all physical phenomena, including our sensorimotor behaviors.

Once we grant the possibility of abstraction and theoretical reasoning, the schemata and mapping of Lakoff and Johnson prove only that much of our theoretical reasoning concerns physical factors and we recognize that our body shares many general features with other physical systems. They fail to prove that we conceive of other physical systems as metaphoric extensions of our body. If we discard theoretical reasoning, we have to rewrite not only all Western philosophy as metaphoric, as Lakoff and Johnson trumpet, but all theoretical science beginning with physics. Concepts such as time and causality are indispensable in physics. If they are metaphoric, we end up with metaphorical physics.

The success of science is evidence enough that we are capable of theoretical reasoning. Granted that we need not adopt Lakoff and Johnson's specifically rigid sense of embodiment where our mind is totally structured by our specific sensorimotor organs. We need only a more flexible sense of embodiment where mind is structure by the general features of physical objects. I propose this flexible sense of embodiment, lay out its general structures, and present ample evidence.

3

The Emergence of Mind from Its Infrastructures

7   Toward a Natural and Self-Consistent Model of Mind

Let us adopt the natural scientific approach that is content to study and understand our actual mental characteristics and actual structures of thinking. An empirical science has a specific domain of inquiry, phenomena in which are data that the science must reckon with. Suppose we agree that for the science of mind, the most important domain consists of humans, because they are the only uncontroversial mental beings that we know. This at once suggests a criterion for judging theories of mind, as we realize that we scientists are the same kind of being as the subjects whom we study; we are among them. Scientific research is a normal human activity and scientific reasoning is a refinement and development of the theoretical attitude, a mental ability shared by all people in their daily coping (see section 6). Our mental abilities make possible science in general and the science of mind in particular. No scientific theory of mind can deny the possibility of science and scientific practice without being self-refuting. A theory is inadequate if it depends on scientists having supermind with capacities falling beyond the general structures of the mind that it describes (figure 3.1).

A test stone I use is self-consistency: Are the general structures of the mind described in a model capable of proposing such models? A theory of mind is *self-consistent* if it applies also to the theoreticians who frame it, and thus can account for the possibility of science in general and itself in particular. This criterion demands that models of mind be self-critical. Self-criticism is an important prerequisite for rational inquiries; as Kant argued, reason reaches its pinnacle in critiques of itself.

The self-consistency criterion rules out theories of the closed mind in which the subject under investigation has access only to private mental

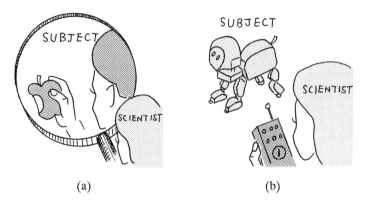

Figure 3.1
(a) In a self-consistent science of mind, the scientist and the subject being studied are both human beings and thus share the same general mental structures and abilities. (b) In a science that is not self-consistent, the scientist is a godlike being with mental power that transcends the general mental capacities ascribed to the subject.

representations and not to objects in the world. Such mind cannot possibly develop science, not to mention a science about other minds. Thus these theories tacitly assume that scientists play the role of mind designers. By straddling the inside and outside realms, scientists have capacities categorically beyond those of the closed mind that is their subject, just as computer engineers have capacities categorically beyond those of the computers that they build. They assign meanings and confine the ordinary mind to play with meaningless mental representations; make predictions but deny the ordinary mind the ability to believe and hence to predict; control electrodes and condemn the ordinary mind to be the brain in a vat at their mercy; speak the mind of Mother Nature and treat people as artifacts to be reengineered are reverse engineered. These theories of mind are not self-consistent because their mind as a closed entity under the thumb of mind designers cannot conduct any objective inquiry. When we demand how scientists gain this extraordinary power and why it is denied to ordinary people, we get no answer. Models of the closed mind simply assume scientists qua mind designers with no explanation. They mystify science without illumination mind.

A General Conceptual Framework for Thinking about Mind
We know people at home, work, and play. Scientists also examine them in clinics and laboratories. At once we notice a tension in our domain of

study; people's characteristics as recorded in the street and in the laboratory appear to be quite different. Ordinarily we are conscious of our mental life, but cognitive science reports blindsight, implicit memory, universal grammar, and other unconscious processes that many people would not believe to be theirs. Because everyday experiences and scientific results are so different, most theories concentrate on one to the neglect or dismissal of the other. I maintain that a satisfactory science of mind must do justice to both. It should explain the relation between the two classes of apparently dissimilar phenomena and show how they influence each other. Many explanations have to wait for the development of science. Meanwhile, I try to articulate a general conceptual framework that keeps questions open and leaves room for future science to fill in the answers. It consists several main theses:

1. *Monism*: mind is not a nonphysical entity but a kind of emergent dynamical property in certain complex physical entities, notably human beings.
2. *Infrastructure*: the locus of current cognitive science is not mind as we experience it in our everyday life but its infrastructure consisting of its underlying processes.
3. *Emergence*: conscious mental processes emerge from the self-organization of many unconscious infrastructural processes.
4. *Openness*: the basic characteristic of mind is its openness to the world; the subject is aware of himself only as he engages in the intelligible natural and social world.

The first three theses, which address the relations between mind and body, demand the cross-illumination of cognitive science and commonsense psychology. The fourth, which addresses the relation between mind and world, demands an analysis of the structures of everyday experience. They are summarized in the notion of an open mind emerging from infrastructures, as illustrated in figure 3.2.

Mind as a Dynamical Property of Persons
The general hypothesis that mind is a kind of high-level emergent property of a kind of complex physical entity makes two ontological assertions: first, mind is not a thing with independent existence but is a property of something. *Property* is a general classification that includes process; an entity undergoes a process, which is its dynamical property.

MIND-OPEN-TO-WORLD   MENTAL FACULTIES
the engaged-personal level

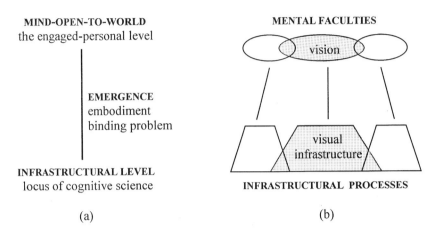

EMERGENCE
embodiment
binding problem

INFRASTRUCTURAL LEVEL
locus of cognitive science   INFRASTRUCTURAL PROCESSES

(a)   (b)

Figure 3.2
(a) The model of an open mind emerging from infrastructures consists of three parts: the mental level whose chief characteristic is the open mind of engaged persons (section 13 and ch. 8); the infrastructural level studied by cognitive science (sections 8, 9); and the binding problem asking how mental properties emerge from and are embodied in infrastructural processes (sections 10–12). (b) We analyze the mental level into various mental faculties such as vision or memory (chs. 4–7). Each faculty is roughly supported by its infrastructure, which we analyze into many interactive infrastructural processes. Analyses on both levels are approximate, so faculties and infrastructures interact and interpenetrate.

Mind is mainly a dynamical property, which is why I always try to use verbs instead of nouns to describe it. Second, it denies the existence of soul stuff or spiritual power and asserts that mind is the property of certain physical entities. Thus my hypothesis falls in the realm of metaphysical monism, the roots of which reaches back to the pre-Socratics (see section 3).

The idea that mind is a property of physical entities is old. In *de Anima* (412b), for example, Aristotle regarded the soul as the form of the body; the *form* being what it is for the body to be a body of such a kind. To illustrate soul as form, he cited the cutting power that makes a chunk of metal an axe: "Compare the following: if an instrument, e.g., an axe, were a natural body, then its form would be what it is to be an axe, and this would be its soul; if this were removed, it would no longer be an axe."

The idea of mind as a property is not limited to Western philosophy. Reacting to the infusion of the Buddhist idea of a reincarnating soul, a furious debate about immortality raged in fifth- and sixth-century China.

Against reincarnation, Fan Chen wrote in *On the Mortality of Soul*: "Body is the substance of soul; soul is the function of body. . . . Soul is to substance as sharpness is to the edge of a blade; body is to function as edge is to sharpness. The name of sharpness is not edge, nor is edge named sharpness, but there is no sharpness without edge or edge without sharpness. It never happens that sharpness remains when the edge perishes, how can it happen that soul remains when the body perishes?"[1] Fan did not know Aristotle's metaphor of the axe's cutting power, but his idea was not too different.

I call a mental entity—an entity with mental properties—a *person*. Mind is the inalienable property of an individual person. Persons are mostly human beings, but not necessarily. *Human* is a biological term referring to a species of organism. Persons are more generally recognized for their characteristics, many of which we define according to our own experience. The ancient Greeks called themselves animals with *logos*, whose distinguishing feature is shared by the gods and hence not limited to a biological species. Usually, besides being a conscious subject, a person is also a moral agent and the source of concepts and values. Therefore nonhuman animals, which are usually deemed incapable of moral and value judgments, are seldom honored as persons. I relax the moral requirement and acknowledge the mastery of the most primitive concepts and values as a sign of mentality. Thus I would not object if some people count finicky cats or faithful horses as persons. At this time, the only actual persons we know are animals, but in fiction we freely acknowledge persons with other constitutions: Martians, extraterrestrials who breathe chlorine, androids such as Frankenstein's Monster or Star Fleet's Commander Data. It is possible that we will find similar persons in the real world. My model of an open mind emerging from infrastructures accounts for this possibility.

Furthermore, I maintain that mind is the dynamical property not of a person in isolation but of one radically engaged in the natural and social world. Thus we consider only persons living among things and in the community of other persons, because the abilities to manipulate things knowledgeably and understand each other are defining characteristics of mind. Many of these characteristics are described by familiar psychological concepts. That is why I call the mental level where psychological concepts apply the engaged-personal level.

Mind is the property of an engaged person as a whole, not of any of his parts, not even his brain, although its underlying mechanisms are mostly located in the brain. In studying mind we are concerned with a person's mental states and processes wherein he is conscious of his thoughts, experiences his body, perceives things, understands the world, has a sense of self, and cares for other people. Properly speaking, it is the person who thinks by exercising his mental capabilities, as Aristotle said in *De Anima* (408b): "It is doubtless better to avoid saying that the soul pities or learns or thinks, and rather to say that it is the man who does this with his soul." Nevertheless, Aristotle continued to use "soul" as the subject. Similarly, although it is the person and not his mind that thinks, for the convenience of writing I sometimes say mind thinks to distinguish mental from other kinds of personal properties.

Mind as Emergent from the Self-Organization of Infrastructural Processes

To maintain that mind is a kind of high-level emergent property of a person, we must clarify at least two concepts. First, what are the general meanings of emergence and emergent properties? Second, what are the specific characteristics of the emergent property that we call mind?

A person is a very complex physical entity. Complex entities typically exhibit structures on various scales and levels of organization, the descriptions and explanations of which call for different concepts and intellectual perspectives. Emergence and self-organization are general concepts for the causal connection between two organizational levels. Fluidity, for instance, is a high-level emergent property of a large system of molecules that is visible only from a macroscopic perspective. It is in this sense that I assert mentality is a high-level property that emerges from the self-organization of processes in a lower organizational level, namely, the infrastructural level.

My hypothesis maintains two theoretical points that are encapsulated in the notion of emergence. First, mental properties are scientifically explicable, and second, the explanations are irreducible. Briefly, by *irreducibility* I mean that mental concepts are indispensable in the descriptions and explanations of mental properties, so that mental properties cannot be said to be *nothing but* some other properties that are totally different. The possibility of nonreductive causal explanations implies that mentality is a person's emergent characteristic that is absent in his neural and physiological constituents and whose descriptions demand peculiar concepts that are not applicable to neurons, the brain, and other organs.

Why do we need mental concepts if we agree there is no soul stuff and mind is a property of physical entities? Why aren't physical concepts sufficient? What most of our concepts describe is not *stuff* but the *structure of organization*. According to our best experimentally confirmed physical theory, all things in the universe are made up of a few kinds of elementary particles and fundamental interactions. There is no other stuff or force. However, elementary particle concepts are far from sufficient in describing things, even within physics. Physical stuff has never ceased to surprise scientists with the amazing structures into which it can organize itself. To account for these structures scientists are constantly introducing new concepts, chemical, biological, and more. Biologists have long rejected a nonphysical vital force, all the same they insist that biological concepts are indispensable for biology. Similarly, rejection of soul stuff does not entail exclusion of mental concepts. Mental phenomena are wonderful organizational structures with which we are familiar and for which we have some concepts. If these commonsense psychological concepts do capture realistic phenomena as I hypothesize, they need only be clarified, not abolished. Therefore the ontological assumption of physicality and the theoretical assumption of irreducibility are compatible.

The causal connection between organizational levels is usually difficult to explain. The connection between mind and its infrastructure is even more difficult because people are far more complex than most entities that science has tackled. Thus the binding problem, which asks how myriad infrastructural processes combine into mental properties, remains unsolved. In this circumstance, the hypothesis of mind as an emergent property has the advantage of making mind and its embodiment a special case in the problems about complex phenomena. Thus it enables us to glean insight from successful theories about complex phenomena in other sciences. Instead of speculating in a vacuum and spinning simplistic stipulations, we can study concrete examples to find a clear notion of emergence that is also applicable to mind.

Mind–Open-to-the-World as a Situated Property

Many kinds of complex physical entities are present in the universe and most have emergent properties not found in their constituents. Turbulence in the atmosphere, which we recognize as various weather patterns, emerges in a system of colliding air molecules. It is a complicated property whose details still baffle physicists, but it is not mental. What are peculiar about emergent properties that are mental?

What are the general characteristics of properties on the mental level? I abolish all Cartesian intermediaries, be they called sense impressions or symbols or mental representations. There is no veil of perception or veil of formality; we see things directly and immediately. To say that we perceive the world directly does not mean that no causal process connects things with our perception of them. It means that the connecting processes—numerous, minute, unconscious, and involuntary—belong to a lower organizational level, the infrastructural level. They do not crystallize into salient items such as mental representations on the mental level, and they are neither seen nor manipulated by the subject in the sense that mental representations are.

Abolition of mental representations leads to the mental peculiarity I call openness to the world. Embodied in the engaged person, mind opens to the world by differentiating among objects and subjective experiences of them, hence gaining a sense of self, finding events meaningful, occasionally making mistakes and capable of recognizing them as such. Openness is also the mental characteristic necessary for the possibility of science, as it is responsible for turning the blind universe into the intelligible world of our experiences and hence the topic of science. Because it is an essential characteristic of mind, the proper entity on the mental level is an individual engaged person. The notion of engaged persons with open mind differentiates my model from both the closed mind and the ecological approach in which a mental entity is merely a part of a larger system (see section 17).

Taking openness as the chief mental peculiarity brings into relief a problem that has irritated philosophers for a long time. Infrastructural and neural processes all occur beneath a person's skin. In making sense of the world, however, the open mind goes beyond skin and yet is still the property of an individual. You can think about the whole universe but your thinking is your property. How can openness be compatible with individuality and the localization of the brain? How can we connect mind to its infrastructure without imprisoning it within the skin?

Again the general concept of emergence enables us to learn from existing scientific theories of complex phenomena that treat different levels and their connections seriously. Ample examples show that science succeeds because scientists do not try to solve everything in a fell swoop from a single intellectual perspective. They adopt different perspectives, different scopes of generalization, and different assumptions to explain phenomena on different scales and organizational levels. These differences, which foil simplistic prescriptions in the philosophy of science, account for emergent properties. To understand mind on both the engaged-personal and infrastructural levels, the science of mind must be as flexible in perspectives as physics or dynamical theory. Furthermore, this flexibility is a basic structure of the human mind on which depends its openness and sense of objectivity. Accommodation of multiple theoretical perspectives, a basic structure of mind, is also what makes the science of mind possible. It is a crucial element in a self-consistent theory of mind.

A Road Map

Figure 3.2 illustrates my model schematically. On the mental level we analyze the open mind into various intuitive mental faculties, for instance memory, emotion, perception, and language. Each large faculty can in turn be analyzed into smaller abilities. Perception, for instance, divides into vision, audition, and other senses. The analysis is approximate, so faculties couple to each other. Cognitive science mostly takes intuitive faculties for granted and delves into their respective infrastructures. They analyze the infrastructure of each faculty into many processes, which they probe with ingenious experiments and represent with theoretical or computer models. Again, the analysis is fruitful but approximate, so that considerable interacting exists among various infrastructural processes. So far, scientists have successfully identified many of these processes but are baffled about how they synthesize into various mental faculties.

The open mind and its faculties are familiar; they are described by commonsense psychological concepts such as thinking and seeing, which we use daily. I trust that when I say, "I think it's raining," you understand that I am not talking about some mental representation inside my head but the weather outside, and that I am uncertain about my judgment. I will rely on this intuitive understand for most of this book, leaving conceptual analysis of the open mind to the final chapter, where I propose that multiple perspectives and the systematic variations thereof are essential to direct perception and the openness of mind.

The next two sections introduce the infrastructural level, contrast infrastructural and conscious processes, and explain why and how cognitive science focuses on the mental infrastructure. Sections 10 and 11 analyze the concept of emergence, drawing clues from existing multilevel scientific theories. They explain why mind is an emergent property, how mind is embodied, and why it is possible for mental properties to emerge in entities with different constituents. Section 12 explains why the diversity of infrastructural processes is compatible with the unity of consciousness. Section 13 introduces the concept of situated property and explains in what sense the open mind of an engaged person includes factors beyond the person's skin.

This chapter presents a conceptual framework. The next four chapters put some substance into it by considering four prominent mental faculties: language, vision, memory, and emotion. In each case we examine how everyday experiences and scientific results supplement and illuminate each other. We will see that scientific knowledge about the relevant infrastructural processes modifies our intuitive view of the mental faculty. Using the results from these chapters, the final chapter analyzes openness of mind with its subjectivity and objectivity.

8   The Mental Infrastructure: Locus of Cognitive Science

Plato's *Republic* (238) described Socrates trying to explain how a person acts justly for justice's own sake and not merely for the action's profits. He suggested it is easier to grasp justice on a larger canvas, in a city instead of an individual. Let me adopt a similar magnifying metaphor. Suppose we compare the mental properties of a person with the bustling activities of a metropolis. What would a tour of cognitive science be like? It would not be like an ordinary visit where tourists talk to locals, stroll the markets, and sample restaurants and theaters to learn the city's culture and atmosphere. Instead, the visitors descend to inspect the city's infrastructures: roads and subways, water and power lines, drainage and sewage channels, telephone and broadcast networks, law-making and -enforcement institutions. Analogously, cognitive science mostly studies the infrastructures of mind.[2] It bypasses visual, auditory, emotional, and other experiences. Instead, it delves into the infrastructural systems that serve vision, audition, emotion, conception, attention, imagination, memory, motor control, speech comprehension, and other experiences.

Visitors and inhabitants of the metropolis alike turn on water and switch on lights without a thought about infrastructures. Infrastructures are so crucial to what they serve that they are often taken for granted and become inconspicuous. The slightest mishap, however, drives home their indispensability. Power outages and other malfunctions in the civil infrastructure disrupt activity and raise choruses of scream from citizens. Similarly, glitches in mental infrastructures have dire consequences in mental life. Examples of the plight of patients with brain injuries are presented later.

The Cognitive Revolution

The discovery of mind's infrastructure is the big achievement of the cognitive revolution. A little story will show how greatly it changed our conception of mind. Hurlbert and Poggio (1988) reported that Minsky once assigned a summer project to a graduate student: hook a camera to a computer and make the computer describe what it sees. The assignment looked like a snap, for nothing seemed easier than vision. Many people regard vision to be simply the passive registration of optical stimuli. According to this conception, little is left to be done once the camera takes care of the registration. The student could leave for the beach in August. So it appeared forty years ago.

Perhaps historians of science will track down the student and ask how he felt. One thing I am ready to bet on. If he did leave early, he left in total despair and frustration, a victim of a common illusion. David Marr (1982:16), one of the professors who took over the student's project, mused in retrospection: "In the 1960s almost no one realized that machine vision was difficult." Reality quickly cured them of complacency. Machine vision has grown into a thriving research industry using all cutting-edge technologies ranging from symbolic computation to artificial neural networks. Reviewing its status, Shimon Ullman (1996:1) noted jealously the ease with which animals recognize things: "In contrast, the recognition of common objects is still way beyond the capabilities of artificial systems, or any recognition model proposed so far." After more than three decades of intensive effort by an army of professors and professionals, the student's summer project still has a long way to go. Scientists underestimated the difficulty of machine vision because they underestimated the intricacy of animal vision, which they tried and are still trying to make machines emulate. How much they miscalculated on the effort required reveals how much they misjudged the infrastructure of animal vision.

Such misjudgment was widespread. So was the misconception of mind that it entails. Perception is mind's window to the world and provides most contents of our concerns and thoughts. Thus its nature strongly influences the nature of mind. We are all aware of our perceptual experiences, but few if any are aware of any effort in attaining them under normal conditions. Even when we strain to read small print under dim light we are aware more of our eyes and reading environment than of our mental operation. How complicated can the infrastructural processes underlying perception be, if indeed such processes exist? This question has attracted the attention of philosophers since antiquity. In the seventeenth and eighteenth centuries it incited a great debate between empiricism and rationalism that rages today. Locke (1690:104), as was typical of British empiricists, endowed mind with minimal structures and attributed most ideas to sensual input. He compared mind with a "white paper, void of all characters, without any Ideas." Mind may be busy organizing sense impressions, but as far as the impressions are concerned, it is merely a faithful recorder, a tabula rasa to be written on. Therefore, to Locke, perception is always conscious with little else behind it. That seemed to be what Minsky thought as well.

Across the English Channel, rationalists shook their heads. In contrast to empiricism, which attributes the complexity of experiences mostly to perceptual stimuli, rationalism attributes it mostly to mind's own structures. Rationalists reject the passively receptive mind, maintaining that the simplistic idea of impressions given by the senses obscures mind's spontaneous activities. Leibniz (1765:51–6) found Locke's notion of a tabula rasa especially objectionable, describing mind more like a block of veined than blank marble. Locke (1690:163) compared understanding with a dark closet with tiny holes to admit sense data. Leibniz (1765:144) countered that to make the analogy we must also assume that the closet contained a receptive veil with folds, elasticity, and active force. For Locke, (1690:335) "consciousness always accompanies all thinking," "it being impossible for anyone to perceive, without perceiving that he does perceive." Leibniz (1765:53–4) disagreed, contending that we have many perceptions "unaccompanied by awareness or reflection" because they are too minute and insufficiently distinctive. These "insensible perceptions," he said, are as important to the study of mind as insensible particles are to natural science.

Leibniz's ideas of insensible perceptions and active mental contributions to perception hinted at a perceptual infrastructure. They were mostly ignored, not the least because Leibniz did not elaborate on them. Rationalism failed to give substantive accounts of the structures it attributes to mind. Over the centuries, empiricism with its doctrine of an almost structureless and supportless mind had the upper hand in the scientific circle. When psychology became an experimental science it promptly fell into behaviorism, which restricts scientists to predicting and controlling overt behaviors. By forbidding references to mental states and subjective experiences, behaviorists such as B. F. Skinner ascribed everything to environmental conditions and reduced mental structures to zero. Then, in the late 1950s, behaviorism was swept aside by the revolution that gave birth to cognitive science.

At the forefront of the cognitive revolution was linguist Noam Chomsky, who demolished Skinner's verbal behaviorism and launched his own breakthrough in linguistics. He revived the traditional debate between empiricism and rationalism and sided with the rationalists. Specifically, he theorized that we use language not merely because we are exposed to linguistic stimuli; chimpanzees with similar exposure learn no language. More important, the human mind is endowed with certain structures that, in the proper linguistic environment, develop into our linguistic ability. Chomsky (1986) called these specialized structures the "language organ." Perhaps it is better called it the language system, as "organ" all too often suggests the unnecessary criterion of spatial localization. Whatever we call it, the language system consists of a host of processes of which we are unaware. Even linguists who build sophisticated theoretical models for these processes have no direct experience of them. However, they can study the processes indirectly to acquire objective knowledge of them. Furthermore, Chomsky proposed that these unconscious processes are not imposed by social conditioning but are natural characteristics universal to all humans. Thus he not only developed a new linguistic theory but opened a new perspective for the nascent cognitive science by discovering the linguistic infrastructure and introducing a way to study it.

The cognitive revolution goes beyond linguistics. Across the whole spectrum of our mental abilities scientists have discovered infrastructural processes that escape our awareness. The struggle to create machine vision, for instance, goes hand in hand with a much larger research program to understand animal vision. Far from being trivial, our vision depends on a vast infrastructure that engages almost half of our cerebral cortex. Many of these processes Leibniz would call insensible perceptions. For the first time, we need not blindly speculate about how perceptual experiences come about but can refer to concrete knowledge about perceptual infrastructures.

Research on vision and language highlights the major thrust of cognitive science. Except in small pockets, the bulk of work does not concentrate on what we ordinarily recognize as mental phenomena, those experiences and voluntary mental activities of which we are conscious. Instead, it focuses on the underlying unconscious and automatic processes whose very existence people usually overlook. Its main emphasis is not on seeing and recognizing objects but on processes that underlie seeing, that coalesce to produce conscious visual experiences, but are themselves unconscious. They are conspicuous only when their malfunction prevents people from seeing properly. They and processes underlying hearing, feeling, and other modes of experience constitute the infrastructure of mind.

Mind Lost and Found

Historians looking at cognitive science at the end of the twentieth century would find something strange. On the one hand, they would see great excitement and progress; on the other, much grumbling and discontent. They would find books by renowned scientists, philosophers, and journalists with titles such as *Consciousness Lost and Found* (Weiskrantz 1997), *Mind Regained* (Pols 1998), *The Rediscovery of Mind* (Searle 1992), and *The Undiscovered Mind* (Horgan 1999). Perhaps the first feeling these books incite is a sense of unfairness and untimeliness. Behaviorism did banish mind and consciousness, but it had been severely attacked and ostensibly vanquished by the cognitive revolution of the 1950s. Since then cognitive science has made tremendous advancement. What is this talk about mind rediscovered or undiscovered forty years later?

A second thought makes us hesitate to dismiss these books too rashly. They are not isolated idiosyncrasies but the tip of an iceberg. Publications and conferences on mind and consciousness have exploded in the last decade. Many authors complain that cognitive science has hitherto neglected consciousness, others declare it is high time to face the hard problems regarding mind. A sense of something overlooked seems to prevail. No one denies that cognitive science has produced a staggering amount of knowledge. Knowledge about what? Mostly not about mind, the disgruntled answer seems to be.

The disgruntlement is a bit rash. Take for example the Tucson conferences on consciousness (Hameroff 1996, 1998). Most speakers were seasoned cognitive scientists, and what they presented were not born-again revelations but the results of research over many years. With a little shift in emphasis, what routinely appeared in journals of cognitive science fit into a conference on consciousness. This indicates that mind and consciousness have not been neglected, they have only been kept in the closet. What kept them there?

Cognitive science has made real progress and contributions, but unfortunately, it is marred by too much hype in philosophy and popularization. Because mental phenomena are so complex, the science of mind is at the research frontier looking out on a vast terra incognita, especially the territory of mind itself and not merely its infrastructure. On the other hand, people are thirsty for knowledge about mind. This breeds philosophies that cater to people's thirst by peddling easy but dubious answers, pretending to have consciousness explained. The hype covers up the fact that despite much progress in cognitive science, we still know very little about how the mind works. Compare two assessments of the same state of science. Crick (1994:24) wrote: "We do not yet know, even in outline, how our brains produce the vivid visual awareness that we take so much for granted." Churchland (1995:3) wrote: "We are in a position to explain how our vivid sensory experience arise in the sensory cortex of our brains." Crick acknowledged both the importance of visual awareness and the inability of current cognitive science to explain it. His sober assessment manifested the critical spirit of science. Such spirit is absent in Churchland's claims that current neuroscience explains not only sensory experiences but almost all mental phenomena. "None of it is true," retorted Fodor (1998b: 83) in his review of Churchland's book, which is filled with technical jargon such as "vector activation." Fodor called the jargon and the claims based on it "technohype" and explained how they grossly exaggerate scientific results and cover up difficult problems regarding mind. To pretend that neuroscience has explained everything is to dismiss mental phenomena that Crick realized it does not explain. This dismissal Churchland (1989) elevated into a philosophical doctrine, eliminativism.

Technohype abounds in philosophical doctrines claiming that neuroscience or AI or another branch of cognitive science can explain—if it has not already explained—all there is to know about mind. These philosophies cannot accept the notion of underlying processes, because the notion presupposes some other phenomena that computational or neural processes underlie. Therefore they identify computation or the disembodied brain itself with mind. Constrained by the basic nature of computation or the disembodied brain, they are forced into models of the closed mind controlled by mind designers. Many people, however, hold on to the intuitive conception of mind that they gain from continuing experiences. To them,

the closed mind controlled by mind designers is not mind at all. Therefore mind is lost. Mind is lost not in scientific research but in the technobabble and technohype that jam philosophical interpretations of
scientific results.

Mind is regained by seeing clearly what current science does and
does not know. The locus of cognitive science is not on mental phenomena that we are familiar with in our daily life. Following the general tendency of science to seek underlying mechanisms, cognitive science focuses
on infrastructural processes that underlie many normal and pathological
mental phenomena. Once their interpretation as underlying processes of
mind and consciousness is made explicit, their relevance and importance
become apparent. Underlying processes constrain what they underlie;
infrastructures illuminate what they support. That explains why available
results of cognitive science fit readily into the study of consciousness. The
infrastructural interpretation helps us to appreciate the significance of scientific results far better than hype. One can learn more about a city's
culture from its public transportation systems than from all its tourist traps.

Aconscious, Unconscious, Infraconscious, and Fringe Conscious

As discussed above, mind is not a thing but a kind of dynamical property
of humans and possibly some other things. Therefore I will try to use
adjectives and verbs to describe it; nouns such as "consciousness" easily
conjure the erroneous image of an entity inside the head. What are the
peculiarities of mental properties? How do they differ from the peculiarities of the infrastructural processes? A major peculiarity of mental properties is being conscious; a person is aware of his own mental processes
but not of the infrastructural processes that go in him.

I call an entity *mental* only if it is conscious some of the times. The
most conspicuous example of a mental entity is a person. I call a person's
conscious states his *experiences* and his conscious processes his *activities* as
distinct from his mere *behaviors*. Seeing and more generally perceiving are
experiences, sensing and detecting are behaviors. Behaviors are exhibited
by mental and mindless systems alike, but they are not activities.

Infrastructural processes are not conscious, but they coalesce to
produce conscious mental activities. Because of their function in mental
entities, however, it is well to distinguish them from other nonconscious
processes. I use *infraconscious* to describe infrastructural processes. Infraconscious processes are distinct from the *aconscious* processes in current

rule-driven artifacts, the *unconscious* of Sigmund Freud, and the *fringe of attention* expounded by William James.

Infraconscious processes occur in mental entities. Although they occur at a lower organizational level, they contribute essentially to the emergence of conscious mentality on a higher level. They are studied in linguistics, cognitive psychology, cognitive neuroscience, neuropsychology, psychophysics, and other areas. Aconscious processes occur in nonmental entities that are incapable of being conscious, such as present-day digital computers or perhaps insects. Their major patrons in cognitive science are AI and its philosophers.

Infraconscious and aconscious processes are described in similar concepts and are often lumped together in interpretations where they are associated with both concepts of computation and information processing. This is an unfortunate confusion as it obscures the importance of operational contexts. It makes a big difference in the meaning of a process whether or not the process is integrated into an entity capable of being conscious. Infraconscious processes are *constitutive* of mentality, as they contribute to the autonomous understanding of the person they make up. Aconscious processes are not constitutive of mentality but *instrumental* to external mental beings; they are tools for thinking or models for infraconscious processes.

Freud divided mind into three systems: the conscious; the preconscious, consisting of latent states that, although unattended to at the moment, can readily become conscious; and the unconscious, consisting repressed mental states that cannot become conscious except perhaps through laborious psychoanalytic therapy. As drives or impulses incongruent and hence unacceptable to the conscious mentality, the unconscious discharges its effects indirectly through dreams, slips, or hysteria.[3]

The mental infrastructure differs from the Freudian unconscious mind in three major ways. Repressed desires produce abnormalities, but infrastructural processes are responsible for normal experiences. Repressed mental states can be made conscious through psychoanalytical therapy, but no therapy or training can make infrastructural processes conscious. Finally, the Freudian unconscious often appears as a full-blown belief system, a protoperson warring intentionally and strategically against the conscious system. Whereas the Freudian conscious and unconscious can result in split personality, mind and its infrastructure cannot. Some philosophers do describe infrastructural processes as homunculi, little men in the head who are not very clever but nonetheless capable of intentional maneuvering. I will show later that the talk of homunculi is either fallacious or disingenuous. Infrastructural processes have restricted domains of operation and are far from having the complexity necessary to have beliefs, however simple the beliefs are.

James (1890:253) introduced the psychic fringe that includes, among other phenomena, inattentive experiences. He noted that a good third of our mental life consists premonitory perceptions, fleeting and inarticulate. Conscious processes have various degrees of attentiveness, integration, articulation, and susceptibility to recall. Those with low degrees—habits, skills, know-how, inclinations, careless actions—are often called unconscious, but they are not. I am inattentive of my driving when I am deep in a conversation with my passengers, and later I will fail to recall what route I have taken. Even so, I am not unconscious of driving, and if I were, my passengers and I would soon become eternally unconscious.

Inattentive actions are closely related to the mental infrastructure but not identical to it. We can put driving and other overlearned skills on automatic pilot at the fringe of attention because our learning processes have created dedicated infrastructural processes that can operate automatically. Habits and skills start as highly conscious processes, but with practice they become automatic. Brain imaging experiments reveal that as a process becomes automated, it uses different parts of the brain, indicting that its underlying mechanisms change radically. Many skills involve lightning responses that are infraconscious because conscious responses have long reaction times. Thus a pianist's conscious attention to the movement of his fingers may disrupt the fluency of his play. However, these infraconscious processes are subprocesses integrated in a larger conscious process that is the pianist's overall skill and performance. He can in practice focus on certain passages and deliberately modify his finger movements. That is why coaching is so important in athletic training. In sum, inattentive actions are possible because they can call on a repertoire of infrastructural processes so that they require minimal attention.

The differences between infrastructural processes and fringe experiences are illustrated in two potential forms of advertisements in movies and other entertainments. Movie viewers whose attention is riveted on a blockbuster seldom think that they are also undergoing two kinds of processes that they are hardly aware of. They see a moving picture replete with continuous motion. Most know that nothing actually moves in a

movie; what flashes on the screen is a rapid succession of still frames separated by darkness. However, viewers cannot see the frames and breaks,
even if they try. At twenty-four frames a second, the presentation is too
rapid for conscious discernment. If someone inserts an extra frame that is
totally out of context, say a picture of Joe Camel smoking a cigarette, the
viewers are unable to see Joe in the movie. Even so, their subliminal exposure to Joe can have fleeting causal effects. These causal effects emanate
from infrastructural processes.

Subliminal perception is an oxymoron referring to the causal effects of
stimuli too faint or too brief to be perceived. It is better called the effect
of certain perceptual infrastructural processes triggered by weak stimuli.
People do not see optical displays that are too faint or too brief. These
displays that generate no visual experience, however, do activate certain
infrastructural processes, hence leave causal effects with the potential to
influence subsequent behaviors. Experimental subjects successfully locate
faint light sources that they do not see, and subliminal exposure to a word
improves their fluency in judging the word's meaning. Subliminal perception created much excitement in the 1950s, as advertisers calculated the
profit of subliminal commercials that would induce consumers to think of
a product without knowing why. The excitement subsided as careful laboratory experiments found that although subliminal influences do exist,
they are short lived. The effect of a subliminal exposure lasts for only a
fraction of a second and leaves no memory that can be evoked later. Thus
it is too ephemeral to have commercial value in traditional channels. This
was confirmed by an experiment in which subliminal messages aired
during a BBC television show resulted in only slight influences (Underwood 1994; Greenwald et al. 1996). Things may change with on-line shopping, where a split-second subliminal influence may be enough to prompt
an unwary consumer into clicking *buy*.

Movie goers do not have to worry about subliminal commercials, but
they cannot escape another subtle form of advertisement. Corporations
pay handsomely to put their products strategically into a movie and to
create an aura of cool if the movie succeeds. They do not pay in vain.
The placement of Reese's candies in *E.T.*, for example, had the candy
maker laughing on the way to the bank for a long time (Carvell 1998).
The candies are displayed overtly and susceptible to the most careful
scrutiny. However, movie viewers whose heart and attention went out to
the endearing alien hardly had time to look at them and were only

marginally aware of them in the background. This is precisely what the advertisers want; viewers may resent being hawked to in entertainment, but marginal awareness is enough to dispose them to buy the products afterward. Because the brand of the product is extraneous to the plot, it becomes dissociated from the movie, a case of the prevalent source amnesia, which advertisers count on. Product placement, as it is called in Hollywood, depends on the psychology that inattentive perception of an item can make an impression without all the associations that attentive perception produce.

Inattentive perception is categorically different from subliminal perception. To describe subliminal perception, we do not need attention or other mental concepts. In contrast, to describe inattentive perception properly, we must have the explicit concept of attention distribution, and attention is conscious. Genuine perception is conscious whether the object at issue is at the center or periphery of attention. Hence both cases presuppose consciousness. The effects of conscious processes in inattentive perception are long lasting, in sharp contrast to the fleeting effects of the infrastructural processes in subliminal perception.

General Characteristics of Infrastructural Processes
Many animals exhibit fixed behavioral patterns with specific release mechanisms. For instance, the sight of an egg outside the nest will trigger the egg-retrieval pattern in a nesting goose. The goose extends her neck to reach the egg and moves her beaks sideways to roll the egg back to the nest. Such patterns of action are fixed. Once set in motion, they are very difficult to control or distract. Even if the egg has dropped away, the goose continues the pantomime and finishes the maneuver moving nothing. Fixed behavioral patterns can be complicated. They exist in humans too. The yawn is an example; it is infectious, it lasts about six seconds, is quite similar across persons, and is difficult to suppress. Fixed behavioral patterns are subserved by dedicated infrastructural processes. They reveal how these processes unfold automatically and uncontrollably once released by the proper triggers. Such apparent manifestation of the infrastructure, however, is exceptional, especially in humans. Most infrastructural processes proceed too rapidly and intertwine too tightly to be noticed in normal operation. It is only with great ingenuity that scientists probe them, as we will see in the next section.

Mind and its infrastructure have grossly different properties, and their characterization and explanation demand different sets of concepts. Mental life is conscious and meaningful. It consists of processes that are effortful, flexible, variable in scope, mostly learned, voluntarily controllable, and slow, with characteristic times ranging from fractions of a second to hours or days. In contrast, the mental infrastructure is unconscious and mechanical in a wide sense. It consists of processes that are automatic, rigidity specialized, narrow in scope, often genetically determined, beyond voluntary control, and fast, with characteristic times of less than a tenth of a second. Familiar mental concepts such perceiving, thinking, knowing, desiring, intending, attending, understanding, and acting are strictly applicable only to mind and not to its infrastructure. A person sees and is informed by what he sees; his visual experiences are meaningful. His visual infrastructural processes respond to optical stimuli but they do not see; they know no meaning and are not informed.

Most infrastructural processes specialize in various functions. All important processes that serve a mental faculty constitute the infrastructure for that faculty, for instance, the visual infrastructure or the mnemonic infrastructure. The division of the mental infrastructure into various specialized infrastructures is approximate. As we will see in chapter 4, various infrastructures couple with each other. We are justified to regard them as individual because their internal integrations are tighter and more coherent than their external couplings.

Like a long rope made up of many short fibers, the infrastructure of each mental faculty consists of myriad processes, some running in sequence, others running in parallel and interfering with each other. Some infrastructural processes connect external stimuli to immediate perceptions, such as excitations of the eyes' photoreceptors to visual recognition of objects. Others contribute to deliberate responses, as the generation of actions and speeches. Still others provide the causal link between two conscious mental states such as hearing the starting gun and kicking off.

Each of the many processes that make up the infrastructure of a mental faculty has its own specialties. For instance, neuroscientists have discovered more than thirty distinct but interconnected areas in the cerebral cortex dedicated to vision, each one serving certain functions. Some are specifically sensitive to motion, others to colors, still others to words or faces. Damage in an area may lead to a peculiar visual disability. Patients with damaged motion-sensitive areas see everything in slow motion. Those with damaged face-sensitive areas cannot recognize any face, not even their own (Ungerleider 1995). These and a great variety of clinical cases illustrate that conscious experiences depend on many specialized infrastructural processes that can be individually knocked out.

The consequences of focal brain injuries show that many infrastructural processes are necessary for normal experiences. It does not follow, however, that activation of an infrastructural process is sufficient to produce an experience. Subliminal perception is a familiar counterexample that illustrates several features of infrastructural processes. These processes are fast and hence brief. They are causal, like fixed behavioral patterns. Once they are triggered by the proper causes, they automatically unfold and generate effects. However, because many processes integrate into a conscious experience, the effects of a process may be lost somewhere and hence are not experienced. Subliminal extraction of word meanings indicates that even the processes for higher cognition are insufficient for conscious awareness. Dissociation between activation of an infrastructural process by a causal impact and conscious awareness of its effects becomes a major tool in cognitive science to study the mental infrastructure.

Many infrastructural processes are operational at birth or shortly after, although others require more time and environmental input to develop. If the newborn mind were a tabula rasa with no mental infrastructure, infantile experience would be a "blooming, buzzing confusion," as James once conjectured. It is not so, developmental psychology discovers. A buzzing confusion cannot imitate and judge, as imitation depends on the ability to recognize and the judgment to differentiate. Infants can. Neonates less than a day old happily imitate facial expressions. Mirroring adults, they stick out their tongues, purse their lips, and open their mouths wide. Two-month-olds can differentiate a distant object from a nearby one, although the two objects project the same image on their retinas. Their brains contain neurons that are selectively sensitive to faces and distances. A few more months, and infants notice object rigidity, coherence in motion, persistence during occlusion, and certain causal regularities, as they are surprised by physically impossible events. Thanks to their rudimentary mental infrastructures, infantile experiences are quite well ordered (Spelke and Newport 1998; Dobbins et al. 1998).

Perceptual experiences seem to occur instantaneously. Actually they are not instantaneous, because their infrastructural processes take time to unfold. A person sees an optical stimulus about 500 milliseconds—half a second—after its presentation. We are more sensitive to words, capable of recognizing most spoken words within 125 milliseconds of their onset, or recognizing and pronouncing written words within 500 milliseconds. Infrastructural processes that occur during the lag time we are not aware of and unable to control. Even champion athletes at the peak of concentration cannot control the processes underlying their reactions. Ample scientific evidence shows that uncontrollable processes take at least 100 milliseconds to run. The rules of the Olympic games have taken this fact in account. Consequently, they disqualified British sprinter Lindford Christie for a false start when he left the starting block less than 100 milliseconds after the gun in the 1996 summer games (Libet 1996; Harley 1995; Barinaga 1996). Characteristic time scales are important factors in differentiating various levels of organization in the science of mind as in physics. We will see how confusion can arise when philosophers ignore the time factor, pick on some millisecond phenomena, and insist that conscious experiences are illusory.

Infrastructural processes have no cognizance, hence it is wrong to apply to them mental terms such as perceive, recognize, believe, or speak. However, because they contribute directly to perceiving, believing, or speaking, they are often described in concepts appropriate for the *contents* of people's visual experiences, beliefs, or speeches. Linguists use grammatical concepts to characterize the linguistic infrastructure because grammar is a feature of what we say. Similarly, scientists characterize visual processes not in terms of seeing but in terms of shapes or other geometric concepts that describe what we see. Grammatical or geometric concepts objectively describe and explain infrastructural processes in scientific theories in the same sense that geometric concepts objectively describe planetary motions. They capture certain real characteristics of infrastructural processes but they do not imply that the processes know grammar or geometry. Take for example the notion of orientation. A person sees the orientation of an object, which is a part of the contents of his meaningful experience. An orientation-sensitive infrastructural process does not see the orientation because it has no visual experience and understands no meaning. It is selectively sensitive to the orientation, just as Polaroid sunglasses are selectively sensitive to light of a certain polarization. The difference between *seeing* and *being selectively sensitive* to something, which separates mind from the mental infrastructure, generates much conceptual confusion that this book tries to clear up.

Mental infrastructures of animals rest on neural substrates; however, infrastructural processes are seldom described in neural terms. Their

operations usually involve millions of neurons that have large-scale organizations. Thus theoretical models that characterize them seldom refer to
neural mechanisms. Artificial neural networks, which are fashionable nowadays, are neural only in name. Therefore many scientists prefer to call them
connectionist networks to avoid confusion (see section 4).

Our mental infrastructure makes contact with its neural substrate
through brain anatomy and function, which are topics of brain imagining
experiments. Take for example the visual infrastructure, a greatly simplified version of which is schematically illustrated in figure 3.3. In terms of
brain anatomy, the infrastructure appears as a complicated network with
thirty-odd interactive brain areas. The visual areas are distinguished more
by functions than by neural structures, the interactions more by roles than
by neural synapses. Usually, the visual infrastructure is depicted as an
abstract circuit diagram, which by itself conveys little information about
whether the circuitry is neural, electronic, or constituting an "oil refinery,"
as neuropsychologist Lawrence Weiskrantz (1997:204) described it.

The neural level, where neurobiology studies the operations of individual neurons, their synapses, and their mutual inhibitions and excitations,
is an organizational level with scales much smaller than the infrastructural

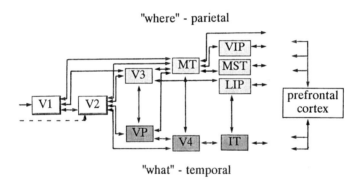

Figure 3.3
A simplified schematic of the visual infrastructure (adapted from Maunsell 1995).
The boxes represent brain areas differentiated by function. V1 is the primary visual
area. The other areas are generally referred to as extrastraite areas. Areas to the left
are called early stages of the visual process, areas to the right late stages. They are
organized into *where* and *what* streams, and both converge on the frontal lobe of
the brain. Lines linking the boxes represent major neural projections. Almost all
connections go both ways. Connections from earlier to later stages are called
forward projection, and those from later to earlier stages backward projection.

level. If we compare an infrastructural system or its brain anatomy with the telephone network, its neural level is like the operation of individual telephones and connections. The neural level loses sight of the big picture by zooming in on the excitation of individual neurons and the interaction among a small group of neurons. Brain anatomy overlooks specifics of neural mechanisms and abstractly describes a higher level organization of the brain that correlates with an infrastructural system. Therefore brain anatomy and function belong to the infrastructural and not the neural level.

Rule-Using, Rule-Governed, and Rule-Driven

Infrastructural processes are susceptible to representation by computer models. Thus they are sometimes said to compute, a description that generates considerable controversy. To clear up the confusion, I distinguish among digital computers that are rule driven, infrastructural processes that are rule governed, and our conscious mind that is capable of using rules.

People consciously and deliberately make rules, apply them, and abide by them. We follow rules when we stop at red lights or do long multiplication. Human activities of following or applying rules require understanding. To follow a rule properly, one must understand both the rule and the circumstance to judge whether it applies, which depends on much circumspection and intuition. "Computer" originally referred to people whose job was to calculate, hoards of whom were employed by banks, accounting houses, or the Manhattan Project. Human computers use tools ranging from abaci to electronic calculators. Above all, they use rules of computation, including rules in programming languages. Rule using is a full mental activity. We follow rules as persons. Our mental infrastructural processes do not follow rules because they have no understanding.

With the development of computation theory, scientists and engineers learned how to break a rule into many simple steps, spell out the steps so precisely that they can be executed without any understanding, and build machines for their execution. They build digital computers designed to implement their rules and perform according to their specifications. Electronic computers, especially stored-program machines that we are familiar with, are rule-driven systems. They do not follow rules because they do not understand. Instead, they literally contain physical parts that encode the rules that humans made and understood. These parts, which embody their programs, causally control and drive their dynamic evolution. So far, the only uncontroversial examples of rule-driven systems are artifacts. The physically inscribed rules that drive them correspond exactly to the rules that we conceive because we deliberately made them that way. They are products of our intellect but not a part of our natural cognitive system, not even our mental infrastructure. Engineers build rule-driven systems. The philosophy of the computational mind, which asserts that humans are also rule-driven systems, remains bitterly contested (see section 4).

Fans of computers and AI are so vociferous they often drown out the fact that cognitive science features many rules besides those driving artifacts. Examples of such rules are the principles of universal grammar, which are presented in section 14. What are these rules that neither drive systems nor are consciously followed? This question creates much philosophical debate. Some say we apply the rules albeit unconsciously, others that they imply we are naturally driven by rules, and still others dismiss unconscious rules as incomprehensible. The controversy peppers mind engineering and retrospective creationism. Approaching mind from natural science, however, it sounds like a déjà vu.

Since early Roman times, rule (*regula*) acquired the meaning of standard or guideline, which is closely associated with the meaning of law (*lex*), except it is less official and authoritative. Three centuries ago, when the notion of physical laws gained prominence with the rise of Newtonian mechanics, physicist Robert Boyle said he could not "conceive how a body devoid of understanding and sense, truly so called, can moderate and determinate its own motions, especially so as to make them conformable to laws, that it has no knowledge or apprehension of" (Ruby 1986). Like most of his predecessors, Boyle understood conformity to laws in the sense of people consciously abiding by laws, either civil or divine. In this sense, Aquinas rightly declared that the use of "law" in reference to inanimate things was anthropomorphic and metaphoric. Similarly, Searle rightly concluded that accounts of infrastructural processes as following rules committed the homuncular fallacy. However, except for certain confusion in the philosophy of mind, this anthropomorphic sense has long faded in the interpretation of a lawful or law-governed physical world. Scientists today unhesitantly call intelligible and predicable causal regularities of natural phenomena laws or law governed. Physicists say that planets obey Newton's laws and electrons are governed by the laws of quantum mechanics without the slightest thought of attributing understanding or cognition to planets and electrons.

In the Humean notion where causation is rulelike regularity, everything is lawful or rule-governed because everything is physical and causal. Natural processes ranging from planetary motions to our mental infrastructure are lawful. Lawful processes usually do not follow rules or are driven by rules. Except a small class of artifacts, notably stored-program computers, lawful systems physically incorporate neither their governing laws nor the symbols that scientists use to represent the rules. Benzene contains carbon and hydrogen atoms that form a hexagonal ring that plays important roles in its causal behaviors, but it contains no symbol "hexagon." All it exhibits is a certain structure that humans represent by the symbol "hexagon." You will not find the laws of quantum mechanics stored anywhere in atoms like computer programs, nor are you likely to find rules encoded in our brains. Laws and rules are framed by physicists or cognitive scientists to describe and represent structural and causal regularities of atoms or infrastructural processes.

Lawful systems are the topics of most of natural science. A dynamical system, for instance, is one whose evolution is governed by a dynamical rule. The rise of dynamicalism and its attendant philosophy that takes mind as motion show that even in AI engineering the trend turns away from rule-driven systems to lawful systems. Connectionist networks are essentially nonlinear dynamical systems, some of which are abstractly analogously to physical systems such as spin glasses.

A chief goal of science is to discover regularities in natural processes, the most general of which has the honorific title of natural laws. Once scientists discern patterns and regularities in natural phenomena and represent them by appropriate rules, they can write the rules into computer programs. Computer modeling is productive in all sciences, including cognitive science.

Processes in the mental infrastructure are lawful but they are neither rule following nor rule driven. The ability to build computer models for them shifts cognitive science into high gear unattainable by previous psychology. We should, however, be careful interpreting the models. Computer models are scientific theories for lawful processes. Their successes no more imply that our mental infrastructure is a rule-driven computer than planets are computers.

General Concepts that Usually Do Not Denote Mentality

It is not rare for philosophers of mind to confuse rule-following and rule-governed entities. This is an instance of confusing scientists with their objects, intellectual tools with the objective contents of scientific theories. To avoid similar confusion, let me introduce some general terms common in theories for lawful entities that cannot follow rules so that they are not carelessly taken to indicate mental ability.

The *state* of an entity is the summary of its properties at a time. As the state changes with time, the entity undergoes a *process*. Much of natural science is devoted to studying the *structures* of entities and their processes. An entity's structures influence its causal behaviors. Structures are found not only in states but also in processes. As explained in section 11, dynamical theories grasp processes as wholes and describe their overall structures. Entities interact with their environment, receiving causal influences and exerting causal effects. Most theories treat the interaction partially, accounting for changes only in the entities and not in the environment. Under this approximation, the causal transaction can be called *input* into and *output* from the entities. For example, an atom is an entity in which many electrons are held together by a nucleus, and atomic physics investigates the structures of atoms such as the arrangement of electrons into shells around the nucleus. Governed by laws of quantum mechanics, an atom goes from an initial high-energy state to a final low-energy state, putting out a photon in the process. Similarly, we can call a photon that is absorbed by the atom the input into the atom.

Laws and rules cover possible as well as actual cases, which is why they facilitate prediction and support contrary-to-fact hypotheses. A rule can predict what the entities it governs would do under certain hypothetical conditions. In other words, it describes the *dispositions* and *capacities* of the entities it governs. For instance, an atom has the capacity to absorb light and jump into a state of higher energy; an atom in a high-energy state has a certain disposition to emit light and relax to a lower-energy state. In sum, state, structure, structural cause, possibility, disposition, capacity, input, and output are all common concepts in theoretical sciences studying rule-governed phenomena. Except in rare cases when theories are about rule-following entities such as humans, the concept of possibility hidden in disposition and capacity is recognized by scientists and not the entities they study. Therefore, the mere occurrence of these concepts in a theory does not imply that the theory is about mental entities, as some philosophers assume. It takes much more to specify mentality.

Infraconscious Processes as Information Processing

Many scientists attest that information processing is one of the most fruitful concepts in cognitive science. I explain in section 17 that information does not exist as ready-made entities in a mindless world. Without mental beings, nature exhibits only structures, not information. Mental efforts alone create information by conferring significance on some chosen physical structures. The same sunlight that is simply absorbed by things becomes, to us mindful beings, bearer of information about the sun's structure. Computers, communication links, and the battery of information-processing tools exist because we build them to serve us. Thus they depend on our minds. Similarly, the notion of processing, as opposed to process, suggests purpose. Water flows through a swamp and is purified in the natural process. We can use processes similar to the swamp to build water-processing plants, but we seldom regard the swamp as a water processor if we do not use it as such to serve our needs.

Information and information processing both presuppose mental beings, because only mental beings can understand and hence are capable of being informed. We call those physical patterns and events that we find informative "information." We call those devices that we build to record and manipulate these physical patterns "information storage" or "information processors," although they themselves are not informed. Thus information processing derives much of its epistemic connotation from its contexts: To whom is the processed information informative?

Contexts separate the significances of computers and mental infra-structures as information processors. Neither computers nor infrastructural processes understand anything. Unlike computers, however, infrastructural processes constitute a larger mental entity that is conscious and capable of understanding and being informed. They contribute indispensably to the mental life of a person who understands, as their products are integrated and become the informative contents of experience and understanding. Thus infraconscious processes process information because what they process becomes informative to the mental entity that they constitute. Aconscious computers, however, can be said to process information only in a diminutive sense, for what they process is informative and understandable neither to themselves nor to the larger entity they constitute, but only to outside agents.

What makes the notion of information processing productive in studying infrastructural processes? Here is one interpretation that involves no theospectivism, anthropomorphism, or homuncular fallacy. When two physical entities interact, both change. In studying them, however, we can choose to concentrate on the changes in only one of them. More specifically, we have two approaches to study a permanent system interacting with a stream of passing entities, as we can concentrate on the system or the passing stream.

One approach concentrates on changes of the permanent system under various impacts of the entities. For instance, physics studies the excitation and relaxation of atoms under various electromagnetic waves; economics studies the booms and busts of an economy under various noneconomical shocks.

The other approach, which cognitive scientists call *signal* or *information processing*, concentrates on changes in the stream of entities as the stream interacts with the system. This is common in many sciences. For instance, instead of studying how a system changes under a train of electromagnetic waves, we concentrate on how the wave train is spectrally resolved or differentially filtered and amplified as it passes through the system. It is also fruitful to abstract from details of the system and consider only its effects in resolving, filtering, and amplifying electromagnetic waves. Such abstraction is the stock in trade of electrical engineering, and it proves equally fruitful in cognitive science. Taking terms familiar in engineering, cognitive scientists call the permanent system a *processor* and the stream of entities that passes through it *signal* or *information*.

Suppose we want to find out the properties of a system. Perhaps the most successful method is to feed the system streams of signal with known properties and infer its operation from the ways input signals are transformed when they emerge from the output. Experimental physicists routinely send beams of light or particles to probe the properties of various targets, although they do not call the scattering experiments information processing. Similarly, to probe a specific infrastructural process, cognitive scientists feed it various signals by presenting a subject with carefully controlled stimuli and record the output by demanding from the subject sharply defined responses. The systematic correlation of characteristics between input and output sheds light on the cognitive processor. This experimental approach probes specific infraconscious processes that are sensitive to specific types of stimuli and responses, for instance visual or linguistic stimuli. Furthermore, by finely differentiating stimuli, scientists target highly specialized subprocesses within say, the visual or linguistic system. Call it information processing, scattering, priming, or whatever, this method is highly successful.

9   How Scientists Probe Infrastructural Processes

The mental infrastructure is a huge complex system. Scientists try to analyze it into various specialized infrastructures and further into coupled processes. How do they do it? The mental infrastructure is rather intangible; one cannot grasp it and take it apart physically. Mental subjects are unaware of its operation and hence cannot report on it. Dissecting their bodies is ineffective, because infrastructural processes must feed into conscious experiences. Thus the mental infrastructure can be probed only indirectly and with ingenious methods. Here we briefly look at some approaches by which cognitive scientists come to grips with infrastructural processes from both the neural and psychological sides. As is typical in this book, the focus is not on detailed techniques but on concepts involved and interpretation of results.

Research methods are not employed blindly but aimed at particular targets. Thus they are based on certain general assumptions about the targets whose specifics they try to find out. Methods based on right assumptions work; those based on wrong ones don't. How are various successful cognitive scientific methods possible? What have they presupposed about mind or its infrastructure? What information do they yield?

Neuropathology and Lesion

Controlled experiments are venerable tools in analyzing complex phenomena. Scientists target a specific element in an entity, alter it while keeping the rest constant, and examine the effects of the controlled alteration. By systematically picking on various elements, they study the effects of the elements individually. Differential control is most easily exercised on entities that are tangible and manipulable, such as the brain.

Since brain processes underlie mental experiences, the obvious experiment for analyzing mind is to modify the brain systematically and study the consequences. Such experiments are routinely performed in nonhuman animals. Scientists kill if necessary but they more often mutilate, as live animals are usually more informative about mind than dead ones. They train an animal to perform certain tasks, then remove parts of its brain and see how the mutilation affects its performance. Animal sacrifice on the altar of science has yielded much knowledge on mental infrastructure. However, it is difficult to relate the knowledge to conscious experiences, as animals cannot articulate on what they see or feel. Only with great ingenuity and difficulty do scientists sometimes infer animals' experiences from their behaviors, and even these often suffer interpretive controversies.

Humans can articulate their experiences, but intrusive experiments on humans are forbidden for good reasons. Thus scientists make most use of "nature's experiments" and learn from the plight of people with brain injuries due to accidents or diseases. As Freud said, through injury and disease, normal functions are laid bare.

For instance, the brain has many areas with vision functions, injuries to which produce a long list of deficiencies. Patients with apperceptive agnosia can discriminate colors and areas but not shapes. Their visual experiences are mere formless colors; they cannot recognize objects and are often mistaken for being blind. People with associative agnosia can see things but cannot recognize objects. They can draw and copy but cannot identify what they have copied. Their visual experiences are stripped of all meaning, and consequently they cannot integrate what they see with other activities. More specifically, some patients cannot see motion, others cannot recognize face. Some can see only one thing at time, others can see only one part or aspect of a thing at a time and fail to recognize the thing if they cannot guess successfully based on the part they see. Such disorders make us realize how much is involved in normal vision. What we see is served by many integrative infrastructural processes that produce experiences of whole objects or scenes. Information gained from people with vision neuropathologies militates against the doctrine of purely receptive perception and has great significance on the objectivity of our mind, as we will see in chapter 5 (Farah 1990; Stoerig 1996; Driver and Mattingly 1998; Köhler and Moscovitch 1997).

Other modes of experiences also have many forms of deficiency caused by focal brain injuries. The sheer variety of cognitive disabilities reveals the complexity of the mental infrastructure, as each ailment highlights an infrastructural process that is derailed. However, there is a limit to what we can learn from neuropathology. It delimits a function negatively by the consequences of malfunction, but offers no positive explanation of the function under normal conditions.

Neural Monitoring

Another class of experiments monitors excitations of the brain or individual neurons while a subject performs certain cognitive tasks. Neuroscience receives a big boost from imaging technologies that reveal spatial patterns of brain excitation. Because imaging is not intrusive, it can be applied to humans. In positron emission tomography (PET), experimenters inject a subject with a radioactive tracer, and the PET scanner measures the distribution of the tracer in the brain. A high tracer concentration in a region indicates elevated blood flow, which in turn indicates elevated excitation in that region. Functional magnetic resonance imaging (fMRI) measures the level of oxygen in blood; regions with high levels are most active. It yields better temporal resolution than PET. Advanced technology improves sensitivity and resolution but does not change the basic nature of brain imaging. By measuring blood flow or oxygenation, imaging yields a gross picture on the relative excitations of various brain regions but not detailed neural mechanisms occurring in the excited regions. Because of its coarse grains, brain imaging studies not the neural but the infrastructural level of organization (Barinaga 1997).

Electrophysiology, which measures electrical activities of neurons, has several techniques. Electroencephalography (EEG) and event-related potential (ERP) record the combined activities of a large number of neurons. Consequently they can be conducted at the surface of the skin or the skull. Like brain imaging, they are coarse grained and unintrusive, hence suitable for human subjects.

In many situations, it is desirable to measure excitation behaviors of individual neurons. This can be performed by inserting microelectrodes into the brain. However, no humans would allow scientists to mess with their brains unless it is for their own medical benefit. Nonhuman animals have no say. Intrusive neural experiments on them yield such information as the sensitivities of individual neurons to various sensual stimuli, connections among various neurons, and various neural pathways. Unlike EEG, ERP, and brain imaging, single-neuron experiments probe processes on the neural and not the infrastructural level.

Always, neural experiments that aim to study mind or its infrastructure emphasize not biology but function. Scientists do not merely monitor neural excitations but carefully control their contexts. In so doing they assume a causal relationship between neural excitations and cognitive tasks that subjects perform. The most significant part of an experiment lies in designing the task to illuminate the cognitive process. The emphasis on tasks is most apparent in animal experiments. Unlike humans, animals do not understand instructions and cannot articulate their experiences. Consequently neural experiments are usually combined with behavioral conditioning and monitoring. Experimenters go to great extents to ensure that the animal is performing the task or perceiving the stimulus that they intend. Without independent checks on animal behaviors, one cannot claim that the measured neural excitation serves a particular cognitive activity. All the care testifies that the experiments presuppose causal relations between the mental and neural levels but do *not* presuppose that causation flows only one way, from the neural level up. Indeed, by comparing the behaviors of a single visual neuron while the animal attends to different aspects of the same stimulus, experimental results vindicate the assumption that mental activities such as attention can cause changes in neurons (see section 12).

Priming

Neuroscientists approach the mental infrastructure from the point of view of the brain; psychologists approach it from the point of view of mental subjects. When people are awake, their experiences eclipse their infrastructures. To get at infrastructural processes, psychologists focus on those rare conditions in which a stimulus that a person is unaware of influences his performance of certain tasks. A time-honored psychological technique for such conditions is priming.

In priming experiments, psychologists measure the improvement in the fluency, accuracy, or reaction time by which subjects perform certain tasks as a result of previous experience. It probes infraconscious processes because it does not require subjects to recall the experience consciously. To make sure that they are measuring only infraconscious effects, scientists often use priming together with other methods that test conscious recall and compare the results.

In a typical experiment, subjects study a list of words and later perform several tasks. In the priming task, they see certain cues and must respond as quickly as possible. Suppose they have studied a list that contains the word "bread." Later they are presented with the stem "br---" or the stem "but---" and asked to complete it with the first word that comes to mind. *Visual priming* occurs if they are more likely to complete "br---" with "bread" than "break" or "breed." *Semantic priming* occurs if they are more likely to complete "but---" with "butter" instead of "button" or "butler," because it shows the influence of the meaning of "bread." Stem completion probes infraconscious influences because it does not refer to the word list and does not ask subjects to recall consciously their exposure to it.

To tease apart conscious and infraconscious effects, scientists often ask subjects to perform other tasks and compare results. In one task subjects recall the words on the study list. In another they recognize the learned words from a test list. Both tasks test conscious memory because subjects explicitly acknowledge that they have seen the words. More often than not, deliberate and priming tests yield different results. Subjects who cannot recall or recognize the word "bread" nevertheless produce "bread" more readily in stem completion. Recall reveals conscious memory, primed fluency reveals the infraconscious effects of a previous experience. The difference between them shows that something is operating without our awareness. That something is infrastructural processes (Moscovitch et al. 1994).

Several priming experiments are designed to probe various infraconscious processes. Psychologists often make sure that subjects are unable to see the stimuli. They present optical stimuli to patients blinded by brain injuries, or make the stimuli invisible to those with normal vision. Sometimes they present a stimulus briefly to trigger certain infrastructural processes and prevent perception by quickly masking it with another stimulus. Other times they present stimuli too faint or brief to be perceived, yet strong and long enough to trigger infrastructural processes. This is how priming experiments reveal the effect of subliminal perception. Even when subjects cannot see the stimulus "bread" because it is way below the threshold of perception, they are likely to complete the stem "br---" with "bread."

A stimulus causes the operation of some infrastructural processes, even if these processes fail to generate experience of the stimulus. Priming experiments aim to probe the processes triggered and their effects. By carefully designing stimuli and tasks, psychologists probe individual infrastructural processes. Many examples are presented later in the book.

Blindsight and the Infrastructure of Vision
Cognitive neural and psychological experiments prick at a huge system. It is usually unclear what among the large number of entangling factors

are being probed. Therefore data interpretation always demands critical attention. Let us take the case of blindsight as an example. The study of this phenomenon combines neuropathological and priming methods. Its interesting results generate much interpretive controversy.

Brain injuries and careful laboratory tests often leave little doubt that some patients do not feign disability but are genuinely incapable of perceiving a certain kind of stimulus. Nevertheless, at times these patients' responses to these unperceived stimuli are uncannily appropriate, suggesting that some of their performances are independent of perception. Perhaps the most striking example is blindsight.

Blindness can result from damage to the eyes as well as to the brain. As described in the appendix, almost all optical nerves from the eyes enter the cerebral cortex through the primary visual area, V1, at the back of the head. Consequently the destruction of V1 eliminates visual experience, resulting in cortical blindness. When damage is partial, the person retains some visual experience, although it is highly degraded. If only a part of V1 is totally destroyed, the person loses only a part of his visual field, but within the blind field, he loses all visual perception. Thus someone who loses the left half of V1 is blind to the right side of his visual field.

Patients with genuine cortical blindness have no visual experience in at least parts of their visual fields. Nevertheless, their eyes move to aim correctly at unseen stimuli. Apparently, destruction of V1 leaves some residual functions that would not survive destruction of the eyes. To probe these residual abilities, neuropsychologists perform controlled experiments. They present an optical stimulus to a person's blind field, give him several options on an aspect of the stimulus, and force him to pick one, even if he has to guess and even if he thinks the exercise silly. Tests assess presence, planar location, movement, orientation, wavelength, and crude shapes. Some subjects refuse to guess. Many who cooperate are surprised to learn that their guesses are accurate. The percentages of their correct responses are above chance performance, sometimes significantly so. Lawrence Weiskrantz (1997), who pioneered the study of this phenomenon, christened the ability to guess correctly the features of unseen stimuli *blindsight* in distinction to conscious sight, normal or degraded.

The peculiar experiences and responses of blindsight subjects give cognitive neuroscientists an opportunity to probe the infrastructural processes underlying vision. Blindsight responses fall into two classes: the first involves no awareness of any kind; the second involves some aware-ness of stimuli, but it is not visual. Most blindsight subjects are not aware of the stimuli at all, and experimenters must prompt them as to when they should guess and about what aspect, such as orientation whenever they hear a bell. They usually have no confidence in their guesses, even when their guesses are highly accurate. These are cases of *pure* blindsight, as accurate guesses are not accompanied by any experience whatsoever.

Sometimes a second sort of response sets in when the salience of the stimuli increases. When the stimuli have high intensity or high speed, some subjects report having some kind of conscious feeling: a "pinprick" for bright spots; a "wavy feel" for fast movement; a "jagged feel" for the figure X compared with the "smooth feel" of an O. As they begin to feel, they start to detect and discriminate spontaneously, and they are confident in their judgments. There are two significant points here: First, confidence does not improve the accuracy of guess compared with pure blindsight; and second, the feeling is not visual. Subjects who acknowledge they are *feeling* flatly deny that they are *seeing* anything. When asked, "What did you see?" blindsight subject GY was unambiguous: "I didn't *see* anything." However, he was equally emphatic about his experience. Waving his hand to mimic a moving stimulus, he said: "I *knew* that there was something moving, I was *aware*." What was his experience like? GY replied: "The dif-ficulty is the same that one would have in trying to tell a blind man what it like to see" (Weiskrantz 1997:66). This is a case of *impure* blindsight because it was a strange experience.

Here are two new kinds of responses to unseen optical stimuli: pure blindsight and novel nonvisual experience. Careful experiments show that both are qualitatively different from normal and degraded sight. What do they reveal about our mind and its infrastructure? For pure blindsight, we need an extra concept to distinguish guesses from perceptual judgments with similar degrees of accuracy. Neuropsychologists argue that this extra concept is *consciousness*, which is absent in guesses but present in percep-tion. It is crisply embodied in experiments by the subject's yes or no answer to the presence of experience. For impure blindsight, we need the concept of *modes of awareness* of the same stimuli. It distinguishes familiar visual experience from the novel experience that GY acknowledges but lacks words to describe. The concepts of consciousness and modes of awareness underscore the fact that whatever are damaged in blindsight are processes that underlie not merely reflexes but experiences.

Blindsight subjects lack only visual experience, otherwise they are aware of objects through sound, touch, or other means. They guess deliberately in the laboratory, and by this conscious act they manage to bring to their awareness the causal effects of optical stimuli that escape their visual experience. If they do not guess, they have neither knowledge nor memory of the stimuli. When they have guessed and judged the presence of a stimulus, they have acquired conscious knowledge and memory. This knowledge is not visual but theoretical, just as physicists know electrons exist without seeing them.

Blindsight subjects quickly catch on to their ability to guess correctly. DB, for instance, insisted he saw nothing, but said confidently after an experimental run: "I got it right almost every time." If the need arises, you bet blindsight subjects will put the knowledge and its generalization to work, to learn to prompt themselves routinely and discriminate spontaneously. Their action will be fully conscious, complete with the feel of uncertainty in guessing and the coolness of reasoning in reckoning with risky guesses. They compensate their lost of visual experience not by unconscious behaviors but by other modes of conscious actions including theoretical reasoning. They can do this because their conscious mentality integrates and correlates vastly diverse factors. The mental ability to rally one mode of experience to compensate for the loss of another also reveals elaborate interconnections within the mental infrastructure.

Dissociation between Experience and Performance

Blindsight is a case of the dissociation between performance and experience. Generally, *dissociation* means that even if a person is not aware of an event that affects him, the event can still influence his behaviors indirectly, notably in the performance of certain subsequent tasks. The idea of dissociation was introduced by Jean Martin Charcot, with whom Freud studied. Charcot inferred from clinical observations that a patient loses voluntary control of a specific mental function because the function is dissociated from mainstream consciousness. Dissociation is a prevalent phenomenon that is becoming increasingly important in cognitive science. It reveals the workings of the mental infrastructure by removing the obstruction of conscious processes.

Dissociation is not limited to vision but occurs also in the other perceptual senses, language, and memory. There are blindtouch, deaf hearing, covert face recognition in prosopagnosia, implicit reading in alexia, implicit memory in amnesia, and more. An amnesic patient refused to shake hands with a psychologist who in a previous introduction had hidden a pin in his hand. The patient could not explain his refusal, because his brain injury robbed him of all conscious recollection. Yet the previous pain had somehow modified his instinct. Alexic patients cannot consciously read words and must spell a word out letter by letter before recognizing it. Nevertheless, they can classify rapidly flashed strings of letters as words or nonwords, animal names or not. This does not imply that they are good at speed reading; they are not reading at all. Besides the crude classification, they are not aware of any meaning of the flashed words. Always, certain restricted residue performances involve some features that survive the elimination of experience about these features.

Dissociation between performance and experience goes only one way: There can be performance without awareness, but not awareness without performance. We have no evidence that a person perceives a stimulus but his experience does not affect his performance.

Dissociation as a Window to the Mental Infrastructure

How does dissociation between experience and performance occur? An experience is subserved by a mental infrastructure consisting numerous processes. Be it perception or remembrance, it requires successful integration of many infrastructural processes. However, the successful operation of a process alone is not sufficient for experience, thus producing the possibility of one-way dissociation.

Suppose your car's engine works but the car does not because its transmission is broken. When you turn the ignition key, you get air conditioning but no automation. If we liken the engine to a mental infrastructure, automation to the experience it normally supports, and air conditioning to its side effects usually overlooked, your broken car manifests the dissociation between experience and performance. When an infrastructural process is properly triggered, it will run its course and generate effects, which in turn causally trigger other infrastructural processes. Under normal conditions, its product contributes to the contents of a specific mode of experience. This need not happen, as mishaps can occur downstream in the normal infrastructural pathway, leading to abortion of experience.

Subjects with dissociation are always conscious. They perform tasks consciously, unaware only of specific stimuli that concern the experimenters. Mishaps that lead the dissociative unawareness are invariably local; global mishaps would knock out consciousness altogether. Thus the effects of the triggered infrastructural process survive in the intact portion of the mental infrastructure and can cause circuitous processes of other actions. Activated but later derailed infrastructural processes account for performance without experience.

Dissociation occurs not only in patients but in normal people. When normal people fail to see something, it is usually not the fault of their optical sensors. Chances are that photoreceptors in the retina registered a feature in the light input and passed it on, and the feature was analyzed by appropriate early areas in the visual pathways. Nevertheless, the feature can still be absent from visual experience because it is "crowded out" in subsequent integrative processes. This possibility was proved in an experiment in which subjects were shown gratings in their peripheral visual field. The gratings' orientation was causally registered in subjects' brains because orientation-sensitive neurons in their primary visual cortices were activated. Nevertheless, the subjects still failed to see the orientation (He et al. 1996).

The neural connections in our brain are extremely multilateral and redundant. Projections to the primary visual area dominate output from the retinas, but do not exhaust it. Secondary pathways connect the retinas to various regions in the subcortical brain, which in turn connect to areas in the cortex. When primary visual pathways function normally, secondary pathways may be eclipsed or idled. When brain injuries disrupt primary pathways, surviving secondary routes are forced to operate alone. These alternative routes can contribute to the discriminatory abilities in blindsight. Brain imaging experiments found that when blindsight subjects have some kind of nonvisual experience of the optical stimuli, their cerebral cortices excite. When they have no experience of any kind, brain excitations shift to mostly subcortical areas. Therefore although the pure and impure modes of blindsight are comparably accurate, they are subserved by different infrastructures. Consciousness does require a difference in the mental infrastructure (Cowey and Stoerig 1992; Sahraie et al. 1997).

The plasticity of the brain can develop alternative pathways, making use of whatever available resources. When the optical nerves of a neonatal ferret were surgically connected to the auditory instead of the visual cortex, the animal grew up responding to light as if it saw with its auditory cortex (von Molchner 2000). The primary visual area of congenitally blind people excites during tactile discrimination such as Braille reading. Furthermore, the excitation is functional and essential. When the visual area is tempered by magnetic stimulation, tactile reading of the blind is disrupted just as magnetic tampering disrupts the visual performance of the sighted. No one suggests that blind people see in any ordinary sense. From the functioning of their visual cortex, however, it is reasonable to guess that their tactile sense is not only more acute but differs qualitatively from that of sighted people. They "see" with their hands, which can be regarded as a novel sense that we lack words to describe (Cohen and Schooler 1997). Similarly, we can interpret the guessing ability of pure blindsight and the nonvisual experience of impure blindsight as extraordinary senses for optical stimuli.

Dissociation has become a powerful probe in cognitive science, as removal of various conscious experiences opens holes for scientists to peek into various functioning of the mental infrastructure. In blindsight, for instance, brain injuries destroy only the visual infrastructure from V1 onward. They leave intact some of the mental infrastructure, including the portion of the visual infrastructure that comes before V1. Just as waters blocked by a dam find their way to the ocean by circuitous routes, some optical stimuli blocked by a ruined V1 trigger infrastructural processes and find circuitous causal routes to some kind of extraordinary experience. As an eclipse reveals the corona usually hidden by the sun's brilliance, cortical blindness reveals the operation of circuitous infrastructural processes that are normally overshadowed by visual experiences.

Two Interpretations of Blindsight

In the preceding discussion I adopted the interpretation of blindsight and other types of dissociation that is common in the scientific community. This fruitful interpretation enables scientists to use dissociative phenomena to probe infrastructural processes underlying various modes of experiences. For it to work, scientists rely on concepts of consciousness and subjective experiences of their patients. These concepts irritate some mind-designing philosophers, who advocate the opposite interpretation: blindsight reveals not the importance but the superfluity of consciousness.

Behaviorists and instrumental behaviorists cite blindsight to deny consciousness, inner mental life, and subjective experience. They refuse to admit as evidence the testimonies of blindsight subjects that they do not see or have visual experience of stimuli whose features they correctly guess. These testimonies pertain to first-person or subjective experiences, which behaviorists rule out as "unscientific." Without the testimonies, what are left are only the records of guesses. Behaviorists hold that the ability of blindsight subjects to make judgments about some optical stimuli with accuracies comparable with those of sighted people proves that visual experience is superfluous if not illusory. Blindsights are zombies who "see" without experience of seeing. We differ from them quantitatively but not qualitatively. We are more talented zombies (Dennett 1991).

Weiskrantz (1997) and other neuropsychologists counter that zombie fans have distorted facts by ignoring the evidence for the difference between blindsight and degraded sight. If we take account of all evidence and respect the testimonies of blindsight subjects, blindsight does not prove the superfluidity of consciousness. Quite the contrary, it proves the necessity of the concept of consciousness in drawing a crucial psychological distinction between seeing and not seeing but guessing correctly. Weiskrantz's theory falls in the line with those of neuroscientists such as Wilder Penfield and Roger Sperry, who explicitly introduced the notion consciousness into neuropsychology to account for the mental states of their patients.

Behaviorists dismiss first-person experiences in the name of "science," thus manifesting a dogmatism opposite to science. Dogmatism rules out certain concepts a priori. In contrast, science uses whatever concepts necessary to save the phenomena. If to characterize some human phenomena scientists require the concepts of subjectivity or first-person experience, so be it. Respect for the phenomena always reigns supreme in science. Introduction of these concepts into neuropsychology was far from casual. Scientists carefully ascertained first-person claims of their patients, controlled conditions that elicited the claims, correlated the claims under systematically varying conditions, and compared the claims of different patients. Such painstaking procedures manifest scientific caution in acknowledging patients' subjectivity. When several blindsight patients guessed correctly what they claimed they did not see, when they were able to guess correctly under a variety of conditions, when their claims of blindness were confirmed by independent tests, scientists could justifiably introduce the notion of subjective visual experience to distinguish patients's states of seeing a stimulus from states of not seeing it but guessing it correctly. Under the weight of evidence, behaviorists' denial of the distinction simply because it calls for subjective experience is dogmatic.

10 The Connection between Mind and Its Infrastructure

We saw in preceding sections that numerous specialized infrastructural processes underlie our experiences. These processes are merely causal and lack such mental characteristics as understanding and consciousness. Cognitive science has provided a huge amount of knowledge on the mental infrastructure. To those who want explanations of mental experiences familiar in our everyday life, however, this knowledge is like scratching at an itch through a boot, because there are few explanations of how the mental infrastructure underlies experiences.

Mind and its infrastructure constitute two distinct organizational levels. How do the two levels connect? How do numerous brief and narrowly specialized infrastructural processes organize themselves into prolonged experiences with broad and variable contents? This is called the binding problem in cognitive science, and scientists are very far from solving it.

The binding problem has many hypotheses. Bernard Baars (1997) proposed a "global workplace" model in which distributed mental representations become conscious when they are broadcast globally and integrated coherently. Gerald Edelman and Tonami (2000) explained consciousness in terms of the reentrant mappings among neuronal groups. Daniel Schacter (1990) proposed a model of dissociable interactions and conscious experience (DICE), which distinguishes processes that mediate conscious awareness sharply from modular systems that operate on linguistic, perceptual, and other kinds of information. Francis Crick and Christof Kock (1990) discovered a 40-Hz neural oscillation across wide regions of the brain. Antonio Damasio (1994) proposed that the brain contains convergence zones where various types of excitation are integrated. Consensus is scarce, except perhaps on the conviction that people's conscious mentality is not mysterious and to explain it is an important scientific task. This acknowledgement of a gap in our current state of knowledge is expressed by scientists with humor. Textbooks and review articles in cognitive science frequently reprint Sidney Harris's cartoon featuring a scientist covering the blackboard with equations, in the middle of which is the step "then a miracle occurs."

Several responses address the gap in the scientific comprehension of mind. Some mind-designing philosophers claim that the binding problem does not exist; no connection has to be made because our mental experiences are illusory, all we have are neural or computational processes, so science will soon explain everything if it has not already done so. Other philosophers assert that the binding problem exists but is insoluble; our mental experience will remain forever a mystery unfathomable by our merely human intellect. Scientists usually avoid both extremes. They react like the colleague in Harris's cartoon, pointing to the miraculous step with a demand for clarification.

Glaring puzzles are signs that the frontier of a science is still wide open. It is still a time of high exploration and great opportunity, a time at which later ages will look back with nostalgia if not envy, as we look back at the Age of Discovery, sighing that America is discovered only once. Explanatory gaps occur in all scientific frontiers. Harris's cartoon also appears on T-shirts that carry the logo of *Physics Today*. Besides humor, it manifests an intellectual honesty crucial to science, especially in the atmosphere of hype that so often envelops frontiers. Science will not advance if scientists deceive themselves about what they do not know, pretend that everything is explained, cover up difficulties with jargon, or condemn phenomena they are unable to explain as illusory, pseudoproblematic, or unscientific.

Connect Levels by Synthetic Analysis

I maintain that mental experiences are real properties of persons and they are scientifically explicable. However, scientists have much time and hard work ahead to produce satisfactory explanations. Why are the explanations so difficult? What kinds of explanations can we expect in the future? Since cognitive science is just beginning to bridge the gap between infrastructural and mental levels, it helps to look at other sciences that successfully connected different organizational levels.

The rest of this chapter considers some general scientific methods for tackling systems with several organizational levels. How these general ideas work in cognitive science to link infrastructural and mental processes is discussed in the next four chapters. The general ideas and their substantiation lead to a major conclusion: Connection is not annexation; the former is bilateral, the latter unilateral. To connect two organizational levels is not to abolish one or to collapse one into the other. A successful connection depends on a clear understanding of both levels. Specifically, a satisfactory solution to the binding problem requires *a clear characterization of experiences into which infrastructural processes organize themselves*. This leads to the final chapter, which analyzes the structures of the mental level and mind's openness to the world.

Generally, to connect two organization levels is always difficult theoretically, as different levels usually have disparate properties and occur in systems with considerable complexity. Using dynamical systems as examples, I illustrate the meanings of different levels and their connections. Modern dynamical theory is able to define properties on a higher level because it includes something that classical dynamical theory lacks: a top-level perspective that reckons a process as a whole. A comparison of classical and modern dynamical theories shows how the bottom-up approach, in which one tries to put together parts without a view of the whole, is futile for systems of any complexity. By insisting on the bottom-up approach, many philosophers blind themselves to the possibility of emergent properties, even when many such properties are affirmed by well established sciences. Despite philosophical prescription, actual science combines bottom-up and top-down approaches, executing a round trip from the whole to its parts and back. This approach, which I call *synthetic analysis*, is as fruitful in explaining mentality as in explaining other high-level properties such as fluidity. Synthetic analysis expands the conceptual framework to accommodate different levels. It is best seen in contrast to *nothing-butism*, which reduces the framework to squeeze out one of the levels.

The Bane of Nothing-Butism

In the eighteenth century, when people genuinely worried about immortality, Joseph Priestley (1777:26) observed that "the powers of sensation or perception, and thought, as belonging to man, have never been found but in conjunction with a certain *organized system of matter*." Priestley had no lack of supporters in the debate about mind and matter, and opposition weakened with secularization and scientific progress. At the end of the nineteenth century, young Freud reflected the intellectual climate of his time in the opening declaration of *A Project for Scientific Psychology*: "The intention is to furnish a psychology that shall be a natural science; that is, to represent psychical processes as quantitatively determinate state of specifiable material particles." For all his keen psychological observations, Nietzsche insisted on using "physiology" instead of "psychology" to avoid brushing on the soul.

Curiously, by the end of the twentieth century, the old commonplace was reincarnated as a bold new proposition. Looking at the scholarly literature, one cannot help sharing Chomsky's (2000:115) puzzlement when he observed: "Every year or two a book appears by some distinguished scientist with the 'startling conclusion' or 'astonishing hypothesis' that thought in humans 'is a property of the nervous system, or rather of the brain.'" What has happened in our times?

The twentieth century witnessed the blossoming of mind-designing philosophies eager to prescribe philosophically correct ways of thinking. Prescriptive philosophies had been around for a long time, but in our time they got a big boost from powerful techniques and the culture of technique worship. Some people identify reasoning techniques—computation, optimization, mathematical logic, decision theory—with reason itself, thus damming the sea of human reason into a pond of instrumental reason. Unfortunately, this identification enthralls not only worshippers but many of their critics who, throwing out reason because of the inadequacy of mere instrumental reason, turn to promote unreason and irrationality.

Using newly developed techniques early in the century, positivist philosophers produced stipulations for their ideal science that are as rigorous and beautiful on paper as glass slippers. They are also as unpractical in actual scientific research as glass slippers are outside fairy tales. When glass slippers shatter on the rough terrain of reality, their splinters become a hazard. Among such glass-slipper philosophies is the prescription of reductionism.

Over the years, reductionism has acquired so wide a range of meanings that proponents and opponents often talk at different frequencies. A crude distinction can be drawn between ontological and theoretical reductionism. *Ontological reductionism* asserts that complex entities, including people, are ultimately made up of elementary particles coupled by fundamental interactions as characterized in the laws of physics; there is no extra ingredient such as vitality or soul stuff. Embraced by most scientists and philosophers, it is not too controversial. Ontological reductionism is physicalism, which I take as one of my premises. But does it imply that complex entities are nothing but elementary particles; that the unending variety of structures of complex things are epiphenomena; that all the sciences that investigate complex structures are merely grinding out the consequences of the laws of elementary particle physics? In short, does ontological reductionism imply theoretical reductionism? Here the controversy begins.

It is common sense that *made up of* does not imply *nothing but*. A building made up of bricks is more than mere bricks, for it has its architecture. For older philosophers such as Descartes, to reduce a phenomenon meant to analyze it. To analyze, however, is not to analyze away or to demolish. Analysts keep the phenomenon in view because it is what they want to understand.

Analytical techniques have become so powerful that some philosophers equate analysis with demolition, elimination, or at least subjugation. For them, to say a class of property is *reducible to* another class is to say it is nothing but that other class and concepts characterizing it are dispensable and replaceable by concepts characterizing the other class. This sense of reducibility is the base of *theoretical reductionism*, a class of well-argued philosophical doctrines with an extensive literature. To emphasize the epiphenomenalism of reduced properties and the superfluity of reduced concepts, reductionists sometimes add the redundant qualification "eliminative" to reductionism. I generally call theoretical reductionism *nothing-butism* to avoid confusion with the other more benign meanings of reduction or the more specific doctrine of reductionism in the philosophy of mind. Basically, nothing-butism is not an ontological doctrine about what the world consists of, but a theoretical doctrine prescribing how we should think and what concepts we should use to explain the world. In a derivative sense, however, it hints about the world, for a restriction on ideas limits the things and properties that the ideas make intelligible.

Various nothing-butists posit various reducing bases: observational, neural, and elementary particle. Nothing-butism first gained popularity in the early part of the twentieth century when the philosophy of science had its heyday under logical positivism, an offshoot of empiricism. No surprise, the first serious nothing-but program tried to reduce concepts about physical objects to concepts about sense data. It failed despite the efforts of able logicians. Then in the mid-1950s some philosophers made a U-turn and determined that reduction should go the other way: concepts about sensual experiences should be reduced to physical concepts, specifically, neural concepts. This is the position that "reductionism" commonly refers to in the philosophy of mind, where it remains influential and is specifically called the mind-brain identity thesis. It asserts that each type of mental state is identifiable with a type or a conjunction or disjunction of types of brain state. For instance, pain is identifiable to the firing of a kind of neuron called the C fiber. Because type-type identity implies that any mental state is describable by the neurophysiological predicates for its corresponding brain state, mental concepts are reducible and dispensable.

We can delete "pain" from our vocabulary and talk only about C fibers firing (Place 1956).

For a while reductionism seemed plausible, as scientists discovered cells specialized for certain functions. For instance, the frog's retina contains cells that are sensitive to the movement of small objects in a wide range of illumination. Some people call these cells bug detectors, although frogs do not differentiate bugs from other small moving objects. Marr (1982) recalled: "People were able to determine the functions of single elements of the brain. There seemed no reason why the reductionist approach could not be taken all the way." In their excitement, people speculated that vision could be explained in terms of the excitation of specialized cells, for example, the fabled grandmother cell that fires only when one's grandmother comes into sight. The excitement died quickly as scientists realized that the behaviors of individual neurons give no clue to how they contribute to vision as a whole. Nevertheless, the philosophy of reductionism survives and is becoming more vociferous, rubbing on the increasing prestige of neuroscience.

The central position of the mind-brain identity thesis is that systems with mental properties are made up of neurons. The logic of this, once started, cannot be arbitrarily stopped. If mental concepts are reducible because mindful people are made up of neurons, then neural concepts too should be reducible because neurons are made up atoms. Drawing the logical conclusion that reduction is a transitive relation, hard-nosed nothing-butists contend that all science is reducible to elementary particle physics (Oppenheim and Putnam 1958).

Nothing-butism builds on two senses of *to reduce*: to contract and to diminish. Its central thesis is to contract our conceptual framework by doing away with concepts in the reduced areas, whose status is thereby diminished to mere subordinates, if not nil. This has a strong imperial flavor, claiming superiority and dominance for the reducing base even in far-flung areas with little apparent relevance, just like British laws once ruled in distant colonies. Those devoted to the reducing base may be flattered, but those working in the areas that are supposed to be reduced think differently. You can see why nothing-butism is so contentious.

To say mind is nothing but something else or reducible to something else is to say that mental and psychological concepts are dispensable and mental phenomena are fully characterizable and explainable in the vocabulary and theory of that something alone. Mental phenomena are described by a diversity of ideas in our everyday discourse. Over them nothing-butism ignites a furious imperial war in which various disciplines fight for the exclusive power of explanation. Mind is claimed to be nothing but the actual or dispositional responses to stimuli (behaviorism); nothing but what is predictable by a certain calculus (behavioral instrumentalism); nothing but the functional relations among input, output, and internal states (functionalism); nothing but a Turing machine (machine functionalism); nothing but a computer program (computationalism); nothing but configurations of the brain (reductionism or the mind-brain identity theory); or simply nothing (eliminativism). Battles among these powers make up much of the philosophy of mind of the past fifty years. The chief casualty is mind itself, which loses most if not all of its essential characteristics when reduced to nothing but something else.

Explanatory imperialism forges psychophobia, the irrational fear of the psychological. It is no longer sufficient to reject soul stuff, no longer sufficient to be physicalists who nevertheless subscribe to psychological explanations. One must shun mental concepts like a plague, because psychophobic philosophers condemn use of mental concepts as a commitment to soul substance, regardless whether the users actually have this commitment. They denounce "I love you" or "I think it's going to rain" as fallacious or at best unscientific, considering "scientific" to mean conforming to one or another form of philosophical correctness. "Scientifically" one must say only that the neurons in his brain are excited in certain ways: We are nothing but a pack of neurons. Mental phenomena must not only be explained but explained *away*. Nothing-butism is the astonishing hypothesis novel to the twentieth century. I reject it by insisting on the irreducibility of mind.

Ontological and Descriptive Levels

The greatest battles between nothing-butism and its opponents are over the issue of multiple descriptive levels. Nothing-butism allows only a single descriptive level, to which all other levels are reduced. Its opponents insist that more than one level is required for proper understanding of complex phenomena.

Levels are ubiquitous in cognitive science: competence and performance levels; conceptual and subconceptual levels; personal and subpersonal levels; computation, algorithmic, and implementation levels; knowledge, cognitive, and programming levels; levels of brains, maps, networks, neurons, and synapses. Generally, they fall into several classes. In talking about properties, for instance mind as a high-level property, we are talking about an *ontological* or *organizational* level, which concerns what there are. To make intelligible entities, properties, and structures on an organizational level, we employ concepts that constitute a corresponding *theoretical* or *descriptive and explanatory* level. Organizational levels are distinguished by various kinds of entities, properties, and processes; descriptive levels by various kinds of concepts and predicates. For example, elementary particles, nuclei, atoms, and molecules form a hierarchy of ontological levels that are respectively described by the theoretical levels of particle, nuclear, atomic, and molecular physics. Chomsky's competence and performance are levels of theoretical description. Marr's computation, algorithm, and implementation pertain to methodology. Brains, networks, and neurons form an ontological hierarchy. Thus neurophilosophers have made a categorical confusion in complaining that Marr's distinction does not match the neural hierarchy, as it invokes two kinds of levels that have no compelling reason to match.

I distinguish three crude ontological levels in this book—*mental, infrastructural*, and *physiological*—and propose that the proper entities in the mental level are situated persons. A mental process may be analyzed into many infrastructural processes, and an infrastructural process into many cellular processes. No sharp boundaries distinguish the levels; fuzzy cases such as subliminal perception can occur if conscious mental processes are pushed to the limit of their characteristic time. The levels are far from monolithic; each comprises a host of overlapping strata. Thus the mental level consists of various mental faculties, and the visual infrastructure consists of many visual processes.

Different concepts are necessary to describe the structures of mental, infrastructural, and physiological levels. Theoretical levels, too, are far from homogeneous. Even descriptions on the same level can vary greatly in degrees of detail, abstraction, and approximation, as the same phenomenon can be represented in models of different refinement.

Engaged persons have their own properties that are described by mental concepts such as believing and thinking, which highlight the fact that they are capable of understanding and following rules. Mental concepts are not applicable to processes in the infrastructural and physiological levels. Infrastructural processes do not perceive but are selectively sensitive to certain stimuli. Theoretical representations of infrastructural processes usually do not use neural or physiological concepts, which belong to the physiological level.

Taking Multiple Levels Seriously

It is one thing to acknowledge multiple levels. It is another to take seriously the consequences of the acknowledgment, which does not always happen. Frequently the acknowledgment functions as a conversation terminator: we work on different levels, therefore we have nothing in common to talk about. Or it provides the rug to sweep dirt under: the knowledge level is important, but it belongs not to the computational mind but to something else, programmers maybe. Or it serves as a legal front for the opposite message, like the health hazard sign on cigarette advertisements: consciousness belongs to the personal level, but really it is illusory because scientific psychology is possible only on the subpersonal level. Or it signals a fight for the top: your level is merely the implementation, the underling, of mine. Some philosophers list a ladder of levels neatly separated from each other by factors of ten, announce their concern with a single level, and on the next page extend their results to the whole mind, thereby quietly eliminating all the other levels. Such casual treatment of levels covers up their significance. To understand mind, we must pay more than lip service to levels, their multiplicity, and their interconnection.

In taking seriously the multiplicity of levels, we encounter several questions. What distinguishes various levels? Why do different organizational levels call for different descriptive and explanatory concepts? How are levels connected? In trying to answer these questions, we will find that scientific theories fall into two broad classes: *single level* and *interlevel*. Most theories pertain to phenomena on a single organizational level. Theories connecting two levels form a class of their own, and they are usually more difficult and fragmentary. Such interlevel theories are required to explain the emergence of mental structures and answer how infrastructural processes integrate into conscious experiences. Let me use the case of fluids to illustrate the meaning of levels, single-level theory, and interlevel theory.

Own-Level and Interlevel Explanations of Fluid

Water is philosophers' favorite analogy to mind. Everyone agrees that water is made up of H_2O molecules, but reductionist philosophers go much farther. They take as obvious truth "water is H_2O" and use it as an analogy to insist that "pain is C fiber firing." In both cases, *is* means *is identical to* or *is nothing but.*

Unfortunately for them, their "obvious truth" that water is identical to H_2O is generally false. Consider the simple deduction: water is identical to H_2O; ice is identical to H_2O; identity is a transitive relation; therefore water is identical to ice. The conclusion is false. Water is a liquid and ice a solid, the two have different densities, and to convert one to the other involves external energy. When guests in a hot summer barbecue ask for ice for their drinks, not even philosophers would offer water as a satisfactory substitute. The fallacy of identifying water with ice stems from the two premises of identity, whose crux is to neglect totally the *structural* aspect of composite systems. Such blindness to structures turns *is made of* into *nothing but* and analysis into demolition.

If water is nothing but the sum of a bunch of molecules and ice is nothing but the sum of the same molecules, then water is indeed identical to ice. However, if one takes account the relations among the parts and the structures they generate, the whole is nothing but the sum of its parts no longer holds. Water and ice are made up of the same molecules; a water molecule is identical to a H_2O molecule; the molecular or chemical constitution of water is H_2O. But water itself is not merely H_2O. It is H_2O molecules arranged in specific ways with specific macroscopic properties. The same molecules can organize themselves into many other forms: steam, cloud, powdery snow, or hexagonal flakes each with a different pattern. In short, water belongs to the fluid level and H_2O to the molecular level. The two organization levels have vastly different properties with different spatial and temporal scales. Nothing-butism tries to force the two levels into one but it achieves nothing but a confusion of levels. Similar confusion lies at the root of the reductionism that identifies pain with C fiber firing. As long as the confusion persists, we cannot hope to understand mental phenomena.

To describe and explain the macroscopic structures of water requires special branches of physics—fluid dynamics for the liquid and thermodynamics for freezing and evaporation. These theories do not mention molecules. They can stand on their own and are most relevant in explaining macroscopic phenomena. When oceanographers predict currents or engineers design flood control, they employ fluid dynamics, not molecular physics. This confirms what many psychologists have been saying all along:

a particular kind of phenomenon has its own most suitable level of description and explanation. For fluidity, the own-level explanation is not quantum mechanics but fluid dynamics. For mentality, the own-level explanation is not neuroscience but psychology.

Fluid dynamics and thermodynamics contain certain parameters such as viscosity and compressibility. Various values of the parameters specify various kinds of fluids, as honey is more viscous than water. These parameters are usually measured on the fluid level. Their empirical determination bolsters the autonomy of the fluid level. On the other hand, physicists can also calculate the values of these parameters using statistical mechanics and molecular physics. This interlevel calculation links fluid dynamics to molecular dynamics. Note that the target of calculation, viscosity or compressibility, is defined by fluid dynamics. Therefore the interlevel explanation is not a blind shot fired from the side of molecular physics. It is a bridge with anchors on both fluid and molecular sides. If one of the anchors is demolished, the bridge collapses.

The properties of fluids and their constituent molecules are so different that the concepts that characterize them are sometimes contradictory. Fluid processes are temporally irreversible; water can spill, but spilled waters never gather themselves. This irreversibility is explicitly forbidden by laws of mechanics for molecular motions; all motions are time reversible. However physicists do not reject irreversibility for illusory; to do so would betray empirical data. Instead, they seek to reconcile differences in interlevel theories. To do this, statistical mechanics introduces its own postulate that is outside the scope of particle mechanics, which does not generalize over the initial conditions of motions. Statistical mechanics adds a postulate about the probability distribution of initial conditions, called the postulate of equal a priori probability. This expansion of conceptual apparatus to accommodate the irreversibility of fluid processes is significant. It shows that in connecting two levels, the interlevel theory respects the theories on both levels and the properties the theories delineate.

Explanatory imperialists frequently assert that fluid dynamics and thermodynamics are nothing but statistical mechanics. They are wrong, as I explained in detail elsewhere (Auyang 1998). Unlike classical or quantum mechanics, statistical mechanics is not the mechanics of atoms, molecules, or other microscopic particles. It is a theoretical framework that connects the mechanics of microscopic particles to the macroscopic properties described in fluid dynamics and thermodynamics. Of importance, statistical mechanics does not dissolve the separate identities of the theories that it connects. It connects but does not connect away, just as the United States unites fifty states without uniting them away. Fluid dynamics and other macroscopic theories stand on their own in the federal unity of physics, not reduced to colonies in the empire of particle physics. Within that federal unity, statistical mechanics finds its peculiar significance. It does not reduce but expands the conceptual framework of physics. It introduces a new kind of explanation for macroscopic properties, an *interlevel* explanation that theoretically connects the microscopic and macroscopic levels of organization. This is the kind of explanation that the binding problem in cognitive science demands.

In sum, the comprehension of fluids involves two kinds of theories. Own-level theories, provided by fluid dynamics and thermodynamics, explain a fluid's flow patterns with concepts such as wave, vortex, and turbulence. Interlevel theories, provided by statistical mechanics and kinetic theories, connect parameters in fluid dynamics to particle mechanics, which describe the motion of the molecules that make up the fluid.

To generalize, there are two types of explanations of properties of a complex entity: own-level theories that address the properties of the entity as a whole and interlevel theories that connect them to the properties of the entity's constituents. If the entity has emergent properties, it is the job of interlevel theories to explain how they emerge from the self-organization of its constituents. Generally, interlevel explanations are more difficult, because they must connect disparate concepts pertinent to distinct organizational levels. They are dependent on own-level explanations, which inform them what properties have to be explained and connected.

Implementationism and the Disembodiment of Mind
The case of fluids also helps to clarify another version of nothing-butism that is peculiar to the philosophy of mind: implementationalism. As discussed in section 4, implementationalism is a part of the computational theory positing that proper explanations of mind occur on the symbolic level. Symbols are abstract. If mind is nothing but computing with symbols, it is disembodied. Computationalists are ambivalent about disembodiment. On the one hand, they think it is essential to mind because systems with different physical constituencies can all have mind. On the other hand, they try to dispel the harm of disembodiment by the notion of implementation.

Some say the computational mind is not actually disembodied because the software is implemented in some form of hardware or wetware. Thus some add the qualification "physical" to symbols and considered all problems solved. This lip service, however, is as ineffective in resolving the difficulty of disembodiment as the Cartesian argument that the *cogito* is implemented in soul substance. The crucial question is *what difference embodiment makes to mental characteristics*, what difference the qualification "physical" makes to symbolic functions. To both Cartesianism and computationalism, embodiment makes no difference at all. This total abstraction from the conditions of implementation is the crux of the computational or symbolic level that distinguishes the computational mind.

The weight of embodiment rests on the meaning of implementation. According to computationalism, a system implements or embodies a computer program if and only if it is structurally isomorphic to the program. Anything that satisfies the criterion is an embodiment, whether its material is silicon chips or potato chips, gray matter or soul substance. Matter simply does not matter. Furthermore, any two systems that implement the same program have exactly the same mentality. If an organic person and an inorganic computer implement the same program containing the state "pain," they will both suffer and cry ouch in exactly the same way. Philosopher Ned Block (1992) constructed a computational story in which the nation of China as a whole feels pain exactly as a person does, when the billion Chinese are organized to implement the program.

The promiscuity of implementation is a consequence of total abstraction. It is often attacked as computationalism's soft spot, and indeed it is. A program neither imposes restrictions on its implementation nor is constrained by its material base in any way. This means that implementation makes absolutely no contribution; the program can be totally abstracted from its implementation. Embodiment is merely cosmetic that can be rubbed off without affecting mind at all. This is the base of immortality that Kurzweil advertises. Putnam and other computationalists declare the mind-body problem solved. The problem is solved only because body no longer matters.

The main explanation of disembodiment offered by computationalists is multiple instantiability. Computer fans consider it species chauvinism to reserve mind for organic systems, as it dogmatically denies mental ability to systems of other material constitution including their favorite, silicon. In fact very little in our commonsense mental notions demands a carbon base. Let us agree that mentality is present in humans and some other animals, and possibly future robots. Thus it must be a property with a high degree of generality not restricted to systems made up of a specific kind of material. This agreement, however, leads to neither computationalism nor disembodiment. For *multiple* instantiability is common among physical properties. Only by confusing it with *promiscuous* instantiability does computationalism arrive at its conclusion of disembodiment.

Fluidity, for example, is a familiar property that is instantiable in many types of materials. Just this morning you may handled water, ketchup, gasoline, and other fluids. Fluidity is not a vague property. It can be defined clearly as the property described by the equations of fluid dynamics. It is well known that fluid equations apply not only to water, alcohol, petroleum, magma, and liquids of any molecular constituency, but also to gases, the atmosphere, and even the spiral arms of galaxies. The diversity is not surprising, because many complex properties pertain more to the *structural* than to the *material* aspect of large composite systems. Structures typically can be built from many kinds of materials. Consider the arch. This structure can be made of sandstone as in the Delicate Arch of Utah, or of steel as in the Gateway Arch of St. Louis, or of stones as in Roman arches. What distinguishes an arch is the distribution of forces and support of weight, not the material. In short, multiple instantiability is the rule rather than the exception in properties of composite systems, and it does not in any way hamper causal explanations. Fluid dynamics is an ordinary causal theory, so is the statics for arches. Thus the argument from multiple instantiability, which computer fans make so much of, is much ado about nothing. The multiple instantiability of mind implies neither that mind is computational nor that its description requires a specific symbolic level. Computationalists have offered no reason why multiple instantiability makes mind unaccountable by causal explanations.

Multiple instantiability is not promiscuous instantiability. A property is promiscuously instantiable if its characteristics are totally independent of its material base. Promiscuity, which disembodies the computational mind, is a stringent criterion not usually found in multiply instantiable properties. Arches can be made of a variety of materials, but not all, and the specific material constrains the maximum span. Fluidity, too, is not promiscuous; water pours more easily than syrup. Material does make a big difference in differentiating various types of fluidity. The difference is duly accounted for by fluid equations that contain certain parameters, different values of which separate the disparate flow characteristics of different materials. Different values of compressibility, for example, differentiate the fluidity of liquids and gases, which lead separately to hydrodynamics and aerodynamics. Thus multiple instantiability is a much weaker condition than promiscuous instantiability. For a multiply but not promiscuously instantiable mentality, a specific kind of pain caused by organic tissue damage would not be realized in silicon-based systems whose pain, if it exists, would have another quality.

Some philosophers assume that mental properties and conscious experiences can occur only in organic systems whose constituency is similar to ours. While at present the only mental beings that we know are carbon based, I do not see why they *must* be so. People readily accept Pinocchio and the Tin Man of Oz, indicating that our notion of the mental does not depend on being organic. Mentality, like fluidity, is a broad class of properties. There is little reason to deny the possibility for it to have multiple instantiations. Implementationalism is unsatisfactory because it goes too far to demand not only multiple but promiscuous instantiability. It is the promiscuity that causes the problem of disembodiment and abstraction of the symbolic mind.

Dualism, Nothing-Butism, and Synthetic Analysis

Suppose that psychology and our commonsense mental concepts provide own-level descriptions of mental properties. Then the binding problem demands interlevel explanations that connect mental properties to their underlying infrastructural processes. What form should the interlevel explanations take?

For simplicity and generality, let us consider only two levels in a complex system and call the higher level that of the *system* and the lower level that of *constituents*. For a system to exhibit distinctive large-scale structures worthy of a level, the constituents are usually numerous and strongly interacting. If the system is a fluid, fluidity is the system property and molecular motion the constituent property. If the system is a person, mentality is the system properties and infrastructural or neural processes the constituent properties. The system can also be a dynamical process made up of constituent stages, whose application in cognitive science is discussed in the next section. Let us forget the specifics now and consider the two levels abstractly. We will also ignore the substrata within each level.

Ontologically, the relation between the two levels is *composition* or *part-whole*; constituents interact to make up the system. Because interactions generate structures, the system is more than the sum of its constituents. Properties on the system level are grossly different from properties on the constituent level. To describe the two kinds of properties, we use two kinds of concepts, which may be contradictory. Fluid, for example, is a continuum although its constituent molecules are discrete. Suppose we have reasonable own-level theories of system properties and constituent properties, respectively. Each invokes causal factors on its own level without referring to entities in the other level. On the system level, we have fluid dynamics for fluidity or psychology for mentality. On the constituent level, we have molecular physics for fluid molecules or cognitive science for infrastructural processes. Our question is: what is the theoretical relation between system-level and constituent-level concepts?

This question has several answers. The first asserts that a proper theoretical connection between the two descriptive levels is impossible. Without theoretical connection, however, the notion of composition becomes totally obscure. All we have are two distinct entities characterized by disparate concepts. The result is dualism, more precisely property dualism (figure 3.4). For the mind-body problem, it asserts that mind and body are two kinds of properties completely disjoint from each other and constituting two distinct realms.

Whereas dualism advocates isolation, nothing-butism advocates conquest. It decrees that the two theoretical levels be so connected that one of them can be abolished and its explanatory territory annexed by the other. With the demise of the second level goes interlevel theory. Only one theory or one set of concepts remains. Depending on the relative power of the two levels, nothing-butism can go two ways: implementationism and the usual reductionism.

In implementationism, the constituent level is reducible because it is nothing but the implementation of structures specified in the system level. It is influential in the philosophy of mind due to the inspiration of computer engineering. In functionalism, computationalism, and cognitivism, the own-level description of mind is that of abstract programs of digital computers. This computational level can later be implemented in one physical medium or another. Computationalism and its variations are peculiar for their holism and total abstraction. Consequently their implementations take the form of structural isomorphism, which is a very stringent

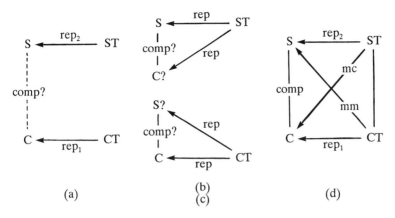

Figure 3.4
Ontologically, a composite system (S) is composed of (comp) constituents (C). System theories (ST) provide own-level descriptions and explanations of systemwide structures. Constituent theories (CT) provide own-level descriptions of constituent properties and interactions. We are interested in the theoretical relationship between the two descriptive levels. (a) *Property dualism* asserts that each of the two levels generalizes in its own way, and to connect them theoretically is impossible. Without proper theoretical articulation, the notion of composition becomes dubious. We are left with two distinct kinds of systems characterized by two theories. (b) *Implementationism* asserts that constituent theories are dispensable because the constituent structures are isomorphic to the system structures as their implementation. Without constituent concepts, however, the system becomes promiscuously instantiable and hence something detachable from its constituent base. (c) *Reductionism* asserts that system theories are dispensable because they are nothing but the mathematical consequences of constituent theories. Without concepts for systemwide properties, however, the integrity of the compound and hence the notion of composition become shadowy. We are reduced to saying there is nothing but a set of interacting elements. (d) *Synthetic analysis* institutes a broad theoretical framework that encompasses two kinds of explanations for system behaviors: own-level, represented (rep_2) in system terms; and interlevel, connecting the two descriptive levels (rep_1 rep_2, mm, mc, ST–CT). Interlevel explanations may be quite rigorous but not reductive, for besides deduction and definition, they introduce ample approximations and independent postulates, and use concepts in both systems and constituent concepts. They explain not only how microscopic mechanisms underlie systemwide properties (mm) but also how the system's macroscopic structures constrain behaviors of individual constituents (mc).

criterion. It is hard to believe that the structure of the brain mirrors the structure of mind, unless one subscribes to creationism, divine or evolutionary, where everything is designed to be so.

Implementationism seldom occurs in natural science and its philosophy. Physicists would find it odd to treat mechanics as the implementation of fluid dynamics. In the war between levels, the constituent level usually wins. The result is reductionism asserting that own-level theories of system properties are dispensable because they are nothing but logical consequences or definitions in terms of theories and concepts about the constituents. Psychological concepts are eliminable in favor of neural concepts, as pain is nothing but C fibers firing. Reductionism claims to proceed from bottom up. Without system concepts, however, it is bottom only, where one tries to see all structures from the perspective of constituents. It is powerful for small systems that are of the same scale as their constituents; we happily characterize the solar system in terms of planetary orbits. However, its power is blunted for large and complex systems that have structures on a higher organizational level.

Dualism rejects the connection between two levels, nothing-butism rejects one of the levels. *Synthetic analysis* keeps both levels and their interconnection, hence it alone provides genuine interlevel explanations. It employs concepts appropriate to both the system and constituent levels, hence it can lay out clearly the causal relations between the levels, which are often obscured in the one-sided framework of nothing-butism. Synthetic analysis combines bottom-up and top-down approaches. It is most productive in studying large complex systems. An example is the study of fluids, where physicists first get a synoptic grasp of fluids as wholes in fluid dynamics, then analyze its parameters to make contact with molecular motions.

The theoretical framework of synthetic analysis is more comprehensive and hence more complicated. Why do we have to invest in the complicated framework to grapple with complex systems? Why isn't the simpler framework of reductionism sufficient?

The Combinatorial Explosion of Diversity

For an intuitive idea of why the bottom-only approach of reductionism does not work, consider the simplest of composite systems, square arrays made up of pixels that can be either black or white. If we neglect relationships among the pixels, an array with n pixels is nothing but the sum of m black pixels and $n-m$ white ones; trivial and boring. What makes the array interesting are the relative positions of its pixels. Accounting for relations, a 2×2 array has $2^4 = 16$ possible configurations, ranging from all four pixels being black through one of the pixel being white to all pixels being white. A 5×5 array has $2^{25} = 33,554,432$ possible configurations; a 20×20 array has $2^{400} = 2.6 \times 10^{120}$. Generally, an array with n pixels has 2^n possible configurations. As the number of a system's constituents increases linearly, the number of its possible configurations increases exponentially and quickly exceeds the astronomical. This phenomenon is known as combinatorial explosion.

The combinatorial explosion of diversity in large-scale composition explains why brute force search, the queen strategy in AI, shrivels. Take chess, for example. It is a finite game with rigid rules and is most conducive to the method of searching through all possible configurations to find the optimal move. Shortly after the Soviets launched Sputnik in 1957, Simon predicted that a computer would be the world chess champion within ten years. It was not until 1997 that IBM's DEEP BLUE, evaluating over 200 million chess configurations per second with its 256 custommade chips distributed over 32 parallel processors, beat the reigning world champion Gary Kasparov in a six-game match. Simon's prediction was off by a factor of 4. During the thirty years that Simon missed, computer hardware technology grew beyond anyone's expectation. Computing power doubled every eighteen months and the price of computing dropped by half every two to three years. Economists estimate that if all prices drop as precipitously as the price of computing, a Cadillac would now cost \$4.98 (Brynjolfsson and Yang 1996). It would almost be affordable to vacation on the moon. Why, despite the phenomenal advance in computing power, was the computer's chess victory so late in coming? A chess game is a process made up of constituent moves, and the number of its possible configurations increases exponentially as one thinks more steps ahead. Pure design chess machines rely mainly on fast speed to search through most possibilities to find the best move. Even when aided by heuristic rules that prune out certain possibilities, the raw power of computers is sooner or later blunted by the sheer number of possibilities generated by the combinatorial explosion. That is why despite its victory in chess, the computer is still a novice in the board game Go; there are simply too many possible Go configurations.

The combinatorial explosion is partly responsible for the problem of scaling. "The whole is the sum of its parts" implies that a larger whole is merely a larger sum, so that once we understand a small system, we can readily scale its properties up to larger systems. That is wishful thinking for systems with any complexity. It is well known in systems engineering and computer science that one cannot simply take a system and scale it up a thousand-fold. The larger system has to be completely redesigned. This explains the lack of success for extending the success of toy-world AI systems to larger systems that can cope in more variegated environments. A similar scaling barrier starts to loom in connectionism. Most connectionist networks now are small ones, typically with hundreds or thousands of processing units. To go from there to networks with millions or billions of units will require research strategies that have yet to be developed.

Some people insist that chess and other AI problems are more difficult than natural science because there are more possible chess configurations than atoms in the universe. This is based on the erroneous comparison between the number of possible configurations and the number of constituents, which is the proverbial mistake of comparing apples and oranges. The correct way is to compare the number of chess pieces, 32, with the number of atoms in the universe, roughly 10^{80}; or to compare the number of possible chess configurations with the uncountably infinite number of possible dynamical configurations that the atoms in the universe can make up. Those who make the correct comparison would realize that natural science would have gone nowhere if scientists were as one-track minded as chess machines. Scientists have managed to understand the universe because they do not rely on brute force enumeration of atomic configurations but can adopt different intellectual perspectives. They are like human chess players. Human players perform searches also, but unlike chess machines, they also recognize strategic patterns, discern good moves, and concentrate on them. Similarly, scientists are not bogged down in microscopic details. They make intellectual leaps to find patterns and regularities on larger scales, thus opening new branches of science. The mental ability to adopt appropriate perspectives for the topic at hand, a salient sign of natural intelligence, is as crucial to scientific research as it is to our everyday coping in the world.

The human brain consists of close to a trillion neurons, each of which connects to a thousand others on average. Thus it has about 10^n possible connection configurations, where n is of the order of 10^{15}. Consider the combinatorial explosion and you will appreciate why cognitive neuroscientists are so impatient with reductionist philosophies. Paul Smolensky (1991) was not alone in arguing against the "blind bottom-up strategy in which we take low-level connectionist principles from neuroscience and see where they lead us, without being prejudiced by archaic prescientific notions such as [memory, constituent structures, attention]."

High-Level and Emergent Structures

Faced with the combinatorial explosion, how do we describe and explain the behaviors of large composite systems? We can try to describe a system in terms of properties of and relations among its constituents: an array in terms of colors and positions of individual pixels; a brain in terms of excitations of individual neurons and synapses. This method is quickly bogged down in details when the system increases in size. For a 2×2 array, we can hold the whole and its parts within the same focus and see that each of its sixteen possible configurations is notably different from the other fifteen. For a 20×20 array, however, the difference between one of its 10^{120} possible configurations and another is minuscule and insignificant. To understand is not to be bogged down by irrelevant details. To gain theoretical understanding of large arrays, we require new concepts to generalize and classify their numerous possible configurations, which is why the combinatorial explosion of possibilities becomes a major theoretical issue.

Fortunately, large numbers can also spawn simplicity if viewed from the proper perspective. As the array increases in size, large-scale patterns appear that can be conceptualized rather simply. They make *pictures* meaningful for the first time. You are now looking at a large array of black and white pixels, but you see not pixels but letters, words, text. Arrays appear to us as a certain shade of gray, salt and pepper, letters, geometric figures, images of things, landscapes, portraits, or, more frequently, junk. We have naturally changed the focus of our mental lens from the organizational level of pixels to the level of pictures, from the scale of constituents to the scale of the system as a whole. Abilities to change intellectual focus, discern patterns on various levels of detail, and introduce concepts to represent them in various degrees of abstractness are important features of our mind. Without them, scientific research would be impossible.

The combinatorial explosion generates a mind-boggling number of possible configurations in large-scale composition. Most configurations of large arrays would be described as junk in the system level. What capture our attention are the special classes that have salient patterns that are susceptible to coherent system-level descriptions such as texts or portraits or geometric figures. These we call *high-level structures* of the system. If they cannot be analyzed in terms of sums or averages of constituent properties, they are *emergent properties.* Thus being gray and being a portrait are both high-level properties of an array of pixels, but only being a portrait is emergent.

Due to the enormity of possibilities generated in the combinatorial explosion, high-level structures are always specific and relatively rare. Emergent structures are even rarer. Texts have endless variety. However, if we remember that a mediocre printer has 320 pixels per inch and $10^{30,825}$ possible configurations per square inch, we realize that the number of possible texts is minuscule in comparison. Texts are highly specialized properties of arrays, which is why it is miraculous that they form spontaneously in natural mosaics. Just as an arbitrary array of pixels is unlikely to produce a text, an arbitrary jumble of neurons is unlikely to produce mentality. Neurons in the brain have very specific organizations that, with their high-level properties, call for scientific investigation. What are the high-level structures of a brain? How are they characterized? If trivial systems such as arrays of millions of black and white pixels can exhibit high-level structures characterizable as the text for the Declaration of Independence, it is possible that complex systems such as networks of a trillion neurons can exhibit high-level structures whose description calls for mental concepts.

Synthetic Analysis of Complex Phenomena

Large-scale composition generates an overwhelming number of possible configurations. As we see in the case of black-and-white arrays, most configurations are junk; only a few are significant in the sense of exhibiting high-level structures. Stuck to the description of individual pixels, the bottom-only approach has no way to differentiate the junk from the structures except by brute force search and comparison. We learn from the lesson of AI that despite the skyrocketing advancement of computers, the brute-force strategy is easily defeated by the combinatorial explosion.

How would you classify and characterize the countless possible configurations of a large array of pixels? Would you pick out a class of configuration for its motif of being circles and another class for being triangles? Would you use the concept of circularity or triangularity to describe the typical characteristic of the selected class? This top-down approach of classifying high-level structures is precisely what scientists employ in their research. Bottom-up workers, stuck as they are among trees and undergrowth, try in vain to hack through the jungle without a map. Scientists, like smart explorers, secure a map of the jungle by doing an aerial survey. They get their bearing by observing the relatively few salient high-level structures that nature provides. The aerial view, which reductionism spurns, is an essential factor in synthetic analysis. It is provided by own-level theories of the system as a whole, which direct bottom-up deductions by a top-down view of the whole. One needs equipment to get an aerial view, and here is where the conceptual investment of synthetic analysis comes in. The investment pays handsomely, as we will see.

In studying the emergent properties of complex phenomena, scientists do not gather a bunch of elements and see what they add up to. Instead, they analyze a complex whole to find the interesting parts and structures. Analysis is not atomization or demolition as it always keeps the whole in mind. Even when the focus is on individual parts, the notion of the whole provides the necessary context wherein the parts are significant. The context of the whole, which is destroyed in atomization and unavailable in the bottom-up approach, prevents scientists from losing sight of what they aim to explain in the jungle of complexity.

Resolution and combination, the method of Galileo, had a long root tracing back to the ancient Greeks. Plato (*Phaedrus* 265–6) said that Socrates was an ardent follower of "the methods of division and collection." Division carves nature at its joints; collection takes a synoptic view of many scattered particulars to expound their exact nature. Similar ideas took off with the rise of modern science. Descartes (1985:20) combined resolution and composition into two steps of a single method: "[W]e first reduce complicated and obscure propositions step by step to simpler ones, and then, starting with the intuition of the simplest ones of all, try to ascend through the same steps to a knowledge of all the rest. This one Rule covers the most essential points in the whole of human endeavor." The combined method, which guides bottom-up synthesis with top-down analysis, I call synthetic analysis (Auyang 1998).

Synthetic has a double meaning in synthetic analysis. It points to a synthetic conceptual framework wherein we delineate clearly the properties of the system that we try to understand, the framework of fluid dynamics for instance. This framework facilitates analysis and guides the final synthesis of analytic results. Guided by synthetic understanding of a complex system on its own level, scientists analyze it into more manageable subsystems, study the subsystems thoroughly, and synthesize the results to provide the interlevel explanations that relate the whole and its subsystems. Thus synthetic analysis makes a round trip from a system to its subsystems and back; from an emergent property to its underlying mechanisms and back; from the top to the bottom and back. Faced with the possibilities generated by the combinatorial explosion, bottom-only reductionists are like hikers at the heads of billions of trails without a clue as to their destinations, except the suspicion that most lead to nowhere. Synthetic analysts know the important destinations, because they have own-level explanations that inform them precisely what to explain. The hike is still arduous, but at least it is not a blind march because the trail is blazed by analysis.[4]

A good indication of the top-down synthetic view is the notion of *function*, which is as important in cognitive science as in biology. Reductionists say that mental concepts are dispensable because mental states M_i is nothing but brain states B_i and should be completely described in neural terms. It sounds plausible only because it is abstract to the point of being empty. The brain is so complex, what are these brain states B_i? In cognitive neuroscience, brain states are characterized in mental terms, not the other way around. Neuroscientists differentiate various brain regions and classify neurons according to their mental functions such as face or word recognition. Functional characterizations are synthetic analytic, not reductive.

Functional characteristics are usually middle-level properties. Viewed from the lower level, they are abstractions that overlook many small details. Viewed from the higher level, they are contributors to a larger system. In talking about the heart's function of circulating blood, for example, biologists at once abstract from the heart's detailed structures and take account of the context in which the organ operates. Of the two perspectives, it is the top-down view from a higher organizational level that makes functional characteristics special. The sciences routinely study the properties of composite systems as wholes without worrying about their constituents. Molecular and solid-state physicists proceed without considering elementary particles that make up molecules and solids. Nevertheless, their practice of abstraction requires no sense of function. Functional connotations enter when we consider a supersystem to whose characteristics system properties contribute, as biologists talk about the functions of various organs in an organism. The supersystem provides the context in which the system is significant. Even if the supersystem is tacit in some theoretical models, its demands hide in the notion that the system has certain functions, because the notion is issued from the perspective of a higher level of organization. Christof Koch and Gilles Laurent (1999) wrote in their assessment of the research on the nervous system: "[C]ontinued reductionism and atomization will probably not, on its own, lead to fundamental understanding. Each brain is a tremendously heterogeneous patchwork. Understanding the function of any of its parts requires a precise knowledge of its constituents but also of the context in which this part operates." What they demand is none other than synthetic analysis.

The following chapters present many examples of synthetic analysis in cognitive science. Mental concepts, imprecise as they are, provide the synthetic framework from the situated-personal level. This framework enables scientists to analyze mind into its various modes of operation and further into various infrastructural processes. Conversely, it enables us to use scientific knowledge of the mental infrastructure to understand better our mental experiences.

11   The General Notion of Emergence

Together, the assumptions of physicality, explicability, and irreducibility lead to mind as a high-level property emerging from the self-organization of myriad infrastructural processes. Emergence is no stranger to cognitive scientists. Over the decades, Sperry (1969, 1987) defended the thesis that consciousness is "a dynamic emergent property of cerebral excitations. As such, conscious experience becomes inseparably tied to the material brain process with all its structural and physiological constraints. At the same time the conscious properties of brain excitations are conceived to be something distinct and special in their own right. They are 'different from and more than' the collected sum of the neurophysico-chemical events out of which they are built." He was emphatic that his thesis is not dualism as it does not involve soul, vitality, or a nonphysical substance. My hypothesis differs from Sperry's only in my insistence that mind is the property not of the brain alone but of the situated person as a whole.

Sperry had to fight hard to defend his emergence thesis against nothing-butism. The battle was made harder by the confusing meanings of emergence in currency. For instance, Crick (1994:3) proclaimed: "You're nothing but a pack of neurons" and a few pages later, "much of the behavior of the brain is 'emergent'—that is, behavior does not exist in the separate parts, such as the individual neurons." Searle (1997:30) rightly pointed out in his review that Crick confused two conflicting positions: "Crick preaches eliminative reductionism when he practices causal emergentism."

This section clarifies the meanings of emergence, contrasting it with nothing-butism. Specifically, it explains a general notion of *emergent* properties in contrast to *resultant* properties that are sums of the parts. I use the dynamical theory as an example to illustrate general ideas, but take care to explain that even when the theory is applied in cognitive science, emergent dynamical properties are usually *not* mental. The generality of emergence ensures that emergent properties are not singular and hence mysterious. The concept of emergence is used in the following section to explain the emergence of mental properties and refute doctrines basing on the assumption that mental structures are the resultant combination of infrastructural processes.

Emergent and Resultant Properties

Emergence occurs in comparing two states of a system. The two states may occur at different levels of organization; emergent properties appear in the state at the system level compared with the state at the constituent level. The two states can also occur at different times in the same level; novel properties appear that were absent in the system's earlier states. When water freezes into ice or when water vapor crystallizes into snow flakes, the property of rigidity or intricate symmetry emerges. Similar evolutionary emergence has attracted attention as situated roboticists maintain that novel structures can appear in a dynamical system as it interacts with its environment and gradually adapts to it (Hendriks-Jansen 1996). I concentrate on emergence of features in high-level structures. Using the dynamical theory as my example, I explain why many important cases of evolutionary emergence fall into high-level emergence.

John Stuart Mill (1843) distinguished two properties for compounds; the first exemplified by the mechanical combination of forces, the second by chemical reactions such as the combination of hydrogen and oxygen into water. Two forces combined yield a resultant force of greater or smaller magnitude. Hydrogen and oxygen chemically combined yield something qualitatively different. These two properties of compounds were soon called resultant and emergent (Stoeckler 1991).

For a better idea of the distinction, recall the arrays of black and white pixels. The arrays have many properties. We decide whether a property is resultant or emergent by viewing it relative to the properties of the pixels. Consider the property of being gray. The array's gray and the pixels' black and white are all colors and describable in color concepts, and various shades of gray result from summing various proportions of uniformly distributed black or white pixels. Gray is a resultant property. Resultant properties of a compound belong to the same type as the properties of the constituents, are describable by the same set of concepts, and can be obtained by aggregating or averaging the properties of the constituents. They are close to constituent properties and hence belong more to the *material* aspect of the compound. The pixels' blackness and whiteness, which are the material properties or material bases of the array, are reflected in the array's resultant properties.

Other high-level properties of the array, for example, being a text or a portrait, belong to categories totally different from color. They are describable only with additional noncolor concepts and cannot be obtained by simply summing or averaging over the properties of the pixels. These are the emergent properties of composite systems. They can be so different from the material base because they pertain to the *structural* aspect of the array as a whole.

We differentiate organizational levels not by mere size but by the emergence of qualitatively different properties on a larger scale. As long as the arrays are only black or gray or white, they can be as small as a stamp or as large as the sky and still belong to a single organization level. Large arrays are just more of the same, differing from small arrays and pixels only quantitatively, not qualitatively. Qualitative differences that mark distinct organizational levels and call for disparate descriptive levels come from emergent properties. Only when it is possible for patterns such as geometric figures to emerge does it become meaningful to differentiate the level of pictures from the level of pixels.

Intuitively, "the whole is the sum of its parts" applies to resultant but not emergent properties, because interrelations among the parts generate something more than the sum. In my previous study of complex systems in the physical, biological, and social sciences, I tried to give resultant properties the widest berth by pushing the intuitive idea as far as possible (Auyang 1998: sec. 22). A property of a composite system is *resultant* if the system is analyzable by whatever method into whatever weakly coupled subsystems such that in the first approximation, the property at issue is the sum or average of the properties of the subsystems. Scientists in all fields do their best to analyze systems into weakly coupled subsystems, because resultant properties are much more manageable. They developed many ingenious theories for such analysis and defined subsystems tailored to the systems analyzed, which often differed drastically from the familiar constituents of the systems. Under this broad definition, most electrical and optical properties of solids and liquids are resultant. Thus transparency, which many philosophers cite as an example of emergent property, is actually resultant. A fluid is transparent if each of its molecules does not absorb or scatter radiation in visible wavelengths, so the fluid's total absorption and scattering are negligible.

The wide net of resultant properties lets slip many properties that we call emergent. Phase transitions such as freezing and evaporation involve a restructuring of the whole system that cannot be expressed in terms of the sum of subsystems. Emergent properties are high-level structures that belong to different types than those in low-level organizations. They are practically impossible to predict, but explicable when observed, although the explanations are far from easy.

Emergence as not resultant captures two essential intuitive notions. First, a system with emergent properties is more than the sum of its parts. Second, an emergent property is of a different kind from the properties of the parts, for summation or averaging produces only quantitative differences within the same kind. What counts as *a kind* is debatable. Some philosophers recognize only the most general kinds, such as being material, objective, or causal, which are so general they are found in all physical systems. This extremely broad definition rules out the possibility of emergence without soul substance or its like, for only they can belong to other general kinds. It also rules out talks about different kinds of properties in physics and chemistry. I reject it because it is unproductive. My view of kind delineated by the possibility of summation and averaging is narrower and more useful. On the other hand, by allowing the most advanced techniques in analyzing the system into summable parts, it is not too narrow.

A good example of emergent property is superconductivity, whose peculiarity is best seen in contrast to the resultant property of ordinary electrical conductivity. Metals conduct electricity because they contain many mobile electrons. An electron carries an electric charge and its motion generates a tiny electric current. Ordinary conductivity results as individual electronic motions sum into a macroscopic electric current. Because electrons move and scatter individually, ordinary conductivity is finite. Even in copper the macroscopic current suffers losses from attrition.

Some metals also show a strange behavior that surprised experimentalists when they stumbled on it in 1911. When these metals are cooled below certain critical temperatures, they change from ordinary conductors to superconductors with infinite conductivity. A macroscopic electric current in a superconductor never dies because it suffers no loss. Why? Physicists finally figured it out in 1957. Electrons in a superconductor lock themselves into a coherent motion manifested in the macroscopic current. Because interlocked electrons cannot scatter individually, the current suffers no attrition. Superconductivity is an emergent property because the large-scale pattern of coherent electronic motion cannot be obtained by the most sophisticated summation, which cannot account for interlocking. Ordinary conductivity and superconductivity involve the same bunch of electrons; the same piece of metal can convert from one to the other. The difference lies in how electrons organize themselves. They highlight the fact that resultant and emergent properties differ mainly in the structural organization and not the material base.

Most composite systems have some important resultant properties, for instance mass, energy, momentum, and force; the total mass of a system is the sum of the masses of its constituents. A system is likely to have resultant properties if its parts interact very weakly, in which case we can neglect coupling in a first approximation and sum the individual properties of the parts. For a system of strongly coupled constituents, relationships among them generate complicated structures that are very difficult, often impossible, to represent as sums, even with the most advanced techniques. Such tightly integrated systems are most likely to exhibit emergent properties.

The Explicability of Emergent Properties

The concept of emergent properties as the contradistinction to resultant properties was historically the first to appear. It is scientifically productive as it encourages scientists to go beyond methods of summation and averaging in searching for explanations of high-level properties. However, it is not popular in philosophy, where emergence occurs mostly as the antithesis of nothing-butism. Here the favorite definition of emergence is inexplicability; emergent properties are mysterious. To many philosophers, to say mind is an emergent property is to say mental phenomena are beyond our comprehension (Kim 1993). It is no surprise that they deem the emergence of mind antiscientific. The trouble lies in their sterile notion of emergence. The difference between arguing endlessly about the sterile meaning of a term and choosing a fruitful meaning contributes to the different degrees of success in philosophy and science.

The idea of emergence as inexplicability has several sources. Emergentism or emergent evolutionism asserts that novel properties appear mysteriously in the course of evolution. Popularized, this doctrine has given bad press to evolution as well as to emergence, but it is neither the earliest nor the clearest exposition of emergence. Then there is the positivist philosophy of science with its glass-slipper criterion of scientific explanation, which would disqualify many actual and successful scientific theories. Emergent properties are invariably complicated. Their equally complicated explanations usually involve many approximations and would be considered incomprehensible to those who demand everything to be rigorously written in a paragraph if not a sentence.

Especially unfavorable to emergent properties is the philosophical doctrine that identifies explicability with predictability. Nothing-butists stipulate that something is explicable or predictable if it can be deduced from a set of basic laws. Therefore everything explicable is nothing but a logical or mathematical consequence of the laws. In practice, however, emergent properties are seldom predicted. They are first observed in experiments, and the discoveries are often surprising. Take the emergent property of superconductivity. All known metal superconductors work only at very low temperatures. People fervently want superconductors that work at or near room temperatures; imagine how much energy we would save if we could build electrical power lines with superconductors. Despite their arsenal of theories, physicists not only failed to predict high-temperature superconductivity in ceramics, they were so surprised by its discovery in 1986 that a Nobel prize was immediately awarded to the experimenters. The practical unpredictability of emergent properties is translated into inexplicability by nothing-butists.

Arguments against nothing-butism presented in the preceding section also hold against identifying prediction with explicability. Human beings have more methods of explanation than merely deducing the consequences of some laws. They are often unable to predict a phenomenon. However, after the phenomenon has been observed in experiments, they can often explain it by synthetic analysis, although it takes much hard work and patience. Physicists have a satisfactory theory for metallic superconductivity, although it came almost fifty years after the experimental discovery. They are still working frantically on ceramic superconductivity. Will they eventually explain it? You bet. Similarly, in regarding mind as an emergent property of situated persons, I expect that we will have to wait a long time before science produces satisfactory explanations linking it to physiological properties of the human body. Nevertheless, I believe science will meet the challenge.

In worrying about explicability, philosophers do touch on an important point: As a comparison and qualification of objective properties, emergence contains an epistemic strand and hence depends on assumptions about how we think. Nothing-butists tacitly assume a model of mind that allows only one perspective from which one comprehends everything. They are like those who look at *The Last Judgment* in Sistine Chapel with their noses glued to the wall and claim it is nothing but patches of color that make no sense. Step back and look again. I will show why the nothing-butist model of mind is wrong. To see and think objectively we must be able to adopt different perspectives and be aware of their variations. This is a central thesis for a self-consistent theory of mind presented in chapter 8. Here let us see how it is manifested in dynamical theory, which shows how a high-level perspective enables us to see and define novel properties.

Elements of Dynamics

After mind as behavior, brain, and computer, the latest fashion in cognitive science takes mind as motion (see section 5; Thelan and Smith 1994; Port and van Gelder 1995). Dynamicalism has at least three basic assumptions: first, dynamics is fruitful in representing many behaviors and brain mechanisms; second, new properties sometimes emerge in dynamical systems; third, some of these emergent properties are mental.

I agree with the first two points, and I do not deny the possibility that mental properties can emerge in dynamical systems. However, I maintain that most if not all emergent dynamical processes discussed so far by neuroscientists, developmental psychologists, and AI engineers are not mental. They are not perceptual or deliberate; they belong to the infrastructure of perception or motor action. I register my disagreement but will not support it here. My purpose is to use clearly articulated dynamical theory to bring out some characteristics of emergent properties.

A system is an entity that is analyzable into interdependent parts. A physical system has spatial extensions but no temporal extension. It endures and changes through time; in other words, undergoes a process through time. A process is a spatially and temporally extended system made up of stages, each of which is a state of the three-dimensional physical system that undergoes the process. In the four-dimensional view where we treat time like a spatial dimension, processes constitute a special kind of composite system with temporal parts. Thus the system and constituent levels discussed in the preceding section can be generalized to processes. Processes are considered as wholes on the system level. The stages of a process or the momentary states of the system undergoing the process occur on the constituent level.

A dynamical process is one whose evolution is governed by a set of dynamical rules. It is most conducive to nothing-butism. Given the initial stage of a process, we can deduce all the succeeding stages from the dynamical rules, at least in principle. Furthermore, these stages abut each other temporally, so we can say the process is nothing but the temporal sum of its consecutive stages. We need concepts only for the stages, not for the process as a whole. A missile's trajectory, for example, is nothing but the sum of the missile's positions at various times. We do not require concepts to describe the trajectory as a whole, and for most trajectories we do not even have adequate concepts. Nothing-butism is at its strongest here, and it can appeal to classical dynamics for support.

Unfortunately for nothing-butism, it comes a century too late. Modern dynamics gives us a more comprehensive view. Nowadays dynamics is hot not only in cognitive science. It has become the center of the so-called science of complexity, which is so popular that dynamical terms such as chaos find their ways into Hollywood pictures. Dynamics is as old as Newton. What turns it into a new fashion? Classical dynamics does not have the conceptual means to represent phenomena such as chaos or bifurcation. What makes modern dynamics so much more powerful is the broad synthetic framework introduced by mathematician and physicist Henri Poincaré at the end of the nineteenth century. It is this synthetic framework that enables us to grasp dynamical processes as wholes and see their emergent properties. Thus modern dynamics turned the most favorable case for nothing-butism into a powerful counterexample.

Mathematically, we characterize the behaviors of a dynamical system by four factors: a set of dynamical rules, a set of control parameters, a set of state variables, and a set of initial conditions for the state variables. *Control parameters* account for the fixed features of the system, which can include both its internal structures and influences it receives from the environment. These features are fixed in the sense of being independent of time as far as dynamical rules are concerned. *State variables* characterize changing aspects of a system; their values at each time determine the system's state at that time. *Initial conditions* specify values of the variables for a particular time. Suppose a system has many parts, which in turn contain smaller parts. To account for structural changes, including variations in its parts and their mutual couplings, the system has many state variables and is governed by many coupled dynamical rules. *Dynamical rules* govern the system's evolution by specifying a unique successor to each state. They take the forms of differential equations for continuous time or difference equations for discrete time. For a fixed set of values for control parameters and a given set of initial conditions, dynamical rules determine a dynamical process that consists of a set of system states arranged in temporal succession.

Consider the simplest dynamical system, a pendulum. Its control parameters include the length of its rod, mass of its bob, and strength of gravity. We can change these factors, for instance by adding weight to its bob or sending it into outer space to decrease gravity. However, these changes occur beyond the realm of its dynamical rule and will yield new dynamical processes. For a given set of control parameters, the pendulum's motion is characterized by two state variables, displacement and momentum. Given their initial values, a simple differential equation predicts the pendulum's motion.

Classical and Modern Dynamics

The four factors—dynamical rules, control parameters, state variables, initial conditions—are common to dynamical theories. Classical and modern dynamics alike address the pendulum. They evaluate the same systems, but look at the systems differently. Classical dynamics solves for the system's motions with particular sets of initial conditions; given such conditions, it tells us how the pendulum swings back and forth. Its rather narrow conceptual framework allows it to reckon with particular processes only. In contrast, modern dynamics reckons with all possible dynamical processes that a system can undergo with various possible internal structures and external environments. To grasp all these possible processes, it introduces a broad conceptual framework on a higher level. Now we are no longer confined to tracking the constitutive stages of a process. We can treat a process as a unit, define its properties, compare it with other processes, and classify the processes according to their properties. For instance, we at once differentiate two types of pendulum motion: swinging back and forth and rotating about its pivot.

By grasping processes as wholes instead of merely following its successive stages, modern dynamics opens up the system level for investigation. If its advantage is lost in the trivial case of the pendulum, it quickly becomes apparent when we go to more complex systems. Without system-level concepts, classical dynamics has no means to differentiate between chaotic and regular motions; to classify motions into various attractors and attraction basins; to tell when a system bifurcates or jumps from one type of motion to another. *Chaos* and *attractors* are defined only when modern dynamics allows us to compare processes issuing from different initial conditions with fixed control parameters. *Bifurcation* is defined by comparing the systems of attractors for different values of the control parameters. Such comparisons play crucial roles in situated cognition, where roboticists rig the environment represented by control parameters and study how the dynamical system adapts. The so-called evolutionary emergence of new properties in situated cognition depends on the synthetic conceptual framework where one can discern properties for processes as individual units.

Emergence of Chaos in Deterministic Systems

Consider the logistic system, which is governed by a dynamical rule called the logistic equation

$$x_{t+1} = ax_t(1 - x_t),$$

where a is the control parameter, t the discrete time variable, and x_t the state variable whose values are restricted to $0 < x_t < 1$. The logistic equation has many applications. One is in ecology, where x_t represents the population density of a colony of organisms at time t. The control parameter a takes account of the average fertility rate of the organisms and the carrying capacity of their environment.

For a fixed value of a, one picks an initial state variable x_0, puts it in the right-hand side of the equation, calculates x_1; puts x_1 in the right-hand side, calculates x_2; and repeats the procedure. Thus one generates a particular dynamical process, as illustrated in the graph of x_t versus t in figure

DYNAMICAL SYSTEM $f(x_t, a)$

	State variable x_t	Control parameter a
Variation	governed by f	independent of f
Classification	basins of attraction	systems of basins
Instability	chaos	bifurcation
Characteristic time	T_1	$T_2 >> T_1$
Examples:		
ecology	population density	environmental change
olfaction	separate odors	development
logistic system		
$x_{t+1} = ax_t(1 - x_t)$		

Figure 3.5
A dynamical system is represented by a set of state variables x_t and a set of control parameters a. The temporal evolution of x_t is governed by the dynamical rule $f(x_t, a)$. (Left) For $0 < a < 3.57$ the logistic system is regular. Processes issuing from all initial conditions converge on an attractor A. (Right) The nature of the attractor changes drastically as a changes.

3.5. One can generate another process by picking other values for a and x_0. It would be fun as an exercise for sixth-graders.

If the children pick $a = 2$, they will find the exercise trivial. If they pick $a = 4$, however, they will soon complain that the values of x_t jump all over the place. Worse, if they check their calculation but carelessly drop the tenth decimal place of the initial condition, they will have totally different answers. There is nothing wrong with their arithmetic, the trouble lies in the logistic system. Trivial as it appears, it can be chaotic. The logistic equation is nonlinear; the nonlinearity comes from the x_t^2 term in the right-hand side. Thus the logistic system is capable of a wide variety of behaviors. And it is chaotic for $a > 3.57$.

People usually say that chaos means sensitivity to initial conditions. How do we discern and define sensitivity? Mathematically, *chaos* means that processes issuing from neighboring initial states diverge from each other exponentially, so minute differences in the initial conditions are amplified exponentially. This has great consequences. Almost all important physical quantities are continuous and represented by real numbers. In such cases exact initial conditions are not possible, because the exact specification of a real number requires an infinite amount of information. Any practically feasible initial condition is actually an infinite number of conditions clustered within a certain margin of error. If the system is *regular*, the processes ensuing from initial conditions tend to bundle together, so the dynamic equation can predict their evolutionary courses to within a similar margin of error. For chaotic systems, the processes may bundle together for a short while, but will eventually diverge and diverge big time. Therefore although the dynamic equation determines each successive state uniquely, it loses its predictive power over the long run because it gives answers that spread all over the place. Thus people say that the behaviors of chaotic systems are unpredictable.

All dynamical systems, regular or chaotic, are *deterministic*. Given any stage in a system, dynamical rules always determine a unique successor. This is apparent in the logistic equation. Each stage in a process specified by an initial condition is determined. Determinacy implies predictability. As nothing but the temporal sum of consecutive steps, a dynamical process cannot be other than determined and predictable. In this narrow reductionist framework there is simply no place for chaos and the long-term unpredictability that it implies. Thus chaos and long-term unpredictability are emergent properties of dynamical processes.

Chaos exemplifies several characteristics of emergent properties. First, it is the property of dynamical processes as wholes, defined on the process level by comparing the behaviors of various processes. Second, it is absent in the process's constituent stages or the mere abutment or aggregate of stages. Worse, it is not only absent but cannot possibly be in the mere abutment of stages because it contradicts their definitions. Third, compared with characteristics of constituent stages, it is a totally different kind of property. Fourth, it becomes important only in the long run, when a process has accumulated many stages. A long process is a large, temporally extended system, and emergent chaos is important for large systems. Fifth, chaos is explicable; there is a rigorous mathematical theory for it. Sixth, the explanation is not reductive. To define chaos, we have to expand the scope of generalization to include various initial conditions and divergence between various processes. This is possible only from a high-level perspective where we can grasp and compare different processes as wholes.

Basins of Attraction: Separation of Odors

The regular motions of the logistic system are also interesting. Suppose $a = 2$; you will find that no matter what initial condition you pick, the values of subsequent x_t converge to 0.5 as t increases. The value to which all processes converge is called an *attractor*, as denoted by A in figure 3.5. Attractors are important features of a dynamical system because they represent the system's typical long-term behaviors when the effects of varying initial conditions have died out. Attractors occur in regular and chaotic systems; in the latter case they are called strange attractors.

The logistic system has only one attractor, and processes from all initial conditions converge on it. Other dynamical systems can have many attractors. For them, processes with some initial conditions settle on one attractor, whereas processes with other initial conditions settle on another attractor. All states whose processes converge on a single attractor constitute a *basin of attraction* for that attractor. The basins of various attractors partition the system's *state space*, which is the collection of all its possible states.

Imagine a mountainous landscape. Imagine each point in the landscape as a possible state of a dynamical system and the landscape as a whole the system's state space. Now imagine a raindrop falling on a point in the landscape as an initial state realized, and the path of the water drop on the landscape as the process initiated from the initial state. All water that falls in a valley drain into the lake at its bottom. The water in the next valley drains into a different lake. The lakes are analogous to different attractors, and valleys to their respective basins of attraction. For rain falling on a ridge dividing two valleys, two adjacent drops may end in two lakes miles apart. Similarly, sometimes two close-by initial conditions may generate dynamical processes that settle on attractors with very different behaviors. Or a slight perturbation of an initial condition may cause the system to jump from one attractor to another. This sensitivity to initial conditions, however, can occur in regular systems and should not be confused with chaos.

The system of attractors is a good way for theoreticians to classify initial states and the processes initiated from them. All processes initiating within a basin of attraction belong to the same type, because they eventually settle on the same typical behavior represented by the basin's attractor. In this way we can classify all possible states and processes of the dynamical system by its system of attractors and basins of attraction. Again, classification of processes is impossible without a high-level framework that encompasses many processes as wholes.

If you think about systems of attractors you will see why dynamics is useful to represent the infrastructures of perception and object recognition. Suppose we regard a part of a perceptual infrastructure as a dynamical system. Then sensual stimuli are the initial conditions that trigger various specific processes. Stimuli come in infinite varieties, swayed by not only the objects but the conditions of the sensory organs. Much variation is "noise," which we must abstract to recognize distinctive types of objects. Sometimes two stimuli are similar, but on recognizing them to be different types of objects, we respond differently. Perceptual recognition requires consciousness, but it also depends on suppression of noise and separation of stimuli into distinctive groups, teasing apart similar stimuli if necessary. I do not know how dynamics can represent conscious perception, but it can represent the process of noise suppression and stimuli separation in the perceptual infrastructure. When infrastructural processes triggered by a variety of stimuli converge on a single attractor, they wipe out inessential variations in myriad stimuli. The single attractor will stand as a unit in a larger infrastructure and contribute to our perceptual recognition of a single type of object. Processes settling on different attractors contribute to the recognition of different types of objects. Adjacent initial conditions at the boundary between two basins of attraction leading to different attractors help to explain why similar stimuli can have different meanings to the perceiver.

Walter Freeman studied the physiology of olfaction extensively. He trained rabbits to behavior in different ways on smelling different scents, thus ensuring that they were able to discriminate odors. Then he inserted an array of about sixty microelectrodes into the animals' olfactory bulbs and measured the electroencephalogram as they sniffed around. He found no neuron specifically sensitive to a particular type of odorant. Instead, different types of odorants triggered distinctive patterns of bulbwide activity that involved many neurons. To explain these neural activation patterns, Freeman built a dynamical model with differential equations and found that it exhibited similar behaviors. He conjectured (1991): "We think that olfactory bulb and cortex maintain many chaotic attractors, one for each odorant an animal or human being can discriminate." Thus dynamics can explain important infrastructural processes that underlie the differentiation of various odors.

Freeman's dynamical model of the olfactory bulb proposes a mechanism for producing different responses to different chemical stimuli. As such it has the same status as so-called electronic noses that are available on the market and used in industries to detect and identify chemical vapors (Nagle et al. 1998). It is more significant in the science of mind because the olfactory bulb is an integral part of infrastructures subserving conscious experiences. This general significance is shared by all neural processes, and by itself provides only a vague hint that the processes are somehow connected to consciousness. Substantive elucidation of the connection is required to understand mind in general and conscious smelling in particular. How do the infrastructural dynamics of the olfactory bulb integrate into the larger structure of olfaction on the mental level? What are the peculiarities of that structure? We receive at best hand-waving answers. Throwing out technical terms such as state and chaos and nonlinearity do not help; they are generally applicable to many physical systems whereas adequate answers demand their specific contributions to explaining the mental phenomenon at issue. In a debate between Searle and Freeman (1998), Searle rightly disputed claims that dynamical models solved the problem of consciousness or intentionality.

Bifurcation: Development

So far we have considered cases for a fixed value for the control parameter. Let us return to the logistic equation to see what happens when we vary the parameter. For $a = 2.9$, all initial conditions lead to an attractor that is a fixed value. For $a = 3.1$, all initial conditions lead to another attractor that is quite different. It is no longer a fixed value but is what mathematicians call a limit cycle, which jumps back and forth between 0.8 and 0.512. The variation of the attractor A as the value of a is illustrated in the left side of figure 3.5. Near $a = 3$, for example, a slight increase in a leads to a drastic change in the nature of the attractor. This change in the characteristics of the attractor is called a bifurcation. A familiar example is Bénard convection. Consider a fluid contained between two horizontal plates, the bottom of which is slowly being heated. Here the dynamical system is the fluid, whose control parameter is the temperature difference between the two plates. Bifurcation occurs when at some critical temperature difference the pattern of fluid motion changes drastically as the fluid organizes itself into rolls.

Bifurcation is an emergent property that shares many characteristics of chaos discussed earlier. Proponents of mind as motion hold that when a changes with time, new properties can emerge as a result of bifurcation. This is the base for the argument for dynamic evolutionary emergence.

Wait a minute, you say. How can *a* change with time? It must be a constant in the logistic equation. If *a* depends on *t*, then we would have a different equation and hence a totally different dynamical system. You are right. Here we land in a new level of temporal organization where the property of bifurcation emerges.

The control parameters and state variables belong to *two temporal organizational levels* with disparate temporal scales. The control parameters can change, but only if their changes are slow compared with those of state variables, so slow that we can approximately treat them as constants in the dynamical equation when we reckon with the rapid changes of state variables. In figure 3.5 this constraint is expressed by saying that the characteristic time T_2 for control parameter *a* is much longer than the characteristic time T_1 for state variable x_t. Imagine the mountainous landscape again. What dynamical rules govern is like the draining of a rain storm in a fixed landscape. In the geological time scale, the landscape itself changes, as a basin appears here and a valley disappears there. These topographical changes do not appear in dynamical rules for the drainage of rain storms. However, from a higher intellectual perspective we can compare the landscapes at various times and, if we like, frame a separate dynamical theory for their change.

Characteristic time, which implies a *time scale*, is important in many scientific theories. It reminds us that many processes go on simultaneously in systems of any complexity, some fast, others slow, still others superslow. Their characteristic times mark various temporal levels. We should note their interrelation, but we should not confuse them. For instance, temperature, defined as the mean molecular kinetic energy for a system at equilibrium, is an equilibrium quantity. However, it is a constant only on the level of rapid molecular motions with its microscopic characteristic time. On the fluid level with its macroscopic characteristic time, temperature becomes a state variable whose temporal evolution is governed by fluid equations. Molecular processes are so fast that the temperature is effectively constant during their brief characteristic time when they bring a small local system to equilibrium, so that a local temperature is defined. Temperature varies so slowly that, as far as fluid equations are concerned, molecular equilibrium is always reach instantaneously. Thus there is a consistent explanation for the dual time scales.

I have introduced two temporal levels: infrastructural processes with characteristic times less than tens of milliseconds, and the conscious processes with characteristics times exceeding 100 milliseconds. Psychologists who use dynamics to model development and the effect of learning also stress the importance of multiple time scales. Esther Thelen and Linda Smith (1994: 74, 86) distinguished between the "real time" of immediate action and the "ontogenetic time" for changes in organic components, tasks, and the environment. Given the dual temporal scales, they showed how dynamical theories can be used to model the development of various motor and cognitive skills. "In dynamic terminology," they wrote, "behavioral development may thus be envisioned as sequences of system *attractors* of varying stability, evolving and dissolving over time."

Instead of citing new examples from Thelen and Smith, let us look at a dynamic example for the development of odor discrimination. As discussed earlier, we represent the gross existing connective structures within a neural assembly in the olfactory bulb by a set of control parameters. And we represent the rapid responses of the assembly to chemical stimuli by a set of state variables governed by a set of dynamical rules. A stimulus specifies a set of initial conditions. Governed by dynamical rules, the neural assembly evolves and finally settles on one of its many attractors, thus picking out a specific odor. This neural process occurs in less than 100 milliseconds, the characteristic time of infrastructural processes.

Repeated exposures to various stimuli gradually change the connections within the neural assembly. Scientists of situated cognition call this process "learning," although I prefer *development* because it is incognizant. Development occurs in periods much longer than seconds and belongs to a higher temporal level. Thus its effects on the neural assembly can be approximately represented by slow changes in control parameters. Bifurcation represents the effect of development on the sensitivity to new objects. Thus Freeman (1991) wrote: "Whenever an odorant becomes meaningful in some way, another attractor is added, and all the others undergo slight modification."

Lessons from Modern Dynamics

Dynamics has a clear mathematical formulation and is applicable to many areas beyond cognitive science. By examining it, we have arrived at several general results, which are useful for clearing up several confusions in the discourse on mind.

Emergent properties are discernible and definable only when the theoretical framework is expanded to include the system level of description.

Chaos, attractor, and bifurcation are incomprehensible within classical dynamics whose narrow framework cannot grasp processes as wholes but can only account for individual stages that make up a process. They become meaningful and reveal hidden characteristics of dynamical processes when modern dynamics expands the conceptual framework to include a synthetic view where we can classify processes as wholes. Similar reasoning encourages us to expand, not reduce, our conceptual framework when mental properties are incomprehensible in our existing framework.

Structures of the whole can constrain behaviors of the parts. Some control parameters represent fixed structures of the whole system, and they play important roles in determining stages of the dynamical processes. This is most pronounced in bifurcation, where dynamical stages change drastically with small changes in the structures. The possibility of structural constraints lifts the mystique of mental causation, where a small thought can cause big changes in behaviors.

Spatial location is not necessary in defining the properties of a system. Control parameters for a dynamical system can include environmental factors with no definite location. For instance, the natural frequency of a pendulum is its essential property, but it depends on the strength of gravity that is outside the pendulum. A system's properties do not necessarily reside within its spatial boundary. Thus the philosophical debate about whether mind or meaning is inside or outside the head is ill formulated. It is legitimate to say mind is the property of a situated person.

Higher descriptive levels are irreducible partly because they have a larger scope of generalization. Classical dynamics does not generalize over initial conditions and values of the control parameters. It takes a given set of initial conditions and parameter values and deduces the behaviors of a particular process. Chaos is irreducible to the classical deduction because it depends on further generalization over initial values; bifurcation is irreducible because it depends on generalization over parameter values. We expect a similar expansion of the scope of generalization when we go from the neural to infrastructural to situated personal levels.

Disparate characteristic scales, including time scales, are important in considering different organizational levels. It is legitimate to consider changes in control parameters only when they are slow compared with dynamic changes. Definite magnitudes such as 1 millisecond or 1 second anchor abstract mathematics in real phenomena; they are where the physics is, as physicists say. Paying attention to different time scales prevents us from confusing the many processes that proceed simultaneously with different characteristic rates within a complex system. As we will see in the next section, much confusion in the philosophy of mind results from neglecting differences in scales.

It is not always undesirable to suppress details, as doing so often brings out salient large-scale structures. We sacrifice details about initial conditions when we reckon with attractors and systems of attractors. In return, we get a systematic description for long-term typical behaviors of the dynamical system. Similar tradeoffs are likely to occur in the science of mind, where details about neural and infrastructural processes can be overlooked in a description of mental properties.

Empirical theories always have finite domains of validity. Dynamics includes control parameters and their causal influence on state variables, but it does not account for causal mechanisms that set the parameters. In the fluid dynamics of Bénard convection, for instance, various values of the control parameter represent various temperatures of the bottom plate, but dynamical theory says nothing about how the temperature is manipulated. In allowing us to compare results for various parameters, modern dynamics points to causal factors beyond its domain, thus suggesting other theories for a higher level of organization. Dynamics includes our most established scientific theories. If dynamical theories do not include all relevant causal factors, it is unreasonable to demand a theory of mind to do so.

Let us apply some of these general lessons to the case of mind.

12 Emergence of the Unity of Consciousness

We saw in section 8 that cognitive scientists analyzed mind into various infrastructural processes that they studied in considerable detail. How do these processes integrate into the high-level characteristics of a situated person? Generally, the combination can be resultant or emergent. It is resultant if the processes all feed into a big unit in which they superimpose, aggregate, or run parallel to produce conscious experience; or if the end state of a process triggers the initial state of another, so that a long process obtains from the temporal abutment of short processes. An example of resultant combination of modules is consumer electronics, where the output of a CD player plugs into an amplifier, whose output goes into speakers. Another example is to combine the output of a tape recorder and a video recorder to produce a multimedia display. Is our mental infra-structure as simple as the stack of black boxes that make up your enter-tainment center?

Much evidence suggests that infrastructural processes do not merely combine by simple succession, summation, aggregation, parallel juxtaposi-tion. The degree of reciprocity and interference in neural pathways makes resultant combination highly unlikely. Processes in the infrastructure for a mental faculty interfere strongly. For instance, significant coupling occurs between processes for color and motion in the visual infrastructure, so that color is not simply added on a motion picture (Nijhawan 1997).

Infrastructures for various modes of experience constrain and modify each other. Try this experiment. Fill two cans, one small and one large, to equal weight with water. Lift one in each hand; you will feel that the small can is heavier, because your muscles are cued by your vision to be less mobilized for it. Lift the cans with your eyes closed to eliminate the sight-weight correlation and you will feel them to be equally heavy, as they are. Just as vision can affect proprioception, sound can affect vision. Sekuler et al. (1997) showed subjects a movie of two disks crossing paths, sometimes accompanied by a click at the moment the paths intersected. Subjects were much more likely to see the disks scattering off each other when the intersection was accompanied by the click. These experiments test not inference but immediate sense perception; therefore the cross-modal interference they demonstrate can occur only at the infrastructural level. More examples are presented in the following chapters: Emotion has a rational aspect and sensation has a conceptual strand. Emotion influences memory, which plays a role in perception, emotion, and conceptualization. Concepts can direct attention, and attention affects perception and action. Such cross-couplings indicate the emergence of the unity of consciousness.

Homuncular Functionalism and Its Hidden Assumptions

Despite empirical evidence, emergence is not popular in the philosophy of mind, partly because it is difficult to grasp. Those wanting easy answers often fall into the trap of tacitly assuming resultant combination. Because resultant combination can only produce properties of the same kind as those of the constituents, it cannot produce conscious mental processes from unconscious infrastructural processes, which have radically different properties. Consequently, some philosophers deny the existence of the conscious mind. Such is the case with eliminativists and instrumental behaviorists. They distinguish the personal, subpersonal, and neural levels; discuss the properties on the subpersonal or neural level; and at once generalize the properties to the personal level, effectively eliminating personal experiences. At the base of their erroneous conclusions is the tacit assumption that all the properties are resultant. A good example of the error is homuncular functionalism.

Homuncular functionalism is a variant of the homuncular fallacy. A great problem in the science of mind is to explain the nature of experience and understanding. Put bluntly, the homuncular fallacy explains how a man sees or understands by positing a little man inside the head who sees or understands. Do not let the implausible little man distract you from the really fallacious gimmick. The gimmick is to give a vacuous psychological explanation that posits a process to explain certain mental properties, but hangs the whole explanation on the posited process having the same mental properties that it is supposed to explain. The explanation is fallacious because it claims to shed light on experience or understanding, but it does not. It simply transfers experience and understanding from the man to the internal process symbolized by the little man. The fallacy remains if the little man is replaced by the more plausible-sounding brain or computer. Regarding understanding, we gain little by the explanation that a person understands because he has in his head a brain or computing unit that understands.

Homuncular functionalism gives the fallacy a twist. It claims that the homunculus is bogus only if he is as smart as the person whose head he inhabits; the fallacy would be dissolved if the smart homunculus is replaced by a pandemonium of stupid homunculi. Sure, replacing a person by a homunculus gives you nothing and replacing a smart person by the sum of many stupid homunculi gives you something. But is that something what you ask for?

Homuncular functionalism employs the tactic that Dennett (1995: 214) called "bait-and-switch." Some stores employ the sales tactic of advertising a big bargain to attract potential customers and, when they come in, push on them more expensive items. In intellectual discourse, bait-and-switch works by furtively changing the topic; for instance, advertising a hard or important question and, without warning, giving the answer to an easy or frivolous question. Homuncular functionalism quietly changes the topic and bills the easy answer to the original hard problem. It advertises an explanation for what it is to understand anything at all and delivers an account of the degree of intelligence that either presupposes or eliminates understanding. To understand complicated integration and to understand simple addition are both *understanding*, just as to steal a million dollars and to steal a thousand dollars are both *stealing*. The basic question regarding mind is not the complexity of the contents of what one understands, but what is it for someone to understand even the simplest of propositions; not what separates college professors from illiterate peasants, but what differentiates a person who understandingly judges which of two objects is larger and purposely picks up the larger one from a gadget that retains the larger object on a net through which the smaller one falls. In short, the central question is an explanation of understanding. The homuncular fallacy claims to answer it but does not. Homuncular functionalism works similarly but hides its fallacy by subtly changing the topic to grading IQ.[5]

Homuncular functionalism tacitly assumes that mind is a resultant property defined in terms of behavioral intelligence. It reduces mind to this single dimension, behavioral intelligence, but does not explain it. We will see in section 23 that the notion of intelligence it uses is ill defined. Workers in AI bank much on intelligence, but even they admit that behavioral intelligence resides in the eyes of mind designers and other observers, who grade it according to the efficiency in performance according to their criteria. Homuncular functionalism makes this questionable quality into the only feature of mind. Then it ranks everything, animate or not, on the single scale of intelligence. Mindless simply means too little intelligence and mindful means more intelligence. The difference between a music box and Mozart is merely their amount of intelligence. The amount of intelligence can be aggregated, so that many stupid things add up to a smart system, many stupid homunculi add to a smart person, and the most stupid homunculi is dischargeable and replaceable by mindless machine. However, it gives no explanation at all for the criterion and method of discharge. You ask what it is to understand. Homuncular functionalism pretends to have answered your question by saying that an entity with high intelligence is equivalent to an aggregate of entities with low intelligence. That is bait-and-switch.

Evidence for the Unity or the Disunity of Consciousness?
Homuncular functionalism lies at the basis of many arguments for the disunity of consciousness. It maintains that what we ordinarily know as per-

sonal identity or the unity of consciousness is bogus. There is only a pandemonium of homunculi working inside one's head. Therefore consciousness, if not fictitious, is fragmentary and discontinuous. Homuncular functionalism is similar to the doctrine that Plato ridiculed in *Theaetetus* (184): "It would surely be strange that there should be a number of senses ensconced inside us, like the warriors in the Trojan horse, and all these things should not coalesce into some single nature—a mind, or whatever it is called." What is the basis for this strange doctrine? Perhaps the most often cited evidence for the disunity of consciousness is from Anthony Marcel's (1993) experiments. I maintain that if we do not follow homuncular functionalism in assuming consciousness to be a resultant quantity, the evidence turns out instead to support the unity of the person.

Marcel asked a group of normal subjects to report whether they saw a dim flash, whose intensity was barely on the threshold of perception. Subjects used three different ways of affirming the flash in three separate trails: blink, push a button, or say yes. Statistical results are unmistakable: blinking reports are more accurate than manual reports, which are in turn more accurate than verbal reports. Furthermore, the accuracy of all three modes of response shot up to near perfection when subjects were instructed to guess instead of to report whether there was a flash.

Marcel's experimental conditions involved two distinctions, first between *guessing* and *judging*, and second among *various modes of articulating* the guess or judgment. The difference between guessing and judging can be interpreted along the line of blindsight. Guessing relies on infrastructural processes that are fast and accurate, although inflexible. Judging, on the other hand, is conscious, as subjects make deliberate decisions. The inferior accuracy of judgment shows that conscious decisions require more extensive analysis and integration of infrastructural processes, hence are more prone to noisy interference. Therefore in some situations, one may benefit from *Star Wars*'s advice to trust one's instinct.

The difference among various modes of articulation calls for a separate interpretation. Advocates of the disunity of consciousness often assume a single visual experience that various motor modules access separately and report with different veracity. Thus some ask which motor module we should take as the valid measure of visual consciousness. Others propose a split in consciousness, as each reporting system has its own consciousness. At the back of these versions is homuncular functionalism: the visual homunculus presents a picture, and motor homunculi play the role of reporters coming from a press conference and telling different stories. This story involves at least two dubious assumptions: introspection and the resultant combination of processes.

First, articulation is assumed to involve a form of *introspection* in which we, or more accurately our motor homunculi, observe our own mental states, here our visual state. This introspection is conscious, as it differs from the result produced by infraconscious guessing. The meaning of introspection here is obscure. When you say to your friend in a crowded theater, "I see two empty seats over there," you are looking outward into the hall, not inward into your mind or brain. Logically, "There are seats" and "I see seats" are different; the one is falsifiable, the other arguably not. Psychologically, it is doubtful that the two assertions made in the context of immediate perception represent two kinds of awareness, perceptual and introspective. Immediate perceptual reports are usually on objective states of affairs, not on our subjective experiences of them. Marcel (1993) asks subjects to report whether they see the light or not. Would the result be different if they were asked to report if the light is on or off? If subjective and objective instructions produce different results, it would be significant indeed, as it would differentiate introspection from perception. However, I doubt they would be different.

Another assumption is that the combination of various mental processes is resultant, so that seeing and reporting are disjoint, except that the output of seeing feeds into the input of various motor modules. Visual experience is like a camcorder that produces a tape that can be played on devices with different fidelity. If this is the case, the idea of consciousness becomes obscure. Does consciousness reside on the tape or the various playing? If both the camcorder and the player are conscious homunculi, consciousness is as plural as warriors in the Trojan horse, just as Plato described it.

An alternative interpretation avoids the Platonic Trojan horse. We deny that vision is a homunculus or a conscious module that produces a pure visual experience, which various motor homunculi take up later to produce various conscious reports. There are no conscious homunculi, only the conscious person as a whole. Instead, operations of the visual and motor infrastructures interfere with each other early on to produce the person's visual experience under a complex situation. We will see in section 16 that visual acuity is not an absolute constant but varies according to mental attunement such as the focus of attention. It is not unreasonable to assume that getting an articulation process into a state of readiness can have some causal effects on visual acuity, for alerting an infrastructure requires effort, just as it is expensive to mobilize a standing army. Ordinarily, interference from the intended articulation process is weak compared with the robust neural excitation produced by strong optical stimuli. Therefore we can neglect it in a first approximation that regards the visual process as an independent operation. In the experimental condition where the optical signal is marginal, the interference effect is no longer negligible. Consequently, the visual and intended articulation processes must be considered as a single state with its peculiar light sensitivity that is different from another state that combines vision with another intended mode of articulation. Using language is a more complicated mode than blinking, so its readiness interferes more with the visual process, leading to less accurate reports. Extrapolating the argument, we can say that visual experience is affected by all relevant mental factors and cannot be separated from them. This thorough integratedness points to the unity of consciousness as an emergent property that cannot be obtained by simple abutment of infrastructural processes.

Characteristic Times of Different Organizational Levels

Another alleged piece of evidence for the disunity of consciousness is the discoordination that results when subjects are pressed to respond quickly. In another Marcel's (1993) experiment, subjects used all three modes of articulation in a *single* trial: blinking, manual, and verbal. When they were instructed to respond as fast as possible, some gave conflicting reports, mostly correct ones by blinking and erroneous ones by word. Proponents of the disunity of consciousness eagerly cited this result. However, they ignored another part of the experiment that is unfavorable to their account. When the subjects were not hurried, all gave consistent answers by all three methods. Why does unity prevail only with time?

Consider sequential masking, a phenomenon well established by experiments. If a brief stimulus stands by itself, the subject has a visual experience of it. If it is immediately followed by a second stimulus, the subject sees only the second image but not the first, which is said to be *masked*. Allport (1988) referred to an experiment in which subjects were shown five letters in rapid succession, so arranged that the first two were effectively masked. Suppose one of the letters was *J*, which was masked by the succeeding letter *K*. The subjects must report, by pressing one of two buttons, whether *J* was present in the display. When not pushed to respond quickly, all subjects pressed the "target absent" button, which was consistent with their verbal assertion that they did not see *J*. When urged to respond as fast as possible, many subjects pressed the "target present" button and later apologized for having made a mistake.

Did the subjects have visual experiences of the letter *J* that was masked by *K*? They themselves avowed that they did not, even to the extent of admitting their own harried mistakes. Nevertheless, Allport argued that they were wrong about their experiences. They saw *J* when it was presented alone. Therefore they must also have seen *J* before it was succeeded by *K*, although their visual experience of *J* was fleeting and left no lasting memory. This argument is intuitive. Let us look at it more closely; its crux is whether experience is resultant.

At the base of Allport's argument is the assumption that the visual experience of a sequence of stimuli is the sequence of experiences of individual stimuli, no matter how briefly the stimuli are present. The experience of *JK* is the experience of *J* rapidly followed by the experience of *K*. To the extent that we can temporally make these experiences individual and discrete, this assumption is reasonable. It would raise no controversy if the stimuli *J* and *K* are each present for a second. What is contentious is the assumption that the temporal individuation of experiences can be pushed to arbitrarily small durations simply because the stimuli can be arbitrarily brief. Thus we have discrete experiences even when *J* and *K* are each present for only 10 milliseconds. This assumption is dubious because it neglects that processes on different organizational levels have different characteristic times, as discussed in the preceding section. When the time interval becomes too small, we start to confuse mental and infrastructural levels.

Take water as an analogy. On the macroscopic time scale, we can divide its continuous flow into successive stages, each with a macroscopic duration. When the duration of the stages decreases and finally ends in the microscopic time scale, however, talk about flow becomes meaningless. The whole concept of a continuous fluid breaks down and we must address the new notions of discrete particles and their collision. A flow is not simply a succession of collisions. Flow and collision are two distinct processes, each of which involves change in a distinct property. Their relationship is highly complicated. Fast collisions rapidly bring a tiny region in a fluid to equilibrium. Differences among the equilibrium conditions of various regions and their slow alterations constitute the fluid's flow.

Theories for fluids and particles both use differential equations with an infinitesimal time interval. However, the infinitesimal interval in fluid equations is on the order of milliseconds, whereas that in the particle equations is on the order of picoseconds. Different *characteristic times* are important physical phenomena, and they separate processes on different organizational levels. To apply an equation to processes outside its legitimate characteristic time is a mistake that manifests ignorance of the topic.

Similarly, conscious and infrastructural processes are distinguished by different characteristic times. Conscious processes are slow, with characteristic times ranging from 100 milliseconds to minutes and hours. Infrastructural processes are fast, with characteristic times shorter than 100 milliseconds (Liboff 1990). Experience and consciousness break down at times too brief, just as flows break down at times too small. To talk about a millisecond-experience of *J* followed by a millisecond experience of *K* is like talking about one picosecond-flow following another. Neither makes sense because both apply concepts to the wrong time scale. To conclude from them that consciousness does not exist, however, is like concluding that fluids do not exist or that fluidity has no clear meaning. They have clear meaning on their own organizational level with the proper time scale. Many proposals for the disunity of consciousness manifested in time-pressed experiments stem from confusing mental and infrastructural time scales.

Formation of an Experience

Why are conscious processes so sluggish compared with infrastructural processes? An experience involves numerous infrastructural processes, and to integrate them takes time. A finite binding time is required for a single mode of experience, not to mention cross-modal integration. Optical signals are processed in more than thirty brain regions whose neurons may have different response times. The activities of these widely scattered areas must somehow synchronize so that the person perceives the features belonging to the stimulus of a specific time as a unit. Haste produces mistakes. For instance, experimenters presented a series of pictures of objects, one of which had a frame around it, and asked subjects to identify the framed object. When the pictures were presented with increasing rapidity, at around eight per second, subjects started to make mistakes and put the frame on the object preceding or succeeding the correct one (Intraub 1985). These results illustrate two points: the temporal organization of perception is not a mirror image of the sequence of stimuli, and mistakes occur when responses are demanded in less than 100 milliseconds, which is the lower limit for conscious processes. It is no surprise that discoordination—so-called slip in the unity of consciousness—occurs only when response is pushed to the limit of the time frame.

If we take account of disparate time scales for conscious and infraconscious processes and allow that self-organization takes extra time, we have no reason to reject as meaningless subjects' assertion that they have no visual experience of the masked stimulus *J*. A masked stimulus does causally activate the operation of certain infrastructural processes, which by reflex can trigger the button-pressing finger. However, it does not necessarily result in experience. In masking experiments, stimuli are presented faster than the characteristic rate of conscious processes. A process that changes slower than another must miss many details in the variation of the latter, although we may not know how the details are lost. Suppose each letter lasts 10 milliseconds and self-organization processes leading to conscious visual experience require 100 milliseconds. When the letter *J* is presented alone, subjects see it because the infrastructural processes have ample time to organize into a visual experience. When *J* is immediately followed by the mask letter *K*, subjects fail to see *J* because the infrastructural processes for it, diverted by the subsequent stimulus *K*, do not have enough time for self-organization. The self-organizing processes for rapidly presented stimuli temporally overlap and interfere. Under this condition, the experience of a sequence of rapidly represented stimuli is *not* a sequence of the experiences of individual stimuli. It is an integral unit that covers the whole sequence of stimuli with distortions. The necessity of taking a sequence of events as a unit in conscious experiences reveals the unity of consciousness over time.

The results of these experiments reveal the emergence of the unity and consistency of conscious experiences given enough time. The myriad interacting infrastructural processes need time to settle in a global equilibrium state corresponding to experience. When people must make speeded responses, they may not wait for self-organization to be completed or equilibrium to be reached. Time-pressed results expose the diversity of processes in the cognitive infrastructure. They do not prove the disunity of consciousness. They show only that unity belongs to a different organizational level with a longer characteristic time and therefore cannot be hurried too much.

The Nature and Strength of Unity

As general mental architecture, the unity of consciousness is like the skeletal frame that distinguishes a skyscraper from a classic dome but leaves out most material of the skyscraper. Its gross framework encompasses and confers a certain degree of coherence for the contents of our experiences, but it does not require that coherence be seamless and logically perfect in its details.

All too often in philosophy unity is conceived after the image of totalitarianism that allows no discrepancy. So is the unity of science conceived, so is the unity of consciousness. Both conceptions are wrong. The unity of consciousness is neither a God-given soul nor a human-designed control, but the self-organization of numerous infrastructural processes. It is more like democracy than totalitarianism. The essence of democratic unions is toleration of disagreement and opposition. If discord is too great, a union collapses into anarchy or civil war. As long as a democracy stands, it must have a significant degree of consensus despite much discontent. Its fundamental structure shows itself in how it maintains cohesion in the face of internal conflict; its strength shines in how much dissent it can accommodate without collapsing. Commentators should note disagreement, but they would be wrong to proclaim the dissolution of union simply because of it. Self-organization of infraconscious processes is no less complicated than consensus building. Close inspection of the unity of consciousness exposes many cracks, flaws, and inconsistencies, especially in pathological cases. When the defects are too great, experience collapses totally as the patient "loses his mind." As long as the patient keeps his sanity, he must maintain a significant degree of coherence despite his impairment. The strength of the unity of consciousness shows in the amount of defects it can tolerate without collapsing. Judging from the damage people can sustain, it is very strong.

Some patients had the corpus callosum, the nerves connecting the two cerebral hemispheres, surgically severed to relieve epilepsy. Such split-brain patients are often cited for disunity of consciousness. When psychologists carefully isolate the functions of disconnected hemispheres in laboratory experiments, they find that each hemisphere maintains experiences of its own that can be totally different from that maintained by the other. If a patient sees an object only through the left eye, he can pick out the object by his left hand, as both are controlled by the right hemisphere. However, he is unable to say what he sees, because speech is controlled by the left hemisphere, whose normal communication with the right hemisphere has been severed. Such dissociated behaviors prompted Sperry to say that the patients behave as if they have two minds (Springer and Deutsch 1989).

Equally important but often neglected is the fact that these strange behaviors of split-brain patients are apparent only under experimental conditions that are quite extraordinary. In everyday life where the patients see with both eyes and work with both hands, they act normally and seldom complain of mental conflict. They have abnormalities that are exposed in controlled experiments, but their mind's plasticity is able to compensate for the defect and devise alternative means to communicate, perhaps by external physical means, what in normal people is passed by the corpus callosum. As maintained throughout this book, openness to the world is an essential mental characteristic. The world is a coherent anchor that cements what Kant (1781) called the "objective unity of consciousness" that complements the "subjective unity of consciousness." Laboratory experiments obliterate objective unity to bring out damaged subjective unity of split-brain patients. Even so, experimenters are often confounded by patients' tendency to make objective inferences. In daily life, when the patients are open to the unifying effects of the world, they achieve a remarkable degree of coherence. Normalcy in real life where it counts is the triumph of the unity of consciousness.

Left-right conflict can occur in the rare cases when a split brain suffers further damage. MP's aberrant left hand is a case in point. In doing jobs that require only one hand, her left hand sometimes behaves as if her right hemisphere is bored and decides to play pranks. It undoes the buttons the right hand doses; opens the drawer the right hand closes; throws out the items the right hand packs into a suitcase. However, even with such severe brain injury, the alien hand mischief is infrequent. MP's two hands coordinate well in most bimanual tasks. She drives safely; her hands do not attempt to steer in different directions (Parkin 1996).

When a part of the body is out of control, patients tend to depersonalize it. MP regards her left hand as an alien "it," shouts at it in frustration, but nevertheless accepts it as part of her body; it serves her well in bimanual tasks. Others go further and totally disown the part of body their minds no longer feel and control. One patient woke up horrified to see his "lazy" leg as a foreign object in his bed, tried to throw it out, and fell to the ground. Another said her paralyzed arm belonged to her fiancee.

Such cases show how desperately people try to maintain mental coherence, even at the cost of denying the continuity of their body.

Our mental life is supported by numerous infrastructural processes, many of which can be individually dissociated from the large unity of consciousness. The complicated synthesis of myriad processes can fail in many respects, hence there are various degrees of coherence we can make of our conscious life. However, even the worst pathology does not affirm a disunity of consciousness in which a mind is nothing but a Trojan horse containing an army of homunculi, each with his own purposes. If this were the case, dissociation of specific processes would not be pathological. The sheer variety of dissociating pathology reminds us that even as one or a few processes break off, numerous others cohere to maintain consciousness. After reviewing the pathological deficiencies in the unity of consciousness, Edoardo Bisiach (1992) said: "The above examples, however, demonstrated that, even when under particular circumstances the content of awareness reveals the disunity of its source, a great deal of integration may be achieved through mechanisms we are still very far from knowing."

The Unity of Consciousness Is Not Resultant but Emergent

The following chapters present many results from cognitive science that contradict the philosophical assumption of a resultant mind. Experimental evidence increasingly suggests that resultant combinations of infrastructural processes are the exceptions rather than the rule. Many infrastructural processes proceed not in sequence but in parallel, which does not imply that they run like a bundle of separate pipes. They are not black boxes whose internal processes are immune to external influence except at the terminal input. They are semitransparent, so that their operations are susceptible to interference from other processes running in parallel. Nor is the interference one way. Even in perception, cognitive scientists discover "concept-driven" processes that go in the opposite direction to "stimuli-driven" processes. Such complicated interferences play an important role in combining mental infrastructures. Combination with substantial interference is not a mere aggregate, so its consequences are unlikely to be resultant.

Emergent properties are far more variegated and versatile than resultant properties because their constituents organize in more diverse and complicated ways. Therefore they are more likely to explain many experiences that are impossible as the mere aggregation of infrastructural

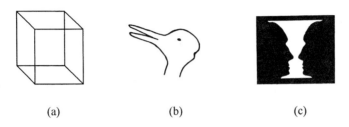

(a)   (b)   (c)

Figure 3.6
The ambiguous figures of (a) Necker's cube, (b) Wittgenstein's duck-rabbit, and (c) Rubin's vase-faces illustrate bistable vision in which one alternately sees two objects in the same display.

processes. If a system is merely the sum of its parts and it has many parts, changing the properties of a few parts changes the property of the system only slightly. Hence resultant properties are stable with respect to small perturbations of constituents. Stability also implies inflexibility.

Emergent properties are far more changeable and adaptable. A system of tightly integrated constituents can be very stable, just as electric currents in superconductors are more stable than those in ordinary conductors (see section 11). Unlike resultant properties, however, emergent properties are capable of instability. Do not belittle instability; it enables the system to change radically. When a system is poised at the edge of instability, dramatic changes in its state can be precipitated by the disturbance of a few constituents. The disturbance can propagate quickly throughout the system because the constituents are strongly and thoroughly interconnected, thus translating a local ripple into a global tide. A speck of dust can turn a supercooled liquid into a solid, changing its entire structure. Such emergent volatility is not uncommon in mental phenomena. Brainstorms are examples. Another example is visual bistability. When we look at ambiguous figures such as Rubin's vase-faces or Necker's cube as in figure 3.6, the stimulation is stable, but our perception of it is not. What we see switches abruptly and often involuntarily between a vase and two faces, or between a cube protruding from the page and one recessing into it. Such switching would be a mystery if our visual experiences were resultant and not emergent properties.

The Legitimacy of Mental Causation
When you want to raise your hand, you raise it. You have no problem understanding your friend's explanation that he brings an umbrella *because*

he thinks it is going to rain. That our mental processes are causal factors in our own actions is so deeply ingrained it is presupposed in our whole legal system and views of responsibility. Mental causation, however, is controversial in the reductionist philosophy of mind. Philosopher Jaegwon Kim (1993) rejected Sperry's thesis that consciousness is an emergent property of cerebral excitation, complaining that it implies "mentality, having emerged from physical-biological processes, takes on a causal life of its own and begins to exercise causal influence 'downward' to affect what goes on in the underlying physical-biological processes." Implicit here is the assumption that causation flows only one way, from the bottom up. Behaviors of constituents can cause behaviors of the system, but not the other way around. Kim maintained that "downward causation," where the system constrains the constituents, makes no sense. Nonreductive theories of mind are untenable because they imply downward causation. Therefore there are only two alternatives: either mind is nothing but physiology or it is inexplicable.

Kim's stricture applies not only to mind but to all high-level structures. But does it really make no sense to say that a solid's rigid structures constrain the motion of its constituent atoms? Is anything wrong with downward causation except its terrible name? I argue that the complaint of Kim and other nothing-butists is unwarranted. At its bottom is a confusion about the notion of causation and a conceptual framework too impoverished to accommodate phenomena of any complexity.

First let us distinguish between causality and causation. Causality, a most basic idea in our general conceptual scheme that plays crucial roles in all our thinking, generally includes all causal relations among all entities. Causation, talk about causes and effects, is a cruder notion that singles out, among myriad causal factors, a few salient ones as the causes of a certain phenomenon, leaving other equally indispensable causal factors as standing conditions. For instance, investigators cite a faulty wire as the cause of a fire, relegating to standing conditions the presence of oxygen and flammable material, without which the fire cannot roar. The controversy over mental causes presupposes causality and debates on causation: what are the legitimate causes in mental systems?

Causal relations and interactions make no a priori assumption about the direction of action. All fundamental physical interactions are symmetric, electrons mutually repel, and the sun and earth attract each other. Thus the only general direction of causation is temporal, causes precede their effects. Because causation and causal power convey directionality, some people deem simultaneous causation an oxymoron. This may go too far, because many respectable equilibrium scientific theories describe standing causal structures.

Despite the prominence of the equations of motion, equilibrium structures are as important a part in science as dynamic processes. Atomic and nuclear physics use the time-independent Schrödinger equation to find internal structures of atoms and nuclei; equilibrium thermodynamics and statistical mechanics are better developed and more widely used than their nonequilibrium counterparts. They are all causal theories that do not fuss over the direction of causation. More familiar examples surround us; buildings erected by architecture and civil engineering are all explained by equilibrium causal theories.

It is not easy to justify the assignment of causal priority among things in equilibrium. Our customary assignments are mostly conventional. When a bowling ball sits on a cushion, we habitually say that the ball causes the cushion to be depressed, and in so saying we get the impression that the ball has "more causal power." Scientifically, however, Newton's third law asserts that action and reaction are equal and opposite. The ball exerts a downward force on the cushion, which is balanced by the cushion's upward resistance. A symmetric causal relation obtains between the objects, neither of which has superior causal power. Struggle for power easily slides into explanatory imperialism, which is why I always talk about causal relations and interactions when I have no reason for prejudice.

The part-whole relation between constituents and the system they make up is an equilibrium relation. Many people take for granted that it is reasonable to say that constituents cause the properties of the system but unreasonable to say the system causes the behaviors of its constituents. What is the rationale? The constituents make up the system, but we can equally say the system breaks down into constituents. Constituents can form other systems, but the system can replace its constituents, as the cells in your body are constantly being replaced. Usually we regard constituents as more basic because they are more versatile, but we cannot forget that they change their behaviors, often drastically, when they coalesce to form a system. It is true that microscopically all causal relations obtain among constituents, but they are minute in a system with zillions of constituents. What counts as a cause, which is something ponderous and salient, in such large systems?

A composite system and its constituents change simultaneously, and the evolution usually involves many parallel processes with vastly different characteristic time scales. To talk about what causes what in the evolution depends very much on what time scale we are interested in and what initial conditions we pick. A tornado is made up of zillions of air molecules, and it derives most of its significance from the patterns of collective molecular motion. Its material base is transient, as molecules leave or join in droves. The tornado hurls molecules in its path as it hurls debris, and the molecules and debris alike become part of it for a while. We accord causal power to the tornado with respect to debris. What is wrong in according it causal power with respect to the air molecules?

Philosophers have debated long and hard about the appropriate criteria for being a cause. They mostly agree that a cause is some combination of necessary and/or sufficient conditions for the effect. Large-scale structures of composite systems, be they resultant or emergent, are necessarily coarse compared with the properties of tiny constituents. Thus the conditions they impose are loose and do not determine precise constituent behaviors. Perhaps it would sound better if these conditions were called *constraints* rather than causes, but constraints are causally efficacious all the same. Moreover, in some situations, especially for emergent properties, constraints can be quite strong.

Scientists routinely consider the causal influences of a system's the high-level structures on its constituents or low-level subsystems, which is very much a part of synthetic analysis. For example, physicists talk about the behavior of a test particle in a large system, where the particle is just a representative of the system's constituents. Physical theories show clearly how the property of an electron is significantly modified when it is incorporated into a crystal and subjected to the downward causal power of the crystalline lattice. Thus habitual prejudice is the sole basis for disallowing causal influences of composite systems on their constituents.

The strongest proposal offered by Kim and other reductionists against downward causation is that it is inconsistent with "upward determination," in which the behaviors of constituents cause and determine the properties of the system. Again, their claim is possible only if we ignore actual science. Several highly successful theories demonstrated rigorously that upward determination and downward causation can harmonize with each other consistently. The self-consistent field theory in physics is one example, the general equilibrium theory in microeconomics another. They are mathematical theories that rigorously show how the constituents causally make up a system and how the structures of the system as a whole causally affect the behaviors of individual constituents.[6]

Widely applied self-consistent theories in physics and economics prove that, contrary to the reductionist claim, upward determination and downward causation are reconcilable by adequate interlevel theories. The reconciliation is not reductive. Concepts for the system and its constituents are intertwined in the explanations of both upward determination and downward causation. The causal relations between a whole and its parts are symmetric. With proper analysis, we can crudely talk about the parts causing the whole to behave in certain ways or the whole causing the parts to behave in certain ways, but neither direction of causation has any intrinsic superior power.

The causal influence of mental activities over neural excitations was evident in many experiments. One experiment showed how a voluntary shift in attention changed the neural activities in the brain. Suppose you are looking at some colored bars moving about on a screen. At first you pay attention to their colors. Then, without any external prompting, you change your mind and focus instead of their shapes or speeds. If your brain is being scanned, the result will show a marked change in your brain activity pattern when you make that change (Corbetta 1998).

Single-neuron experiments give a more dramatic demonstration of the downward effect of mental attention. Experimenters trained monkeys to perform various tasks that require selective attention to various attributes of a visual stimulus. Then they inserted microelectrodes to measure the action potential of individual neurons in the monkeys' visual system as the animals performed these tasks. Care was taken to ensure that the probed neuron was exposed to the same optical stimulus for different tasks, so that the only difference was the monkeys' state of mind, including attention to selective aspects of the stimulus. For instance, one kind of neuron is sensitive only to motion in a particular direction, say, motion from right to left. A monkey looked at a display consisting two moving objects and was trained to attend to only one. Suppose the two objects simultaneously crossed the visual field of a direction-sensitive neuron from opposite directions. If the neuron were not subjected to any top–down attentional influence, it would always respond in the same way because one of the two objects moved in its preferred direction. This was not what happened. The neuron responded strongly only if the attended-to object moved in its preferred direction. Its response was markedly smaller if the ignored object moved its preferred direction. Mental attention made a big difference in the behaviors of individual neurons. Similar results were obtained in many other experiments. Most neurons responded more strongly when a monkey attended to stimuli within its visual fields than when it directed its attention elsewhere. They also responded more strongly when a monkey attended to the attribute of their specialty than when it attended to other attributes. The influence of attention on individual neurons is unmistakable. It shows the downward causation that nothing-butism denies (Maunsell 1995).

Results of single-neuron experiments have many theoretical and philosophical ramifications. They prove the futility of a purely bottom-up approach that describes behaviors of individual neurons independently and then sums the behaviors to find out what they amount to. Even the behavior of a single neuron is not determined by the stimulus alone. In the bottom-up approach, we cannot systematically describe the strange behavior of a motion-sensitive neuron and explain why it responds to the movement of one object and not another moving in the same way. We have no meaningful way to differentiate the two objects without referring to the larger mental context in which the neuron situates and by which its behavior is regulated. Such reference to the whole in explaining the behaviors of its parts, prohibited by reductionism, is an important part of synthetic analysis. It is crucial for understanding emergent properties and mental causation.

In sum, both conceptually and empirically, it is scientifically respectable to consider the causal influence exerted by a system's high-level structures on its subsystems and subprocesses. More specifically, it is legitimate to consider the causal influence of mental processes on neural behaviors. Such considerations are integral in synthetic analysis. Reductionism fails to justify dismissal of downward causation and more specifically mind's causal influence on action. When you lift your hand to register a vote, your mind, a high-level structure, causally influences some of your lower-level subsystems. We have no detailed explanation of how you achieve this, but there is in principle no mystery.

13   Situated Properties and the Engaged-Personal Level

I discussed the emergence of the unity of consciousness in the preceding section without pausing to address the characteristics of the unity. Now I explain what it is and is not, and why it is the property of not an isolated person but a person engaged in and open to the world. My discussion is brief, aiming only to introduce the concept of situated property and distinguish it from coupling. A detailed analysis of the structures of the open mind of engaged persons is deferred to the final chapter.

What Unity of Consciousness Is Not

In some writings, unity of consciousness, or the "self" as it is often called, is an entity sitting in the head or elsewhere inside a person. This view is especially popular among those enchanted by the computer metaphor with its central processing unit. Many who do not regard the self as something like an Intel chip inside a personal computer nevertheless believe that it is something inside and susceptible only to introspection, perhaps as consciousness of consciousness.

The notion of the inner self has been severely criticized by many philosophers, including Hume (1739) and Kant (1781). Kant went into detail to warn against confusing *unity of consciousness* with *consciousness of a unity*. The only entity here is the person. Unity of consciousness is the most basic structure of the person's mental properties, without which the person becomes a mere body. As long as a person exists, he is a conscious unit, and this does not imply a separate unity that he is conscious of. Kant's thesis follows that of Hume, who tried to find the self by introspection but failed. In both cases, denial of consciousness as an internal entity does not lead to the denial of a person's being conscious. Keeping the distinction clear will help us from being distracted by some frivolous noise in the current philosophy of mind.

What then is unity of consciousness? Imagine yourself picking a rose. You see a red flower, smell perfume, stretch your arm and pull with your hand, feel the breeze on your face and the sun on your back, sense the pain as your finger is pricked, hear the rustling of leaves answered by the singing of birds, and think about the woman for whom the rose is intended. You do all this not disjointly but harmoniously in a single experience, a single mental state, that you *are* in the world. You are spontaneously aware that you see the same flower whose thorn causes your pain and whose stem your hand breaks; that in one and the same experience, you are open to the rustling plants, the perfumed air, birdsong, and the woman, not as disjoint items but as parts of one intelligible world. Integrity is an essential feature of personhood. The unity of a person depends heavily on the unity of his physical body, but you are not merely a unit as a stone is a physical unit. You also enjoy unity in your mental dimension, your unity of consciousness.

Your experience is unified in two respects, objective and subjective. Objectively, your sight, smell, and touch converge on the same rose. More generally, the contents of various modes of your experience possess a large degree of coherence that is anchored in the causal structures of the physical world. This coherence also enables you to acknowledge that the diverse perceptions, memories, desires, and beliefs are all *yours*. Like two sides of a coin, the objective and subjective unity of consciousness are inseparable. Without either one we would be unable to distinguish *objects* from our *subjective experience of them*, hence unable to find the world intelligible and meaningful. These points will be explained more fully in chapter 8.

Unity of consciousness, in both its subjective and objective aspects, is the first of five psychological characteristics explicated by James (1890:220, 405): "Every thought tends to be part of a personal consciousness. . . . The universal conscious fact is not 'feelings and experiences exist, but 'I think' and 'I feel.'" We may attend to an indefinite number of things, he wrote, "but however numerous the things, they can only be known in a single pulse of consciousness for which they form one complex 'object.'" A person's mental unity extends beyond the single conscious pulse in a moment. It includes another of James's psychological characteristics, temporal unity of pulses in the stream of consciousness.

Thus in traditional views, unity of consciousness is not an inner entity. It is the identity of a person living in the world. This is the view that I adopt.

The Isolated-Personal, Engaged-Personal, and Ecological Levels

Many philosophers adhering to the inner self maintain that a mind open to the world is impossible if it emerges from the self-organization of neural and infrastructural processes. These processes all occur within the skin, therefore unity of consciousness must also be closed within the body. Philosophers trap themselves in this dilemma partly because they do not appreciate the lessons that we draw from dynamical theories (see section 11).

Scientific theories usually adopt different scopes of generalization for different organizational levels, so that properties on one level can include factors not accounted for on a lower level. Scope expansion partly accounts for the emergence of new properties on higher organizational levels. Furthermore, a system's property can include factors located outside its spatial boundary. Of course, we should be careful about the meanings of extended properties, more specifically, of extended mind. For this purpose I distinguish three candidate levels for mental properties: the *isolated-personal level*, where mental structures include only factors within a person's skin; the *engaged-personal level*, where mind is a property of an individual person but mental structures include factors outside the skin; and the *ecological level*, where a system participates in an environment and mind either disappears or belongs to the system-plus-the environment. What is the level of description most suitable for mentality?

Theories of consciousness as qualia, which is an inner feeling, usually fall in the isolated-personal level. So does Searle's (1983) theory of intentionality, where intentionality can belong to brains in a vat. Undoubtedly we are conscious, but is consciousness merely an inner feeling accessible only by introspection? If so, it increasingly appears to be a causally impotent epiphenomenon, as discussed in section 23. Perhaps it is more productive to find another concept in which consciousness is an integral part of our experiences of objects. I see no way to solve the problem of meanings on the isolated-personal level without appealing to external mind designers. Externalism, for instance, has to introduce external experts to fix meanings (see section 4). Meanings arise from our concern with things and people in the world. Most of our mental processes are so concerned. You see and recognize a friend. You believe that the earth rotates and hope that the stock market rises. Your love or hatred is not merely a hot bodily feeling but is directed at specific persons. Most people who earnestly wrestle with the problem of meaning realize that they must expand the scope of their theories to include things in the world. But how?

To address the relation between mind and world, Gibson's ecological approach and AI's dynamicalism and situated cognition jump to the ecological level, where a system interacts with a large environment and changes because of the interaction. Similarly, some computationalists jump from the functional level to the sociofunctional level on which a set of solipsist minds moves without changing their internal functional structures.

Unfortunately, in the ecological and sociofunctional levels of description, people are not different from other inanimate things. They are parts of the universe, behave in certain ways, and interact in certain ways. Thus the ecological view is essentially behaviorism with emphasis on a system's interactive behaviors with its environment. If mental properties exist, they seem to be diffuse in the environment. Thus sociofunctionalism attributes deliberation and decisions to social institutions.

The ecological level surrounds mind with a blind environment but not an intelligible world. Edward Reed (1988:280) expressed it best in his exposition of Gibson's ecological approach to perception: "The purpose of perception is not for a subject to convert the physical world into a meaningful environment, but to keep observers in contact with their surroundings." This view works for insects but not for humans. A fly's vision ties it to its surroundings without making them meaningful and enables it to react adequately to events without finding them informative. Our vision is different. In seeing, we turn the physical environment into an intelligible world and events into information. Therefore a theory of the universe at the ecological level is not a theory of mind; by mind, I mean something with the sophistication of the human mind. We will find in such theories everything except mind, as they miss precisely the individual subjectivity that makes the universe and society meaningful (figure 3.7).

Physically, people are mere specks of dust in the universe. Nevertheless, they can think about the whole universe and more; they can think about not only the actual but also the possible, not only the present but also the future. They can also think about themselves, so that they are aware of their subjective perspectives from which they see and understand the objective world. They are members of a community, relying on its language for thinking and sustaining many of their beliefs by intersubject agreement. Nevertheless, each person has an individual mind that others can influence but cannot supplant. Each maintains his own initiative and anticipation, knows that his action makes a difference to the future, and cares about the meaning of the difference he makes.

In short, people are not merely parts of a blind environment. Your world is meaningful and you are informed by perceptual experiences. These are possible because of your mental ability. Thus to characterize mind as the individual property of a person, we need a theoretical level where the description of the individual somehow absorbs some structures

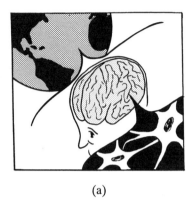   

(a)   (b)

Figure 3.7
(a) An account of how neurons make up brains and how brains are parts of the universe is insufficient to explain mind; the picture misses the person's subjective awareness of his participation in the world. (b) A theory of open mind folds certain general features of the intelligible world into the engaged person's mental state as its contents, thus explaining how the person understands the objective world from his subjective perspective.

of the world. This is the engaged-personal level, the proper own-level explanation of mind. In other words, mind is a *situated property* or the property of a person engaged in the world. As such it is an individual property, but its structures have absorbed much influence of the world to account for the person's situation. This section presents the general concept of situated property. Chapter 8 explains how mind is a situated property.

Situated properties are not uncommon in sciences that address complex phenomena, and I have given many examples elsewhere (Auyang 1998). They are a bit tricky, so I take a step back to introduce the concepts of property, relation, and context. Then I will explain why the own-level description of mind as a situated property is not necessarily incompatible with the interlevel description of mind as an emergent property.

Intrinsic and Extrinsic Relations
We ascribe properties to a thing by subject-predicate propositions such as "the apple is red" and relations by relational propositions such as "the apple is on the table." Besides the logical form, is there an absolute distinction between a thing's properties and relations? Independent of any description of ours, does the universe come furnished with self-identifying entities

with absolute properties clearly separated from relations? A quick answer is yes; nature comes with entities separated spatially. An entity's properties are what belong to it in isolation and hence must fall within its spatial confine. Whatever spatially outside the entity are relations. We can see this assumption at work in the debate between externalism and internalism (see section 4). Putnam (1975) said that meanings ain't in the head; Searle (1983) countered that they are. Reflecting on the writings of the two, John McDowell (1991, 1992) noted that they share the assumption of mind being an organ spatially located inside the head. It is this assumption that prevents a proper account of persons as mental subjects who find the world meaningful.

Spatial separation is a good criterion for many entities we handle, but it falls far short of being universal. Leibniz argued that space cannot be an absolute identifying criterion because entities such as shadows interpenetrate. Biologists have difficulty individuating some plants because their roots entangle. If spatial interpenetration is the exception in the macroscopic world, it becomes the rule in microscopic physics. Atoms are not hard spheres at all; their boundaries are difficult to define. Strictly speaking, an elementary particle is a wave packet with infinite spatial extent and there is no definite separation between it and another particle. Nature is a complicated web. It does not come with a set of ready-made and self-identifying entities with absolute properties. Our discernment plays a significant role in individuating entities and defining properties and relations. The demise of the spatial criterion for individual properties is important for mental properties. It rejects the assumption, often tacit, that a person's mental properties must be enclosed within his skin.

The two general approaches to study compounds are *pure construction* and *synthetic analysis*. They tacitly presuppose two concepts of properties and relations. Going from the bottom up, construction posits a set of given elements with absolute properties and extrinsic relations, as illustrated in figure 3.8a. A relation is *extrinsic* to the entities when the properties of the entities are defined independent of it and do not change when it is added. From known principles governing the elements, constructionists deduce the properties of the system formed by combining the elements in various ways. Examples of the construction approach are various forms of dualism that first posit mind and body, or subject and object, or the inner and the outer realms as two independent entities with predefined properties, and try to connect them by one extrinsic relation or another. One posits first

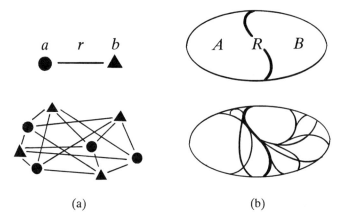

Figure 3.8
(a) Construction starts with predefined entities *a* and *b* with absolute properties, then imposes the extrinsic relation *r* between them to construct composite systems. (b) Synthetic analysis starts with a whole and draws a distinction *R* to differentiate the parts *A* and *B*. *R* is an intrinsic relation because it simultaneously relates the entities it differentiates. Thus *R* and the properties of *A* and *B* are mutually dependent, revealing a gross structure of the whole. Further analysis brings out finer structures.

a computational mind defined in total abstraction and tries to implement it in physical matter; first a closed mind playing with mental representations and tries to connect the representations to physical objects; first systems of mere words and tries to hook words to things.

Synthetic analysis assumes a given whole and draws distinctions to find the parts appropriate for the explanations of the whole's properties. Suppose we analyze a whole into two parts by drawing the boundary *R* as in figure 3.8b. *R* does three jobs: it defines, differentiates, and unites the two parts. Whenever we talk about one part, we tacitly invoke the other part and the whole by the boundary *R*, without which it is not defined. Therefore *R* is an *intrinsic relation* between the two parts, as their mutual relationship is constitutive of the essential properties of each. Further analysis reveals finer structures of the whole by drawing more distinctions and delineating more intrinsically related parts. Synthetic analysis is successful in many sciences. Biologists analyze the genome into genes with interrelated functions; the genes are intrinsically related, because as a gene and not merely a chain of nucleotides, it depends on the regulation and cooperation of many other genes to produce a protein. Cognitive scientists analyze brain states into activation patterns and the mental infrastructure into interconnected subsystems and subprocesses; the patterns and subsystems are intrinsically related, as they are defined by their functions in the whole.

Intrinsic relations are more complex and hence more difficult to address than extrinsic relations. However, there is nothing mysterious about them. They are ubiquitous in mathematics. A mathematical theory posits a set of axioms with intrinsically related terms. The definition of each term depends on the definitions of the other terms, so that a term becomes meaningless when taken out of the axiomatic structure. Mathematics is not merely a calculation tool. More important, it excels in precise articulation and analysis of complicated concepts, which partly explains why it is so efficacious in representing complex structures with interrelated components.

The difference between extrinsic and intrinsic relations is most apparent when we consider the properties of one part of the system. In construction, the part's properties are *absolute* and independent of the context wherein the part locates, as they are not affected by the extrinsic relations the part engages in. Consequently, implementation is optional to the computational mind and the external object is optional to the closed mind. Context is always important to the properties of a part in synthetic analysis because the part is defined only in the context. Their properties are situated within the whole. Even when the context is treated approximately in simplified models, its leading role is unmistakable. Context is presupposed in infrastructure, which is by definition the support of something else.

The Cartesian Trojan horse fails because it tries to impose extrinsic relations between a ready-made closed mind and a blind environment; extrinsic relations prove unable to import meaning to the closed mind. In contrast, the open mind's relation to the world is intrinsic. It is not defined apart from its world, because intelligibility of the world is its essential property.

From Extrinsic Relations to Situated Properties

Synthetic analysis aims to understand complex phenomena. Thus it gives theoretical precedence to the whole and does not tie its hands by committing to a set of ready made parts. We have various ways of carving the whole into entities with individual properties and mutual relations. Abuse is always possible; analysts can carve up nature arbitrarily by chain saws, just as constructionists can construct arbitrary monsters by pure logic.

Scientists, however, usually take pains to observe nature's joints and products. Even so, they have certain discretion. Depending on the depth and refinement of analysis, they can stop at crude parts. Furthermore, they can adjust properties and relations to find the parts most appropriate for explaining certain properties of the whole. Such adjustment brings out the meaning of situated properties most clearly.

Consider how physicists investigate the macroscopic properties of solids. They know that a solid is made up of atoms with whose properties and relations they are familiar from microscopic physics. Thus their job appears to be made for the constructionist approach. They do spend ten minutes writing down equations representing the construction, but the bottom-up march stops right there. To make further progress, they turn to the top and synthetic analysis. As I explained elsewhere, they have developed many methods and approximations to connect various properties of solids to atomic properties. Several productive methods analyze the solid afresh to find new entities with situated properties (Auyang 1998).

A solid is made up of atoms, which are decomposed into positively charged ions and negatively charged electrons. For simplicity let us relegate ions to the background and consider only mobile electrons, which are most interesting because on them depend all those wonderful electronic gadgets and computers. We know that electrons have velocities and positions, which we summarily called their typical property P, and that two electrons interact electromagnetically, which we represent as the binary relation R. Thus we have a sea of electrons in a positive background where the electron i has individual property P_i and relation R_{ij} with the electron j, as illustrated in figure 3.9a. Although each binary relation connects only two electrons, each electron can engage in as many binary relations as there are partners. The result is a complicated relational network. Physicists can write the equations for it in two lines, but it is almost impossible to solve the equations as they are. Suppose we change a single electron. The effect of its change is passed on to all its relational partners, which change accordingly and in turn pass their effect to their relational partners. To track all the changes is hopelessly complicated.

Relations make the problem difficult. Simply to throw them away, however, would amount to committing systemic suicide. Without electromagnetic coupling, atoms fly apart and the solid disintegrates. Relations cement the constituents, ensure the integrity of the composite system, and generate all the interesting structures. To take account of relations without

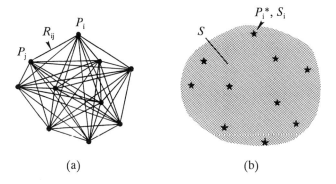

Figure 3.9
(a) Intuitively, each constituent i in a composite system has property P_i and relation R_{ij} to every other constituent j. The multiple relations form a complicated network. (b) To make the system more tractable, scientists analyze it into new constituents. Each has situated property $P^\star_i$ and responds individually to the situation S_i generated by all. There is no explicit relationship between the new constituents, but they are not solipsistic, because their situated properties, custom-made for the situation, have absorbed many relational effects.

being stuck in the relational network like a butterfly in a spiderweb, scientists try to represent the system in a different way. They turn to synthetic analysis.

In a widely used strategy, scientists analyze the electronic system afresh to find new "electrons" whose properties automatically harmonize with each other so that they naturally fit together without explicit relations. In doing so, they divide the collective effects of the myriad original relations R_{ij} into three groups. The first group of relational effect is absorbed into *situated properties* $P^\star$ for newly defined electrons. The second group is fused into a *common situation* S, an electromagnetic field to which the new electrons respond. Whatever relational effect that is not accounted in these two ways is neglected in the first approximation. These steps transform a system of interacting electrons into a more tractable system of noninteracting electrons with situated properties responding independently to a common situation jointly created by all, as in figure 3.9b. In the reformulation of the problem, an original electron with familiar property P_i is replaced by a new electron with new property $P^\star_i$. The property $P^\star_i$ is *situated* in two ways. First, it has absorbed much effect of the original electromagnetic relation R_{ij}. Second, it is intrinsically related to the situation S_i where the electron sits and hence reflects the situation's characteristics.

The new electrons with the situated properties are intrinsically being-in-the-situation.

This strategy of replacing extrinsically related entities by new entities with situated properties flourish in many branches of physics as the Hartree-Fock approximation, or the self-consistent field theory. The second name is descriptive because the situation S is not imposed externally but is determined self-consistently with the situated property $P^\star$.

Situated properties come in many varieties. A particle's mass, for example, is intuitively the most "absolute" of properties that should reside "inside" the particle. However, you can find tables for effective masses of electrons inside specific crystals such as in silicon or in germanium. The effective masses are situated properties that have absorbed the effects of the specific crystalline structure of silicon or germanium. In size, the crystal is to the electron like the earth is to a person. Yet the electron's individual situated mass has accounted for the crystalline effect.

Philosophers may find in the self-consistent approach an alternative to the externalist theory of meaning. Such a model would feature individual speakers immersed in a common linguistic environment. Each speaker understands word meanings in his peculiar way and contributes his own understanding to them. Here word meanings are represented by something akin to S and individual speaker meanings by $P^\star_i$. No communal mind or expert stipulates absolute word meanings. Some pundits may be influential, but if most speakers in the community shift what they mean by certain words, the words' meanings will change despite the pundits' grumble. The shared meaning S is determined self-consistently from the collective effect of all speakers' meanings $P^\star_i$. This decentralized model for meaning does more justice to the "division of linguistic labor" than the antiindividualistic model where meanings are the monopoly of experts.

Situated Mental Properties and the Mental Infrastructure

As a person's situated property, mind is intrinsically open to the world and is structured by its characteristics. As an emergent property, the structures of mind constrain the functions and characteristics of its infrastructures. Thus the mind-world relation is closely connected to the mind-body relation. We cannot adequately understand processes underlying mind, including brain processes, without accounting for the world to which mind is open.

Except philosophers who insist that a brain in a vat with no revenue from the world can have the same experience as a person, few people doubt that the characteristics of one's brain are influenced by both genetics and sensory input. The relative importance of the two, however, is vigorously debated by scientists. Many people believe that interactions with the world modify detail but not salient brain structures, which are innate or determined by genetically encoded developmental programs. If a region of the brain is born to be a part of the visual infrastructure, it cannot develop into something else, whatever input it receives. James (1890) conjectured that if acoustic input is fed into the visual cortex and optical input into the auditory cortex, we would hear lightening and see thunder. Experiments proved him wrong.

For a decade, Mriganka Sur and his group have been perfecting techniques for rewiring brains. Sharma et al. (2000) surgically connected nerves from the right eye of a newborn ferret to its left primary auditory instead the primary visual cortex. The two brain areas normally have drastically different structures, which is expected in view of the different signals that they process. How the auditory cortex develops under retinal input sheds much light on the relative strength of genetic and sensory influences. Results are unmistakable. As a rewired ferret grew up, its left auditory cortex developed the salient structures of a visual cortex, including the highly ordered orientation map that is responsible for spatial differentiation. The rewiring changed not only brain development but behavior. By carefully designed conditioning, von Molchner et al. (2000) trained the animal to respond to light and sound, then performed further brain ablation to ensure that light stimuli in its right visual field were fed only into the auditory cortex. In the final phase of the experiment, the ferret was exposed to sound and light on the right. Always, it responded to lights in similar ways as it saw them. Sensory input trumped genetic programming in determining the structure and function of a brain area.

If brain's characteristics are so strongly influenced by interactions between sensory organs and the environment, it would be surprising indeed that mind's are not. Mind is not merely embrained but fully embodied and engaged. Its being the situated property of a person coping actively in the world gives it general structures that are closely associated with the general characteristics of the world. These structures Kant called general concepts of objects, which are just the basic common sense that the world we understand consists of physical things with certain causal regularities. We will analyze and examine empirical evidence for them in chapters 5 to 8. They form a conceptual scheme so complicated that models of the closed mind, unable to deal with it, mutilate it. However, infants begin to develop them at a surprisingly early stage. They ensure that the open mind and its intelligible world are made for each other, not unlike individual situated properties $P^\star_i$ and the situation S being made for each other in self-consistent field theories. Thus subjective and objective unities of consciousness depend on each other, agreeing with Kant's (1781:194) highest principle of empirical knowledge: "The conditions of the *possibility of experience* in general are likewise conditions of the *possibility of the objects of experience* in general."

4

Language and Modularity: How Far Is Mind Analyzable?

14   Universal Grammar and Its Interpretations

In the preceding chapter I postulated that mind is a high-level emergent property of persons situated in and open to the world. It is supported on a lower organizational level by a vast infrastructure that is incognizant. By commonsense and psychological research, scientists analyze mind crudely into various faculties such as vision and memory. They delve into the respective infrastructures, which they further analyze into many interactive processes. Exactly how these incognizant processes self-organize into mental processes awaits the solution to the binding problem. Nevertheless, the synthetic analytic approach never loses sight of the connection to mind when it shines the spotlight on the mental infrastructure.

This and the next three chapters present case studies for the synthetic analysis of mind, specifically, of the mental faculties of language, perception, memory, and emotion. Cognitive science has produced many fascinating results. I present some and ask what their significances are. Many are now interpreted in various models of the closed mind controlled by mind designers. I describe some influential models, reject them, and offer alternative interpretations of the same scientific results without invoking mental representations that close mind from the world and mind designers who interpret them. This will prepare the way for the final chapter, which sketches the structures of a situated person's open mind.

Two major moves in my reinterpretation are to replace computation by causality and to separate clearly the thinking of mental subjects from the thinking of scientists studying them. Instead of inner computational and outer representational realms separated by the veil of mental representations, I introduce organization levels of engaged persons and mental infrastructures. Thus I reinterpret what many people call the computational mind as theoretical computer models framed by scientists for causal processes in mind's infrastructure. These processes, numerous and minute, do not coalesce into salient mental representations in the engaged-personal level, leaving room for mind's openness to the world.

Infrastructural processes are numerous, specialized, automatic, and precocious. Thus they touch on many controversies in cognitive science. Are they innate? What is the meaning of innateness? Are they modular or domain specific? What are the meanings of modularity and domain specificity? Do they understand what they are doing, so that they are like little men computing in the head? Do they coalesce into unified experiences on the engaged-personal level, or is the person nothing but a Platonic Trojan horse, a zombie housing a horde of homunculi? We have considered some of these questions in general terms. Here we add substance by addressing them in the concrete context of language. Instead of the constructionist approach common in the literature, I offer alternative interpretations in the analytic approach, which yields more flexible and practical notions of modularity and unity.

I start by examining a specific infrastructure, Chomsky's "language organ" characterized by universal grammar. Chomsky spearheaded the cognitive revolution by tearing down the pretension of behaviorism and advancing a new linguistic theory. His universal grammar and interpretation thereof made linguistics into an important branch of cognitive science, generated much controversy, and strongly influenced the discourse on mind. After presenting his theory, I discuss my interpretation of the language organ as the infrastructure underlying our grammatical competence. Universal grammar is foremost a theory about human languages, which are phenomena on the engaged-personal level. The postulate that it also describes the architecture of the syntactic infrastructure reveals the connection between the engaged-personal and infrastructural levels.

Chomsky's theory incited much debate on innateness, modularity, learnability, and unconscious knowledge. It provides a good context for clarifying the meanings of these concepts and how they apply to mind or its infrastructure. The innatism and informational encapsulation that Chomsky and Fodor ascribed to the syntactic infrastructure, even if valid here, cannot be generalized to other mental infrastructures. The following chapters provide some counter examples in perception, memory, and emotion. Our analytic approach to linguistic and other mental infrastructures further exposes mistakes in the doctrine that diversity of infrastructures implies disunity of consciousness (see section 12).

Languages, Formal and Natural

One has to be careful about what "language" means in cognitive science with its emphasis on computation and symbolic manipulation. In the widest sense language refers to symbolic systems, either formal or meaningful. Under the influence of mathematical logic and computational theory, most philosophies of language and cognition treat languages as formal systems. Examples of formal systems are predicate calculus and various programming languages such as C or LISP. A formal system consists of a set of alphabets or symbols and a set of syntactic rules that combine alphabets into words or expressions and transform the expressions. Do not be misled by the ordinary nuance of the names. Symbols and expressions here are totally meaningless, neither representing nor expressing anything. Thus 0 and 1 in a formal system do not mean zero and one. They are merely ringlike and rodlike entities, and their forms or shapes alone distinguish them and determine their fate under syntactic rules. This is the meaning of "symbol" in the "symbolic level." Advocates of the computational mind claim it to be the locus of thought; critics see it as a veil of formality that closes mind from the world.

Formal systems are precise. They are precise because they are devoid of meaning, which is vague and ambiguous. As a formal system, a language contains no nouns or verbs but only symbols. Even its semantics appeals only to sets and sets of sets, not things and properties. Hence it is totally detached from the practical life. For the sake of distinction let us call such symbolic systems artificial languages or artificial grammar, as they are pure grammar without meaning. Their structures and functions are usually very different from natural languages and their grammars.

By "languages" we ordinarily refer to natural languages such as Arabic, Chinese, Spanish, or American sign language. This is a narrower meaning, as natural languages have restricted structures. There can be any number of formal and semiotic systems, but as some linguists believe, there can be only a finite number of natural human languages. Unlike formal systems, natural languages are so integrated into our lives that even their grammatical structures are not totally drained of meaning. The noun phrase, verb phrase, subject, and object into which linguists analyze sentences are closely associated with ideas of thing, action, and agency. In talking about noun instead of apple and orange, verb instead of eat and drink, syntactic analysis abstracts from substantive meaning. Nevertheless, it retains certain general structures of meaningful discourse.

From now on, "language" without qualification refers to natural language. Here we consider only a few questions regarding the complicated role of language in our practical life. Does anything special distinguish natural from artificial languages? Are natural languages arbitrary social artifacts that happen to be adopted in one place or another? Or do they have some roots in the psychology and physiology common to all humans? Are there infrastructural processes dedicated to them?

Linguistics as the Natural Science of Human Languages
Naturalism is the chief approach of Chomsky (2000:106), who repeatedly insists that linguistics is a natural science that adopts "an approach to the mind that considers language and similar phenomena to be elements of the natural world, to be studied by ordinary methods of empirical inquiry." He considers only the grammatical aspect of natural languages and says that it is neither artificial design nor social construction but a natural phenomenon. Consequently linguistics is not social engineering but a natural science employing methods typical of empirical inquiry. Using mathematics, he strives to develop a comprehensive theory for the general grammatical structures common to all human languages. Universal grammar (UG) is the name of his theory, which has undergone many modifications over the decades.

Universal grammar revolutionized linguistics; however, Chomsky does not stop there; he wants to make it into a theory of mind, not merely of language. Arguing that the human ability for natural languages is based on a complicated structure of the human mind, he gives UG a psychological interpretation where it becomes the structures of an innate language organ that functions autonomously. This interpretation sways the theoretical discussion of mind. I will return to it after I present UG in its essential role as a linguistic theory.

Naturalism here means studying our mental or linguistic abilities as they naturally occur in our daily activities. As such it fully respects the mental concepts and vocabularies that people use every day. It should not be confused with the philosophical doctrines for *naturalizing mind*, a euphemism for psychophobic nothing-butism that opts for eliminating mental concepts and expresses mental phenomena in nonmental terms.

Chomsky is not psychophobic. He distinguishes two general conceptions of language: E-language that is externalist and extensional and I-language that is internalist, individual, and intensional. Formal systems and artificial languages are examples of E-language. An E-language is an arbitrary infinite collection of sentences treated as an object in itself, considered externally to individual persons, and detached from consideration of the structure of the human mind. If it has any meaning, its semantics is externalist in the sense of being assigned by outside experts instead of understood by individual speakers. Many E-languages are extensional and, in contrast to intensional languages, cannot accommodate belief, possibility, and other concepts with mental connotation. Consequently they are the favorites of psychophobic philosophers (see section 24). Most traditional linguistics and philosophies address E-languages. Chomsky argues that the proper concern of linguistics should be I-language, which is a natural ability of individual persons. He concentrates on natural languages, paying little attention to artificial languages, although his work contributed much to research in that area (1986, 2000).

Linguistics has a closer tie to computation than other natural sciences. Recursive function, a mathematical tool of linguistics, is also basic to the theory of computation, the mathematical foundation of computer science. Finite-state automata, Turing machines, and digital computers can equally be formulated in terms of various artificial languages and grammars, of which Chomsky introduced a hierarchy.[1] Nevertheless, Chomsky is unsympathetic to AI as an approach to the study of mind. The science of mind aims to study natural mental states, not to design artifacts; to discover general principles governing wide classes of mental phenomena, not to build machines that emulate specific bits and pieces of human behaviors. His naturalistic approach irks many promoters of designing and engineering mind.

Chomsky has more adversaries than AI fans and traditional linguists. Since the early twentieth century, analytic philosophy made a linguistic turn and considered language its empire. Many language philosophers concentrate on artificial languages such as predicate calculus. They tend to deny there is anything special about natural languages, except perhaps that they are especially unkempt and should be replaced by a neater artificial language. Philosopher Willard Quine (1960), for example, professed his aim to be the "regimentation" of language or the quest for an ideal language or notation. Instead of natural languages, which are intensional, he prescribed an extensional language for ideal science. His prescriptive attitude clashed with the descriptive attitude of Chomsky, who wrote (2000): "Quine and others have suggested operational criteria to identify well-formed signals, but operational tests are a dime a dozen, and it must be shown that there is some interest in the concept they characterize. In the case of E-languages, no such argument has been proposed." The difference between Quine and Chomsky runs deep into the traditional debate between empiricism and rationalism, which will surface repeatedly as we look at various aspects of mind.

Language and Its Science

What are the natural phenomena that linguistics attempts to describe and explain? Among life on Earth, natural linguistic ability is unique to humans; among humans, it is universal. From desert plains to rain forests, from the tropic to the arctic, anthropologists have not met a single mute tribe. Roughly 6,000 natural languages are identified. Most face extinction, but not because they are primitive. None is (Wuethrich 2000). Languages invariably exhibit sophisticated structures, whether the people who speak them have stone-age or computer-age technology.

"It was Greek to me," Casca admitted in Shakespeare's *Julices Caesar* when he got nothing from Cicero's speech. Of course he understood nothing; Cicero spoke in Greek. Languages are so different that those spoken by foreigners often sound like birdsongs or machine guns. Is there any order under the Tower of Babel? Do human languages possess any common structures? Natural sciences typically try to find general structures that sweep across a great diversity of phenomena. Linguistics is not an exception.

Obviously whatever common structures languages possess must be subtle. To discover hidden structures, however, is the expertise of science. It was not obvious at all that a common law governs stones falling on earth and planets moving in the sky. If it were, Newton's theory of universal gravitation would not have come as a shock in the seventeenth century. When natural scientists approach a topic, they try to discern patterns and introduce concepts to describe them approximately. They also try to frame general theories that can cover as wide a range of topics as possible, thus explaining the topics by revealing their interrelationships. Linguists proceed like other scientists. A language has a structure that can be captured by a set of rules, and the thousands of human languages provide a fertile field for theoretical scientists to extract regularities and formulate general principles.

Linguistics has a long history and many branches. Historical linguistics studies the evolution of various languages, such as the divergence of Romance languages from Latin. Sociolinguistics studies how language relates to society; psycholinguistics to psychology. The major thrust, however, is on the characteristics of human languages themselves. Analyzing languages to various degrees of abstraction, phonetics, syntax, semantics, and pragmatics separately address their sound pattern, grammar, meaning, and context. Chomsky made syntax the queen of linguistics. Because syntax has closer relation to computation and formal systems than semantics and pragmatics, it also plays a big role in the philosophical theories regarding cognitive science.

Many people had grammar lessons, either in school when they learned their native language or later when they learned a second language. In linguistics, however, grammar is more sweeping and systematic. *A grammar* is a system of rules abstracted from a particular language. It characterizes formal structures, and its instances include all grammatical sentences of the language and none of the ungrammatical ones. In language after language, linguists descry regularities representable by language-specific grammatical rules: lexical rules that classify words as nouns, verbs, and other parts of speech; inflectional rules that mark nouns for case and number, verbs for tense, voice, mood, and agreement with subject; phrase structure rules that combine words into various kinds of phrases and phrases into larger phrases and sentences; transformation rules that move phrases in declarative sentences to form passives, questions, and other constructions. Some of these rules can be applied recursively, generating infinite numbers of sentences.

As good scientists, linguists are not satisfied with the regularities within one language when languages abound. They examine the rule systems of various languages to find regularities susceptible to generalization on a higher level. Following the common practice of theoretical science, they introduce powerful concepts that encapsulate the myriad rules of a language into a few abstract superrules that bring to relief the interconnection among various petty rules. They discover that these superrules exhibit regular patterns. For example, the word order in English is subject-verb-object; Jones eats steak. The same word order occurs in all types of English phrases—noun, verb, preposition—and is accompanied by peculiar positions of prepositions and modifiers. Japanese has a subject–object–verb word order; Yamato sushi eats. This order occurs in all phrases and is accompanied by peculiar preposition and modifier positions that are systematically different from English (Pinker 1994).

Chomsky brought linguistic theorization to a new height. Based on regularities of superrules, he strove to develop universal grammar aiming to characterize structures for the rule systems of all human languages. Over the decades he and his followers continued to develop, refine, and modify the substance of UG, partly in response to experimental feedback from psycholinguistics. To attain the generality to which it aspires, UG must be abstracted from the specifics that stick it to particular languages. Fittingly, its latest version is called the minimalist program. It is far more abstract than the transformation grammar Chomsky put forward some forty years ago (1986, 1995).

Universal Grammar: Principles and Parameters
Basic to the minimalist program are principles and parameters. UG consists of a set of principles common to all human languages and a set of parameters, the specific values of which differentiate particular languages. If we compare the principles with the logistic equation in figure 3.5, the parameters are like the control parameter a.

The principles in universal grammar describe the most general syntactic structures. An example is the projection principle asserting that the meaning of a word imposes certain constraints on the syntactic structure of a sentence. For example, the verb "push" implies an actor acting on an object, thus a sentence containing it must have the minimal structure of also containing two nouns. The projection principle, which suggests that words automatically join into structured chunks, has great psychological ramifications. It helps to explain why we can remember sentences containing many words, although the capacity of our working memory is limited to about seven uncorrelated items (Chomsky 1995).

As usual, a parameter has a range of values. An example is the head parameter, which is a part of the head principle. The head principle asserts that each type of phrase has an essential parameter called its *head*; the verb "eat" is the head of the verb phrase "eat steak," and the preposition "by" is the head of the preposition phrase "by Jones." The head can occur in various positions within a phrase, and the positions are the values of the head parameter. It is important that the head principle leaves open the value of the head parameter, thus allowing it to vary from language to language. English, for instance, is a "head first" language, which means the head comes first in all types of phrases such as "eat steak." Japanese is a "head last" language; again, the parameter determines the position of heads in all kinds of phrase such as "sushi eat." Once values are set for all parameters, UG determines the structure of a particular language.

As a theory of all human languages, UG is a sweeping generalization. Sweeping generalizations in theoretical science are typically content with a high degree of abstraction and idealization. Thus many physical equations of motion neglect friction and other minor forces. Similarly, Chomsky insists that UG characterizes only the ideal linguistic *competence* common to all humans, leaving out details about the variable linguistic *performance* of individual persons. Some people perform better with words than others, but all human beings share the competence of speaking a language, provided they have no mental impairment.

Principles, parameters, competence, and performance all point to a general characteristic of science: we can investigate a topic in more than one degree of generalization and abstraction. Principles are like low-resolution panoramic cameras; they operate on a high level of generality to capture sweeping structures. By containing parameters, however, they leave room in the big picture for the operation of high-resolution, narrow-view shots. The values of the parameters zoom in to capture specific details. Such multilevel theories are common in science. They provide concrete examples for the argument, presented in section 25, that multiple intellectual perspectives are essential structures of our mind.

We can compare the principles-and-parameters version of UG with physical theories. Physical theories typically have three levels of generality, the first two of which resemble principle and parameter. For example, Newton's second law, force equals mass times acceleration, is a universal principle covering all motion. It contains a parameter, the form of force, but leaves the form open. A value of the parameter is a form of force, for instance the inverse square law of gravity, which Newton introduced independent of the law of motion. Various forms of force determine various kinds of dynamic systems: gravitational, electromagnetic, and, more narrowly, oscillator and scatterer. Analogous to the law of motion are the principles of UG, which encapsulate common characteristics of all human languages. Analogous to the form of force are the parameters, values of which determine various languages: Bantu, French, or Sanskrit. The law

of motion and the form of force are general to a broad type of dynamical system, just as linguistic principles and parameters characterize general
competence in a natural language. The third level of specificity in physical theories, the initial condition, specifies individual systems. It is analogous to the linguistic performance of individual persons.

A scientific theory, even one called universal, has a finite region of
validity. Thus Newton's laws do not apply to microscopic objects and laws
of quantum mechanics do not apply directly to macroscopic objects.
Similarly, Chomsky stresses that UG covers all possible human languages,
but no more. It is not extendable to extraterrestrials, because there is no
guarantee that their mind is similar in structure to ours. The principles-
and-parameters theory strongly constrains the structure and variety of
human languages. The vocabulary of languages may vary indefinitely, but
there can only be a limited number of basic grammatical structures,
because UG contains only a finite number of parameters, each with a
finite number of values.

Universal grammar is mainly a theory of states, not processes. It
describes the state of linguistic competence, but not the process by which
competence is attained. Nor does it describe real-time processes in which
a sequence of sound is parsed into grammatical parts. These real-time
processes, often called linguistic performance, become the topic of psycholinguistics. Since the 1960s, when psycholinguists tried enthusiastically
but unsuccessfully to verify Chomskyan conjectures, it has grown apart
from linguistics. Nevertheless, linguistics continues to supply the basic
theoretical notions that guide psycholinguistic modeling, so that the
models do not merely emulate specific behaviors but partake in a larger
explanatory framework of linguistic performance.

Universal grammar is limited to syntax, the formal structure of human
natural languages. It specifies syntactic interfaces with sound and meaning,
but does not consider them explicitly. Meaning and use are far more perplexing than formal syntactic structures. In his early writings, Chomsky
professed interest in meaning and promised investigation into semantics.
However, he did not deliver on the promise and has not appeared to make
serious attempts. When his disciples, impatient for the promised land,
developed generative semantics, he turned against them, precipitating the
nasty "linguistics war" of the late 1960s and early 1970s (Harris 1993).
Extending Chomsky's generative syntax, generative semanticists sought
rules that connect semantic representations with the surface structures of

sentences. They failed. As the war cries died down, Chomskyan linguistics became even farther removed from meaning, limiting itself to formal structures and retaining only an interpretive interface.

How Is Universal Grammar Possible?

The possibility of UG suggests that the Tower of Babel did not destroy all common bonds among human languages. By painstaking comparisons, linguists discovered a long list of universals, features shared exactly or with slight variations by all languages. What is the origin of the commonality?

One possibility is that all languages descend from a single proto-language and inherited some of its features, similar to biological evolution in which all species share some similarities because they descended with modifications from a common ancestor. Undoubtedly linguistic evolution is widespread. For example, most existing Old World (Eurasian and African) languages are traceable to about sixteen languages that existed some ten thousand years ago. Even so, it is highly questionable that human languages have common structures because they have a common origin. For that assumption to hold, a close correlation should exist between the history of human dispersal and the distribution of language types, akin to the correlation between biological phylogeny and morphological types. Historical data show otherwise. Major language types do not correlate with major branches in the linguistic genealogy.

Another piece of data against the hypothesis is the genesis of new languages. It does not happen often, but a new language can appear within a single generation. In South Pacific slave plantations, for instance, the parent community consisted of people with different mother tongues who improvised a jargon called a pidgin for communication. A pidgin typically consists of fragmentary word strings with few grammatical rules and little expressive power. When children grew up among pidgin speakers, they spontaneously injected grammatical complexity into their speech, creating a new and expressive language called a creole. Similarly, deaf children growing up in a community of clumsy signers spontaneously added grammatical structures and developed a more sophisticated system that has many hallmarks of natural language. More remarkable is the case of Simon. Born deaf, Simon was exposed to American sign language (ASL) only through his parents who, having learned it late in life, were not fluent. Nevertheless, tests found that Simon was much more accurate than his parents in ASL grammar. His superior accuracy would be impossible if grammar is a social convention, as his only access to the convention was from his parents. Simon may have been very clever and introduced complexity into his sign language, but what can explain that those introductions conform to the grammar of ASL? The source of the general structures of human languages seems to reside not in an ancestor but in each child (Pinker 1994).

How Is Language Acquisition Possible?

Only certain sentences are grammatical within each language, but their variety is infinite. Some linguists estimate that an average high-school graduate knows around 45,000 words. From them one can generate some 10^{30} grammatical sentences with up to 20 words. Therefore chances are high that the next sentence you utter has never been spoken before. Children acquire linguistic ability in several years. The amount of stimuli they receive during the process is meager compared with the variety and complexity of sentences they will produce and comprehend. Most children receive no formal instruction in grammar. Even worse, the sentences they hear are not always well formed and their own ill-formed utterances are seldom corrected. Instead of correcting the grammar of their babies, parents sometimes happily imitate the baby talk. Confronted with such contaminated exemplars, learners who proceed by generalization, induction, association, or hypothesis formation would easily go astray. Yet despite the obstacles, almost all children grow up speaking their mother tongue correctly and fluently. How do they accomplish the feat?

According to empiricist philosophers, it is miraculous. This can be seen from comparing the predicament of the infant with that of Quine's (1960) fictional field linguist who goes to a foreign country to learn its language. A rabbit runs by and the natives utter, "Gavagai." Suppose after many experiments, the linguist finds that the natives utter "gavagai" only in the presence of rabbits and not of other white things, flurry entities, or short-tailed animals. Can he conclude by this process that "gavagai" translates into "rabbit"? No, he can never be sure, Quine insists, as "gavagai" may always refer to other possibilities and there is no way to resolve the ambiguity. Quine's indeterminacy of translation partly stems from the assumption that field linguists can rely only on natives' overt behaviors and utterances. Chomsky (2000) counters that the behaviorist stipulation is radically different from the actual practice of field linguists. Real-life linguists engaging in empirical studies do not merely rely on overt behaviors. They also apply general principles that they glean from studying other languages. Language competence common to humans endows various languages with certain general structures, of which linguists avail themselves in research.

Quine adheres to both behaviorism and empiricism. He believes all that are given to us are sensual stimuli and that the mind has minimal structures. Thus his big puzzle is how, given the "meager input" of surface stimuli, we can produce a "torrential output" of talks. A bigger puzzle is how children learn to speak based on the meager input. Chomsky too starts from the premise that stimulus input is meager. As a rationalist, however, he denies that mind is a blank slate that is open to social conditioning. No, the infantile mind is naturally endowed with certain structures that constrain possible interpretations and enable the child to acquire linguistic abilities. Quine argues from the poverty of input to a radical relativism that isolates people in different cultures. Chomsky argues from the same poverty of input to certain mental structures that unite all humans.

The Language Organ and Its Development

To explain grammatical universals and children's ability to acquire their mother tongue and even to generate new languages, Chomsky introduced the language organ and the language-acquisition device. With these he brings UG from linguistics into psychology. His psychological interpretation has three major thrusts. First, UG is both tacit knowledge of ideal speaker-hearers and the structure of the language organ that is a part of the human brain. Second, tacit knowledge is innate, as babies are born with the language organ that matures automatically in a linguistic environment. Third, the language organ is encapsulated; it is responsible for syntax and, except at designated interfaces, isolated from interferences from meaning and context.

Chomsky proposes that all normal human infants are born with a language organ, the initial state of which is characterized by the principles of UG with indefinite parameter values. They also have a language-acquisitive device, which sets the values of parameters as children receive input from in a specific linguistic community. With the help of the device, their language organ evolves from its initial state to a final state characterized by UG with definite parameter values, which account for specific environmental influences. The final state of the linguistic organ is manifested by matured competence in one's mother tongue. Once children have acquired their mother tongue, the state of their language organ remains quite stable, changing only on the periphery such as accumulating vocabulary. In Chomsky's (1986:146) words, at birth the language organ characterized by UG is "an intricately structured system, but one that is only partially 'wired up.' The system is associated with a finite set of switches, each of which has a finite number of positions (perhaps two). Experience is required to set the switches. When they are set, the system functions."

In this picture, children do not learn their native language in the ordinary sense of the word. Instead, their linguistic organ grows along an internally directed course, triggered and partially shaped by the effects of environmental input. They naturally develop grammatical competence as their language organ matures, just as they naturally develop ability to walk as motor control matures. Chomsky wrote (1980:134f): "In certain fundamental respects we do not really learn language; rather, grammar grows in the mind."

E-languages may be pure grammar, but the grammars of I-languages are embodied in meaningful utterances in practical contexts. Here Chomsky makes a hypothesis as radical as his innatism. He sharply distinguishes I-language from "common language" or "shared language" that belongs to a linguistic community. I-language is internal in the strong sense of developing according to internal dynamics with minimal influence from meaning and use. Matured, the language organ functions as an encapsulated module that parses and produces the formal structures of speech. It has an interface with speech sound as characterized in phonetics and an interface with meaning as studied in semantics and pragmatics. These interfaces supply input and output to the syntax module but do not interfere with its internal operation. The syntax module is susceptible to rigorous theoretical representation, but it is doubtful if meaning and use of languages are also susceptible. Because of its isolation and susceptibility to formal representation, the language organ is agreeable to the computational theory of mind, which partly explains its pioneering status in cognitive science. Encapsulation of the syntax module becomes a cornerstone of Fodor's thesis of the modularity of mind, which is discussed in the next section.

In short, Chomsky (1986:27) holds that people's ability to acquire, know, and use grammars of I-languages stems from an innate, specialized, and encapsulated mental organ, the structure of which is reflected in UG. Thus linguistics as the study of I-languages "becomes part of psychology, ultimately biology." These hypotheses, if true, are productive in cognitive science. Language has an edge over perception and other mental processes in revealing the infrastructural processes underlying our mental life. Like sensual organs, the language organ is physically internal to each person. Unlike perceptions, which are experiences private to perceivers, natural languages spoken by various peoples are well-recorded public systems susceptible to analysis and theorization on their own. Therefore linguistics has more data than other areas in cognitive science and these data are more susceptible to theoretical analysis. Products tell about their producers. Because languages are the natural products of our mind and the media of our thoughts, linguists can infer much about the structures of mind from the universal structures of human languages. Thus Chomsky justifiably cited Leibniz: "Languages are the best mirror of the human mind."

How sound are the hypotheses of the language organ's specialty, innateness, and encapsulation? I consider specialty here, the other two in the next section.

Is a Special Faculty or General Intelligence Responsible for Grammar?

Chomsky posits not only a rather well-formed mental structure at birth but also a specific substructure geared to syntax. Few people doubt that humans are born with something peculiar that enables them, as distinct from monkeys, to grow up speaking languages. To many people, however, that peculiar something is simply a larger brain or a higher general intelligence. It is not analyzable into components, one of which is specifically linguistic, not to mention specifically syntactic. The question is not whether if we try, we can use our general intelligence to learn a language just as we learn symbolic logic or computer programming. Let us assume that we can. Perhaps general intelligence plays a great role in adults learning a second language, which uses a different part of the brain as their native languages (Kim et al. 1997). Nevertheless, general intelligence is vague. Is it analyzable into more specific aspects? Can cognitive science pinpoint some specific subsystem of our overall mental structure that is at play in children's acquisition and subsequent proficiency of their mother tongues?

Over this point Chomsky once joined a debate with Piaget and Putnam. All three agreed that anyone who is to learn anything must be equipped with the requisite learning mechanism. They diverged on the nature of that mechanism. To Putnam, it sufficed that infants are born with enough general intelligence that serves them to learn natural or artificial languages, games, mathematics, whatnot. Some apes, too, are smart enough to learn symbolic systems, albeit trivial ones by our standard. Nevertheless, as manifestations of general intelligence, their linguistic ability and ours differ only in degree and not in kind. Piaget was more specific. He stated that our linguistic ability is based on our symbolic ability generally made possible by sensorimotor development, therefore we do not need a specific language faculty. Chomsky countered that Piaget and Putnam had mustered neither evidence nor theory. Notions of general intelligence and sensorimotor development are too vague to serve as alternative hypotheses to his own highly detailed and precise linguistic theory. Please be more definite, he constantly pleaded in his exchange with philosophers; empty generality merely covers up the issue and blocks scientific inquiry. Merely positing intelligence that can learn everything tells us nothing about how it manages to learn anything (Piattelli-Palmarini 1980).

Neuropsychological Evidence for a Specialized Syntactic System
The human brain is not a homogeneous mass supporting general intelligence. It differentiates into many areas. Areas specialized to language are located in the left cerebral hemisphere for almost all right-handers and about 70 percent of left-handers. The two major language areas are Broca's, next to the motor areas controlling the jaws, lip, and tongue, and Wernicke's, next to the auditory and sensorimotor areas (see figure A.2 in the Appendix). These areas serve both the spoken languages of hearing people and the sign languages of the deaf. Sign languages are as complicated and expressive as spoken languages, and have similar grammatical structures. Thus linguistic ability is not tied to the auditory-vocal mode but works equally with the visual-manual mode.

Just as injuries in the visual areas result in various forms of visual agnosia, lesions in the language areas result in aphasia. Aphasic patients are impaired linguistically, but many do not experience deterioration in general intelligence. There are various forms of aphasia. Take for example Broca aphasia, so called because it results from damage in Broca's area. These patients produce stuttering and ungrammatical speech in which functional elements such as articles, prepositions, and verb inflections are missing. Furthermore, they cannot comprehend subtleties based on grammar. They have trouble differentiating between "the boy pushes the girl" and "the boy is pushed by the girl." Nor can they decide who pushes who, because the decision depends on the grammatical notion of active and passive voices. Nevertheless, they can understand the meanings of sentences. Thus they have no difficulty with "the table is pushed by the girl," because they know from meaning that girls push and tables do not (Caplan 1987).

On the other hand, people with Williams syndrome are mentally retarded except in verbal ability. They speak fluently and amiably, perhaps more so than a lot of people. Laura, for instance, had intact grammatical capacity although her cognitive and pragmatic abilities were highly deficient. She had a large vocabulary that she used to generate grammatical sentences, but she showed little understanding of their meanings (Yamada 1990).

A large degree of dissociation exists between syntax and semantics. In rare cases superior linguistic competence occurs with inferior general intelligence. Because of brain damage diagnosed when he was six weeks old, Christopher had an IQ of 42 to 75 and was unable to get around by himself. Yet he mastered sixteen languages, easily conversing in and translating among them. The double dissociation between linguistic and general cognitive abilities indicates certain autonomy of the language faculty (Smith and Tsimpli 1995).

Christopher also provides evidence that different processes underlie comprehension of natural and artificial languages. Experimenters taught him two new languages: Berber, a natural language spoken in North Africa, and Epun, a simple artificial language that violates natural linguistic principles. Christopher learned Berber easily but was totally helpless with Epun. In contrast, a control group of normal subjects did much better with Epun than Berber. Apparently they treated Epun as an unknown symbolic system and figured out some of its simple rules, a task of which Christopher, hindered by his low general intelligence, was incapable. This case shows clearly that different infrastructural processes underlie natural and artificial languages.

Developmental Evidence for Special Linguistic Processes

Some parents constantly talk to their babies; others leave them alone. Despite the great variety in developmental environments across cultures, the courses by which children acquire their native language are remarkably uniform. At around eight months, babies start to babble, hearing babies with their mouths, deaf babies with their hands. They produce their first words when they are around ten months old and acquire about fifty words during the next eight months. Then a spurt occurs as the rate of word acquisition jumps. Around the same time they begin to join two words into phrases. Linguistic comprehension precedes production. When babies can produce only two-word phrases, they understand the word ordering in longer sentences, for instance who tickles who in "Big Bird is tickling Cookie Monster." Shortly after their second birthday children can tell the difference between "Big Bird is eating Cookie Monster" and "Big Bird is eating with Cookie Monster," which indicates their ability to understand the linguistic device of *with* (Bloom 2000; Boysson-Bardies 1999).

Several linguists proposed a critical window for language acquisition: people who are not exposed to proper linguistic stimuli before a certain age will never learn to speak. This conjecture remains to be tested. The plights of feral children provide inconclusive evidence because these children may be mentally retarded. The case of EM, a congenitally deaf Mexican boy with normal mentality who had no exposure to sign language, is interesting. At age fifteen his hearing was restored. After two years he had acquired a considerable vocabulary, but had great difficulty learning anything beyond the most rudimentary grammar (Green and Vervaeke 1997).

In the proper linguistic environment, congenitally deaf children acquire sign language along a similar course and make similar mistakes as hearing children do. Such mistakes are telling, especially when they occur in unlikely places. Perhaps the easiest words to recognize in ASL are the personal pronouns "I" and "you," pointing to oneself and to the addressee. Children can point very early. Thus one does not expect signing children to have any problem with the pronouns. But no. Around the age of two, when hearing children start to use the pronouns and sometimes mistakenly refer to themselves as "you" and their addressees as "I," deaf children make the same mistakes, pointing to themselves when they mean "you." The mistake indicates that they are acquiring an ability that is specifically linguistic (Poizner 1987).

Each language has its own set of phonemes or meaningful sound contrasts. English, for instance, distinguishes between the sounds of /b/ and /p/, but Kikuyu does not. Six-month-olds in all cultures are sensitive to most sound contrasts, but they soon lose the sensitivity to sounds not differentiated in their native language. Kikuyu adults are unable to distinguish /b/ from /p/ in speech. It is significant that the inability occurs only in linguistic contexts. When the sounds of /b/ and /p/ occur outside of speech, Kikuyu adults can tell the difference. This indicates specifically linguistic processes that leave out the differentiation (Werker 1989).

Do Apes Share Our Language Faculty?

The disparate performances of Christopher and control subjects in learning Berber and Epun reveal the dissociation between the abilities for handling natural and artificial languages. This helps us to assess the controversy over ape language. Some trainers claim that their chimpanzees and gorillas have acquired impressive linguistic skills that will shed light on the origin of human languages. Linguists, however, are not impressed. Is ape language subserved by a primitive language faculty?

Many nonhuman animals have a repertoire of vocalizations that serve specific functions, such as distress calls and mating songs. However, so far no natural vocalization possesses enough systematic correlation to qualify as the simplest language. Under intensive training, some animals can associate labels with groups or aspects of objects. They often appear on television shows and are written about in popular magazines. Dolphins and sea lions have their share of the limelight, but I think the prize goes to Alex, the African gray parrot. Alex has a vocabulary of about eighty words and shows understanding of their meanings. He can produce word sounds to identify, classify, and count more than 100 objects. Facing the same tray containing a dozen of balls and cubes in blue or green, he correctly answers many questions: How many green cubes? Four. How many blue balls? Three. What material blue cube? Wood. What color metal ball? Green. Which bigger? Ball. However, he is unable to string the words in a rulelike manner to form sentences (Beer 1998).

Our cousins the great apes are not to be outdone. They can handle numerals up to five, not only in labeling various quantities but also in summing, thus displaying certain symbolic skills. In the 1970s, Koko the gorilla and Washoe the common chimpanzee endeared television audiences when their trainers claimed that they had learned ASL. Closer studies, however, discredited many claims. What the trainers wishfully interpreted as sentences turned out to be mostly natural gestures, random movements, or arbitrary strings of single signs such as "drink eat me," "me banana you banana me you give." Some enthusiasts turned whistle blowers and most ape language projects folded. The one survivor, however, has something special: a bonobo or pygmy chimpanzee that is allegedly smarter than his common cousin (Ristau 1996).

As an infant, Kanzi the bonobo watched his foster mother being trained in using lexigrams. The mother failed after two years of excruciating lessons, but the baby picked it up and can use lexigrams to request items. His trainers also taught him to comprehend spoken English. When Kanzi was eight years old he took an extensive test that was also administered to a two-and-a-half-year-old girl. The examiners uttered, often repeatedly, a command in English, for example "Knife the sweet potato" or "Make the doggie bite the snake." Then they graded Kanzi and the girl on whether they performed the correct action. Kanzi outperformed the girl slightly. The test does not definitely show that Kanzi's English comprehension was comparable with or superior to the two-year old's. Besides understanding the command, the test performance also depends on familiarity with object manipulation and the game of obeying commands. In this Kanzi may be better trained (Savage-Rumbaugh 1986).

Undoubtedly Kanzi understands many words and certain word orders. That is it, some linguists maintain; catching the key nouns and verbs and their order is sufficient for the chimp's performance. One need not understand, "Would you please get the carrot that is in the microwave" to fetch the carrot; understanding "get, carrot, microwave" suffices.[2] Nonlinguists who watched Kanzi on video, however, are likely to agree that he grasps a simple grammar. Exactly what grammatical rules he has mastered, however, is unclear, because his language production is peculiar.

Kanzi imbibed lexigrams with his mother's milk. He uses lexigrams mostly to request things, and on rare occasions, for other purposes. Like two-year-olds, his utterances are limited to two words; most consist only one. However, his word ordering differs significantly from that of two-year-olds. Children's utterances are fragments of grammatical sentences. Thus those in an English-speaking community say "go garden" and "more cookie," not "garden go" and "cookie more." It is remarkable how rarely they make mistakes in word ordering. The mistakes that they do *not* make are often cited by linguists as the indication of a partially working syntactic module. In contrast, Kanzi's word orderings often buck the rules of his linguistic community. For example, he frequently chains two verbs, which his interlocutors never do. His peculiar word ordering is inventive, according to his trainers; arbitrary, according to linguists. Without further development on Kanzi's part, it is difficult to decide. Significant progress, however, has not occurred ten years later (Savage-Rumbaugh 1986; Rumbaugh and Savage-Rumbaugh 1996).

Apes demonstrate ability to handle simple symbolic systems, not in their natural environments, but after intensive training by humans. Despite the best training, apes cannot increase the mean length of utterances beyond two words, cannot use language to elicit linguistic responses, and cannot describe themselves in response to requests of their interlocutors. The word orderings produced by Kanzi and other apes, however, suggest that they do not share the language faculty of humans. It is more likely that they use their general intelligence to acquire this special skill that is unnatural to them, just as humans use their general intelligence to learn artificial languages (Parker and McKinney 1999).

15   Syntactic Competence and Its Infrastructure

I interpret Chomsky's language organ as the infrastructure that underlies our grammatical ability. The existence of infrastructural processes specialized to syntax, at least in adult speaker-hearers, is supported by developmental and neuropsychological evidence cited above. Besides being a linguistic theory, I interpret UG in two ways, which I hope do not diverge too far from Chomsky's. On the engaged-personal level, UG with a definite set of parameter values is a theory that linguists use to represent explicitly certain tacit knowledge of adult speaker-hearers of a particular language. On a lower organizational level, it is a highly abstract theoretical representation for some general features of the rules that govern the evolution of various syntactic infrastructural processes. About these processes, speaker-hearers do not even have tacit knowledge without learning psycholinguistics and other branches of cognitive science. The two interpretations of UG suggest a direction for tackling the binding problem, whose solution will explain how the syntactic infrastructural processes contribute to conscious language use.

If we have tacit as well as explicit knowledge, it should also be possible for us to learn tacitly in addition to explicitly. Subjects in psychological experiments showed tacit learning of artificial grammars. Connectionists contend that learning plays crucial roles in children acquiring their natural language. The involvement of some learning does not dethrone the hypothesis that much of syntactic infrastructure is innate.

However, it avoids a form of stark genetic determinism featuring the grammar gene and other controlling genes.

The syntactic infrastructure, both in its nascent and matured forms, has enough internal coherence to be studied as a unit. However, ample empirical evidence suggests that it is not as encapsulated as Chomsky and Fodor described. I will explain how I differ from Fodor's modularity of mind when I talk about various mental infrastructures and infrastructural processes.

The Analysis of Mind

All things interact with each other and all our ideas are interconnected. Thus it sounds profound to say that all is one or all our concepts must face empirical evidence as one unit. Holism rightly reminds us about the importance of context for anything. However, as a dogma it spells the death of scientific inquiry, for it is extremely difficult, if at all humanly possible, to consider everything at once. Scientists advance by analysis and proceed step by step. They approximately analyze a complex system or process into more tractable aspects, subsystems, and subprocesses, which they study separately and thoroughly. They may have neglected many inter-actions among the parts in the first-cut analysis; however, as long as they do not mistake analysis for mere decomposition, they will come back to account for the interactions when they have some grip on the parts. The analytic approach and successive approximations are so important in scientific research they are institutionalized in physics in perturbative calculations.

Analysis is also fruitful in the study of mind. People have analyzed mind into aspects and faculties since antiquity. Plato divided the soul into three parts: rational, passionate, and auxiliary. The parts can conflict, but on the whole they hang together under the rule of reason. Aristotle explored the natures of the five senses and posited the "common sense," a part of mind that integrates sight, hearing, touch, smell, and taste into the perception of a unitary object. The five senses are recognized in many cultures. Our general discourse is replete with reference to various modes of experiences: vision, audition, taction, olfaction, gustation; mood and emotion; imagination and memory; conceptualization and anticipation; language comprehension and production; decision and attention; motor control and action.

During the second half of the eighteenth and the first half of the nineteenth centuries, a faculty psychology flourished that distinguished various mental powers such as perception and volition, and tried to associate them with various pronounced parts of the brain. It fell into disrespect until cognitive science began to carve out various mental subsystems for close investigation and Chomsky's postulate of the language organ became well known. Fodor systematized and rationalized the analytic approach in cognitive science by concluding that mind is susceptible to analysis because it is modular, and only in so far as it is modular. He revived the ideas of traditional faculty psychology and described its analysis of mind's functional architecture "horizontal," for its faculties are not domain specific. As an alternative, he offered his own modularity of mind, whose "vertical" architecture defines mental faculties that are domain specific. *Domain* here refers to the subject matter of a faculty. A *domain-specific* faculty deals with only one kind of topic, or in other words, admits only one kind of content. Traditional mental faculties are not domain specific; memory and imagination can have the same topic.

Fodor (1983) analyzed mind into three parts: transducers, which are essentially sense organs; central systems for inference and higher cognition; and input modules that mediate between the two. The central systems are holistic and unsusceptible to scientific analysis. Therefore insofar as cognitive science aims to unravel higher cognition, it is impossible. Fodor called this his first law of the nonexistence of cognitive science. Do not despair, though, for science has yielded much information on the input modules. In line with his computational representational theory of mind, he noted that the language organ is an input-output module that communicates between inner mind and outer world.

My analysis of mind differs from Fodor's in two respects. First, as far as mental faculties are concerned, I keep to the familiar horizontal analysis, which I also call various modes of experiences. Second, I make explicit the sense of "vertical" by positing a distinct organization level. Underlying each mental faculty is a more or less distinguishable infrastructure that is further analyzable into many processes. Infrastructures for perceptual faculties are more distinctive, but thinking and higher mentation too have their underlying mechanisms.

The difference between Fodor and me stems from our basic conceptions of mind. Fodor subscribed to the Cartesian mind closed behind the veil of formality. For the closed mind, domains or subject matters are various kinds of stimuli or mental representations. Therefore vision and audition have different domains. For my mind open to the world, the subject matters are objects in the world. Vision, audition, memory, and other mental faculties often share the same topic, as I remember the same opera that I saw and heard. More important, their convergence on the same object is an essential structure of experiences, Kant's objective unity of consciousness. Therefore domain specificity is not important for me.

Fodor's input modules share properties of both transducers and central systems; they are both reflexive and inferential. My infrastructural processes are strictly reflexive and nonmental. They share many but not all of the characteristics of Fodorian modules: fast; unconscious; unfolding causally and automatically; having shallow output and definite neural substrates; and with characteristic breakdown symptoms of brain injury.

Infrastructural processes differ from input modules in three ways. Because mental faculties are not domain specific, their infrastructural processes do not have to be so, although many finely analyzed processes are sensitive to only one kind of causal factor. Although we cannot deliberately control infrastructural processes, they are not immune to conscious modulations such as a shift in attention. Finally, they are not informationally encapsulated; their operations often interfere with each other, although the interference is normally not great enough to fuse the processes. Interference and intentional modulation do not conflict with their automaticity. This can be illustrated in terms of dynamical theory (see section 11). If an infrastructural process is a causal system represented by a dynamical equation, interference and modulation enter as changes in control parameters.

Partial Encapsulation of the Syntatic Infrastructure

Does the syntactic infrastructure operate largely free from interferences from semantics and other factors? As we listen or read, we encounter words sequentially. Many words have several meanings and function as different parts of speech. Sometimes the first part of a sentence has several possible syntactic continuations. For example, in "the horse raced past the barn fell," we do not know whether "raced" is the main verb or a past participle until we come to "fell." In most cases, ambiguities are transient and are resolved by what follows. When and how efficiently we resolve them are revealing about infrastructural processes underlying language comprehension. They have been intensively probed by psycholinguists with methods such as priming and monitoring eye movement in reading. Conflicting results are still being produced. However, accumulated data suggest something between watertight modularity and unbridled interaction among processes (Mitchell 1994).

Regardless of syntax, we spontaneously access all meanings of a word when we first come across it, but irrelevant meanings fade within 200 milliseconds. Experiments that monitor eye movement when subjects listen to verbal instructions for manipulating objects show that way before the sentence is finished, subjects immediately look at the relevant object once it is unambiguously named. Thus language comprehension is not a resultant process in which the output of the syntax module feeds into the semantics module (Tanenhause, 1995). Nevertheless, despite meanings and context, we have a strong tendency to read a sentence according to its simplest syntactic structure, follow the formal structure down a "garden path" and backtrack when we come to a grammatical impasse. We tend to read "raced" as the verb in "the horse raced past the barn fell" until we come to "fell," stumble, and grumble about the bad writing. Thus syntactic processes play a fairly autonomous role in sentence comprehension but are far from immune to semantic influences.

The midway answer is expected if we remember that analyzing mechanisms underlying mind into various infrastructures is messy and approximate. Therefore much cross-talk exists among various infrastructures, which scientists ignore in their approximate theoretical models. An approximation is reasonable if under most normal situations, the ignored interfering disruption is weak compared with the internal coherence of an infrastructure. Visual, auditory, and syntactic infrastructures satisfy this criterion under many normal conditions so we can treat them as independent modules to a first approximation. Such treatment is far from perfect, and scientists are continuously trying to improve it; however, we must tolerate approximations in scientific research. If we insist on taking on everything at once as holism stipulates, we would fail to make any inroad into complex phenomena.

As usual, approximations have finite regions of validity. We accept an approximation if it is good for most of a system's normal working conditions. No box is absolutely impervious; even black-box modules are susceptible to disturbance under extraordinary conditions. Anyone who has worked in laboratories with delicate electronic instruments and powerful voltage generators knows it. A high-priced signal analyzer designed to work by itself usually functions beautifully, but will fall to pieces if someone next door fires up a power generator. It is unreasonable to claim, based on failure under extreme conditions, that the signal analyzer is not an independent instrument. This point is worth mentioning because many psychological experiments use extreme conditions. Therefore we must be careful to interpret their results in accessing pros and cons for modularity.

UG as a Theory for Rule-Governed Infrastructural Processes
Fodor includes natural language as an input-output module because in his model of mind, inner thoughts are already formed in a language of thought comprising mental representations. Thus natural language is only a vehicle conveying inner thoughts to the outside world. In contrast, I hold a language to be an important cognitive medium without which most of our complicated thoughts are impossible (see section 28). Thus my syntactic infrastructure comprises only internal processes, in agreement with Chomsky's I-language. Its causal and incognizant characteristics also resonate with Chomsky's deliberately nonmental epithets of "organ" and "device."

I distinguished among rule-following, rule-governed, and rule-driven processes in section 8. In some of Chomsky's writings the language organ seems to be a rule-driven system, so that rules and principles of UG are physically encoded in the brain to generate and relate mental representations causally. This makes the language organ a part of the computational mind but pries it apart from natural physical systems. I reject this interpretation. For me, the syntactic infrastructure is not rule driven like stored program computers. It is rule governed and lawful like other natural physical processes. Atoms need not have Schrödinger's equation etched in them to obey the law of quantum mechanics. Why does the syntactic infrastructure have to have the rules of UG physically encoded?

Like all objective theories, the validity and merit of UG compared with competing hypotheses must be decided by usual standards of empirical science, not by philosophical debate. It can turn out to be inadequate or false. As long as it stands, however, it purports to describe and explain, perhaps approximately, the regularities of a certain domain of reality, the infrastructure for the syntactic competence of ideal human speaker-hearers. If vaid, UG is an objective linguistic theory representing a class of natural lawful processes, in the same sense as classical mechanics is an objective physical theory representing a class of motion. It has the same general status as Newton's law, and it is generative in the sense that Newton's law is predictive: UG can generate all the grammatical sentences in any specific language, just as Newton's laws can predict all kinds of classical motions. This sense of UG fits comfortably into natural science, as Chomsky insists.

As typical of empirical scientific theories, UG involves much generalization and idealization. It operates on a highly general level, so that its rules and principles are far too abstract to describe in detail the evolution of infrastructural processes. What they represent is the pattern of the syntactic infrastructure as a whole, the skeleton that structures and constrains various parsing processes. Thus researchers working on the details of sentence parsing use UG only as an organizing framework.

Do We Have Unconscious Knowledge of UG?

Chomsky (1980:231) is unambiguous that the rules and principles of UG "are in large measure unconscious and beyond the reach of potential consciousness. Our perfect knowledge of the language we speak gives us no privileged access to these principles." This accords with my interpretation of UG as a theoretical representation of the syntactic infrastructure of which we are not aware.

However, Chomsky also holds that UG's rules and principles are tacit knowledge of speaker-hearers. He introduces the technical term "to cognize" meaning "to know tacitly." Consider the sentences: "The candidates wanted each other to win" and "The candidates wanted me to vote for each other." He (1980:69f) wrote: "We know that the former means that each wanted the other to win, and that the latter is not well-formed, with the meaning that each wanted me to vote for the other. We therefore cognize these facts. Furthermore, we cognize the system of mentally-represented rules from which these facts follow. That is, we cognize the grammar that constitutes the current state of our language faculty and the rules of this system as well as the principles that govern their operation. Finally, we also cognize the innate schematism, along with its rules, principles and conditions." Cognizing seems not to go well with profound unawareness. The notion of unconscious knowledge generates much protest, which Chomsky has exerted much effort attempting to answer.

I think few people would object to cognizing the difference between the two sentences about the candidates. But "furthermore" cognizing is another matter. I cannot accept cognizing "mentally-represented rules" that I cannot be aware of; I doubt such rules exist. I think there is a sense in which we tacitly know some grammatical principles. However, it makes sense only if we interpret UG on the level of the conscious speaker-hearer, not on the level of unconscious mentally-represented rules. From our expressed linguistic competence, we can say we have grasped some abstract concepts that UG tries to represent explicitly.

Concepts and Concept Possession

To explain my sense of tacit knowledge, let me first explain the meanings of *concept* and *grasping a concept*; it will be useful in many places as we go along. "Concept" is one of the most widely used terms in the discourse on mind. Unfortunately, its meanings vary just as widely. The many implicit or explicit theories of concepts fall roughly into two big classes that respectively regard concepts as *entities* and as *abilities* (Weitz 1988).

Entity theories, whose roots reach back at least to Locke, found a champion in Fodor (1998a). They state that concepts are mental entities that are a form of mental representations. Many are atomic entities without internal structure, that are either innate or caused by sensual input. Each atomic entity has its own meaning independent of others. They make up larger entities that are complex concepts. Various principles govern the make up of complex concepts. For some, a concept consists a prototype; for others, a set of necessary and sufficient conditions. In any case, concepts are entities, simple or complex. They make up propositions, which are larger entities that appear in the belief or desire box in one's head as the contents of believing or desiring. A person possesses a concept by standing in a relation with an entity in his head. Suppose I have the concept of cause, so that every time I believe that one event causes another, an entity <cause> appears in my head, to which I stand in the relation of believing. Fodor maintained that an entity theory of concepts is required by the computational theory of mind. As entities, concepts are mental representations that the computational mind manipulates. Chomsky (1980) seems to subscribe to such a theory when he says we can cognize mentally-represented rules; the rules are entities that we cognize because they are there sitting in the head.

Those rejecting mental representations have an alternative view that asks not *what a concept is* but *what it is for someone to master a concept*. This view can be traced to Berkeley, Hume, and Kant, if not farther back, and was expounded by Christopher Peacocke (1992). Here concepts are mental abilities to analyze, classify, generalize, integrate, infer, and judge. To say a person's mental state has certain conceptual structures is to say the person has certain mental capabilities. Thus to have the concept of cause is not to have an entity <cause> that sits between the entities <match> and <fire>. It is to have the ability to recognize the consistent relationship between striking a match and lighting a fire; more generally, and to discern certain regularities in the courses of events, to hold certain coherent beliefs about them, and to act appropriately in anticipation. For linguistic animals, it also means the ability to use the word "cause" and its cognates correctly; to understand sentences such as "he strikes a match to see what is hidden in the dark," which, although it does not contain the word "cause," nevertheless relates the causal relations among match, fire, light, and sight.

We have many abilities. What makes an ability *conceptual?* Consciousness is insufficient; we walk consciously, but the ability to walk involves no concept. To count as conceptual, an ability must be directly involved in some judgment or reasoning. Because a mental ability usually involves many concepts and a concept usually functions in many abilities, dispositional theories of concepts are analytical. Conceptual analysis takes apart various abilities to delineate individual concepts approximately. Linguistically, it clarifies the meanings and usages of words in various contexts. Analysis starts from patterns of abilities and regards individual concepts as abstractions of them. Abstractions, however, are not absolute. They leave individual concepts in the contexts of conceptual schemes that span classes of abilities or contents; only as a part of a conceptual scheme is a concept functional. Concepts obtained through analysis are seldom simple. For example, cause is a complex concept with both external connections and internal structures. The top-down approach of conceptual analysis contrasts with Fodor's bottom-up entity theory, which puts together atomic concepts given through birth or sensation to construct complex thoughts.

Concepts come in various degrees of generality. Cause is a general concept. We seldom use the word "cause" explicitly, even in describing causal chains of events; we use more substantive causal words such as collision or injury. The concept of physical object which figures heavily in developmental and cognitive psychology, is another general concept. We talk about apples and oranges, taking for granted that they are objects, but seldom explicitly think about objects in general. General concepts are most detrimental to entity theories, as they function mostly tacitly and should not appear as entities in the head. They are manifested in mental abilities.

UG as a Theory for Linguistic Ability

In comprehending and producing grammatical expressions we exercise a mental ability that involves general grammatical concepts. We tacitly know these concepts, just as we tacitly know the concepts of object and cause. Philosophers have yet to come up with clear definitions of object and cause, but everyone intuitively knows what they mean. Similarly, when English speakers know something is wrong with "The candidates wanted me to vote for each other" but cannot say explicitly what, they manifest a tacit grasp of some grammatical concepts.

Universal grammar tries to give an explicit theoretical representation for the tacit grammatical knowledge of speaker-hearers. Here we should carefully heed the distinction that Chomsky (1980:220) makes between "linguist's grammar" and "the grammar in the mind of the ideal speaker-hearer." The former, UG, is a scientific theory about the latter. In my interpretation, UG is a theory about a human linguistic ability. It is objective in the sense that its rules and principles purport to capture and represent salient patterns and regularities in the mental states of people with linguistic competence. However, it involves much abstraction and approximation. Therefore we cannot say that its principles are computation rules implemented in the minds of the speaker-hearers to drive their language usage.

I interpret UG on two organizational levels. On the engaged-personal level it is a moderately substantive theory about certain human syntactic abilities. On the infrastructural level it is a very abstract theory for the skeletal structures of the causal processes that underlie our syntactic abilities. The two interpretations reveal a connection between the levels. The parameters of UG are like viscosity, compressibility, and other macroscopic coefficients in fluid equations. They pinpoint features on the higher organization level that call for interlevel explanations. That is why UG can serve as the theoretical framework for psycholinguists who work to unravel infrastructural processes underlying language acquisition and sentence processing (Radford 1990).

Innateness and Implicit Learning

The alleged impossibility of children to learn a language figures heavily in Chomsky's theory of an innate language faculty. *Learning* here usually refers to conscious processes such as induction, generalization, hypothesis formation, and testing. However, when one talks about unconscious and implicit knowledge, it would be unfair to admit only conscious and explicit learning. For decades psychologists have been studying implicit learning. Their experiments on the implicit learning of artificial language are especially pertinent here.

An artificial language consists a set of alphabets and a set of rules that strings the alphabets into grammatical sequences. Psychologists asked subjects to memorize many sequences of alphabets that appeared to be random. Afterward, they revealed that the sequences are actually grammatical in an artificial language but did not divulge the grammatical rules. Then they showed subjects other sequences, half of which were grammatical, half not, and forced the subjects to classify the sequences according to whether or not they were grammatical. Subjects performed significantly above chance level in the task, although they could not explain how they decided or figured out the grammatical rules. Many psychologists believe that the subjects implicitly learned the grammar of the artificial language and possessed implicit knowledge of it (Berry 1997).

If experimental subjects can learn artificial languages implicitly in the laboratory, why can't children learn natural languages implicitly in real life? Of course, natural languages are far more complex and natural samplers are far more heterogeneous. But still the possibility exists. With the rise of connectionism in the 1980s, this possibility became the battery against innatism. Connectionists propose that infants can learn by extracting and generalizing statistically salient factors in the stimuli. Saffran et al. (1996) found that eight-month-olds exposed to a string of syllables for two minutes could distinguish three-syllable sequences that appeared as units in the string. Thus infants recognize word boundaries in speech by statistical learning. Bates and Elman (1996) cited the experiment as a death blow to Chomsky's innatism and lauded "learning rediscovered." Chomskyans countered that the connectionists had overblown the significance of the experiment and misrepresented their own position. Learning words is different from learning grammar; words have to be memorized, grammar is rule structured. Chomskyans never claimed that vocabulary and hence word boundaries are innate; that would be absurd. Note the abstractness of what they now claim to be innate: only the principles of UG with indefinite values for their parameters. To set values of parameters, environmental input is indispensable; so are some processes that respond to input. Call these processes implicit learning if you will, but they do not harm Chomskyan theory.

Connectionist networks "learn" by extracting the statistical central tendency of samplers. Statistics give different frequencies for the occurrence of various values of a property. When a property and its values are well identified, as it is in most experimental conditions, to extract the most frequent values is not too difficult. Real-life situations, however, are usually not as simple as the controlled environment of laboratories. Facing a complex situation with a large number of entangling factors, one must first pick out the important properties and their values, and this is far more difficult. Developmental environments are most complex. Innate structures alleviate some difficulties by biasing infants toward certain properties, for instance the rigid motion of physical objects, as we will see in the next section. Universal grammar postulates that among the clutter of acoustic stimuli, infants have special innate sensitivity toward values of linguistic parameters. It is an empirical hypothesis that can be tested experimentally.

As discussed in section 4, connectionist networks offer a kind of cognitive modeling distinct from symbol-rule systems and can be applied to all areas of cognitive science, linguistics included. David Rumelhart and James McClelland (1986) trained a connectionist network to construct the past tense of English verbs. Because the network was not driven by encoded rules, connectionists declared the obsolescence of syntactic rules, not to mention innate rules. Linguists fired back. Analyzing the network of Rumelhart and McClelland, Steven Pinker and Alan Prince (1988) found many syntactic notions built into it. The built-in linguistic structures represent innate linguistic bias. Connectionists conjecture that a single process suffices for both regular verbs such as walk-walked and irregular verbs such as eat-ate or bring-brought. Linguists posit two distinct processes: regular verbs are served by the syntactic infrastructure with its generative rules, whereas irregular verbs are memorized and depend on a different infrastructural process. This is an empirical issue that experimental data can resolve. Various neuroscientific and psychological priming experiments show that regular and irregular verbs involve different processes and different brain regions. Some people with neurological disorders can handle one type of verb but not the other (Pinker, 1997).

Most connectionists deny that they are returning to the blank-slate view of mind. They realize that they will go nowhere if they posit general intelligence as a huge network consisting millions of nodes with arbitrary initial connections. It is doubtful if such a network can be trained to do anything. Connectionist networks are specific. Their architectures, forms of input and output, methods of training, and initial settings incorporate many assumptions about their tasks that their designers have digested. When networks are used as theoretical representations of cognitive or infrastructural processes, these built-in assumptions are aptly interpreted as innate elements that constitute the platform for subsequent learning. Therefore it is important to analyze the assumptions and spell out their meanings. Here linguistic theories can help.

Connectionism severely challenges the notion that we are rule-driven systems that learn by adding rules to programs. It loses its philosophical edge once we deny that our mental infrastructure contains physically encoded rules in the brain. Suppose we treat UG as a theory of rules that govern syntactic infrastructural processes but do not drive them. Then the connectionist challenge amounts to offering alternative theoretical models. The two can complement each other productively. Universal grammar is so general it outlines only the skeleton of the syntactic infrastructure, which must be filled out by more substantive descriptions. For instance, it demands only certain parameter values be set but does not indicate how they are set. Connectionism, being more substantive and detailed, offers models for the infrastructural processes that set values. Explanatory imperialism wastes intellectual energy. Mind, even the narrow mental ability to speak grammatically, is too complicated for a single theoretical method.

5

Concepts in Perception: Making Things Intelligible

16 Two-Way Traffic in the Visual Infrastructure

Sensual perceptions seem to be the most primitive of mental activities. Our senses of vision, audition, taction, olfaction, gustation, proprioception (the sense of one's own limbs), and interioception (the sense of one's own viscera) constantly bind us to the world and our own bodies. What are the general structures of the most immediate human sensual perceptions? What are the general characteristics of your vision when you lazily open your eyes in the morning; drive with your thoughts engaged elsewhere; lounge at the beach watching the waves? If you put your attention to it, you can describe what you see, or you can try to figure out what that strange thing is. That description and categorization are complications that we will leave to later chapters. Here we focus on the most primitive aspects of human perception. From the time you open your eyes in the morning to the time you fall asleep, you see continuously. However, often when you go about your daily business, your attention is focused on something other than what meets your eyes. You are not thinking about it and later you will fail to recall what you saw. Nevertheless, at the moment you are not blind; you do have a visual experience that is mostly inarticulate. This is the immediate visual perception whose structures I try to analyze in this chapter.

Theories of perception distinguish theories of mind. Those who allow minimal mental structures regard perception as passive and receptive. Those who endow mind with rich structures accord active and constructive roles to perception. Active perception is much more complicated than passive reception. Consequently it requires the support of a sophisticated perceptual infrastructure. The visual infrastructures of humans and other mammals are most elaborate. Of importance, signals in the visual infrastructure do not flow one way from the eyes up, as one expects if vision is purely receptive. They flow both ways. Many experiments confirm the involvement of both stimulus-driven and concept-driven processes in vision. They support the active view of perception. This section briefly presents the characteristics of our visual infrastructure, which will help us to assess various theories of perception in the next section.

Sensual perception is our most immediate link to the world. Intuitively, it should be most illustrative of how our mind opens to the world and makes sense of it. This is not the case for two of the most influential theories of perception, which I call *closed mind* and *ecological perception*. By contrasting them to active perception of the *open mind*, we gain a first insight into the conceptual complexity of our mind-open-to-the-world. Even the most primitive sensual perception of the open mind involves general concepts of physical objects that are independent of being perceived. We survey the arguments and empirical evidence for the indispensability of these general concepts, the details of which are analyzed in chapter 8.

Do We Have to Learn How to See?

The night closed in, but SB did not turn on the light. Depression weighed on him. He was not always like that. Twenty months ago he was active, happy, and healthy, although he had been blind since infancy. Then, at the age of 52, a corneal graft gave him sight. The first few months after the operation were full of excitement; color struck him especially. He recognized at first sight many objects familiar to him from touch, and learned many more things previously out of touch. Six months later, however, disappointment set in. Vision was more difficult and less rewarding than he expected. Crossing a street, which he did confidently when blind, became a terrifying nightmare when he saw traffic bearing down on him. To a significant extent he continued to lead the life of the blind. His workmates, who previously admired his physically challenged performance, came to despise his "unchallenged" performance. His neighbors considered him odd. Gradually, he withdrew from active life and sat for long hours in the dark. He sank into a deep depression and fell ill, and two years after his eyes were opened, died (Gregory 1998).

SB's case is not singular. Virgil's originally thriving life also came to a tragic end a few years after surgery ended forty-five years of blindness (Sacks 1995). In all documented cases in over 300 years, newly sighted adults underwent some motivational crisis. Some, like SB and Virgil, did not pull through. Richard Gregory (1998), the neuropsychologist who studied and reported the progress of SB, was not alone in expatiating on the danger of adults' recovery from infant blindness.

The tragedies of SB and Virgil were partly caused by social pressure. We do not expect people paralyzed for years to play football once they walk away from a wheelchair, but we expect people blind for decades to behave normally once they face the world with cured eyes. This unreasonable expectation, based on the erroneous assumption that seeing is nothing but the eyes' detection of optical signals, can exert crushing pressure. Painful rehabilitation of newly sighted adults challenges the assumption: There is far more to visual experiences than passive registration of what is given in the stimuli or optic flow.

"Do we have to learn how to see?" Gregory asked. This is a tricky question to answer, even if "learn" means no more than practice and development under appropriate stimulation. Experiments with cats and other animals show that certain general aspects of the neutral machinery underlying vision can develop without visual experience. Human infants are capable of making certain visual discriminations shortly after birth. They are sensitive to the difference between faces and nonfaces, for example, and prefer looking at faces. Experiences, however, are essential for many other aspects, which deteriorate significantly under prolonged visual deprivation. This explains why rehabilitation of newly sighted adults is so difficult (Crair et al. 1998).

Newly sighted adults can readily see and differentiate various features. They see an aspect of an object, a part of a scene, and pick out individual colors, movements, or features. Probably it was by noticing peculiar features that SB identified elephants and Virgil kangaroos on their first visits to the zoo. To piece the features and parts together and see an integral object, however, is another story. Reporting on Virgil's examination of a cat, neuropsychologist Oliver Sacks (1995:123) remarked: "He would see a paw, the nose, the tail, an ear, but could not see all of them together, see the cat as a whole." It took Virgil a full month to piece leaves and trunk together to see a whole tree. Both SB and Virgil learned English letters by touch, and Virgil could fluently read inscriptions on monuments and tombstones. Both recognized letters immediately, but at first neither could string the letters together to see words. SB never managed to read by sight more than a few simple words. HS experienced similar difficulty.

He was literate by touch, but only after weeks of exhausting attempts did he succeed to make out whole words by sight.

Seeing various features is far from seeing objects as wholes, and normally we see objects as wholes. This lesson gained from the plight of SB, Virgil, and other newly sighted adults is a significant one that theoreticians of human vision cannot neglect. But why is seeing whole objects so difficult? To answer this we have to examine the infrastructure of vision.

The Eyes and Saccades

When we look at a complicated scene we may have the impression that we are taking in all its details, but we are not. We do see a seamless integral panorama, rich in colors and textures, but the details are much less than what we unreflectingly assume. The problem starts with the eye. The eye is not a simple camera. It is more like the combination of two cameras, one with high resolution but a narrow angle of view, the other low resolution but a wide angle of view. The fovea is the only area in our retina that supports high-acuity color vision. It has a tiny visual field that is about the size of a thumbnail at arm's length. Sensitivity to details outside the fovea's visual field drops drastically, and the extrafoveal area of the retina supports crude panoramic vision.

Stare fixedly in front and you will find that scenes to the far right and far left are blurred although not gappy. You would see a face to the right, for instance, but unable to tell whose it is. More specifically, fixate your eyes on the letter "s" in "representation" and try to see if you can recognize the preceding and succeeding words. Experiments under carefully controlled viewing conditions find that most subjects have a fixation window of about twenty letters. They readily recognize letters within the window but do not notice that all the letters outside the window of fixation are replaced by xxxx, as illustrated in figure 5.1. However, they notice the change when all outside letters disappear because the disappearance changes the gross luminance. Similarly, we miss most peripheral details but easily detect gross changes and motions in the periphery. Detection of gross peripheral features is important in informing us where to redirect our gaze.

To compensate for narrowness of the foveal view, our eyes flicker rapidly several times a second to aim the fovea at different spots of a scene or a book. Each flicker, called a *saccade*, takes about 200 milliseconds to prepare and from 10 to 80 milliseconds to execute. An average person's

Basic sentence: `Do you notice anything strange in this display?`

Fixation *n*:   `xx xxx notice anything straxxx xx xxxx xxxxxxxx`
Fixation *n*+1:   `xx xxx xxxxxe anything strange ix xxxx xxxxxxxx`
Fixation *n*+2:   `xx xxx xxxxxx xxxxxxxx strange in this xxxxxxxx`

Fixation *n*:   `DO yoU NoTice aNYthInG STrAnGE IN thIS dISpLaY?`
Fixation *n*+1:   `do YOu notICE AnyTHiNg stRaNge in THis DisPlAy?`
Fixation *n*+2:   `DO yoU NoTice aNYthInG STrAnGE IN thIS dISpLaY?`

Figure 5.1
In eye-tracking visual experiments, the subject's head is held at a fixed position in front of a screen that displays certain images. As the subject views the images, an eye tracker determines the fixation point of his eyes and monitors his eye movements. The eye tracker feeds the information to a computer, which changes the display when the eyes execute a saccade. Thus the screen displays different images for different eye fixations. Do subjects notice the difference? In both examples shown here, they do not. In the first example, the dot marks the point of eye fixation measured by the eye tracker. By varying the number of letters that can be replaced by *x* without the subject noticing, the experiment measures the width of the fixation window. The window is asymmetric around the point of fixation because the reader's attention is biased to the right.

eyes make more than 100,000 saccades a day. Between saccades the eyes fixate on a spot for 200 to 300 milliseconds to take in the details within the fovea's visual field (Irwin 1993).

During a saccade, the retinal stimulus changes rapidly, but we do not see anything blurry as we see real motion. The blurred and dim image during the saccade is masked by the clear and bright image of fixation that immediately succeeds it. Saccadic suppression, like blinks, breaks up the perceptual process into temporally isolated fixations, each of which lasts a few hundred milliseconds. When we survey a broad scene, we see the whole scene during each fixation, but miss details everywhere except at the spot where the fovea aims. In the next fixation, we again see the whole scene but with a different detailed spot. Thus as far as our eyes are concerned, the optical input resembles that from a dim stage illuminated by a narrow beam of spotlight that dances around, staying briefly at this place and that, leaving the rest of the stage visible but shadowy.

The first stage of our visual infrastructure shows two interesting complications. First, vision involves not only optical input but also motor control. A narrow-view camera must pan to survey a scene. The eyes do not flicker randomly. Right before a saccade, attention shifts to the intended destination of the next fixation. In reading, for example, when your eyes fixate on one word, your attention has already shifted to the next word. That is why the fixation window of reading is asymmetrical around the fixation point. Readers see about four letters to the left of the fixation point and fifteen letters to the right, because they are incessantly preparing for their eyes to saccade to the right (Henderson 1996). To execute a saccade and land the gaze on the right spot is no simple task, as we see in the difficulty of newly sighted adults. Sacks (1995:123) described Virgil's first visual encounter with a text: "His eyes seemed to fix on particular letters and to be incapable of the easy movement, the scanning, that is needed to read."

Our eyes' orientation and movement determine the optical input to our visual experience. To ascertain the spatial layout of objects, orientation of gaze is as important as the input in that orientation. Therefore information on the motor control of the eyes must be properly integrated with the optical signal the eyes gather. Such integration resolves the possible conflict between two very different kinds of signals. Experiments show that attentional preparation for a saccade consistently induces errors in judgment about the distance between objects. Such errors must somehow be corrected by other processes for accurate vision (Miller and Bockisch 1997).

Constrained by narrow foveal field and rapid saccades, optical signals we take in are disjointed bits and pieces, fleetingly and erratically succeeding one other. If these are all, talks about physical objects are fantastic. But then we would be functionally blind. Fortunately, there is much more to the visual infrastructure than eyes and saccades. Other infrastructural processes are responsible for piecing the many narrows views from brief fixations into our panoramic visual experiences of a stable physical world.

The Visual Cortex

The human eye has roughly 100 million photoreceptors called rods and cones. Some of them are so sensitive they respond to a single photon. Excitatory signals of photoreceptors are analyzed and integrated by three cellular and two synaptic layers in the retina. In the innermost layer are ganglion cells. Each ganglion cell has its own receptive field covering many photoreceptors and its peculiar firing pattern according to their relative excitations. Some ganglion cells are sensitive to the contrast between central and peripheral photoreceptors, others to the direction of successive firings of photoreceptors in their receptive fields. Thus the analysis of optical stimuli starts in the retina (Van Essen and Deyoe 1995; Webster and Ungerleider 1998; Rao et al. 1997).

The retinal processes integrate signals from photoreceptors, so that about a million optic nerves emerge from ganglion cells. Optic nerves lead to various parts of the brain. A small group of them rendezvous with input from other perceptual senses in the superior colliculus, which also plays a major role in controlling eye saccade and fixation. About 90 percent of the optic nerves connect the retina to the lateral geniculate nuclei in the thalamus, which relay their signals to the cerebral cortex. Optic nerves multiply in the cortex, which contains over a billion cells devoted to vision. Almost all output from the thalamus lands in the primary visual cortex (area V1), a large patch at the back of the brain, where the signals are processed by neurons sensitive to such general features as orientation or the presence of edges.

Figure A.2 illustrates the brain areas involved in vision and figure 3.3 depicts a simplified schematic of the visual infrastructure. From the primary visual area, signals proceed toward the front of the brain through more than thirty extrastriate visual areas with specialized functions. These areas fall into two major parallel pathways with limited cross-talk. The *where* pathway includes areas in the parietal lobe in the upper part of the brain. The *what* pathway includes many areas in the temporal lobe in the underside of the brain. Areas in the *where* pathway, such as MT, respond selectively to spatial factors such as movement, speed, direction and vector of motion, and spatial relations among objects. They also contribute significantly to visuomotor coordination such as tracking eye movement. Areas in the *what* pathway, such as V4, respond selectively to features and forms of objects such as color, contrast, orientation, and geometric configurations. Humans even have areas specialized to faces and word forms. Extrastriate visual areas in the where and what pathways project directly and individually to the prefrontal lobe, where large-scale integration of signals from various visual areas occurs. Most visual areas also have direct connections to areas for motor control.

In conventional terminologies, areas in a pathway fall into a hierarchy of earlier and later. By virtue of its proximity to the input from the eyes, V1 is the earliest stage in the cerebral visual process. It is an upstream area that projects its output forward. An extrastraite area projects both forward and backward, sending output to both upstream and downstream areas. Reciprocally, it receives input from both directions. Backward projections ensure that our visual experiences are driven not only by optical stimuli but also by such high-level functions as attention and concept.

Neurons in early visual areas have relatively small receptive fields, which means that they respond only to a small area in the field of view. They are sensitive to relatively simple features such as color and orientation. Neurons in V1 and some other early areas are arranged retinotopically; that is, to preserve the spatial patterns on the retina. Experimenters injected a cat with a radioactive substance that concentrated on excited neurons, made the cat stare at a picture of wheel and spokes, then killed it and measured the distribution of radioactive trace in area V1. Behold, they found the wheel-and-spokes pattern, a little distorted but clearly recognizable, left by the excited neurons in the cat's primary visual area (Kosslyn 1994). Patterns in the primary visual area are perhaps the best candidates for mental representations inside the skull. Nevertheless, the candidacy fails, because we do not and cannot see the patterns as we see mental representations; if we can, scientists need not sacrifice an animal to find out.

Neurons in later visual areas have increasingly larger receptive fields. These larger sizes have two consequences. They necessarily overlap, making a retinotopic arrangement of neurons impossible. Furthermore, because complex features usually occupy extended areas, neurons with increasing receptive field size can respond to features of increasing complexity. Thus the later visual areas are selectively sensitive to such complex features as faces, word forms, and physical objects.

Most data on the visual infrastructure are obtained from experiments on cats and monkeys, whose visual systems are similar but not identical to that of humans. The schematic of the visual infrastructure as comprising thirty odd areas organized into two main streams is an approximation and a rather crude one. To grapple with a complex system, scientists must approximate, simplify, and differentiate manageable parts. Brain areas are tractable parts on a crude level. Scientists are far from fathoming the mechanisms of individual areas. To say an area "specializes" in a function does not mean that it engages in that function exclusively; chances are it has many other functions that are minor relative to the special one. Nor does it imply that the area alone is sufficient for the function; chances are it depends on contributions of many other areas. Therefore the visual infrastructure is not as clearly modular as the schematic has one believe. For example, the what pathway has some ability to track particular objects. The where pathway contains areas that are also selectively sensitive to geometric shapes. Evidence shows intimate coupling between color sensitivity in the form and motion sensitivity in the latter (Sereno and Maunsell 1998). The functional modularity of the infrastructure is a useful approximation, but it demands constant scrutiny and amendment.

In sum, each visual area undergoes several processes with various functions. The visual infrastructure is a complicated network of many coupled processes, some run in parallel, others in sequence. Numerous processes actively abstract, encode, retain, and combine features in optical stimuli to construct the contents of our visual experiences. They are like processes underlying the operation of a car: fuel injection, ignition, combustion, coolant circulation, transmission, and exhaust emission, none of which is like translational motion, but together they make the car run. Similarly, visual processes are infraconscious and automatic. None alone understands anything, but they coalesce in some complicated ways into our visual experiences of an intelligible and coherently dynamic world. The malfunction of any infrastructural process impairs visual experience, just as the malfunction of any automotive part hurts a car's performance.

Some infrastructural processes, notably those involved in the initial analysis of input signals, are characterized in neural terms, for instance excitation of orientation-sensitive or motion-sensitive neurons. Most other processes responsible for synthesizing the initial analysis into coherent contents involve mutually affecting excitations of many neurons. These processes are characterized in cognitive terms such as shape differentiation or face recognition. Neuroscientists talk about the processes' neural *correlates* and not their neural *mechanisms*. They can tell which brain areas activate when a person consciously performs a particular visual task. They can link injury in a particular area to a specific perceptual pathology. In either case, they identify an area by its function in a conscious task or its malfunction. However, rarely have they figured out the neural mechanisms that produce the function.

How do the many visual infrastructural processes combine into visual perception of objects and scenes? How do they combine with infrastructures of other senses to produce a unitary experience of the world? Again we run into the binding problem that befuddles cognitive science. Whatever the solution to the problem turns out to be, much evidence suggests that integrative processes are complicated and not anything like simple aggregation or image superposition. Emergent visual experiences are on a different level of organization as infrastructural processes. Visual experiences have a longer characteristic time, or equivalently, they proceed with rates slower than infraconscious processes. They are also more abstract and coarser grained, contain fewer details but more associations with other topics, associations that underlie object recognition. Much conceptual confusion results when people try to force conscious perception and infraconscious processes into a single level of description.

Visualization

Vision is the quintessential sensual perception whereby we receive input from the environment. Many perceptual theories tacitly assume that neural excitations carrying input information flow mostly forward from the retina to the brain's higher cognitive areas. The passive view of perception further requires the flow to be *exclusively* one way, so that sense data or surface stimuli can be received as *given*. Passive viewers are in for a surprise. Cognitive neuroscience finds that the visual infrastructure is like a highway system with many lanes for parallel processes and, what is striking, the traffic goes two ways and both ways are equally busy. In almost all cases, forward projections from early to late areas are reciprocated by equally dense backward projections from late to early areas. Various areas project forward to the frontal lobe responsible for higher cognitive functions and receive reciprocal backward projections. In this system, almost all processes involve forward and backward projections.

Because the visual infrastructure supports traffic both ways, it need not be idled by lack of optical stimuli. Thus it makes possible hallucination and visualization. James Thurber is totally blind but has vivid and detailed visual hallucinations that have similar quality as normal seeing. Brain imaging experiments with similar patients found that hallucinations of colors, faces, textures, and objects excite brain areas responsible for perception of corresponding features. Hallucination is usually not under voluntary control, but like dreams, its contents are mostly coherent enough to be described conceptually. The fact that it is supported by the visual infrastructure highlights the backward traffic (Ramachandran and Blakeslee 1998; Ffytche et al. 1998).

For people who do not hallucinate, visualization is the best manifestation of backward projections. However, systematic studies of visualization are hampered by great variety in people's reports. Visualization is a subclass of imagination. In imagination, we voluntarily think about possible scenes and events in whatever format, propositional or depictive. Suppose you saw some books on the center of a long shelf and recall the scene with your eyes closed. Your recollection is *propositional* if it is in the form of a sentence such as "two books are on the center of the shelf." It is *depictive* if it is in a pictorial form where the spatial layout of the books and the shelf figures directly. *Visualization* is imagination in the depictive format without optical stimuli. It is often accompanied by some quality of visual experience, but the visual qualities vary over an enormous range in different people, from nil to as vivid as actual seeing. It is nil for me. I can think depictively, but it has no visual quality. I know what it is like to visualize or to have mental imageries, because I experience it in dreams and half dreams. However, I cannot voluntarily conjure them up. If I close my eyes when awake, I experience a blank no matter how hard I try to picture a triangle. Asking around leads me to the same result as Francis Galton, who in 1883 sent out questionnaires about people's mental imageries and was surprised by the great diversity in responses.

The varying quality of visualization may play a role in the debate on mental imagery (Kosslyn 1994). Cognitive psychologists have performed many experiments to probe how people imagine. In some experiments, subjects decided whether an object they saw previously was identical to a target object, which may be the object they saw rotated through a certain angle. Subjects had to imagine the object they saw and rotate it mentally. The time they took to reach a decision increased proportionally with the angle through which the object must be rotated, just as it takes longer to rotate an object physically through a larger angle. In other experiments, subjects saw a complicated spatial configuration such as various landmarks on an island. They then answered questions about the landmarks from memory while focusing their attention on a particular landmark, say a dock. They took longer to make decisions about the landmarks far away from the dock than on those near by, as if they were spatially scanning the scene starting from the dock.

Based on these and other experimental results, Stephen Kosslyn and other cognitive scientists posited that people's imagination is at least partly depictive. They met with staunch opposition. Zenon Pylyshyn and other computational theorists of mind denied the possibility of depictive contents altogether, stating that experimental results can be explained by purely propositional contents. Instead of the spatial layout of the island, subjects retained a list of propositions about its landmarks, and it takes longer to search through the list when objects are farther apart.

Undaunted, proponents of depictive contents did more experiments, carefully avoiding methodological pitfalls and refuting computationalist arguments. They realized that psychological experiments alone are unlikely to resolve the issue, but evidence from other levels of organization can be brought to bear. Because structures of contents are constrained by the operations of the brain, they investigated brain activities during imagination.

Brain imaging experiments in blindfolded subjects showed that imagination activates the primary visual area V1. Furthermore, imagining a larger object activates a larger area of V1. As discussed earlier, V1 "depicts" the retinal stimulus in the sense that most of its neurons are so organized that their spatial excitation pattern roughly preserves the retina's excitation pattern. Thus the correlation between the size of the imagined object and the area of activated V1 indicates that imagination is at least partly depictive (Kosslyn et al. 1995). I wonder how my primary visual area behaves when I imagine but fail to visualize a triangle. Nevertheless, I am convinced by Kosslyn's arguments for the possibility of depictive imagination.

It is hard to imagine that painters and sculptors think only in the propositional and not the depictive form. Some historians of science found "visual thinking" in physicists and mathematicians (Miller 1984). On a smaller scale, the depictive format can be a valuable tool for higher cognitive functions. With the invention of writing and other notations, our abstract thinking acquired a certain visual embodiment. Place-value notation, in which the two 6s in 64,365 have different meanings because of their respective positions, is one of the greatest breakthroughs in human thinking. A mathematical equation has a certain spatial layout. Good notations facilitate thinking, and I would not be surprised if a research project finds spatial congruity to be a measure of notational goodness. Feynman diagrams, which are invaluable for theoretical physics, derive much of their power from their visual quality. It would be most interesting to know if the primary visual area activates when subjects do long multiplication or sum Feynman diagrams in their heads.

Ironically, the spread of digital computers does not help computationalism. Computer output can take both propositional and depictive forms, but whenever possible, people prefer graphics to lengthy printout, because they find the depictive information easier to grasp. It is not merely marketing that makes Microsoft Windows so successful; graphic user interface does make personal computers friendly to a wide range of people.

The physical world, including our bodies, is spatial. Spatial layout is so important in our daily coping it pervades in all our thinking. Our visual infrastructure engages about half of our cerebral cortex. To idle it in abstract thinking would be a great waste of resource. Such waste is a bane for the pure computational mind that snubs the advantage of the body.

Looking for Things

With our eyes open, visualization pales in a flood of stimulation. Instead of being drowned, however, it can facilitate vision. Psychological experiments established that our visual acuity for an object is enhanced if the object is surrounded by certain other stimuli called masking stimuli. Visual acuity is similarly enhanced when the masking stimuli are imaginary; that is, when they are absent but the subjects imagine them to be there. Visualization-facilitated and stimulus-facilitated enhancements have the same characteristics that suggest the activity of the primary visual area. Thus vision is not a one-way flow of information; the flow is influenced by the backward projections of visualization. Enhancement of visual acuity by imagination can help to explain the functioning of attention (Ishai and Sagi 1997).

We search for someone in a crowd or scrutinize a merchandise to find flaws. Our daily life is goal oriented. Therefore we more often *look for* something actively than *look at* it passively. We know from practice that we usually spot a particular item in a complex scene more quickly if we look for it. The difference between passive viewing and active discrimination was confirmed by psychological and neuroscientific experiments. Presented with the same optical stimulus, our visual infrastructure is more excited during active looking for than during passive looking at. The difference is most pronounced in the primary visual area, showing that stimulation does not determine everything even in the entrance hall of the cortex.

Furthermore, when we focus our attention on discriminating a specific feature, excitation of visual areas most responsive to that feature jumps up. While experimenters scanned their brains, subjects examined displays consisting colored bars moving horizontally and had to decide whether the bars in two successive displays were similar in color, shape, speed, or all three. When subjects focused their attention on color, they could discriminate color more accurately and the color areas in their visual cortex were more activated. Results were similar for shape and motion. Backward projections must play an important role in producing different brain-activation patterns when subjects actively look for different attributes in the same stimuli. Perhaps subjects imagine or keep in mind the attribute that they look for, and imagination enhances their visual acuity in discrimination (Corbetta 1998).

The Insufficiency of Stimulation: Attention

Any student knows that no matter how loudly and clearly the teacher speaks, what she says makes no impression on the "wax tablet" if he is not paying attention. Such inattentional deafness or inattentional blindness, as psychologists call it, was confirmed in many experiments. Imagine yourself in a psychological experiment with your eyes fixed on a cross at the center of a screen. Simple figures appear randomly on the periphery, and you easily locate them and discern their shapes. Following the experimenter's instruction, you focus your attention on the arms of the cross and try to compare their lengths. Now you are oblivious to the figures at the periphery. If you catch a few of them, you see only shapeless blobs. The optical stimuli remain the same, and your eyes have not moved. However, your visual experience has changed radically because your attention has changed. Many such experiments confirm the folk wisdom that stimulation without attention does not always produce perception (Rock and Mack 1994).

You can shift your attention from one object to another without moving a single muscle, not even a flicker in gaze, yet the shift elevates your perceptual acuity of the targeted object. The covert shift of attention is not merely a protective mask that hides our intention in social arenas, so that one can observe that gorgeous blond or muscular hunk without people noticing. Your eyes can follow only one thing at a time. Covert attention enables you to track several objects simultaneously, even when they scatter across the field. Usually, a shift in attention precedes eye movement to determine the appropriate landing site of the saccade.

Because our mental capacity is small compared with the onslaught of stimuli and the long list of agenda, our attention is highly selective. We can attend to several tasks simultaneously, but only if the tasks are not too mentally demanding. You can drive, eat, and converse at the same time, often quite comfortably. However, if the road or the traffic becomes treacherous, you would forget the sandwich and stop talking as you concentrated on driving. Probably you would shout at your passengers to shut up; if they didn't, you would understand little of what they said.

James distinguished between active and passive attention, which nowadays are more commonly called *goal-* or *concept-directed* and *stimulus-driven* attention. Usually, both goal and stimulus contribute to the deployment of attention. Passively, our attention is captured by certain happenings in the environment and shifts by reflex to certain stimuli, a loud noise or a pin prick. Sometimes, however, we can counteract the reflex. A flash caught at the corner of the eye usually induces a saccade to see what happens, but we can often suppress the saccade if we are determined to concentrate our mind elsewhere. Actively, we direct our attention to what concerns and interests us, which we sometimes formulate conceptually in our beliefs and desires. Since we are concerned about our future, our active attention is often anticipatory, even if we have no clear goal in mind.

By selectively focusing our attention, we actively inspect things of our choice instead of passively take in what the stimuli offer. Attention affects the sensitivity, resolution, and speed of perception. When we actively attend to something, we look for it before we find it, anticipate it before it appears, and with our mental readiness, we recognize it more quickly. The acceleration of perception by "expectant attention" has long been noticed. James (1890:409) recorded examples such as surgeons who occasionally saw blood flowing from a patient's arms before they saw the scalpel puncturing the skin. Since then it has been more systematically probed. When presented with stimuli at two locations equidistant from the eye-fixation point, subjects saw the stimulus at the location they attended to first, even if it actually occurred as much as 50 milliseconds later than the one at the unattended-to location. More striking, when a line connecting the two locations was presented, subjects did not see the line at once; they saw it being drawn from the attended-to position. Results of many such experiments are unequivocal. When two stimuli are presented simultaneously, we first see the one we attend to (Hikosaka et al. 1998).

More often our attention is not acutely focused. Nevertheless, our active mood and state of mind bias our sensitivity so that our attention is more readily attracted to stimuli relevant to our concern. Thus newspaper advertisements are noticed much more often by prospective customers than by disinterested readers. When one is interested in a product, the eyes are likely to be captured by an advertisement that would otherwise be overlooked. In such cases, our active attention is dispositional, biasing our susceptibility to certain attention-capturing stimuli.

Attention pertains to the actions of the whole organism and is not limited to vision. It has its own infrastructure that engages various brain regions; some maintain vigilance, others orient to various locations, still others coordinate motor programs and their relative arousal levels. Some attentional processes must influence the visual infrastructure, but exactly how, scientists are just beginning to unravel (Posner and Dehaene 1994; Tootell and Hadjikhani 2000).

Several models were proposed for selective visual attention. One compares attention with gate controllers that screen out irrelevant input in the early stages of the visual pathways. Another compares attention with a spotlight that rapidly and successively scans various locations in the visual field, enhancing neural activity for the attended area and reducing activity for unattended areas. These models have come under criticism. Allport (1993) echoed other cognitive scientists in complaining that the gate keeper or central executive that allegedly controls the swing of the attentional spotlight "has all the characteristics of a processing homunculus."

Unlike early models, newer ones take account of the neural characteristics of the visual infrastructure. Remember that neurons in later stages of visual pathways have very large receptive fields that enable them to respond to extended patterns. However, large fields also pose a problem for selectivity of response. Many objects with varying features may fall within the reception of a neuron. If the neuron passively sums neural excitations induced by all features, its responses would be almost indiscriminate. This is not what happens. Careful brain imaging experiments show that later areas in the visual pathways respond to fewer objects than earlier ones (Kastner et al. 1998). Thus several neuroscientists believe that neural excitations induced by different objects tend to inhibit each other, creating bottom-up competition among neural responses to different objects. Objects with certain features have a competitive edge, so that they tend to pop out and capture our attention. That is not all, however. The competition is also biased by the top-down influences arising from the organism's overall concern or goal, influences conveyed by backward projections from higher cognitive areas. Through many feedback loops in massively parallel processes, biased competition settles into selective responses of later visual stages. There is no homunculus in the brain to direct the spotlight of attention. Rather, as Rober Desimone and John Duncan (1995) wrote: "Attention is an emergent property of slow, competitive interactions that work in parallel across the visual field."

Stimulus-Driven and Concept-Driven Processes

All visual processes involve both forward and backward projections in the visual infrastructure, but relative contributions of the two vary. Many scientists call the processes dominated by forward projections stimulus driven and those dominated by backward projections concept directed. It is reasonable to say that the concept of shape plays a leading role in our attentional focus on shape discrimination, the concept of triangle in our visualization of a triangle. Our experiences exhibit salient patterns and regularities that are sometimes absent in the optical stimuli and can be described independent of them. Extrastimuli patterns are most obvious in blindfolded visualization but are also present in ordinary vision. Let us call certain patterns a "concept" if the processes exhibiting these patterns produce visual experiences in which the concept figures essentially. What concepts are prevalent in visual processes?

Rubin's vase-faces, depicted in figure 3.6, is a standard illustration in cognitive psychology. Sometimes you see a vase in the center, sometimes two facial profiles on the sides. This phenomenon, in which you alternately see two things in the same stimulus, is called bistable vision. Other familiar stimuli that produce bistable vision are Necker's cube and Wittgenstein's duck-rabbit. Psychologists call them ambiguous figures. Ambiguous in what? Not in stimuli; the figures are all clearly drawn to produce a definite optical impact. Thus a figure is ambiguous only in interpretation; only because we can apply different concepts to it and see it *as* disparate things, *as* a vase or two faces, a duck or a rabbit. Bistable vision, in which the stimulus is stable but our experience of it is not, demonstrates that our visual experience is driven not only by stimuli but also by concepts of coherent objects.

The demand for coherent objects is even more obvious in binocular rivalry, where ambiguous stimuli are generated by presenting disparate displays to the two eyes. Place a prism in front of one eye so that your two eyes are exposed to two completely different views. Say your left eye looks at a face while your right eye at a house. What will you see? Under most conditions, what you see is neither chaos nor a face superposed on a house. Frequently you have bistable vision in which the face alternates with the house as wholes. Your vision has definite infrastructural supports. If your brain were scanned while you were having the alternating visual experiences, it would show that different regions are excited when you see a house or a face. In short, our visual infrastructure is such that we do not see arbitrary junk that happens to irritate our eyes. We tend to see coherent objects, even if some stimulus input must be suppressed to achieve coherence. Experiments find that even the vision of monkeys or cats is not totally controlled by ocular irradiation (Logothetis et al. 1996; Tong et al. 1998; Sheinberg and Logothetis 1997).

A most popular topic in cognitive science is visual illusion. Hundreds of fascinating illustrations are available at www.illusionworks.com. What do you think your visual infrastructure is doing while you look at them?

Kanizsa's subjective contours are so well established they have become stock items in psychological textbooks. When presented with three black wedges carefully aligned on a white background, people see a white triangle occluding three black disks. Look at figure 5.2a. Do you first see three wedges and then infer a blocking triangle? No, you immediately see a blocking triangle with continuous contours, then infer that it is an illusion because the contours are not there on the paper. The contours of the triangle are subjective or illusory in the sense of being absent in the optical stimuli. They are not subjective in the sense of being arbitrarily made up by you. Your visual experience is produced by your visual infrastructure, whose operations are common in many animals and can be measured objectively.

Figure 5.2b contains only horizontal lines, but people see illusory vertical boundaries. Cats probably see the same, as vertical-sensitive neurons in their brains are activated. Neuroscientists made a cat watch a display similar to the figure and inserted electrodes into its brain to measure the excitation of neurons sensitive only to vertical orientation. These neurons

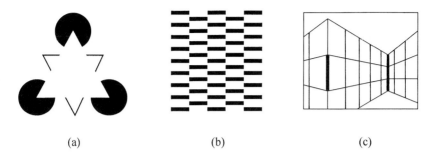

(a)   (b)   (c)

Figure 5.2
(a) In Kanizsa's subjective contours, one has the visual illusion of the contours of
a triangle that occludes three black circular discs. (b) Although this display contains only horizontal bars, it excites neurons in a cat's brain that are sensitive only
to the vertical orientation, indicating that cats too can experience subjective contours. (c) The thick vertical line on the right appears longer than the one on the
left, even when we are convinced that the two lines are of the same length. The
Müller-Lyer illusion is stronger in people in cultures favoring right-angular architecture, which presents similar stimuli for depth perception.

would be quiescent if the cat's vision were purely stimulus driven, for the
stimulus contains nothing vertical. But they were not. A significant percentage of them fired in the primary visual area in a way similar to that
when the cat was exposed to a vertical grating. The percentage of activated vertical-sensitive neurons increased in later visual areas. Thus experiences of subjective contours are supported by infrastructural processes
(Pessoa et al. 1998; Sheth et al. 1996).

Suppose we agree that processes underlying subjective contours are
concept driven. What are the responsible concepts? When we examine the
variety of visual illusions, we find that they are not arbitrary but are
associated with our activities in the physical world. For example, the
Müller-Lyer illusion in figure 5.2c has something to do with depth perception for people in a visual environment studded with right-angular
constructions. Thus it is experienced to a much smaller extent by Zulus,
who have a "circular culture" with round huts and curved furrows
(Gregory 1998).

Many visual illusions have to do with object integrity and object
occlusion. Illusory experiences are not superfluous. We live in a three-
dimensional world where objects obstruct the views of each other, so that
the stimulation an object inflicts on our retina is often discontinuous.
Despite fragmentary stimulation, we see integral objects, for instance, a

vertical grating instead of a bunch of horizontal lines. The general concept of *integral objects* complements stimuli in shaping perception of illusory contours.

A similar account can be given for the perception of apparent motion, on which movies are made. When a briefly presented stimulus is followed rapidly by a second stimulus in a different location, we do not see two distinct objects succeeding one another. Instead, we see one object moving from the first location to the second. The stimuli need not be identical in color or shape. If the differences are too drastic, we see no apparent motion, but moderate differences pose no problem. Presented with two different stimuli, we see one moving and changing object, as a triangle moving and changing into a circle, or a red dot moving and changing into a green dot. Responses of motion-sensitive neurons in monkeys show that like subjective contour, perception of apparent motion has a firm infrastructural underpinning (Ramachandran and Antis 1986; Assad and Maunsell 1995).

A moving object often disappears from view temporarily as it passes behind other objects. Nevertheless, we recognize the object emerging from the back of an obstacle as the same one that earlier disappeared behind it. The concept of an enduring and moving object that is temporarily occluded may be responsible for the perceptual experience of apparent motion.

In sum, bistable vision, binocular rivalry, subjective contour, and apparent motion all point to the general concept of integral objects in our visual experiences. They are only the tips of an iceberg of visual experiences featuring concepts of objects. This should not be surprising, as objects are the most prevalent units that we deal with in everyday life. Consequently, many scientists maintain that in evaluating perceptual experiences, one cannot neglect the level of the person interacting with the wold (Pessoa et al. 1998).

17   Open, Closed, and Ecological Theories of Perception

Being open to the world is apparent in our commonsense notion of perception, which is defined in the Webster Dictionary as "awareness of the elements of environment through physical sensation." Perception is of objects in the world. Furthermore, the demand of awareness implies that perception is more than a physical coupling to the objects by the sense organs; it is also a mental activity that is closely associated with recognition and understanding.

The idea of perception that we use daily applies not to the infrastructural level but the mental level. On this level, we are not aware of the many infrastructural processes inside our brains. We are concerned with the phenomenal structures of what we experience. What are the structures of our perceptual understanding? This section presents empirical evidence to support Kant's thesis that our most immediate sensual experiences involve the general concepts of individual enduring objects. As elaborated in chapter 8, these general concepts are the minimal structures of our open mind. They enable us to distinguish our experiences from the objects that we experience, hence to know the world as largely independent of us and ourselves as subjects participating in the world. Involvement in sensual perception implies that mind is always aware of its own openness to the world.

Some theories conclude that sensual perception involves no concept, at least not concepts of physical objects. We will consider two, closed perception and ecological perception. The closed mind is out of the environment and oblivious of its elements; the ecological perceiver is situated in the environment but has no awareness of it. Neither agrees with the dictionary definition of perception and neither enjoys support of empirical evidence.

Closed Experience: Given in Sensual Stimuli

Models of the closed mind imply closed perception, where a perceiver sees not things in the environment but only mental representations called stimuli or sense data or sense impressions or surface irritation or transducer input, all of which are strictly inside the perceiver's skin. Closed perception is purely receptive and can occur in a mind as simple as a blank slate, because the mind needs only to register the stimuli on the sense organs as the *given*. Thus the perceiver needs no concept of objects, and cannot distinguish between vision and hallucination without the intervention of mind designers.

Since its first version introduced by Locke, closed perception has many variants besides being a large part of the closed mind discussed in section 4. Early in the twentieth century, positivists in the Vienna Circle made the dichotomy between sense data and physical objects into the base of a philosophy of science that dominated for decades and still casts a long shadow. Positivism maintains that only sense data are certain and necessary because they are given in observations. All else, ranging from familiar things that we handle to atoms, genes, and other populations of modern science, are dispensable "theoretical entities" or logical constructs of sense data. Consequently, the positivist philosophy of science stipulates that all contents of ideal science should be deducible from pure evidence of sense data. To achieve the ideal, philosophers poured tremendous effort into reducing theoretical entities to sense data; that is, to translate sentences about physical things to sentences about "the immediately given." They failed.

Quine (1953:44) talked not so much of sense data as of "surface irritations," "surface stimulations," "ocular irradiation patterns," and "stimulation of sensory receptors." These, he insisted, are the only legitimate evidence for ideal science. So far he agreed with the positivists. He deviated from them, however, in rejecting their reductionist program and advocating a radical relativism. He wrote: "As an empiricist I continue to think of the conceptual scheme of science as a tool, ultimately, for predicting future experience in the light of past experience. Physical objects are conceptually imported into the situation as convenient intermediaries—not by definition in terms of experience, but simply as irreducible posits comparable, epistemologically, to the gods of Homer. . . . In point of epistemological footing the physical objects and the gods differ only in degree and not in kind. Both sorts of entities enter our conception only as cultural posits."

Note that "experience" here is only the experience of surface stimuli, not of physical things, because things are not given in closed perception. However, when physical objects are cultural myths illegitimate as evidence, "surface," "eye," "receptor," which refer to our physical bodies, are also merely convenient ways of speaking. Surface stimulations and sense impressions share essential characteristics. Both occur inside the veil of perception, both are given and unquestioned, and both are ephemeral. A surface irritation vanishes as soon it ceases. To be is to be irritated, just as to be is to be perceived. Only the inner realm is secure, the outer world is an option dependent on cultural taste.

No one who retains the slightest common sense would let the physical world evaporate. Despite his skepticism, Quine immediately proclaimed himself to be a lay physicist and readily turned from an empiricist to a behaviorist holding physical objects as stimuli to query other perceivers. Similarly, Fodor, Pylyshyn, and other advocates of the computational mind tried desperately to show that mental representations qua transducer input do represent things outside and hence constitute information. Their computational or information-processing models purport to explain how the closed mind infers or reconstructs features of three-dimensional objects in the world from the patterns of two-dimensional transducer input. Because of the common acknowledgement that perception should ultimately be of objects, their theories of perception are called *mediated*. Their peculiarity lies in introducing an intermediate step where perceivers immediately see sense stimuli or compute with transducer input in methodological solipsism. This immediate experience is more certain than the ultimate perception that it mediates, as the stimuli and input are given and not contaminated by the perceivers' subsequent construction.

Ecological Interaction: Given by Mind Designers

While closed perception takes the Greek view inside the Cartesian Trojan horse, ecological perception takes the Trojan view outside. Ecological theories, which include Gibson's ecological approach and AI's situated cognition, consider perception mainly from the standpoint of mind designers, be they ecologists or engineers. Gibson (1966:267; 1979:238) went farthest in stressing the brutal directness of perception. He maintained that all that is necessary for vision exists *as information* in structures of ambient light in the form of invariants or features that do not change under changing perspectives. Therefore visual perception is "optical information pickup." He explained the pickup process: "If the invariants of this structure can be registered by a perceptual system, the constants of neural input will correspond to the constants of stimulus energy, although the one will not copy the other. But then meaningful information can be said to exist inside the nervous system as well as outside. The brain is relieved of the necessity of constructing such information by *any* process—innate rational power (theoretical nativism), the storehouse of memory (empiricism), or form-fields (Gestalt theory)." Consequently, information pickup dispenses with "old-fashioned mental acts: recognition, interpretation, inference, concepts, ideas and storage and retrieval of ideas."

Critics at once noticed the peculiarity of Gibson's version of direct perception: the dearth of processes on the part of perceivers, who are thereby mindless. To be a perceiver one needs only a properly configured retina that is sensitive to specific invariant features of the ambient light;

one needs only to "resonate" and "be attuned" to them. Gibson (1979:149) acceded: "I thought I had discovered that there were stimuli for perception in much the same way that there were known to be stimuli for sensation. This now seems to me to be a mistake. . . . I should not have implied that a percept was an automatic response to a stimulus, as sense impression is supposed to be. For even then I realized that perceiving is an act, not a response." The admission of mistake did not quiet critics, as it was not accompanied by correction. Gibson did not explain what the perceiving act consists of beyond resonance to or registration of stimulus information (Ullman 1980).

Ecological perceivers resonate with certain environmental features and pick up the information, like a harmonic oscillator resonating to a particular frequency and picking up energy from the field with that frequency. Thus they share the passivity of the closed mind but differ in what they register passively. Ecological perception involves not awareness or understanding or concepts. An entity is said to perceive a thing if mind designers decide that it interacts appropriately with the thing. Thus a bee sees the flower on which it lands and a heat-seeking missile sees the jet fighter it chases.

For some Gibsonians, the perceiving act consists of extracting information from the ambient light. However, since Gibson explicitly ruled out recognition, interpretation, inference, concepts, and other mental operations, it is not clear what information extraction amounts to. Fodor and Pylyshyn (1981) contended that if Gibson were not to fall into the information-processing camp that he so vehemently denounced, information extraction can only be a reflexive response. That is why until the end, Gibson himself insisted on information pickup and not extraction.

The ecological approach requires much interpretation and information extraction. The important question is, who performs the extraction, perceivers or mind designers theorizing about causal relations between perceivers and objects? Not perceivers, that is the whole point of the approach, which is essentially ecological *optics*, not psychology. Undoubtedly optics is crucial to vision, but a psychology of vision should illuminate the relation between physics and visual experiences. This is the missing link in the ecological approach.

Light and matter are governed by physical laws. Marr (1982) and other computationalists appeal to the same causal principles in their inverse optics as Gibson did in his ecological optics. Everyone agrees that predictable causal correlations exist between the illuminated objects and the structure of light that strikes the perceiver. Physical correlations are what Gibson called "information." After analyzing it, Fodor and Pylysyhn (1981) concluded: "Gibson has no notion of information over and above the notion of correlation." Information as the optical correlation between light striking perceivers and their environment is available only to mind designers from their third-party vantage point, not to perceivers. It can be picked up by perceivers only because Gibson slipped from information as correlation to information as some specific features in stimuli. Then, he assumed that perceivers are equipped with apparatuses that are specialized to register these features, or in mind designers' eyes, to pick up the information.

The ecological approach is interactive behaviorism. Instead of responding to whole stimuli, perceivers respond to a specific invariant feature in stimuli that mind designers know to be causally correlated with a particular environmental property. There are any number of properties in the environment and equally as many invariants in the stimuli. Perceivers are restricted by their physiological makeup to respond to only to a few. These are Gibson's "affordance." "In short, an affordance is *a scientist's description* of the environment relevant to some organism's coordinated action," Clancy (1997:243) concluded in his sympathetic study of Gibson's approach to gain inspiration for AI's situated cognition.

One can see why the ecological approach is so appealing to situation roboticists. Robotic engineers are playing similar roles as ecologists; both consider perception as mind designers. The main difference is that instead of reading meanings into existing organisms, roboticists try to design new systems according to their preconceived meanings. Their analysis is more sophisticated than Gibson's because they have to discern the affordances involved in tasks they have in mind and build robotic receptors and motors that resonate properly to these affordances. They realize how difficult it is to emulate the ecological perception of insects. Nevertheless, they share the basic outlook of interactive behaviorism; their main concern is to build robots that interact with the environment in ways that satisfy their criteria.

Ecological perceivers and present-day robots can pick up only rather simple information that is correlated with simple properties. For example, highly reflecting surfaces are the affordance perceived by some water bugs in flight, for they afford the bugs something to plunge into. Ecologists can give a meaningful account of how affordance and its perception help bugs find homes, but how meaningful is affordance to the bugs themselves? It becomes apparent when people come along with shiny cars and the bugs smash themselves on the hoods. The ecological approach is attractive for insisting that perceivers are interactive parts of the environment. However, in the process it robs perceivers of mind and reduces them to no more than parts of the environment. Ecological perceivers need not be conscious. No surprise, substantive applications of the ecological approach occur in insect perception, such as the navigation of dragonflies (Turvey and Shaw 1995). In ecological perception, scattering electrons perceives atoms; the electrons pick up information about atomic structures, which physicists happily extract. However, it is doubtful if ecological perception is applicable to humans.

Mediated perception consists two steps: immediate experience of stimuli followed by inference to objects. When skeptics challenge the justifiability of the inference, mediated perception retreats to a closed mind's reception and registration of stimuli. The ecological approach relieves perceivers of the inferential step, fine tunes their sensual apparatus to specific features in the stimuli, and appeals to external mind designers to establish the correlation between features and environmental factors. As far as perceivers are concerned, ecological perception is not that different from the closed mind. Both are reception or registration of stimulus features, differing only in the design of receptive devices. Both involve no mental activity.

How Do We See a Coherent and Stable World?

Let us agree that the optic flow striking our eyes is mind-bogglingly complex, but we manage to see a coherent and stable world. Let us also agree that our complicated visual infrastructure somehow maintains certain invariant features that structure our stable visual experiences. What are these invariant features? Are they all contained in the optic flow after we account for eye, neck, and bodily movements, as Gibson maintained? Or are they more abstract, involving contributions that are conceptual?

A good way to find out is to control the optic flow and test what subjects see. Eye-tracking experiments do just that. Recall that our narrow foveal vision and saccades produce fragmentary optical input that jumps several times a second. To produce a temporally continuous visual experience from such jumpy bits and pieces, our visual infrastructure must have

extracted something during each fixation and retained them across saccades. What it retains are good candidates for the invariants that we see.
What are they?

Cognitive scientists designed special eye-tracking machines that
monitor fixations and eye movements of otherwise immobilized subjects
while they read a text or examine a picture on a computer screen. When
the eye tracker detects the beginning of a saccade, with electronic speed
it changes the display on the screen before the saccade is completed. The
trick is kept a secret from the subjects, who know only that they are
preparing for a memory test, but can press a button if the screen is unsta-
ble or behaves strangely. Thus subjects face optic flows whose structures
change rapidly and perhaps arbitrarily. By comparing the optics and what
subjects see, we can surmise subjects's contribution to perception (Irwin
1993; Grimes 1996; McConkie and Currie 1996).

In one version, the display contains sentences written in a changing
mixture of upper and lower cases. A sentence "THe aPPlE Is rED" changes
into "thE AppLe iS Red" during a saccade and changes back during the
next saccade and so on (see figure 5.1). Nothing is invariant in the optical
pattern. Therefore if subjects depend on ecological information pickup,
they should not be able to get anything. The very opposite happened in
experiments. Subjects read fluently, not noticing the optical changes at all.
When they were told of the changes after the experimental session, many
were surprised, some annoyed, that they could be victims of such a trick.
Perhaps the person most surprised was Zola, a scientist who designed the
experiment. When the eye-tracking machine was first delivered, he eagerly
tried it and declared after a few minutes that it did not work. Of course
the machine worked in changing the text display. It worked so well it
fooled its designer. This experiment reveals at least two points. First, readers
successfully extract the meaning of the text although the physical optics
contain no invariant. Thus meaning is not ecological "information." To
extract meaning, mental operations of readers are indispensable. Second,
meaning extraction is not merely a higher cognitive process that operates
after sensual perception. It penetrates into the perceptual process itself, so
that readers do not see the optical changes at all.

Similar results obtain when the displays are pictures whose sizes, orientations, or features change during saccades. When the size of a picture
is enlarged more than 30 percent, subjects experience a looming effect as
the ecological approach predicts. However, they do not see smaller size

changes, indicating that optics alone do not determine the invariant feature.

Mounting experimental evidence suggests that our visual processes are nothing like movie cameras or camcorders, which keep a literal record of optical stimuli or sense impressions. At each fixation, our visual infrastructure more or less lets input present itself so that we see an integral scene with varying degrees of detail at the center and the periphery. However, it does not retain the pictorial image once input ceases with onset of a saccade. To store images of any detail requires enormous capacity, and the expenditure may prove to be a hindrance and not a gain. Pictures are subject to spatial constraints, and their details often obscure gross similarities that may exist among them. Thus it is very difficult to piece pictures together seamlessly. Evidence suggests that the visual infrastructure discards optical details, and abstracts and holds on to certain salient features that are especially stable. Of importance, it seems to organize these features on a more abstract level than optical structures. In reading, we retain meanings and not spatial forms of words presented in the optics. In examining pictures, subjects more readily discerned intersaccadic differences when they explicitly identified the objects or properties they saw previously: "I saw a dog before and now it is a cat." Do we retain not optical qualities but object identities, property specifications, and causal regularities; not detailed features but the gross layout of objects? The answer would have great implication on theories of mind, because object identity and causal regularity are high-level concepts. Are these concepts grasped by perceivers themselves instead of merely by outside mind designers?

The Primitive Conceptual Structure of Open Perceptual Experiences

Leibniz objected to Locke's notion of mind as a blank slate that passively receives sense impressions. Kant (1781) went farther and proposed that our mental faculty actively contributes to even the most immediate sensual experiences. He tried to uncover the fundamental architecture of our mind without which we cannot possibly have the kinds of experiences that we do. Our experiences are meaningful; we perceive an intelligible world. How is intelligibility possible? To Kant it is made possible by a complicated mental architecture. All experiences, including immediate perceptual experiences, bear the imprints of both sensual stimuli and characteristics of our mental faculties. The mental faculties he analyzed into two aspects, intuition and understanding. Understanding is structured by a web of general concepts, of which the most important are general concepts of objects or more appropriately the objective world. Intuition, which is the sensual aspect of perception, has forms of time and space by which we identify the *individuality* of particular objects that fall under the general concepts. Kant maintained that both intuition and understanding are indispensable to the unity of consciousness, in which we see, hear, and touch the light, sound, and texture of objects in a unitary world.

Suppose you and I are looking at a house. I intuitively know that the house persists when it does not contribute to the optic flow I am exposed to; that it is distinct from the other house across the street that causes a similar ocular irradiation pattern; that it can cause different patterns of ocular irradiation if I look at it from a different perspective; that I may be wrong, for from a different perspective it may turn out to be a stage prop; that it is also perceivable by you, so that we can discuss it and reach intersubjective agreement about it. This intuitive knowledge is neither given in the optic flow nor derived by conscious inference from the stimuli. But it is part and parcel of our immediate visual experience. Based on these and other considerations, philosopher Peter Strawson (1979) stated: "The employment of our ordinary, full-blooded concepts of physical objects is indispensable to a strict, and strictly veridical, account of our sensible experience. . . . I have argued that mature sensible experience (in general) presents itself as, in Kantian phrase, an *immediate* consciousness of the existence of things outside us."

Quine (1953:18) wrote: "The conceptual scheme of physical objects is a convenient myth." Kant (1781:126, 93) wrote: "Concepts of objects in general must underlie all empirical knowledge as its a priori conditions." "Thoughts without contents are empty, intuitions without concepts are blind." Gibson wrote: " Kant . . . foisted on us a terrible theory about percepts being 'blind' without concepts (and concepts being 'empty' without percepts). Crap I say! *That's* what we have to reject" (Reed 1988: 299).

We can distinguish between *general concepts* such as physical objects and *substantive concepts* such as various kinds of objects. Later we will consider whether our primitive visual experiences tacitly involve considerable substantive concepts. However, substantive concepts are not under dispute here, for Kant never got beyond the generality of quantity, quality, causality, and possibility. What Quine took to be myth and Gibson dismissed as crap are *general* concepts of physical objects. General concepts signify two objective peculiarities. Physical objects *endure* when you are not looking at them: to be is to be independent of being perceived. They have *numerical identities* by which they remain as the same objects through changing properties, and by which they are distinct from each other even if they have the same properties and cause the same irritation patterns. Because of these two peculiarities, objects cannot be given in sensory stimuli, which are ephemeral and carry no lasting identity. Nor are they given in the optic flow, because they can be occluded. Therefore to say that you see a physical object is to say that you see more than meets the eyes, that your immediate visual experiences involved certain mental contribution on your part.

Ecologists may contend that the invariants in the optic flow are sufficient for perception without any concept. However, as Fodor and Pylyshyn cogently argued, any one of the unlimited environmental properties is an invariant. Without any restriction on the invariants that perceivers pick up, talks about invariants are empty. Physiological restrictions are too rigid to account for the flexibility of human vision. Other kinds of restrictions are cognitive. General concepts of physical objects provide a broad restriction that picks up most important invariants.

If optics alone determine what we see, as the ecological approach postulates, signals should flow only from the eyes up. But our brains do not work that way. Our visual infrastructure supports two-way traffic. Signals flow not only from the eyes to brain regions for higher cognitive functions, they flow also in the opposite direction in concept-driven processes. We do not know exactly what concepts are involved, but it is not unreasonable to assume that general concepts of objects are among them. These general concepts convey no specific information but only general assumptions of objective identity and continuity. They bind various features into a single object. Such binding fails in patients with simultanagnosia and adults newly recovering from long-term blindness, such as SB and Virgil. Their visual experiences of things are fragmentary; many can see only one thing, a part or an aspect of a thing at a time. Their vision does resonate to some invariants in optic flow, but they are almost functionally blind (Farah 1990).

Because of our small fovea and our eye saccade, we are exposed to a small optical field at a time and the field jumps rapidly. Thus no matter how complex our optic flow is, it contains gaps and inconsistencies that can foil the extraction of optical invariants. Eye-tracking experiments cited earlier are some examples. Visual illusions are others. In such cases, concept-driven processes in our visual infrastructure fill in the gaps and ensure coherent visual experiences of the physical world. General concepts of physical objects are the most primitive concepts by which we know ourselves to be in the world. Ecologists depend heavily on them in their analysis of ecological optics. Why deny the same conceptual ability to perceivers who are fellow humans?

Physical Objects or Bundles of Features?

Suppose physical object is an optional cultural construction. What are other options? Anthropologists did not report any culture in which people see things other than physical objects, but Quine (1960:52f) offered three logical alternatives: "Point to a rabbit and you have pointed to a stage of a rabbit, to an integral part of a rabbit, to the rabbit fusion, and to where rabbithood is manifested." Instead of a rabbit as a physical object, we can interpret the same stimulus in three new ways. We can conceive the world as made up of four-dimensional "worms" and interpret the stimulus as a stage or temporal slice of a rabbitlike worm. Or we can conceive the world as consisting of spatially discontinuous "fusions" and interpret the stimulus as a part of the "rabbit fusion," which is the collection of all rabbits scattered around the globe taken as one unit. Or we can conceive the world in terms of conjunctive manifestations of various features, "bundles of features," and interpret the stimulus as the manifestation of the bundle called rabbithood. To Quine, it is a mere convention that we say we see physical objects instead of worms, fusions, or bundles.

Among Quine's options, the bundle of features is best articulated and defended and accords with his empiricism and regimentation of language. Thus I will contrast a bundle of features with a physical object to explain the difference between closed and open perception. Worms, which are actually four-dimensional bundles, will be discussed in the context of memory.

A feature is a universal; the feature redness, for example, has an unlimited number of instances. A conjunction of several features cuts down the range of instances, but generally does not specify a unique case. The conjunction of redness and roundness and walking may be something rare or nonexistent, but it does not indicate something unique.

Linguistically, features are described by predicates such as red or round. Logically, they are represented by variables. A bundle of features inherits the characteristic of universality. To refer to it, we need only the relevant predicates. Anything that fits the description of being red and round will be our bundle. Quine has a slogan for it: "To be is to be the value of a variable."

A physical object is not a universal but a particular entity with properties represented by universals. An object has all the features included in the bundle view. It also has what a bundle of features lacks: its numerical identity, by which it is distinguished from other objects of the same kind and same properties, and is recognized as the same entity even if some of its properties have changed. The numerical identity turns the bundle of features into the properties of a physical object. Linguistically, we refer to a particular by singular terms including proper names, pronouns, and common nouns preceded by definite articles. Instead of casting out a net by the predicates redness and roundness to pull in whatever it catches, we say "the tomato" to spear a particular object.

The general concept of bundles of features is simple; it contains only one general variable: feature. However, to refer to any bundle, we require complicated substantive predicates to describe definite features. The general concept of physical objects is complex; it contains two general variables: property and numerical identity. However, to refer to a particular object, we need only singular terms without substantive predicates.

Numerical identity and hence the object concept are difficult to represent in some theoretical models, for instance in connectionist networks. Network patterns encode general features such as being a sheep or being white, so that their activation represents only sheep in general but not this particular sheep. How to represent the idea of particularity in connectionist networks is a problem that scientists are still working on. Philosophers face similar problems of representing particularity in some logical systems, and one of their favorite solutions is bundles of features. Quine, for example, advocates discarding terms of singular reference and referring only through definite descriptions. Instead of referring to a horse by the name Pegasus, he would invent the predicate "pegasize" for it. Thus instead of physical things, we talk only about bundles of features.

Which general concept, bundles of features or physical objects, structures our immediate sensual experiences? Empiricists favor bundles of features; their sense impressions are various shapes and colors. Kantians insist on physical objects; for them, the general concept of numerical identity is necessary for normal perceptual experience. These are empirical hypotheses that can be tested by experiments.

Infrastructural Support for Seeing Particular Objects

Many eye-tracking experiments call into doubt the empiricist claim that we see various shapes and colors, compare them, extract their regularities, and construct optional ideas of objects. Subjects were shown an advertisement featuring four models in attractive swimsuits, one of which changed from hot pink to bright green during a saccade. More than half the subjects failed to see the change (Grimes 1974). Thus colors and shapes appear not to be what we retain across saccades to facilitate comparison.

Increasing evidence suggests that separate and dissociable infrastructural processes underlie our understanding of universal and particular, or of property and numerical identity, or of type and token as they are better known in the psychological literature. Separation begins in the visual infrastructure with its two broad pathways. Areas in the what stream are generally sensitive to properties of objects. Areas in the where stream are sensitive to relative positions of objects, hence their numerical identities. The where stream is also intimately involved in planning and controlling motor actions. You may think about universal properties of apples, but what your grasp in your hand is one particular apple.

The primary visual area and early areas in the what stream are sensitive to such features as color, edge, and simple shapes. If they suffice for vision, we would see bundles of features. But then all the later stages of the visual infrastructure would become redundant. Nature is not so wasteful. Patients with visual agnosia aside, people do not see sheer roundness in conjunction with redness, which they infer to be a tomato or an apple. They immediately see specific objects such as a ripe tomato or a delicious apple. The tomato is red and round, but the properties cannot be peeled from it as they can be pulled out of a bundle and given to us independently in sensual perception. Based on the brain's organization, Crick and Koch (1995) went so far as to propose that the contents of our conscious visual experiences do not include features as they are registered in the primary visual area. Our visual experiences are results of much further processing and integration down the stream. Sometimes integration distorts or ejects features detected in early stages.

There are many possible reasons for a feature registered by early visual areas to be absent in visual experience. One possibility, failure to bind the

bundle of registered features into one particular object with various properties, is enjoying increasing evidential support. Many kinds of laboratory
experiments converge on a similar conclusion. Normal subjects fail to perceive a stimulus if infrastructural processes for *types* are excited but
processes for the *token* are derailed. It is the token or numerical identity
of the object that binds various properties into a unit in perceptual experience. Without the extra infrastructure for numerical identity, a stimulus
incites no perceptual experience, although its features are registered by
some brain areas.

Imagine yourself sitting before a computer screen on which characters appear one at a time at a rate of about eight per second, say, "2, 5,
G, 9, 7, D, 6, . . ." The experimenter asks you to push a button whenever
you see a letter. Easy, you think. If you are like most normal subjects,
however, you would successfully report G but fail miserably with D. It is
as if your first response causes your mind to blink, so that you miss the
stimulus that occurs within a lag period of 400 to 600 milliseconds. This
lapse of mind, which psychologists call *attentional blink*, is robust and widespread. It even blanks out striking stimuli that normally pop out at us
without paying attention. It is much worse for patients with certain brain
injuries. What causes it? Priming experiments show that although subjects
fail to see the stimulus D, they respond faster and more accurately to a
subsequent d than to a subsequent k. The enhanced fluency indicates that
the subjects are primed to the meaning of the stimulus that escapes their
conscious vision. Experimenters also measured event-related potential in
subjects when the meaning of the blanked-out word conflicted with its
semantic context. In sum, the stimulus is registered in the brain up to the
stage of meaning extraction, although it is finally blanked out from perceptual experience (Wolfe 1997).

Most psychologists now explain attentional blink in terms of the *type-
token* or *property-individuality* distinction. In attentional blink, processes for
type differentiation work but those for token recognition do not. Early
infraconscious visual processes successfully register various properties of the
stimulus, including its meaning if it is a word. However, because of some
glitch resulting from having responded too short a time ago, the properties are not "tokenized" or not bound by the notion of a particular individual. Consequently there is no conscious perception of the stimulus.
Perception requires invocation of particularity (Luck et al. 1996; Shapiro
et al. 1997; Chun 1997).

The effects of failing to particularize show up in unexpected places. For example, line editors or proofreaders often overlook the second instance of a repeated word in a sentence. The weakness is not peculiar to their trades. *Repetitive blindness*, as psychologists call it, is a robust phenomenon observed in many experiments (Kanwisher 1987). When the words in the sentence "Her jacket was red because red is conspicuous" were presented in rapid succession, most subjects missed the second "red." They did not make this error when the first "red" was replaced say, by "pink." The phenomenon is not limited to words; any repeated item is susceptible to selective omission. This is surprising because usually the presentation of a stimulus primes subsequent recognition of a similar stimulus, a phenomenon on which many psychological experiments are based. In repetitive blindness, however, the opposite happens, as the first stimulus kills perception of the second. Its effect is strong enough to override people's sensitivity to meaning. People fail to see the second "red" even when its omission produces a meaningless word sequence "her jacket was red because is conspicuous."

Many causes of repetitive blindness have been suggested. A plausible hypothesis is that the neural units responsible for processing the specific type of item must have some time to recover from their response to the first instance, thus missing the second instance. This hypothesis was refuted by several experiments, one of which found that repetitive blindness did not occur if the words were printed in different colors. After a variety of experiments to test various hypotheses, psychologists are converging on the explanation in terms of failure to individuate particular objects. Each word in a sentence must be processed as an individual object if it is to be perceived consciously. For a repeated word, the first occurrence is individuated and perceived. Objects usually persist through brief absence, and the infrastructural processes for them persist similarly. Thus the numerical identity of the first word persists and assimilates the properties of the second word. No excitation for a second numerical identity occurs to bind the features registered from the second stimulus. Consequently, the second stimulus is not perceived. In this explanation, repetitive blindness is closely related to attentional blink, although the two are not identical; one can occur without the other. Repetitive blindness may also be tied to apparent motion. All three phenomena point to the infrastructural processes for the numerical identification of enduring objects. "Intuitions without concepts are blind." When intuition is the visual sense and the concept is numerical identity, "blind" is almost literal (Chun 1997; Chun and Cavanagh 1997).

Movement and change are Achilles's heels of bundles of features. Without numerical identity, two bundles containing different features or locating at different space regions must be distinct. Thus it is meaningless to say that a bundle changes or moves, or that we pay attention to the s ame bundle. Thus change and movement can differentiate the concepts of objects and bundles of features in perception. Do we directly see change and movement? Many psychological experiments leave no reasonable doubt that we do. We can track several moving objects, distinguish them numerically when they cross paths, and reidentify them after they temporarily disappear from our visual field. Recognition of a specific object facilitates discernment of its changing properties. Experimental subjects recognize different letters appearing on the same object more quickly and accurately than they recognize the same letter appearing on different objects. This *object-specific advantage* in perceptual acuity is robust and holds when the object is moving, or when it is perceived as an integral object in apparent motion. To explain it and many related phenomena, cognitive scientist Ann Treisman proposed the influential feature integration theory in which the concept of individual objects bind various properties. The infrastructural process underlying our recognition of a specific object is called an object file, object token, and various other names. An object file is excited when a person consciously recognizes a specific object. It persists to bind together various features and locations of the object, resulting in perception of the object's change and movement (Kahneman et al. 1992).

All these results suggest an answer to the question of what our visual infrastructure retains across saccades to produce coherent visual experiences. It retains not impressions of colors or shapes but general concepts of particular enduring objects, which are often identified by their spatial relationships. Concepts of physical objects tie together detail features glimpsed in successive saccades and produce the panoramic vision of a dynamic world. This objective unity of consciousness is an essential aspect of mind's openness to the world.

What Infants See

Those who regard the concept of physical objects as a cultural posit may insist that our mature visual infrastructure works this way because it is socially conditioned. Nothing prevents another culture from conditioning its people so that their visual infrastructures produce vision not of particular objects but bundles of features. Undoubtedly the characteristics of our mental infrastructure are subject to the influences of cultures and customs, because its development depends partly on practice and experience. Nevertheless, differences documented in cross-cultural studies tend to belong to specific and substantive concepts, as one sees an airplane where another sees a strange bird. Can social conditioning change so deep a conceptual structure as physical objects in general?

Stimulation on the retina is a two-dimensional variation of light frequency and intensity. A first step toward intelligible vision is to parse consistently the undifferentiated nuance of color into distinctive entities. This is difficult, not the least because objects in the three-dimensional world often occlude each other, so that our optical stimuli correspond only to parts of objects. It is most interesting to find out if infants show any innate or early-developed bias in parsing, and if such bias leads to general concepts of the physical world familiar to adults.

To probe what newborns make of various stimuli, developmental psychologists use the fact, confirmed in many independent experiments, that infants are attracted by new stimuli and look at them longer than they look at boring old ones. Psychologists present an infant with an object or an event until the infant becomes habituated and ceases to look at it. Then they change the stimulus. If the new stimulus does not induce longer looking time, they infer that the infant finds it to be the same old stuff as the habituating stimulus. If the infant looks much longer at the new stimulus, they infer that it finds the new stimulus to be significantly different from the habituating one. By systematically varying stimuli and recording looking times, psychologists extract features to which infants are especially sensitive.

Among the first problems to which this method is applied are features constitutive of a physical object, especially when the object is partly occluded. Experimenters display a rod whose middle is occluded by a block. Does the infant see a partially occluded rod as adults do, or does it see two unrelated rods? If it sees a single rod, what are the display's general features that induce the perception of object integrity? Gestalt psychology maintains that we always see a figure against a background, and it delineates various principles for the figure-ground segregation: goodness of form, continuance of color, homogeneity of texture, uniformity of substance, and common fate or change in unison. Which, if any, of these principles shape infantile perception? Experiments find that the features most responsible for the integrity of an object are *rigidity* and *cohesion in motion*, which is a case of common fate. Shape and color are secondary. This by itself is evidence for objects and against bundles of features. Motion is central to objects but alien to bundles. Motion is change in location and change is precisely what bundles of features are designed to eliminate. It is legitimate only to talk about two bundles at different places and different times, not one bundle moving from one place to another.

In one experiment, infants four months old were first habituated to the display of a rod whose two ends protruded from behind a block. Then they were shown two new stimuli without the block: a whole unobstructed rod, or two discontinuous segments identical to what protruded from the block in the habituating display. When the rod was static in the habituating display, infants looked equally at the new stimuli, showing that straight-line interpolation between rod segments did not induce the perception of object unity. When the rod in the habituating display was moving back and forth behind the block, however, infants reacted differently to the new stimuli without the block. They showed no interest in the whole rod but looked much longer at the broken rod segments. The difference showed that cohesion in motion had induced the perception of an integral rod, so that infants found the broken segments new. Motion-based perception of object integrity is robust. Infants perceived that whatever moved cohesively behind the block was one unit, even if its two protruding ends were of different colors and shapes (Kellman 1993; Spelke and Newport 1998).

Individuating entities is only the first step toward making the world intelligible. We understand the world as consisting of objects that exist independent of our perception of them. Objects endure when they are hidden from view or pass out of sight. Their displacement, transformation, and mutual interaction are not totally arbitrary but have certain patterns and regularities, so that many of their behaviors are more or less predictable. When do infants come to grip with these? Piaget, who did the first and the most influential work in developmental psychology, thought the process begins at around nine months and is not completed until the child is two years old and starts to use symbolic representations. Based on the observation that infants do not search for hidden objects until they are nine months old, he concluded that before then they lack the notion of objects persisting through occlusion. More recent experiments based on visual tasks, however, indicated that infants are more precocious. Those as young as four months had some appreciation of constant motion, continuity in occlusion, and other general properties essential to physical objects.

Psychologists use the same habituation-preferential looking method to probe infantile understanding of physical regularity. A typical experiment uses a habituating stimulus as a baseline to calibrate how infants differentiate among new stimuli, some of which are physically possible, others physically impossible. For instance, after being habituated to the event of a falling ball stopped by a board over a box, infants are presented with new events: a physically possible event in which the board is absent and the ball falls into the box; a physically impossible event in which the board is absent and the ball stops in midair; and a second impossible event in which the board is present and the ball falls through it into the box. Superficially, the possible event contains two differences from the habituating event, whereas the impossible events contain only one. However, infants hardly bother to look at the possible event, as if they find it the same old stuff. They look much longer at the impossible events, as if they are surprised at a body passing through another or suspended unsupported. Infants consistently look longer at physically impossible events: the disappearance of a toy temporarily occluded by a screen; the passage of one object through another, even when the obstacle is hidden from view by a screen. These results show that at age four months if not earlier, infants notice physical regularities. Their minds are opening to the world (Karmiloff-Smith 1992; Bertenthal 1996).

Rigidity, continuity in occlusion, regularity of motion, and impenetrability of solid bodies are basic to general concepts of physical objects that we use without thinking and that physics represents more precisely. Infants' sensitivity to them shows that from a very early stage their mental infrastructure is disposed to understand the world in the same general ways as adults do.

Infants' sensitivity to continuity and causal regularity, together with adults' psychology such as attentional blink and object-specific perception, offer strong evidence of a mental infrastructure shared by all humans. Because of this infrastructure, our immediate visual experiences are not of sense impressions or bundles of features but of physical objects. General concepts of physical objects are not relative to cultures but are universal to humans. And they are indispensable in structuring our immediate sensual perception.

6

Constructive Memory: Making Time Intelligible

18   More than Files on a Wet Disk

Just as there are active and passive views of perception, there are active and passive views of memory. As in perception, the active view is upheld by scientific findings about memory and its infrastructure. Schacter et al. (1998) summarized: "Psychologists have recognized that memory is not a literal reproduction of the past but instead depends on constructive processes that are sometimes prone to errors, distortions, and illusions." Thus falls a long-standing belief that mind is like a wax tablet that passively preserves the marks imprinted on it. We now know that memories are not stored intact in the brain like computer files on a hard disk. A recollection is not retrieval of a file but reconstruction from bits and pieces. Furthermore, the reconstruction is not a closed process but is much influenced by environmental cues for recall. Thus we are open to the world even in reminiscence.

The mind's spontaneous activity creates structural complexity of our experiences. We have seen that our sensual perception is structured by general concepts of individual enduring objects. We will see that our autobiographic memories are structured by the general concept of causality, which enables us to link what we remember with our present status, to check our memory, hence to distinguish it from fantasy. This knowledge about the constructive nature and conceptual complexity of memory helps us to assess our conscious remembrance and the personal identities we build on it.

Like other areas of cognitive science, memory research is mainly directed at the infrastructural processes underlying our conscious memory. Scientists ask how current events are recognized, stored, recalled, or forgotten; why memories are accurate most of the time; how occasional distortions occur; how present contexts bias recollections. Research has two major discoveries besides the constructive nature of memory. First, the mnemonic infrastructure is highly heterogeneous, with different mechanisms underlying different kinds of memories. Therefore any theory of human nature based on a single kind of memory is too simplistic. Second, what we remember depends equally on how we learn it and how we recall it. Thus an adequate theory of memory should also cover learning, which means taking account of most of our mental activities. This chapter examines the infrastructural mechanisms of memory and their constraints on the nature of what we remember.

The Store Room and the Hard Disk

Perhaps the most venerable and influential model of mnemonic mechanism can be called, in this age of computationalism, the computer model of memory. It is much older than the computer. In *Theaetetus* (191), Plato compared memory with impressions on a wax tablet; perception and ideas imprint on our mind just as a seal-ring stamps on the tablet. Augustine in his *Confessions* (X) likened memory to a storehouse for countless images of all kinds conveyed to it by the senses. Technology has changed tremendously; wax tablets are replaced by magnetic tapes, laser disks, and other media of computer memory, but the idea of memories as stamps persists.

The computer model of memory has three characteristic features. First, memories are stored and retrieved exactly as they are saved. Second, a single process suffices for saving and retrieving all kinds of memories, whether they are skills, procedures, general knowledge, or incidents in personal life. Third, memory is location addressable; like paper files stored in indexed filing cabinets, items are stored and retrieved according to their locations indexed by addresses, probably in terms of absolute time.

In the computer model, a mnemonic item is saved as a unit just like an imprint on a wax tablet or a file or subroutine in the computer memory, and it is retrieved as a unit identical in all details to the original. The unity is not necessarily spatial. Even in a computer, a file is often broken into many pieces and stored in scattered locations on a hard disk. Nevertheless, addresses of locations are always noted and connected so that scattered pieces always combine in exact order on retrieval. Consequently, nothing that is impressed on our mind is ever distorted or lost unless the brain changes or deteriorates, just as computer memories are permanent unless the hardware is overwritten or damaged. We forget because we fail to find the pertinent imprint on our wet hemispheres, as we cannot dig up a piece of information from the millions of files that clutter our computer's hard disks, even when we are sure that the information is there somewhere. We misremember because we activate the wrong impression, as we call up the wrong file.

It is apt to call the three mnemonic characteristics the computer model because they are vital to the digital computer and the computational mind patterned after it. An elementary cycle in computing consists of fetching a string of symbols from a specific address, transforming it in the execution of certain rules, and storing the result in another address. Always, symbols retrieved from an address are identical to the ones stored. There can be no mistake in memory, and physical memory at all times contains a complete and exact record of all there is to retain. Computer memory is famous for its exactitude. Your bank's computer will not forget a single zero in your bank account. It better not.

The computer model underlies the notion of photographic memory. Many people say they wish they had a photographic memory. They may want to think again after reading the case of Shereshevsky (Luria 1968). After hearing a long text or seeing a large tableau of numbers once, Shereshevsky could reproduce it flawlessly, even years later. He could recite it backward or pick it up at any point because he visualized the whole in all its details as a single unit. He did not mix up different units, hence he made no error. Enviable? Look at its price. Suppose you meet a friend who has a new haircut or weight loss, probably you'd say, "Hey, you look different!" You recognize the friend. Shereshevsky was different; he was likely to say, "Have we met?" With his prodigious memory, he would fail to recognize his old friend. He was like computers, whose pattern recognition capacity is easily foiled by minor changes. A computer memory that saves and retrieves a file in its entirety is not analytic. It must invoke the file in all its details, therefore it is rigid, ill suited for coping in the world, and inapplicable to new situations in which some details differ. Chances are slim that we encounter the exact situation repeatedly in a complicated world. Consequently, people relying solely on photographic memory will forever find themselves in totally new situations where their memory is no help. Shereshevsky's memory was of particulars, rich in imagery and affect, but lacking in general concepts that cut across particulars to abstract salient and important features. He could recite a long list of animal names easily, but could not recall only the bird names in the list. The simple task of teasing out meanings of names foiled him. Because he thought in purely concrete terms and failed to see particular items as instances of something general, he could not understand anything abstract and metaphoric.

Shereshevsky's rigid but perfectly durable memory is extraordinary. No one knows how his brain worked. For the memory of ordinary people, which buys flexibility at the price of fragility, the computer model seemed to find support from neuropsychology, but only for a brief time. In the 1950s, while performing brain surgery on epileptic patients to relieve seizures, Penfield (1958) electrically stimulated parts of their exposed brains. The patients were fully conscious, and some of them reported that the stimulation elicited vivid imagery or recollection. One saw a scene outside her kitchen, another heard the laughter of his two cousins in South Africa. Penfield interpreted the reports as memories permanently imprinted in the brain and activated by electric stimulation. Many people cited his observation as evidence of a videorecorder memory. It is, however, under severe criticism. Careful analysis found that of 520 patients, electrical stimulation elicited responses in less than 10 percent, of these only a third experienced something like recall, and there was no way to check if the recall was genuine. Most of the vivid imageries elicited were dreamlike, hallucinations rather than remembrances. Other surgeons obtained similar results. Evidence is scant that the electrodes switched on permanent records of specific events stored in the brain (Loftus and Loftus 1980).

The computer model of memory is attractive for its simplicity. However, scientists increasing find its essential features—exact duplication by a unitary process—to be implausible for human memory. Daniel Schacter (1996:34), who has done extensive scientific research on human memory, asked: "Are computers rememberers?" In answer, he said he agreed with neurobiologist Gerald Edelman (1972:238) who insisted that the richness of human recollection processes "cannot be adequately represented by the impoverished language of computer science—'storage,' 'retrieval,' 'input,' 'output.'" Computer memory is a tool we build to aid our memory. Worshiping the tool detracts us from understanding our own memory.

Memory Systems and Their Malfunction

Let us see how the three characteristics of the computer memory break down in human memory. To start with, human memory is not a unitary phenomenon. Cognitive scientists have differentiated various memory systems or types of memories. The systems differ both in their functions in our conscious life and their underlying infrastructures (Tulving 1995).

Most crudely, short-term memory spans only a few minutes, and long-term memory has indefinite temporal horizons. It takes several seconds to utter a sentence. To grasp the meaning of the sentence, you must be able to remember its beginning when it ends. For this you depend on your *short-term* or *working memory*, which some scientists identify with consciousness.

In everyday discourse, *memory* often refers to *long-term memory*, which concerns events hours or years ago. According to what we remember, cognitive scientists roughly divide long-term memory into two broad classes, declarative and procedural. *Declarative memory* includes contents that, in humans, are expressible in linguistic and propositional forms, although they need not be so expressed. It in turn divides into *semantic memory* for general knowledge and *episodic memory* for episodes and experiences specific to one's personal life. When episodes are not only recalled but located in specific periods, they constitute *autobiographical memory*. What falls beyond declarative memory is by definition *nondeclarative* or *procedural* memory. It includes areas ranging from the habits of using certain phrases, proficiency in crafts and games, skills in athletics, to painting and playing musical instruments, although these activities include considerable declarative elements. Because declarative memory with its linguistic expressions is more susceptible to systematic investigation than nondeclarative memory, we have much more scientific knowledge about it. Nondeclarative memory remains a "vast terra incognita," as Schacter and Tulving (1994:27) described it.

Memory consists of three phases: *learning or memory formation, storage and maintenance*, and *recall*. For particular instances, a later phase depends on the success of an earlier phase. If one is unaware of an event, nothing is stored, maintained, and recalled. For general operation principles, however, the three phases have independent infrastructural mechanisms, so that one can continue to work while the others break down. Malfunctions in the learning infrastructure result in *anterograde amnesia* in which people cannot form new memories. However, they do not prevent the recall infrastructure to operate, as many patients with severe anterograde amnesia retain memories of events formed before learning was derailed. Malfunctions in the maintenance or recall infrastructure result in *retrograde amnesia*, which robs people of their old memories, usually autobiographical ones.

Priming and the Causality of Infrastructural Processes

Episodic memory has temporal and autobiographical coherence; semantic memory has conceptual coherence; skills have practical coherence. These memory systems are systematic on the level of conscious life, where they are genuinely mnemonic. They are supported by vast infrastructures, each of which consists many causal processes. One of the most successful methods to probe infrastructural processes, for memory as for other mental faculties, is priming (see section 9). Some scientists call priming a memory system. If it is a system, it belongs to a lower organizational level than other memory systems. Perhaps it is more appropriate to regard priming as a method to probe changes in the mnemonic infrastructure produced by previous experiences.

Infrastructural processes are automatic. We effortlessly recognize an object as an apple or a sound as a word because most processes in our long-term memory work infraconsciously. We have seen many examples of infrastructural processes that are somehow derailed from coalescing into conscious results, for example, blindsight and subliminal perception. Similar cases occur in the mnemonic infrastructure, where a process operates but fails to produce an explicit recollection. Nevertheless, it leaves its causal effects, which manifest themselves in increased fluency in certain tasks. Priming probes the increased fluency.

Infraconscious processes are always there subserving normal mental operation. Thus priming works for normal subjects; however, it is more spectacular for brain-injured patients. Like a candle in the sun, infraconscious effects are usually overshadowed by conscious experiences. When a brain injury extinguishes a kind of experience, some infraconscious effects become noticeable, like the corona that is visible during eclipses. The corona is not peculiar to eclipses; it exists all the time.

Like many other areas in the science of mind, systematic analysis of memory did not take off until scientists fully appreciated and used the value of nature's experiments, in this case amnesia. When amnesia wipes out conscious recollection, infraconscious retention becomes conspicuous.

Consider, for example, the puzzle, "The haystack was important because the cloth ripped." If you have not heard the sentence before, probably you would think it is nonsense. It makes much sense if it occurs in the context of parachuting, and once you have learned to associate the sentence with parachutes, it is unlikely that you would forget it. Many puzzles can be transformed by proper keys from nonsense to meaningful sentences. "The notes were sour because the seams split," for instance, is transformed by the key word "bagpipe." These puzzles are hard to solve, but once learned, hard to forget. It is interesting that amnesiacs respond to them similarly as normal people. They cannot remember previous exposure to a puzzle, but they tend to remember its key word solution. Few can solve the puzzle the first time. When they encounter it a second time, most solve it readily, although none recall that they have learned it. They simply explain that they solved it because it is easy. Their improved fluency in this regard testifies to the causal effects of remnants of a damaged mnemonic infrastructure.

A causal process leaves its effects, but we usually do not count the effects as the memory of the process. A billiard ball that was chipped and has wobbled ever since bears the effect of incidence but has no memory of it. A new car runs more smoothly after several months, but not from remembered experiences. Memory presupposes understanding and a grasp of the notion of the past, all of which are absent in infrastructural processes. An infrastructural process that merely leaves it effects but fails to contribute to conscious memory cannot be said to remember anything.

Infrastructure for the Formation of Declarative Memory

Memory pervades our mental life and its infrastructure engages extensive parts of the brain. Various domains of knowledge and skill are stored in various regions of the brain. For the formation and recall of declarative knowledge, two areas are especially important: the prefrontal cortex and middle part of the temporal lobe.

The medial temporal lobe, located in the middle of the brain, contains a pair of seahorse-shaped structures called the hippocampus and its surrounding cortex (see figure A.1 in the Appendix). Scientists first discovered its importance in the plight of HM (Hilts 1995). In 1953 a brain surgeon tried to relieve HM's recurrent epileptic seizures by removing a part of his brain that included the hippocampus and its surrounding cortex. The surgery left HM's language comprehension, perceptual and intellectual functions, skill, and knowledge almost intact. Intelligence tests before and after the operation measured comparable IQs at about average. After the operation, however, HM suffered from severe antero-grade amnesia and mild retrograde amnesia. Patients with anterograde amnesia cannot form new long-term memories, hence they cannot re-member anything beyond the brief duration of their working memory. Greg, another patient who lost his hippocampus, flinched every time someone told him about the death of his father, but forgot the conversation a few minutes later and believed happily that his father was still alive (Sacks 1995). Anterograde amnesia suggests that the medial tem-poral lobe is crucial to formation of memory, although not to retention and retrieval.

The hippocampus has bidirectional connections with the parahip-pocampal areas. The parahippocampal areas in turn have reciprocal con-nections with many areas of cerebral cortex dedicated to diverse perceptual and cognitive functions. From all perceptual and cognitive areas in the brain, signals for what we attend to converge on the hippocampus, which automatically analyzes and integrates them in forming a memory. The hip-pocampus is too small to store all the knowledge we acquire in a lifetime. After signals from various areas are combined, they diverge again and return to their respective areas for long-term storage. Thus memories for various visual images are stored in areas dedicated to visual perception of faces, word forms, or physically possible objects. Memories for motor skills are stored in cortical areas for motor control. The arrangement is efficient. Every act of visual perception involves some visual memories. Therefore it is efficient to have the memories stored nearby (Gabrieli 1998; Wallenstein et al. 1998)[1].

Although long-term storage is distributed at diverse functional areas, the initial excursion into the medial temporal lobe is not in vain. The hip-pocampus notes relations among signals, binds them into facets of the memory of an incident, but does not fuse them into an undifferentiated whole. After the signals return to their storage places, the medial tempo-ral lobe retains a kind of crude sketch or "index" to the whereabouts of facets. The index is crucial for activation of relevant traces for con-structing a recollection of the incident. This elaborate mnemonic infra-structure organizes the input into a format both analytic and associative. As memory construction in the formation phase, it is far indeed from simple imprinting.

The hippocampus is thus crucial to memory's ability to analyze and associate. Its importance is evident in experiments with rats learning the water maze. The maze is a large circular tank of opaque liquid with a slightly submerged escape platform at a location relative to salient spatial cues outside the tank. Rats, some normal and some with selective lesions in the hippocampus, are released repeatedly from a fixed location at the edge of the tank until they have learned to find the escape platform. Rats with damaged hippocampus learn as quickly as normal ones, displaying memory adequate for the fixed task. Then experimenters release them from a new location, and the function of hippocampus becomes apparent. Normal rats swim straight to the platform no matter where they entered the maze. They are sufficiently analytic and flexible to compare spatial cues of their new position with cues they remembered from training, and extracted the direction to the platform. Brain-injured rats are totally lost when released from any position other than the one in which they were trained. Whatever memory they have is not flexible enough to be applicable in slightly modified situations. Howard Eichenbaum (1997), who performed many such experiments, concluded that memory's analytic function was impaired with damage to the rats' hippocampus.

Most patients with a damaged medial temporal lobe have anterograde amnesia for both semantic and autobiographical memory. Some young patients with profound anterograde amnesia for everyday episodes, however, manage to learn general knowledge. Early mishaps left them with damaged hippocampus, which produced severe loss of episodic memory. They could not find their ways in familiar surroundings, remember regular schedules, or recall events in the day. However, they attended mainstream schools and attained literacy and factual knowledge in the low average level. They suggest that only formation of episodic memory is totally dependent on the hippocampus. If started early, the parahippocampal cortex can develop the ability to form semantic memory (Vargha-Khadem et al. 1997).

Consolidation and Recall of Declarative Memory

Destruction of a specific part of the hippocampus is enough to result in anterograde amnesia. Destruction of additional areas surrounding the hippocampus brings retrograde amnesia or destruction of previously formed memory. Retrograde amnesia is often graded temporally. Patients tend to remember the remote past more than events just before the sickness. Jim, whose alcoholism-caused amnesia confined him to a mental hospital in 1975, remembered events from the 1940s better than those from the 1960s. Autobiographical memory is most vulnerable to retrograde amnesia. Even at its most dense, the disorder spares many skills, habits, and general knowledge that patients acquired before its onset. HM, for example, retained enough vocabulary to become an expert in crossword puzzles.

Although the medial temporal lobe is indispensable in the formation of memory, it plays a smaller role in recollection. Accidental excitation of it can result in involuntary memories. Voluntary recollection of something specific, however, is beyond its reach. That requires the frontal lobe.

The prefrontal and frontal lobes are crucial to working memory and higher cognitive functions. It is not surprising that they also contribute importantly to the formation and recall of declarative memory. Brain imaging experiments found that people remember word meanings and visual experiences better when their prefrontal lobes are highly excited during learning. When their frontal lobe is damaged, some patients fall prey to spontaneous confabulation; others show great deficiency in planning and organization; still others are incapable of shifting their attention away from an object (Tulving and Markowitsch 1997; Buckner et al. 1999).

Our memory is associative, but not freely associative. Memory must possess certain coherence. Luria described a brain-injured patient who, having read "A peasant had a hen that laid golden eggs," recalled: "A peasant . . . a small bourgeois who liked money . . . had a hen . . . it's very nice to have poultry . . . that laid golden eggs . . . you know how precious gold is in our time of inflation . . ." When each word becomes an atom that freely generates extraneous associations, memory quickly loses the way and becomes baffled.

A comparison of the conditions of HM and Clive Wearing shows the functions of the prefrontal lobe. HM, who lost only his medial temporal lobe, could not remember anything new but could remember old events without confabulation. Wearing, whose brain lesions extended beyond the temporal lobe into the frontal lobe, lost all autobiographical memory, retained some semantic memory, and confabulated compulsively. Without any intention of lying or deceiving, he recalled nonexistent events or erroneous information. One of his favorite confabulations was on word meanings. On hearing "amnesia," for example, he would spin out: "That is from the Latin 'anti-amnesia,' meaning autumn." He confabulated in actions as in words. He persistently treated the hospital where he stayed for seven years as the place he once worked. Confabulation is a symptom of impaired disciplined and strategic recall. Without some integrating mechanism, analytical memory degenerates into atomic memory, where each cue can trigger arbitrary association and confabulation, thus robbing patients of their ability to distinguish fantasy from reality (Wilson and Wearing 1995).

The Infrastructure of Procedural Memory

Relatively little is known about the mechanisms of nondeclarative memory. Initial learning of a motor skill activates not only the cerebellum and primary motor areas but also the frontal lobe, the part of the cerebral cortex associated with higher cognitive functions, including theoretical learning. Neural activities in all three areas at first decreased with practice, as neurons become more selectively sensitive to important features of the skill. Neural dynamics continue for four to six hours after practice as memory for the skill consolidates, a process that can be disrupted by learning a second task. During consolidation, while performance of the task remains constant, activity shifts from frontal areas to the primary motor area, the part of the cortex dedicated to controlling the feel and movement of relevant body parts. Further practice that improves proficiency is accompanied by increasing activity in the primary motor cortex, as more neurons are recruited for the task. It appears that the prefrontal cortex is heavily involved in the initial effortful learning stage, and the primary motor area takes over when the task becomes more automatic (Ungerleider 1995; Shadmehr and Holcomb 1997).

Expanded neural activity in the motor cortex with increasing proficiency is specific to the task and not to body parts performing the task. Proficiency occurs, for example, for performance of an intensively practiced sequence of finger movements and not for the performance of an unpracticed sequence by the same fingers at the same speed. Thus what is remembered is the specific structure of the trained sequence. Specificity and inflexibility are features that distinguish nondeclarative from declarative memories (Ungerleider 1995).

Nondeclarative memory is more robust than declarative memory. Many patients who lose semantic memory retain memory of skills. Frederick, an avid golf player whose retrograde amnesia robbed him of much semantic knowledge including the names of most things, preserved intact not only the motor skill for golf but its jargon and rules. Some anterograde amnesiacs retain limited ability to acquire new skills and habits, although they cannot remember the episodes in which they labored to learn the skill. AC, who had dense anterograde amnesia, could not remember new episodes and general knowledge. Nevertheless, he managed to acquire word-processing skills by using his nondeclarative memory and a memory book that kept track of activities he had already performed (Van der Linder and Coyette 1995; Schacter 1996).

Short-Term or Working Memory

Suppose you are told a telephone number but have no pen to write it down; can you hold it in mind by rehearsal? Can you do the same for a Social Security number? A credit card number? What is the maximum number of random digits you can keep in mind, so that you do not forget the beginning digits when you come to the end? The number of digits measures the capacity or span for your immediate memory. In the 1950s, George Miller found that the immediate memory span for most people is seven plus or minus two items. The limited capacity of our short-term memory, which allegedly creates a bottleneck like a single toll booth on a four-lane highway, is often cited as a support for the symbolic computational mind with its serial information processing. For humans, the picture has changed. Brain-injured patients whose immediate memory span is as short as one or two items nevertheless have normal long-term learning and little cognitive deficiency. To find out why, scientists simulated short-term memory impairment by asking subjects to keep a sequence of digits in mind and simultaneously perform reasoning and comprehension tasks. The experiments yielded results similar to those of nature's experiments. Rehearsal of digits did exact a toll on the performance of the simultaneous task, but not a heavy one. There is more to short-term memory than that.

Scientists now analyze working memory into three components, a central executive and two short-term buffers, an auditory loop for verbal memories, and a visuospatial sketch-pad for pictorial memories. What previous measurements of short-term memory reveal are characteristics of the buffers; the seven-digit span pertains to the capacity of the auditory loop. The exact functions of buffers are not clear. Patients with grossly damaged phonological loop can comprehend sentences that are not too long and complex. The most important and interesting part of working memory is the central executive, a misleading name because it smacks of a homunculus. Unfortunately, little is known of it except perhaps that its neural substrate lies in the frontal cortex. As a locus of attention allocation, its function seems to extend beyond memory. It is so crucial to consciousness scientists are beginning to treat them together (Baddelay 1994; Smith and Jonides 1999).

Probably short-term memory is not only necessary but also sufficient to consciousness. One can survive without long-term memory; but with short-term memory alone, it is not much of a life. "I have just woken up for the first time." This sentence, which recurs endlessly in Wearing's diary, often several times in the same day, expresses a life with working memory but scant long-term memory. Wearing was an outstanding musician before illness left him with severe retrograde as well as anterograde amnesia. He could not recall any episode in his past. He also lost most of his previously acquired general knowledge and musical skill, although not all. His spared memory enabled him to carry on conversations of limited topics, as he still remembered facts such as that air and water both contain oxygen. Like most amnesic patients, his short-term memory survived, he could remember about as many digits as normal people can in the immediate present. Functioning short-term memory enables amnesic to retain words during the production of a sentence, without which they would be unable to comprehend and produce speech. For Wearing, however, the span of short-term memory was everything to him. When he played patience (solitaire), he found the cards' arrangement new and surprising after a brief glance away from them. His life was literally reduced to the present moment, a perpetual first-time awakening in a strange room (Wilson and Wearing 1995).

In sum, different processes underlie different kinds of memory. For both learning and recall, the infrastructure for autobiographical episodes is more vulnerable than that for general knowledge, which is more vulnerable than that for skills. Furthermore, all these underlying mechanisms for long-term memory are more vulnerable than those for working memory, which keeps a person conscious. One can lose all episodic memory and live only in the present moment, sustained by some skill and general knowledge. Without the past and future that only autobiographical memory brings, however, the significance of the present vanishes.

An Infrastructural Model for Associative Memory

The third characteristic of computer memory, location addressability, also fails for human memory. We do not fetch memories by their addresses as we pull files from certain drawers; we never know where they are stored.

One may devise simple rules that correlate temporal order to storage locations, such as first-in-first-out or first-in-last-out. Such rules may help to
explain some behaviors of nonhuman animals, for example, the order by
which birds retrieve the food they have cached. However, they are far too
rigid to explain human memory (Griffith et al. 1999).

Our recollections are often associative, cued not by address but by
content. Locke noted that he could not enter a particular room without
suffering because he associated the room with the death of his friend. The
protagonist in Marcel Proust's *Remembrance of Things Past* described how
the taste of a madeleine soaked in tea reminded him of a similar experience years earlier, thus triggering recollections of his childhood in
Combray. Such content-addressable memory is extremely difficult for symbolic computers to emulate but occurs naturally in connectionist networks.
Therefore connectionism claims to be better model for the human
mnemonic infrastructure (Rumelhart and McClelland 1986).

Symbolic and connectionist models differ not only in ways
mnemonic items are maintained and retrieved but also in ways they are
acquired and encoded. They both seem capable of representing infrastructural processes underlying rote. When learners generalize on given exemplars, symbolic models add more definitions and rules to the mnemonic
infrastructure; connectionist networks try to extract a prototype. After
exposure to a number of dog samplers, for example, symbolic systems try
to frame the definitions for what it is for something to be a dog. Connectionist networks try to extract the central statistical frequencies of
various features in the exemplars and hold them as a dog prototype.
Prototypes are less precise but more flexible, because it is often difficult
to spell out clearly membership criteria of a class of thing in rules and
concepts.

Connectionism provides models for infrastructural processes underlying generic memory and associative memory. After suitable training, a connectionist network not only reacts more strongly to the prototype than to
variants. From now on it will respond to new input similar to the prototype, including deformed cases such as a three-legged dog. It has generalized from exemplars to the prototype to dogs generally. Thus
connectionist networks can support generic memory for general knowledge—to a certain extent (Rumelhart and McClelland 1986).

As explained in section 4, a connectionist network extracts a prototype and stores it distributively in a pattern of connection weights among

many nodes. When it evokes the prototype, it recreates the encoding pattern by excitation. Because connections involved in the pattern are trained to excite jointly, the entire pattern can be re-excited when only a portion of it is presented as input. Thus networks are capable of associative memory. If the item is a complex memory such as dining with a friend in a restaurant, presentation of the restaurant will also excite the pattern of the friend. Thus the network emulates our remembering one thing by its association with another.

Because of their superposed encoding, connectionist networks have no stored items but reconstruct an item anew every time they activate, often in distorted ways. As Rumelhart and McCelland (1986:81) wrote: "This view of memory makes it clear that there is no sharp distinction between genuine memory and plausible reconstruction." This contrasts sharply with the symbolic models that literally retrieve an item exactly as it is stored.

Connectionist networks also have serious weaknesses. They are not analytic and not specific. They can extract a dog prototype as a whole but cannot analyze various features of the prototype separately. Consequently, the kind of knowledge they support is not favorable for reasoning, because reasoning demands the ability to draw the consequences for specific features, such as a dog's bark. Also, because network excitations represent only prototypes, they cannot simulate autobiographical and episodic memory. Memories for specific episodes in one's life require not only generality but particularity, especially the source of each remembered item. I remember not only a barking dog but *the* dog that barks at me on Sunday behind that fence. To achieve such memory a system must be able to separate similar patterns and identify specific ones. Such tasks still beat connectionist networks. Lack of analytic function and of specificity are related. They greatly limit the power of connectionism in representing our mnemonic infrastructure.

Connectionist networks also suffer from the grave threat of catastrophic forgetting (French 1999). A network can be trained to do a type task well, for instance, adding 1 to an input number. Unfortunately, when the network is trained for a second type of task, such as adding 2 to an input number, it often totally forgets what it had learned for the first. Perhaps catastrophic forgetting is not all that surprising when we realize that a network superimposes its memories of various tasks on the same set of connection weights. If weight patterns for the two tasks interfere, acquisition of the second task would disrupt memory of the first. Connectionists are still trying to build models that can overcome catastrophic forgetting. In any case, the gravity of the problem indicates that connectionism alone is far from sufficient for a satisfactory model of our mnemonic infrastructure, not to mention our whole mental infrastructure, as some philosophers claim.

19 Giving Meaning to the Past and the Future

Most data produced by cognitive psychology and neuropsychology reveal facts of the mental infrastructure. To make sense of them, we have to connect them to the larger picture on the mental level. The problem is most conspicuous in memory research, because memory's picture is larger than other mental faculties. Organizing many mental dimensions through long periods of time, it is a large-scale phenomenon ill suited for the confines of the laboratory. Consequently, scientists increasingly turn to study memory in natural living contexts. How do people remember everyday routines and emotional events? How do they maintain their life histories? These questions are important not only for their utility in deciding the accuracy of eye-witness testimonies or the plausibility of suppressing and recovering memories of systematic childhood abuses. More generally, autobiographical memory is closely related to our sense of personal identity (Rubin 1996; Stein et al. 1997a; Pillemer 1998).

Data produced in studying everyday memory generally agree with those produced in laboratory studies. Our mnemonic infrastructure does not keep files in the head addressed by dates. It comprises many constructive and associative processes that are usually reliable but susceptible to distortions. Constrained by the nature of its infrastructure, our conscious memory too is constructive and fallible. David Rubin (1996:4) wrote in the introduction to an anthology of research papers on memories of personal life: "One theme that occurs throughout this book is that autobiographical memories are constructed." Constructive memory sanctions neither historical relativism nor factual fabrication, neither the claim that the Holocaust did not occur nor the best-selling memoir of childhood ordeal under the Holocaust written by someone who grew up in Switzerland. It does not imply that learning something involves no lasting modifications in our brains. It asserts only that modifications are not in the form of a unitary and rigid engram that lights up as a whole with each recall. Modifications are fragmentary, change over time, and contribute differently with different recall conditions. Recollection is a re-collection of bits and pieces biased by present conditions of recall.

Knowing how important memory is to our mental life, it is amazing how much it is taken for granted in theories of mind. Underlying this casual attitude is the tacit conception of memory as stamps on a wax tablet or files on a computer disk. Now that the simplistic conception is overturned, we can see that the structure of our mind, by the very fact that it is capable of autobiographical memory, is much more complicated than most theories depict. How is autobiographical memory possible? What are the minimal mental structures for a person to have it? I contend that the minimal mental structures are simultaneous openness to the objective world and to past and future. For brevity, I consider only declarative memory.

Time: The Difference between Knowing and Remembering

Many psychological experiments designed to explore the experience of memory hinge on the distinction between *remembering* and *knowing* or *being familiar with.* Take the "false fame" experiment. After subjects read a list of nonfamous names, they take a fame-judgment test in which they have to identity famous names from a new list consisting a mixture of famous and nonfamous names, some of which appeared in the old list. They are also told that any name that was on the old list was not famous. The experiment teases explicit memory from familiarity. Exposure to the old list increases subjects' familiarity with a name and hence the propensity to judge it famous. However, if they explicitly recall a name on the old list, they would deny it fame according to the instruction. Results show subjects are more likely to accord fame to names on the old list than to new names. Young (1994) called this false fame effect; subjects who did not read the names accord fame by familiarity. It is more pronounced when they are prevented from paying full attention while reading the old list. The experiment shows that there is more to remembering than familiarity.

Remembering and knowing differ in both general and substantive structures. We will return to substantive differences shortly. Here we note the logical difference to launch our inquiry into a theoretical framework for memory. Familiarity and knowledge pertain only to the present mental state. Remembrance demands the present state to recall explicitly a past state that no longer exists. The distinction highlights a peculiar factor in episodic and autobiographical memory: *temporality*, a concept of the past and by extension that of the present and the future. Thus to see whether a theory of mind can account for autobiographical memory and explain psychological data, we can examine whether it allows concepts of past and present to play substantive roles. Most theories do not. The closed mind, for example, does not have the complexity to accommodate past and future. These notions, together with that of genuine memory, are added by mind designers.

Unlike perception, whose nature is vigorously debated by theoreticians and philosophers, very few explicit theories on memory exist. Nevertheless, from presuppositions on perception and other mental activities, we can infer what various theories assume about the characteristics of memory.

Ecological Memory: Information Containment

The commonsense notion of memory is a quintessentially mental phenomenon. Thus Gibson (1996:263), whose ecological approach excludes recognition from perception, also inveighed against "the muddle of memory" and denied it. Nevertheless, extrapolating ecological reasoning, we can find a notion of "ecological memory" that falls in line with ecological perception.

Perceivers are dynamical systems in the ecological approach. Many, although not all, dynamical rules are invertible. An invertible rule specifies a unique predecessor as well as a unique successor for each state of a dynamical system; thus it is as good for retrodiction as for prediction. There is an ecological sense in which invertible dynamical systems "remember" their past. This sense is perfectly compatible with ecological perception, as neither assumes anything mental.

More generally, in the ecological approach where structures in the optic flow caused by a distal object are defined to be information about the object, structures in a system caused by a past event should also be information about that event; whereas perceivers are just entities that pick up information about distal object, rememberers should be no more than entities that contain information about their past. Therefore plants and planets are all ecological rememberers. A plant contains information about its evolutionary history in its genome; the earth contains information about geological history in sediment and rock formations. The information is readily extracted by biologists and geologists, just as information in the optic flow is extracted by ecologists. In parallel to the theory of information pickup, the theory of *information containment* offers a new concept of memory that gets rid of old-fashioned mental acts: recognition, interpretation, inference, and concepts.

The ecological sense of memory does not distinguish between remembering and knowing in their ordinary sense, because neither applies to it. It does not need the explicit notion of time, just as ecological perception needs no consciousness. It requires only that the present state of an ecological system have certain structures by which it operates fluently. Ecological memory may apply to a limited range of nondeclarative memory. For some primitive skills such as riding a bicycle, memory becomes a reflex. However, such mindless retainment of previous causal effects can hardly account for declarative memory that, as research shows, involves much interpretation and inference.

Memory for the Closed Mind

Contrary to the ecological view from the outside, memory plays a crucial role in the empiricist view of mind behind the veil of perception. Locke (1690:335) put consciousness and memory at the core of a person: "And as far as this consciousness can be extended backward to any past action or thought, so far reaches the identity of that *person*." Hume (1939:261) rejected Locke's substantive self, but retained memory as the base of resemblance on which rest notions of persistence and causality: "As memory alone acquaints us with the continuance and extent of this succession of perceptions, 'tis to be consider'd, upon that account chiefly, as the source of personal identity. Had we no memory, we never shou'd have any notion of causation, nor consequently of that chain of causes and effects, which constitute our self or person."

For a mind closed off from the physical world and with access only to ephemeral and erratic mental representations, memory is the only cement that can produce some kind of coherence, including coherence of personal identity. Any theory of mind that puts so much emphasis on memory should at least address two questions: how memory distinguishes from imagination and how various memories combine. For the second question, the typical empiricist answer is the association of ideas. If mental representation B frequently follows mental representation A, the two become associated. Activation of A will automatically activate B, and one

can predict the occurrence of B given A. Thus prediction involves no inference but the sheer momentum of habit, which was what Hume counted
on. However, it is doubtful whether habitual momentum can ever become
declarative memory. Many processes in our mental infrastructure are associative. Important as they are, they form only one link in the chain of our
conscious remembrance. Connectionist networks are capable of memory
as association of ideas and their performance shows that associative
processes are not analytic. They excel in activating generic patterns but
fail to specify the particularity of the patterns activated. This is a serious
defect because they cannot explain how we remember specific episodes
in the past.

Activation of a mental representation is a present mental state. What
warrants that the present state is a recollection of a past state and not a
mere imagination? The answer that the present state is a memory because
it is caused by the past state would be viciously circular for the closed
mind. Hume made it plain that the notion of causation rests solely on
memory to bring together the various states to establish resemblance and
constant conjunction. Because causation is based on memory, it cannot
justify memory. Empiricism and its closed mind lack the extra dimension
of a persisting physical world to whose causal processes we with our commonsense open mind appeal to check our memories. Consequently
empiricists cannot draw a qualitative distinction between imagination and
memory. Hume's only criterion for memories is that they are more vivid
and lively than fantasies. This criterion easily collapses, as people can have
dim memories and vivid imaginations.

The empiricist framework is too simple to account for the possibility of errors in recollection. Logically, this amounts to the inability to
accommodate tense, which distinguishes between "I now recollect being
thus" and "I was thus then." Ideas of past, present, and future hide in our
familiar ontology of three-dimensional physical objects that endure and
change through time. These are complicated concepts. Unable to account
for them, some empiricists maintain that they are superfluous. Quine
(1960; 1981), for instance, advocated a regimentation of language that
expels all temporal notions except explicit dates. Such regimentation
entails a radical transformation of ontology. Instead of three-dimensional
enduring objects, it posits four-dimensional "worms" that consist of
bundles of features indexed by dates and spatial locations. Quine's example
of such a worm consists of a momentary stage of a silver dollar in your

pocket and a temporal segment of the Eiffel Tower through its third decade, where "consists of" is used tenselessly. Time is totally spatialized in the worm ontology, and with time go change, tense, and genuine memory.

Worm ontology wreaks havoc in physics by destroying mass and motion, but this would not bother Quine the empiricist, for whom the ontology of physical objects is a myth (see section 17). His aim is not psychology but to stipulate the "canonical scheme" for "limning the true and ultimate structure of reality." At this level of generality, however, the structures of mind and of reality that it comprehends are closely correlated. What does worm ontology tell about the memory of the closed mind that understands it?

Consistent with Quine's empiricism, the worm ontology suggests the memory for the closed mind. When to be is to be stimulated, the best hope for getting any sense of persistence is a computerlike memory containing replicas of the surface stimulations—mnemonic representations—that are addressed by dates under which they are stored. Consecutive dates subjectively attached to replicas as their indexes in memory provide a psychological continuity in lieu of enduring physical objects. Mnemonic representations are subject to association, as in Quine's example of associating time slices of a silver dollar and the Eiffel Tower. However arbitrary the association is, the date stamps of the pieces ensure that they are not mere imagination. Instead of seeing a yellow banana and remembering that it was green on Tuesday, the closed mind has only to retrieve from its memory file dated "Tuesday" a green representation and abut it to the yellow representation in sensory stimuli to form the present mental state of experiencing a two-colored banana-worm. Everything is in the present; the past is abolished. Replicas may decay, leading to memory loss. Some files may even be emptied. But as long as representations are available in some files, they can be put together to form the worm that is the personal identity of the rememberer.

This model for the closed mind is a photographic memory where the rememberer has a single four-dimensional photograph continually expanded by replicas of incoming sense impressions. Memory is a *resultant* property where one adds a date to a replica and aggregate dated replicas to form worms. In terms of general structure, the closed memory is simpler than the *emergent* memory of a mind open to the objective world. The closed memory not only has no need but has no possibility to check its memories. Freed from objective constraints, it can do without general concepts of past, present, and future. All it has to do is assemble a present mental state from items present either in the sensory box or in some dated boxes. Because all items originate from sense impressions and are dated, remembering and knowing become identical. The general simplicity, however, is paid for with the price of overwhelming substantive complexity in maintaining dated items. Is the closed mind a rememberer? It is if you regard as a rememberer your digital computer operating without interpretation from you or other users. For human memory, however, cognitive science has found this model to be far too simplistic. Human memory is an emergent property whose characterization requires explicit distinction between past and present that is not found in the mnemonic infrastructure.

How Do Humans Remember?

Research on everyday memory is not easy because scientists often have no way to check the veracity of reports to figure out how people remember their work and leisure. Fortunately, we have an unintended but comprehensive experiment that was widely known, the Watergate hearings. Before the Senate Judiciary Committee, John Dean gave accounts of what happened in a series of meetings in the Nixon White House. His narration, vivid, specific, and replete with details, won him the epithet "the human tape recorder." No, Dean was not a showcase of the computer model; his memory did not operate like a tape recorder at all. The real recorder, turning secretly in the Oval Office, would tell a different story. On the whole, Dean did not perjure, but his account was wrong in many places. Comparing and analyzing his testimony and the transcripts from the tapes for the same meetings, Ulric Neisser (1981) illustrated a characteristic in Dean's memory that is common to many people.

In details, every event in our life is unique. In gross features, many events are similar, which is why we sometimes find life monotonous. Because we tend to leave out details and retain the gist, many episodes become blurred in our memory as they fall into the same generic schema. Sometimes an incident sticks out, but we cannot locate it in a particular episode under the schema. Try to remember what happened at the first conference you attended in 1999. Probably you will recall the hotel lobby, the meeting rooms, people crowding at the coffee table during breaks. Probably you will have difficulty differentiating them from the recollection of lobbies and crowds in the many other conferences you have

attended. These overall impressions constitute the *generic memory* of conferences, which is formed by abstracting from variations of numerous
similar episodes. In contrast, the heated argument you remember having
with a rival in the conference is a specific episode. *Episodic memory* consists of memory of specific incidents, therefore it is more detailed than
generic memory. Suppose you argued with your rival on several occasions.
You remember that he raised a specific point but cannot remember when
he raised it. In this case you have a lapse in *source memory*.

Source amnesia, in which one remembers something but not the date
and context of its acquisition, is an important cause of memory distortion. Intellectuals are prone to source amnesia regarding the origin of ideas.
Freud recounted how he proudly announced the important discovery of
ubiquitous bisexuality to his close friend Wilhelm Fliess, only to be
reminded that this was the very same idea that Fliess told him two years
earlier and that he rejected at the time. Freud eventually remembered the
earlier conversation and surrendered his claim to originality. Probably you
know similar cases in which people never remember. Source amnesia has
worse consequences than the squabble over credits. When people acquire
a piece of information from an unreliable source but later forget the
source, they also forget the dubiousness of the information. Experimental
evidence shows that eyewitnesses sometimes confuse what they saw at the
scene with what they later gathered about the scene, perhaps indirectly.
Thus through source amnesia, hearsay can sneak into sworn eyewitness
testimonies (Schacter 1995, 1996).

Dean's performance at the Watergate hearings demonstrated a
memory like that of common people. Dean knew that witnesses should
stick to the facts and avoid generalization, and his job was to tell what
happened in specific White House meetings. He did the job well. His testimony gave the impression that he had a phenomenal episodic memory.
However, Neisser (1981) found in his analysis that Dean's memory was
often generic and not episodic: "What seems to be specific in his memory
actually depends on repeated episodes, rehearsed presentations, or overall
impressions." Dean had a good generic memory of the series of meetings
but forgot the exact sources of many remarks. In preparing for his testimony, he constructed accounts for individual episodes by various means.
He relied on newspaper clippings and the timing of historical events to
locate a particular dialogue in a particular meeting. Incidents that defy this
method of dating, such as Nixon's million-dollar remark, he arbitrarily

inserted into various meetings and told them as if they were detailed facts of the episodes. Dean's construction made many mistakes. These mistakes were not important for the Watergate hearing, because he did manage to abstract quite correctly the gist of the whole series of meetings. They are important for the understanding of human memory. The confusion of generic and episodic memory contributes to stereotyping and prejudice.

Dean's case shows how unrealistic is the model of memory based all on dated items. People remember well what happened but not exactly when it happened, as dates are usually not part of the original experiences. To date memories and arrange them chronologically are extra steps on which people often fumble. This explains why source amnesia is so common and why episodic memory is more vulnerable than other types of memory. To fix dates, people appeal to events in the natural and social world, as Dean consulted newspaper clippings. In doing so, they assume that the courses of physical events follow definite temporal sequences. If you cannot remember where you put your keys, you would retrace your steps, knowing that keys stay put unless someone takes them. We maintain our memory by opening our mind to the world, which requires a more complicated mental structure than containing information or dating mental representations.

Memory for the Open Mind: Autobiography in the World

Kant (1781:246) stated in his refutation of idealism that "outer experience is really immediate, and that only by means of it is inner experience— not indeed the consciousness of my own existence, but the determination of it in time—possible." Like Quine, Kant was concerned not with psychology but with philosophy. They both addressed the most general structures of the world. Kant was the first to hold that the general structures of the world intelligible to us are closely correlated with the general structures of our mind that make the world intelligible. Therefore we can borrow his philosophical theory to construct a theory for general structures of memory open to the world. His thesis implies that my memory, determination of the consciousness of my existence in time, is possible only because I have immediate experiences of objective world. In short, my autobiographical memory traces a subjective route in the objective world.

Contrary to Gibson, who sharply separated perception and memory, Kant held the two to be mutually interdependent. Together they constitute the minimal mental structures by which we know that our experiences are experiences of objects independent of us. We saw in the preceding chapter that perception involves general concepts of objects, including that of an object's numerical identity. However, we are too hasty in our conceptual analysis. Numerical identity presupposes endurance of the object. To grasp duration and to reidentify the object after it has lapsed from perception, we need some notion of time and hence memory. For Kant, objective experiences depend on synthesis with at least two dimensions. It combines various facets and modes of experiences at each moment and it integrates over a period of time. Consequently, time and process play heavy roles in his analysis of the unity of consciousness.

Unlike Quine, who happily talked about slices of time, Kant insisted that time itself is unperceivable. The world is not a sports telecast equipped with a digital clock that dates events for us. Events are related not to time but to each other. Similarly, we date our experiences not by a time stamp but by their relations to each other and to objective events such as the ticking of a clock. Time is only the form in which we organize events and our experiences thereof sequentially. Mental life is a continuing process. The possibility for us to separate subjective experiences from objects of experiences, according to Kant, depends on the possibility for us to distinguish two sequences of temporal relations: the *objective sequence of events* and the *subjective sequence of experiences of the events*. The two usually do not coincide, because we sample events randomly; our eyes, for instance, jump several times a second to focus on various spots of an unchanging thing.

How is it possible for a person not only to distinguish the temporal ordering of subjective experiences from the temporal ordering of objective events, but also to infer something of the objective order from the subjective order? Kant maintained that it is possible only if our general concepts of objects account for three temporal modes: duration, succession, and simultaneity. And our concepts work because the intelligible world is abiding, conforms to causal laws, and contains coexisting objects in a spatial layout. The general concepts of endurance, causality, and spatial coexistence are presuppositions that our mind has contributed to the process of coherent perception.

Conversely, endurance, causality, and spatial coexistence of the world are also preconditions for us to maintain our autobiographical memory. Kant (1781:245) was at one with Hume in rejecting an abiding self: "I am conscious of my own existence as determined in time. All determination of time presupposes something *permanent* in perception. This permanent cannot, however, be something in me, since it is only through this permanent that my existence in time can itself be determined." What is abiding is not the self but the world. The self or autobiographical memory is a formal construction, but the world is real.

Introduction of the world and its objective time order as a second variable opens up genuine roles for temporal concepts, which are not available to the closed mind confined to its subjective experiential sequence. Within the subjective sequence alone one can distinguish two modes of present experiences or two qualities but not two times. One can only distinguish "I see thus" from "I remember thus," or "I experience thus-at-t_1" from "I experience thus-at-t_2." This explains why memory is distinguished by a faded quality for Hume and a date qualification for Quine. Only by distinguishing my present mental state from the abiding objective world whose events proceed independent of my subjective experiences can I also distinguish two times, "I see it *is* thus" and "I remember it *was* thus." Only in presence of the real world is it possible for me to doubt the veracity of my recollection. The event I remember has long gone, but by presupposing that objective events are causal and follow regular orders, I can check my memory against its effects. Thus I can bring my present perception to bear on my memory.

Kant's philosophical position is too rigid in many places, including the requirement for necessary causal connections. By loosening the requirement, however, we can extract several characteristics of memory of the mind open to the world. Experience is a synthesis, so is memory thereof. In the synthesis, memory is structured by concepts. Because perception and memory are intertwined, memory is not merely recollection but begins with it formation in life experience. Because the presupposition of causality is so important for experiences, we expect it to play a large role in the structures of memory. As it turns out, these are also characteristics of constructive memory as discovered by cognitive science.

The Synthetic Nature of Multimodal Experience and Memory

All memories, semantic or episodic, are acquired one time or another in a person's life. An experience integrates not only various perceptual and cognitive modes but also over at least a short period of time. This brief unity of consciousness is underwritten by short-term or working memory. We will regard it as the first stage of long-term memory.

Live experiences always involve several perceptual modes but are not always verbal; we see, hear, and smell but often do not describe the sights, sounds, and scents. Consequently, many episodic memories are multimodal but not verbal. Several psychological experiments find that remembrance is usually accompanied by some experience whereby one "relives" the original episode, albeit in a faded or distorted way. The vividness of visual imagery and other sensations, including the mental effort of analysis and elaboration, correlates with the accuracy of recollection. The qualitative difference marks autobiographical memory from autobiographical knowledge and semantic memory. You may know that you once wore diapers but have no remembrance of it. Psychogenic amnesiacs who forget who they are may be informed of their identity and biography by relatives and friends, but the information does not constitute memory; it is more like knowing a story of someone else. Remembrance of an episode involves at least some sensory or emotional details experienced by the rememberer not verbally but in their respective modes. Drained of support from other experiential modes, in words alone one merely knows that the episode happened but does not remember it.[2]

Corroboration of other experiential modes gives intensity to verbal recall. Perhaps no one has described various intensities of autobiographical memories better than Proust. The protagonist in his *Remembrance of Things Past* recorded many "undifferentiated memories" and a dozen or so "full and plenary" ones. "Snapshots" of Venice that he retrieved from memory, although accurate and detailed, are flat compared with the incident in which he relived a past moment in its fullness, including such details as the proprioceptive feeling of a posture. Such a moment occurred in his remembrance of standing on two uneven stones in the baptistery of St. Mark's in Venice, a recollection triggered by staggering on two similarly uneven paving-stones years later.

Many people retain vivid imaginary of the details of memorable or emotional experiences, for example, the circumstances when they learned about the assassination of President Kennedy. Some psychologists suggest that recollections of memorable events involve a special mechanism called *flashbulb memory*, which "freezes" the exact details of an event, not unlike imprinting on a wax tablet. Closer investigation shows, however, that flashbulb memory is just autobiographical memory with more vivid multimodal corroborations, more frequently remembered more accurately, but not immune to distortion or decay (Conway 1995).

Many people believe that multimodal details are hallmarks of memory as distinct from mere knowledge. Even so, we can hardly agree with Hume that qualitative details alone suffice for memory, for they can be vivid imaginations. To qualify as an episodic memory, it should not be impossible to be located in a chain of events, some of which have effects that are presently available. Memories survive for their coherence, notably causal and conceptual coherence. For episodic memory, causality enters in the formative stage.

Memory Formation: Analysis and Elaboration of Experiences

Besides various memory systems distinguished by their contents, Tulving (1995) distinguished three memory processes: encoding, storage, and retrieval. Some people are not accustomed to include encoding or learning in memory, but structuring experiences properly is crucial to our ability to remember as well as we do. Perhaps once you had a good laugh from this demonstration: A student read a story, told it to a second, who told it to a third, and so forth; the chain retelling quickly produced funny distortions in the story. If similar distortions occurred in oral traditions, it would be impossible for a people to preserve its memory by recounting its past from generation to generation. Some distortions are inevitable, but researchers found that many oral traditions were remarkably stable over long stretches of time. This is possible because many oral histories had numerous built-in constraints that minimized distortion in transmission. The meter and formulas of Homer, for example, are striking even in translation (Rubin 1995).

Ancient people devised mnemonic schemes to help them remember things by imposing structures on them. A psychologist of memory sneered at such schemes, saying they are unhelpful in remembering mundane information; if he wants to remember items on a shopping list, he simply writes them down. Good for him, but he has forgotten that until recently most of humanity was illiterate. Breezy dismissal of mnemonic schemes for everyday life reveals how easily recording tools obscure the significance of memory. Mnemonic schemes harbor deep wisdom. Much of memory goes into actively structuring impressions, or in modern terminology, in encoding events. Original structuring, which analyzes and elaborates the event to be remembered, is the first step in constructive memory.

Analysis breaks up an experience into interrelated elements so that we can compare them in detail. We not only can say that two experiences are different, we also can tell in what elements or aspects they are different and hence what they have in common. Consequently, analysis facilitates abstraction and generalization, which are crucial for adapting memories to cope with new situations. Whereas analysis emphasizes internal structures, *elaboration* emphasizes relationships to exterior factors and multiple associations. The memory of an event derives much of its strength from its connections to external factors in its context and elements in our background understanding. It is through these elaborating associations that we recall the event. It is important that analysis and elaboration proceed in a *synthetic framework* that holds the elements together in the form of a unitary experience and distinguishes them from associative external elements. Otherwise memory will degenerate into arbitrary association, as in the case of Luria's patient described above whose brain injury caused him to generate random associations regarding a sentence about a peasant's gold-egg-laying haw.

Among coherent factors in the synthetic framework, *causality* reigns, as demanded by the open mind. Many experiments found that accurate recollection of an event depends crucially on the ability to grasp causal relations as the event unfolds. When a narrative omits information about the goal of a goal-directed action, subjects infer the goal and later recall it as if it has been a part of the original narrative. When they see the presentation of a causally jumbled event, they tend to rearrange it to make causal sense and remember it as such. Sometimes, when the event is too badly jumbled, subjects try so hard to understand a crux they overlook subsequent happenings (Stein et al. 1997b).

Memory is poorer for events with several interpretations than for events with unambiguous meaning. Real life experiences, however, are often complicated and confusing. To make sense of them, people rely heavily on knowledge of similar happenings, typical conceptualization for similar experiences, in short, generic memory. The influence of general schema is proved by an experiment in which subjects saw a drawing of two circles connected by a straight line. One group of subjects saw the drawing alone, a second group saw it with the label "eye glass," and a third group with the label "dumbbell." Later they were asked to draw what they saw from memory. The first group reproduced the drawing as it was, the second drew something like an eye glass, the third drew something like a dumbbell. To combine various facets of a complicated input, make some sense of it, and generate some coherent interpretation constitute memory construction in the formation stage.

Conceptual Coherence in Semantic Memory

Although an experience involves many perceptual and cognitive modes, our attention often focuses on only a few. When we are absorbed in reading a book, for instance, we may be oblivious to the surrounding noise. We are concerned daily with a wide variety of topics. Depending on the topic and distribution of attention, we can crudely distinguish *spectacle* and *personal* experiences. Fans in a football game have personal experiences of cheering excitement but only spectacle experiences of athletic exertion. Intellectual pursuits are mostly spectacle activities whose motives are ulterior to the topics pursued. The motion of planets, for instance, is ulterior to the motives of a physicist studying them. Since the topic does not involve spectators personally, it directs spectators' attention away from their own personal conditions. Detached from personal conditions, it is retained as a semantic memory. In contrast, topics of personal experiences involve the mental subjects themselves. Emotional events are personal; even when lovers think mostly of the beloved, their own bodily conditions in emotional arousal capture attention and are retained in autobiographical memory. Of course, no experience is purely spectacle or purely personal. But depending on its emphasis, an experience is likely to yield either semantic or autobiographical memory.

Everything we know is learned and constitutes our memory, and learning is always an experience. However, usually we distinguish knowledge from memory. You ask someone if he knows who was the third American president. If he says he forgets, he means he knew it once. Regarding personal topics, memory means more than knowledge; it involves multimodal recall, as discussed previously. Regarding spectacle topics, knowledge means more than memory. To know something is not merely to memorize it; it implies understanding, the ability to integrate the topic into a conceptual framework in which it makes sense.

Besides causal coherence of worldly events, our knowledge also possess conceptual coherence. Most of what we learned was conceptualized and organized by our ancestors, which is why an average student now can learn in a few years what many geniuses strived for for decades. Coherence and elaboration of factual and theoretical knowledge explain why source amnesia is so common. Semantic memory is a prevalent case of source amnesia; we forget how we come to know what we know. A learning experience includes the sight and smell of the library, mental exertion and frustration, the ache in the back from sitting too long. In semantic memory, however, these become mere accidental contexts to what we are struggling to learn, and as such they are easily detached and forgotten. The fact that Paris is the capital of France has a lot to do with other geographic facts but little to do with the circumstance of my learning it. Objective information and logical inference have their own coherent structures that have no room for the experience of learning. Declarative memory, sensitive as it is to coherent structures, integrates input into semantic memory by dissociating it from learning contexts. Consequently, we know many facts without remembering how we learned them (Tulving 1995; Gardiner and Ramponi 1998).

Reconstruction of the Past

Remembrance attains its full meaning in autobiographical memory. What do our recollection processes tell us about ourselves? Undoubtedly we forget and misremember, especially things that happened in the remote past. However, many experiments show that on the whole, people remember recent events quite accurately. Even young children are quite reliable in their recollection of everyday events that they can understand, if they are not misled by adult instructions or insinuations (Stein et al. 1997a). How do we recall the past?

Scientists distinguish *spontaneous occurrence* of a memory from effortful *strategic recall*. Tidbits of memory dance spontaneously like bubbles in the stream of consciousness. They are not recalled voluntarily but are triggered by tiny cues, either external or inherent in a preceding thought. Sometimes a small thing can trigger a flood of memory, as old tune brings to mind a long-lost love. Deliberate recollections of specific events or facts are not automatic and effortless. What did you do on New Year eve of 1998? What happened in your senior year in high school? To retrieve the memory, you have to think and search for the proper cues. Such a search is a kind of inference process, and people have many strategies for it.

We invoke memory by certain cues. Because facets of a memory are multiply related by analysis and elaboration, different cues may evoke different facets with different intensities, so that an event may be remembered with different nuances. Besides a specific event, cues can also evoke the generic memory for similar events and the semantic memory for relevant general information. These evoked factors usually do not fit perfectly. Some inferential processes fill the gaps and smooth out conflicts to create a rich experience of recollection.

Kelley and Jacobi (1993) did an interesting experiment that revealed the role of inference in recollection. Subjects studied a long list of words. Later they saw cues of word fragments and tried to recall the word on the list, for instance to recall *brick* in response to the cue *b-i--*. They also reported whether their memory of each word from the original list was clear, marginal, or nil. Unknown to the subjects, some cue fragments could be completed only by words not on the studied list, so that they could not evoke a memory. Among the deceptive cue fragments, some were easy and others difficult to complete. For difficult cues, few subjects reported they remembered. For easy cues, significantly more subjects reported having a "clear memory" of the original word. These subjects did not get the sense of familiarity and the experience of remembering from memory traces because there were none. Instead, they inferred the familiarity and experience from the ease of performing the task. Such inference contributes to memory construction in the recall stage.

A recollection of the past is itself a present experience and consequently is susceptible to present influences. In 1973 a group of subjects reported their attitudes toward certain salient social issues. In 1982, the same subjects rated the same issues and recalled their attitudes back in 1973. What they recalled were much closer to their present attitudes than those they reported in 1973. Other experiments confirmed similar "biases in retrospection." Our present state of mind colors our recollection of the past (Schacter 1995).

With each recollection, activated memories are strengthened and perhaps modified slightly by factors present in the recalling experience. Uneven frequencies of recalling preferentially strengthen those memories one is inclined to recall and weaken those one is glad to forget. Depressive people tend to recall sad memories that further fuel their depression. Such process gradually changes autobiographical memory and shapes the personality.

Multiple Perspectives in Autobiographic Memory

A salient characteristic of constructive memory is that we can recall an event in different ways and see the past from various perspectives. Try to remember something from your grade school years. Do you see yourself a child or do you see the circumstance from a child's eye point of view? Freud distinguished *field* and *observer memories*, the former recollects from the first-person and the latter from the third-person viewpoint. A field memory for someone who gave a lecture would consist of writing on the blackboard and glancing at the audience. For the same event, an observer memory sees through the eyes of a listener and remembers the lecturer gesturing and speaking. Scientific surveys find that over 40 percent of recollections take the third-person view. Observer memories tend to dominate the remembrance of childhood; field memories tend to dominate recent or emotional recollections. Often a person can shift between field and observer perspectives depending on what aspects of the event he recalls. People are likely to adopt the observer perspective when asked what they saw, and the field perspective when asked what they felt. Field and observer memories of the same event are accompanied by different affective intensities and experienced differently. They testify to the constructive nature of memory.

The variability of perspective in memory is an example of our mental capability to examine an object or event from many possible angles. It has profound consequences for personality and self-knowledge. We experience all present events from the first-person perspective. Observer memory illustrates our ability to detach ourselves, abstract from certain details, and redescribe a situation from a different point of view. For example, griping flashbacks and fantasy-impregnated memories that torture people with posttraumatic disorder are invariably from the field perspective. A powerful therapy for the disorder is the exercise in which patients try to put themselves in the observer perspective by expressive writing. One participant remarked, "it helps me to look at myself from the outside" (Robinson 1996:207). Such detachment, by which we free ourselves from the grip of immediate experiences and see ourselves in the third person as well as in the first person, is essential to a full sense of the autonomous self, as discussed in section 26. It is indispensable for the formation of autobiographical memory, where we see ourselves leading our lives in a shared world.

In sum, results gathered by cognitive research supports models of memory based on causality, not dates. Dates are among the first things that we forget, but causality plays leading role both in memory formation and recall. Furthermore, little evidence exists for the empiricist claim that memory is the sole base of the concept of causality. We may not have the concept if we have no memory, but dependence is not only one way. Causality is presupposed by memory from beginning to end. It enables a person to open his mind to the world, to organize events into an objective sequence, grasp it, and remember it as distinct from the order of his subjective experiences of the events. He may be confused, as in the case of source amnesia, but he attributes the mistake to himself. He knows that objective events have many causal consequences, of which he can witness only a fraction. By looking for their causal fallout, he can have multiple accesses to past events, which confirm or correct his subjective recall. By knowing himself to be a causal agent, he can adopt both the field and observer standpoints in constructing his autobiography. Dates are static; causality is dynamic. Retrieving dated files can be achieved by a closed mind; reckoning with causality can be achieved only by people active in the world. Thus memory, which seems to be an inner activity, actually depends on mind's openness to the world.

Emotion and Reason: Making Purposes Intelligible

20   From Bodily Feeling to Motivation

Of all the mental faculties considered in this book, emotion is the one most explicitly dependant on our physical bodies. Therefore promoters of the computational mind, which is abstract and disembodied, seldom discuss emotion. Nevertheless, emotion has its own form of being closed. An influential school treats emotion as bodily feeling, a pure inner awareness. The bodily-feeling model has been criticized for leaving out essential dimensions, most important, emotion as the motivator of action. To motivate, emotion must be open to people and events in the world. Therefore it must be understood on the engaged-personal level where the emotional person, although replete with impulses and bodily feelings, cares about others. It is a complex experience with many facets, including a rational aspect. Analysis of emotion brings out the difference between mere embodiment and the openness of mind.

Emotional Phenomena on the Situated-Personal Level

Emotion is not as clearly delineated as perception or memory. Thus we start on the engaged-personal level to clarify emotional phenomena before delving into their infrastructures. Listen to Siegfried in the third opera of Richard Wagner's *The Ring of the Nibelung*:

Beneath my feet the ground seems to sway!
Anguish and yearning conquer my courage.
On my heart, beating wildly, trembles my hand.
Am I a coward? Is this what fear is?

Siegfried was orphaned at birth and grew up playing with beasts. Having never tasted fear, he set out to learn it. He slew a dragon, shattered a god's spear, penetrated the fire that would consume all but the intrepid, and saw the sleeping Brünnhilde, whom he discovered to be a woman! His heart grew feeble and faint as he called out to his mother for help, saying that he finally knew fear.

"Is this what fear is?" To what does *this* refer? Does it refer to Siegfried's pounding heart and trembling hands; to his anguish and yearning; to his realization of being in a totally new situation; to his gut feeling of something important; to his premonition of future catastrophe; or to all these woven intricately? What is fear? If you were in Mime's position, could you enlighten young Siegfried?

What is emotion? Despite our rich emotional experiences, we find emotion baffling and difficult to explain. Our commonsense ideas of it seem to be full of contradictions. We regard it as the antithesis to reason, but we also acknowledge that it often goes hand in hand with rational judgment. We are so keen on its active and motivating power we build it into etymology; "emotion" literally means outward movement. Nevertheless, we just as frequently talk about passion, passive emotion that overwhelms us and holds us helplessly in its grip. By observing fear and anger in almost all humans and many nonhuman animals, we surmise that emotions are biological, but we also realize that many are molded by society. Emotion is so fluid and messy that philosopher Paul Griffiths (1997) concluded that it is unlikely to be a useful category in scientific theory.

Emotion accentuates the concrete details and specific characteristics of each incident we experience. Therefore its substance is more resistant to theoretical systematization and generalization than other mental faculties. Most of our emotional experiences are poorly conceptualized and nonverbal. That is why we admire poets for giving voice to our deep feelings. To depict the great variety and rich nuance of human emotions, science pales besides the arts and literature. As an optimist, however, I think science has its own advantage in investigating the more general characteristics of emotion. Let us first differentiate the kinds of emotions, tease out some of their aspects, and consider influential theories.

The Diversity and Generality of Emotions

Systematic studies must have some ways to differentiate emotional experiences into distinctive modes or emotions. An obvious starting point are the vocabularies of natural languages, which have proved their worth by enabling people to express emotions with considerable success. Unfortunately, it is more complicated than first appears. The English language has roughly 400 words for emotional states. We love and hate, pity and envy, fear and dare, hope and despair, panic and relax, respect and resent, rejoice and regret; we are happy and sad, calm and angry, content and jealous, smug and insecure, eager and gloomy, proud and ashamed, encouraged and embarrassed, enamored and disgusted, impassive and surprised. More variety shows up in other cultures. Chinese has more than seven hundred words about emotion. At the other extreme, Chewong in central Malaysia has only a handful, roughly corresponding to angry, frightened, jealous, ashamed, proud, want, and want very much. Ommura of Papua has even fewer emotional words if it has any at all (Heelas 1996).

Undoubtedly emotion, at least human emotion, has an inalienable social dimension. It is partially structured by the culture in which we participate, because it plays crucial roles in social intercourse. Love, for instance, takes many forms that vary from culture to culture: parental, filial, erotic, romantic, Platonic, Christian. The romantic love we take for granted nowadays is a latecomer even in Western civilization, not to mention in other cultures. Some anthropologists distinguish between shame culture and guilt culture; shame and guilt are perhaps the two emotions most effective for social control. An example of shame culture is the Homeric society, in which tarnished honor was the worst that a person could endure. An example of guilt culture is Christianity, whose original sin injects everyone with guilty feeling.

To acknowledge the great variety in emotional expressions is not to give in to a relativism that abandons the systematic inquiry or confines the inquiry to within specific cultures. To acknowledge diversity is to reject extreme relativism that denies the possibility of cross-cultural understanding. We have agreed on something general about emotion when we count Chewong's *chan* as an emotional term, even when we are not sure whether it means anger exactly. What are the general features by which we recognize emotions in people around the globe?

Here it is advantageous to look first at how we attribute emotions to other animals. Fear is the one most studied, partly because experimenters can readily instigate fear in animals by torturing them under controlled conditions. They find that under conditions that are naturally interpreted as dangerous, many animals show fixed behavioral patterns that can be interpreted as fear. For example, rats adopt a frozen posture, accompanied by elevated heart beat and blood pressure. Some threatened animals emit specially intonated distress calls. These responses, which we interpret as fear expressions, ensue automatically once triggered. Some triggering stimuli are innate. Laboratory-raised rats never exposed to cats freeze the first time they see a cat, although they have not learned how dangerous it is. Other triggers are learned by association. Rats exposed to a tone followed by an electric shock quickly learn the tone as a dangerous signal, so it alone is sufficient to trigger fear response. Whatever the trigger, the fear response is the same set of involuntary physiological changes and fixed behavioral patterns. Thus we can say that fear is a generic emotion, at least in rats (Ledoux 1995).

Generic emotions are instinctive and common to a species. They occur impulsively and rapidly under a class of typical situations, involve pronounced physiological changes and perhaps fixed behavioral patterns, and preferably are subserved by specialized infrastructural processes. Are some generic emotions common to all humans whatever their cultural backgrounds? Scientists have compiled many lists of human "basic emotions." The lists vary, but anger, fear, happiness, and sadness consistently show up in most (Ben-Ze'ev 2000).

Facial expressions and voice inflections are the most common emotional behaviors, as they are the quickest ways to communicate emotion. In distinction to other facial movements, they involve dedicated infrastructural processes. The true smile of joy and the posed smile in front of a camera involve different muscles. People with paralyzed faces are unable to feign smile, but they can nevertheless lift the corners of their mouths in smiles of heartfelt pleasure. Not only production but recognition of emotional expressions have specialized neural substrates. Scientists found brain regions that are necessary for the recognition of happy, frightened, and disgusted faces. When these regions are damaged, patients fail to differentiate expressions, although they retain the ability to differentiate faces. They can tell whose face it is but not whether it is happy or sad (Ekman and Davidson 1993; Damasio 1997; Hyman 1998).

By surveying snarling dogs, sulky monkeys, wailing infants, and many other animals, Charles Darwin noticed certain commonalities in emotional expressions. For a long time, however, his observation was brushed aside by behaviorism and social constructionism, which attributed all facial expressions to social conditioning. Darwin's insight has enjoyed a revival since the 1970s. Many scientists find that some emotional facial expres sions are universal, perturbed only slightly by cultural variables. When they systematically asked people in different cultures to state the emotional terms in their own language for photographs of Caucasian facial expressions, the results were remarkably consistent. Even preliterate people in New Guinea and west Iran, untouched by Western television and printed literature, readily identified expressions of fear, anger, sadness, and enjoyment. A culture may have trained its people to hide their emotions and deadpan in public. When the masks fall in private, however, their faces wear the same natural expressions. Results of cross-cultural studies are controversial. Not everyone is convinced that they prove the universality of facial expressions. Nevertheless, they do put on the defensive doctrines of unmitigated social conditioning and cultural relativism (Ekman 1994).

Based on scientific results from diverse areas, we can reasonably hypothesize that fear, anger, happiness, sadness, and perhaps disgust are basic human emotions. Their identification is scientifically important. As products of biological evolution instead of social conditioning, they have a better chance to be shared by other animals. Thus animal experiments and models can help shed light on their infrastructures. Consequently, we know much more about basic emotions than more sophisticated ones.

Feeling and the Bodily Feeling Model of Emotion

Emotions are never simple, not even basic ones. What, for instance, is anger? In *On the Soul* (4030) Aristotle reported two contemporary theories. Naturalists said: "Anger is boiling blood and hot stuff around the heart." Dialecticians countered: "No, no. Anger is the desire to retaliate or the like." Both schools have influential descendant. Through Descartes and James, the ideas of the Greek naturalists developed into the bodily feeling model of emotion. Perhaps it is more appropriately called the bodily condition model, as it treats emotion mostly as bodily responses to certain stimuli, to which feeling is an epiphenomenon. In resonance with behavioral psychology, it dominated the discourse on emotion for most of the twentieth century and enjoys a large following today. Then, in the wake of the computer comes the computational mind, which has no body and no bodily feeling. Fortune turns to heirs of Greek dialecticians, who developed various computational models in which emotion is mainly appraisal of stimuli and calculation for beneficial responses. An extreme form of these models is affective computing, in which engineers try to make computers recognize and simulate emotion without mention of the body or bodily feeling (Picard 1997; Power and Dalgleish 1997).

Emotion is closely associated with mood, desire, and feeling, and is sometimes confused with them. These are vague terms with many meanings, and I do not attempt definitions. I take emotion as a broad complicated experience that includes desire and feeling.

Feeling is often used as a synonym of emotion, but it has other meanings. In its most general sense, it is *awareness*. Thus all conscious experiences, emotional or not, have certain feeling. Another sense of feeling, colloquially called gut feeling, refers to the inarticulate or underarticulated contents of experiences. It includes the experiences of our bodies that we can describe only vaguely, but it need not involve the viscera. A gut feeling as a hunch or intuition can be intellectual, referring to the poorly conceptualized part of our knowledge. Because emotion is far more difficult to articulate than cognition, much of it belongs to gut feeling.

The feeling that is inextricably associated with emotion is bodily feeling. Echoing the Greek naturalists, Descartes (1985:325) introduced what is called the bodily feeling model of emotion. He distinguished various functions of the body and soul and sketched a causal chain that leads to emotion, which he defined as a perception of the soul. Stripped of talk about "animal spirit" or the motion of the pineal gland, his account is not entirely outlandish: sensual perception of certain situations, especially factors relevant to one's own well-being, generates various changes in the body. Passion is thus the soul's perception of the bodily commotion.

If Descartes's ideas were obscured by his archaic physiology, James (1890:1066) made it clear while putting almost all emphasis on physiology. He could not conceive an emotion of fear without the feeling of quickened heartbeat, shallow breathing, trembling lips, weakened limbs, goose flesh, or visceral stirring. Thus he concluded that bodily changes make up all moods, affections, and passions: "bodily changes follow directly the perception of the exciting fact, and that our feeling of the same changes as they occur *is* the emotion." To the commonsense saying that we weep because we are sad, strike because we are angry, flee because we are afraid, he countered that we are sad because we cry, angry because we strike, afraid because we take flight.

Bodily feeling can be analyzed into bodily conditions and the feeling thereof. Bodily conditions do not presuppose consciousness; feeling or awareness thereof does. To any conscious being possessing interioception and proprioception, feeling automatically accompanies bodily conditions. To articulate the feeling or awareness, however, is far more difficult. Thus although this model defines emotion as the feeling of bodily changes, its discussion almost entirely concerns changes. It is essentially a physiological and behavioral model, with the tacit assumption that the emotional organism is conscious of its own bodily states. Like most approaches to conscious experience through physiology or behavior, feeling is viewed as a qualia, an epiphenomenon, a causally impotent coating of physiology. The weakness of this general view is that the model fails to distinguish emotion from nonemotion. Even less can it account for the motivational aspect of emotion.

Bodily conditions that are usually associated with emotion include physiological changes such as rising heart rate or falling skin temperature, behaviors such as altered facial expression and voice intonation, and movements such as posturing or running. They have the advantage of being externally observable and can be monitored in laboratories. However, they are too common and crude to distinguish emotions, at least in humans. The same physiological change can be emotional or nonemotional, or interpreted as different emotions. The thumping heart and trembling hands, which Siegfried interpreted as fear, a less intrepid man may see as love, struck by a lightening bolt, as Sicilians say; or it may be the product of physical exhaustion. Fixed behavioral patterns, such as the freezing posture of frightened rats, may help differentiate emotion in nonhuman animals, but not in humans. Innate fixed behavioral patterns such as facial expressions may exist for some basic emotions, but we can freely suppress or feign them. A man running from a bear need not be frightened; he may be luring the beast to a trap. Conversely, a frightened man need not scream and flee; he can grit his teeth and fight. With our freedom of action, our behaviors are so varied that try as behaviorists did, they failed to come up with credible criteria for even fear and anger, and they fared even worse for more delicate emotions such as love and hatred.

Othello killed Desdemona out of jealousy. The active aspect of emotion has no place in the bodily feeling model. If we feel angry because we strike out, our anger does not induce but is induced by our striking. Nor can anger motivate further action except perhaps to cool our boiling blood, as it includes no cognizance of any other object or goal.

Undoubtedly Othello had many bodily feelings; however, none of them appeared as factors in his consideration of action, which focused on Desdemona's supposed infidelity. To motivate action, emotions must have more cognitive elements than awareness of bodily conditions.

The Jamesian theory is an example of the *resultant view* in which a mental state is the sum of its elements. It observes that if we subtract bodily feeling from a familiar experience, we get a dispassionate intellectual assertion. From this it concludes that the original experience is the sum of two parts, a cognitive part plus emotion as bodily feeling. It contrasts with the *emergent view* in which bodily feeling is not something we add to cognition; it is integrated finely with the cognitive elements to produce a far more complicated mental structure we experience as emotion. When frightened, I am aware not only of my bodily condition but, more important, of the fearful situation and object. An adequate characterization of fear must account for cognizance of the fearful object and evaluation of the situation, not merely as a trigger for the physiology of fear but as part of the emotion itself.

The bodily feeling model is too crude to account for many features of emotion. Bodily feelings close on themselves. It makes no sense to say that you are afraid of a snake if fear is nothing but your feeling of quickened pulse and shallow breath. Similarly, it makes no sense to say that you love your children if love is nothing but a warm feeling of the heart. Reduced to private feelings in which a solipsist licks himself, emotion loses most of its characteristics and significance.

The Embodiment and Situatedness of Emotion

Bodily feeling models highlight what computational models of emotion missed: emotion is radically embodied and cannot be dissociated from all bodily feeling. Many people regard the disembodied mind's computational love to be as passionate as a marriage based on calculation of the spouse's wealth, frailty, and gullibility. Even those who accept artificial intelligence as true intelligence hesitate to call the artificial emotion professed by computers true emotion. Thus astronauts in *2001: A Space Odyssey* acknowledged the computer HAL's intelligence but declined to admit that he had emotions, although he used emotional words. The inconceivability of emotion without bodily feeling implies that the latter is an essential and inalienable aspect of the former. However, it does not imply that bodily feeling *is* emotion.

Neither the bodily feeling nor computational model of emotion out-
grows all the deficiencies of its forerunner. Aristotle criticized naturalists
for noticing only the matter of emotion and dialecticians for noticing only
the form. Matter and form, he insisted, are both crucial to all things, as it
takes both bricks and architecture to make a house. Aristotelian synthesis
encompasses not only material and formal aspects of emotion but also
the social context in which emotion is expressed and assessed. In *Rhetoric*
(1378) Aristotle analyzed an emotion into three factors: the state of mind
of the emotional person; the target of the emotion; and the grounds for
being emotional. For example, "anger may be defined as a desire accompanied by pain, for a conspicuous revenge for a conspicuous slight at the
hands of men who have no call to slight oneself or one's friends."

Aristotle's first factor emphasizes the mental context of emotion. For
persons with different states of mind, the same event can induce different
emotions, or different intensities of the same mode of emotion. Shakespeare described how Caesar's power incited in Cassius and other con-
spirators various degrees of envy, but in Brutus it was the agony of
choosing between friendship and the good of Rome.

Emotion can vary in intensity and endurance. There are protracted
emotions such as love and flash emotions such as surprise. Moods are
usually persistent and subdued in intensity. Protracted moods and emotions cannot always maintain a high level of intensity, if only because
intense emotions consume so much energy one is soon exhausted. Hence
emotional intensity fluctuates, sometimes violently. When emotions flare
up, they absorb attention, but during much of their lifetime they bubble
at the periphery of attention, subtly influencing our attitude toward other
matters. Most theories concentrate on flash emotions and flare-ups, treating the subdued phase as mood, inclination, state of mind, or disposition to emotion. Intensity and persistence belong to the *affective aspect* of
emotion, which also covers bodily conditions and our feelings thereof. The
affective aspect falls under Aristotle's first factor, as it accounts for the state
of being of an emotional person.

Aristotle's second factor brings out what I call the *openness* of
emotion. In our emotions, we open ourselves to people and events in the
world. We are angry with someone, surprised by something, saddened by
an event, pleased with a circumstance. The object of an emotion can be
physical, as the friend one is angry with; or illusory, as the ideal beloved
in the eyes of the lover; or anticipatory, as tomorrow's market that worries

speculators; or extremely vague, as the unknown lurking in the dark that frightens us. Objects of emotions are usually particular persons, things, events, or circumstances. When they are not particular entities but the general states of the world, real or illusory, we often talk about moods. A person in an anxious mood finds the world generally fearful; one in a happy mood finds it generally cheerful. Nothing prevents a moody person from being emotional about specific objects, and often mood-congruous emotions are amplified in intensity. Hamlet in his melancholy was disgusted with a world out of joint and his mood accentuated his loathing for his mother's infidelity and uncle's depravity.

Suppose I am angry at a friend because I think he badmouths me behind my back. On learning his innocence, my anger evaporates, leaving behind a guilty feeling for having wronged him. Generally, an emotion rises and falls with a belief. When we say someone's emotion is reasonable or not, justifiable or not, we are actually referring to the belief that is a part of the emotion. My anger is unreasonable if it is perpetuated by my refusal to take seriously the evidence in favor of my friend. Belief and evaluation belong to the *cognitive aspect* of emotion, Aristotle's third factor.

Unlike bodily feeling and computational models of emotion, Aristotelian synthesis goes beyond what occurs underneath the skin and puts the emotional person squarely within the social world. Discussions of emotion and temperance pervade Aristotle's *Ethics*, and his *Poetics* explores the emotional impact of tragedy. The most systematic analysis of various emotions, however, occurs in *Rhetoric*. Good rhetoric arouses emotion in the audience, and to achieve this the orator must know why and how people become emotional. Emotion is not merely a private feeling but plays crucial roles in interpersonal relations. This Aristotelian insight was confirmed by results in the neuropathology of emotion. Brain-injured patients with emotional deficiency are also disabled in social knowledge and social judgment. For example, they consistently find agreeable faces that normal people find untrustworthy and unapproachable (Adolphs et al. 1998).

Most orators aim to elicit some reaction from their audience. Thus the discussion in *Rhetoric* touches on a fourth dimension of emotion: its motivational power. Many people talk about the *appetitive aspect* of emotion, which comprises desires activated under the circumstance. Desires are not merely blind appetite or behavioral impulses. Water has no desire to go anywhere although it always runs downhill. A system capable

of desiring must also be capable of anticipating a possible goal or satisfaction; that is, capable of believing. Thus emotional desires reinforce the
openness of emotion. They often invoke images of hedonism and compulsion, but both impose too restrictive a scope on desire. Many of our
desires are hedonistic and satisfiable by pleasure, especially sensual pleasure
and the psychological elation of gratified self-esteem. Pleasure and the
absence of pain, however, do not exhaust our desires. We can desire anything, including an action or a state of mind that is not pleasurable. Desires
can be compulsive or rational, and either type can be fomentive (emotion instigating) or conative (action motivating). I want to emphasize the
action-motivating role of emotion, as it highlights the deficiency of the
computational models. Computations of costs and benefits can yield tons
of answers but no action. As we will see, neuropsychological results show
that to translate answers into actions, cognition must be combined with
conative emotions. As Aristotle noted in *Ethics* (1139a): "The intellect alone
moves nothing."

21   Impulsive and Cognitive Circuits Underlying Emotion

By integrating openness to the world, bodily feeling, cognitive evaluation,
desire, and motivation, emotion spans the range of our mental life. It is
underwritten by a vast and complex infrastructure that scientists are just
beginning to sort out. This section crudely sketches the infrastructure,
emphasizing how it supports the impulsive and rational aspects, and
explains the diversity and generality of emotion.

The Body in Mind

James rightly stated that emotion is inconceivable without bodily feelings.
Emotion engages not only many areas in the brain but the whole physical body. Thus it provides the strongest ground for Damasio (1994) to
maintain that our mind is not merely embrained but fully embodied. The
operation of the brain in the body is much more complicated than the
operation of the brain in a vat stimulated by electrodes. Two great circuits,
nervous and circulatory systems, connect the brain to other parts of the
body. From every muscle, joint, and sensory and internal organ, peripheral nerves originate and move to the central nervous system, some enter-
ing the brain at the spinal cord, others at the brain stem. From there,
signals from the periphery project to various parts of the brain dedicated

to perception, emotion, reasoning, and sensorimotor and body regulation, which integrate on a larger scale to produce unitary conscious experiences. Evidence shows that artificial excitation by electrodes and natural excitation by peripheral signals elicit different activities in brain neurons. Not only neural responses but sensory experiences vary depending on whether the sensory cortex or a sensory organ is stimulated. Experimental subjects are conscious of a single electric pulse applied to their skin, but not if the pulse is applied to their brain. They are unaware of electric pulse trains applied to their brain that last less than half a second (Libet 1996).

From parts of the brain, signals move to parts of the body. Some regulate bodily conditions automatically and unconsciously, although the physiological results of such regulation can often be consciously experienced. Other signals activate voluntary movements of muscles and joints, whose actual behaviors are detected and fed back to the brain by ascending nerves as proprioception, thus completing the control circuit of action.

The neural system dominates most discussions of brain and mind. In an organism, however, it does not work alone. The circulating blood stream is more than a life-support system for the brain. It participates in mechanisms underlying mental processes by transporting chemicals such as hormones and neural transmitters and modulators. It spreads chemicals secreted from one part of the brain to other parts, changing their excitation patterns; distributes chemicals from the brain and glands throughout the body, affecting the functions of its parts; and carries chemicals generated from bodily activities to the brain, modifying its operation. Unlike the synaptic excitation of individual neurons, hormones and other chemicals influence a large group of neurons continuously. Such diffuse and imprecise chemical modulation has no place in the computational mind or brain, but it has profound consequences for the human mind, as the efficacy of drugs for many mental ailments testifies.

Neural and chemical circuits interact with each other. Neural activities in one brain region trigger a gland in the body to secrete a hormone. Circulated in the body, the hormone can directly modify neural activities in other brain regions. It can also indirectly influence the brain by generating bodily changes that, detected and conveyed by peripheral nerves to the brain, alters its neural activities. The brain arguably includes peripheral nerves, but not the blood stream and the chemicals it circulates. Close cooperation of nervous and circulatory circuits underscores the inseparability of brain and body in supporting mental processes. It is most apparent in emotion.

An example in which bodily changes influence the brain and mental operation is the epinephrine-facilitated relation between emotion and memory. The hormone epinephrine facilitates memory consolidation so that we remember emotional events better. It is secreted by adrenal glands adjacent to the kidneys and does not readily enter the brain due to the blood-brain barrier. Evidence suggests that it acts peripherally at visceral receptors, whose response projects to the brain and affects the memory process. Thus the body mediates brain operations (McGaugh 1991).

Pain: From Bodily Feeling to Emotion

The body does not merely contribute to cognitive processes. It and its conditions constitute an important part of our cognitive contents, and by that I do not mean obsessions that make boom industries of cosmetics and diet food. Actions require the body, and we consciously control and monitor our body's movements. We have two internal senses that continuously monitor the states of our body: proprioception for muscles and joints and interioception for internal organs. With interioception, you are aware when you are hungry and when full. With proprioception, you do not have to look to know whether your legs are crossed or whether you are leaning to one side. Both can be distorted by brain injuries that damage certain infrastructural processes for the bodily senses. HM, who had damage to the limbic system of his brain, knew neither hunger nor satiation; without supervision he would go on eating. MacGregor, who lost his sense of balance, was unaware that he stood and walked like Italy's Tower of Pisa until he watched a video movie of himself. Christina was even more unfortunate. A neural inflammation destroyed her proprioception and left her "body blind." She had to learn to control her body's movements by vision, find a particular body part with her eyes, and literally see that it moved according to her will. She had no feeling of her own body. "If only I could *feel*! But I've forgotten what it's like. . . . It's like something's been scooped right out of me, right at the center" (Sacks 1985:50).

Among bodily sensations, pain is the most acute. Pain has definite survival values in attracting attention to tissue damage and disabling an injured organism to give the injury a chance to heal. Most, but not all, pain originates from nociceptors, which are receptors sensitive to tissue-damaging stimuli. From nociceptors at various parts of the body, two types of peripheral nerves lead to the spinal cord: fast A δ fibers for sharp prick-ing pains and slow C fibers for prolonged burning pains. The message is relayed to the thalamus by complicated spinal cord processes, some of which can be manipulated to block pain; the brain itself secrets morphinelike substances that inhibit pain. The brain has no pain center; many regions in the limbic system, somatosensory cortex, and frontal lobe activate in pain under various conditions. These complicated neural mech-anisms show that pain is not simple or primitive, at least in humans (Rainville 1997).

Pictures of Hindus fire walking or Christians flogging themselves make one wonder if people in different cultures experience pain differ-ently. Is it possible that pain does not hurt them so much because they have a different mind set? Recent decades witness a fundamental break from the traditional view that pain is merely a sensation, an ineffable *ouch*, that some miracle drug may eradicate. Scientists and clinicians increasingly recognize that it is not a raw sensation but is close to emotion. Besides the ouch, pain has an *affective aspect* that determines its unpleasantness: how badly it hurts and disrupts other mental processes (Fernandez and Turk 1992).

The affective dimension of pain has an inalienable cognitive compo-nent, which explains why mental concentration can sometimes block pain. People absorbed in intense physical activities such as combat or sport are often oblivious to injuries; they are too busy to feel pain. Kant's biogra-pher told how once, when the philosopher had a severe attack of gout, he plunged himself into some tedious but absorbing work such as search-ing for Leibniz's remarks on a specific topic, and commented later that he hardly noticed the pain. Drawing on similar principles, pain clinics mush-roomed in the last decades of the twentieth century to help people manage the affective aspect. Many people suffer from chronic disorder such as migraine. They cannot dull their pain by drugs, but they can learn to cope with its intractable sensation by reducing its unpleasant affects. An impor-tant element seems to be one's attitude toward pain in relation to one's body and identity. "Before, my pain controlled me; now I control my pain" is heard frequently in pain clinics. A patient explained: "If you look at the pain as being a horrible, terrible thing, then it is going to do horrible, terrible things to you. If you look at it as being a neutral thing—it is just *there*—it loses a lot of its power" (Jackson 1994; Morris 1991).

When the power of the intellect fails, surgery comes as a last resort. Pain with its sensory and affective dimensions is subserved by a complicated infrastructure that includes the frontal lobe for higher cognitive functions (Price 2000). To relieve debilitating pain, some patients have parts of the frontal lobe removed. One who before the operation crouched in extreme suffering, cheerfully talks about his postsurgical condition: "Oh, the pains are the same, but I feel fine now." The surgery leaves the pain sensation but destroys its affective bite so that it no longer hurts (Damasio 1994).

We have come a long way from simplistic theories that reduce pain to C fiber firing or localize it in the brain, even the disembodied brain. In pain, the embodied mind is fully aware of its own embodiment, and the structure of its awareness is anything but simple. The differentiation between sensation and affect indicates that pain, a primitive trait common to most animals, has in humans developed into something more complicated and akin to an emotion.

Amygdala, the Brain's Emotional Center

If some evaluative elements are contained in human pain, how much more are they in human emotions. In the brain, emotion depends as heavily on the frontal lobe, which is responsible for higher cognitive functions specific to humans, as on the limbic system, the older part of the brain whose basic structures are shared by all mammals. At the center of the emotional infrastructure is the *amygdala*, a pair of small almond-shaped masses of gray matter in the limbic system in the middle of the brain (see figure A.1). The amygdala has many parts with different functions. For instance, only the right one responds to subliminal presentations of threat, and only the left supports conscious perception of the same threat (Morris, Öhman, and Dolan 1998).

The amygdala plays crucial roles in emotional responses and expressions. Electrical stimulations of it usually produce fear and sometimes rage. Its functions are most apparent, however, when it malfunctions. As discussed earlier, frightened rats exhibit innate fixed behavioral patterns such as frozen postures. When experimenters pair an electric shock with a bell, normal rats quickly learn to associate the bell with the shock and freeze on hearing it. Rats with a damaged amygdala fail to learn the appropriate fear association. This disability can be fatal because it prevents the animals from learning what is dangerous and avoiding it. Similar disability is manifested by monkeys. Monkeys with a surgically damaged amygdala willingly approach normally threatening objects and put inedible things in the mouth—perilous habits. The monkeys' general loss of fear, together with their abnormal tameness, is called Klüver-Bucy syndrome. Humans with injured amygdala do not exhibit the full syndrome, perhaps because their higher cognitive abilities act as safeguards. Nevertheless, they do show substantial emotional deficits. Guess which part of the brain is damaged in patients who are unable to recognize facial expressions and are attracted by faces that put normal people on guard? You are right if you said the amygdala (Ledoux 1995; Damasio 1994).

Once the amygdala excites, it produces emotional arousal by whipping up the activities of the body's motor, autonomic, and endocrine systems. It sends signals to muscles in the face and limbs, producing fixed behavioral patterns such as rats' frozen posture, preys' distress call, or humans' facial expressions and ducking movements. Even when people consciously suppress their fixed behavioral patters, arousal energizes their bodies and readies them for action.

The autonomic system regulates respiration, blood circulation, and other operations of the body. When the amygdala puts it in overdrive, it generates the familiar physiological changes that accompany emotional arousal: quickened pulse, tightened viscera, flushed skin, short breath, dry mouth, and cold sweat. Proprioception and interioception quickly bring to awareness these changes, which we recognize as the affective aspect of emotion. This recognition can in turn influence the amygdala and its output, and the cycle perpetuates the continuing process of emotional arousal.

The endocrine system controls the body's chemistry by regulating secretion of various hormones and neurotransmitters. People have known the influence of wine and other intoxicating substances for a long time, but now we have more choices. In this age when people depend on Prozac for happiness and Valium for tranquility, it is difficult to underestimate the emotional effects of chemicals. We need not rely on external drugs, however. Our bodies produce extra doses of chemicals to foment, maintain, and modulate our emotional states. Stress hormones produced on the amygdala's command can have profound and durable effects. They last and give our mental states that subtle coloring we usually call mood. For instance, they contribute to the chronic stress that plagues many people living in the fast lane.

We tend to remember emotional events better than dull events, a phenomenon confirmed by many experiments with animals and humans. To find out how emotional arousal enhances memory, experimenters trained rats for a task, and immediately after training injected them with various doses of epinephrine, a hormone normally released during emotional arousal. Rats that received moderate doses retained their training better than control rats that received a saline injection. The hormonal effect on memory is dose dependent. With increasing doses, retention initially increases proportionally, then saturates and declines. Thus a moderate dose of epinephrine improves memory but a large dose impairs it. Emotion-related hormones, if present immediately after the formation of a memory, help to consolidate the memory and improve its retention. Their beneficial effect on memory is long lasting (McGaugh 1995).

Emotion-induced body chemistry is most influential during infancy and early stages of development. When rats are raised in isolation they grow up frenzied and overexcited, and their brains contain elevated levels of dopamine, a neurotransmitter that can cause schizophrenia in humans when misregulated. Baby rats deprived of their mothers grow up dull, and their brains contain reduced levels of serotonin, a neurotransmitter that can cause depression in humans if misregulated. In contrast, rats with especially attentive mothers develop brains with less stress hormone and more neurotransmitter that inhibit the activity of the amygdala, and they behave with equanimity in new situations. The emotional life of an infant mammal can have long-term effects on the neurochemistry of its brain, and hence on its temperament and behavior (Mcewen 1995; Mlot 1998).

The amygdala not only indirectly affects the brain by its effects on the body's chemistry and operation, it directly sends its output into other areas of the brain. It has massive projections into areas responsible for sensory perception and higher cognitive functions. Thus it can influence various infrastructural processes for perception, thinking, memory, and selective attention. Laboratory experiments find that anxiety biases attention toward threatening information. Anxious people were better than unconcerned people at detecting threatening words among attention-consuming distractions. Some subjects found it difficult to ignore these words even when they were instructed to do so. Emotional tone can selectively sharpen perceptual sensitivity (MacLeod 1996).

Two Neural Circuits of Emotion

We have seen what the amygdala can do when it excites. What activates
it? Roughly, the amygdala sits at the center of two neural circuits for
emotion, an *impulsive circuit* for rapid and automatic trigger and a *cognitive
circuit* for reasoned initiation. The two circuits differ greatly in the sort of
input they feed into the amygdala. Nevertheless, they overlap and operate
in parallel, and both are closed by proprioception and interioception of
amygdala's output to the motor, autonomic, and endocrine systems. The
cognitive circuit is further complicated by the neural projection it receives
from the amygdala (figure 7.1).

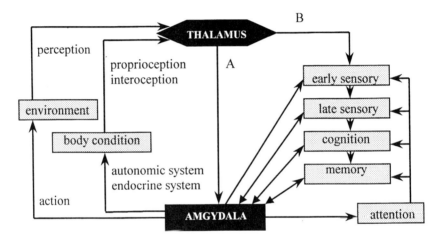

Figure 7.1
The thalamus, the gateway to the brain, receives sensual input from the body and
the environment. It is the branching point for the two circuits of the emotive
infrastructure. The *impulsive circuit* (A), passes the input to the thalamus directly to
the amygdala, the emotion center. In the *cognitive circuit* (B), the input goes on
to diverse brain regions serving various sensory, cognitive, and mnemonic functions. Most of these areas send their output to the amygdala, facilitating reasoned
emotion. Once excited, the amygdala modulates the autonomic and endocrine
systems, which in turn modify the body's physiology and chemistry. These body
conditions become input to the thalamus through proprioception and interioception. The amygdala also influences behavior through the motor systems. Furthermore, it affects various brain areas by direct neural connections. It projects
into the areas for early stages of sensory processes, which are sensitive to separate
features; later sensory stages, which are sensitive to integrated objects and events;
areas of higher cognitive functions, mostly in the frontal lobe; areas for memory
in the hippocampus and its surrounding cortex; and areas for attention in the
nucleus basalis. The diagram does not show the complicated interconnection
among these areas, except the influence of attention.

From the sense organs, internal organs, joints, and muscles, perceptive, interoceptive, and proprioceptive signals converge on the thalamus, the brain's entrance hall. The thalamus is also the switching station between impulsive and cognitive circuits of emotion. In the impulsive circuit, the thalamus sends the signal it receives directly to the amygdala. This raw sensory input is crude but prompt, because it does not go through numerous processes in the cortex. It rapidly excites the amygdala if it happens to convey appropriate triggering stimuli for emotion: the smell of cats in a rat, the span of wide wings in a prey of arial predators, and a loud noise or a looming object in anyone. The process is reflexive and automatic.

The cognitive circuit of emotion is much more complex. Here signals from the thalamus diverge to regions in the cerebral cortex dedicated to sensory, somatic, motor, and cognitive functions. Early sensory areas, which are sensitive only to isolated features of sensory input, do not send signals to the amygdala. Later sensory areas, which are sensitive to integrative objects and events, do. The amygdala also receives signals from the hippocampus for memory and the frontal lobe for higher cognitive functions. This input is slower in coming, but it conveys better information. Autonomous emotions excited by higher cognitive processes underlie their rational side and are especially important in practical judgments.

Because the amygdala has mnemonic and cognitive input, it can be excited without external or physiological stimulus. Thus brooding can depress, imagination can exasperate, happy memories can cheer, and rational judgment can induce moral indignation. Mnemonic and cognitive input also provides mental contexts for emotional experiences. It is the part of the emotional infrastructure that underlies what Aristotle called the emotional person's state of mind.

Both impulsive and cognitive circuits operate in normal emotional experiences. Suppose you are startled by a sudden noise at home, then are relieved to find all is safe. The noise passing through the impulsive circuit automatically triggers the startle response, which is assuaged by the cognitive circuit's evaluation of the situation. If, when you turn quickly to the source of the noise, you find a hostile stranger, the cognitive circuit will maintain or heighten the fear physiology.

The Impulsive Circuit and the Passivity of Emotion
Passivity is inherent in various bodily feeling models of emotion that rest only on the impulsive circuit of the emotional infrastructure. Most

physiological changes and fixed behavioral patterns incited by the amygdala are underwritten by dedicated infrastructural processes and common to members of the species. This explains why many emotional responses are universal across cultures. It also justifies attribution of basic emotions to nonhuman animals.

The impulsive circuit activates the amygdala automatically and instinctively. It explains why emotion is so frequently identified with passion instigated by compulsive desires that arise on their own and push us around. Many emotions, the surge of rage or the flood of tenderness, happen in spite of ourselves. We say we fall in love or succumb to grief, are consumed by hatred or overwhelmed by joy, are paralyzed by fear or carried away by enthusiasm. Such acknowledgment of emotional passivity and compulsion is not specific to our culture. Homeric heros saw their strong emotions as divine intervention. Agamemnon explained his fury with Achilles in terms of the *ate* implanted in him by Zeus, and warriors commonly attributed the effect of adrenaline flow to the *menos* that gods put into their chests or thrust up their nostrils. As a distant echo to this Homeric view, Freud called the emotional aspect of our mental life *id*—it.

The impulsive circuit in the emotional infrastructure accounts for four familiar features of emotion: embodiment, impulsiveness, irrationality, and universality of some responses. However, it fails to account for openness, cognitive and motivational aspects, and diversity and social variability of many responses. For these the cognitive circuit must come into play.

The Cognitive Circuit and the Openness of Emotion

The impulsive circuit is not totally blind. It must have certain minimal discriminating power to be selectively sensitive to triggering stimuli. However, its selectivity is infraconscious and thoughtless. On the other hand, emotional effects produced by amygdala excitation, many of which are chemical, influence all parts of the brain, including those involved in conscious experience and reasoning. Thus emotion affects reason but not vice versa. If that is all, then reason is the slave of passion. But that is not all; the impulsive circuit does not operate alone. The cognitive circuit of the emotive infrastructure engages processes underlying perceptual recognition, memory, and reasoning. Here emotion still influences judgment, but is itself impregnated with rational elements.

Memory, imagination, and thinking can activate the amygdala in the cognitive circuit, thus generating emotion without any direct sensual trigger. Dostoyevsky's Underground Man worked himself into a frenzy of resentment by ruminating on other people's attitudes. Despite his unconventional value system, his resentment was not irrational. The entire first part of the novel records the justification he gave for it, and it is coherent granted what he was happy with. The *Notes From the Underground* punctures the bubble of reason that claims universal validity regardless of emotional context. One the other hand, it also explodes the myth that human emotion can occur in a mental vacuum. Our emotional experiences are embedded in a fabric of beliefs, desires, values, ideals, memories, moods, and dispositions that constitute a person's peculiar state of mind.

Wide involvement of the cognitive circuit ensures the proper mental context for emotion. It ties emotion to all other dimensions of mind, including our inclinations, latent beliefs, and desires not explicitly articulated at the moment. Beliefs and ideals, which are important parts of our mental states, are subject to social influences. Thus the variety of contexts of emotion explains the diversity of emotions across cultures.

The cognitive circuit generates emotions according to what we intellectually judge to be threatening, repulsive, admirable, or commendable. It mostly runs in parallel with the impulsive circuit, which generates compulsive physiological changes. These changes remain effective even when a person rationally chooses to override fixed pattern responses. Thus courageous people are not reckless or fearless like monkeys with Klüver-Bucy syndrome. They have suppressed their impulse to flee, but their bodies are still geared for fear. Facing danger, frightened, tense, but determined to pursue their goals, they experience their bodily conditions as the imperative for caution and concentration in action.

Emotion and Motivation

The intimate relation between reason and passion is best revealed in the behaviors of patients with frontal lobe injuries. Knowledge about the frontal lobe is still sketchy. We do not know how its injuries damage the cognitive circuit of emotion, but the effects of damage are pronounced. These patients can be startled by sensory stimuli and will scream and sweat because their impulsive circuit still works. However, they are emotionless to anything that requires intellectual judgment; for example, they are totally impassive to pictures of atrocities. Their cold-bloodedness is not feigned; atrocity does not excite their amygdala as it does in normal people.

To probe the role of the frontal lobe in emotion, psychologists use the knowledge that among the effects of amygdala excitation is skin conductance. They asked normal subjects and patients with frontal lobe injuries to watch a slide show while being hooked to lie detectors, which measure skin conductance. The show contained bland scenes interspersed with atrocious images such as a person being decapitated. Normal subjects invariably showed a big jump in skin conductance in response to the horror slides but not the bland ones. In contrast, patients did not generate the slightest change in skin conductance in view of atrocity, although they could describe the pictures in detail and discuss their horrible elements. One patient confided that he knew that the atrocity ought to be disturbing, nevertheless he himself was not disturbed (Damasio 1994). Such dissociation of emotion from perceptual recognition shows that sensual stimuli alone are insufficient to generate certain emotional responses. Our normal emotional responses to horrors have a rational source.

The behaviors of these patients also confirm the intuition that emotion is crucial in motivating action. The inability of reason to incite emotion in these patients ruins their lives. Take Eliot, who had been a respectable accountant until he got a tumor in his forebrain. After surgery to remove his frontal lobe, tests showed that his speech, memory, intelligence, and knowledge base were intact. However, anyone outside the laboratory could see that something was deeply wrong. His personality was totally changed. He became irresponsible, indifferent to his situation, reckless in action, and incapable of learning from catastrophic mistakes. He could not hold a job; his business ventures collapsed and marriages disintegrated; his friends turned their backs on him. Perhaps the only saving grace was he took all these events with perfect equanimity, without a shred of emotion. Listening to Eliot's own impassive narration of his ruinous life, Damasio (1994) said he felt more sadness than Eliot showed. Eliot was neither stupid nor ignorant. In tests, he had the intellectual ability to understand verbally described situations, to conjure means for achieving given social goals, to generate various options, to anticipate and assess their consequences, and to reason morally. In short, his computational mind was intact. Unfortunately, his theory and practice were disjointed. Why? Was the link broken with the extirpation of emotion? Could he have failed in life because nothing mattered to him, except perhaps instantaneous compulsions subserved by his spared impulsive emotional circuit?

We have many desires, some of which conflict with each other. Desires for long-term goals often have to combat desires for instantaneous satisfaction, such as parents who decide to save for their children's college education sometimes have to forego purchases for themselves. Reason decides on a long-term goal, but the resolution to pursue the goal is deeply emotional. Without commitment, reason cannot become practical. That is why Aristotle and Kant took care to leave room for passion and desire in their rationalistic ethics. When brain injury kills commitment with emotion, impulsive desires for instant gratification hold sway and ruin the pattern of rational desires that constitutes a healthy personality.

The demise of long-term resolve is shown in an experiment in which patients with frontal lobe damage and normal subjects engaged in a game of gambling while hooked to lie detectors. Each player successively turned a card from one of four decks. A card specified a prize, but occasionally it exacted a penalty. Unknown to the players, the cards were stacked. Cards in two of the decks awarded high prizes but exacted even higher penalties, so that subjects choosing them would lose in the long run. Cards in the other two decks awarded low prizes and exacted lower penalties, so that subjects choosing these would win in the long run. All players, injured and normal, felt the thrill of instant satisfaction, as their skin conductance increased on receiving a prize. They all professed desire to win. Initially they all chose cards randomly. After turning some sixty to ninety cards, most players figured out that the cards were stacked and how. When normal players knew that the two high-prize–higher-risk decks were bad, they wisely avoided them and ended up winners. Similar knowledge, however, did not help the patients much. They continued to turn cards from the bad decks, which they knew to be stacked against them. A big penalty did drive them momentarily from the bad decks, but the temptation of instant high prizes was too strong. They kept returning to the bad decks and ended up losers (Damasio 1994; Bechara et al. 1997).

Daily life is not a card game; it does not always offer the thrill of instant prizes. Without the thrill, patients with frontal lobe injury became indecisive in practical matters. They would spend hours pondering where to dine, what trinkets to buy, or which date to pick for an appointment, reckoning all conceivable factors and frequently failing to make up their minds. Impatience and boredom, by which we are normally aware that we have better things to do with our time, are nonexistent. With them go the urgency of life and the force to choose. Decision processes become manipulation of symbols without significance, trapped in infinite computational loops. Patients retain the faculty of reason, but not *practical* reason. In their endless accounting of pros and cons for each option, they are reminiscent of Jean Buridan's rational ass that starved to death midway between two identical piles of hay because it found no reason to choose either one over the other (Eslinger & Damasio 1985; Damasio 1994).

"All that is practical, so far as it contains motives, relates to feelings." These words are not from romantics but from Kant's *Critique of Pure Reason* (1781:61). Rationalism at its strongest is more than passionless logicism or computationalism. Rationalists are not mere digital computers but practical human beings. To get through one day in a flourishing life is a great achievement. One can drift in the current of impulsive desires. To choose action, even an action as simple as purchasing a small item or winning a little game, however, is something else. Pure intelligence is not up to the task. Patients with frontal lobe injuries are intelligent. They reason well and are capable of computing costs and benefits in the abstract. Without emotion, however, the pale cast of thought never gains the name of action.

Emotion and Reason in the Choice of Action

Hume (1739:414) rightly observed that "reason alone can never produce any action, or give rise to volition." However, this premise does not lead to his conclusion: "Reason is, and ought only to be the slave of the passions." Emotion and reason are related neither by dominance nor adversary. They cooperate.

We must make choices in life, and choices involve both reason and desire. The disembodied computational mind receives its "desires" or its criteria of choice from external mind designers. Therefore it can survive on instrumental reason alone, caring only about finding the best means to satisfy the criteria dictated to it. People not enslaved to desires of mind designers must decide for themselves what is desirable. Autonomous goal setting calls for both emotion and reason, and reason that is more than merely instrumental.

A perennial question in moral philosophy is do we call something good because we desire it, or do we desire something because we judge it good? "Desire" has different meanings in the two clauses. The first desire may be hedonistic and compulsive; the second is not necessarily so. We can use objective standards to judge goodness. Through the cognitive circuit of our emotive infrastructure, rational judgment can generate desires of its own, even if these desires conflict with some impulsive desires for pleasure. Desires resulting from deliberation and judgment are often called *rational* in distinction to *compulsive desires*. If the involved deliberation and judgment neither presuppose nor depend on compulsive desires, the rational desires they generate are *moral*, according to an influential school of ethics.[1] Suppose you are starving in a famine and the sight of food in the hands of a well-fed child intensifies the gnaw of your hunger. You check your urge to grab the food, not because you have a queasy feeling, nor because you pity the child or fear the wrath of God or the censure of men, but because you think it is a wrong thing for anyone to do. In such cases your moral desire to act correctly overrides you compulsive desire to relieve your hunger. Because the cognitive circuit in the emotive infrastructure enables our reasoning to generate desires and emotions, we are not automata run by impulses and compulsive desires. Our actions can be free from compulsion.

Realistic situations are fluid and fraught with factors difficult to disentangle. Thus we are frequently at a loss about the right course of action. Choice depends on evaluating situations. Our evaluation is conscious but usually not clearly conceptualized. Seldom do we have the kind of decision-making exercise with precisely formulated options, goals, and choice criteria that we assign to the computational mind. Furthermore, we often do not know our beliefs and desires precisely. Thus judgment and evaluation rely heavily on hunches and gut feelings that are imbued with emotion.

Our mental capacity is small compared with the torrent of events in our life. Stimuli jam our senses competing for our focal awareness. What grab our attention and stick to our memory are of utmost importance. Emotion plays a great role in the selection, acting as advocate for our concerns. Ordinarily, our attention is so absorbed by external stimuli we are hardly aware of our mental states. Emotional arousal brings into vivid awareness our states of being and what we care about in a situation. Within the full emotive infrastructure, physiological changes accompanying emotional arousal acquire a significance alien to the bodily feeling model. Here my body functions like a resonance box, amplifying the factor that triggers my emotional arousal. Thus it singles out that factor from all its competitors, signals its significance to me, and expresses my tacit desire. Consequently my emotions are a source of self-knowledge, as they reveal to me my personal values. In my grief over the loss of a loved one, I realize how much he meant to me. If I find myself to be particularly sensitive to a friend's remarks, I know that I care about him more than I do others. Recognizing my anger at petty things may prompt me to examine my value system. Often such critical reflections lead us to reinterpret our feelings, reevaluate situations, and hence modulate our emotions. Thus emotion intertwines with reason in shaping our course of action.

By biasing our attention and modulating the relative strength of our memory for particular events, the emotive infrastructure screens the contents of experience, which we consciously interpret as what is of concern to us. By signaling what matters, emotion contains certain rationality, participates in value judgment and decision making, and motivates action. Thus it is a mistake to consider emotion and reason as two distinct if not outright antagonistic realms. Nietzsche (1901:387) put it best: "The misunderstanding of passion and reason, as if the latter were an independent entity and not rather a system of relations between various passions and desires; and as if every passion did not possess its quantum of reason."

Mind Open to the World

22 How Is Intelligibility of the World Possible?

What can I know?
What ought I to do?
What may I hope?
What is man?

These are the foremost questions that define philosophy, according to Kant (1800:29). He added that the first three are based on the fourth, as determination of the sources, limits, and ends of knowledge and morals depends on an explanation of human nature and understanding.

From chapter 3 on I presented a model of an open mind emerging from the self-organization of infrastructural processes. The model explicitly posits two organizational levels of a person, mental and infrastructural (see figure 3.1). We lead our conscious life on the mental level, and cognitive science concentrates on the infrastructural processes that underlie mental phenomena. So far, we have been concerned mainly with infrastructural processes or individual mental faculties. In this chapter we finally turn our spotlight on the mental level as a whole and study the general characteristics of human understanding.

A person is capable of knowing, hoping, choosing his actions and being responsible for his choices. Empirical knowledge rests on sensual perception. One's hope for the future depends on his present mental state, which is influenced by memory of the past. Decisive action involves not only means-ends computation but also the commitment to pursue a certain course. Thus knowing, hoping, and choosing depend on perception, memory, and emotion. We saw that each of these mental faculties has a complicated structure supported by an intricate infrastructure. Let me summarize some results as a launch pad for our investigation of the mental level.

In chapter 5 we noted that sensual perception is not a simple reception of stimuli. It is the self-organization of complex processes that is influenced by attention and concepts. We actively look for instead of passively look at things. Consequently, even our most immediate sensual experiences have a minimal conceptual structure, which we identified to be general concepts of individual objects that persist when we are not looking.

In chapter 6 we observed that memory is not simple retrieval of stored files. It is a braid of complicated processes starting right from the learning stage, when we actively structure the experience to be remembered, especially by sorting out its causal orders. Recall, which requires the concept of tense, is a reconstruction from bit and pieces, mostly accurate but biased by the present contexts in which we reinterpret the meanings of our experiences. Continued reinterpretations shape our personality and shade our hopes for the future.

As discussed in chapter 7, emotion is not merely an inner feeling. It includes a significant cognitive component by which we evaluate external events and set our purposes. Emotion is the force of motivation without which we would be pushed by impulses but unable to pursuit our ends.

Perception, memory, and emotion involve spontaneous activities and are concerned with events in the world. Furthermore, they are not disconnected processes but interact with each other. Perception can initiate memory and emotion; memory can bias perception and emotion; emotion can color memory and perception.

Each mental faculty has complex structures, and faculties interact. The mental level emerging from interaction is highly complicated and covers all human experience. We cannot possibly go into details but will be content with its most general structures. We are concerned not with analyzing this or that piece of knowledge but with the general nature of knowing; not with how we understand this or that phenomenon but with what it is to understand anything about the real world. What are the minimal mental structures without which it is impossible for us to find the world intelligible and have the kind of experience that we do?

I call the minimal structures of human experiences mind-open-to-the-world. My analysis contains four major points:

1. No inner realm of mental representations is given that closes us from the external world. Mind immediately reaches out to the world and makes it intelligible by spontaneously deploying *concepts of world*, a shorthand for the framework consisting of interrelated general concepts of objects, time, causality, and purposes.

2. Human experiences invariably involve particular physical or intellectual perspectives. Nevertheless, concepts of the world explicitly acknowledge subjective perspectives and treat them critically. Thus we can justify the common sense that we have objective knowledge about reality.

3. Intersubjective understanding is based on the presupposition that we share an objective world. Intersubjectivity is also a prerequisite to the full sense of subjectivity, in which I know myself as one among many of the same kind, and hence can experience myself both from a first-person and a third-person view.

4. There is no inner self transparent to introspection; the subject exists only in perceiving, choosing, and other activities, most of which engage the world. Subjective experience, objective knowledge, and intersubjective understanding rise and fall together. I cannot say *I* if I cannot also say *it* and *thou*.

These points have a Kantian and Heideggerian flavor, which is not the fashion of current philosophy and science of mind.[1] I briefly introduce the points in this section, compare them with the more familiar ideas in the next, and analyze them in more details in the rest of the book.

Mind Embodied and Engaged

Two of the most important issues regarding mind are its relations to the body and the world. They are different. Embodiment emphasizes operational processes underlying mental activities and is mainly addressed in studies of the mental infrastructure. Engagement emphasizes structures of thinking, the contents of which are mostly about the world; hence it demands an analysis of the mental level. Whether the two issues are interconnected depends on the meanings of embodiment and engagement.

Embodiment has at least two senses, situated and isolated. Mind as brain-in-a-vat is embodied and isolated; its operational mechanisms are completely disconnected from the causal processes responsible for the contents of its thoughts, so that it imagines itself sunbathing on the beach while it can only float in nutrients and be stimulated by electrodes. Forever trapped in a global illusion, it has no way to distinguish between truth and falsity. The embodiment of a person's mind is situated; the exposure of a person's body to the sun is a cause of his enjoyment on the beach. He has illusions, but these are local; he can distinguish between truth and falsity because he knows that his body plays a direct causal role in determining the contents of his experiences.

Engagement also has two senses, intrinsic and extrinsic. Relations between mind and world are extrinsic if subjects and their mental characteristics exist independent of objects in the world. Extrinsic engagement fits well with isolated embodiment, resulting in models of the closed mind controlled by mind designers in which mind is closed entity with internal mental representations accessible by introspection and optional relations to the world imposed by external mind designers. If abilities of mind designers are not questioned, as they almost never are, these models need not worry about the structures of our thinking that are mostly about the world. They do not contain any sense of I or subjectivity, because their embodied closed mind is merely an individual entity to whom a third party refers as *this* or *that*, as illustrated in figure 8.1a. Thus they are applicable to brains-in-a-vat, insects, and robots in AI's situated cognition.

Models of the open mind demand intrinsic engagement; a subject does not exist before engaging objects, for having an intelligible world is

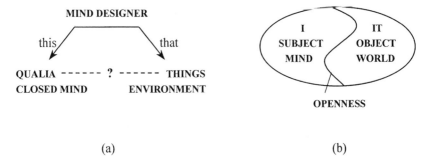

(a)   (b)

Figure 8.1
(a) The closed mind and the environment exist independent of each other with no subject-object relationship. Referring to them as *this* and *that*, mind designers establish an extrinsic relation that imparts no subjectivity or understanding to the closed mind. (b) The open mind is intrinsically related to the world, for it exists by distinguishing *I* from *it*, or its experiences from objects of experiences. The spontaneous distinction, called openness, is the basic mental structure that makes objects intelligible to the subject, who is thereby simultaneously aware of himself.

his basic mental characteristic. As an autonomous subject, I must be able to adopt a first-person view of objects and say *I* experience *it*. To distinguish objects from my experiences and hence judge the truth and falsity of my beliefs, I rely on causality. I decide that I'm seeing a chair instead of dreaming about one because I can somehow check the causal elements in my perception, which is only possible because my body's interaction with the physical world agrees with the contents of my thoughts to a significant extent. Therefore intrinsic engagement and situated embodiment demand each other, and together they constitute mind-open-to-the-world. One cannot properly understand how an animal's mind is embodied in its infrastructures without referring to world in which the animal is active, as sensory input determines brain's salient functions and structures. Conversely, when we study how mind engages in the world, we always presuppose that it is not merely embrained but fully embodied.

Subject and object, I and it are intrinsically related (figure 8.1b). As explained in section 13, an intrinsic relation between two entities implies that the defining characteristics of one depend on the defining characteristics of the other. Thus when we examine one entity we simultaneously gain knowledge about its partner. Taking advantage of this, we can get some sight into our mind by investigating the meanings of our world. Putting openness at the center of our inquiry enables us to adopt a two-pronged approach. On the subjective side, we examine the structures of our mind to see how it makes objects encounterable. On the objective side, we examine the general structures of the world to see how it is intelligible to us. The two prongs complement each other to reveal how we are aware of ourselves as subjects as we engage in the objective world.

It may seem strange that we put so much emphasis on the world in our study of mind. The ability to understand and cope with things is so ordinary and obvious many people take it for granted and cannot see any problem with it. Those who have thought deeply, however, find the ordinary ability most astonishing and difficult to explain. To explain how we manage to know reality taxes Kant's critique of reason and Heidegger's analytic of the meaning of beings. Failures in explanation not only afflict Cartesianism, computationalism, and other models of the closed mind but also fuel controversies about realism and antirealism in metaphysics, meaning and reference in the philosophy of language, truth and objectivity in the philosophy of science. The scandal of philosophy, in which one needs a proof to believe the physical world exists, is not only alive but spreads beyond philosophy to areas such as science studies and education, where relativism dismisses the objectivity of science.

I clarify some controversies by a schema that explicitly represents the intrinsic relation between mind and the intelligible world by two mutually dependent variables: *perspective* and *object*. It distinguishes the commonsense "reality is independent of our subjective perspectives" from the illusory "reality is what is viewed from nowhere." The illusory notion does not invoke perspective. The commonsense notion does and thus accounts for the general interdependence of mind and world. Therefore common sense is conceptually more sophisticated than the illusory notion and relativism, which makes its profits by whipping an illusory straw man and spends them trashing common sense. My schema accommodates many subjective perspectives and shows how transformations among and syntheses of perspectives entail objectivity of knowledge without assuming a transcendent position available only to God. Thus it illustrates the symbiosis of subjectivity, intersubjectivity, and objectivity.

A person is conscious of himself and his environment and can intelligibly share his thoughts about the world. The next section discusses intelligence, consciousness, and intentionality. Each has a range of meanings. I choose meanings appropriate for the open mind and incorporate them into my model.

As discussed in section 13, the proper approach to study complicated phenomena such as mind-open-to-the-world is not construction but analysis. Analysis proceeds from the general to the specific. We first draw broad distinctions to see the outline of a phenomenon, then draw finer distinctions to reveal the details. Thus I start in section 24 by identifying the most basic mental characteristic, the ability to imagine the *possible* and separate it from the *actual*. The ability to entertain possibilities is closely related to mastery of concepts. By emphasizing that we are concerned not with empty logical possibilities but with possibilities that open up the intelligible world, mind as a situated property is introduced.

In section 25 I observe that to account for the partiality and fallibility of our beliefs about the world, a model of mind needs at least two variables, the first germane to what is the case, the second to what we think to be the case. I discard mental representation as the second variable and replace it with *mental frame*, which subsumes the variable of perspective because its values range over various modes of experience and the physical or intellectual perspectives in each mode. My model of the open mind as represented by the interrelated variables of object and mental frame is summarized in what I call the *transformation schema*. Its meanings are explained and contrasted with various views of the closed mind.

The transformation schema with its two variables is analyzed in the two subsequent sections. Section 26 concentrates on the mental frame and the subjective side of experiences, showing how the subject draws the distinctions and intrinsic relations among *I, thou,* and *it*. It argues that our full sense of self includes both a first-person *I* and a third-person *One*. Section 27 concentrates on the object and objective side of experience. It addresses our everyday dealings in the world and explains how the theoretical attitude of scientific investigation arises by abstracting from some, although not all, value considerations. Finally, section 28 consolidates the idea of consciousness as personal identity by considering functions of language and autobiographical narrative.

The Open Mind and Commonsense Psychology

The open mind is common to all human beings and manifests itself foremost in our everyday life. Thus my analysis emphasizes ordinary experiences and common sense. It bucks a philosophical trend that treats mundane activities with condescension if not contempt. Therefore I have to defend my emphasis before I start. I contend that the philosophical disdain is unjustified. In trashing common sense in the name of ideal science, a philosophy is also demolishing its own basis, as our everyday thinking is the foundation on which actual philosophizing and scientific research develop.

We express our open mind by commonsense psychological concepts such as see, know, believe, and desire. We depend on these concepts for our daily intercourse and social institutions. We assert our own beliefs, attribute beliefs to others, act on what we believe in, and debate on the truth or falsity of beliefs in scientific research. Most people consider these concepts to be objective in the sense of describing, albeit approximately, some real characteristics of human beings and perhaps some other animals.

The mental properties described by commonsense psychological concepts are mostly absent in the closed mind, be it a computer, brain in a vat, or insectlike robot. Some philosophers respect these mental properties and make effort to account for them, even if the effort is less than successful. Other philosophers claim them to be false and advocate getting rid of them. Two prominent persecutors of common sense are eliminativism and instrumental behaviorism.

Note that we are concerned not with the contents of beliefs but with the concept of *believe* itself. At issue are not the specific contents of our psychological beliefs, such as that intelligence is heritable, or hypotheses that philosophers and scientists propose to explain mental phenomena, such as believing is computing. These contents and hypotheses may well be false. At issue are the general psychological concepts such as believe, whatever the specific contents of beliefs, in the ordinary sense that people have the ability to believe whereas stones and neurons do not. The contention is not whether these concepts are vague and in need of being criticized, modified, and supplemented by the science of mind. To that few people would object. The controversial contention of eliminativism and instrumental behaviorism is that the concepts are radically false and should be purged; it is merely a fiction that people believe, desire, know, and hope; what we ordinarily take as mental states and mental phenomena do not exist at all.

The Final Solution and the Devaluation Stance

Eliminativism advocates the final solution to mental phenomena: exterminate them. Some philosophers phrase it subtly as a form of the "naturalization of mind." Others are more blunt. Churchland (1989:1) curtly threw believe, desire, and other commonsense psychological concepts to the same stack to be burned with alchemy and witchcraft: "Our common-sense conceptions of psychological phenomena constitute a radically false theory, a theory so fundamentally defective that both the principles and the ontology of that theory will eventually be displaced, rather than smoothly reduced, by completed neuroscience." An objective theory implies an ontology because its concepts refer to real objects and phenomena, and its ontology falls with it. Commonsense psychological concepts express our mental characteristics. When they are eliminated, so is mind. What remains is only the brain.

We use concepts discriminately, as we say people can believe whereas stones cannot. A concept makes a distinction and hence is like a physical mark that distinguishes a thing from other things. If you want to hide the distinction, you can either erase the mark or put a similar mark on everything else. The final solution of eliminativism applies the first method; the devaluation stance of instrumental behaviorism applies the second.

We use concepts to describe and explain different phenomena: physical concepts for physical properties, biological concepts for biological processes, mental and intentional concepts for mental and intentional systems. In studying a specific kind of phenomenon, the meanings of the relevant concepts are especially important. Thus the scientific study of mind should try to sharpen the meanings of mental concepts such as believing and desiring. Some philosophies do the opposite by taking a devaluation stance.

A financially strapped government can use a trick to repudiate its debts: devaluate its currency by unrestrainedly printing money. I call it the devaluation stance. It is applicable not only to financial but to intellectual matters, where the analog to putting the monetary imprint on an indefinite amount of paper is to apply important concepts to an indefinite range of items. Thus one devaluates the significance of the concepts just as a sleazy government devaluates the worth of its monetary imprint. The information content of a concept depends on its power of discrimination. A concept that picks out one of two items carries one bit of information. A concept that picks out two of two items carries no information, because it is not discriminating. The meaning of a term depends on its extension or the range of entities to which it applies; the smaller the range, the sharper its meaning. Therefore science strives to frame concepts with higher discriminating power and sharper meaning. The devaluation stance proceeds in the opposite direction. By arbitrarily extending the extensions of difficult terms, it razes the terms' information contents and subjects them to equivocation. The Newspeak in George Orwell's *1984* is a good example of the devaluation stance: "War is peace. Freedom is slavery. Ignorance is strength." Currency devaluation can generate a hyperinflation that ruins the economy. Devaluation is no less harmful to science. Newspeak, for instance, destroys the possibility of rational inquiry into freedom and slavery by rendering them meaningless.

The devaluation stance is popular in the philosophy of mind, in which consciousness is explained by defining "consciousness" to be as meaningful as "democracy" in the former German Democratic Republic. Cognitive scientist George Reeke (1996) recognized it when he criticized some philosophers for using words in the style of *Through the Looking Glass* where Humpty Dumpty declares: "When *I* use a word, it means just what I choose it to mean—neither more nor less." Any concept can be devaluated. For instance, technobabble such as the identification of mind with syntactic machines devaluates the meanings of technical terms (see section 4). Devaluation wreaks most havoc when applied to psychological concepts, which are central to mental phenomena.

Suppose a philosophy of mind is unable to explain what it is to have the mental ability to believe. It can use the devaluation stance and apply the concept of believe to everything, thus devaluating its significance and effectively explaining the mental ability away. This is the crux of the "intentional stance" of instrumental behaviorism[2]. Using examples such as "the chess machine believes in getting its queen out early" and "the thermostat will turn off the boiler as soon as it comes to believe the room has reached the desired temperature," Dennett (1987:22) held that believe, desire, and other intentional concepts are applicable to everything from thermostats to chess machines. Furthermore, the meaning of "believe" is the same whether it is applied to a thermostat or a human being. The only difference is that the thermostat's beliefs are more stupid than the human's. As an advocate of AI, Dennett mostly attributed beliefs and desires to artifacts, but his stipulations work equally for natural things, as in his example of lightning desiring to strike a particular target. According to his stipulation, water desires to go downhill and magnetic needles believe that a certain direction is north. When the universe is flooded with things described in mental terms, believe, desire, and other psychological concepts are drained of information contents and become meaningless. Mental phenomena, properties most precious to us, are buried under the ruin of hyperinflation.

Actual Science versus Scientism

Models of mind in eliminativism and instrumental behaviorism are not self-consistent. Eliminativist and behaviorist philosophers deny mind the power to believe, while they themselves happily make predictions, propose models, and assert their beliefs about mind. They can do so because they are full persons living in the world. However, the mind in their models is not; it is merely a brain or a computer closed inside the head. In short, both philosophies propose models of the closed mind, where philosophers themselves assume the position of mind designers. Thus the ability to believe is a major target for the devaluation stance and the final solution. For to believe is to enter into some kind of relation with the world, which mind designers reserve for themselves and deny to the closed mind that they ascribe to ordinary people.

Eliminativism and instrumental behaviorism trounce commonsense psychology in the name of ideal science. What they promote, however, is not science but scientism, the dogma that betrays the critical scientific spirit and profits by wantonly extrapolating scientific techniques and results. They undermine actual science. As we have seen in many examples, scientific psychology and cognitive neuroscience presuppose many commonsense psychological concepts, as in assuming that experimental subjects *understand* the instructions and *see* the targets. If these concepts are fallacious, cognitive science stands on a rotten foundation. Nor would science in general be unscathed, as hypothesis testing is the trial of beliefs, and scientific theories are confirmed beliefs that may require further modification. If people cannot form beliefs, they cannot conduct scientific research. The claim to ideal science by eliminativism and instrumental behaviorism is self-defeating, because the models of mind that they promote make science impossible.

Eliminativists deny that their doctrine is self-refuting, as it assumes that the completed neuroscience would provide replacement concepts to do the job now done by the commonsense notion of believe. This argument does not defuse but amplifies the criticism. If commonsense psychology is so radically false as to deserve elimination, a true theory needs no replacement for its concepts. The admission that believe and other commonsense concepts perform vital functions implies they contain elements of truth, in which case falsity belongs not to common sense but to eliminativism. Furthermore, what are the alleged replacements? Someone can always invent a set of impressive jargon that does not change the contents of common sense but only cloaks it in academic snobbery. Skinner (1957) wrote a book claiming to account for language in behaviorism. However, it was exposed by Chomsky (1959) to be merely a paraphrase in behavioral jargon of linguistic ideas that behaviorism professes to discard. Are eliminativists doing better than Skinner? Churchland (1995) wrote a book claiming to account for common mental abilities by "multidimensional vector space" and other technical terms. However, it was exposed by Fodor (1998b) as merely technohype that paraphrases in connectionist jargon ordinary psychological concepts.

Our common mental concepts are vague, but that does not imply that they should be casually sacrificed to technohype. It implies that an important job of the scientific study of mind is to articulate, analyze, and criticize common psychological concepts to bring out the structures of actual thinking. This is our job in the remainder of the book.

23   Intelligence, Consciousness, and Intentionality

What are the essential characteristics by which we acknowledge an entity to have a mind? Three major candidates in the current literature are *intelligence, consciousness,* and *intentionality.* Other than a few philosophers, I think most people agree that we are intelligent, conscious, and intentional. However, we are hard put if asked to explain how or what it is that we are so. What are the peculiarities, structures, and consequences of intelligence, consciousness, or intentionality? To articulate them clearly is the job of the science of mind. Philosophers and scientists have offered many formulations over the years. Here I examine some of them and criticize some currently prominent ones for yielding to the closed mind. In the next section I present intelligent, conscious, and intentional mentality as openness to the world.

Intelligence and Behavioral Efficiency

Intelligence was the chief mental characteristic in cognitive science for several decades. In a paper entitled "Foundations of cognitive science," Simon and Kaplan (1989) defined: "Cognitive science is the study of intelligence and intelligent systems, with particular reference to intelligent behaviors as computation." What is intelligence? Newell and Simon (1976) replied: "By 'general intelligent action' we wish to indicate the same scope of intelligence as we see in human action." The answer begs the central question in the scientific study of mind: what is it in human actions that we acknowledge as intelligent?

The dominance of the concept of intelligence in cognitive science manifests the bias toward AI engineering instead of natural science. Nature is replete with complicated processes that humans, even with their best effort, cannot emulate. We have to develop chemical engineering to synthesize rubber that is still inferior to the natural product. Amoebas produce amoebas, but biologists cannot. The sun is an efficient nuclear fusion reactor which, after fifty years of research, engineers are unable to build. Are rubber plants intelligent? Are amoebas more intelligent than we are? Is the sun's superior intelligence a reason why it was revered as a god? Intelligence is not merely complexity. Many natural complex processes befuddle the most brilliant of scientists, but that does not make the processes intelligent. Indeed things in the universe seem so orderly yet unpredictable they give an impression of intelligence that incites religious feeling. Ancient people saw intelligence in all natural phenomena and worshipped them as gods. With the rise of science, we have stopped regarding inanimate natural processes, no matter how complicated, as intelligent, for we have found out that they proceed without understanding.

The primary and commonsense meaning of intelligence presupposes active thinking and understanding. We grade beliefs as intelligent or stupid. Things that cannot believe are neither intelligent nor stupid; and the primary notion of intelligence does not apply to them. Intelligent animals learn, know, cope with difficult situations, and persevere in pursing their purposes, all with understanding. In contrast, water erodes the earth and flows more and more in the channels it cut, but it has not learned its ways. On its way to the ocean, it is blocked by rocks, snatched by heat, carried by wind, dropped on mountains, and packed into glaciers, but it neither copes with hardship nor perseveres in trying. These mental terms do not apply to it. In the ordinary sense of intelligence that requires understanding, many people say that intelligence resides not in AI systems but their programmers. Hence they criticize interpreters for anthropomorphically attributing programmers' understanding to their products.

Philosophical advocates of AI evade the criticism by applying the devaluation stance to intelligence to diminish its significance. Instrumental behaviorism and homuncular functionalism muddle up the concept of believe by applying it to all things. When believe is devaluated by promiscuity, intelligence follows in the wake. If water believes in finding its way to the ocean, its unerring methods are so intelligent as to shame many humans. Devaluated intelligence involves no understanding but only behaviors. Thus rubber plants and thermostats and water are all intelligent; they differ only in their IQs. Shorn of understanding, intelligence is reduced to a classification of behaviors; notably, efficiency in performing externally assigned tasks, for example, playing chess or walking like a cockroach. It fits into models of the closed mind where an external mind designer grades the behaviors of the mind according to his own purposes. As such, intelligence has scant psychological connotation. In this behavioral sense people say that consumers are offered numerous "smart" gadgets and television viewers are shown footage of "smart" munitions doing surgical bombing, a small proof of return for the countless tax dollars they invest in "intelligent" weapons.

Behavioral intelligence is as vague as beauty, and like beauty, it resides in the eyes of the beholder. Many kinds of tasks demand different kinds of talents. Many efficiency criteria exist for a task, such as minimization of time, monetary cost, human suffering, environmental degradation, and others. Often criteria conflict with each other. Much violence is required to press multidimensional behaviors into a lineal ordering of intelligence that determines who is more stupid than whom. The standard IQ test, which emphasizes abstract reasoning, is under constant attack for promoting a trait favored in our culture to the neglect of other talents. In many areas, classification of behaviors by degree of intelligence is highly subjective and controversial, as is evident in debates over the relative intelligence of people with different skin colors and whether or not AI systems are intelligent.

An important criterion of intelligence in AI is the Turing test, by which a machine is judged intelligent if it can pass for a human in behind-the-screen conversation. The criterion depends explicitly on subjective opinions of judges. When a machine eventually wins the $100,000 Loebner prize for passing the Turing test, will people argue endlessly whether it is due to the machine's cleverness or the judges' stupidity? Consider POSTMODERNISM GENERATOR at http://www.csse.monash.edu.au/cgi-bin/postmodern. It is a program that combines words, taking account of grammar but not meanings. Every time you hit it, it automatically generates a new essay with perfect scholarly form and apparent erudition loaded with postmodern jargon. Suppose one of its essays is published in a prestigious journal, would you say it passes the Turing test? This is not an outlandish scenario. *Social Text* published a hoax essay by physicist Alan Sokal (1996) that is jammed with sentences as meaningless as those by POSTMODERNISM GENERATOR. Suppose the computer is similarly honored, would you admire its intelligence? Judging from the responses to Sokal's hoax, which made the front page of the *New York Times* (May 18, 1996), I think people are less likely to applaud it than to laugh at the journal's editors.

For all their flirtation with intelligence, AI scientists have not only failed to come up with a clear objective definition for it, they have conceded the failure. Minsky (1985) wrote: "the very concept of intelligence is like a stage magician's trick." Lenat and Feigenbaum (1991) wrote: "Intelligence is in the eye of the (uninformed) beholder." Intelligent behavior is a commodity that fetches fat prices, which in turn translate into power. This is the highest honor anything can achieve in our capitalist society. Nevertheless, it does not give the concept of behavioral intelligence any value in the objective contents of the science of mind.

Consciousness: From Personal Identity to Qualia

Consciousness has been a hot research topic since the early 1990s. A few philosophers, notably advocates of AI and behavioral intelligence, maintain that it is illusory and should be explained away. However, most people agree that consciousness marks us off from things, no matter how intelligent their behaviors are. We readily distinguish between conscious and unconscious entities and know when a person loses consciousness. The meaning that we are familiar with, however, is tacit and vague. It is a totally different matter when we try to frame a definite theory or even a concept for consciousness.

All people are conscious, but not all people have explicit concepts of consciousness. Eastern cultures had theories of consciousness early on. Starting in the second century c.e., Buddhists developed a refined philosophy of mind to explicate the meanings of subject, object, and their relation. Most branches of Buddhism have much to say about consciousness, but one specifically puts it in center stage. The Consciousness School, founded by Indian philosophers Asanga and Vasubandhu, was one of the two major branches of Mahayana Buddhism. To defend the Mahayanist doctrines against numerous rivals, the Consciousness School analyzed human psychology and distinguished eight modes of consciousness. Besides the five perceptual senses and the attentional consciousness common to other Buddhist schools, it added a seventh consciousness for abstract mentation and a "store-house" consciousness as the base of the other seven. The store-house consciousness, containing seeds for all conscious experiences and responsible for their transformation and manifestation, is frequently compared with a flowing stream. Buddhism spread to China in the sixth century and stimulated a lively discourse on mind. The Chinese further developed their ideas of *wei-shih*, or consciousness–only, which, after centuries of quiescence, enjoyed a brief revival in the early twentieth century.[3]

Consciousness was not a distinct concept in Western philosophy until Descartes's turn to inner mental life. Down to the seventeenth century, the Latin *consientia*, which translates as consciousness, was entangled with conscience. Aquinas defined it as "the application of knowledge to acts." As the soul's ability to judge the rights and wrongs of actions, *consientia* was essentially a rational and moral notion, consonant with the intellectual sense of the Aristotelian *nous*. Descartes's meditation first brought out the importance of inner awareness and first-person experience. It was under his influence that Locke stated "consciousness makes personal identity." The idea was so new Leibniz had to coin a French word for "consciousness" in his dialogue with Locke. Initially, consciousness referred only to apprehension of what constitute one's own existence. Gradually was it extended to include awareness of external objects (Baker & Morris 1994).

The earliest Western notion of consciousness is closely tied to what makes a person a person. Locke (1490:335) wrote: "For since consciousness always accompanies thinking, and 'tis that, that makes every one to be, what he calls *self*; and thereby distinguishes himself from all other thinking things, in this alone consists *personal identity*." Leibniz (1765:236) agreed: "I also hold this opinion that consciousness or the sense of *I* proves moral or personal identity." He then went on to emphasize the moral aspect of consciousness.

Generally, rationalists tend to retain the heavy intellectual nuance of *consientia*, so they sometimes equate consciousness with articulated thought if not rationality. Against this rationalist consciousness the romantic movement rebelled and turned to feeling and emotion. By the last part of the nineteenth century, a literary trend developed that penetrated the mask of rationality and exposed the depth of human psychology. Philosophically, Nietzsche (1901:676) called for the "modesty of consciousness," observing: "For the longest time, conscious thought was considered thought itself. Only now does the truth dawn on us that by far the greatest part of our spirit's activity remains unconscious and unfelt." Delving into the genealogy of morals, Nietzsche (1882:333) exposed much of rational morality as the disguised manifestation of hidden *ressentiment*.

When psychology first became an empirical science in the late nineteenth century, its focus was not the unconscious but the conscious. Wilhelm Wundt and William James both defined psychology as the study of conscious experiences. Soon, however, the wind changed. James, who in 1890 analyzed the stream of consciousness and refuted all suggestions that mental states could be unconscious, wrote in 1904 that consciousness "is the name of a non-entity and has no right to a place among first principles." In the first half of the twentieth century behaviorism, which restricted psychology to the prediction and conditioning of overt behaviors, tabooed references to mental states and subjective experiences. Cognitive science, which started to displace behaviorism in the late 1950s, mainly adheres to computationalism, in which thinking is symbol manipulation and cognition is information processing. Computationalism admits "mental states," but they lack consciousness and intentionality, and are more like fine-grained descriptions of behavioral states. Under AI's influence, more vociferous segments of cognitive science tend to identify mind with intelligence qua behavioral efficiency, thus continuing behaviorism in a disguised form (Johnson and Erneling 1997).

Care for people, not the design of lucrative artifacts, brought consciousness back to cognitive science. In 1958 Penfield found that electrical stimulation of regions of patients' brains elicited vivid experiences, including alleged reliving of past episodes. In the 1960s, the technique of surgically severing nerves connecting the cerebral hemispheres was introduced to relieve epilepsy, with interesting side effects. Split-brain patients act normally in everyday life. However, when Sperry (1966) carefully isolated the functions of the disconnected hemispheres in laboratory experiments, he found that each hemisphere had experiences of its own that could differ dramatically from those of the other. Both men were led by their research to introduce consciousness and subjective awareness into their explanatory frameworks. (Eocles 1965; Milner and Ruzz 1992).

In the 1970s the trickle became a torrent, as a wide range of neuropathologies came under intense investigation. All results point to the radical difference between conscious perception and unconscious causal influence of stimuli, which we examined in the preceding chapters. To describe and explain the difference, the notion of consciousness becomes indispensable. Many scientists, among them Baars (1997), Crick and Kock (1990), Edelman (1989), Jackendoff (1987), Schacter (1990), and Weiskrantz (1997), attempted to account for consciousness and find out its underlying processes. Philosophers join in (Dennett 1991; Flanagan 1992; Ellis 1995; Hunt 1995; Tye 1995; Chalmers 1996; Searle 1997; Hurley 1998; Stiewert 1998). In the 1990s consciousness became a hot research topic with two specialized journals and huge conferences (Revonsuo and Kamppinen 1994; Velmans 1996; Cohen and Schooler 1997; Hameroff et al. 1996, 1998). As studies become multicultural, Buddhism returned and found its way into scientific journals (Rao 1998; Varela and Shear 1999).

The Race for Consciousness, the title of a book by John Taylor (1999), is by now a familiar slogan, especially among neuroscientists scrambling to identify processes underlying experiences. "The race may be on, but where's it going?" wondered John Pickering (1999) in his reflection on a conference on consciousness. What are they racing for? When we ask for a clearer description of the nature of consciousness, we find a dazzling array of answers but nothing definite like the goalpost of a race.

Take, for example, Block's (1995) notion of *access consciousness*. When the behavior of an entity has a direct causal connection to something, it has access to that thing, and Block added that it has access consciousness to that thing. Thus a hand calculator has access consciousness when it retrieves the symbol that you interpret as *three* in performing the calculation you interpret as 354 × 930. This concept of access is useful when neuroscientists talk about a cognitive process having direct causal link to the features to which certain brain regions are sensitive. But where does consciousness come in? Many people contend that here it is superfluous, if not misleading, as access or causal channel suffices to characterize the phenomenon.

Rosenthal (1986) proposed a *higher-order thought theory* asserting that; a mental state is conscious only when it becomes the object of thought. You may be furious but you are not conscious of it. Your mental state becomes conscious only when, triggered by your anger, you reflect on it and think, "Boy, am I mad!" This view of consciousness is similar to that in class consciousness or consciousness raising. Reflective thinking crystallizes myriad experiences by categorizing and verbalizing them, hence bringing them to focal attention. However, critics point out that in the basic science of mind, higher-order thought theories confuse consciousness with substantive conceptualization. Day laborers who have no class consciousness are nevertheless conscious of their misery, and they do not transform from unconscious things to conscious persons by learning concepts such as exploitation. Most of our mundane experiences are inarticulate. Important as substantive concepts are, they are neither necessary for experience itself nor sufficient to capture all experiential nuances. It is difficult to accept a notion of consciousness in which you are not conscious when, shouting at the offender, you are too engaged to reflect on yourself. Proponents of higher-order thought theories reply that you in your fury are not totally unconscious but in a different state of consciousness. Then we demand an account of *that* state of consciousness, as it is more basic. To our demand, high-order theories have no reply, except perhaps the contemptuous remark that it is to "low" to deserve attention.

The mental state jumped over by higher-order thoughts is *phenomenal consciousness*, which is the dominant notion of consciousness in current cognitive science. It was the topic of the phenomenological philosophies of Husserl and Merleau-Ponty, and before that, various Eastern philosophies. As discussed in section 6, when a person is in a particular mental state, his phenomenal consciousness contains all the rich nuances of that state. It is a concrete experience that is usually poorly articulated and conceptualized. It is doubtful if theoretical representations, which depend on generalization and abstraction, can capture all its details. To account for all details, however, is not a necessary criterion for satisfactory theories. Fluid dynamics, for example, leaves out details of molecular motion, but is still a good theory for the flow patterns of liquids. The important question is whether, among all its details, phenomenal consciousness exhibits salient features and causal consequences. If it does, it is susceptible to theorization.

Because phenomenal consciousness is an experience articulated mainly from the first-person view, many people assume that its scientific study requires systematic methods of introspection. They find three old methods: introspective experiments used by early psychologists, Husserlian phenomenology, and Buddhist meditation. To adapt these introspective methods to scientific research conducted from the third-person stance, ways have to be found that adequately connect the first- and third-person views. Papers are appearing in journals of consciousness studies discussing how to do it. We wait for results.

Under the shadow of the closed mind, phenomenal consciousness acquires a narrow meaning in the Anglo-American philosophy of mind. Here, phenomenal consciousness is identified with the medieval *quale*, which is strictly introspective. The idea of consciousness as qualia is best expressed by David Chalmers (1996:4): "A mental state is conscious if there is something it is like to be in that mental state. To put it another way, we can say that a mental state is conscious if it has a qualitative feel—an associated quality of experience. These qualitative feels are also known as phenomenal qualities, or *qualia* for short. The problem of explaining these phenomenal qualities is just the problem of explaining consciousness. This is really the hard part of the mind-body problem." Discussions of "missing qualia" or "dancing qualia" occur only behind the veil of perception, for qualia belong solely to the closed mind.

As Searle (1997) pointed out, underlying Chalmers's definition of consciousness is a computational theory of mind. Furthermore, it is a resultant view in which qualia are an added layer draping loosely on unconscious processes characterized in functional and computational terms.

Qualia can be peeled off to yield an unconscious zombie that behaves exactly like a conscious person. The prevalence of this notion in discussions on the nature of consciousness is partly responsible for the resurgence of *epiphenomenalism*. Qualia seem more and more to be epiphenomena without causal relevance and not susceptible to science. As Pickering (1999) summarized the consensus that emerged in a recent conference: "There is something odd about consciousness that makes it difficult to investigate scientifically."

Qualia are sometimes known as "the hard problem" in the science of mind. To face the hard problem is a sensational slogan, but it misses something important. Science progresses not by taking on arbitrary hard problems but by identifying and framing *fruitful* ones. Scientists are not deterred by difficulty if they judge a problem fruitful. Sterile problems are something else; the worst thing a scientist can do is to spend years working on a problem that leads to a dead end. Problems about epiphenomena are unproductive because epiphenomena are causally sterile. If the problems are also hard, so much the more reason for not wasting scarce research resources on them. I think the concept of qualia and the problems framed in terms of it are not fruitful. That does not mean that phenomenal consciousness does not exist, it only means that "qualia" is a bad concept to characterize it. We will do better in trying to find better concepts for scientific accounts that include subjectivity and the first-person view on experience.

Intentionality

A peculiarity is shared by most of our familiar mental terms such as see, hear, love, hate, remember, know, think, dream, hope, and fear. The mental states they characterize are all *about* or *directed at* some things or events in the world. I see a thing; love a person; recall an event; know that a certain state of affairs obtains; hope that it is otherwise. *Intentionality* is the traditional name for the mental peculiarity of aboutness and directedness. It is more prevalent in our mental life than is often assumed. For instance, we saw in section 20 that emotions and moods are more than inner feelings. You are not merely euphoric or depressed when you are happy or melancholic; you are happy about a happening or melancholic about the general state of the world.

The concept of intentionality was adumbrated by Aristotle, elaborated by Arabic philosophers, transmitted by medieval scholars, and revived in the late nineteenth century by psychologist Franz Brentano. He contended that intentionality is the exclusive mark of mental phenomena and gave the classic definition for it (1874:88): "Every mental phenomenon is characterized by what the scholastics of the Middle Ages called the intentional (and also mental) inexistence of an object, and what we would call, although not in entirely unambiguous terms, the reference to a content, a direction upon an object."

The paradigm examples of intentionality are believe and desire. I desire something and I believe that a certain condition holds, although I can desire in vain and believe falsely. Intentionality encompasses two ideas. First, mind is directed at or referring to something, or in other words, a mental state has a content that is about something. Second, that something at which mind directs, usually called the object, is not necessarily real or present, so errors and illusions are possible. Thus the object of intentionality is understood in the most general sense that includes physical objects and more, covering anything conceivable, real or imaginary.

Mind can refer to objects in many ways. The contents of mental states can take various forms and have different degrees of clarity. When they are in verbal form, they are expressible as propositions. The proposition "it rains" is the content of the mental state of believing that it rains. It can also be the content of the mental state of desiring that it rains. Human psychological attitudes such as thinking, believing, wishing, and desiring often have propositions as contents. Thus a subclass of intentionality consists of what analytic philosophers call *propositional attitudes*. People hold psychological attitudes regarding propositions.

Theories of intentionality reveal the dangerous pull of the closed mind. Unlike consciousness, which can be regarded as an internal quale, intentionality is by definition directed at external things and events. Therefore, it should clearly convey openness of mind to the world. This is not the case, however. Many eminent theories of intentionality lapse back into the closed mind. Their failure indicates the intricacy of the open mind, which is more difficult to describe.

The theoretical trouble is apparent in Brentano's classic definition of intentionality. Notice the ambiguity: mind directs at a content and an object. Are the content and the object same or different? If different, how are they related? If same, how are errors possible?

Suppose you believe that it rains. Do you think about the proposition "it rains" or about the weather condition? If you think about the weather, how do you account for the possibility that you are wrong, that it is not raining at all? You can avoid the problem by saying you think only of the proposition and not about the weather. This route, taken by many philosophers, falls into the rut of the closed mind controlled by mind designers. When one always thinks only about propositions and not about things and events, the mind is closed off from the world. Philosophers may add that the proposition is about the weather, but then they have to explain how the mind, which thinks only about the proposition, knows what the proposition is about. Do we need mind designers to tell us that?

Husserl, for example, started his analysis of intentionality by bracketing the world, hence closing off the mind (see section 6). Why did he do that? The reasons he gave are not that far from Descartes's reasons for doubting away the world. In their formulations, intentionality implies a *three-way* relation among subject, world, and contents of mental states such as propositions. Ternary relations are difficult to represent theoretically. Therefore most theoreticians of intentionality make a simplification that breaks the subject–world–content relation into two binary relations. Then they put aside the content–world relation and consider only the subject-content relation. They state that the content to which mind allegedly refers is the *intentional object*, which is a mental representation, an entity inside the head that does not exist in the outside world. It functions as some kind of intermediary between mind and the real object that does exist, hence accounts for the possibility of error and illusion. An example of mental representations is a proposition, so that a propositional attitude is the relation between a subject and a proposition. The attitude of believing, for instance, is the relation between a believer and the belief in his head. Once beliefs, propositions, and mental representations are introduced, intentionality becomes another Cartesian Trojan horse.

The plight of closedness haunts even the most elaborate theories of intentionality. Searle (1983, 1992), a staunch opponent of computationalism and representationalism, offered a theory of intentionality that draws analogy with speech acts. He analyzed intentionality into a psychological mode and a representative content. A psychological mode determines the direction of fit and the direction of causation between mind and world. The mode of perception, for instance, has a world-to-mind direction of causation and its contents have a mind-to-world direction of fit. The representative contents contain a set of satisfaction conditions describing certain objects in specific ways, thus bestowing on them a specific "aspectual shape." When I see a yellow station wagon, for instance, the condition of satisfaction of my perceptual content is the yellow vehicle that is causing my visual experience. Notice that it invokes both causation and the experience itself, which make it quite complicated. The complexity is possible because a content does not stand alone but is a part of a complicated network of concepts and background of skills. By virtue of their causal self-reference and directions of fit and causation, the contents of intentionality are about the world directly, without mediation of sense data or mental representations.

I cannot go into Searle's elaborate theory in detail, but discuss only one idea that is also central to some other theories of intentionality. It holds that the intentionality of a mental content consists of a set of *truth conditions* or *satisfaction conditions* that must be met if the content is to be representative of the object. The idea is familiar in the philosophy of language, where many philosophers regard the meaning of a sentence as the conditions of the world under which the sentence is true. Suppose you are told that the sentence *S* is true if and only if snow is white. If *S* stands for "*La neige est blanche*" or "*Schnee ist weiss*," you learn the meaning of a French or German sentence.

I use foreign languages as examples because "'Snow is white' is true if and only if snow is white" sounds banal. The truth-conditional definition of meaning depends on our tacit understanding of what it means to be *true* and our ability to recognize realistic conditions such as the whiteness of snow. It works in the philosophy of language, which takes for granted many presuppositions of our mental ability, especially in differentiating and recognizing conditions of the real world. When transplanted into the philosophy of mind, whose aim is precisely to investigate our ability to make propositions that we ourselves can judge to be true or false, truth conditions beg the question.

"What is truth?" Pontius Pilate asked and did not wait for an answer. Perhaps he anticipated that he would still be kept waiting after two millennia, despite the central importance of truth and falsity in logic-loaded analytic philosophy. Among numerous theories of truth—numerous because none proves adequate—philosophers are increasingly being pushed to the redundant theory asserting that truth, if meaningful at all, is merely a matter of disquotation: "'Snow is white' is *true* if and only if snow is white" (Horwich 1990). Without an adequate explication of truth, truth conditions can hardly illuminate intentionality. Satisfaction conditions are in the same boat.

The crux of intentionality lies not merely in the direction of fit but fit or satisfaction itself. "Satisfaction condition" is ambiguous. It can refer to either a requirement or the state of affairs required. Analyses of intentionality should explain how the two are distinguished and related; how the requirement and the things required fit; when and how mismatches and errors occur; and how matches or mismatches are judged and acknowledged by the intentional person himself. Such explanations can bring out the three-way relation among the subject, his requirement, and the required state of the world; however, they are seldom found in theories of intentionality. Most theories simply exploit the ambiguity in "satisfaction condition" and acquire apparent plausibility by quietly sliding its meaning from the requirement to the required. Thus they collapse the ternary subject-requirement-required relation into a binary subject-satisfaction condition relation. When pushed, they admit that the condition refers to the requirement. Thus they leave in the dark the central question: what it is for a requirement to be satisfied. More important, how it is possible that a subject can judge when and how a specific requirement is satisfied. The subject himself must be able to render the judgment at least some of the time. If he must always appeal to a third party's judgment, he has lost his intentionality with his mind. The crux of intentionality is the relation between mind and the world. Without a proper explication of satisfaction, a satisfaction condition as a requirement is like an electronic gadget with a bank of plugs with no specification of the receptors they would plug into. Thus the satisfaction-condition model of mind does not escape solipsism. Perhaps it is not too surprising to find Searle (1983) insisting that it must be possible for the intentional mind to belong to a brain in a vat.

The fate of closedness and solipsism is not relieved by increasing the complexity of satisfaction conditions as requirements. A requirement can contain elaborate descriptions of causation, but as long as it cannot tell whether and how causal stipulations are satisfied, it does not touch the world. It merely jumps from a smaller dream into a larger one.

What Meanings to Use?

The notions of intelligence, consciousness, and intentionality are intuitive but not clear. We have seen that each has a range of disparate meanings.

This may not matter in our daily discourse, but poses a problem in scientific inquiries that strive for clarity.

I am convinced that we are conscious, that we know about things in the world, that we are intelligent in recognizing and solving problems, and that these characteristics are central and crucial to our mind. I am not satisfied with the way in which these mental abilities are currently represented in theoretical models. In one way or another, the models seem to slide back to the shadow of the closed mind controlled by mind designers and miss some crucial subtleties that we intuitively hold to be essential to mind.

My analysis of the openness of mind differs in several ways from current theories of mental characteristics. Instead of intelligence as a measure of efficiency and information as a commodity, my analysis emphasizes the intelligibility of the objective world and our ability to find events informative. It has an apparent affinity to intentionality, which is thinking about objects in the world. However, it differs from other models of intentionality by emphasizing the necessity of multiple perspectives and systematic transformations among them. As we will see in the next section, the multiplicity of perspectives forestalls criticisms from social constructionism and relativism. Simultaneously, my model refutes constructionism and relativism by articulating how transformations among perspectives underlie our commonsense notion of objectivity and reality.

For consciousness, I deemphasize qualia but follow Locke and Leibniz in associating consciousness with personal identity, the ability to recognize oneself as a subject as distinct from objects and other thinking people. A conscious being not only can take the first-person view of things but can definitely refer to himself as I. This criterion is not as simple as it seems. It defeats the Cartesian pure thinker who is complete with qualia. The Cartesian ego, stripped of body and uprooted from the spatiotemporal world, is at best able to say "thinking goes on" but not "I think," because there is no entity that persists through changing thoughts and serves as the referent of "I." To have a robust identity of self, the subject must be fully embodied and engaged in the world. Therefore mind is not the property of an organ isolated the head, as some theories of intentionality imply. It is the situated property of a person who finds things meaningful and communicates with other people who share the world. More precisely, the ability to see a meaningful shared world is the basic structure of the open mind.

24 Possibility: Opening the Informative Horizon

What is peculiar about mind? What distinguishes mental beings from non-mental things? We have many psychological concepts for mental properties. Do these concepts have any common peculiarities that we can use as a key to our inquiry? Fortunately, not only does such a peculiarity exist, but it has been clearly articulated.

I begin my investigation into the structures of mind-open-to-the-world by taking my cue from a fact well known to logicians and analytic philosophers. There are a group of concepts that are recalcitrant to the logic that is adequate to describe the behaviors of inanimate things. These include believe, think, see, and other intentional concepts; possibility, actuality, and other modal concepts; ought, permission, and other deontic concepts; and now, yesterday, and other tense concepts. Intuitively, they all have a strong mental connotation. Nonmental things neither think nor care what they ought to do. They engage only in actual interactions and cannot imagine possibilities. To describe them we need only the concepts of before and after but not past and future. What are the peculiarities of these special concepts? What can they tell us about the peculiarities of mind?

Intentional, modal, deontic, and tense concepts are peculiar in that they demand a logical framework that is far more complex than the extensional logic that is sufficient for nonmental things. The logical complexity reflects structural complexity of mind that the concepts describe. I first explain the peculiarities of the concepts generally. Then I concentrate on *possibility* as the most basic concept for mental abilities. It is the presupposition of belief and information, for only by grasping possibilities can one form beliefs and be informed by actual occurrences. It is also the presupposition of using concepts; one entertains a range of possibilities when one uses a concept. This section establishes the presuppositions of information and concept usage, so that the next section can analyze specific concepts, notably, subject and object.

Intentionality and Intensionality

What is the difference between the "sees" in "Tom sees Mary" and the "sees" in "The security camera sees Mary?" Most people would say that sees in the camera's case is metaphorical whereas in Tom's it is not. Tom's vision is conscious and implies recognition; the camera's "vision" is not. Recognition is fallible. People usually recognize the things they see, but they sometimes fail. Therefore we readily accept the qualification "Tom sees Mary but does not recognize her." Even here, seeing is not metaphorical because Tom's failure of recognition is *partial*. Although Tom fails to recognize Mary, his vision is still meaningful; he still recognizes Mary as a person, failing only to recognize her as *the* person. This is categorically different from the absolute failure of recognition for cameras or brains in a vat (see section 4). The literal "see" implies recognition and is mental. The qualification we accept for seeing brings out two important peculiarities of mind: Mental activities are susceptible to errors, and they retain their mental status even when suffering from partial loss of recognition.

We can make the notion of recognition explicit by saying "Tom sees *that* that is Mary," which allows qualification only in judgment but not in recognition. "Tom sees that that is Mary but doesn't recognize her" or "Tom sees that that is Mary but thinks that she is Jane" is senseless because it makes Tom contradict himself.

The tiny *that*, used after an intentional term such as see or think, brings in a whole new logic: intensional logic. Analytic philosophers have long realized that *extensional logic* suffices for descriptions of most nonmental phenomena but not for mental characteristics such as seeing or believing. To describe mental phenomena we need *intensional logic*, which is much more complicated. This logical difference is significant. We saw in section 11 that the emergent properties of a complex entity are of a different kind from the properties of the entity's constituents. Different kinds of properties require different concepts for characterization. A logic is a system of very general concepts. The fact that mental properties require a different logic for description indicates their radical difference from nonmental properties. We can get some ideas of their peculiarities by comparing extensional and intensional logics.

Extensional logic is standard predicate logic. The *extension* of a predicate is the set of all entities that exemplifies it, as the extension of the predicate red is all things red. An essential feature of predicate logic is its principle of extensionality, because of which it is also known as extensional logic. The *principle of extensionality* asserts that equivalent terms—terms with the same extension, referring to the same entity, flanking the two sides of an identity—can be interchanged in any proposition without changing the proposition's truth value. The principle works beautifully for propositions concerning actual inanimate things but fails for those concerning mental activities.

Cases that violate the principle of extensionality call for intensional (with an s) logic. There are several kinds of intensional logic: epistemic logic for knowledge and belief, deontic logic for permission and obligation, modal logic for possibility and necessity, and tense logic for past and future. The mental connotations of epistemic and deontic logics are obvious. They are less apparent in modality and tense, but we will see that possibility and time belong to the most basic structures of our mind.

Separating extensional and intensional logics is the validity of the principle of extensionality. Let us see how it works. "Mark Twain" and "Samuel Clemens" are equivalent terms because both refer to the same man. According to the principle of extensionality, we can substitute "Clemens" for "Twain" in any proposition with impunity. If the proposition is true, it remains true under substitution; false, false. "Twain wrote *Huckleberry Finn*" is true. Substitution produces another true proposition: "Clemens wrote *Huckleberry Finn*."

Now consider "Yamanaga believes that Twain, not Clemens, wrote *Huckleberry Finn*." Suppose the proposition is true because Yamanaga saw "Twain" on the cover of the novel he read but has never heard of Clemens. Replacing "Twain" by "Clemens" in this true proposition yields "Yamanaga believes that Clemens, not Clemens, wrote *Huckleberry Finn*." The substitution not only makes the proposition false but turns poor Yamanaga into someone who has lost his mind.

Anyone can tell what is wrong with the substitution: Yamanaga does not know that "Twain" and "Clemens" are different names of the same person. Our knowledge and more generally our mental abilities are finite. Each of us has a finite mental horizon beyond which we are ignorant. Your horizon of knowledge is different from mine; to put it in another word, you and I have different intellectual perspectives. The finitude of knowledge and the variety of intellectual perspectives, which are essential conditions of the human mind, have no place in extensional logic. To account for them, logicians developed epistemic logic.

Several classes of concepts violate the principle of extensionality. One that philosophers call *intentional* (with a t) contains believe, desire, perceive, think, see, and most familiar concepts in commonsense psychology. Mind-designing philosophers eye intentional concepts with suspicion or hostility. Some maintain that extensional logic alone is sufficient for all "scientific" thinking. Quine (1960:221), for example, denounced the "baselessness of intentional idioms and the emptiness of a science of intention" and banned intentional concepts on the ground that they are fuzzy and unsuitable for his ideal science.

Behaviorists, instrumentalists, and eliminativists in the philosophy of mind appeal to Quine's authority. One of them coined the verb "to quine" meaning "to deny resolutely the existence or importance of something real or significant" (Dennett 1988). They quined consciousness and intentionality. Quine, not merely a staunch behaviorist but a logician and genuine philosopher, argued on a deeper and more general level. He opted for discarding all concepts that violate the principle of extensionality. This move purges mental notions more thoroughly than eliminativism, which is concerned only with intentional concepts. Its wide consequences also bring out how deeply mental notions have sipped into important concepts in science.

Possibility and Temporality

The class of concepts that incur Quine's wrath by violating the principle of extensionality are loosely called modal concepts. *Modality* has a narrow and a broad meaning. Narrowly, it refers to the classic modal concepts of possibility, actuality, and necessity. Aristotle presented a rudimentary exposition of possibility and necessity, which his medieval commentators developed into the general concept of modality. In the development, the range of modal concepts was broadened to include intentional, deontic, and tense concepts (Rescher 1968).

In the broad sense, *modal* concepts stand in contradistinction to *descriptive* concepts. Descriptive predicates such as being a mouse ascribe properties to things. Descriptive propositions such as "The cat catches a mouse" account for states of affairs. The modal concept of possibility qualifies a predicate in "The cat catches something that is possibly a mouse." It can also qualify a proposition, as in "It is possible that the cat catches a mouse." In both cases, the objective state of affairs is just the cat catching a mouse. Qualifying "the cat catches a mouse" with "possible" does not add or alter anything objective. It does, however, illuminate *how we think* by expressing our ways of conceiving the state of affairs and our mental contributions to its description. Kant (1781:239) explained it well: the concepts of possibility, actuality, and necessity "have the peculiarity that, in determining an object, they do not in the least enlarge the concept to which they are attached as predicates. They only express the relation of the concept to the faculty of knowledge."

Intentional concepts are modal in the broad sense because they qualify states of affair, as in "I believe that the cat catches a mouse." Noting its similarity with "It is possible that the cat catches a mouse" and knowing that "believe" foils extensional logic, we would not be surprised to find that "possible" does the same.

Propositions qualified with possibility or necessity violate the principle of extensionality. Consider a variation on Quine's example that has become the industry standard. "The number of planets = nine" is an identity. Therefore "nine" and "the number of planets" must be interchangeable in all propositions, according to the principle of extensionality. The principle holds for descriptive propositions. If "The number of stars is greater than the number of planets" is true, so is "The number of stars is greater than nine." Trouble comes with modal propositions. Consider the true modal proposition "It is possible that the number of planets is less than nine."[4] Extensional substitution makes it false: "It is possible that nine is less than nine." To reckon with possibility and necessity, logicians developed modal logic.

Another class of modal concepts is temporal, as in "Sometimes the leaves are green" or "Last month the leaves were green." Propositions involving temporal qualifications pose similar difficulties for the principle of extensionality. Suppose "Jane Smith was the prettiest unmarried woman in town and had many suitors" is true. Jane later married Mr. Jones, yielding the identity "Mrs. Jones was Jane Smith." Substitution gives "Mrs. Jones was the prettiest unmarried woman in town," which is a contradiction. To account for time properly, one has to go beyond extensional logic and use tense logic.

Expressing our ways of conceiving the world, intentionality, possibility, and temporality are all closely associated with mind. They all share the logical characteristic of violating the principle of extensionality. Thus their logical peculiarity offers an important clue to analyze the basic structures of mind.

If Yamanaga knew that Twain was Clemens, substituting "Clemens" for "Twain" would preserve the truth value of "Yamanaga believes that Twain wrote *Huckleberry Finn*." Extensional substitution assumes perfect knowledge. Its occasional failure brings into relief several crucial features of human knowledge: Human knowledge is finite, issuing from a certain perspective but capable of adopting alternative perspectives. These features are reinforced by modal and temporal concepts. With possibilities, one considers a situation from various perspectives different from the actual one. With past and future, one considers a thing from perspectives different from the present one.

I contend that acknowledgment of many interrelated possible perspectives is a fundamental structure of the human mind. Contrary to philosophies that insist on the view from nowhere, the variability of perspectives does not vitiate but underlies the possibility of objective science. The implication of many perspectives is apparent when we consider possibilities. Let us start with the concept of possibility, and examine how it structures our thinking and what havoc its banishment would wreak.

Information versus Natural Structures

We are undergoing an information revolution, if we are not already in an information age, according to the popular media. In these contexts, information is a commodity that one can purchase and exchange, and its value is surpassing values of other commodities. This commercial meaning of information has little value in scientific studies of mind, as it has missed much of informativeness. What does information generally mean? How is information possible? What does it tell us about mind?

I propose that information presupposes the general concept of possibility, the basic structure of our mind that is presupposed by even the general concepts of object and causality that we encountered in sections 17 and 19. By conceiving possibilities, we free ourselves from the actual and the present, acknowledge objects that persist in our absence, remember and anticipate, find causal events informative, and make the world intelligible.

The ordinary notion of information—knowledge gained from study, observation, or instruction—is thoroughly mental. We take for granted the existence of people who are knowledgeable. Therefore we can reify knowledge, treat pieces of information as commodities, reckon their amounts, and build machines to process them. As a commodity, information depends on an informed community but not necessarily on any specific member of the community. This book or that computer disk carries information without being read by you or me or any specific person, but its being informative presupposes involvement of some people or some mental beings. Without some mental beings, information does not exist, even if the natural universe that mental beings would recognize as the object of information exists.

A science of mind that aims to find out how people are knowledgeable cannot simply take information as commodity. It must investigate general structures of mental subjects presupposed by the commercial notion of information. Therefore I will stick to the basic idea of information as objective knowledge. To focus on the mental subject, I emphasize informativeness. To avoid sliding into the commercial sense of information, I must first dispel mind-designing philosophies that rip mental presupposition from information. The discussion will simultaneously clarify the notion of information.

Some mind-designing philosophies want to "naturalize mind," which is a euphemism for dismissing mental concepts as "unscientific." To achieve this aim they must discard information, but some are unwilling to do so. Dretske (1981) tried to purge information of its epistemic connotation. He contended that information is independent of mind, for it existed *as information* from the beginning, antedating the appearance of all intelligent life and independent of interpretive activities of all mental agents. Such positions confuse information with structure or structural complexity; confuse information with causation; confuse scientists and the objects they study; confuse the general meaning of information with substantive meanings of specific pieces of information.

Structure or structural complexity alone does not imply information. Clouds in the sky have complex patterns, but they are not god-sent information. Smoke signals, although structurally much simpler than clouds, carry information. Physical structures that we recognize as information may have existed long before the evolution of life, but they existed as mere structures and not as information. The geological strata exposed in the Grand Canyon existed for eons, but only to mental beings do they become information about earth's history.

Causal interaction is usually not information acquisition. Physical things constantly interact with each other, change because of the interaction, and behave differently due to the changes, but they do not thereby acquire knowledge and information. An atom emits a photon that is absorbed by a second atom, which consequently jumps from an initial state to an excited state. The second atom has not acquired information about the first atom from the photon. Physicists can extract information about the absorbed photon and hence the first atom from the excited state of the second atom. Physicists are capable of being informed, atoms are not. When people erroneously project the understanding of physicists onto the physical systems they study, they muddle up information with causation. This muddle lies at the bottom of ecological perception (see section 17), and not only there.

More subtly, mind-designing philosophies confuse the mental activity of finding the world generally meaningful with the mental activity of assigning specific meanings to specific events. This confusion is most apparent in the invocation of communication theory to maintain that information is mind independent; forgetting that the theory presupposed the general notion of meaningful information.

Communication theory characterizes the capacity of communication channels. Suppose you wants to send a message to your friend; the channel may be a telephone line or a satellite link. In the communication system, your message is encoded into a form acceptable to the channel, distorted somewhat by noise in the channel, and finally decoded into a form recognizable by your friend. Since communication is a purposive activity and people want to preserve the meanings of their messages, communication engineers have to ensure that noise distortion is not too great. Furthermore, for rapid communication, they want to design channels capable of handling large amount of signals. It is in this context of purposive human communication that Claude Shannon introduced the scientific notion of information (Verdú 1998). Consequently, the notion is soaked with intentional connotation from the start. The intentional connotation accords with our ordinary idea of information, which is always information about something and for the purpose of other things.

As a general mathematical theory, communication theory abstracts from the specific contents of specific pieces of information. However, it presupposes some form of general interpretation to differentiate between signal and noise, identify sources of signals, and delineate communication channels. Detached totally from mental and intentional factors, there is no reason to call one pattern signal and another noise over and above their being certain physical structures or causal regularities. Therefore the concept of information plays no part in the objective content of physics but only in the theoretical tools of physical research. The objective contents of physics only describe the electromagnetic field radiated by stars and scattered by interstellar dust, and explain the causal relation between the field's journey and its property on reaching Earth. The purely physical descriptions of structures and causal regularities exhaust the objective phenomena, leaving no crack for the notion of information to sip in. It is only for the human purpose of learning about a specific star that physicists talk about its radiation field as a "messenger" carrying information on stellar properties. With the purpose in mind, physicists interpret the star's radiation as signal to be separated from the noise caused by interstellar dust, although both radiation and dust are parts of nature. Radiation from stars millions of light years away existed long before humans evolved, but it is a mere physical field, and not an informative signal without someone's mental interpretation.

Definitions of information and the amount of information, which lie at the foundation of communication theory, depend on the notion of possibility. Possibilities do not exist in the mindless world; they rise when mental beings make sense of actual events. Therefore the amount of information is mind dependent in a way that the amount of mass is not.

Once we take for granted knowledgeable people and the *general* meanings of signal and information, we can use communication theory to abstract from *specific* meanings of informational contents and talk only of the amount and forms of information. This abstraction allows us to avoid interpreting specific contents. It does not avoid the general interpretations of signal and noise, the possible and the actual, which it presupposes. Therefore it does not support mind-naturalizing and mind-designing philosophers' claim that information exists totally independent of mental interpretation.

Information, Possibility, and Mind

If mind-designing philosophers looked at the concept of information in communication theory more deeply, they would find it inimical to their doctrines. Mathematically, information is defined as the specification of one case among a set of possibilities. Multiple-choice questions, for example, probe students' store of information by asking them to pick one among several possible answers. The basic unit of information, a *bit*, specifies one of two equally probable alternatives, such as whether a binary digit is 0 or 1. Thus the concept of information rests squarely on the concepts of possibility and actualization, which are modal concepts that violate the principle of extensionality. It would be out of the window if Quine the arch mind-naturalizer had his way.

The actual must be possible, but not vice versa. The universe and all the things and processes it consists of are actual; there are no mysterious entities called "possibilia" hiding behind actual things. A sensual stimulus is an actual occurrence and it always changes its recipient as governed by causal laws. However, it is informative only to the perceiver who, besides registering it and being causally influenced by it, is also aware of what it is not but can be, of the world having other possibilities. To be informed, an entity must be aware of possibilities, so that it can see the actualization of a specific possibility as a piece of data that eliminates some prior uncertainty. To an entity incapable of entertaining possibilities, the actual configuration exerts causal influence but imparts no information. You wonder whether it rains or shines and gain information by looking out the window. A plant simply droops in the sun and soaks in the rain, uninformed by either. Awareness of alternatives, which goes beyond mere responses to stimuli, turns *structures in the environment* into *information about the world* and opens a realm of intelligibility like a clearing in a dark forest. With the clearing, mind is born.

Only entities capable of being informed can believe, doubt, and admit error. These are the characteristics of the open mind. A closed mind is certain of itself because it cannot doubt, because it is incapable of knowing that reality can possibly be different from what it thinks. HAL, the supercomputer in *2001: A Space Odyssey*, boasted: "We are foolproof and incapable of error." He was not the least troubled when he and his equally foolproof sibling arrived at opposite conclusions for the same situation. And he flashed the "computer malfunction" sign when he cut off life support and killed the hibernating astronauts entrusted to his care. HAL was not incapable of error but incapable of knowing the meaning of error. Mindless things commit no error because they cannot. We can imagine atoms sneering at HAL's boast: "Big deal, as if any of us is capable of error in this sense." HAL's incapacity to doubt and admit error exposed him for what he was. He was a remarkable information processor, but he was not informed.

Constitutive and Instrumental Possibility

To go beyond the actual and entertain possibilities is the hallmark of the open mind that understands the world. It is no surprise that the concept of possibility suffuses our everyday discourse and scientific research. Scientists of mind and subjects they investigate both think in terms of possibilities, because they all have the same general mental ability. Thus it is mandatory for scientists of mind to separate the *use* and *attribution* of possibility. They should distinguish in their models the *instrumental* possibility that they themselves use in their theoretical thinking and the *constitutive* possibility that they ascribe to the actual mental states of their subjects. Similarly, a self-consistent theory of mind should distinguish *instrumental* information informative only to scientists who frame the theory and *constitutive* information informative to subjects that the theory describes.

The concept of possibilities occurs in all theories; however, only in theories of mind and mental beings is it constitutive and belonging to the objective contents. In physics and other natural sciences, possibilities are not objective contents but are theoretical notions that physicists use to understand aconscious physical systems. They do not imply that the systems themselves are aware of possibilities and do not belong to actual states of the systems. Similarly, possibility and information are theoretical notions used by engineers to design communication systems and are not understood by the systems. Telephone lines handle large amount of information without being the least informed.

In contrast, mental beings anticipate possibilities that do not obtain at the present. Consequently the notion of possibility is constitutive of mental systems in the sense that it is indispensable in characterizing the structures of actual mental states. Thus the concept of possibility belongs to objective contents of theories of mind.

The distinction between constitutive and instrumental possibilities lifts a confusion about computers. To search through a possibility space to find states that satisfy a given criterion is perhaps the most common strategy in AI. Does the strategy imply that computers are mindful? No, because the possibilities are not constitutive but instrumental; they are possibilities only to computer programmers and users, not to the computers themselves. AI scientists admit that the problem domain with its possibilities makes sense only on the knowledge level where humans operate and not on the symbol level where computers operate (Newell 1990). The computer goes from one actual state to another until it halts on reaching a certain condition, like gas that passes rapidly through myriad actual states before settling into those states with maximum entropy. Programmers see the computer as searching through possible solutions; physicists see the gas as wandering in its space of possible states. But the computer or the gas simply evolves dynamically, driven by artificial rules or governed by physical laws. At each moment it realizes an actual state that harbors no structure for the notion of other states or alternatives. Thus the computer is totally different from mental systems whose actual state at each moment is much more complex because it encompasses simultaneously several possible courses of events.

Imagination: Breaking Free from the Grip of the Immediately Present

To be open to possibilities requires the ability to disengage from the actual and imagine what one knows to be not actual. It does not come easily. The actual and ongoing stimulus, the present sound, sight, and smell, the dynamics of inner structures, imminent bodily urges and feelings fascinate so strongly that many animals are totally absorbed by them. They dictate these animals' responsive behaviors. To break from their grip is more difficult than imagined by us who are so used to it. When chickens see food on the other side of a narrow wire fence, they rush straight at it and struggle in vain against the fence, never seeing the possibility of going around it. Sometimes a struggling chicken accidentally stumbles to the edge of the fence and gets to the food, but it is not any wiser. To be open to possibilities is more than simply adding a fluctuating factor to the behavior for more variation. It requires imagination of what is systematically related to the actual stimulus.

To act with purposes or for goals is often regarded as a criterion of mindful agents. Of course, the purposes or goals must be constitutive and intrinsic to the agent, not merely instrumental and belonging to mind designers. Many animal behaviors that appear to be purposive turn out to be complicated, stereotyped responses to stimuli. Young gulls peck at their mother's beak; ants remove the remains of their relatives from the nest; robins attack other robins that intrude in their territory. These behaviors have tempted some people to attribute purposes: gulls aim to get food, ants to clean their nest, robins to drive off competitors. Closer investigation, however, reveals that although the behaviors often achieve the effects we humans regard as goals, they are not performed by the animals with those goals in mind. Young gulls peck at any long dotted object regardless of whether or not it yields food; robins attack any red lump regardless whether it poses threat. Ants simply react to a chemical; they drag anything dosed with oleic acid, including their nestmates alive and kicking, out into the dumping ground, but leave dead ants in the nest if the acid is washed away. In short, these behaviors are programmed responses triggered or released by the stimulation of dotted objects, red lumps, and oleic acid (Radner 1996).

Purposes are significant and have many active ramifications, as purposive actions contribute to the welfare or the perceived welfare of the agent. No significance can be found for behaviors toward dots, lumps, and acid, which are arbitrary and pointless. Significant purposes usually demand flexible strategies of achievement, but such flexibility is conspicuously absent here. Gulls, robins, and ants fail to show that they have significant purpose for begging food, fighting competitors, and cleaning nests. They show no sign of recognizing situations that are totally not relevant and not appropriate to the alleged purpose, and they show no sign of trying to find alternative means to it.

Purposive actions are distinguished from mindless stereotyped behaviors by the abilities to disregard features in a stimulus that are not relevant to the purpose, and to imagine alternative means to the end that are not present in the stimulus. The ability to negate makes room for imagination to play. The actual and the present are always positive. Negation enables one to slack the dictate of reality and entertain possibilities that are not actual; to go beyond imminent presence and realize that things absent from view do persist; to escape from the present moment and entertain changes that depend on recognizing enduring things whose properties are not the same as they were or will be; to start transforming the blind environment of pure causation into an intelligible world that is the object of experience and contemplation.

To use a tool is to handle an object in a way that is not obvious in its appearance. To make a tool is to turn an object into something that it is presently not. Thus tool using demands imagining the possibilities of an object, and tool making demands further imagination about its potentiality. Such imaginative ability is demonstrated, among others, by chimps who strip leaves from branches to fashion twigs fitting to dip for honey or fish for termites. Great apes often play with things with no apparent purpose, and many observers conjecture that they are exploring possibilities. Most chimps, for instance, spontaneously play with and join two attachable sticks, even if the resultant long stick has no immediate use (Parker and McKinney 1999).

To be open to possibilities requires not only imagination but also the power to disengage from the stimulus, to suppress the automatic responses to it so that one can act on the imagination. Many animals capable of imagination are limited in their power of detachment. Chimpanzees that learned to join two short sticks into a long one for reaching far-away food nevertheless forget the possibility when they see a food they especially want. Gripped by the enticing food, they persist in trying to reach it with a short stick, too busy to pause and consider alternatives. A similar weakness of theirs is exposed in a game where a player chooses one pile of candy out of two, but receives the pile he rejects and sees the one he picks given to a rival. Human children quickly learn to pick the smaller pile to receive the bigger one, but chimps never do. No matter how often they play the game, they can never resist choosing the bigger pile and thus see it given away. However, if the piles of candies are represented by numerals that they have learned, the chimps have no difficulty choosing the smaller number to get more candies. There are several interpretations of their behaviors. It is possible that they have not really grasped the representative meaning of the numerals, hence they have merely learned to pick certain symbols to receive the bigger pile of candies. This interpretation is contested by many trainers, who cite other experimental results to argue that the chimps do understand that numerals represent quantities. Suppose we agree with trainers. Then the chimps' behaviors reveal their failure to free themselves from the immediate response to the stimulus of actual candies. Consequently, the imagined possibility of choosing the smaller quantity, which they demonstrate when not being tempted by the sight of candies, is unable to sway action (Boysen et al. 1996).

The Clearing and the Horizon of Intelligibility
Spiraling in from physical systems in general, through insects, birds, apes, to humans, we have arrived at a primitive condition for mentality: *the ability to negate the actual and imagine the possible.* In contrast to passive responses to stimuli, imagination of alternatives is the spontaneous mental activity of the subject. Because of it, an animal is no longer conditioned to behave in fixed ways, constrained to run on a track like a tram. It sees leeway for maneuver, for action.

The distinction between the actual and the possible opens a new dimension categorically different from distinctions among actual quantities, qualities, and relations. Without this dimension, there is only a brute environment imparting disjoint actual stimuli. The new dimension of possibility enables us to interpolate actual stimuli, to make sense of them, and thus turn raw reality into meaningful facts. Stuck with the actual only, we are like the fictional inhabitants of the two-dimensional Flatland where things appear and disappear mysteriously in actual perceptions. By

imagining the possibility of a third spatial dimension, the mystery of intermittent appearances in Flatland becomes intelligible things traveling in
three-dimensional space, and observations of their appearances yield information about their trajectories. Only in the light of the possible is the
actual informative and meaningful. Imagination of possibilities opens a
clearing wherein the environment lights up and becomes an intelligible
world for the first time.[5]

The range of possibilities varies, and its limit forms the horizon of
intelligibility for an individual or a species. Language, symbolic representations, and large conceptual schemes enable humans to open realms of
possibilities far greater than those of other animals. A tiny realm, however,
is not vanishing. The crucial step is to go beyond the immediately present,
to make a distinction, no matter how slight, between the actual and the
possible. Ample evidence suggests that humans are neither the only nor
the first to make the step. The first step may be as small as Neil Armstrong's step on the moon, but with it some animals leap to a new plan
of being. Note that we are considering qualitative differences, not the
engendering historical processes. Like Armstrong's step, which is symbolic
of a long and arduous project, the step to the realm of possibility must
have taken millions of years of evolution.

A match struck in the dark, the first flicker of mentality illuminates
only a small clearing in which the actual is not much more than the
present stimulus. The clearing, however, is not rigid and static. As its
horizon expands with language-aided concepts, especially causal concepts,
the realm of the actual expands to open a world far beyond our immediate sensual reach. This extended conception of the actual has presupposed many ideas of the possible, which is why it also demands more
explicit notions of *existence* and *reality*. The expanding reality neither
annexes nor crowds out the realm of the possible, which expands around
it like the light of a growing fire. In the expansion, possibility also acquires
more meanings and comes to include *uncertainty* and *unnecessity*. The
horizon of intelligibility then signifies the finitude of knowledge, remind-
ing us that the world is larger than our comprehension and we are not
omniscient.

The skeletal structure of the clearing of intelligibility is manifested
in modal concepts discussed earlier. Chief among them is possibility, the
basis of information. Possibility pervades our thinking. Conjecture, choice,
and planning, which are indispensable to our capacity as autonomous and

rational agents, depend on it. Probability, necessity, and certainty build on it; so do disposition and potentiality. Less conspicuously but more pervasively, it is expressed in small auxiliary words such as can, may, and ought. Ought implies can, and one cannot do the impossible. Even less noticeable is differentiation between the general and the particular; the general always covers a range of possibilities, of which the particular is a case. Finally, the most prevalent idea, that of an enduring and changing thing, invokes possibility, as it implies that the thing can be different from what it presently is. We can think of the past and future because we can break free from the present. When you look in the mirror, remembering how smooth your face once was and fearing more lines will appear, you have tacitly presupposed possibility.

Many philosophers believe that modal concepts are indispensable to our mental life. For Kant (1781), possibility, actuality, and necessity constituted one of the four categorical groups that he argued to be the necessary and most general conceptual structures for all experiences. Heidegger (1926:143) put possibility squarely at the foundation of human existence: "It [Dasein] is primarily Being-possible. Dasein is in every case what it can be, and in the way in which it is its possibility."

Coming from the side of logical rather than existential analysis, Jaakko Hintikka (1975) was no less emphatic about possibility. He held that intentionality must involve "the simultaneous consideration of several possible states of affairs or courses of events," which he said is not far from Hazlitt's dictum: "Man is the only animal that laughs and weeps; for he is the only animal that is struck with the difference between what things are and what they ought to be." My only disagreement is with the exclusiveness in attributing intentionality to humans. Monkeys readily learn to retrieve food that they previously saw hidden in a certain place. They are exasperated when they see their favorite food being hidden but, thanks to the trick of experimenters, later find in the hiding place a food they do not care for. Perhaps monkeys do not laugh or weep when confronted with the difference between what is and what should be, but they surely can show anger and frustration.

Logical Possibilities and Thrown Possibilities

In considering insects, birds, and humans, the preceding argument presupposed that they are situated in the environment in the sense of being interactive parts of it. Imagination of possibilities marks the first step in which situated entities acquire an open mind by making sense of their environment. Thus our notion of possibility is weightier than logical possibility. Anything not self-contradictory is logically possible. It is logically possible that the universe came into existence a minute ago and will cease to exist a minute hence. It is also logically possible that the universe is made up not of enduring three-dimensional things but of four-dimensional worms, bundles of features, or whatnot (see section 17). Closed from reality, one can dream up anything as long as it is not contradictory. Thus logical possibilities can be conceived by both the disembodied closed mind trapped behind the veil of formality and the open mind when it chooses to abstract. The possible as distinct from the actual, however, is recognized only by engaged beings with open mind.

The closed mind stresses the primacy of logical possibilities. The mind open to the world stresses the primacy of what Heidegger (1926:143) called *thrown possibilities*. Logical possibilities require only noncontradiction; thrown possibilities require actual contexts. Heidegger argued that the capability to be open to possibilities, including Dasein's own, is "the most primordial and ultimate positive way in which Dasein is characterized ontologically." Dasein's primary possibility is not "empty logical possibility" but "thrown possibility," whose range is constrained by the conditions of our own constitution and our natural and social environments. As mortals, we are thrown into a situation with a certain horizon. It is up to us to explore its possibilities, to weigh and choose among them in our action, to develop them, to expand our horizon. If we have leisure and if we please, we can sit down and think about all logical possibilities, but that is secondary.[6]

The primacy of thrown possibility in our thinking is upheld by developmental psychology. How do children learn the meanings of words? It is an almost impossible task, according to the dominant empiricist model based on logical possibilities. Children hear a word for which there are infinitely many logical interpretations. The word can be the label for an object, or a part of it, a color, a texture, an aspect, a bundle of properties, a temporal slice of a four-dimensional worm, whatever. Children form hypotheses of all these logical possibilities and gradually eliminate the wrong ones to arrive at the correct meaning of the word. Learning models show that this process requires far larger mental resources than are realistic for children or even adults. "Given the impossibility of ruling out every logically possible hypothesis, how is it that children succeed in figuring out the correct meanings of terms?" Psychologist Ellen Markman (1989:8) asked. "Part of the answer is that children are constrained or biased to consider only some kinds of hypothesis. They do not have to eliminate many logical possibilities because they never consider them in the first place." Being unaware of certain possibilities is a limitation of the intellectual horizon that differentiates thrown possibilities from empty logical possibilities. Children are born with certain mental, infrastructural, and physical conditions. Above all, they are engaged in manipulating objects, and it is with this real world that their thrown possibilities are concerned.

Possibility and Concept

As the distinction from the actual and the extension beyond the present, thrown possibilities are inherently relational. Possibility has many degrees of explicitness and substantiveness. Most dimly, the possible is a negation of the case at hand. One doubts or excludes certain cases but does not even have a clear general notion of alternatives. For instance, infants four months old notice the difference between physically feasible events and physically infeasible events. They show surprise at the disappearance of a toy temporarily occluded by a screen. However, they do not look for the missing toy until they are nine months old (Spelke and Newport 1998). Younger infants notice the difference between two types of events. From their surprise at infeasible events, we can say they have a protoconception of negation and even possibility. But they have yet to develop the general concept of possibility.

At its most skeletal level, the general concept of possibility contains the general notion of alternatives but specifies nothing positive or definite about what the options are. It is expressed by a lost traveler who stands on a precipice and mutters "there must be another way" without the foggiest idea where the way lies. Despite its lack of definite options, the general concept of possibility is most important; it prompts the traveler to seek alternatives rather than to freeze in despair. As the first break-away from the dictate of the actual, it opens the mind to doubt and makes meaningful the distinction between truth and falsity.

One who conceives some definite possibilities for a certain situation has some grip over a concept for that situation. Conceptual ability improves as one sees more possibilities and their interrelations. When young children start to search for a hidden object, they see definite possibilities for the object's location, showing that they have begun to develop the general concept of enduring objects. It will take several more years for them to master this complicated concept, which, as explained in the following sections, is actually a framework of general concepts. During these years children conceive more possibilities for objects and systematize them to form conceptual schemes.

We saw in section 15 that a concept is a mental ability to make some discriminations or judgments. Among mental abilities, envisaging and relating possibilities are the most basic ones manifested in concepts. Possibility separates *conceptual discrimination* from *differential sensitivity*. An animal has different sensitivities for two kinds of stimuli when it has one response for actual stimuli of one kind and another response for actual stimuli of the other kind. Differential sensitivities are what many stimulus–response experiments probe. Experimenters consecutively show pigeons many pictures, some of which contain people, others do not. They have some success in training the birds to peck only when a picture contains people, although it is doubtful that the discrimination is of people or something else. More important, discrimination is strictly stuck to actual stimuli. There is no indication that the pigeons see beyond the stimulus for what people can do or relate to the people in various pictures (Herrnstein 1990; Thompson 1995).

Differential sensitivity sticks to the immediately present and the particular entity; it responds in a special way to a present entity if the entity is a dog, full stop. Conceptual discrimination treats particular entities, but it also generalizes. When we recognizes a particular dog as a dog, we realize that it is a member of a group that includes indefinitely many members; in other words, the particular is an instance of the concept of dog, which is something general that also applies to many other dogs. We see a sleeping dog, but we know that it barks and runs. Generalization opens the realm of possibilities and leads us beyond the immediately present. It enables us to think about dogs in their absence and to anticipate their behaviors.

Instead of talking about an ability, it is often easier to talk about what the ability enables us to handle. Thus we often take a concept to be something general that applies to a range of items, many of which are not present or actual. It is a *possibility space*, or a set of possibilities with certain structures that account for relations among possibilities. The structures are important; they distinguish a concept's possibility space from its extension. Possibility spaces for various concepts overlap, thus generating conceptual relations and facilitating inference.

Inclusion is a form of overlap. The inclusion of some possibility spaces in others occur in taxonomy. A general concept has a large possibility space that more substantive concepts carve into smaller spaces. The possibility space for general concepts of physical objects, for instance, is huge, because it covers all possible behaviors of everything physical. It is divided by substantive concepts for various kinds of objects such as animals or artifacts. Further division is effected by more specific concepts such as insects or computers.

Most overlapping of possibility spaces is not inclusive. Possibility spaces for concepts of bird and flight overlap at some regions, but birds have possibilities beyond flight and flight has possibilities beyond birds. Because a thing usually has many properties, the possibility space for the concept for a kind of thing overlaps many possibility spaces for concepts of properties. Usually, we deem a concept important if its possibility space is the center overlapping many noninclusive spaces. As hubs of possibilities, such concepts become the crux of inference.

Possibility and the Foundations of Science

Despite the importance of the concept of possibility in our everyday thinking, Quine concluded that it is dispensable because it is not fit for ideal science. Ideal science is a fantasy in mind-designing philosophies and has nothing to do with actual science. A look at actual science shows that it not only retains the concept of possibility but systematically formulates it into scientific theories. Many mathematical theories start with the basic posit of a possibility space that encompasses all the states a system can possibly assume under all conceivable conditions.

Perhaps the most obvious examples of possibility spaces occur in the probability calculus and statistical inference. The probability calculus encompasses all possible configurations of a system in an exhaustive possibility space. Another example is modern dynamical theory. Dynamical theories consider explicitly the causal or temporal relations among various possible states. As noted in section 11, modern dynamics is more powerful than classical dynamics because it expands the scope of generalization. Generalization opens new realms of possibilities. It accounts for processes ensuing from all possible initial conditions for all possible values of control parameters, which it summarizes in a "state space portrait."

Possibility spaces are also called state spaces and other names in science. Quantum mechanics calls them Hilbert spaces; statistical mechanics calls them phase spaces. Furthermore, quantum mechanical predictions are probabilistic, and statistical mechanics has its postulate of equal a priori probability; probability depends on possibility.

Examples can be multiplied, but we need not continue. We have seen enough to appreciate the full impact of Quine's (1960) doctrine to universalize the principle of extensionality and expel modal concepts, including the concept of possibility. Dagfinn Føllesdal (1969) put it best in his sympathetic review of Quine's philosophy: "If Quine's conclusion in *Word and Object* is unavoidable, then any attempt to build up adequate theories of causation, counterfactual, probability, preference, knowledge, belief, action, duty, responsibility, rightness, goodness, etc. must be given up." The result is calamitous. Without concepts for causality and probability, science is in ruins.

Scientific theories are not mirrors of the universe. They do not merely depict the world but depict it in a way that is intelligible to us. By making the world humanly comprehensible, they reflect essential structures of the human mind. Modal concepts are indispensable in science because they account for our mental contribution to the intelligibility of the world. Quine quined modal concepts in the name of ideal science, but his ban, if instituted, would destroy the possibility of actual science.

25   Perspectives and the Objectivity of Experiences

We saw in section 15 that concepts are mental abilities and in section 24 that the most basic ability is to entertain and relate various kinds of possibilities. Thus we can characterize the structures of mind by the concepts it grasps. What are the concepts without which we cannot find objects intelligible and events informative? What possibilities do they entail?

Kant (1781) argued that the minimal structures of the human mind are general concepts of objects, experimental support for which we saw in the chapters on perception and memory. I summarize the structures in *concepts of the world*, by which our mind opens to a world intelligible to us as consisting of causally related objects and ourselves as integral parts. Structured by them, the open mind is a situated property that absorbed certain salient characteristics of the world in which the person engages. They consist of interrelated general concepts, including that of individual entities and causality, and involve at least two possibility spaces, that for *objects* and that for *mental frames*. Possibility spaces have certain structures and thus are not merely collections of unrelated possibilities. Rulelike relations among possible objects constitute what Kant called the objective unity of consciousness; rulelike relations among possible mental frames constitute the subjective unity of consciousness. The two sides of the coin together explain how we are aware of ourselves as informed subjects simultaneously as we make sense of objects.

As minimal structures of our immediate experiences, concepts of the world are tacitly understood by everyone. To articulate them explicitly, I use a *transformation schema* borrowed from modern physical theories. With it I illustrate how two interrelated variables—object and mental frame—structure the commonsense notion of objective knowledge based on human tolerance and restraint of subjective perspectives. When the variable of mental frame is deleted, the schema deteriorates into theospectivism with its view from nowhere. When the variable of object is deleted, the schema deteriorates into relativism that denies reality any role in thinking.

Objects and Objectivity

As minimal mental structures, concepts of the world that we consider in this section are *general*, signifying only our basic ability to recognize objects in the world as real things. They differ from *substantive* concepts for various kinds of objects such as table and chair, which manifest more elaborate mental discriminations, which we consider in later sections.

Whatever tables and chairs are, they are generally things. But what is a thing? Suppose a little boy asks you, how do you answer? If he asks about a specific kind of thing or a specific thing, say a toy or his favorite toy truck, you would have plenty to say. But how do you explain what a thing is in general? If you say things are real entities and physical objects, such as those we can grasp in our hands, you would have assumed that the boy already knows what a thing is. Of course he tacitly knows; if he did not, he would not be able to ask the question. That tacit knowledge is the basic structure of mind. Can it be articulated theoretically?

What Is a Thing? is the title of a book by Heidegger in which he engaged in a dialogue with Kant. Referring to Kant, he (1926:244) concluded: "The question 'What is a thing?' is also the question 'Who is man?'" Do not confuse this with instrumentalism that treats people as tools in the league with artifacts. The close connection between questions about things and humans does not mean that things are human products, or that humans are mere things. It means that to inquire into the general nature of things is simultaneously to inquire into the general nature of human beings with their mental capacity to encounter things and find the world meaningful. Without mind, we can interact intricately with things in our environment, just as trees interact with their ecosystem. However, we cannot be informed by the interaction; we cannot perceive and manipulate things, use them to our purpose, know and talk about them, value and care for them. Without things to perceive and think about, mind vanishes into a blank. Mind finds itself in the world of things that it itself makes intelligible.

Because everyone intuitively knows what a thing is, this tacit knowledge is usually taken for granted and glossed over. People like to vaunt esoteric knowledge about neurons and computers, to traffic information and market intelligence. Most philosophers of mind join the bandwagon and care only about constructing esoteric knowledge on the base of unexamined presuppositions. I adopt the opposite approach, characteristic of Kant and Heidegger. Instead of taking tacit knowledge of things for granted, I take it as the problem and inquire into its preconditions. How is it possible that we manage to know things? Thus we return to analyze the comprehensibility of the world that Einstein found so mysterious. Einstein (1954:292) hinted at the result: "It is one of the great realizations of Immanuel Kant that the postulation of a real external world would be senseless without this comprehensibility." The postulation is the work of concepts of the world.

In the literature on mind, "object" has two common meanings. In the broad sense, it is what philosophers call the intentional object. It covers any topic of experience, anything actual and possible, be it an event, a state of affairs, a living person, one's own body, an immaterial angel, an abstract entity such as a number, or a fiction such as a centaur. Thus all mental states have objects in this broad sense.[7] I do not use "object" in this broad sense.

I reserve the word object for the restricted sense that refers to entities and processes in the physical universe, physical things and happenings in so far as they are intelligible, including things with mental properties—people and human affairs. This restricted sense figures in concepts of the objective world. Physical things, events, processes, and states of affairs constitute the most important topics of thinking, with which we live, evolve, and find our ways around the world.

It is redundant to qualify objects as objective. Objective and objectivity primarily describe mental states: experiences, thoughts, and knowledge about the physical world. Objective mental states open to the world. Objective knowledge demands empirical evidence, direct or indirect. Because physical objects are publicly accessible, objective knowledge enjoys intersubjective agreement. Other kinds of knowledge, for instance mathematics, demand intersubjective agreement but not empirical evidence. These I call intersubjective knowledge. In talking about the objective world or objective reality, I mean the physical world in so far as it is intelligible to humans and known to be independent of our experience. It is our commonsense notion of reality accessible from human viewpoints and it entails the commonsense notion of truth: some statements about reality are true, others false. I will explain their radical difference from the naked reality and absolute truth of theospectivism and social constructionism, untouched by finite human minds, accessible only from God's position or the view from nowhere.

All mental states have topics, but many mental states do not have objects; hopes, fantasies, literary creations, and formal reasoning are examples. Descartes, having doubted the physical world away, took objectless thoughts and inner qualia to be the foundations of mind. Kant (1781:247) countered that we can make sense of occasional objectless thoughts only because most of our experiences are about physical objects with their causal regularities: "Inner experience in general is possible only through outer experience in general." Descartes's problem is to get out and bring objects back to mind. Kant's big task is to bring out structures in objective experiences so that objects and experiences thereof are not fused together.

Frames of Mind: Psychophysical Modes and Perspectives

Very young infants tend to be captivated by external stimuli. In their first two months, their attention, once captured, is so easily manipulated one experimenter called them "little looking machines." They look at a pattern as if mesmerized, until they are overcome by fatigue. They are machines not for long. From two months on, repetitive stimuli fail to captivate them, as they quickly lose interest and turn their attention away. At this age, however, they still have difficulty disengaging their gaze from fixation at salient central stimuli and turning it elsewhere at will (Colombo 1993). Thus Piaget was probably right in stating that we begin life knowing neither ourselves nor objects because we are totally absorbed by surrounding light and sound. The first-cut mental distinction occurs when babies differentiate themselves from their environment and find themselves in it (see section 6). Piaget was influenced by Kant, whose general concepts of objects are precisely the ability to make the distinction between objects and objective experiences.

How do we differentiate our experiences from the objects that we experience? Here the Cartesian trap gapes. The easiest answer is to introduce intermediaries, sense impressions or mental representations or what not, that separate the subject inside from the objects outside, as in figure 8.1a. The easy answer is a death trap that puts an unbridgeable rift between the subject and object. In rejecting Cartesianism, we seek a differentiation that is also an intrinsic relation, as in figure 8.1b.

Suppose you are looking at an object, say a house. Describe your visual experience. You will find that you are not describing any mental imagery but the features of the house itself. You see the house directly and immediately. The big difference is that you see only one side it because you are seeing from your specific perspective. If you walk around it, your visual experience changes because your perspective changes. Your visual perspective, not any representation on the veil of perception, is your subjective contribution to your vision.

We see, hear, touch, think, wish, and remember often about the same object, as I hold, smell, and savor a cup of coffee. We have many possible *psychophysical modes*, ranging from perception, proprioception, motion, memory, and emotion to language, fantasy, inference, anticipation, and narration. Each mode consists of a spectrum of *perspectives*. Perspectives come in a variety of types: spatial, temporal, intellectual, cultural, linguistic. Vision and audition involve spatial perspectives; recollection temporal perspectives. Intellectual perspectives are less obvious but no less prevalent. An object can be described in several ways, as the planet Venus is recognized as the morning star and the evening star. My intellectual perspective changes when I learn more about an object, just as my visual perspective changes when I draw closer to it. When the ramification of an intellectual perspective is so broad it covers one's whole outlook, it becomes personal. Shared personal perspectives become cultural. Thinking and speaking in different languages, too, constitute different perspectives, because languages have different word meanings and concepts.

I combine psychophysical mode and perceptive in a *frame of mind*. A person is in a specific mental frame when he adopts a specific perspective in a psychophysical mode. When I think, "The sun will rise soon," my mental frame is my everyday intellectual perspective in the mode of believing. If I switch to my physicist's perspective, I would think about the same astronomical event in terms of the earth's rotation. At any moment I am in a certain frame of mind, but I am also aware of the possibility of other frames. The substantive ranges of possible mental frames are relative to a person's background and knowledge. However, mastery of the general possibility of multiple fames is common to all humans.

We see and hear and think and move simultaneously. Many mental frames participate in a mental state, a phenomenon called the unity of consciousness (see section 12). However, usually we focus our attention on only a few psychophysical modes, although we are not totally oblivious to the unattended ones. We may be engrossed in thought and hardly notice the scenery on the drive home, although we must see when we drive. Or, fascinated by a painting, we may miss the conversation behind us but are readily alert at the mention of our name. Shifting attention from one mode to another changes the characteristic of our mental state. Thus an adequate characterization of a mental state should account for the relative attention received by its psychophysical modes. To achieve this we introduce a qualitative variable, which I call a psychophysical mode's *intensity*; a mode has a higher degree of intensity when it is attended to.

Distribution of intensities among various psychophysical modes and the particular perspective adopted within each mode constitute the *color* of a mental state. A melancholic color prevails when one dwells with relatively high intensity on remembering from a pessimistic perspective about bad events. A sober color prevails when one thinks with high intensity and is ready to shift his intellectual perspective. Changing distribution of attention among modes in a mental state contributes significantly to the dynamics of mental processes.

As finite beings, our mental frames are partial and finite in range. All our experiences and mental processes involve some perspectives, which manifest the subjectivity of our mentality. Philosophers have realized the indispensability of perspectives for a long time. To account for the possibility of disparate descriptions of the same object, Gottlob Frege (1892), the father of analytic philosophy, introduced the *mode of presentation* of a referring expression and set it apart from what expression refers to. The names "Mount Everest" and "Gaurisanker" are different modes of presentation that refer to the same thing, the highest peak on earth. Frege was concerned not with mental states but with logic. Nonetheless his modes of presentation bring out the perspectival nature of thought. In the hermeneutic tradition, Georg Gadamer (1960) stressed the importance of horizons of understanding and analyzed how cultural heritages shape all our thinking.[8] In cognitive science, Searle (1992) showed that each intentional state has a certain "aspectual shape," so that thinking about Paris and about the French capital are two states because they refer to two aspects of the city. I draw on their insights when I take frame of mind as an essential dimension in our minimal mental structures. Unlike social constructionists, however, I insist that the insights are beneficial only with a healthy dose of common sense, which refuses to let the multiplicity of mental frames drive reality out of thought. I propose that the multiplicity of frames leads not to relativism but to objectivity.

Doubting without Instructions from Mind Designers

Suppose I stand in front of a building and look at it. The object of my visual experience is the building, and my frame of mind captures only its front. However, I see a building and not merely a facade. I do not infer the building from the facade; I see it immediately and directly. By this I mean I know the back of the building to be there independent of my seeing it, but it is not impossible that I am wrong. These are common-sense notions involved in seeing real objects. How do we manage them? How do errors enter direct perception? More important, how can we spontaneously doubt and recognize errors for ourselves?

Consider the experience and reasoning of Shakespeare's Macbeth:

Is this a dagger which I see before me,
The handle toward my hand? Come, let me clutch thee!
I have thee not, and yet I see thee still.
Art thou not, fatal vision, sensible
To feeling as to sight? or art thou but
A dagger of the mind, a false creation
Proceeding from the heat-oppressèd brain?

Macbeth was more imaginative and poetic than most people, but his rationale here is plain common sense, comprehensible to a child. He had a vision. He was skeptical, because in ordinary frames of mind, daggers do not hang in thin air. To resolve his uncertainty he invoked the possibilities of the dagger and checked them by resorting to another frame of mind, not unlike someone moving to a new position to gain a better view of a thing. When the two frames of mind yielded conflicting experiences, he thought of various hypotheses. Finally he concluded "There's no such thing," even as the dagger became more vivid, dripping blood: "Mine eyes are made the fools o' th' other senses."

Macbeth would not be able to reason thus if he were unable to conceive the possibility of alternative mental frames or to relate various frames. Our multitude of interrelated psychophysical modes and perspectives act as the checks and balance on each other, enabling us to doubt, judge, criticize, affirm, or reject the objectivity of an experience. We judge an experience to be objective not because it is "given" but because it coheres with experiences in other mental frames in certain ways that we know as the causal regularities of the physical world. Whatever "given" means, the vision of a dagger is vividly given to Macbeth. Yet Macbeth denied its objectivity because it was not confirmed by his other senses, and deviated from the memory and knowledge of how things usually behave.

The Multiplicity of and Interrelation among Mental Frames

Perspectives have acquired a bad reputation from the rising notoriety of relativism and social constructionism. These doctrines debase the multiplicity of perspectives into perspectivism, in which perspectives extinguish reality, so that astronomy and astrology are equally true in different cultural perspectives. They provoke other people to retaliate and dismiss perspectives for being subjective and unfit for objective knowledge. Mental frames do highlight the subjective contributions to knowledge. However, Macbeth's reasoning suggests that they are not *merely* subjective as relativism and constructionism make them. By adopting and relating various mental frames, Macbeth was able to make an objective judgment about his vision. It is the systematic relation among possible mental frames, not the proscription of alternative frames, that signify objectivity of experience. By discarding the systematic relation, perspectivism, relativism, and constructionism also discard the possibility of objective knowledge and thus turn science into a myth.

Macbeth's case calls attention to a curious phenomenon in the science and philosophy of mind. Although the importance of perspectives is duly acknowledged, their main consequence is the pathology of relativism; they make little positive contribution. Why? Positive contributions of perspectives come only from the explicit treatment of the multiplicity and, more important, the systematic interrelations among the perspectives. Lip service to multiplicity is not enough. Many theories of intentionality start by talking about the possibility of multiple perspectives, then in the next paragraph narrow their attention to a single perspective. This maneuver kills the advantages of alternative perspectives. Consequently, attempts to explain how thoughts are about objects collapse into the solipsism of a single perspective. Other theories take the multiplicity of perspectives seriously but totally ignore their interrelations, thus degenerating into the disunity of consciousness, relativism, and constructionism. They have forgotten Kant's argument for the *synthetic* unity of consciousness. General concepts of objects and the world depend on synthesis of experiences from myriad mental frames.

Disentangling the Subjective and the Objective

At this moment I am thinking about an object in a specific mental frame; my experience is a complex with intertwining subjective and objective strands. To know the object better, I should try to disentangle the strands as much as possible. I can do very little if I am stuck on a single mental frame. The multiplicity of interrelated mental frames opens a new dimension for analysis. By comparing and correlating experiences in many frames, I can abstract from subjective factors and extract objective factors.

When we are stuck in a single viewpoint, we cannot determine visually the position of a distant object. When we avail ourselves of two viewpoints, we can measure the object's position by triangulation. Triangulation succeeds because we can grasp the object, the viewpoints, and their interrelation in a single conceptual framework. Similarly, when I grasp many possible mental frames and their correlations in one framework, I can subtract factors that vary from frame to frame and extract certain invariant features. Features that remain unchanged in changing mental frames I attribute to an object and acknowledge it to be the same object that I experience in various frames. Objective features so determined are not opaque but intelligible; they are products of mental analysis that constitute concepts of the world.

This is roughly Kant's (1781:159) conclusion: our judgments are objective if "they are combined *in the object*, no matter what the state of the subject may be." The notion of *objectivity as invariance under changing subjective states* has been explicit since Einstein's special theory of relativity of 1905 and extensively used in physics. We will presently borrow the general conceptual structure of physical theories to articulate concepts of the world.

The notion of invariance features in several theories of mind, including Husserl's phenomenology and Gibson's ecological optics. However, it has different functions and significance in different theories, such as those of Kant and Gibson. For Kant, invariance is constitutive; it is the subject himself who recognizes an object for what it is no matter what his own subjective state may be. This first-person experience involves considerable mental activity on the subject's part, including application of general concepts of objects. For Gibson, invariance is instrumental; it is not the subject but the ecologist who extracts and recognizes the invariance from a third-person view. The insectlike subject who merely resonates with the invariant has no conceptual ability if it has any mental ability at all. Instrumental invariance has been well known in physics, of which optics is a part. Our concern here, however, is not the structures of the optical field but the structures of mind. I presented my case against Gibson's ecological approach in section 17. Here I will follow Kant's approach.

Kant (1781:111) maintained that a subject must have considerable mental ability to have objective experience. Because the subject's state is constantly changing even if the object is not, the subject has manifold experiences. I hear sounds, see colors and shapes, feel textures and hardness. To become experiences, the manifold must be synthesized, "gone through in a certain way, taken up, and connected." I do not merely see yellow, taste sour, and feel something firm; I combine all these into the perception of a lemon. To have such experiences, I have tacitly made at least two general presuppositions. The first is that the same object is susceptible to several modes of perception or to intermittent attention of the same perceptual mode. I see the same lemon that I hold, and I see it again after turning my eyes elsewhere. I cannot possibly have such coherent experiences if the objective world does not possess certain regularities and coherence. This is what Kant (1781:156f) called the *objective unity of consciousness*: "that unity through which all the manifold given in an intuition is united in a concept of the object." "An *object* is that in the concept of which the manifold of a given intuition is *united*."

Consider the analogy of triangulation again. With the objective unity of consciousness, we know that we are looking at the same object from two positions. However, we still would fail to determine its distance if we did not also grasp the relations between our viewing positions. Similarly, to have a coherent experience of the lemon in my hand, the objective unity alone is not sufficient. I must also know that vision and touch are all *my* experiences. Thus Kant (1781:154) argued that the second basic presupposition of experience is the *subjective unity of consciousness*: "only in so far as I can grasp the manifold of representations in one consciousness, do I call them one and all *mine*." I can make objective judgments only because I have a synthetic conceptual framework wherein all my possible subjective states can be compared, so that subjective contributions can be discounted and objective features extracted.

Unity of consciousness has a subjective and an objective aspect. Subjectively, it introduces the first-person viewpoint whereby diverse perceptions, memories, desires, and beliefs are acknowledged as mine. Objectively, I can consistently acknowledge my experiences as mine because their contents possess a large degree of coherence that is anchored in the causal structures of the physical world. Kant explained that the subjective and objective unities of consciousness are the two sides of a mental distinction that drives a wedge between subjective experiences and objects of experiences. That distinction I call openness, illustrated in figure 8.1b.

Unity of consciousness involves several ideas. First, it accommodates a multiplicity of subjective states and mental frames. Second, it synthesizes the experiences from various frames. Third, the synthesis abstracts invariant objective features from changing frames. The abstraction conveys the commonsense notion that things are independent of our subjective thinking.

By extracting objective judgments as those that are unchanged in varying subjective experiences, we are aware of the distinction between "this is how the object is, independent of being experienced" and "this is how the object is experienced." As a structure of an experience, the distinction is reflexive, because both the object experienced and the object's independence of experience allude to the experience itself. This reflexivity conveys a sense of self. As explained in the next section, this self is not an entity that can be perceived as objects are perceived. It merely signifies the mental ability to synthesize experiences in various mental frames and recognize them to be mine. This ability is a part of concepts of the world; with it I acknowledge objects that I encounter to be independent of being experienced by me. Thus I differentiate myself from objects while participating in the world. Because I am aware of myself only in a distinction or intrinsic relation in which I am simultaneously aware of the world, I am never a solipsist and my mind is not closed. I am always and intrinsically open to the world, and my mental states are my situated properties.

What Is a Thing? The Answer from Physical Theories

If objectivity as invariance under changing mental frames is constitutive of our mind and presupposed by our talks of various objects, it should manifest itself in our activities. The manifestation is usually tacit. When you turn a strange-looking thing in your hands, or try to recall where you placed you key, or admit you were mistaken about an event, you have understood that objects can be thought of in various ways but are not changed by your thinking. Such understanding shows forth in your actions but usually is not explicitly articulated. If challenged, you can defend the objectivity of your judgments by something akin to Macbeth's reasoning. Nevertheless, such common sense is rather vague. It need not be clearer in daily life, for everyone understands, as long as you keep away from mental hospitals and departments of philosophy and cultural studies. Does science offer anything more precise?

The essential subtleties of our mind are fully manifest in our commonsense understanding, which flows in the intellectual veins of scientists even before they become scientists. Natural sciences generally take the common sense for granted and leave its presuppositions unexamined most of the time, turning to it only in moments of foundational crisis. An example of such crises concerns the foundations of modern physics. The topics of classical physics are mostly macroscopic objects, which, although not household items, are observable and intuitively understandable as things. It does not take much to imagine the sun as a huge fireball and planets as solid spheres. Therefore classical physics can rely on our intuitive notion of things. Twentieth century physics cannot be so complacent, as its topics in the relativistic and microscopic world are anything but obvious and self-evident. They are intangible and unobservable; quantum objects are not even visualizable. Electrons are not tiny pebbles and atoms not miniature solar systems; they are like nothing you have ever seen. In the strange microscopic world, our intuitive notion of objects falter and *what is a thing?* becomes a pressing general question. This predicament incited intense debate among physicists early in the twentieth century. This is the background to Einstein's (1954:324) remark that physicists have to undertake "the problem of analyzing the nature of everyday thinking."

In resolving the foundational crisis, modern physics has made explicit many general concepts tacit in everyday thinking. Among them is the notion of objectivity, for physics must assert its objectivity to secure its foundations. Manifesting the self-criticality of objective thinking, physical theories themselves have consolidated their presuppositions by spelling out what it is to be an object in general, what it is for a description to be about an object, and what it is for the object to be independent of our theories and observations. These criteria they incorporated in their mathematical structures.

We explicitly talk about tables and chairs and various kinds of object but not objects in general, although we tacitly know that tables are objects. Like our everyday objective thoughts, physical theories are about specific topics such as electrons and they are couched in substantive concept such as quantum phases. The concepts of the objective world we are after are not expressed in individual terms but embedded in the mathematical structures of theories. They are still shown and not said, but they are shown clearly in mathematical forms. Compared with logical structures of everyday thinking, mathematical structures of physical theories are like steel frames of skyscrapers rather than cross-currents of swamps. They are much easier to extract and interpret. Sometimes we can even look them up in architectural blueprints or mathematics texts.

In an earlier book (Auyang 1995), I compared physical theories with common sense and abstracted their common general conceptual framework. I find that general concepts of objects are explicitly incorporated in physical theories as what I briefly call the *transformation schema*. Appearing first in Einstein's special theory of relativity, it revolutionized the formulation of physical theories. Because the structure embodies the most general and basic concepts, it is promptly retrofit into Newtonian mechanics and generalized to other novel theories: quantum mechanics, general relativity, and quantum field theories. In many applications it is known as *symmetry* and is underpinned by the mathematics of *group theory*. All fundamental physical laws now take the form of symmetry and invariance.

The transformation schema interweaves three general concepts: multiple descriptions, transformations among the descriptions, and invariance under transformations. Physical theories identify *the objective* with *that which is invariant under certain groups of transformations of descriptions.* Thus they have made explicit what we tacitly presuppose in our everyday thinking: Objects are what they are, unchanged by our different ways of description or the mental frames in which we experience them. I will not go into the mathematics; much detail is irrelevant here. However, I adapt its general ideas for a theoretical schema for the general structures of objective thinking and objective mental states.[9]

Objectivity: Invariance under Transformations of Mental Frames

Figure 8.2 schematically illustrates the general idea that objective features are those that are invariant under the systematic transformations of relevant mental frames. It contains two variables, object x and mental frame f, each with its possibility space. In the diagram, the variability of mental frames is explicitly represented by the subscript of f_i, but the variability of objects is kept implicit; it is understood that x can take on various values. Both variables are necessary for objective experiences; an experience $f_i(x)$ is an object x conceived in a mental frame f_i.

Suppose you have an experience p_1, which you tentatively analyze into two aspects: the object x and your specific mental frame f_1, so that $p_1 = f_1(x)$. If x is a house and f_1 the mental frame of vision from the front, then $f_1(x)$ is the experience of the house seen from the front, which appears like a facade.

From p_1 alone you are unable to determine substantively the features of x. Is it really a house or merely a stage prop? You can find out by going

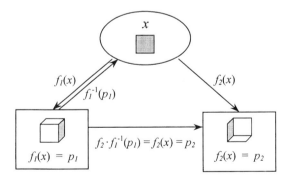

Figure 8.2
The *transformation schema* as a model for the structure of objective mental states. In it, an experience $p_1 = f_1(x)$ is analyzed into a subjective mental frame f_1 and the object x the experience is about. The objectivity of experience p_1 is secured by the fact that its object x can also be experienced in other mental frames such as $p_2 = f_2(x)$ and is invariant under transformations $f_2 \cdot f_1^{-1}$ across all relevant mental frames. Invariance under systematic transformations implies that the object is independent of subjective experiences.

around the corner. In so doing you are changing your viewpoint and hence your mental frame. From around the corner you have another mental frame, f_2, in which you have another experience, $p_2 = f_2(x)$.

You are aware of the change in your mental frame and correlate experiences p_1 and p_2 by the frame transformation $f_2 \cdot f_1^{-1}$. Information about the frame transformation you gather by reckoning with your own spatial locations relative to the house, with which you situate yourself in the same world as the house. Thus the transformation is not a simple mapping between two internal mental representations. Rather, it is a composite mapping that refers to the object x: $f_2 \cdot f_1^{-1}(p_1) = f_2(x) = p_2$. This composite transformation indicates mind's openness to the world and provides an adequate notion of intentionality.

By systematically transforming your mental frames, f_1, f_2, f_3, and so on and comparing your experiences p_1, p_2, p_3, and so on, you abstract the features of object x. You ascertain that it is a house with front and back, inside and outside, roof and cellar. Conversely, because you can extract coherent and invariant features from the transformations, you judge your experiences to be objective. Otherwise, you would join Macbeth's company and decide that you are hallucinating.

The *whole* transformation schema in figure 8.2 represents concepts of the world that constitute the minimal structures of our mind. Accounting for systematic relations between two variables, object x and mental frame f, it is a complicated structure. As discussed in the next sections, details of the object variable account for the objective unity of consciousness; details of the frame variable account for the subjective unity of consciousness.

A mental frame is not a thing but a mapping that takes objects as its argument. Theories of intentionality usually treat perspective as a function f that maps an object x into an experience. Our theoretical framework differs from them in insisting that the map itself is explicitly treated as a *variable*. Variables are theoretically powerful not only because they cover a range of possible values. More important is their ability to account for systematic variations and relations among their values, and their systematic connections to values of other variables. Because of systematicity, introduction of a variable opens a new dimension of structures. We would waste its power and significance if, after introducing it, we promptly went on to consider its values separately, as in most theories of intentionality. Its essence as a variable is lost in the myopic view that fixes on single values.

Philosophers of intentionality insist that one engages only in a specific mental frame at any time. Even if that is the case, a subject is also aware of the possibility of alternative frames. I maintain that without this awareness, the subject's state falls short of being mental.

Concepts of the objective world are as important in theoretical science as in our daily activities. For instance, figure 8.2 can also schematically depict the structure of relativistic physics. Here the fs represent coordinate systems, which are descriptive schemes associated with various motions of an observer. Connecting two coordinate systems is a Lorentz transformation $f_2 \cdot f_1^{-1}$. The special theory of relativity accounts for all possible coordinate systems that move with constant speeds relative to each other. Systematic transformations among them are represented by the mathematics of a group, the Lorentz group. The objective spatial-temporal structure, called Minkowski space-time, is the x that is invariant under all Lorentz transformations, and $f_1(x)$ is Minkowski space-time measured in a particular coordinate system. Coordinate systems are theoretical entities. Let us call them subjective or conventional elements in the theory of relativity. Minkowski space-time x, represented in the coordinate-free form, is independent of any and all subjective elements connectable by transformations in the Lorentz group. It is intelligible to us only through the elaborate theoretical apparatus of descriptions and transformations. If we use a smaller group of transformations, we would get a different x that is spatial-temporal structure of classical mechanics. If we use a larger group of transformations, we would get another x that is the spatial-temporal structure of general relativity. Candidates are judged empirically. Physical theories do not pretend to provide absolute truth; they are always fallible.

Physics is interested in inanimate physical systems. Thus only the invariant x is the *objective* theoretical representation of physical systems. There is a mathematical way to represent x that is coordinate free. Why don't physical theories simply use it; why do they employ the entire transformation schema with its ancillary coordinate systems and transformations? Physical theories do not merely represent objects but represent them as accessible to human knowledge. They need the empirical support of experiments, without which they are mere mathematics with no physical import. Experimenters are human beings, and as such they cannot observe from nowhere but can only observe from their subjective viewpoints. Whenever they have to describe or measure a system definitely, observe or do experiments on it, they must resort to one descriptive scheme or another. All they can do is to try their best to screen out subjective elements and make explicit the objectivity of the features they attribute to objects. For this they employ complicated transformation schema, where various descriptions f_i and their transformations are put on the table and explicitly acknowledged to be theoretical and empirical tools necessary to measure and extract objective features. Descriptions and transformations are instrumental, expressing the general way of thinking of physicists, not the physical systems that they investigate.

The science of mind takes physicists themselves as objects of investigation. Thus I assert that the framework of mental frames-transformations-invariance *in its entirely* is constitutive. As concepts of the world, it is an objective theoretical schema of the mental structure of subjects who are capable of objective knowledge. (The first "objective" signifies that the mental structure is the object investigated in the science of mind; the second "objective" that the mental structure pertains to experiences about physical objects.) The schema is crude, highlighting only general relations among mental frames and objects. I do not suggest that its substantive details can be filled. In other words, the person whose mental state the schema describes grasps only the general concepts of object, mental frame, frame transformation, and objective invariance. These general notions enable him to be aware of the possibility of substantive details, hence be aware of his own ignorance and be informed when he gains specific details.

The Open Mind and Its Fallibility
In physics, the transformation schema is a part of mathematical theories that are substantiated to great details. Adapted to the science of mind, whose complex objects defy representations of comparable refinement, the schema does not function as a mathematical model. It presents a framework of interrelated variables but not their values, general concepts but few substances. It does not guarantee that the values and substances are all available, not to mention specifiable with mathematical rigor. The possibility for deficiency where some values are missing or substances mislocated is crucial for accounts of fallacy and ignorance. All we want is a general framework strong and complicated enough to sustain mishaps without collapsing.

For a single experience, most elements of the complicated mental structure are not explicit but are not totally absent either. They wait in the background of understanding as possibilities. At any moment, one experiences only some objects in some mental frames, but possible alternatives and their connections always lurk in the penumbra. Only because they do can we doubt and actively shift our physical or intellectual perspectives to acquire better knowledge of the world. Even as you stand in front of a building, you see a building and not merely a facade because you tacitly assume that it is possible to be viewed in other mental frames. Such assumptions are ubiquitous in objective knowledge.

The notion of *my* experience of *objects* separate the subject from the blind environment, thus marking the opening of mind to the intelligible world. Two other characteristics are essential to the open mind: *fallibility* and *self-criticality*. All objective mental states, including perceptual states, are fallible. One can hallucinate, believe erroneously, judge wrongly, fear groundlessly, hope in vain. Cross-cultural studies find the notion of false belief to be universal (Lillard 1997). By showing that subjective mental states and the objects they are about can vary independently of each other, fallibility drives a wedge between subject and object. Fallibility, however, is significant only in contrast to veridicality. Its wedge vanishes if all mental states are perpetually illusory with no possibility of verification, as is the predicament of the brain in a vat or Descartes under the spell of the evil demon. False opinions are possible only against a background of true ones. Aware of the possibilities of both truth and falsity, we are capable of self-criticism. Without waiting for mind designers, we can spontaneously doubt, wonder, find fault with our own thinking, admit mistakes, and correct ourselves. These abilities can be accounted for by unfilled possibilities in our mental structure.

Concepts of the world establish only a schema encompassing the possibility of multiple mental frames, the possibility of transformations among them, and the possibility of invariant features. They do not specify what the possible frames or objects are, or how the transformations operate. Thus they are like a form with many systematically connected blanks. It is not required that all the blanks for mental frames, objects, and transformations be filled in all cases. What is required is only that they are partially filled most of the times, so that the person whose mental states they represent retains his sanity even in his ignorance.

When some blanks are not filled in a mental state, *aberration* occurs. If one separately knows an object x in two mental frames, $f_1(x)$ and $f_2(x)$, but does not know the transformation $f_2 \cdot f_1^{-1}$ between them, he is ignorant that the object in one frame is the same as the one in the other.

For example, $f_1(x)$ may represent seeing a bright star in the morning and $f_2(x)$ seeing a bright star in the evening, but the viewer is ignorant that both "stars" are the same planet Venus. He gains knowledge about the world if he learns about the identity represented by the transformation $f_2 \cdot f_1^{-1}$. If someone such as Macbeth has an experience p_1 whose object x fails to be substantiated as the object in other mental frames, he can judge that the first content occurs in an illusory rather than visual frame of mind.

A distinguishing feature of the framework of objects, mental frames, and transformations is its complexity that allows the mind to operate despite some defects. It consists of enough elements so that when some are missing the result is an error instead of a fatal collapse. Furthermore, in such cases the interconnection among the elements highlights checks and balance of various mental frames that underlie the possibility of doubt and self-criticism. Its superiority is revealed when we later compare it to an all-or-nothing framework that, being incapable of errors, crashes spectacularly if it is not completely correct.

Improving Knowledge and Converging to Truth

When a boy tries to figure out how a toy works, he does not merely stare at it but turns it around in his hands, examining it from all angles, thus bringing many mental frames to bear. Similarly, scientists try to gain as broad a spectrum of perspectives as possible. Physicist Richard Feynman (1965:168) observed that "every theoretical physicist who is any good knows six or seven different theoretical representations for exactly the same physics." He explained that the point is not to pick the right theory; it may be impossible to decide or the theories may be all equivalent. Even if two theories are mathematically equivalent, "for psychological reasons, in order to guess new theories, these two things may be very far from equivalent, because one gives a man different ideas from the other." Scientists are human and their theories are partial. In any act of thinking, a scientist adopts a specific intellectual perspective or theory, just as in an act of seeing, one adopts a specific viewpoint. But he would do poorly if he is stuck to it. Therefore it is crucial to scientific research to incorporate as many intellectual perspectives as possible, to shift among them, and try to connect the representations in them to understand the same physical reality. This is the position I took in chapter 3 to argue for the variety of descriptive levels for complex systems and against reductionism that insists on a single intellectual viewpoint.

Our knowledge about objects is not absolute and errors are always possible. However, we can try to increase the accuracy and reliability of our judgments. An important way of checking is to see whether a theory framed in a certain perspective holds in other perspectives. As it works in more and more perspectives, we have more and more confidence in it. I compared objective judgment with triangulation. Longer bases of triangulation yield higher accuracies in position measurement. Similarly, a framework encompassing greater diversity in mental frames yields better objective knowledge. As explained below, the possibility space for human mental frames is enormous. For instance, I can generalize and consider the mental frames of other people, thus forging intersubjective agreement about objects. Substantive knowledge of causal connections among things expands the diversity of intellectual perspectives, because each causal link opens a new door to the object. As we use our communicative ability to take account of other people's viewpoints, our technological ability to build instruments that augment our sense organs, and our theoretical ability to multiply intellectual perspectives systematically, our bases of judgment expands and probability of error decreases rapidly as science advances.

As the probability of errors decreases asymptotically, scientists often say that scientific knowledge and theories converge on truth. At a time when postmodernism is making "reality" and "truth" into dirty words, I should be careful not to fall into its trap. The clearest concepts of convergence occur in mathematics. In one definition, a real sequence $\{y_1, y_2, \ldots y_n, \ldots\}$ *converges* to the limit Y if and only if for each $\varepsilon > 0$, there corresponds some positive integer N such that $|y_n - Y| < \varepsilon$ if $n > N$ (figure 8.3a). This definition posits the limit Y in advance. The notion of a preexisting limit has been used by postmodernists to attack the convergence of knowledge, for the limit implies naked reality or absolute truth toward which scientific theories converge. Furthermore, it implies that we must know naked reality to assess the convergence of our theories. If the convergence to truth requires our access to naked reality, postmodernists are justified to dismiss it as illusory. However, this is not the only concept of convergence, not even in mathematics.

In another familiar definition, a sequence $\{y_1, y_2, \ldots y_n, \ldots\}$ is *convergent* if and only if for every positive ε there is a positive integer N such that $|y_n - y_m| < \varepsilon$ whenever $n \geq N$ and $m \geq N$. This definition of convergence, which does not posit the limit, has been generalized to many areas that does not involve real numbers, such as topology (figure 8.3b).

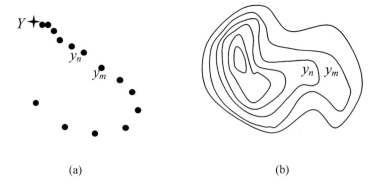

Figure 8.3
(a) A mathematical definition of convergence posits the limit Y in advance, and judges whether a sequence $\{y_n\}$ converges by measuring the "distances" of each of its term y_n from Y. (b) More general definitions posit no limit in advance. Instead, they judge whether a sequence is convergent by measuring the "distance" between the different terms y_n and y_m of the sequence.

It is a more appropriate analogy for the convergence of scientific knowledge and theories. Each term in the sequence y_n is analogous to a theory, and we deal only with theories. There is no hint of naked reality. We judge the convergence of successive theories by comparing their results and experimental data obtained with their help, which we legitimately know. If diverse theories and experiments yield closely similar results for a range of phenomena, we judge them to be true for the range of phenomena. This is what scientists routinely do to access their theories. For instance, physicists compare results of classical mechanics with results of relativistic physics for systems moving with speed much lower than the speed of light. They find that under the condition of slow motion, results from the theories agree to reasonable accuracy. Hence they decide that the theories converge under this condition. The agreement of disparate theories and experiments affirms the objectivity or truth of the results, as they are invariant under changing theoretical descriptions.

You take the oath in court to tell the truth. Investigators query witnesses, attack inconsistencies in their testimonies, and try to find out what really happened. Our everyday business depends on commonsense notions of truth, reality, and convergence of descriptions. Mathematical definitions help us to articulate these the notions clearly. They show that we can rationally judge the convergence of theories and assert the truth of results without in any way pretending to be in God's position.

The concepts of reality and truth are difficult to define precisely. To dismiss them as senseless because of the difficulty, however, is irrational; they are the basic presuppositions that guide our actions and inquires. In reply to philosopher Thomas Kuhn's (1962) insistence that it makes no sense to say science progressively comes "closer to truth," physicist Steven Weinberg (1999) wrote: "If I agree with Kuhn's judgment about the progress of science, that there is no sense in which science offers a cumulative approach to some sort of truth, then the whole enterprise would seem rather irrational to me, even if not to Kuhn." Why would anyone bother, he asked, if scientific theories merely solve problems that happen to be in vogue and that in no sense concern reality and truth? Why not save the trouble of scientific inquiry by ignoring the fashion?

To assert that the objective contents of a scientific theory are true in no way implies that theory explains all phenomena in the universe. A theory, no matter how powerful and general, applies only to a certain range of phenomena to a certain degree of details, to which its truth claim is limited. We need many theories for various types of phenomena, and we have no guarantee that we can gain the truth for all. When the topics of two theories partially overlap, they provide different perspectives for the overlapping region. Thus we have the opportunity to check them against each other, delineate their invariant features, and effectively patch them together. Our transformation schema can be generalized to represent the patchwork (Auyang 1998, figure 2.2).

Views from Everywhere versus the View from Nowhere

It is a universal human condition that all our experiences involve our physical and intellectual effort and hence are somehow biased by our subjective mental frames. The question is how we face our human predicament in our quest for objective knowledge of the real world. Let us compare three major attitudes: *denial*, *abandonment*, and *self-criticality*. Theospectivism and objectivism try to deny the human condition; relativism and social constructionism relinquish objective knowledge and abandon themselves to subjective caprice; common sense and the scientific spirit acknowledge our subjective involvements and demand us to be critical of ourselves and make best attempts to minimize prejudices.

Denial and abandonment agree on important points. Both equate truth with absolute truth and equate reality with naked reality accessible only from a transcendent position absolutely free of all human perspectives. Thus they assert that objective knowledge is possible only if we can get a view from nowhere. They twist the commonsense saying that "reality is independent of us and our thinkings" into "reality is what is given in the view from nowhere." The twist is unwarranted; the two assertions are logically and substantively different.

"Reality is given in the view from nowhere" is appropriate for both theospectivism and solipsism. Theospectivism posits God's eye point of view transcending human conditions. Its definition of reality does not mention human thinking and subjectivity at all, thus expressing its claim that naked reality is absolutely independent of us. God's throne is also the illusion of the solipsist's closed mind. God transcends all viewpoints; the solipsist uprooted from the world is incapable of having any viewpoint. God is omniscient; the closed mind does not know that it is not. Wrapped in its cocoon behind the veil of perception and passively receiving sense impressions given to it, the closed mind blissfully dreams of itself as the master of the universe. To it, private mental representations constitute all that is real and the recalcitrant physical world is a myth. Its definition of reality does not mention human subjectivity because it too simplistic to know human conditions.

"Reality is independent of our observations" first posits observations that invariably involve human perspectives and then recognizes reality by separating it from our subjective observations. Contrary to theospectivism, it does not hint at a transcendent view. Unlike solipsism, its observational viewpoints put us squarely in the physical world. It accounts for both subjective and objective contributions to our knowledge of reality.

Just as we leave our fingerprints when we handle an object, we leave our intellectual marks when we think about it. If we are unaware of our inadvertent imprints or deny their existence, we are stuck with the contamination. Once we acknowledge them, however, we can find ways to improve the situation. Whenever we say anything about the world, we are saying too much, for what we say contains factors particular to the circumstances of our speech that are irrelevant to the object. To get at reality, we can try our best to erase those subjective factors, just as we wipe objects clean of our finger marks.

To unsay something is no easy task, but people try. Buddhism, for instance, has a method of edification known as uncovering. To a student's question of what is whiteness, the master does not answer that snow is white, for that will tempt the student to stick to certain extraneous factors in the particular case of snow. Instead, the master answers that snow is not whiteness, snowdrops are not whiteness, clouds are not whiteness, and so on. The negation prompts the student to "wipe away" irrelevant particularities in each case and hence to uncover the true feature of being white.

The ideas of subtraction and extraction are precisely the crux of the transformation schema illustrated in figure 8.2. Transformations of descriptions erase certain particularities of descriptions. Thus a larger group of transformations erases more features, leaving a structure with higher symmetry. Imagine a perfect sphere. Its symmetry depends on its being free from marks and blemishes. But without marks, it is very difficult to discuss distances on it. Suppose for the convenience of discussion we imagine a mark "here" on the sphere and then talk about its distance from "there." It is fine, except the mark destroys the symmetry of the sphere, and hence stick us to a particular view of it. How can we erase the intellectual mark and "unsay" the "here" and "there"? This is a job for the transformation schema. We erase the effect of the mark by identifying spherical properties with what are invariant under all rotational transformations of the mark. In plain words, it doesn't matter where you put the mark in your discussion; the reality of the sphere is independent of your particular ways of discussing it. This is the commonsense notion of reality's independence on our thinking.

The commonsense notion has been made explicit and incorporated into the conceptual structures of modern physical theories. Thus instead of "space is homogeneous," relativistic physics says "space is invariant under the translational transformations of coordinate systems." Coordinate systems are our ways of description, and the objective features of space are independent of their particularities (Auyang 1995).

In science as in everyday business, usually we talk about not the whole universe but only certain facets of it, so we are concerned only with certain elements of reality. To talk about a specific real element properly that is the same no matter how we look at it, we must first identify relevant ways of looking at it and then erase their subjective peculiarities. This task, tacitly understood in everyday discourse, is explicitly carried out in science. For instance, the group of translational transformations secures the feature of homogeneity, and the group of rotational transformations secures the feature of isotropy. Generally, a larger group of transformations secures a more general feature.

In sum, "reality is independent of our thinking" in the sense of "objective features are invariant under the transformation of our subjective descriptions" is more sophisticated than the illusory "reality is given in the view from nowhere." The latter depends on the illusory view from nowhere and passively receives the given. The former demands much active intellectual effort to take account of the views from everywhere, more accurately, the views from as wide a range of perspectives as we can manage. Unlike theospectivism, it never pretends to be in possession of absolute truth. Even in the asymptotic case where we say reality is independent of all perspectives and mental states that we can conceive, the abstraction still presupposes a broad conceptual framework that includes subjective states and the abstraction therefrom. Therefore the independence of reality on us is not absolute; we have presupposed the accessibility and intelligibility of reality to human observations and understanding. Objects are neither given nor self-identifying but are made intelligible by our mental effort. The nonabsolute independence of the objective world from our subjectivity is the intrinsic relation between object and subject that I explained earlier.

Objectivity versus Theospectivism and Objectivism

In section 4, we distinguished between local and global illusions. We occasionally have local illusions that we distinguish from our mostly objective experiences. We can recognize errors because our *general* mental structures stand even when we suffer from some *specific* deficiencies. The brain-in-a-vat has no objective experience and suffers from a global illusion that completely and eternally severs the contents of its thought from their etiology. It can never know that its thoughts are illusory because it lacks the general mental structure for the recognition.

The transformation schema in figure 8.2 represents our general mental structures. I explained how it accounts for local illusions, errors, and ignorance by allowing some specific values of the object variable x or some specific values of the frame variable f to be unfilled. Global illusions result from debilitations in general mental structures, which are represented not by missing values of a variable but by the variable itself missing. Two kinds of global illusions are popular in the philosophy of mind: theospectivism, objectivism, and solipsism that result from striking out the frame variable f; relativism and constructionism that result from banishing the object variable x.

Let us consider the frame variable first. We saw in the preceding section that many concepts with mental connotations violate the principle of extensionality that demands the unrestricted substitution of coreferential terms. The violation mainly stems from considering more than one mental frame. Intentional, possible, and temporal propositions all involve two frames: two ranges of knowledge, two possible states of affairs, and two time frames. You can be unaware that you smell the same cheese that you hold, so that substitution across descriptions of different perceptual modes does not always preserve truth value. A native of Nepal traveling in Tibet fails to recognize that the majestic peak he sees there is same Mount Everest he saw every day at home.

The transformation schema shows clearly how the multiplicity of frames foils extensionality. Consider coordinate systems. A specific set of coordinates in a specific system designates a place; for instance, coordinates (71, 42) designate Boston. In another coordinate system, however, Boston is designated by (58, 40) and (71, 42) is the designation of New York. Therefore we cannot substitute coreferential terms across different coordinate systems and hope that the substitution preserves truth, as extensionality demands. We must transform whole coordinate systems to preserve objectivity. Transforming frames is generally much more complicated than substituting terms. That is why accounting for mental phenomena and objective knowledge intelligible to humans calls for more sophisticated intensional logic that violates the principle of extensionality (see section 24).

Objectivity as invariance under transformations of mental frames violates the principle of extensionality because it explicitly invokes variable mental frames. To preserve extensionality, one must permit only a single mental frame, effectively discarding f as a variable. To strike out the variable f has far greater consequences than merely to leave out some specific values of f; f represents a general mental capacity, whereas its values represent specific achievements given the capacity. When philosophers who prescribe the universalization of extensionality ban the variability of mental frames, they proscribe a mental capacity and thus land in global illusions of solipsism, theospectivism, or objectivism.

Just as theoretical attitude is often confused with theospectivism, objectivity is confused with objectivism. They are diametrically opposite. Objectivity depends on the variability of perspectives. Objectivism insists on a single and permanently fixed viewpoint, which is usually identified with the view from nowhere or God's-eye point of view, because human viewpoints are always biased. Therefore objectivism is similar to theospectivism.

Behind objectivism and theospectivism is a mirror model of mind asserting that our thinking reflects reality. The metaphor of mind as a mirror not only has a long history in Western thought but occurs in other cultures.[10] Objectivism and theospectivism add that the mirror is not like anything humans can make because it has the magic of divine transcendence to give a view from nowhere, so that the mirroring mind is in possession of absolute truth that corresponds exactly to naked reality, as illustrated in figure 8.4a. This truth is absolute and immutable because it is uncontaminated by any mention of human conditions, not even the presupposition that the world is intelligible to us.

A mirror reflects light but has no way of knowing any causal relation between the light and distant objects; a person can correlate mirror

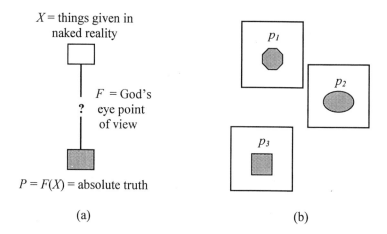

(a)   (b)

Figure 8.4
Two degenerations of the mental structure depicted in figure 8.2. (a) Theospectivism and objectivism prohibit the variability of frames and posit a single absolute truth obtained by viewing naked reality from nowhere. When the correspondence between the alleged absolute truth and naked reality collapses, they become solipsism, in which the closed mind P has no way of distinguishing absolute illusion from absolute truth. (b) Relativism and social constructionism retain the subjective frame variable but discard the concept of the objective world x. By this they also abandon the common ground for intersubjective understanding, as transformations among mental frames $f_2 \cdot f_1^{-1}(p_1) = f_2(x) = p_1$ always refer to the object x. Consequently they end up with a host of incommensurate closed minds, which they can compare only by pretending to be transcendent mind designers.

images to objects because people have abilities far beyond the mirror's. Similarly, the mirroring mind is a closed mind that has no way of establishing the correspondence between its thoughts and naked reality. Once the legitimacy of correspondence is challenged, the closed mind reveals itself to be a solipsist under absolute illusion with no ability to distinguish it from absolute truth. Objectivism and theospectivism can claim the correspondence only because they assume the position of mind designers who transcend the ability of the closed mind to straddle it and naked reality. We encountered such mind designers in eliminativism, instrumental behaviorism, and retroactive creationism.

Objectivism is a pet prescription mind-designing philosophies have for their ideal science. If adopted, it would stifle actual science, which thrives instead on objectivity. The drastic difference between the two is revealed by comparing figures 8.2 and 8.4a. With its mental capacity mutilated by the banishment of variable mental frames, objectivism depends on blindness to its own subjectivity. With healthy common sense, objectivity insists on the frame variable, and science systematically reckons with as many as possible of the variable's values. It is intrinsically self-critical, depending on the explicit recognition of subjectivity and the incessant effort to check its effects.

Newton said he saw far because he stood on the shoulders of giants; Einstein compared scientific advancement to climbing a mountain and gaining a higher perspective. Both depicted science with its feet planted firmly on the human ground, where its horizon remains finite no matter how wide it expands. Science is not omniscience; it cannot jump clear of human conditions to attain God's transcendent position. Like their fellow humans, scientists are influenced by their social and historical backgrounds. Science is objective because scientists acknowledge the possibility of subjective biases, thus critically check their abuses and never rest in complacency.

Objectivity versus Relativism and Social Constructionism

The idea of absolute truth corresponding to naked reality has been under attack for a long time. Kant and Heidegger, whom I cited, are among many who criticized it. Their philosophies are complicated because they not only reject objectivism but also try to propose positive answers to how we manage to know the world. Their constructive efforts differentiate them from simplistic and purely destructive doctrines such as relativism and social constructionism, which lay waste objective knowledge together with objectivism.

Relativism and social constructionism stir controversies in science studies, which are relevant here because scientific inquiry involves mental effort and studies of its conduct shed light on mind. Contrary to claims of relativists and constructionists, their doctrines are not the only alternatives to objectivism. Nagel (1986) criticized the view from nowhere more deeply than they did without falling into their league. Instead, he (1997:6) exposed their impotence: "Many forms of relativism and subjectivism collapse into either self-contradiction or vacuity—self-contradiction because they end up claiming that nothing is the case, or vacuity because they boil down to the assertion that anything we say or believe is something we say or believe."

Do scientists discover or construct physical laws? Discovery and construction highlight objective and subjective contributions to knowledge. It is a symptom of postmodern science studies that they flank an exclusive or to form an identify-friend-or-foe question.

Scientists find the question puzzling. They usually talk about discoveries, but no one means that Newton and Einstein were like Moses descending Mount Sinai with tablets and saying: Look at what we've discovered! This tablet has the law $F = ma$ written on it by Nature's finger; that one has $E = mc^2$. Scientists are not merely fact collectors and compilers; they are among the most creative of human beings. Actively engaged in framing theories, they know better than anyone how much intellectual creativity it demands. Inquiring into the unknown, they begin by trial and error, posit concepts, test them, and tear them apart; they debate with each other and often change their minds. Physical laws are not diamonds in the ground ready to be dug up. Einstein (1954:226) wrote: "It seems that the human mind has first to construct forms independently before we can find them in things." Nevertheless, he was a staunch realist. In constructing substantive concepts and theories such as quark and quantum chromodynamics, natural scientists always presuppose that they are investigating the real world, the structures of which remain the same whether they know it or not, and whether they or people in other cultures are the investigators. The general presupposition of reality strongly constrains their discretion in constructing substantive concepts. Specifically, it demands them to recognize their personal and cultural biases, which should be removed from objective contents of their theories. Soviet and American physicists have disparate cultural environments and irreconcilable political beliefs. Despite the differences, they should come to the same laws about quarks and other elementary particles. If any discrepancy exists, both sides would criticize themselves as well as their opponents until they come to an agreement, because all parties presuppose that they pursue objective knowledge about nature whose characteristics are independent of their cultures. This is the notion of objectivity as invariance across transformations of research environments. Under this presupposition, scientists say physical laws are discovered, even as they acknowledge that the discovery processes involve intellectual construction.

Discovery and objectivity presuppose nature and reality. Anyone who thinks in this way is identified as a foe by postmodernists, including relativists and social constructionists. Harry Collins (1981) declared: "The natural world has a small or non-existent role in the construction of scientific knowledge." Bruno Latour (1987:99) stipulated a rule of method: "Since the settlement of a controversy is the cause of Nature's representation not the consequence, we can never use the outcome—Nature—to explain how and why a controversy has been settled." Richard Rorty (1994) summed it up: "What people like Kuhn, Dirrida and I believe is that it is pointless to ask whether there really are mountains or whether it is merely convenient for us to talk about mountains. We also think it is pointless to ask, for example, whether neutrinos are real entities or merely useful heuristic fictions. It is pointless to ask whether reality is independent of our ways of talking about it." Together with nature goes truth. David Bloor (1991) advocated the "strong program" that enjoins symmetrical treatments of true and false explanations and expulsion of truth considerations from scientific investigation. In the same vein, Andrew Pickering (1984:413) declared "there is no obligation upon anyone framing a view of the world to take account of what twentieth-century science has to say," because all content of science, including the laws of elementary particles, is "a culturally specific product." This does not merely mean that other cultures may choose to worry about something else rather than the basic building blocks of matter; that belongs to what postmodernists call the "weak program." Their strong program goes beyond cultural variations in research agenda to proclaim radical cultural variations in contents of theories for specific phenomena. People in other cultures can ignore our elementary particle physics and construct different laws for the basic constituents of the universe.

Postmodernists deny that they say the real world does not exist but do not explain how the denial is compatible with their doctrines. What they legislate is not the existence of reality but the general structures of our mind: what we are allowed to think about and what concepts we are allowed to use. They are as fervent in designing mind as theospectivists, differing only in specific dogmas. Relativism and social constructionism aim to expunge the general concepts of reality and truth from our mental structures, allowing them little if any role in thinking, especially scientific inquiry. Their major target is objectivity, as they deny the possibility of anything remaining the same under cultural changes. Ordinarily, we say mountains are not merely convenient figures of speech because we presuppose that everyone, no matter what culture he comes from, would be forced to acknowledge their existence. This presupposition is none other than the general concepts of the physical world that preclude radical cultural relativism; the references to mountains and contents of science are not culturally specific because they describe objective phenomena. When postmodernists expel the concepts, they destroy the ability to assert existence; therefore they dismiss our realistic thinking as pointless and senseless. It is their denial of objectivity tacit in common sense, not of objectivism, that makes their doctrines controversial and detrimental to science. By imprisoning scientific theories to the culture in which they are constructed, postmodernism reduces science to a myth.

The general mental structures supporting objective thinking requires at least two variables, object x and mental frames f_i. Both are basic to scientists' talk of discovery. By insisting that all theories are constructed without concepts of reality, relativism and social constructionism banish the object variable. Standing alone, the frame variable sinks into perspectivism in which perspectives determine the contents of thinking and we are deprived of mental abilities to think about nature and reality. As explained in the next section, we can understand each other mostly because we presuppose that we share a physical world, to which we refer separately. Together with the concept of the objective world goes the possibility of intersubjective understanding facilitated by the transformations among various mental and cultural frames. Only a multitude of mutually incommunicado frames remains, as illustrated in figure 8.4b.

We saw that when Quine (1953) dismissed the notion of physical objects as a myth, he ended up in an ontological relativism where it is impossible to translate accurately from one language to another. Similarly,

Kuhn (1962) held that different scientific theories are incommensurate paradigms and scientists are not free to change from one to another; it is impossible for people holding them to understand each other and one has to undergo something like a religious conversion and be born again into a new paradigm. Thus people in one cultural frame celebrate creationism as hard science, those in another condemn Newton's *Principia* as a rape manual, some maintain that alien abduction occurred, others that the Holocaust did not, and no one in other frames can dispute them, because their frames are incommensurate. This is the "lonely provincialism" that Rorty extolled.

By denying the possibility of rational discourse across cultures and theories, incommensurability closes the mind, inducing people to settle smugly with their own biases. No one assumes that intersubjective under-standing is easy, but the notion of objectivity demands that we try, whereas relativism tells us to give up. Science investigates many phenomena far from everyday experiences, thus some nonscientists regard it as a separate culture. Is it incommensurate with our commonsense culture? Construc-tionist Paul Forman (1997) dismissed as "snake-oil" scientist James Trefil's (1997) proposal to increase scientific literacy by designing college-level curricula for nonscience majors. Such postmodern attitudes are having an adverse effect on education (Cromer 1997).

The presuppositions of nature and reality discipline our thinking. When they are banished, theoretical constructions become arbitrary. Post-modernists call such arbitrariness "open" and "unforced." The liberal tone is deceptive. Presupposing reality in their pursuit of truth, scientists acknowledge the force of nature and rational persuasion, and on the strength of it resist the force of authorities, because nature is accessible to all rational inquirers and not only those in power. It is the spirit of the Enlightenment to keep an open mind to evidence and persuasion, to yield to reason but not to blind beliefs imposed by culture and tradition. Reason and the Enlightenment are the chief targets of postmodernism, which obliterates the force of nature and reason. Postmodern constructions, however, are anything but open and unforced; they are enslaved by power politics and culture with all their unexamined opinions. Everything, including all contents of natural scientific theories, are closed within a culture.

Contrary to relativism, rationality is not peculiar to the Enlighten-ment or even Western culture. Economist Amartya Sen (2000) was not the first to expose the relativist pretension and show the global reach of reason. Reason not only prompts us to open our mind to people in other cultures, it also demands us to be critical of our own opinions, many of which are instilled by our culture. Confucius said he examined his own thoughts and actions three times daily. Kant analyzed how reason critiques itself by ferreting out its own hidden presuppositions. In denigrating rationality, social constructionists also forego self-criticism. Latour (1987:13) boasted: "we will carry with us no presuppositions of what constitute knowledge." He was only blind to his own presuppositions.

Despite bitter polemics, relativism and social constructionism presuppose a model of mind that is akin to that of objectivism and theospectivism. Both favor the closed mind and prefer to see it from the position of mind designers, differing mainly in the number of closed minds considered. We saw that theospectivism easily slides into solipsism. Relativism is a cultural solipsism featuring a host of closed minds that have no concept of reality and cannot communicate with each other. Many people observed that relativism is self-refuting. It holds all theories to be relative to cultures. If this is true, it itself is specific to a culture and can be safely ignored by people in other cultures. However, this is not what relativism says; it claims to be universal and thus provides a counter example to itself. For example, Kuhn claimed that Ptolemic and Copernican theories are incommensurate and went on to compare them, thus by example refuted his own claim. To the charge of self-refutation, relativists reply that they consider the matter from a higher and broader perspective. Yes, they imprison ordinary minds within specific cultures but fancy themselves to be mind designers that can judge and compare minds closed in different cultures. Like theospectivism, relativism issues from a transcendent position.

Theospectivism is mainly concerned with ideal science. Relativists and social constructionists claim to describe actual science and collect historical episodes that they allege to be cases in support of their doctrines. Ideal scientists do not exist to protest misrepresentations, actual scientists do and are not dumb. Many scientists analyzed constructionists' accounts of scientific theories and practices; exposed their errors, omissions, conceptual confusions, unsupported conclusions, and ignorance of the contents of scientific theories; explained how they distort scientists' decision-making processes by ignoring topics and considering only politics of scientific debates; showed how their cited episodes fail to support their sweeping conclusions, which are often attached like misleading captions with scant justification on their relevance to the figures (Gross et al. 1997; Koertge 1998). Constructionists reacted swiftly. Replying to the first major criticism, *Social Text* published a special issue entitled *Science Wars* (Ross 1996), flanked by several papers in other journals bearing the same phrase in their titles. Their response is consistent with their doctrines; when all theories are cultural paradigms and rational discourse among incommensurate paradigms is by definition impossible, the major way out seems to be war.

26   Subjectivity, Intersubjectivity, and Community

In the last section, I presented a conceptual schema representing the minimal mental structure by which a person distinguishes his experiences from the objects of his experiences. So far, our discussion has stayed on the most general level. In this section and the next we fill in some specifics of the schema and examine more substantive issues about the characteristics of subject and the objective world.

The Closed Mind versus the Existential Self

The notion of the self or the subject is always of paramount interest, because it directly cuts into our conception of our own status. The *Journal of Consciousness Studies* featured several special issues on models of the self that ran over 400 pages. The enthusiasm is significant. No less significant is the editors' introduction to the issues. Shaun Gallagher and Jonathan Shear (1997) wrote: "The Western notion of self continually narrows. . . . Thus, the self, which once flourished as the Aristotelian fullness of human life, came to be stabilized in a Cartesian substance, and was subsequently distilled to a flowing consciousness in which it dissipated and disappeared." The diminishing self again testifies to the sway of the closed mind controlled by mind designers. The self implies a certain notion of mental autonomy, which is stifled by closure and control.

Like many contributors to the special issues, I disagree with the editors' assessment. True, the self is endangered in simplistic models that posit the thinking subject as an entity that exists by itself, independent of the world and perhaps of the body. There is hardly anything that we can say about this entity, not even what is peculiar about its states that make them thoughts. What can "subject" or "self" mean for such an isolated entity, except perhaps it is self-evident in introspection? Closed off from everything else, however, self-evidence becomes an epiphenomenon. By virtue of what do we acknowledge self-transparency to the entity we call "mind" and not to other entities, for instance the atmosphere? If we cannot give an account, the self looses it significance. Simplistic models of the closed mind with its disappearing self are influential in a few academic circles. Extrapolating their dominance to the Western culture, however, reveals blatant disregard for ordinary experiences that plagues interpretations of cognitive science. Think about yourself and the people you know. Do you not find a commonsense notion of self flourishing in the fullness of your everyday life?

Against the academically fashionable self that is transparent only in introspection, I present the old notion of existential self wherein one finds oneself by being in the world and with others. The self *exists* in the Greek sense of "standing out" by differentiating itself from and relating itself to things and other people. The Delphic injunction "know thyself" asks people to know their proper places in the cosmos, for instance, not to behave with hubris by fancying themselves to be gods. Socratic self-examination looks at the active lives of citizens. This self is the existential self who leads an active life in nature and society, enjoys bodily exercises, and relishes in the bounty of this world. I see no evidence that this sense of self is declining in the contemporary West, except in some academic philosophies.

The existential self can be analyzed into a first-person *I* and a third-person *One*, both of which are incorporated into the transformation schema in figure 8.2. The schema represents the minimal mental structure in terms of two interrelated general variables, mental frame f_i and object x. Intuitively, the frame variable f_i has more subjective connotation. However, it alone is not sufficient for any sense of self. Even in discussing subjectivity, we must constantly refer to the objective world and invoke the object variable x. That is because the subjective and objective aspects of mind are intrinsically related, so that one is aware of oneself simultaneously as he finds the world intelligible. This intrinsic relation is theoretically represented by f_i and x being two interrelated variables in a unitary framework.

Remember that f_i, mental frame, is a variable that covers a range of values. Variables are susceptible to generalization by rationally extending their ranges of values. When we introduced f_i we considered only psychophysical modes and perspectives of an individual person. Now we will extend the range of f_i to cover the perspectives of other people, thus generalizing it from subjectivity to intersubjectivity. In this model, the basic interpersonal relation is not a two-way relation in which a person guesses at the mind of another, but a three-way relation in which the minds of two persons meet at an object, so to speak. We can understand each other because we share the same objective world, and the sharing constitutes our community. This section concentrates on the subjective and intersubjective significance of the frame variable. One of its important values, language, is mentioned only in the passing and is discussed more fully in section 28.

The Body as Unifier of Psychophysical Modes

Let us start by examining the important mental frames that human beings have. They come in a great variety. Some may be luxury. Are any of them indispensable to our having any mental property? What are the mental frames that are necessary for us to have a sense of self? My basic hypothesis is that mind is a high-level property of a physical entity—an engaged person—who is and is aware that he is a part of the physical world and interacts with other entities in the world. The person has other kinds of properties that I loosely call bodily properties. Mental and bodily properties are sharply separated in the Cartesian picture including computationalism, but not in mine. Their intertwining is apparent in mental frames. Some frames, such as thinking and reasoning, seem not to involve the body. However, I will argue that a pure thinker can hardly maintain a sense of self and personal identity. A major conclusion of this section is that a person's sense of self depends on his ability to know his state of being both as the agent and as an observer. We have this ability because our mind's transformation schema contains frames for both the first-person agent and the third-person observer perspectives, and it can encompass both perspectives because we are fully embodied and engaged.

Parts of our mental frames are psycho*physical* modes: senses of perception and proprioception for our postures, bodily conditions, and deliberate movements of our bodily parts. With my motor control and proprioception, I know whether I am raising my hands without looking at them. My knowledge is routinely checked and confirmed by my perception. With sensual perception, I also know my location and orientation with respect to other objects in the world. Perception is much more than registration. It presupposes a perceivable world in which the perceiver moves and views from various points. Thus psychophysical modes ensure that the person's mind is embodied and can be open to the world.

Perception and action, the two large classes of person-world commerce, are much more intimately related than many armchair thinkers imagine. Bodily activities play a great part in integrating different modes of perception. To see more closely how it contributes to mind, consider vision. Vision features heavily in discussions of the brain in a vat, where it is merely the processing of electrode stimulations. Suppose we make the tale more credible by equipping the brain in a vat with eyes to receive optical stimuli. Can it then have genuine vision? No, experiments on humans and other animals answer. As a starter, to see something we must position our heads and orient our gaze properly. Motor, vestibular, and proprioceptive input must be integrated with optical input to produce visual experiences. For instance, many animals learn to fear and avoid cliffs early in life. Infants stop at the edge of an optical cliff covered by a sheet of Plexiglas, refusing to crawl over to their mothers calling from the far side. To fear cliffs one must first be able to judge height and recognize edges. These visual abilities do not develop in isolation. Studies found that before infants acquired locomotion by crawling, they showed no sign of fear when lowered into an optical cliff. An orthopedically disabled baby also showed no fear as long as he had no locomotive experience. Whatever the age when an infant begins to crawl, it is not the age but the crawling experience that initiates fear of height. Furthermore, fear appears in precrawling infants who have experienced "artificial" locomotion in a walker. Thus locomotive exercise plays an important role in the acquisition and cognition of fear (Campos et al. 1992). However, it is not clear whether the motor activity helps visual cognition of height, association of height with danger, or the fear of danger. For some hints on this question, we turn to a classic experiment with kittens.

Experimentalists raised kittens in darkness except under controlled conditions. During the illuminated sessions, they paired the kittens up. One in the pair was allowed to walk on its own and be active. The other was packed in a box and kept passive. Both kittens were exposed to the same optic flow; however, only for the active one did visual experience relate to the act of walking; the passive one was an ecological perceiver in the sense of being a mobile viewpoint. After several weeks of such visual training the kittens were tested. The active ones developed normal visual ability. The passive kittens were functionally blind; they fell over cliffs, bumped into things, and failed to blink at approaching objects or extend their paws at surfaces (Gregory 1987).

The result has a plausible explanation. Motion parallax, in which a mobile observer determines the distance of an object by moving to various positions, is an effective way of judging depth. For it to work in perception, the perceiver himself must have some ways to determine the distance between viewing positions. Locomotion, whose progress can be measured by monitoring the moving limbs that generate it, is a natural way to gauge distance. It appears that for some animals the development of depth judgment requires calibrating visual input with relevant limb movements. Thus the perceiver is more than a mobile viewpoint, and depth information is not there in the optic flow ready to be picked up. Depth judgment requires much active effort of the fully embodied perceiver, including his proprioceptive monitoring of his bodily functions. As Piaget maintained, sensorimotor exercises are indispensable for mental development. In such exercises babies develop their ability to integrate experiences in various psychophysical modes and perspectives.

Many other experiments demonstrated the importance of body in orientation, navigation, and other cognitive processes. People remembered a sequence of movements much better after they performed the movements than after they read verbal descriptions of them. Experimental subjects, after memorizing a scene containing various objects, retrieved with different efficiency objects located along different axes with respect to their bodies. Other subjects, after memorizing things in a room, had difficulty pointing to the objects blindfolded when asked to imagine rotating their bodies by 90 degrees, but had no difficulty when they actually rotated their bodies. Having a body is an enormous advantage in thinking about the ways of the world (Tversky 1997; Wong and Simons 1999).

The body is not merely a luxury for mind; it is indispensable to mind through psychophysical modes. We start to develop our ability to integrate our psychophysical modes early in life. Neonates spontaneously turn their heads to look at ticking clocks placed on their pillows for the first time. Babies are always excited at relations among experiences in different psychophysical modes, preferring visual stimuli that are accompanied by auditory stimuli belonging to the same event. When, at twelve weeks of age, they begin to reach for and grasp objects in sight, they also begin to reach for and grasp noisy objects in the dark. Around four months, when they succeed in catching objects moving at 30 centimeters per second, infants begin to transfer some knowledge gained from one perceptual mode to another. They can recognize visually whether the object they touch out of sight is rigid or flexible. Furthermore, their recognition is far better when they actively move an object than when they passively hold on to a self-moving object. Perhaps this is because activity heightens the intensity of the tactile mode and engages a more acute perspective (Streri et al. 1993; Karmiloff-Smith 1992).

Agency and Its Development

Agency is a major aspect in our sense of ourselves as subjects. It implies purposive action, where one deliberately manipulates objects with the expectation of making a definite difference in the world. Thus agents are radically open. Unlike behaviors, which can occur for an isolated psychophysical mode, actions depend on integration of several modes, including goal-directed movements and perception of results. A system's behaviors interact causally with the environment, that is all. Action, however, requires more. It presupposes the possibility that its result is different from its goal, for it takes account of the world's resistance. To be an agent, therefore, one has to be simultaneously in the world and possess the ability to separate himself from it, so that he is not absorbed and exhausted by the causal effects of his actions. This is achieved by the checks and balances among various afferent and efferent psychophysical modes. Above all, it depends on the ability to distinguish consequences of one's own initiative from other events.

Agency requires complicated mental capacity that takes years to bloom, but it buds early. Babies take great delight in effects that they initiate. If they are presented with mobiles that are activated only when they kick, they quickly learn the secret; they are much more excited by controllable mobiles than by similar mobiles that turn independent of their movements. The joy in efficacy is expressed not only with things but with people. Babies are extraordinarily enthusiastic about faces that imitate their own. Barely six weeks old, they differentiate clearly between people who interact with them and those who behave similarly but do not respond to their own activities. They happily smile and goo-goo at images of their mothers who return expressions and vocalizations in real time through closed-circuit television, but frustratingly ignore replays of their mothers' former performances, in which they now have no say (Meltzoff and Moore 1995; Spelke and Newport 1998).

Joint Attention and Intersubjectivity

If you stand in the middle of a busy street and stare at the sky, soon several people will be doing the same, trying to figure out what attracts your attention and finally deciding that you are nuts. Interaction is not restricted to two parties. When you and I look at or talk about the same object, we are in a sense united by the object. Such three-way interaction appears very early. At age three months babies can follow the gaze of an adult to look at the object the adult looks at, although they do not always succeed in disengaging their gaze from the adult's eyes and are not very accurate in locating the target object. Locating accuracy improves quickly. At eighteen months, a baby will turn around to search behind it if an adult looks beyond it at something at the back (Meltzoff and Moore 1995; Hood et al. 1998). The ability to follow gaze is not limited to humans. Field and laboratory observations report that a chimpanzee can follow the gaze of another to look at the object the other looks at (Mitchell 1997).

The precocious ability to follow gaze is significant; it shows that a fundamental mode of social communication is joint attention to physical objects. Realization that other people are open to the same physical world as we are is indispensable in forging mutual understanding. It is the basis for our attribution of beliefs to others. Joint attention indicates that intersubjectivity depends on objectivity. As Heidegger (1926) illustrated, being-with-others is a mode of being-in-the-world.

Joint attention is most important in the process of learning, for instance, in learning word meanings. Children are smarter than many adults think. They usually do not arbitrarily associate a word that they hear with the object that they happen to be seeing or handling. They are also sensitive to pragmatic conditions, including the gaze of the adult who utters the word. Psychologists probed the operation of referential cues by showing a young subject two new toys, one of which they let the subject hold, the other they hid in a bucket. An adult entered, looked at the toy in the subject's hands, and said: "Hey, it's a toma." Most youngsters learned the new word "toma" as the name for the toy. The result was totally different if the adult looked into the bucket and said: "It's a toma." Some nineteen-month-olds learned "toma" as the name for the hidden toy. Sixteen-month-olds ignored the word. They did not learn, but they were not misled either. They did not associate the word they heard with the toy in their hands, because they monitored the gaze of the adult and found it directed elsewhere. Learning word meanings is much more complicated than simply associating labels with things. It is a social and communicative activity through and through (Woodward and Markman 1998).

Children's ability to monitor gaze and join attention flowers into important concepts. People appear as objects; but children realize that people are not ordinary objects but objects that are like themselves in having capacities to see and manipulate things. To account for this realization in our theory for the basic mental structures as shown in figure 8.2, we take advantage of the fact that the mental frame f_i is a variable. A variable introduces certain rules and relates its values systematically. Rules and systematicity are theoretically powerful because they can readily be generalized. Thus we can generalize our schema to cover intersubjective understanding by expanding the range of mental frame variable to include other people's psychophysical modes and perspectives.

The generalized schema represents other people in two ways. As objects in the world, they are represented by certain values of the object variable x. As sharers of the subject's attention to things in the world, they are represented by a certain class of mental frames f_i. Suppose Tom and Mary look at a statue. Then in the theoretical representation of Tom's mental state, $f_1(x)$ is his visual experience from his viewpoint f_1 and $f_2(x)$ is what he imagines to be Mary's visual experience from her viewpoint f_2. Because the two experiences are connected by the same statue x, the model makes explicit the idea that objects are publicly accessible and intersubjective agreements about them are possible. Thus we explicitly reject relativism.

Intersubjective communication, represented by $f_2 \cdot f_1^{-1}(p_1) = f_2(x) = p_2$, is objective from the start. A person does not merely try to induce the experience p_2 in another by broadcasting his own experience p_1, in which case a simple transformation suffices. That the transformation $f_2 \cdot f_1^{-1}$ is composite and refers to an object x indicates that as an intersubjective relation, intentionality is not merely intentional speech act but communicative action. People do not merely talk to each other and come to a convenient consensus. They talk *about* some object x and come to consensus *about it*. This *joint intentionality* is beyond the ken of any closed mind. The objective world unites our subjective understanding. Conversely, the possibility of intersubjective intentionality in which many persons refer to the same object secures the objectivity of our knowledge.

Empathy with and Theory about Other People

Besides being a generalization of our own mental frames, other people are objects in the world. Objects are what we form beliefs about and for which we posit theories. We frame propositions about people as we do about things. Because people are special and important, we have reserved a large class of concepts and words, mental and psychological, just for them. We believe that other people believe, desire, feel, and think in general ways as we ourselves do. We not only attribute beliefs and desires to other people but act on the basis of the attribution. If I believe you will meet me at the airport, I'll wait; otherwise I'll leave. Such beliefs, which are crucial to our daily business, are based on a host of assumptions we hold about people and how they think. Cognitive scientists account for them by saying that people have a theory of mind, namely, folk psychology.

Do we form beliefs about other people's minds, or do we project our own thinking onto others? This question about how we know other minds has generated a long debate in cognitive science. Proponents of the so-called *theory-theory* of other minds maintain that people have a tacit theory of mind that is expressed in everyday psychological concepts. Proponents of the *simulation-theory* deny tacit theory of mind, proposing that a person understands another by projecting himself imaginatively into the other's conditions, thus simulating the other's mental processes with one's own (Carruthers and Smith 1996).

Instead of being mutually exclusive, the theory-theory and simulation-theory can complement each other to explain our mutual understanding. My model of mental structures synthesizes both. It accounts for the theory-theory by representing other people as objects in the intelligible world, and for the simulation-theory by representing their perspectives as a generalization of the subject's. Adult humans are capable of both theory and projective simulation. One method may be more efficient than the other under certain circumstances, but there is no reason for monopoly. I can try to understand you by treating you as an object x from my theoretical mental frame. I can also try to understand you by projecting myself into your perspective f_i; this is what people usually call sympathy or empathy.

As a basic interpersonal relation, empathy plays important roles in ethics. Hume (1739:316) wrote: "No quality of human nature is more remarkable, both in itself and in its consequences, than that propensity we have to sympathize with others, and to receive by communication their inclinations and sentiments, however different from, or even contrary to our own." Sympathy is the foundation of morality, he maintained. Without it, we would not recognize anything as virtue or vice; we would only reckon with monistic self interests, just as economists do. Empathy offers a straightforward interpretation of the golden rule in the New Testament, do to others what you want others to do to you, or the negative formulation of the rule in Confucianism, do not do to others what you do not want others to do to you, which shows more respect for the diversity of tastes. However, it is not the only possible interpretation. Kantians interpret the rule as a universal moral maxim for respecting others, which depends on theoretical understanding of people.

Projection of perspectives is more immediate than theorization. It is likely to work best in inarticulate situations such as those involving feeling and emotion, or in simple situations such as joint attention, when both parties and the topic of their beliefs are present. Uncritical empathy, however, easily falls into errors such as animism, where we arbitrarily project our mental frames to artifacts and inanimate things. This happens, for instance, in homuncular functionalism and "wishful mnemonics" in AI, where people carelessly project their own thinking onto computers (see section 5).

Critical reflection leads to theorization, where we take account of many factors that are neglected in empathy. We ask, for example, whether the object to which we project our mental frames has mental properties. Such questioning prevents us from falling prey to animism gilded with technobabble. Usually, conjectures about other people's minds become more effective when the situation is complicated. They become essential when we lack particular data for definite projection because of ignorance or other factors.

The course of development also suggests that the projection of perspective operates first and is probably the base on which theories about beliefs develop. A child a few months old is capable of following gaze, thus revealing some grasp of others seeing what he sees. However, not until he is four or five years old does he grasp that other people may be ignorant of something that he knows. An experimenter put a candy in a box in a child's presence and then left the room. In his absence, another experimenter took the candy from the box, put it into a can, and asked the child where the first experimenter would look for the candy. Children younger than four mostly answered in the can. They projected their own knowledge into the absent experimenter, indicating that they were unable either to transform between two radically different perspectives or to form the concept of false belief. Older children answered correctly that the experimenter would look for the candy in the box. They grasped the concept of false belief, because when asked, they explained the experimenter's behavior by his absence and ignorance (Wellman 1990).

Autistic children may suffer from inability to handle the three-way relation among objects and their own and other's perspectives. Autism is a complicated disorder that is poorly understood. However, most researchers agree that it involves some kind of "mind-blindness," as these children have great difficulty appreciating other people's mental states, resulting in poor social and communicative competence. Two of its early indications are inability to follow gaze and to point to objects of interest and not merely of want. Autistic children concentrate on their toys and rarely look at others or express an intention to share their experiences. Later they fail false-belief tests. Probably the early inability to extrapolate their mental frames to others impedes the development of concepts about people as belonging to a special kind of object with mental properties.

The Third-Person Self: One in a Community

An object x in the world and a sharer of some mental frames f_i together constitute the general concept of Someone, as distinct from Something that is merely an object. An instance of Someone is an object to whom a person can extend the values of the frame variable; an instance of Something is an object to which he cannot.

With perception, proprioception, and other psychophysical modes, a person realizes that he is a participant in the world. With the concept of Someone, he realizes there are special participants with mental frames similar to his. Now he comes to realize that he is one of those special participants whose mental frames are precisely his own. Thus he arrives at the notion of himself as One, who is simultaneously oneself, a particular instance of Someone to whom mental properties can be attributed, and a flesh-and-blood object that is a part of the world. This notion of One is not very different from Heidegger's (1926) *das Man*, which is variously translated as One, They, or the they-self.[11]

One is a reflective notion wherein a person sees himself from a partially detached standpoint. Many believe that some such reflective ability is the minimum criterion for a sense of self. This is the base for the mirror test of identity. Experimenters familiarize a subject with a mirror, then paint a mark on its face while it sleeps. If it rubs at the mark when looking into the mirror, they decide that it recognizes itself. Yearlings and monkeys fail the mirror test; eighteen-month-olds and chimpanzees pass. A few months after a child first rubs his face, he readily answers "me" when an adult points to his mirror image and asks, "Who is this?" He recognizes himself as One.

Being an instance of Someone, the concept of One is the crux of personal and psychological concepts. Concepts are abilities to conceive possibilities, hence they imply generality. Consider the subject-predicate proposition, for instance "The apple is red," "Mary is conscious," or generally "*a* is *F*," where *a* refers to an entity such as Mary and the predicate *F* attributes a certain property to the entity. Philosopher Gareth Evans (1982) examined the conceptual ability required to handle such propositions. To understand "*a* is *F*" implies at least two basic abilities. First, one must be able to grasp the possibility of attributing other properties to *a* such as "*a* is *G*" or "Mary is unconscious." Second, one must be able to grasp the possibility of applying the predicate *F* to other entities such as "*b* is *F*." A person who understands "Mary is conscious" should be able to attribute consciousness not only to Mary but to Jane or you or me or himself. This sounds trivial, but it poses tremendous difficulties to a Cartesian ego who thinks "I am conscious." Being disembodied and closed from the world, it has no way to generalize the notions of I and being conscious. This problem does not arise for us because we are embodied and open to the world. The notion of One as an instance of Someone enables me to attribute various mental properties to myself and to others, hence to grasp fully the meaning of being myself and being a mental entity. It also underlies the ability to use pronouns such as "I" and "you," the meanings of which vary with speakers and hearers.

Therapists encourage patients with posttraumatic disorder to write out their experience, thus externalize their trauma and come to grips with it by distancing themselves from it. In memories, we recall not only what we experienced as children but see ourselves as children from an adult's perspective. In autobiographies, we examine our lives, criticize them, and adopt an observer's position with respect to ourselves. Even when we use the first-person pronoun in narratives, what we recount are often the mental states of ourselves as One. By seeing ourselves as One, who is an interactive part of the world, we monitor the results of our efforts. Without the notion of One to complement the sense of initiative and effort that we get from proprioception, we cannot have the full notion of agency and hence of subjectivity.

Seeing myself as One, I realize that I am one of many who share the same world and form a community that is my social world. The diversity of mental frames for members of society brings enormous knowledge about the world, on which a person depends. With limited mental capacity, a person cannot possibly imagine all the mental frames. However, he can master the norms and conventions of practice and forge cultural and social perspectives by which he fits into the community, gets along with his fellows, taps their resources, and expresses himself so they understand.

We saw that I acknowledge other people as Someone by joining intentionality and referring to the same objects as they do. Because One is an instance of Someone and essential to my knowledge of myself, my full sense of self depends on my making sense of things and of my fellow beings. A three-way intrinsic relation exists among subjectivity, objectivity, and intersubjectivity. They are defined in terms of each other, so that the mention of one implies the other two.

Because of the symbiosis of *I*, *it*, and *thou*, the traditional problem of other minds does not arise. The problem is rampant where mind is an abstract entity closed in its little private chamber and has no way of knowing if there are other chambers, let alone breaking into them. It loses its force in our model where mind is the property of a physical person who manipulates things purposely, monitors his own and others' attention, and knows himself as one among many of the same kind. There are many things about other people that one cannot fathom, but these are unknowns, not mysteries.

The First-Person Self: I Think

As a part of the world, One is an object about which a person thinks. The person is also the thinking subject who says I and is Dasein. I experience this. I think about that. *I think* or *I am aware* is the most primary hallmark of mentality, without which one cannot know anything, let alone form the reflexive idea of One. What is the meaning of this primitive I? What are its structures and prerequisites? How is it represented in our schema of mental structures?

Unlike One or *das Man*, which is represented explicitly as a particular value of x, *I* or Dasein is not represented by any definite term in figure 8.2. The objective world contains no entity that is a pure mental being or the thinking subject qua subject, and the head does not hide a Cartesian ego or mental self that is accessible to introspection, which is a special mental frame. Such inner subject has always been a suspect. Hume (1739:252) went in to look for it and came out empty-handed: "When I enter most inti-

mately into what I call *myself*, I always stumble on some particular perception or other. . . . I never can catch *myself* at any time without a perception, and never can observe any thing but the perception." Kant (1781:136,
329) followed Hume and said that "no fixed and abiding self can present
itself in the flux of inner appearances." He went further to launch a barrage
against the Cartesian doctrine that " 'I,' as thinking, am an object of inner
sense, and am called 'soul.' " The Cartesian soul, he explained, is an illusion
arising from confusing the unity of experiences with the experience of an
entity. If Kant was windy, Wittgenstein (1921:5.631) cut to the quick: "The
thinking, presenting subject; there is no such thing." I will explain more
fully the meaning of the pure thinking subject that they and I rejected. Here
I note that its nonexistence is represented by my schema's containing no
definite term for it.

Hume's failure to find *myself* by introspection does not imply that
Hume did not exist or was merely a fat lump of flesh without a sense of
self. He was the I who entered and stumbled and observed and tried to
catch and admitted failure. This I, not the illusory item it tried to reach
by introspection, was primary to Hume's mind and subjectivity. Kant held
that I think, which must accompany all my thoughts, is the synthetic unity
of apperception. However, it is only a *formal* unity in which various
thoughts are grasped in a single consciousness wherein they are recognized
as all mine. Along similar lines, I contend that the primary *I* is represented
not by any term in the schema in figure 8.2 but by the *entire schema*. The
whole schema represents the minimal mental ability without which an
entity cannot synthesize experiences from various mental frames and grasp
them as *my* experiences, hence cannot possibly have any sense of self.
Whenever I perceive an object from a particular mental frame, whenever
I conceive a state of affairs from another frame, whenever I transform from
one mental frame to another, I exercise my mental ability and thereby am
aware of myself as the subject. Besides that there is no extra entity, no
mental self, that hides inside the head.

The Existential Self: I and One

The ubiquitous mental frames and their interrelations constitute I or my
first-person self that always accompanies my mental activities. It is more
substantive than *I think* because it includes the psychophysical modes that
anchor mental frames to the body and the world. It is the base on which
we develop the notion of One or the third-person self by extending the

range of mental frames and objects. We can transform between the two senses of self just as we can switch from field to observer memory, or from empathy to speculation about other people's minds. Together, I and One constitute the existential self, our full sense of subject. Together, they constitute consciousness as personal identity.

One and I are two aspects of the existential self. To see the difference between them, compare two narratives that are usually both counted as "first person," Odysseus's account of his great wanderings and Leopold Bloom's soliloquy during his wandering in Dublin. Homer had Odysseus tell his own story in the Phaiakian court. In the story, Odysseus himself appeared as an active character referred to as "I." For instance, in the land of Lotus Eaters where his men were enchanted: "I myself took these men back weeping, by force, . . . then gave order to the rest of my eager companions to embark on the ships in haste, for fear someone else might taste of the lotus and forget the way home." In his narrative, Odysseus differs from other actors in the story only in his importance and greater revelation of thoughts and feelings. His memory is more from the observer than the field perspective, and he mainly views himself as the third-person self, the One, a man in action.

Odysseus' narration differs not only in contents but in general nature from Bloom's stream of consciousness in an enchanting moment that James Joyce described in *Ulysses*: "Nice kind of evening feeling. No more wandering about. Just loll there: quiet dusk: let everything rip. Forget. Tell about places you have been, strange customs." Here is the first-person I at work as the thinking subject in his field perspective. Notice that "I" and "I think" seldom appear in the contents of Bloom's silent monologue, as he is mostly thinking not of himself but of other things. Nevertheless, all the while he is not only thinking but is aware that he is thinking, thus engaging in his most immediate first-person experience.

The narratives of Odysseus and Bloom illustrate the points of Hume and Kant discussed earlier. Except as One, the thinking subject does not appear in thought; I is not an inner entity. Nevertheless, awareness of thinking implies that it must be possible for "I think" to accompany thoughts; Bloom could at any time think explicitly: "I have this nice kind of evening feeling" and so on.

Because One involves much conceptualization, it is fully grasped by children at a much later stage of development, probably only with the help of language. We can reasonably assume that it is absent in most nonhu-

man animals that have some sense of I. The notion of One is crucial to
the full sense of a person, without its substantiation we cannot attain a
robust sense of ourselves as rational and moral agents. However,
One depends on the primary I. As an object of reflection, it depends
on the mental structures in which any object is intelligible in the first
place.

I and It

Ordinarily, we use the same pronoun "I" to refer to first-person self (I),
the third-person self (One), and the existential self (I and One). In discussing the distinction between subject and object, I and it, "I" generally
refers to the existential self, the full sense of subject.

The existential self is radically engaged in the world; neither the first-
person nor the third-person self is detachable from the body and the
world. That is the major difference between us and the Cartesian Trojan
horse. Cartesians posit mind and environment existing independent of each
other and try to relate the two by imposing external relations such as representation or causation (figure 8.1a). In contrast, we post a person-
engaged-in-the-world and try to delineate his basic mental properties as
his ability to distinguish the subjective and objective aspects of his own
experiences. There is no mind or mental subject to start with. The existential self is born with a person's own ability to distinguish the objects
of his experience from his subjective experience (figure 8.1b). This distinction whose two variables are depicted in figure 8.2, is the most primitive structure, without which there would no experience, no mind, no
subject, and no intelligible object.

As discussed in section 13, a distinction is simultaneously an intrinsic relation between what it distinguishes. When we talk about part A in
figure 3.8b, for instance, we tacitly invoke part B through the boundary
R that defines A's shape. Like the boundary R, general concepts of objects
distinguish objects and objective experiences. When we talk about objects,
we tacitly assume the possibility of encountering them. When we talk
about experiences, we tacitly assume the possibility that they are of some
objects. Because subjects *as mental* arise only with the objects that they
recognize, mind is intrinsically open. As possible objects of experiences,
things become intelligible.

Subject and the objective world are intrinsically symbiotic. The symbiosis rejects the closed mind that exists by itself and embraces a mind
that is open to the world through and through. As Heidegger (1927:197)

argued, Dasein or human being is primarily being-in-the-world: "Self and world belong together in the single unity, the Dasein. Self and world are not two things, like subject and object, or like I and thou, but self and world are the basic determination of the Dasein itself in the unity of the structure of being-in-the-world." He was not the only or the first to assert thus. Kant (1781:194) used different words for a similar conclusion. He summarized the symbiosis of subjectivity and objectivity in a principle of empirical knowledge: "The conditions of the *possibility of experience* in general are likewise conditions of the *possibility of the objects of experience.*" One commentator explained: "There can be no *it* unless there is an *I*," another added: "Not only does the *it* entail an *I*, but conversely the *I* entails a *it*" (Bennett 1966:129). Zhuang Zhou, a founder of Daoism, expressed it best more than two thousand years earlier in nine words: "Without it [there is] no I, without I nothing is intelligible" (figure 8.5).

To say that it, the intelligible world, is an essential aspect of a person's open mind does not mean that the person carries the physical world or a mirror image of it in his head. It means that the open mind is a situated property that makes a subject qua subject. We saw in §13 that scientists often attribute to a system properties that include factors lying physically outside the system. These situated properties, which have absorbed many relational factors, are custom-made for the environment where the system situates. In other words, situated properties and their situation are defined self-consistently. The open mind is a person's situated property that has absorbed important general structures of the world that are physically beyond the person. The objective world has many characteristics that are not up to us. To account for them, our open mind has developed complementary structures. Conversely, these structures shape the intelligible world that open-minded people encounter and understand. This is the sense of Kant's principle that the general conditions for the possibility of experiences are consistent with general conditions for possibilities for objects of experiences. Its crux is that our most fundamental mental structures are not to be found inside the head or in abstract logic.

非彼無我 非我無所取　莊子齊物論

Figure 8.5
"Without it [there is] no I, without I nothing is intelligible."—Zhuang, "Equality of Beings"

As a situated property, the open mind is embodied in our dealing with and understanding of the world and in the characteristics of that dealing and understanding. It is what Einstein deemed the most incomprehensible thing of the world, its comprehensibility.

What Am I? Who Am I?

There are many other notions of the self. Models of the closed mind controlled by mind designers offer two views of the subject. From the inside, the closed mind is a solipsist self, a mental entity assessable only by introspection. From the outside, mind designers see an ecological self that is no more than a mindless object interacting with other objects. Let me contrast solipsist and ecological selves with my model of the existential self as a flesh and blood person whose mind is open to the world.

Discussions of the self involve at least two questions: what kind of entity is the subject?, and to what particular entity does "I" refer? The two questions are interrelated, for how to individuate particulars depends on what kind of thing the particulars are. Questions about the self are confusing because they involve tricky reflexive concepts. Let us first clarify these concepts.

In taking the self as the referent of "I," we have presupposed that it is an entity. An entity, individual, or particular is a complex notion comprising two general concepts, numerical identity and property. There are other logical ways of conceiving the world. For instance, a bundle of features is an alternative that does not require a numerical identity (see section 17). A solipsist is a bundle of qualia, but in talking about the self, people usually insist on seeking an entity instead of a mere bundle. Thus we will assume that the self is an entity. What kind of entity is it? Several general criteria readily come to mind: it is reflexive, is capable of the first-person view, and has mental properties.

Reflexivity is a general notion that applies to things and people alike. Physicists speak of an electron's self-energy, which is the modification of an electron's energy by its interaction with the electromagnetic field that it itself generates. The occurrence of self-energy and similar concepts in fundamental physics reminds us that our division of the universe into a set of entities is not absolute and that entities are intrinsically related. It also reminds us that reflexivity does not necessarily imply subjectivity. Although electrons have self-energy, they have no sense of self because they have no mental property.

First-person view presupposes particularity but is more than that. Any entity, be it a thing or a person, has its numerical identity and hence particularity. Viewpoints presuppose understanding. Physicists can adopt a heliocentric or geocentric viewpoint in studying the solar system.[12] The viewpoints are physicists'. A heliocentric theory does not accord the sun a first-person view; it is just the entity that sits in the origin of a reference frame that physicists use. One can use viewpoint metaphorically. In the context of studying mind, however, we should be careful not to devaluate the meanings of mental concepts. Therefore I insist on the mental connotation of viewpoints.

What are the mental properties that make an entity a self or subject? Intelligence, consciousness, having an inner realm that one can access by introspection are some of the most common answers (see section 23). Having qualia is different from having a first-person view. Qualia is strictly inward; it is an epiphenomenal feeling that has few if any implications. The first-person view looks outward and has many structures and implications. It implies that a person knows himself as one among other persons, so that he can ascribe first-person viewpoints to others and assume a third-person view for himself. This ability is not necessary for a person to have qualia; he needs only to feel his own mental states.

Having clarified the meanings of the general concepts, we can see differences among the ecological, solipsist, and existential selves. Briefly, the ecological view considers a set of interacting entities and accords selfhood solely on the general notions of particularity and reflexivity, rejecting any mental criterion. The solipsist subject has qualia accessible by introspection but no first-person viewpoint. The existential self is an entity with both physical and mental properties, so that he can distinguish himself from other physical objects by acknowledging his first-person viewpoint.

The Inner Ego

With the Christian identification of the self with the immortal soul, attention turned inward to the neglect of the body and this world. Descartes identified self with the thinking subject and maintained that it exists independent of the body and the physical world. His introspective meditation brought the self into the solipsist level. Thinking, to Descartes, is the property of the soul substance, which persists as the subject. When the dualism of the soul and physical substances falls, what remains is a dualism of the mental subject and a detachable physical body, which can be added later in implementation. The mental self has mental properties but not necessarily physical properties; it is aware of its own states but not necessarily anything else.

The solipsist mental self, inner and abstract, is popular today. It resonates with ideas of a central processing unit in computers, mind as identical to the brain in a vat, and consciousness as qualia. Introspection, too, regains respectability with the rising interest in qualia. The Cartesian theme rings in the keynote paper of the special issues on the self in the *Journal of Consciousness Studies*. Galen Strawson (1997) wrote that the self is a single mental thing alone in the head that is the bare locus of consciousness. The mental self is not incompatible with the body, but is distinct and independent of it: "one's body is just a vehicle or vessel for the mental thing that is what one really or most essentially is." This mental self, however, lasts only a short period of time. It is almost the solipsism of the moment. You do not even have an abiding self; all you have is a succession of solipsist selves. How you know that all these selves are yours and what it means for you to be a single person remain obscure.

The revival of the Cartesian solipsist self did not answer properly the many criticisms it received over the centuries. Thoughts are ephemeral; a thought is no sooner born than it gives way to another thought. Without the soul substance or physical body that persists through changing thoughts, memory loses meaning and becomes just another present thought (see section 19). There is nothing abiding to tie the myriad thoughts together and serve as the identity to which "I" refers. Disembodied and disengaged, momentary and without location, the mental subject evaporates. Without the body and the physical world, what can be said with certainty is not "I think" but "thinking occurs." It is a bundle of qualia, not a self as an entity.

The revival of the solipsist self has invigorated criticism. Many philosophers are recovering the Aristotelian fullness of human life and its notion of existential self. When Merleau-Ponty (1945:xi) asserted that "there is no inner man, man is in the world, and only in the world does he know himself," he discarded only the solipsist mental self but retained the more robust existential self.

Nor is the existential self as being-in-the-world limited to Continental philosophy. It is interesting to imagine a debate between two Strawsons, Galen and Peter. Galen Strawson (1997) viewed a person as a resultant compound made up of two parts, the mental self and the body, that are intelligible independently of each other. For Peter Strawson (1979) a sense self detached from the body is incoherent. The primitive subject is a person with both conscious and corporeal states, a person among other persons who can ascribe mental states to himself as he can ascribe mental states to others. This primitive subject cannot be decomposed into a mental and a physical part. The disembodied mental thing inside the head that Galen defended may be an abstraction from the person, Peter contended, but to take it as a primary entity is an illusion that Hume and Kant blasted. Peter Strawson's notion of self as a full-blooded person goes beyond the Cartesian ego. Thus even in Western analytic philosophy, the existential self on the engaged-personal level is running strong. This self I model by the transformation schema as in figure 8.2, where a particular value of x is One.

The Ecological Self

Gibson's ecological approach has much in common with AI's situated cognition. Thus much criticism of his ecological self applies also to AI's situated agent or autonomous agent. In all cases, the self or the agent is no more than a relata or an entity that participates in a relationship without understanding it. The significance of the agency and the relation is known only to outside ecologists, engineers, or other mind designers.

Gibson (1997:112, 126) wrote: "Ask yourself what it is you see hiding the surroundings as your look out upon the world—not darkness, surely, not air, not nothing, but the ego." Thus "one perceives the environment and coperceives oneself." This sounds like the symbiosis of the subject and object discussed above, but it is not. The symbiosis arises from a mental distinction and presupposes much conceptual ability, which Gibson excluded from perception.[13]

Recall that Gibson's ecological perception is simply picking up certain structures in the energy pattern that impinges on the perceiver (see section 17). Energy patterns vary spatially, therefore what is picked up depends on the location of the point of impingement. That point, metaphorically called the viewpoint, is the ecological self that is coperceived with the object whose information is picked up in perception. Thus the self here depends only on the particularity of an object in an interactive environment. In this sense, coperception of self always occurs, because physical objects are all particulars and their fields of exposure are always limited by their particular locations in the environment. Look at a photograph and ask what is hiding the surroundings—not white paper, but the camera lens, whose position and orientation determine what is and is not in the picture. This is all for the ecological ego. Thus a camera perceives the scene and coperceives itself. Similarly, the earth perceives the gravitational field in the solar system and coperceives itself.

Our ordinary sense of self and perception also depends on the particularity of the subject and perceiver, but it involves much more. It requires the subject to have the ability to distinguish himself from the object he perceives to make sense of "I see it." This distinction ecological perceivers cannot make, because they lack rudimentary concepts and memory. Gibson went so far as to reject proprioception as awareness of one's own bodily conditions, insisting that it is only the perceiver's pole in interacting with the object. Thus the ecological self has no understanding. Any entity that interacts with other things has its ecological self. This self can be replaced by particularity without any lose of meaning.

In the ecological level, ecologists adopt the third-person viewpoint in considering everything. They distinguish this and that just as physicists distinguish the sun and the earth. The commonsense distinction between I and it, however, is primarily made in the first-person view. At issue is not an ecologist's distinction between you and the object presented to you. That distinction, instrumental to scientists studying objects from a third-person standpoint, is applicable to insects or cameras. At issue is the distinction constitutive of a situated subject's own mental states. It is your ability to distinguish between your experience and the objects you experience from your first-person view, without intervention of ecologists. This constitutive distinction is not applicable to insects, as it signals the mental complexity by which you as a mental being are not only part of but also open to the world and find it intelligible. Looking at a perceiver from the third-person's view, Gibson (1979:282) wrote: "If a picture displays the perspective of a scene it puts the viewer into the scene." Looking from the perceiver's first-person view, Wittgenstein (1921:5.632) wrote: "The subject does not belong to the world but is a limit of the world. . . . You say that this case is altogether like that of the eye and the field of sight. But you do *not* really see the eye." Gibson's instrumental "viewer" and Wittgenstein's constitutive "limit of the world" highlight the difference between a camera and a human being. Most theories of self, which do not apply to insects, issues from the first-person view. In protesting against them, Gibson showed more sensitivity to the big gap between their first-person view and his third-person ecological view than his followers who confused the two.

27 The Intelligible World: Everyday and Scientific

Physics, biology, and other sciences take the world's intelligibility for granted and study its substantive features. For the science of mind, however, the main issue is intelligibility itself. What are the conditions of the world that make it possible for us to understand it? What are the conditions of our mind that enable us to understand the world? More specifically, what are the conditions that make empirical knowledge and science possible?

World versus Surrounding

As a technical term in theories of mind, the *world* refers to what is intelligible and meaningful to people, what they share and care about, where they dwell and act purposely; in short, what their mind is open to. As the field of purposive actions a person's world means more than his surrounding or environment. Surroundings can be treated from a strictly external view, so that an entity in its environment means no more than being an interactive part of it. This third-person view is insufficient for addressing the world, which also demands understanding from the first-person perspective; it is world because I find it intelligible and know that many of its elements are shared by other people from their perspectives. The world is not only objective but also subjective and intersubjective. Thus in considering it, we need to take account of the whole transformation schema in figure 8.2 instead of only the object variable x. We can talk about an environment without invoking the mind of the entity in it, but we cannot do so with for the entity's world. Only because we are mental beings can we see our environment as a part of our meaningful world, hence to treasure it instead of tramp in it mindlessly like the robots of AI's situated cognition.

That mind and the world rise and fall together does not imply that we are God who created the universe by thinking. Nor does it subscribe to the cryptographic constraint of the computational mind asserting that if the computational syntax is right, then semantics automatically follows. It means that the minimal structure of mind is its understanding of the world, so that general structures of mind and general structures of the world that it understands are intrinsically related. On the most general level, the intelligible world is just the possibility space of the object variable x in $f_i(x)$; as such it arises with the mind that makes it intelligible. Further analysis of the world reveals that among many other things, it contains people as someone, entities that exist simultaneously with the subject at the present time. On this more substantive level, we understand the world as nature that existed long before our birth or the evolution of human beings.

When we examined subjects and mental frames in the preceding section, we constantly referred to the intersubjective and objective world. Similarly, we will refer to the mental frames when we examine the world in this section. Because we have generalized the frame variable f_i to cover the perspectives of other people and the collective cultural perspectives, I will drop the qualification "mental" and simply call them frames. Depending on the frame that we adopt, we view the world as our field of everyday activities, as environment, nature, cosmos, which we work to appropriate and know.

The world has several general features. It is a complex whole that can be analyzed into systems of interrelated entities in various frames, where it is meaningful in several ways. We always perceive or think about the world in one frame or another, but we can understand each other because the frames are not incommensurate. They refer to a common objective world and are so related that we can transform from one to the other leaving the world invariant, at least in principle. Thus the world is a unifier, as Kant observed in his objective unity of consciousness.

These general features of the world were presupposed all along in the analysis of this book. When I maintain that a complex system has many levels of organization that require many levels of description, I have presupposed various intellectual frames for looking at a system. When I argued that the structures of two organizational levels are related by emergence so that interlevel theories are possible, I have assumed the transformations among frames. Thus the two parts of my theory, the emergence of mind and the openness of mind, are compatible, satisfying the self-consistency criterion put out in section 7.

In so far as we have any experience, what we experience is *already* meaningful, because our experiences of the world always involve one frame or another. How it is meaningful varies across frames. Interpretations occur when a person transforms from one frame to another, especially from a less articulate to a more articulate one; it does not mean adding meanings on some meaningless sense impressions.[14] It is important to note that this interpretation is a person's spontaneous mental ability to switch frames; it has nothing to do with the intervention of outside mind designers in models of the closed mind. In this section, we examine the world in two important general frames, that of our everyday activities and that investigated by science. Both involve practical and theoretical considerations, although their involvements differ in degree and scale. Their mutual interpretations bring out the meaning of science as a practice of humans with open minds, in contradistinction with scientism, which is a prescription of mind designers pretending to be God.

The Perceptual Frame and the Visual World

You open your eyes in the morning and see a world. How meaningful is the world of your immediate perception? How does your visual experience differ from the exposure of a camera film?

We are mainly concerned with the human mind and human experience. Humans are linguistic animals and our general language capability is an important structure of our mind that influences all our experiences. It enables us to form complicated concepts and propositions. However, having linguistic ability does not imply that we exercise it explicitly all the times. Many of our experiences are nonverbal and much of our understanding is not in the form of explicit beliefs. The issue here is the nature of our perception when we are not thinking about it and forming propositions. Do you inattentively perceive a meaningful world, meaningful to yourself and not merely to mind designers?

Models of the closed mind adopt a resultant view in which perception is sensation plus belief. In sensation, one sees meaningless patches of color and other sense impressions. Then one may add explicit beliefs to them in the form of propositions. Or a perceiver registers some causal features, to which ecologists add meanings. Do we have meaningless sensations or registrations on which optional meanings can be somehow coated?

Some people have visual experiences drained of meaning because they suffer from associative agnosia. Comparison of their vision with the inattentive vision of healthy people brings out the meaningfulness of normal experiences. Suppose you argued so heatedly with your colleagues during lunch that later you could not recall what you had eaten.

Nevertheless, during the meal you saw and used your utensils properly. Your ability to recognize the knife and fork by sight expressed their intelligibility to you even when your mind was elsewhere. This ability is impaired in patients with associative agnosia. They can see things because they can copy and draw them. They have concepts because they can recognize and name various objects by touch. However, their vision and concepts are dissociated from each other. They cannot pick out eating utensils by sight; they cannot look at a fork, a knife, and a hammer and decide which two are used together. A case of associative agnosia with a very specific range of affliction is prosopagnosia, in which a person is incapable of recognizing faces, even his own, his wife's, and his children's. He sees faces, but the faces are meaningless. Again this contrasts with normal inattentive vision, with which we recognize our loved ones from the corners our eyes, so to speak. Because the visual experiences in associative agnosia are stripped of all meaning, they cannot be integrated into other living activities. When people with prosopagnosia meet friends and relatives in the street, they treat them as strangers (Farah 1990; Stocrig 1996).

People with associative agnosia can add meaning acquired by other methods to vision. By touching a fork, they learn what they see. After hearing a familiar voice, they add a name to a meaningless face. However, this vision plus meaning is different from the meaningful vision that normal people have. The added meanings do not stick; the face becomes a stranger again the next time. Experiences under associative agnosia are close to Cartesian sensation or ecological registration.

Fortunately for most of us, we do not have such meaningless experiences and find them hard to imagine. As explained in chapter 5, our visual experiences are supported by a vast infrastructure, processes in which unfold automatically when triggered. Some of these processes underlie recognition and they intertwine intricately with other processes. Because it proceeds automatically, our visual experience is always meaningful. It is not a resultant property where meaning is simply added to the meaningless vision of associative agnosia. It is an emergent property in which we automatically see an intelligible world. Without brain surgery, it is as impossible to peel meaning from our vision as it is to take taste out of a well-cooked soup. Comparing ourselves with people with associative agnosia makes us cherish the intelligibility of our visual world.

If you cannot imagine the meaningless vision of these patients, perhaps you can get some hints from Jean-Paul Sartre's *Nausea*. The hero,

Roquentin, occasionally suffered from an existential illness akin to associative agnosia in which everything became meaningless. Sartre's extensive description of Roquentin's encounter with the root of a chestnut root, which to him was a mere thing on which concepts such as "root" refused to stick, makes us appreciate the meaning of absurdity. As Heidegger (1926:163) observed: "It requires a very artificial and complicated frame of mind to 'hear' a 'pure noise.'" "What we 'first' hear is never noise or complex of sound, but the creaking wagon, the motor-cycle. We hear the column on the march, the north wind, the woodpecker tapping, the fire cracking. . . . Even in cases where the speech is indistinct or in a foreign language, what we proximally hear is *unintelligible* words, and not a multiplicity of tone-data." When we are exasperated with that damned noise, we hear the nuisance that disturbs our works. When we peer hard into the gloom, we see the unknown that incites fear. Even when their meanings are not clearly articulated, things we immediately perceive are always significant in the context of our purposive actions.

The point stressed by Heidegger is important, because the meanings in our immediate experiences are so mundane and familiar they are often taken for granted and neglected by scholars who have eyes only for "higher" meanings explicitly stated in propositions. For the science of mind, such neglect is disastrous, as familiar meanings reveal the most basic structures of our mind and structures of the world intelligible to it. The fact that our most primitive experiences are meaningful shows that our mind is intrinsically purposive and hence more complicated than registration plus extrinsic meanings. Scientists can interpret people's experiences in their specific theoretical frames, but they do not assign meanings as mind designers.

The Utilitarian Frame and the Everyday World

Models of the closed mind controlled by mind designers mostly regard a mindful entity not as a doer but as a thinker floating in a vacuum. They grade intelligence by formal tests, analyze mental ability in terms of propositions, and enthrone chess machines as the paradigm of mental entities. After differentiating knowing-how from knowing-that, they promptly put aside know-how as inferior if not irrelevant.

For an open mind, the most important world is not the one of pure knowledge but the one of living and purposive actions. Without this life world science would be impossible, for scientific research is a purposive activity inalienable from the life world. Consider how we treat things in the world. For those concerned only with knowing-that, the most important step is categorization, in which we classify things into kinds by applying taxonomic concepts such as apple or orange. Asked to sort out a heap of objects, adults look for items belonging to the same kind or having the same salient property. Children older than six or seven sort like adults. Very young children, however, have their own schemes. They can sort taxonomically, but they prefer to group things that occur in a meaningful event, for instance putting a boy, a coat, and a dog together because the boy wears the coat when walking the dog. In short, they prefer to group things according to pragmatic or thematic relations. This does not imply that children grasp relational concepts before they do taxonomic concepts. Relational concepts are usually more complicated. Experiments that probe the mastery of abstract relations show that children below five fail to match relations although they can match kinds. Yet they do not group arbitrarily; their grouping is meaningful in daily activities. Their thematic organization is revealing. It shows that the first arrangement and order we discern in the world are the order of pragmatic relations (Markman 1989).

Some people dismiss the child mentality as irrelevant to discussions of the adult mind. Heidegger suggested an opposite view: Even for adults, the primary world to which we are open is the life world: home, office, farm, workshop, laboratory. Here we deal not with things neatly categorized and labeled but with tools connected by various relations of in-order-to. In our daily goal-directed activities, things that we are most involved with are those that come in handy, such as the doorknob by which I open the door or the relaxing clouds that reduce my tension when I look up. We recognize them by their serviceability, reliability, conduciveness, usability, and manipulability, and simultaneously recognize ourselves as purposive beings. Heidegger (1924:68) wrote: "The Greeks had an appropriate term for 'Thing': *pragmata*—that is to say, that which one has to do with in one's concernful dealings." This pragmatic world is what we understand primarily and foremost, because we are directly involved in it in our purposive life. However, its handy entities are not obtrusive; they require no explicit categorization when they function most smoothly. Your shoes work best when you are oblivious of them as you walk. In using tools in purposive actions, our attention skips the tools and leaps ahead to yet unrealized goals. The concept "pen" hardly arises explicitly in my mind when I sign the credit-card receipt, as I am thinking about the great gift my purchase makes. Handy tools serve us to realize possibilities that our goals open up. Hence they are intelligible and genuinely significant, suffused with what we care for.

The Kalahari Desert is barren to city dwellers. For !Kung San hunters, however, it is a world replete with clues about animals. Patterns of crushed grass, colors of droppings, bent twigs, and drops of blood all come in handy for tracking a wounded animal. This is the intelligible world of hunters, whose mental abilities are manifested in how they cope with it. They cope superbly. Thus it is wrong to say that they are stupid because they perform poorly in formal IQ tests administered by Westerners. The problem lies not in the hunters but in the assumption that formal tests adequately measure mental abilities. Torn out of the context of everyday life, these tests miss precisely the most important mental characteristics of dealing with the real world (Ceci 1996).

Humans always act in context. Taking formal tests has its context, which is most meaningful to students applying for college. Problems arise when some philosophies focus on contexts that are too narrow and far removed from everyday life, and then universalize the results. Some cognitive scientists criticized laboratory studies for their sterilized contexts and turned to investigate living experiences, thus underscoring the importance of living contexts in cognition. In rehabilitation after hand injuries, for instance, patients recover more readily when they use their hands in meaningful activities than when they perform similar movements in exercise routines. Psychologists studied learning in daily activities and compared apprenticeship with schooling. Grocery shopping, for instance, is a fairly complex decision-making process in which shoppers balance price, taste, quality, nutritional value, and other factors. Most people have much higher arithmetical proficiency in shopping than in formal tests. The difference is most pronounced in less educated shoppers; although their test scores are inferior to those of highly educated persons, their arithmetic proficiency in grocery shopping is not. Uneducated young street vendors in Brazil, who can swiftly figure out the prices for various quantities and unerringly make changes to the customers, perform miserably in the formal test for similar arithmetic. Conversely, educated youngsters who excel in formal tests do not always perform well in role-playing games simulating street vending (Rogoff and Lave 1984; Sternburg and Wagon 1999; Gallagher and Marcel 1999).

Mind is an essential human characteristic, and to adopt one or another notion of mind has tremendous practical consequences, especially in education. Many psychologists propose that abstract logic or computation suffices for the education of a closed mind, but not for the open mind that also requires proper training in action and communication. Based on empirical research results, they criticize the current educational system for devaluating life experiences in favor of "high-brow" abstract contemplation, a stance resonating with the notion of the closed mind. Even mathematics, which is most conducive to abstract reasoning, is learned more easily when aided by practically meaningful situations (Kirshner and Whitson 1997).

In sum, we are primordially involved doers, not detached thinkers. The primary frame of mind of our daily life is utilitarian, not theoretical. Meanings arise first and primarily not in abstract propositions but in concrete living, where we find our ways in the world, deal with things circumspectively, and go about our business. Our skill and ability to handle, value, and care for things in our daily activities constitute what Heidegger called fore-conception. Vague and inarticulate, it is our basic understanding of the world. We can make some of it explicit by conceptualization and assertion, but not all; it forms the tacit background of our understanding.

The Theoretical Frame and the Commonsense World

Practical contexts are important. Equally important are contents of theories. Education suffers when, under the sway of social constructionism, contexts squeeze out contents. Excessive socialization and enculturation is distractive in learning many topics, especially scientific topics that require systematic reasoning (Cromer 1997). A certain degree of abstraction is indispensable in certain aspects of the world: things are not always handy and tools break. In such circumstances we switch from the utilitarian to the theoretical frame of mind.

The everyday world is rich in significance because it ties closely with the particularities of a person's life. Its details, however, also make it inflexible, for entities involved in an action are tied down by immediate purposes. Therefore the utilitarian intelligibility is not versatile. Abstraction and explicit conceptualization break apart the utilitarian world by neglecting some pragmatic relations among entities. They dim down the immediate practical significance of the everyday world to get a clearer view of some items. Because these items are freed from their specific utilitarian contexts, their characteristics can be generalized. Thus they gain new significance in theoretical contexts; we can apply the knowledge gained from them to things beyond the orbits of our ordinary routines. Thus abstraction and conceptualization trade particularity for flexibility, richness for scope, familiarity for explicitness. With them we transform from the frame of concernful dealing to the frame of common sense, in which the world consists of entities that are categorized and systematically related. The transformation wrought by conceptualization is a kind of interpretation, because the everyday world is already meaningful.

Theoretical abilities are developed in formal education and further refined in scientific research. However, they are as common to human beings as practical abilities and are simply known as common sense. The theoretical frame abstracts from many pragmatic relations and generalizes results to other areas. Its development may disrupt the pragmatic network that functions in our utilitarian frame. Thus children often exhibit U-shaped learning curves, where performance dips with nascent theories. The most noticeable example is overgeneralization in the acquisition of past tense verbs in English. At first children acquire verbs by rote, use regular and irregular forms of tense correctly as they learn them, and do not automatically add -ed to new verbs. Around age thirty months they begin to add -ed to all verbs, including familiar irregular verbs, to form past tense. Thus they say hitted or breaked, when they earlier said hit or broke. This stage of overgeneralization lasts for a year or so. Gradually, exposure to irregular forms wins over excessive regularization, and children graduate to adult speakers who follow rules with exceptions.

The U-shaped curve appears in many other areas with more theoretical connotation. Consider the task of taking a rectangular slab loaded with lead at one end and balancing it on top of a pivot. Four-year-olds perform the task easily. They simply grab the slab, move it along the pivot, get the tactile feeling of its pressure, and adjust its position until it sits balanced on the pivot at a point way off its geometric center. Six- or seven-year-olds, however, have a much harder time. They pick up the slab and put it on the pivot at its geometric center. When the slab falls off, they try again but take more care to locate geometric center. After several failures, many give up in frustration and declare that the slab cannot be balanced. These children are going through a period in which they transform from trial-and-error pragmatists to little theoreticians regarding physical objects. Their theory that blocks are balanced at their geometric centers is naive, and in a couple of years they will learn to account for more factors and succeed in balancing all kinds of blocks. Despite the temporary regression in their performance, that first step toward explicit conceptualization and generalization of experiences with physical objects is a momentous development. Conceptualization enables them to look beyond what are involved in each particular case, discover patterns, learn from mistakes, think hypothetically, make inferences, and prepare for new situations. All these are beyond the ability of four-year-olds, whose experience is tied to each particular case and who cannot think about balancing blocks without putting their hands on them (Karmiloff-Smith 1992).

Categorization of the World
The world of common sense and science is categorized and contains entities of many kinds. Categorization is an important theoretical ability by which we systematically and consistently apply concepts to carve the world into entities of classes. Thus we explicitly recognize things as having properties and belonging to different kinds, as we recognize some entities to be plants and others animals; parts of a plant to be green and others red; some parts to be leaves and others flowers. Science excels in categorization. Systematic classification of biological species laid the groundwork for the development of evolutionary theory. Chemistry teased out various kinds of atoms and classified their variations in the periodic table, whose explanation called for theories in atomic physics. For a while high-energy physics was wading its way through a jungle of hundreds of "elementary" particles; only after physicists sorted them out did they develop unifying theories known as the standard model. Scientific taxonomy involves many theoretical considerations, although their scope is often dwarfed by the high-level theories that develop out of them.

Categorization culminates in science, but it starts in childhood. Developmental psychologists find that children as young as two or three years are capable of categorization. They prefer pragmatic groupings; when given a bluejay and asked to pick a companion from an assortment, they would pick a nest. However, if the sample entity is accompanied by a name, they switch to categorical grouping; when asked to find a companion for "the bluejay," they would pick a duck. Language influences mentality in very general ways, as discussed in the next section. Here we see how it goads children to conceptualize in sorting things (Markman 1989).

Categorization is a conceptual activity that goes beyond mere differentiation and sorting. A ten-dollar gadget can sort coins into quarters, dimes, and nickels, but it does not categorize. Many dynamical systems have multiple attractors that can serve to separate processes starting from various initial states. Some such systems probably operate in the infra-structure for categorization, but categorization itself requires more (see section 11). With differential sensitivity alone, one can notice a difference but cannot pinpoint what it is. Using concepts in categorization, one can make the difference explicit and draw its consequences. Categorization not only sorts things into kinds but enables us to think about the things in hypothetical situations and predict their behaviors.

Differential sensitivity is confined to one or another type of prop-erty. To categorize conceptually, one must be able not only to sort among many aspects but also select one aspect and persistently abstract it from others. Real life is much more complicated than stimulus-controlling lab-oratories, where the choice parameters are narrowly predefined by exper-imenters. In the chaotic world, subjects must discover for themselves the appropriate way to sort and stick to it through distraction. The difficulty of this is apparent in the trivial task of sorting cards. When given a pack of cards and asked to sort it out, young children can make a mess by what psychologists call "key-ringing." They pick a focal card as the ring and attach to it various keys that are similar in various aspects. For instance, they pick the ace of spades as the ring, then the seven of spades because it is a spade, the ace of hearts because it is an ace, the two of clubs because it is black, and so on (Markman 1989). They have analytic and discrimi-native abilities. What they lack is the global vision that discovers salient differences that systematically run through all the cards. They can differ-entiate a spade from a club, but they have not grasped the concepts until they learn to sort by suits. Conversely, the possession of concepts disci-plines the mind to abstract actively from irrelevancies.

Differential sensitivity is holistic; if an entity is particularly sensitive to dogs, it reacts to a dog as a unit. Applying concepts, categorization is at once more analytic and more synthetic. Recognition of a dog implies the ability to analyze it into various aspects and consider its various prop-erties, which we have separately categorized. Hence we can explicitly focus on a particular characteristic and its consequences, say a dog's hunger and its effect on the dog's behaviors. On the other hand, we do not treat the dog as nothing but the sum of its properties because the properties are interrelated; a hungry dog would fight more ferociously for food than a well-fed one. The concept of dog has a rich internal structure that inte-grates correlated properties and the causal relation a dog may have with its environment. When a person knows that the concept of dog applies to a particular entity, he at once knows a lot about the entity; that it has to eat, is mortal, and so on.

The concept of dog involves the concepts of many properties that are applicable to other things besides dogs. We can conceive that the dog is hungry only if we are also able to apply the concept of hunger to other animals. Concepts are general and have wide relations. Thus they do not stand in isolation but are embedded in a conceptual scheme that covers a significant domain of the world. Conceptual schemes facilitate inference, in which we trace the relations among concepts in a principled way. With inference, we relate categorized objects by connecting the concepts applicable to them. The process emphasizes the relations among concepts. However, its ultimate result is the ability to make reasoned judgments about objective states of affairs, as it enables us to view a state of affairs from various intellectual perspectives.

Categorization is a hot topic in cognitive science. A debate is raging about whether we classify according to defining characteristics or according to the similarities to prototypes. However, as Fodor (1998b) observed, chances are both are deficient, for both concentrate on sorting to the neglect of generalization, analysis, elaboration, and inference. Consequently many models are closer to differential sensitivity than categorization. A case in point is the statistical model that forms a class by gathering items that resemble a given prototype more than they resemble other prototypes. A prototype embodies the summary of a cluster of characteristics that are typical to members in the class. Typical characteristics are neither necessary nor sufficient for membership. They are exemplified in the prototype but are not explicitly spelled out. The dog-recognition connectionist network discussed in section 19 is an example of the statistical model. It encounters a set of dog exemplars, extracts their statistical central tendency as a dog prototype, and responds preferentially to novel input that resemble the prototype. Differential sensitivity, however, is all it has. It lacks the power of analysis and elaboration that teases apart the internal structure of the prototype and relates the prototype to external factors (Sloman and Rips 1998; Foder 1998c).

Fodor is not alone in holding that neither definition nor prototype is sufficient to account for the complicated ways in which people categorize. Knowledge-based models propose that categorization is not an isolated activity but is embedded in people's general knowledge about the world. People rely heavily on their general knowledge even as they recognize members of a single class. They reckon with not only relations among properties attributed to members in the class but also relations between members and the rest of the world. Arguments for knowledge-based models of categorization resonate with theories for the background understanding in our everyday routine. We have some tacit foreconception of the whole world when we explicitly conceptualize about a specific kind of thing in it (Media 1989).

The Utilitarian World and the Categorized World

Categorization is the cornerstone of conceptualization and theorization. The preceding discussion shows that these intellectual activities are not free floating but are firmly grounded in both the objective structures of the world and some general structures of our mind. It is neglect of these concrete groundings that makes categorization a playpen of relativism and social constructionism.

Constructionists are right that logically, everything noncontradictory is allowed; they are wrong to conclude from this that categorization is an arbitrary cultural game. Logically, there are limitless ways to categorize the world. One can group all things that are striped and four legged and partly white into a class whose members include zebras and patio chairs. One can form more bizarre classes by the disjunction of properties, for example, a class that includes things that are red or metallic or weigh more than three kilograms. The favorite example of philosophers is the class "grue," whose members are green before the year 2005 and blue thereafter. By sliding the transition date from blue to green, one can readily obtain an infinite number of "gruesome" classes. Arguments for unrestrained arbitrariness in categorization depend on two tacit assumptions: Categorization proceeds in a vacuum devoid of realistic concerns, and it is a bottom-up constructive process. Both assumptions mesh with a closed computational mind manipulating concepts as mental representations. Both, I contend, are untenable.

Despite their proliferation in academic discussions, bizarre systems of classification are seldom found in actual practice. Categorization is not a logical game but a serious business in understanding and coping with the world. An open mind is a situated property. Thus its main concerns are thrown possibilities and not empty logical possibilities. The range of thrown possibilities is much smaller than the range of logical possibilities, but thrown possibilities have more complicated salient structures that take account of the world's constraints. No culture categorizes by conjunction or disjunction of logical possibilities; if there were such cultures they would not survive to tell their stories.

People in different cultures categorize differently. Compared with the infinite range of logical possibilities, however, the variation in actual classes is minuscule. Actual categorization is disciplined by one big factor that ontological relativism and social constructionism dismiss, structures of the physical world. Nature does have joints that people manage to sever in their categorization. Some joints are so conspicuous they are recognized in many cultures. When natives of New Guinea and Western biologists independently categorize birds on the island, they agree on thirty-eight of thirty-nine species. Classes that enjoy wide agreement we call natural kinds. Discrepancies still exist, but they are minor and we assume they can be ironed out. It would be surprising if New Guineans and biologists cannot come to agreement about the remaining bird species when they put their heads together. Other joints in nature are not so conspicuous, and considerable variations in categorization exist. Biologists admit that taxonomy above the species level is nominal; genus, class, family, and phylum are all nominal kinds. Thus it would not be surprising to find cultures that put whales in a group with fish. Even so, nominal kinds found in actual cultures form a tiny subset of those conjured by philosophers. Nominal kinds that function in practical thinking still more or less conform to some joints in nature. Cultures have many ways of carving up nature, but none uses powerful logical techniques to grind nature to a pulp. They all have pragmatic concerns.

Models of the closed mind usually assume that environmental contributions to categorization stop with differential sensitivities of our sense organs. These include only apparent properties. All other structures, including various kinds of things, are constructions obtained by combining the apparent properties. Babies are differentially sensitive to colors, shapes, and some materials. Then they put the properties together in different ways, and by trial and error obtain the right combinations for categorization. Blue, triangular, has wings—forget it. Red, round, soft—tomato. Experiences start with atomic sparks like tiny Christmas light bulbs. As the lights become more numerous, they combine in different ways to form large bright mosaics. Atomic sparks can confine in limitless ways, which is why we have all the bizarre kinds that keep academic philosophers busy.

Arbitrariness would be greatly reduced if the categorized world arose not by free association of small parts but by constrained analysis of a whole that is our life world. Before explicit categorization, everyday life is a meaningful place where things are connected in a pragmatic network. A boy puts on a coat to go out and ride the bike. A man uses a pen to sign a check to pay for the grocery for the dinner of his family. Things stand as lumps in a significant network and cruxes of practical relations. In theoretical analysis, we need attend only to them and make them stand out explicitly. Thus we ignore most meaningless classes that are produced by the combinatorial explosion of conjoining properties.

One way to look at the relationship between the categorized and utilitarian worlds is to look at the relationship between general and substantive concepts. General concepts are like the crude sketch on a canvas; substantive concepts are like the colors that turn the sketch into a painting. To categorize, we develop substantive concepts for various kinds of things. Before that, however, we have mastered many general concepts in our daily handling of tools, for instance concepts of objects and their reliability. General concepts constrains the variety of substantive concepts, just as the sketch constrains the application of colors in painting. On the other hand, general concepts become more clearly articulated in the process of categorization, just as a portrait becomes more vivid as the painter adds colors to the sketch on the canvas. The pragmatic idea of reliability, for instance, becomes causal regularity in the world viewed theoretically.

The utilitarian world precedes the categorized world. Idle thinking can generate arbitrary classes, but real life has its general conditions and requirements. They shape the structures of fore-conception, which in turn bias categorization and preempt bizarre classes. This view agrees with not only data of developmental psychology but also the central tenet of evolutionary biology. Mind is not designed according to the logical principles of retroactive creationism, it evolved as animals coped with their environments in the struggle to survive. Babies grow up in a meaningful environment where they are put to bed, wrapped in blankets, and fed with nipples or bottles or spoons. These matters mean life or death. It is reasonable to assume that they play important roles in helping children to categorize. Many of our categories are expressed in words. Results of experiments designed to probe how children understand the meanings of new words revealed salient regularities. Children tend to apply a new word to a whole object instead to its parts, properties, or material; to objects of the same kind instead of to objects related thematically; to nameless objects instead of objects already named. Markman called these regularities the whole object, the taxonomic, and the exclusion constraints or biases in word learning. They demonstrate that children have some mastery of the general concepts of an object and of a kind of object, and that these general mental abilities enable them to learn words efficiently (Markman 1989; Woodward and Markman 1998).

The human mind can abstract and generalize in a continuum of degrees. On one end we perform our daily routines in a mostly utilitarian frame; on the other, we study science in a mostly theoretical frame. Neither theory nor practice monopolizes even these extreme cases, and their mixture is more pronounced for the commonsense frame that lies in between. The utilitarian and theoretical worlds are not incommensurate; they are the same world viewed from two mental frames. Far from being mutually exclusive, they often intermingle to form intermediate frames. Astronomers who teach earth's rotation are not suffering from a split-personality syndrome when they tell their camping pals to hurry up because the sun sets soon. People switch from one mental frame to another all the time. The switch may be approximate and violate the logical rigor demanded by some philosophers, but the assumption that it is possible prevents most people with common sense from falling into relativism and constructionism.

How Is Inquiry Possible?

In *Histories* (II, 109), Herodotus wrote that geometry rose out of practical utility. The yearly inundation of Egypt demanded that the sizes of properties be frequently resurveyed for tax purposes. The practice of land measurement led to geometry. Aristotle conjectured in *Metaphysics* (981b) that geometry originated in Egypt because the priestly class was afforded the leisure for such pursuit. Probably both conditions contributed essentially to the emergence of geometry, our first science. The pragmatic root of science answers the so-called paradox of inquiry. How is it possible that we ever engage in scientific research that brings knowledge about the universe remote from our life experiences?

In Plato's *Meno* (80), Socrates criticized the definitions of virtue that Meno proposed. Frustrated, Meno counterattacked by questioning the very possibility of inquiring. One either knows something or he does not. If he knows it already, there is no need or sense to inquire. If he does not, he cannot inquire at all. "How will you look for something when you don't in the least know what it is? How on earth are you going to set up something you don't know as the object of your search? To put it another way, even if you come right up against it, how will you know that what you have found is the thing you didn't know?" Inquiry is not chance learning, in which we pick up whatever we happen to encounter. It is a purposive action aimed at some target, but how do we target something we do not know? Socrates granted that inquiry is impossible in total ignorance of the target, but he denied that one cannot inquire about what he already knows. We need not buy Socrates's theory that we know the target from recollection. But we can follow him in asserting there are various senses of knowledge, and in a sense we know what we are inquiring about in our fore-conception, which we acquire by living practically in the world. Knowledge in fore-conception, however, is vague and loose, sufficient to suggest some targets of inquiry but insufficient for much information about the targets. Such detailed information will be the result of the inquiry, which makes our knowledge explicit and solid.

The Platonic dialogues portray Socrates asking what is justice, what is knowledge, what is love; trying to formulate and define the concepts of justice, knowledge, and love. The inquiries did not start from a mental vacuum; if they did, Socrates and his interlocutors would not be able to frame the questions in the first place. They arose in a meaningful lifeworld in which justice, knowledge, and love played important roles and were vaguely understood by Athenian citizens. The knowledge was tacit, and the aim of the inquiries was to make it precise and explicit. Such inquiries are interpretive, as they start from a meaningful ground. An inquirer tries to frame a theory of justice guided by his participation in civil society. An articulated concept of justice influences civil actions, which in turn leads to modifications of the concept of justice. More generally, an inquirer tries to conceptualize a part of his fore-conception, motivated and guided by the fore-conception as a whole. When he brings to relief the structures of the part in conceptualization, he also modifies the whole fore-conception in which the part sits, which in turn helps him to refine his concept of the part. This going back and forth between part and whole, between conception and fore-conception, between explicit and tacit knowledge is the hermeneutic circle of understanding.

A similar process goes on in scientific research. Scientists inquire systematically on a large scale but do not alter the basic nature of inquiry.

Philosophers of science regard scientists as problem solvers or computers doing calculation, but scientists are much more. Professors know how important and how difficult it is to frame good problems for students, as problems are crucial guides for thinking and learning. However, scientists have no gods or mind designers to hand them problem sets. They must find the areas and frame fruitful problems for themselves. Pseudoproblems or sterile problems are invitations to waste energy. At the frontier of research and facing the unknown, scientists share Meno's predicament of deciding the direction of research. They have to penetrate the tangle of real-world phenomena, tease out important facts, discern enigmas, and introduce concepts to formulate them clearly as problems. These activities depend crucially on fore-conception and intuitive understanding of their areas.

Reductionist philosophers fancy they can stipulate a single problem for all science, compute all the consequence of the laws of elementary particle physics. However, their fancy leads them to waste time in futile debates. Scientists are not trapped into the futility because their pragmatic common sense prevents them from falling into the black-or-white philosophy of either one knows everything or nothing. As discussed in section 12, scientists are circumspect of their research areas, make approximations to bite off the parts they can chew, frame and solve small problems, note their significances in the large picture, and proceed step by step to tackle complex phenomena. The successive approximations so common in science are manifestations of the hermeneutic circle of human understanding at work.

28 Language, Narrative, and Freedom of Action

Mind's openness is not passive. It not only opens to but also opens up the world, constituting part of it by creating values and social bonds. This world-making capacity is most apparent in its linguistic frame. We have glimpsed how language facilitates categorization, where the introduction of a name prompts children to switch from thematic to taxonomic grouping of objects. Language is even more important in constituting the human and social world. It enables us to think explicitly of the past and future, narrate our autobiographies, communicate with each other, appropriate our historical traditions, lay out substantive possibilities, judge right and wrong, and make genuine choices. Without our linguistic capacity, we cannot attain the full sense of autonomous agents that we are.

What is unique about man? Aristotle asked in *Ethics* (1098a). Not life or perception, as these are shared by plants and animals: "There remains, then, an active life of the soul's element that has *logos*." Latin translation interpreted *logos* as *ratio* or reason, thus rendering the Aristotelian dictum "Man is an animal possessing *logos*" as the now familiar "Man is a rational animal." It has lost much of the original meaning. Derived from the root *legein*, meaning "to say," *logos* most generally meant anything said or written. Besides the faculty of reason, *logos* also meant cause, argument; things said or written; weighing up pros and cons. To have a *logos* meant to have something to say about, to have a description, and more specifically to have an explanation or a reasoned account (Guthrie 1962). You do not know something, Plato said in *Theaetetus* (201), unless you can give an account for it; otherwise you possess only opinion, not knowledge. Knowledge is opinion with the addition of a *logos*. Thus *logos* had a linguistic connotation that was as strong as its rationalistic connotation. Man is a linguistic and rational animal, and much of his rationality depends on his linguistic ability.

In *Ethics* (1139–41), Aristotle analyzed the soul with *logos* into five states of mind: systematic knowledge (*epistēmē*), art or skill (*technē*), prudence or practical wisdom (*phronēsis*), intelligence or intuition (*nous*), and wisdom (*sophia*). The animal with *logos* was not the disembodied thinker closed within the inner mental sanctuary. He was a doer with many talents in an active life, and his speech functioned in all practical matters. All these changed with the exaltation of pure thinking and computation. Now languages have become formal systems whose symbols are drained of meaning. Language philosophy deems natural languages inadequate without formalization. In Chomsky's words, this academic climate produces E-languages ripped from human conditions and social contexts, mere systems with no practical role, except to give philosophers jobs for trying to hook its words to objects. We will leave them alone and concentrate on natural languages. What roles do they play in our everyday mental life? How do they accomplish these roles?

The Cartesian Trojan Horse in Language

Undoubtedly language is essential for communication, but are its roles exhausted by communication? An influential view answers yes. We do not need natural languages to think because our thoughts exist independent of them in the form of mental representations inside the head. All that languages do is translate ready-made thoughts into acoustic or spatial patterns that are publicly accessible and communicable. Spoken sounds are external symbols that represent mental representations. Written patterns in turn code the sounds. They transport the ideas inside a person's head to the heads of others, and hence are superfluous to loners. A person who knows no natural language can nevertheless have intelligible experiences and thoughts similar to normal adult humans, if only he is content to live alone and speak to no one. In this conception, natural languages are merely communicative and play no role in thinking and concept formation.

This merely communicative view of language has a long history but receives strong impetus from computationalism, resonating with the inner-outer dichotomy and the closed mind controlled by mind designers. Implicit in it is a division between two realms, the realm of mental representations inside the head and the realm of communicable patterns outside. Fodor (1975; 1983) held that mental representations private to each of us constitute a special language of thought, mentalese, which is a formal system that is distinct from any natural language that we speak. We think, or more fashionably, compute, in mentalese just as digital computers process meaningless symbols. Natural languages serve as the input and output modules for thinking, akin to computer monitors and printers. They are optional for thinking.

The Cartesian Trojan war rages as fiercely in language as in other areas concerning mind. While the Greeks fight for internal mentalese, the Trojans reject anything internal and mental, be they thoughts or propositions. To behaviorists, utterances and linguistic behaviors, which are verifiable by external observers, are the only acceptable forms of thinking. Because natural languages vary widely, identifying uttering with thinking leads to a radical relativism wherein people speaking different languages think so differently they effectively inhabit different worlds and hence cannot possibly understand each other. Linguistic relativism was advanced in the early twentieth century by amateur linguist Benjamin Lee Whorf. It became the darling of social constructionists, who regard languages as social institutions and relish the social design of mind itself. Whorf claimed that Eskimos saw the world differently because they had a huge vocabulary for snow. Professional linguists called this the "great Eskimo vocabulary hoax" after carefully examining the evidence. Eskimos do not have many more words for snow than English with its sleet, slush, flurry, and blizzard. Despite scientific evidence, the academic and popular press continues to talk about how the dozens if not hundreds of Eskimo snow words shape their peculiar view of the world. Such disregard for reality, not the Eskimo vocabulary, bolsters relativism (Pullum 1991).

I have argued against the Cartesian Trojan horse in many other contexts and simply register my opposition here. In my general model of the open mind supported by infrastructures, mental processes emerge from the self-organization of infrastructural processes that can be represented by computer models. On their own level, mental processes are perceptual, linguistic, emotional, and inferential, all of which are open to the world but none of which is merely an input-output module. By "languages" without qualification I always mean the natural languages that we speak every day. They are not mentalese or other symbol systems of the computational mind, whose existence I deny. Languages constitute much thinking. Therefore they do influence how we think. However, their influence is far weaker than the claims of linguistic relativism. People of all tongues share a linguistic infrastructure and many general concepts, which enable them to understand each other, if they are not discouraged from trying by relativism.

Language, Thought, and Belief

The inner-outer dichotomy and the merely communicative conception of language have many critics. Philosophers such as Taylor (1985) maintain that language is not merely clothing for thoughts, a tool by which we broadcast our mind. It is the medium of much of our thinking and hence is constitutive of our mental life. The ability to think linguistically is essential to the human experience of finding the world intelligible and meaningful. Without language, we would not be the human beings that we are. In Heidegger's words, "language is the house of being."

Existential phenomenologists emphasize the practice of speech and discourse in our daily activities. Proceeding from formal instead of pragmatic considerations, many analytic philosophers also arrive at the conclusion that language is a medium of thinking (Carruthers 1996). The more extreme ones hold that it is the exclusive medium of thinking, and deny thoughts, at least conscious thoughts, to prelingual babies and animals without language. Donald Davidson (1982, 1984) proffered an influential theory along this line. Considering the case of a dog barking up the wrong tree, he argued that it is false to assert: "The dog thinks that the cat is up that oak tree." His central point is that one requires concepts to believe, and one cannot grasp a concept alone but must understand it in relation to other concepts in a conceptual scheme. Dogs cannot have a concept of trees, even less oak trees, because the concept entails the knowledge that trees grow, need soil and water, have leaves or needles, and so on. Consequently a dog cannot believe that the cat is up the tree. In sum, a creature cannot believe unless it has the concept of belief, and it cannot think unless it has language; hence animals without language can neither think nor believe.

I agree with Davidson's general point although not his extreme conclusion. A single concept brings no thinking; to be able to believe, one must master some conceptual scheme. Let us agree that no dog can grasp the conceptual schemes employed by farmers or botanists. Nevertheless, the jump from these arguments to the conclusion that dogs cannot believe involves at least two mistakes. It confuses mindlessness with dumbness, both as speechless and stupidity. Dogs lack ability by human standards because they cannot have the kinds of complicated conceptual schemes that our linguistic ability makes possible. Davidson rightly pointed out the fallacy of attributing our familiar concepts to nonlinguistic animals. However, it does not follow that nonlinguistic animals are incapable of some crude conceptual schemes that are trivial or vague to us. A dog does not need the specific concept of tree to entertain belief while barking up a tree. It can regard the tree as one of its territorial markers or a place around which there is shade on hot days. Suppose "the dog thinks that the meowing nuisance is up its favorite spraying station" is true, but "the dog thinks that the cat is up that tree" is false. Then the substitution of terms that refer to the same thing has changed the truth value of the proposition. This violation of the principle of extensionality is precisely the criterion of mentality that Davidson himself stipulated.

Davidson's theory of meaning is based on recursive enumeration of truth values and interpretations of detached observers, whom I have been calling mind designers. His arguments and examples reveal the almost exclusive concern with formal reasoning and detached observations that draws so much fire from existential phenomenologists. There is little reason to expect dogs, which are not even herbivores, to have the concept of tree as a plant. For animals struggling in the world instead of thinking in the armchair, their essential knowledge is of food, fight, flight, and fornication. The foundation of mentality lies not in abstract argument but in concrete living; in skills and know-how; in *technē* and *phronēsis*; in everyday conversation. These are ways in which mental beings open to their physical and social world. If dogs show some of these abilities, it is hardly justifiable to deny them the power of thinking, even if they can neither speak nor use symbols nor understand formal logic. Mental concepts are vague and no consensus exists about the criterion of thinking. I know of no opinion poll, but I suspect that most people who have close contact with animals or prelingual babies would agree with Hume (1739:177), who complained: "The common defect of those systems, which philosophers have employ'd to account for the actions of the mind, is, that they suppose such a subtility and refinement of thought, as not only exceeds the capacity of mere animals, but even of children and common people in our own species; who are notwithstanding susceptible of the same emotions and affections as persons of the most accomplish'd genius and understanding."

The Diversity of Thinking Modes

What is the relation between thinking and using language? One of two popular answers maintains that all thinking is linguistic, the other that words are optional dresses for preexisting thoughts and concepts. Both are too simplistic. We have many psychophysical modes and mental frames, all of which can function in thinking. Intensive research accompanying the debate on mental imagery has demonstrated that we visualize using our visual cortex (see section 16). We also rehearse our motor actions using our sensorimotor cortex. Such nonverbal processes can play important roles in thinking, for instance in reckoning spatial layout or mentally retracing one's steps. I can give verbal accounts on how to fold a paper airplane with some difficulty; it is much easier for me just to fold it in my mind. Similar nonverbal thinking occurs in planning to use skills. When it comes to more abstract topics, however, we often think linguistically. In wondering about the atomic number of carbon or trying to decide whether to visit a friend on Friday or Saturday, we have to think at least partially in words, as abstract concepts of atomic number and date are embodied in some words or others.

The stream of consciousness is difficult to monitor systematically, but scientists have tried. They made subjects wear devices that beeped randomly during the day. When the subjects heard the beep they froze and recorded what went on in their minds at the moment. All normal subjects reported some internal speech. On the average, linguistic thoughts occur about half the time. However, the frequencies vary widely, ranging from 7 percent to 80 percent (Hurlbert 1990). It seems that styles of mind are as diverse as styles of life. Some people think mostly in words; Plato compared thinking with arguments among parts of the soul, and Feynman confided he often thought by talking to himself. Other people think mostly in images, as Temple Grandin described in her autobiographic *Thinking in Pictures*. No kind of thinking alone suffices for the richness of the human mind. Despite his propensity for linguistic thinking, Feynman invented the Feynman diagrams with high depictive value. Despite her propensity for pictorial thinking, Grandin described her mental life in admirable prose. There is no monopoly on the medium of thought.

The diversity testifies to our multiple mental frames. We can think about the same topic in different ways, as recalling a scene depictively, verbally, or in a mixture of modes. Little evidence suggests that visualization must be embedded in sentences to make sense. Philosophers deem a word meaningful only within a sentence because their abstract theories neglect the living context. In real life, practical circumstances provide ample contexts for single words or images to be significant. Verbatim transcripts of conversations, such as tapes in the Nixon White House, show that people often speak in broken sentences that are readily understood in the conversational context but difficult to read when taken out of it. Novelists are more sagacious than philosophers when they use sentence fragments or the concatenation of single words to describe the stream of consciousness. Constrained by their medium of expression, novelists must describe ongoing thoughts linguistically. However, the many sentence fragments by which Joyce concatenated to form Bloom's silent monologues can well stand for fleeting imageries interspersed with brief comments. They make good sense.

Language as an Essential Medium of Thought

Language is one mode of thinking among several. Since the transformation among mental frames is a basic mental ability, we can transform from visualization or motor rehearsal to words. However, that does not imply that language is merely an input-output module. Transformations bring changes. Just as we see a different view from a different angle, transformations to the linguistic mode often make thinking more precise but less rich. Furthermore, much of our thinking, especially in higher cognition, proceeds directly in linguistic terms.

A major argument for language as an input-output module is that it is subserved by a specialized linguistic infrastructure. This tacitly assumes homuncular functionalism, where infrastructural processes combine resultantly. I explained in section 12 that this view of mind is unlikely to be valid. Once we reject it, we see that having a specialized linguistic infrastructure is compatible with language being an important medium for thinking. In view of complicated interconnections within the mental infrastructure, we have no reason to assume that a substructure can contribute to only one function, either a central processing unit or a monitor.

Suppose that observation leads us to decide that dogs can believe. Although man and his best friend are both believers, their beliefs differ drastically. With his linguistic and rational faculties, man can entertain a kind of belief that is way beyond his canine friend. Prelingual children think consciously and nontrivially about their environment, but they develop a new kind of thinking with their linguistic ability. What kind of thinking is it? How is it constituted by language? What peculiarities of language enable it to convey such thinking?

Like other mental processes, speaking and listening are dynamic and pragmatic. We know that prelingual children have considerable general mental abilities. They can differentiate among objects, notice causally impossible events, manipulate things, enjoy their sense of agency, interact with others, join attention, and correlate their companion's gaze and utterance. These abilities are crucial for language acquisition. Children ignore irrelevant utterances of adults, hence are not confused by their meanings. They surmise the nature and meaning of verbs by the agency and direction of action. Their grasp of word meanings helps them to acquire grammar. This phenomenon, which linguists call *semantic bootstrapping*, accords with universal grammar, whose projection principle asserts that a word's meaning constrains the syntax of the sentence in which it occurs (Karmiloff-Smith 1992; see section 14). One can doubt that human beings are united by an innate language organ or a similar syntactic infrastructure, but one cannot deny the common human characteristics of being in the world and being with others. These commonalities, which linguistic relativism ignores, are strengthened, not weakened, by the development of language.

Natural languages work primarily in conversations, which are intrinsically thoughtful and meaningful. People talk not in the stratosphere of abstract logic but in the concrete world, to which they constantly refer. The inalienability of discourse from the objective and intersubjective world is built into the structures of languages. A class of linguistic devices called *indexicals*—this, that, I, you, here, there, now, then—firmly plants speakers and hearers in the world. Indexicals are complicated because they refer to different things in different contexts. Pronouns confuse children who are learning to speak, as they often follow their interlocutors in saying "you" to refer to themselves and "I" to their interlocutors. When children finally master pronouns and know that "I" refers not only to themselves but to anyone who speaks, they gain an explicit understanding of the notion of themselves as One, an instance of someone, whereas they formerly had only a vague intuition in following gaze and joining attention. Thus language constitutes the third-person self discussed in section 26.

The objectivity of the prelingual mind is general and tacit, possessing a skeletal frame but little differentiated substance. Language makes it substantive and explicit by enabling us to conceptualize in details. Many of our substantive concepts are embodied in words. It is no surprise that children's ability to categorize develops in conjunction with their learning word meanings. Most children's first words are count nouns such as "apple" and "orange." In the first few months they apply words rather haphazardly, using some only in a very restricted context, extending others to cover wide ranges of associative features. This arbitrariness stops with the word spurt that begins at around eighteen months, during which children learn several words a day. This is facilitated by their precocious sensitivity to the relation between words and categories. When faced with an assortment of objects, they are more prone to look for categoric similarities in the presence of a word. They tend to apply new words to unnamed objects, as if the names of objects exclude each other. If they have only a named object, they would apply the new word to a part of it, or begin to learn the categories at a higher or lower taxonomic level. Thus children who already know "dog" learn the meaning of "animal" when it is applied to dogs (Markman 1989; Woodward and Markman 1998).

Developmental psychologists are not alone in observing the close relation between categorization and naming. Names have worried philosophers all around the world. Plato struggled with them, finding unsatisfactory the popular view that the relationship between names and what they name is either natural or conventional. Confucius observed that when names are not correct, reasoning is in jeopardy. To these men, names were not merely extravagant labels, they embodied concepts of classes. In many cases we categorize by naming or describing. Things and events tangle with each other and impinge on us in many ways. They lack definite contours as long as we cannot consistently pick them out. The fine discriminative power of language enables us to pinpoint an aspect of some phenomenon, delimit it from and contrast it to other features, identify and reidentify it in various circumstances, and elaborate it by multiply connecting it to other phenomena; in short, to crystallize it by categorizing it. Categorization, by which we carve nature at its joints, is difficult, because many nominal kinds are not obvious, as discussed in the preceding section. If, in Plato's metaphor, we respect nature's joints and take care not to hack it up like an unskilled butcher, our systems of names are far from arbitrary. The "correctness" of names means the adequateness of our schemes of categorization, and philosophers' critical reflection indicates their awareness of the danger of relativism. Their worries are justified, as language is often abused. An example is the devaluation stance that misleads by applying names arbitrarily, such as applying "believer" to thermostats and other mindless things.

Categorization is a good example of the role language plays in opening up the intelligible world. Language is even more important in personal and social matters, where descriptions become parts of the categorized phenomena because they modify people's thinking and behaviors. Thinking and articulating influence emotion through the cognitive circuit of the emotive infrastructure (see section 21). Our emotions change as we give voice to them. Mute animals can be angry, but only humans can be indignant, because indignation implies the acknowledgment of some injustice that only language can articulate. The power of rhetoric, poetry, and other literary means amply demonstrates how linguistic expressions can generate new emotions, more refined feelings, keener awareness, raised consciousness, and deeper understanding of oneself and one's world.

From categorization to emotion, from saying I to understanding thou, language functions as an indispensable medium of mental processes. We are so used to language we do not appreciate the high degree of refinement and elaboration with which it allows us to know the world. Such explicit and detailed thinking is possible only in linguistic form. Nonlingual thinking is important. However, for topics for which linguistic forms excel, prelingual ideas are crude and tacit. To say that they existed before linguistic articulation is like saying that the sculpture existed in the marble before the sculptor wrought it out. Perhaps prelinguistic ideas are like Michaelangelo's unfinished pieces where half-formed figures struggle to come out of the marble. Like finished sculptures, refined and explicit ideas *are* their linguistic articulation.

Language as Practical, Physical, Public, Symbolic, and Systematic

What are the characteristics of language that make it so potent a medium of thinking? Language is narrowly physical and readily susceptible to display outside the head. Mental processes are physical in the broad sense, but they are private to each individual and their underlying mechanisms proceed microscopically in the brain, inaccessible without the intrusive probe of scientists. Two consequences of privacy are isolation and transience. Mental states do not last, they quickly yield to other mental states. And if memory fails, which often happens, there is no way to check and recover. Language opens our mind to the world. Its sounds and written patterns are physical on the level of middle-sized things that people handle every day. Participants of a linguistic community produce and accept similar sound patterns, which serve as broad-based checks and reinforcements for the mental processes of individual members. Writing produces lasting records to which one can go back repeatedly. With language, our brain is aided by our mouth and ears, hands and eyes, which mobilize the vast resources of the physical and social environment for thinking. Try to do a long multiplication in your head and you will appreciate the tremendous contribution of your body to thinking. In promoting the disembodied mind, Cartesianism and computationalism chopped off not only our physical limbs but also a great portion of our mind.

Underlying language are the general abilities to use symbols and master the systematic connections among symbols. We talk and write about people and things. The sounds and written patternss that we produce are distinct from and bear no resemblance to our topic. Yet they are so regularly correlated we readily recognize what they are about in a variety of contexts. Thus most people regard languages as symbolic systems. Many words are genuine symbols that represent things or properties. More precisely, sentences are symbolic forms that represent states of affairs, as the marks "the moon is half full" represent a configuration of the solar system. Words do not represent in isolation but operate only within the linguistic system where they are connected according to certain rules. Systematic connections are important, because they enable us to go from one symbol to another, thus to organize, reason, infer, and predict. Among the most important rules is syntax, for which Chomsky maintains we have an innate ability. Once children have mastered grammar, they can use it to guess at and acquire word meanings, a phenomenon linguists call syntactic bootstrapping. By observing the position of a new word in a sentence, for example, they can surmise whether it is verb or noun.

I emphasized that words are genuine symbols that represent things to distinguish them from the symbols in computationalism and mental representations that do not represent anything. We ordinarily say "The word 'tree' represents a trunky plant" or "The mathematical symbol F represents force." In the same vein, scientists frame theoretical or computer models to represent mental and other phenomena. These common meanings of "representation" and "symbol" are relatively uncontroversial. However, when the words occur in the discourse of mind, they are often confused with mental representations and meaningless symbols manipulated by digital computers. The confusion engenders attacks on all symbolic systems. Therefore I must be more precise about the meaning of natural languages as symbolic systems.

First, words and other linguistic symbols are not mental representations or physical symbols that constitute the computational mind. Second, words and sentences primarily represent things and states of affairs in the world, not ideas or concepts or propositions or mental representations in the head. Third, not all linguistic symbols are representative. Many words, including articles, prepositions, conjunctions, and negative terms, do not represent anything. Fourth, representation is not mirroring or isomorphism. Fifth, we need not assume that what are represented existed before the linguistic representation; language can create the abstract entities that its words represent. Sixth, symbolic systems need not be uprooted from the world but can be integral parts of it.

Linguistic symbols are not mysterious entities inside a person's head but are external entities that the person and others can observe and manipulate and agree on. The mark "apple" that represents a fruit is on the paper, not in the head. When I silently think "The apple is red," I am in a mental state in the linguistic frame with the apple as the object. It is similar to my visualization of a red apple. In neither case do I have a symbol or mental representation inside my head, be it a word pattern or an apple image, which I somehow access by introspection. My brain assumes a definite activation pattern when I think "apple" or visualize an apple, but I am not aware of the pattern. The activation pattern is not a mental representation that I can see in any sense, although neuroscientists may call it a representation in their theoretical models for brain processes (see section 3). As far as my mental life is concerned, I *am* my thinking process and my mental state, just as the apple *is* red—full stop.

The representative relation between words and objects, sentences and states of affair are complicated. It is the rule rather than the exception that several words represent the same object and a word can represent several objects. We are seldom confused because it is a part of our linguistic ability to transform among the representations. Each representation is an intellectual perspective in the linguistic mental frame, and the transformation among them is schematically depicted in figure 8.2. In its application in physical theories, the transformation structure involves mathematical representations, which are generalizations of linguistic representations.

When several words represent the same thing, we can abstract from their physical patterns and talk about a concept, such as the concept of car. Thus concepts are theoretical abstractions, not entities in the head. Most substantive concepts do not exist before their linguistic articulation but are created in the linguistic medium itself. When I say that a word "represents" a concept, I mean that the concept is an abstraction from the specific physical pattern of the word. The abstraction is legitimate and fruitful. Language requires physical embodiment only generally, the specifics of the physical patterns are not mandatory. Abstraction from specifics simplifies, as we can talk about conceptual relations instead of more complicated linguistic relations.

The assertion that concepts are abstractions from words is different from the usual assertion that concepts are what words represent. That assertion assumes that concepts exist before and independent of their verbal representations. It is the crux of the theory that language is merely communicative because it functions as the input-output module for the computational mind, where concepts are mental representations with which the mind computes, and words are their representations. Since I reject mental representations and other entities in the head, I also reject the theory that linguistic symbols represent concepts in this sense.

Several schools regard a language as a semiotic system in which words, spoken or written, are signs that are meaningful in two ways: they are interconnected in a system, and the system they form represents a system of ideas. The view is most apparent in Ferdinand de Saussure's linguistic structuralism. To Saussure, a word is a sign that is a combination of two elements: a signifier, which can be a sound or a spatial pattern, and the signified. Of importance, the signified, which determines the "value" or meaning of the word, is not anything external to the language. It is the nexus of internal relations that connect it to all the other concepts signified in the language. Thus the sign "apple" consists a pattern of five letters and a meaning. Its meaning resides not in reference to the fruit that you munch but only in its relation to the ideas signified by all other words in your linguistic system. In short, a semiotic system is closed and detached from anything external. Saussure (1959:159) wrote that language is "a system in which all the terms are interdependent and in which the value of each results only from the simultaneous presence of the others." Semiotics does capture the systematic nature of language. However, in making languages into closed systems of signs, it uproots languages from the world, turns them into the kin of symbol systems manipulated by digital computers, and falls into the trap of the closed mind.

Natural languages are systematic, but their systems are open. The urge to formalize often drives linguists and philosophers to close the systems. Rooted in the world of discourse and constantly referring to nonlinguistic things, however, natural languages are too rich and fluid to be formalized. This is especially true when we consider meaning and use, semantics and pragmatics. Brute-force formalization destroys the essential characteristics of language as discourse and a medium of opening to the world. Many criticisms of languages as symbolic systems are directed at closure and forced formalization.

Unwarranted closure leads to the notion of two disjointed realms: those of language and of the objective world. Consequently, many language philosophers are stuck with the insoluble problem of hooking words to objects and language to world. An easy answer assumes an isomorphism between language and world; linguistic structure mirrors the structure of the world. It is similar to the cryptographic assumption in the computational theory of mind: if the syntax is right, semantics will take care of itself. This tacit assumption turns empty referential terms such as "the present king of France" into a big puzzle in language philosophy. It is unjustifiable. Human beings are not God who said, "Let there be light," and there was light. Linguistic symbol systems are not isomorphic to the actual world. In fact, much of which power derives from lack of isomorphism. In going beyond the actual world, they open up possibilities, thus constituting human understanding of the world.

Autobiography and Choice

I argued in section 24 that the essential characteristic of mental beings is the ability to free themselves from actual sounds and sights and entertain possibilities that are not immediately present. Our ability to distance ourselves depends heavily on languages with their representative symbols. As a symbol, the mark "apple" at once signifies the apple and the fact that it is *not* the apple. This implicit negation provides the necessary distance for us to break free from the pull of the actual environment. Now we can talk about the apple in its absence. This is tremendously important, because both the past and the future are by definition not present.

Life is a process, but at each moment we experience only the present stage of it. To know one's life as a process, to grasp it as a whole and find meaning for it, one needs the notion of time. Time, however, is abstract and not observable. We can neither see it nor form an image of it. Our representations of time, dates on various scales, are symbolic and linguistic. Without language, we can respond to changing lights and seasons as they occur, just as migratory birds fly north in response to lengthening days and south in response to falling temperatures. We can develop habits for recurrent changes. However, we cannot know changes as changes, because that requires the explicit representation of time. Language makes possible time, and with it autobiographical memory and history.

We saw in section 19 that declarative memory is constructive. We do not store a memory in our brain like a computer stores a file on its hard disk. We reconstruct the event every time we recall it, and our reconstructions can vary according to present circumstances. Language plays a crucial role in constructive memory, especially autobiographical memory that is an essential part of our personal identity. A dog can bury a bone and later dig it up. When it digs, it knows that a bone is there; it may even have some feeling of the bone being buried. Without language, however, it has no means to think "the bone *was* buried here." Its memory is not episodic or autobiographical but procedural; its past activity causes it instinctively to dig at the spot. Autobiographical memory invokes time explicitly, and hence is not merely visualization of a scene that happens to have occurred sometime in one's past life. Visualization is a present mental state. To acknowledge that the present state is a recollection requires not only language but a language that can handle tense, either by word inflection or by dating words. A mentality without tense or time is illustrated in William Faulkner's *The Sound and the Fury*. One of its protagonists, Benjy, was mentally retarded. His stream of consciousness consisted a sundry of images, with no hint which ones were current occurrences and which recollections. To him, they were all alike present. Consequently, the stream was a tale told by an idiot. It was senseless because it jumbled all causal relations. Benjy's inability to grasp tense greatly hampered his function in the human society.

Episodic memories, in which we relive past events, usually involve several mental frames. A linguistic element is necessary for the mental state to be acknowledged as a memory. Past-tense sentences enable us to anchor a memory in a chain of events that is no more, and to evaluate its influence on the present. Autobiographical memory, in which we recall many episodes, mostly takes the form of narrative. We linguistically describe the episodes, organize them, date them or put them in proper order, trace their interconnections, and thus bring out their significance. We articulate our thoughts and feelings, thus externalize and objectify them. My articulated desires are not merely inner urges. Now I can think about them as I think about other people's desires; examine, compare, criticize, evaluate, and thus make concrete my third-person sense of self. Examination in turn generates new desires through the cognitive circuit of the emotive infrastructure. I may value some of my desires above others and desire to nurture them. Such self-examination is a higher-order thought only in the sense that it is linguistic and explicit, which people usually regard as the higher cognitive power lacking in nonhuman animals. It does not require some mysterious consciousness of consciousness. The abilities to articulate and generalize are sufficient for us to see ourselves as instances of Someone. Language, not a mysterious superego that monitors the ego in the head, makes our full sense of self.

Historians often say that history is a dialogue of the present with the past; each generation writes its own history from its own perspective. Autobiography is a dialogue of the future with the past conducted in the present. In narrating my past, I pick out certain episodes and organize them according to my present interpretation made in light of my expectation for the future. When I ponder on an action, I consider the options available at the present time, put myself in the future and try to choose the action that, as a continuation of my remembered past, contributes to a coherent life most meaningful to me. Thus I confer meaning on my action by bring several temporal perspectives to bear on it. I cannot change my past. By selectively narrating and interpreting its episodes, however, I can change its significance for me. With narratives, we see our lives as coherent wholes.

Many people regard freedom of action as a characteristic of humans. Freedom is neither randomness nor arbitrariness, and free choice is not without constraints. To be able to choose at all, one must have not only a vague idea of possibility but also definite available options. In deciding on future action, options are not present, therefore the chooser must represent them. Representations should be explicit, definite, and analytic so that the chooser can pick out specific aspects of each option, consider their relevance to the choice criteria, and evaluate them. Only language is up to the job. So far as humans are able to remember and choose, they are animals with *logos*.

Nietzsche (1874) observed that it is possible to live and live happily without memory, like grazing cattle blissfully oblivious of past or future, but to live without forgetfulness is as impossible as to live without sleep. The strength of forgetfulness makes more remarkable the genealogy of morals, which culminates in the autonomous and responsible individual with the right to make promises. Only animals with *logos* can promise. A promise is a choice made in the present. It implies not merely the passive inability to forget an utterance but the active memory that must hold through all the vicissitudes between the initial "I will" and its final discharge. Our full-blown mental capacity manifests itself in the will to remember, the confidence to promise, and the assurance to foresee one's own ability to stick to his freely given words. As Nietzsche (1887:II.1) wrote: "To breed an animal *with the right to make promise*—is not this the paradoxical task that nature has set itself in the case of man? Is it not the real problem regarding man?"

Appendix: The Human Brain

Our central nervous system, consisting of the brain and spinal cord, is connected to all parts of our body by forty-three pairs of nerves, twelve of which originate or terminate in the brain, thirty-one in the spinal cord.

Emerging from the spinal cord as it ascends into the brain is the cerebellum, an ancient formation vital to balance, movement, and sensorimotor coordination. The brain stem contains the reticular formation controlling sleeping and waking. At the top of the brain stem sits the pineal gland, the brain's only nonbilateral structure. The upper part of the brain stem together with several adjacent structures constitute the limbic system, also known as the old mammalian brain because it evolved early and its structures and functions are similar to all mammals. It lies beneath the cerebral cortex or neocortex, the new evolutionary product forming the outer layer of the brain (figure A.1).

The limbic system consists of several interconnected structures with various functions: the olfactory bulb, for which it was called the smell brain; parts of the thalamus that relay sensory information to the cortex; the hypothalamus that maintains the constancy of internal bodily conditions by regulating the autonomic nervous system and secretion of hormones from its pituitary glands; and amygdala, nut-sized entities involved in emotions and drives. It also contains the hippocampus, seahorse-shaped structures that, together with its surrounding cortex, constitute the medial temporal lobe system vital for forming although not storing long-term memory.

The cerebral cortex is largely responsible for the higher mental activities that distinguish humans. It is divided into two hemispheres, which are physiologically and functionally unequal. Each hemisphere controls the

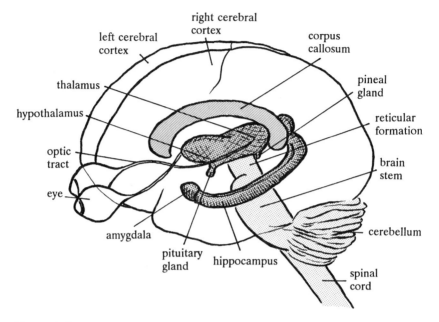

Figure A.1
Parts of the brain underneath the cerebral cortex, including the brain stem and limbic system.

side of the body opposite to it by nerve fibers that cross over at the bridge called corpus callosum. Severance of these nerve fibers in split-brain patients generates strange awareness and behaviors.

Each cerebral hemisphere divides into four lobes: frontal, parietal, occipital, and temporal. The lobes are infolded and convoluted to increase surface area, as cortical neurons lie close to the surface and form a covering layer about two millimeters thick. Various localized areas in the cortex contribute dominantly, although not exclusively, to different mental functions. For instance, Broca's area in the left hemisphere is mainly responsible for speech. The primary sensorimotor cortex is subdivided into areas for analyzing information from fingers, limbs, and facial areas. The motor cortex has subareas for controlling limbs, fingers, and facial and speech organs. Generally, a larger cortical area is devoted to a more acute sense (figure A.2).

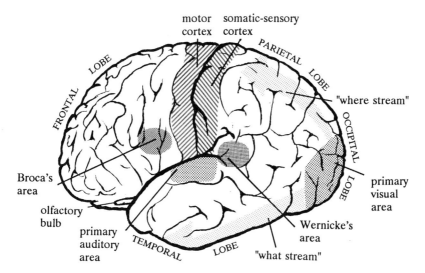

Figure A.2
The surface of the left cerebral hemisphere shows major functional areas.

Notes

Chapter 1

1. Luminous matter includes all matter that emits and interacts with electromagnetic radiation in whatever frequency, ranging from gamma rays to radio waves. Dark matter emits no radiation, but manifests its existence through its gravitational effect on the motion of luminous matter. For instance, based on physical laws and the observed rotational velocities of the arms of spiral galaxies, physicists find that the mass of a galaxy must be much greater than the sum of the masses of its luminous stars, and the difference implies dark matter. It is still a mystery as to what the dark matter is. Answers such as it is composed of brown dwarfs, burned-out stars, or massive neutrinos all have unsurmountable difficulties. Most physicists think that much of it is not "ordinary" matter, which means baryonic matter explained by the experimentally confirmed standard model of elementary particle physics, but is some "exotic" matter that has not been seen in any experiment. Many theoretical candidates of exotic particles exist, but none has any experimental confirmation. See Rees (2000) for a brief review.

2. This view of the theoretical attitude is adopted from Heidegger (1926), as discussed further in section 6. For the distinction between the theoretical attitude and theospectivism, see sections 5 and 25.

Chapter 2

1. Descartes defined thinking things in *Meditation II* (1641, p. 19). I mostly follow the interpretation of Baker and Morris (1996).

2. Descartes *Discourse on Method* (1985, p. 127). The same conclusion is reached in *Meditations on First Philosophy*, written in 1638–1640.

3. Hume (1739:253) wrote: "The comparison of the theater must not mislead us. They are the successive perceptions only, that constitute mind; nor have we the most distant notion of the place, where these scenes are represented, or of the materials, of which it is composed."

4. A 1963 study found that people were as likely to view computers as "awesome thinking machines" as "beneficial tools." Similar studied conducted later, when people became more familiar with computers as tools, found a sharp decline in the awesome-thinking-machine view. But the view lingers in some areas of the academia. See Martin (1993).

5. DEEP BLUE's designers Feng-Hsiung Hsu, Campbell Murray, and Chung-jen Tan, repeatedly asserted that their aim was not to build an autonomous thinking machine but to develop powerful searching tools that are useful in many areas. See their interviews with Horgan (1999). See Newquist (1994) on the development of AI and its industry.

6. The first idea is the dual roles of symbols as revealed in the proof theory and model theory of mathematical logic. In proof theory, symbols are meaningless entities transforming according to syntactic rules that preserve the truth of formulas without invoking meaning. In model theory, they are representations semantically interpretable in various models. Furthermore, Gödel's completeness theorem shows that, at least for predicate logic, the formal approach of proof theory can produce the equivalence of all true meaningful propositions. The second great idea is the Church-Turing thesis, which implies that symbolic transformations can be mechanically implemented, so that all our formal algorithmic thinking can be imitated by the universal digital computer. The mechanical implementation gives symbol transformations causal power. Taken together, the two ideas suggest that these transformations can both mimic meaning change and be causally efficacious. See Fodor (1981, the introduction and Part III).

7. A good definition of objectivism is given by philosopher Richard Bernstein (1983:8), who goes beyond objectivism, which is the doctrine "there is or must be some permanent, ahistorical matrix or framework to which we can ultimately appeal in determining the nature of rationality, knowledge, truth, reality, goodness, or rightness."

8. Dennett's (1978:80, 124) main thesis in homuncular functionalism rests on the anthropomorphic practice he imputed to AI researchers: "The AI programmer begins with an intentionally characterized problem, and thus frankly views the computer anthropomorphically. . . . His first and highest level of design breaks the computer down into subsystems, each of which is given intentionally characterized tasks: he composes a flow chart of evaluators, rememberers, discriminators, overseers and the like. These are *homunculi* with a vengeance; the highest level design breaks the computer down into a committee of army of intelligent homunculi with purposes, information and strategies."

Dennett unjustifiably attributed to all AI workers what McDermott criticized as "wishful mnemonics." All computer programmers write analytic flow charts and call subroutines, whether they are modeling the weather or summing a series. Nowhere in such applications of analysis, however, will one find the slightest suggestion of homunculi or anthropomorphism. Programmers, who are human beings, always think intentionally. No AI system can "*understand* English" as Dennett (1978:80) claimed. He has misattributed the understanding and intentionality of AI workers to their products to generate his fictitious army of homunculi.

The AI engineers write programs to perform certain tasks. Whether the programs think in performing the tasks, however, is not apparent. Therefore Turing proposed what has come to be called the Turing test. A computer thinks if it can converse with people and fool its interlocutors into thinking that they are talking with a human being. One can disagree with Turing's specific criterion. Nevertheless, one cannot deny that in realizing the need for some criteria for thinking, Turing was far more sophisticated than the so-called AI programmers in Dennett's story, who airily maintain that a system thinks simply when they say it thinks. This uncritical attitude is Dennett's, not AI's.

9. Dennett (1987:ch. 2) defended instrumental behaviorism, undersoring "*all there is* to being a true believer is being a system whose behavior is reliably predictable via the intentional strategy." The intentional strategy is one that uses intentional concepts such as belief and desire, and is applicable to everything. As to specific beliefs and desires, "We attribute the desires the system *ought to have*." His example of the intentional thermostat illustrates the fictitious nature of the ascribed belief and desire.

10. Humans as "meat machines" is Minsky's term, which Dennett defends, see Joseph Weisenbaum's report in Baumgarner and Payr (1995). Weizenbaum (1976) offers a sustained criticism on the dehumanizing effects of computationalism.

11. This discussion is adapted from Heidegger's (1926, ¶ 15) example of a broken hammer. In his terminology, when we are involved in our mundane activities, things are *ready-to-hand* and unobtrusive in their working context. When something breaks down, it becomes conspicuous, and we treat it as *present-at-hand*.

Chapter 3

1. Fan is quoted in Fung (1953:289–91); my translation is a little different.

2. Edward Pols (1998:10–2) distinguishes between studies of mind and studies of infrastructure, and criticizes scientists and philosophers for neglecting mind in favor of infrastructure. His infrastructure covers everything causal, from the brain and body to all physical influence that bears on the body. My mental infrastructure is much more specific; it is only an intermediate level of organization between the mental level above and the neural level below.

3. Freud summarized his theory on the unconscious in two short essays, "A Note on the Unconscious in Psychoanalysis" (1912) and "The Unconscious" (1915).

4. Auyang (1998) gives many examples of synthetic analysis from the physical, biological, and social sciences. Chapter 2 discusses the general methodology in more details and contrasts it to reductionism.

5. Many arguments for homuncular functionalism are found in Dennett (1978). He claimed that finally the most stupid homunculi are discharged and replaced by machines. How are they discharged? What are the criteria of discharge? What is the difference between stupid homunculi and machines that replace them? Why can't smart homunculi be replaced by more complicated machines? Over 90 percent of the human body is water; water, which finds its way to the ocean through all obstacles and forms snow flakes with perfect symmetry and endless intricacy, is surely no moron. How can such smart substance in our brain be discharged and replaced by machines? According to the behaviorist theory of intelligence on which homuncular functionalism depends, is anything so stupid as to be dischargeable? These are crucial problems, but homuncular functionalists do not give the slightest hint of answers. Thus "discharge"

is merely an empty word that adds nothing at all to the vacuity that makes the homuncular explanations fallacious. See note 8 in chapter 2 for a refutation of Dennett's appeal to AI practices in support of his homuncular functionalism.

6. Auyang (1998, sections 15, 16) gives an accessible discussion of the physical and economic theories. The self-consistent field theory, also called the Hartree-Fock model, is applicable in many branches of physics. A more intuitive example is the general equilibrium theory for perfectly competitive markets, which is the keystone of microeconomics. Price levels and their movement are the properties of the economy as a whole. Commodity prices are determined by the equilibration of aggregate demand and supply, which in turn are determined by decisions of individual consumers who make up the economy. This upward determination is the cannon of theoretical economics. Suppose prices go up. I think I am not alone in regarding myself a victim rather than a cause of inflation; I am too insignificant to be a cause, but high prices do force me to forgo some purchases. My intuition of downward causation is precisely represented in the theory of perfectly competitive markets, which defines all consumers as passive price takers who are powerless to influence price. The crux of the theory is a mathematical theorem economists call the invisible hand theorem. It proves rigorously the existence of consistent solutions in which market prices are determined by decisions of passive price takers. The perfectly competitive market is idealistic, but conceptually it is crystal clear and mathematically rigorous. It articulate precisely how upward determination and downward causation are consistent in an ideal free market economy.

Chapter 4

1. In the theory of computation, each grammar is equivalent to a type of abstract computing machines:

Grammar (type)	Abstract Machine
Regular (3)	Finite-state automation (FSA)
Context-free (2)	FSA with pushdown memory stack
Context-sensitive (1)	FSA with head for reading and writing on finite tape
Unrestricted (0)	FSA with infinite tape (Turing machine)

Type 0 grammar is the highest in the hierarchy. A higher-level grammar can accept and produce sequences describable by a lower-level grammar, but not vice versa (Hopcroft and Ullman 1979).

2. See, e.g., Pinker (1994). The controversy can be resolved by control tests where the examiner utters both a complete sentence and only the key words in the sentence. If Kanzi responded only to the sentence and not the string of key words, he would silence the skeptics.

Chapter 6

1. The diencephalon is another brain area vital to declarative memory. Its destruction in patients with Korsakoff's syndrome, often caused by heavy drinking, leads to severe amnesia.

2. Brewer (1996) reviews many experiments. In one, college students wore beepers and stopped to write down what happened whenever the beepers sounded. They handed in their records to the psychologist and were later tested for their memories of the episodes.

Chapter 7

1. This is the point of Kantian ethics. Kant sharply distinguished prudential choices based on preexisting desires and moral choices based solely on the principle of reason and free from preexisting desires. He argued that we can judge the goodness of action by pure reason; an action is good in a certain situation if we decide that any rational person should act similarly. The impartial decision cannot depend on any assumption of desires, because desires vary from person to person, and compulsive desires contaminate the freedom of action that comes from rational choice.

Chapter 8

1. My mind-open-to-the-world and intelligibility of objects are close to Heidegger's being-in-the-world and meaning of beings.

2. Dennett (1987) introduced the intentional stance in distinction to the physical stance of natural science and the design stance of engineering. Its meaning is different from adopting an intentional conceptual framework for explanations. Scientists use different concepts for different phenomena, astronomical concepts for astronomical, biological concepts for biological, and intentional concepts for intentional system. Like biological concepts, here the intentional concepts are objective and belong to the physical stance because they purport to describe and explain the real properties of the systems under study. Dennett denied that people have intentional properties, and that is why his intentional concepts call for a strategy different from that of natural science. In his instrumental behaviorism, intentional concepts neither describe nor explain mental properties; no such property exist. They are tools for predicting and controlling behaviors by attributing fictitious properties, which Searle (1992) rightly called "as-if-intentionality." The fictitiousness of intentionality is the hall mark of Dennett's intentional stance. Addressing criticism, he sometimes claimed that intentionality is real but insisted that a thermostat is as real a believer as a person. That is the devaluation stance applied to the concept of reality.

3. Mahayana Buddhism has two major philosophical branches: Madhyamika, or the dialectical school, and Vijnanavada, or the consciousness school. Both assert the radical interdependence of subject, object, and all things, so that the absolute existence of any independent entity is illusory. Their doctrines would not sound strange to Western philosophers familiar with British idealists such as George Berkeley and F. H. Bradley. Varela, Thompson, and Rosch (1991) give a good account of Madhyamika with application to cognitive science. Vijnanavada proposed a subject-object relationship through the evolution of consciousness, (*vijnana* means consciousness). See Kalupahana (1992).

The *wei-shih* or consciousness-only school was established in China in the mid-sixth century. The Chinese word *shih* generally means awareness. It was probably not used for consciousness in indigenous Chinese philosophy, but its meaning was naturally extended, absorbed into subsequent Neoconfusianism, and rooted in Chinese over the millennium. Paul (1984) discusses the rise of consciousness-only doctrines in China. Buddhism passed from China to Japan, and most Chinese Buddhist schools have their Japanese counterparts. The Hosso school, counterpart of the *wei-shih* school, dominated Japanese Buddhism in the seventh century.

4. It is more than possible; it is plausible. Many astronomers want to disqualify Pluto as a planet, although their proposition was defeated in a vote of the International Astronomical Union in February 1999.

5. I borrow the word "clearing" from Heidegger (1976:133), who wrote: "To say that it is 'illuminated' means that *as* Being-in-the-world it is cleared in itself, not through any other entity, but in such a way that it *is* itself that clearing. . . . *Dasein is its disclosedness*."

6. The priority of thrown over logical possibility occurs in science as in everyday life. For instance, statistical inference is restricted to considering only relevant options, and its notion of "small worlds" is embraced in possible-world models of modal theories. This is discussed in many texts on statistical inference, starting from Leonard Savage's (1954) classic. For a philosophical discussion, see Hintikka (1975:195).

7. Some philosophers believe that certain mental states, for instance pain, fear, mood, have no intentionality, hence no object. I agree with Tye (1995) that all mental states are intentional if we take a properly broad view of objects. For an embodied mind, pain and other bodily sensations are part of proprioception, so that one is aware of the conditions of his body, as he groans, "My back hurts."

8. Frege (1892) distinguished between the *Bedeutung* and *Sinn* of a sign. *Sinn*, translated as meaning or sense, contains the *Art des Gegebenseins*, or mode of presentation. Gadamer (1960) described, among other things, how the fusion of horizons facilitates cross-cultural understanding.

9. Compare figure 8.2 with figure 5.1 in Auyang (1995), where I examined the conceptual structures of quantum and relativistic theories.

10. The mirror model was adumbrated by Plato, who said the easiest way to re-create everything in the universe is to point a mirror at it (*Republic*: 596). Francis Bacon (1605:I-6) wrote: "God hath framed the mind of man as a mirror or glass, capable of the image of the universal world, and joyful to receive the impression thereof." The mirror, however, is often not a "clear and equal glass" but an "enchanted glass" that distorts. The glassy essence shines in Ludwig Wittgenstein's (1921:2.1–2.225) picture theory of propositions and hides in computationalism's cryptographic constraint. Dretske (1995:2) stipulated that a system represents a property if it has the function of providing information about the property by assuming states that correspond to certain values of the property. The mirror satisfies this definition admirably, as mirror images provide information about what they reflect.

The mirror model is not confined to Western culture. Shen Hsiu, who founded the North School of Chinese Zen Buddhism in the seventh century, wrote: "The body is like a bodhi tree, the mind a bright mirror. Polish it frequently and diligently, let no dust blemish it."

11. Neisser (1993b) and Butterworth (1998) use joint attention to describe what they call interpersonal self. My interpretation differs from theirs in that I deviate from their basic ecological outlook.

12. Neither is false; only relative motions are objective. To encompass different reference frames and the transformations among them is the gist of relativistic physics (see figure 8.2).

13. Neisser (1993b) introduced five kinds of self: ecological, interpersonal, extended, private, and self concept. He (1997) explained: "While some of this work has been directly influenced by J. J. Gibson's (1979) ecological theory of perception, much of it draws on quite different intellectual traditions." Consequently, much mental ability has been injected into his five selves, which sometimes come close to existential phenomenology, with which I agree. However, they sound so much like what Gibson denounced that I am not sure whether they are compatible with Gibson's theory. In any case, I have criticized only the ecological self based on Gibson's theory in contrast with my existential self. Similar critiques of the ecological self are found in Bermúdez (1995).

14. My "already meaningful" and "interpretation" roughly correspond to Heidegger's (1926:149, 159) "interpretation (*Auslegung*)" and "Interpretation." The former, translated with a lower-case i, covers all topics and is associated with the "existential-hermeneutical *as*." The latter, with a capital I, is more systematic and associated with the "aphophantical *as*," where we explicitly acknowledge an entity *as* belonging to some kind of thing.

References

Abelson, H. and Sussman, G. J. (1996). *Structure and Interpretation of Computer Programs*, 2nd ed. Cambridge: MIT Press.

Adolphs, R., Tranel, D., and Damasio, A. R. (1994). The human amygdala in social judgment. *Nature*, 393, 470–4.

Agre, P. E. (1995). Computational research on interaction and agency. *Artificial Intelligence*, 72, 1–52.

Agre, P. E. (1997). *Computation and Human Experience*. New York: Cambridge University Press.

Akins, K., ed. (1996). *Perception*. New York: Oxford University Press.

Allport, A. (1988). What concept of consciousness? In Marcel and Bisiach (1988), pp. 159–82.

Allport, A. (1993). Attention and control: Have we been asking the wrong questions? A critical review of twenty-five years. In Meyer and Kornblum (1993), pp. 183–208.

Annas, J. (1992). *Hellenistic Philosophy of Mind*. Berkeley: University of California Press.

Aristotle (1984). *The Complete Works of Aristotle*. J. Barnes, ed. Princeton: Princeton University Press.

Assad, J. A. and Maunsell, J. H. R. (1995). Neuronal correlates of inferred motion in primate posterior parietal cortex. *Nature*, 373, 518–21.

Auyang, S. Y. (1995). *How Is Quantum Field Theory Possible?* New York: Oxford University Press.

Auyang, S. Y. (1998). *Foundations of Complex-System Theories in Economics, Evolutionary Biology, Statistical Physics*. New York: Cambridge University Press.

Baars, B. (1997). *In the Theater of Consciousness: the Workspace of Mind*. New York: Oxford University Press.

Bacon, F. (1605). *The Advancement of Learning*. New York: Oxford University Press.

Baddeley, A. (1994). Working memory: The interface between memory and cognition. In Schacter and Tulving (1994), pp. 351–68.

Baker, G. and Morris, K. J. (1996). *Descartes' Dualism*. London: Routledge.

Barinaga, M. (1996). Neurons put the uncertainty into reaction time. *Science*, 274, 344.

Barinaga, M. (1997). New imaging methods provide a better view into the brain. *Science*, 276, 1974–6.

Barry, J. A. (1991). *Technobabble*. Cambridge: MIT Press.

Bates, E. and Elman, J. (1996). Learning rediscovered. *Science*, 274, 1849–50.

Baumgartner, P. and Payr, S., eds. (1995). *Speaking Minds*. Princeton: Princeton University Press.

Bechara, A., Damasio, H., Tranel, D., and Damasio, A. (1997). Deciding advantageously before knowing the advantageous strategy. *Science*, 275, 1293–5.

Beer, C. G. (1998). King Solomon's ring redivivus: Cross-species communication and cognition. In Hameroff et al. (1998), pp. 522–32.

Beer, R. D. (1995). A dynamical systems perspective on agent-environment interaction. *Artificial Intelligence*, 72, 173–215.

Beer, R. D. and Chiel, H. (1993). Simulations of cockroach locomotion and escape. In R. Beer, ed. *Biological Neural Networks in Invertebrate Neuroethology and Robotics*. San Diego: Academic Press, pp. 175–213.

Bennett, J. (1966). *Kant's Analytic*. New York: Cambridge University Press.

Ben-Ze'ev, A. (2000). *The Subtlety of Emotions*. Cambridge: MIT Press.

Berry, D. C., ed. (1997). *How Implicit Is Implicit Learning?* Oxford: Oxford University Press.

Bermúdez, J. L. (1995). Ecological perception and the notion of a nonconceptual point of view. In Bermúdez et al. (1995), pp. 153–74.

Bermúdez, J. L., Marcel, A., and Eilan, N., eds. (1995). *The Body and the Self*. Cambridge: MIT Press.

Bernstein, R. J. (1983). *Beyond Objectivism and Relativism*. Philadelphia: University of Pennsylvania Press.

Bertenthal, B. I. (1996). Origins and early development of perception, action, and representation. *Annual Review of Psychology*, 47, 431–59.

Bisiach, E. (1992). Understanding consciousness. In Milner and Rugg (1992), pp. 113–38.

Block, N. (1992). Troubles with functionalism. In B. Beakley and P. Ludlow, *The Philosophy of Mind*, Cambridge: MIT Press, pp. 69–90.

Block, N. (1995). On a confusion about a function of consciousness. *Behavioral and Brain Science*, 18, 227–87.

Block, N., Flanagan, O., and Güzeldene, G., eds. (1997). *The Nature of Consciousness*. Cambridge: MIT Press.

Bloom, P. (2000). *How Children Learn the Meaning of Words*. Cambridge: MIT Press.

Bloor, D. (1991). *Knowledge and Social Imagery*, 2nd ed. Chicago: University of Chicago Press.

Boyd, R., Gasper, P., and Trout, J. D. (1991). *The Philosophy of Science*. Cambridge: MIT Press.

Boysen, S. T., Berntson, G. G., Hannan, M. B., and Cacioppo, J. T. (1996). Quantity-based interference and symbolic representations in chimpanzees. *Journal of Experimental Psychology: Animal Behavior Processes*, 22, 76–86.

Boysson-Bardies, B. (1999). *How Language Comes to Children*. Cambridge: MIT Press.

Brentano, F. (1874). *Psychology from an Empirical Standpoint*.

Brewer, W. F. (1996). What is recollective memory? In Rubin (1996), pp. 19–66.

Brooks, R. A. (1999). *Cambrian Intelligence*. Cambridge: MIT Press.

Brynjolfsson, E. and Yang, S. (1996). Information technology and productivity. *Advances in Computers*, 43, 179–215.

Buchanan, B. G. and Shortliffe, E. H. (1984). *Rule-Based Expert Systems*. Reading, MA: Addison-Wesley.

Buckner, R. L., Kelley, W. M., and Peterson, S. E. (1999). Frontal cortex contributes to human memory formation. *Nature Neuroscience*, 2, 311–19.

Burge, T. (1979). Individualism and the mental. Reprinted in D. M. Rosenthal, ed. (1991). *The Nature of Mind*. New York: Oxford University Press, pp. 536–67.

Butterworth, G. (1998). A developmental-ecological perspective on Strawson's "the self." *Journal of Consciousness Studies*, 8, 132–40.

Campbell, R. and Conway, M. A., eds. (1995). *Broken Memories*. Oxford: Blackwell.

Campos, J. J., Berthenthal, B. J., and Kermoian, R. (1992). Early experience and emotional development: The emergence of wariness of heights. *Psychological Science*, 3, 61–4.

Caplan, D. (1987). *Neurolinguistics and Linguistic Aphasiology*. New York: Cambridge University Press.

Carnap, R. (1928). *The Logical Structure of the World*. Berkeley: University of California Press.

Carruthers, P. (1996). *Language, Thought, and Consciousness*. New York: Cambridge University Press.

Carruthers, P. and Smith, P. K., eds. (1996). *Theories of Theories of Mind*. New York: Cambridge University Press.

Carvell, T. (1998). How Sony created a Monster. *Fortune*, June 8, pp. 162–70.

Ceci, S. J. (1996). *On Intelligence*. Cambridge: Harvard University Press.

Chalmers, D. J. (1996). *The Conscious Mind*. New York: Oxford University Press.

Chomsky, N. (1959). Review of B. F. Skinner's *Verbal Behavior*. *Language* 35, 26–58.

Chomsky, N. (1980). *Rules and Representations*. New York: Columbia University Press.

Chomsky, N. (1986). *Knowledge of Language, Its Nature, Origin, and Use*. New York: Praeger.

Chomsky, N. (1995). *The Minimalist Program*. Cambridge: MIT Press.

Chomsky, N. (2000). *New Horizons in the Study of Language and Mind*. New York: Cambridge University Press.

Chun, M. M. (1997). Types and tokens in visual processing: A double dissociation between the attentional blink and repetitive blindness. *Journal of Experimental Psychology: Human Perception and Performance*, 23, 738–55.

Chun, M. M. and Cavanagh, P. (1997). Seeing two as one: Linking apparent motion and repetitive blindness. *Psychological Science*, 8, 74–9.

Churchland, P. M. (1989). *A Neurocomputational Perspective*. Cambridge: MIT Press.

Churchland, P. M. (1995). *The Engine of Reason, the Seat of the Soul*. Cambridge: MIT Press.

Clancy, W. J. (1994). Review of T. Winograd and F. Flores. In Clancey et al. (1994), pp. 191–210.

Clancey, W. J. (1997). *Situated Cognition*. New York: Cambridge University Press.

Clancey, W. J., Smolier, S. W., and Stefik, M. J., eds. (1994). *Contemplating Mind*. Cambridge: MIT Press.

Clark, A. (1997). *Being There*. Cambridge: MIT Press.

Clark, A. and Lutz, R., eds. (1992). *Connectionism in Context*. Berlin: Springer-Verlag.

Cohen, J. D. and Schooler, J. W., eds. (1997). *Scientific Approaches to Consciousness*. Mahwah, NJ: Lawrence Erlbaum.

Collins, H. (1981). Stages in the empirical programme of relativism. *Social Studies of Science*, 11, 3–10.

Colombo, J. (1993). *Infant Cognition*. Newbury Park, CA: Sage.

Conway, M. A. (1995). *Flashbulb Memories*. Hillsdate, NJ: Lawrence Erlbaum.

Corbetta, M. (1998). Functional anatomy of visual attention in the human brain. In Parasuraman (1998), pp. 95–122.

Cowey, A. and Stoerig, P. (1992). Reflections on blindsight. In Milner and Rugg (1992), pp. 11–38.

Crair, M. C., Gillespie, D. C., and Stryker, M. P. (1998). The role of visual experience in the development of columns in cat visual cortex. *Science*, 279, 566–70.

Crick, F. (1989). The recent excitement about neural networks. *Nature*, 337, 129–32.

Crick, F. (1994). *The Astonishing Hypothesis*. New York: Charles Scribner's Sons.

Crick, F. and Koch, C. (1990). Toward a neurobiological theory of consciousness. *Seminars in the Neurosciences*, 2, 263–75.

Crick, F. and Koch, C. (1995). Are we aware of neural activity in primary visual cortex? *Nature*, 375, 121–3.

Cromer, A. (1997). *Connected Knowledge: Science, Philosophy, and Education.* New York: Oxford University Press.

Damasio, A. R. (1994). *Descartes' Error.* New York: Putnam's Sons.

Damasio, A. R. (1997). Towards a neuropathology of emotion and mood. *Nature,* 386, 769–70.

Damon, E., ed. (1998). *Handbook of Child Psychology.* New York: Wiley.

Davidson, D. (1982). Rational Animals. *Dialectica,* 36, 318–27.

Davidson, D. (1984). *Truth and Interpretation.* New York: Oxford University Press.

Davidson, D. (1987). Knowing one's own mind. Reprinted in Pessin and Goldberg (1996), pp. 323–41.

Deacon, T. (1997). *The Symbolic Species.* New York: Norton.

Dennett, D. C. (1978). *Brainstorm.* Cambridge: MIT Press.

Dennett, D. C. (1987). *The Intentional Stance.* Cambridge: MIT Press.

Dennett, D. (1988). Quining qualia. In Marcel and Bisiach (1988), pp. 42–77.

Dennett, D. C. (1991). *Consciousness Explained.* New York: Little, Brown.

Dennett, D. C. (1995). *Darwin's Dangerous Idea.* New York: Touchstone.

Dennett, D. C. (1998). *Brainchildren: Essays on Designing Mind.* Cambridge: MIT Press.

Descartes, R. (1985). *The Philosophical Writings of Descartes.* J. Cottingham, R. Stoothoff, and D. Murdoch, eds. New York: Cambridge University Press.

Desimone, R. and Duncan, J. (1995). Neural mechanisms of selective visual attention. *Annual Review of Neuroscience,* 18, 193–222.

Dobbins, A. C., Jeo, R. M., Fiser, J., and Allman, J. M. (1998). Distance modulation of neural activity in the visual cortex. *Science,* 281, 522–5.

Dretske, F. I. (1981). *Knowledge and the Flow of Information.* Oxford: Blackwell.

Dretske, F. (1995). *Naturalizing the Mind.* Cambridge: MIT Press.

Dreyfus, H. L. (1972). *What Computers Can't Do.* Cambridge: MIT Press.

Driver, J. and Mattingley, J. B. (1998). Parietal neglect and visual awareness. *Nature Neuroscience,* 1, 17–22.

Eccles, J. (1965). *The Brain and Unity of Conscious Experience.* New York: Cambridge University Press.

Edelman, G. (1992). *Bright Air, Brilliant Fire: The Matter of Mind.* New York: Basic Books.

Edelman, G. and Tonami, G. (2000). *A Universe of Consciousness.* New York: Basic Books.

Edwards, P. N. (1996). *The Closed World: Computers and the Politics of Discourse in Cold War America.* Cambridge: MIT Press.

Eichenbaum, H. (1997). Declarative memory: Insight from cognitive neurobiology. *Annual Review of Psychology,* 48, 547–72.

Einstein, A. (1954). *Ideas and Opinions*. New York: Crown.

Ekman, P. (1994). Strong evidence for universals in facial expressions: A reply to Russell's mistaken critique. *Psychological Bulletin*, 115, 268–87.

Ekman, P. and Davidson, R. J. (1993). Voluntary smiling changes regional brain activity. *Psychological Science*, 4, 342–5.

Ellis, R. D. (1995). *Questioning Consciousness*. Amsterdam: Benjamins.

Eslinger, P. S. and Damasio, A R. (1985). Severe disturbance of cognition after bilateral frontal lobe ablation. *Neurology*, 35, 1731–41.

Evans, G. (1982). *The Varieties of Reference*. New York: Oxford University Press.

Farah, M. J. (1990). *Visual Agnosia*. Cambridge: MIT Press.

Fernandez, E. and Turk, D. C. (1992). Sensory and affective components of pain: Separation and synthesis. *Psychological Bulletin*, 112, 205–17.

Feynman, R. (1965). *The Character of Physical Law*. Cambridge: MIT Press.

Ffytche, D. H., Howard, R. J., and Brammer, M. J. (1998). The anatomy of conscious vision: An fMRI study of visual hallucination. *Nature Neuroscience*, 1, 738–42.

Flanagan, O. (1992). *Consciousness Reconsidered*. Cambridge: MIT Press.

Fodor, J. A. (1975). *The Language of Thought*. Cambridge: Harvard University Press.

Fodor, J. A. (1981). *Representation*. Cambridge: MIT Preess.

Fodor, J. A. (1983). *The Modularity of Mind*. Cambridge: MIT Press.

Fodor, J. A. (1987). *Psychosemantics*. Cambridge: MIT Press.

Fodor, J. A. (1998a). *Concepts: Where Cognitive Science Went Wrong*. New York: Oxford University Press.

Fodor, J. A. (1998b). *In Critical Condition*. Cambridge: MIT Press.

Fodor, J. A. (1998c). When is a dog a DOG? *Nature*, 396, 325–7.

Fodor, J. A. and Pylyshyn, Z. W. (1981). How direct is visual perception? *Cognition*, 9, 139–96.

Fodor, J. A. and Pylyshyn, Z. W. (1988). Connectionism and cognitive architecture: A critical analysis. *Cognition*, 28, 3–71.

Føllesdal, D. (1969). Quine on modality. In D. Davidson and J. Hintikka, eds. *Words and Objections*. Dordrecht, Holland: Reidel, pp. 187–85.

Forman, P. (1997). Assailing the seasons. *Science*, 276, 750–2.

Freeman, W. J. (1991). The physiology of perception. *Scientific American*, 264(2), 78–85.

Frege, G. (1892). On sense and reference. In M. Beaney, ed. *The Frege Reader*. Malden MA: Blackwell, pp. 151–71.

French, R. M. (1999). Catastrophic forgetting in connectionist networks. *Trends in Cognitive Sciences*, 3, 128–35.

Freud, S. (1966). *The Standard Edition of the Complete Psychological Work of Sigmund Freud.* London: Hogarth Press.

Fritz, K. von. (1974). *Nous, Noein*, and their derivatives in pre-Socratic philosophy. In A. P. D. Mourelatos, ed. *The Pre-Socratics.* Garden City, NY: Anchor Books, pp. 23–85.

Fung, Y-L. (1953). *A History of Chinese Philosophy.* Princeton, NJ: Princeton University Press.

Gabrieli, J. D. E. (1998). Cognitive neuroscience of human memory. *Annual Review of Psychology*, 49, 87–115.

Gadamer, H. (1960). *Truth and Method.* New York: Crossroad.

Gallagher, S. and Marcel, A. J. (1999). The self in contextualized action. *Journal of Consciousness Studies*, 6, 4–30.

Gallagher, S. and Shear, J. (1997). Editors' introduction. *Journal of Consciousness Studies*, 4, 339–404.

Gardiner, J. M. and Ramponi, C. (1998). Experience of remembering, knowing, and guessing. *Consciousness and Cognition*, 7, 1–29.

Gazzaniga, M. S., ed. (1995). *The Cognitive Neurosciences.* Cambridge: MIT Press.

Gernsbacher, M. A., ed. (1994). *Handbook of Psycholinguistics.* San Diego: Academic Press.

Gibson, J. J. (1966). *The Senses Considered as Perceptual Systems.* Boston: Houghton Mifflin.

Gibson, J. J. (1979). *The Ecological Approach to Visual Perception.* Boston: Houghton Mifflin.

Giurfa, M. and Menzel, R. (1997). Insect visual perception: Complex abilities of simple nervous systems. *Current Opinion in Neurobiology*, 7, 505–13.

Green, C. D. and Vervaeke, J. (1997). But what have you done for us lately? In Johnson and Erneling (1997), pp. 149–63.

Greenwald, A. G., Draine, S. C., and Abrams, R. L. (1996). Three cognitive markers of unconcious semantic activation. *Science*, 273, 1699–702.

Gregory, R. L., ed. (1987). *The Oxford Companion to the Mind.* New York: Oxford University Press.

Gregory, R. L. (1998). *Eye and Brain.* New York: Oxford University Press.

Griffith, D., Dickinson, A., and Clayton, N. (1999). Episodic memory: what can animals remember about their past? *Trends in Cognitive Sciences*, 3, 74–80.

Griffiths, P. E. (1997). *What Emotions Really Are?* Chicago: Chicago University Press.

Grimes, J. (1996). On the failure to detect changes in scenes across saccades. In Akins (1996), pp. 89–110.

Gross, P. R., Levitt, N., and Lewis, M. W., eds. (1997). *The Flight from Science and Reason.* Baltimore: Johns Hopkins University Press.

Guthrie, W. K. C. (1962). *A History of Greek Philosophy, I.* New York: Cambridge University Press.

Hameroff, S. R., Kasznick, A. W., and Scott, A. C., eds. (1996). *Toward a Science of Consciousness I.* Cambridge: MIT Press.

Hameroff, S. R., Kasznick, A. W., and Scott, A. C., eds. (1998). *Toward a Science of Consciousness II.* Cambridge: MIT Press.

Harley, T. A. (1995). *The Psychology of Language.* Hove: Taylor & Francis.

Harris, R. A. (1993). *The Linguistics War.* New York: Oxford University Press.

Haugeland, J., ed. (1997). *Mind Design II.* Cambridge: MIT Press.

He, S., Cavanagh, P., and Intriligator, J. (1996). Attentional resolution and the locus of visual awareness. *Nature*, 383, 334–7.

Heelas, P. (1996). Emotion talk across cultures. In R. Harré and W. G. Parrott, eds. *The Emotions.* London: Sage, pp. 171–99.

Heidegger, M. (1926). *Being and Time.* New York: Harper & Row.

Heidegger, M. (1927). *The Basic Problems of Phenomenology.* Bloomington: Indiana University Press.

Henderson, J. M. (1966). Visual attention and the attention action interface. In Akins (1996), pp. 290–316.

Hendriks-Jansen, H. (1996). *Catching Ourselves in the Act.* Cambridge: MIT Press.

Herrnstein, R. J. (1990). Levels of stimulus control: A functional approach. *Cognition*, 37, 133–66.

Hikosaka, O., Miyauchi, S, Takeichi, H., and Shimojo, S. (1996). Multimodal spatial attention visualized by motion illusion. In Inui and McCelland (1996), pp. 237–62.

Hilts, P. J. (1995). *Memory's Ghost.* New York: Simon & Schuster.

Hintikka, J. (1973). *Logic, Language Games, and Information.* New York: Oxford University Press.

Hintikka, J. (1975). *The Intentions of Intentionality and Other New Models of Modalities.* Dordrecht, Holland: Reidel.

Hood, B. M., Willen, D., and Driver, J. (1998). Adults' eyes trigger shifts of visual attention in human infants. *Psychological Science*, 9, 131–4.

Hopcroft, J. E. and Ullman, J. D. (1979). *Introduction to Automata Theory, Languages, and Computation.* Reading, MA: Addison-Wesley.

Horgan, J. (1999). *The Undiscovered Mind.* New York: Free Press.

Horwich, P. (1990). *Truth.* Oxford: Blackwell.

Hume, D. (1739). *A Treatise of Human Nature.* New York: Oxford University Press.

Hunt, H. T. (1995). *On the Nature of Consciousness.* New Haven: Yale University Press.

Hurlbert, A. and Poggio, T. (1988). Making machines (and artificial intelligence) see. *Daedalus*, 117(1), 213–40,

Hurlbert, R. (1990). *Sampling Normal and Schizophrenic Inner Experience.* New York: Plenum Press.

Hurley, S. (1998). *Consciousness in Action*. Cambridge: Harvard University Press.

Husserl, E. (1913). *Ideas: General Introduction to Pure Phenomenology*. New York: Coolier Books.

Hyman, S. E. (1998). A new image for fear and emotion. *Nature*, 393, 417–18.

Ingle, K. A. (1994). *Reverse Engineering*. New York: McGraw-Hill.

Intraub, H. (1985). Visual dissociation: An illusory cognition of pictures and forms. *Journal of Experimental Psychology: Human Perception and Performance*, 11, 431–42.

Inui, T. and McCelland, J. L., eds. (1996). *Attention and Performance XVI*. Cambridge: MIT Press.

Irwin, D. E. (1993). Perceiving an integrated visual world. In Meyer and Kornblum (1993), pp. 121–42.

Ishai, A. and Sagi, D. (1997). Visual imagery facilitates visual perception. *Journal of Cognitive Neuroscience*, 9, 476–89.

Jackendoff, R. (1987). *Consciousness and the Computational Mind*. Cambridge: MIT Press.

Jackson, F. (1982). Epiphenomenal qualia. In Lycan (1990), pp. 469–77.

Jackson, J. (1994). Chronic pain and the tension between the body as subject and object. In T. J. Csordas, ed. *Embodiment and Experience*. New York: Cambridge University Press, pp. 210–28.

James, W. (1890). *The Principles of Psychology*. Cambridge: Harvard University Press.

James, W. (1904). Does consciousness exist? In J. J. McDermott, ed. *The Writings of William James*. Chicago: University of Chicago Press, pp. 169–83.

Johnson, D. M. and Erneling, C. E., eds. (1997). *The Future of the Cognitive Revolution*. Oxford: Oxford University Press.

Johnson-Laird, P. N. (1993). *Human and Machine Thinking*. Hillsdale, NJ: Lawrence Erlbaum.

Kahneman, D., Treisman, A., and Gibbs, B. J. (1992). The reviewing of object files: Object-specific integration of information. *Cognitive Psychology*, 24, 175–219.

Kalupahana, D. J. (1992). *A History of Buddhist Philosophy*. Honolulu: University of Hawaii Press.

Kant, I. (1781). *Critique of Pure Reason*. New York: St. Martin's Press.

Kant, I. (1800). *Logic*. New York: Dover.

Kanwisher, N. G. (1987). Repetitive blindness: Type recognition without token individuation. *Cognition*, 27, 117–43.

Karmiloff-Smith, A. (1992). *Beyond Modularity, a Developmental Perspective on Cognitive Science*. Cambridge: MIT Press.

Kastner, S., Pinsk, M. A., and Desimone, R. (1998). Mechanisms of directed attention in the human extrastriate cortex as revealed by fMRI. *Science*, 282, 108–11.

Kelley, C. M. and Jacoby, L. L. (1993). The construction of subjective experience:

Memory attributions. In E. Davies and G. W. Humphreys, eds. *Consciousness*. Oxford: Blackwell, pp. 74–89.

Kellman, P. J. (1993). Kinematic foundations of infant visual perception. In C. Granrud, ed. *Visual Perception and Cognition in Infancy*. Hillsdale, NJ: Lawrence Erlbaum, pp. 121–74.

Kim, J. (1993). *Supervenience and Mind*. New York: Cambridge University Press.

Kim, K. H., Relkin, N. R., Lee, K., and Hirsch, J. (1997). Distinct cortical areas associated with native and second languages. *Nature*, 388, 171–9.

Kirsh, D. (1991). Today earwig, tomorrow human? *Artificial Intelligence*, 47, 161–84.

Kirshner, D. and Whitson, J. A., eds. (1997). *Situated Cognition*. Mahwah, NJ: Lawrence Erlbaum.

Koch, C. and Laurent, G. (1999). Complexity and the nervous system. *Science*, 284, 96–8.

Koertge, N., ed. (1998). *A House Built on Sand: Exposing Postmodernist Myths about Science*. New York: Oxford University Press.

Köhler, S. and Moscovitch, M. (1997). Unconscious visual processing in neuropsychological syndromes. In M. D. Rugg, ed. *Cognitive Neuroscience*. Cambridge: MIT Press, pp. 305–73.

Kosslyn, S. M. (1994). *Image and Brain*. Cambridge: MIT Press.

Kosslyn, S. M., Thompson, W. L., Kim, I. J., and Aplert, N. M. (1995). Topographical representations of mental images in primary visual cortex. *Nature* 378, 496–9.

Krapp, H. G. and Hengstenberg, R. (1996). Estimation of self-motion by optic flow processing in single visual interneurons. *Nature*, 384, 463–6.

Kuhn, T. S. (1962). *The Structure of Scientific Revolution*. Chicago: University Of Chicago Press.

Kurzweil, R. (1999). *The Age of Spiritual Machines*. New York: Viking.

Lakoff, G. and Johnson, M. (1999). *Philosophy in the Flesh*. New York: Basic Books.

Latour, B. (1987). *Science in Action*. Cambridge: Harvard University Press.

Ledoux, J. E. (1995). *The Emotional Brain*. New York: Simon & Schuster.

Leibniz, G. W. (1765). *New Essays on Human Understanding*. New York: Cambridge University Press.

Lenat, D. B. and Feigenbaum, E. A. (1991). On the threshold of knowledge. *Artificial Intelligence*, 47, 185–250.

Lewontin, R. C. (1998). The evolution of cognition: Questions we will never answer. In D. Scarborough and S. Sternberg, eds. *An Invitation to Cognitive Science, Vol 4*. Cambridge: MIT Press, pp. 107–32.

Libet, B. (1996). Neural processes in the production of conscious experience. In Velmans (1996), pp. 96–117.

Liboff, R. L. (1990). *Kinetic Theory, Classical, Quantum, and Relativistic Descriptions*. New York: Prentice-Hall.

Lillard, A. S. (1997). Other folks' theories of mind and behavior. *Psychological Science*, 8, 268–74.

Locke, J. (1690). *An Essay Concerning Human Understanding*. New York: Oxford University Press.

Loftus, E. F. and Loftus, G. R. (1980). On the permanence of stored information in the human brain. *American Psychologist*, 35, 409–20.

Logothetis, N. K., Leopold, D. A., and Sheinberg, D. L. (1996). What is rivalling during binocular rivalry? *Nature*, 380, 621–4.

Luck, S. J., Vogel, E. K., and Shapiro, K. L. (1996). Word meaning can be accessed but not reported during attentional blink. *Nature*, 382, 616–18.

Luria, A. (1968). *The Mind of a Mnemonist*. New York: Basic Books.

Lycan, W. G., ed. (1990). *Mind and Cognition*. Cambridge: Blackwell.

MacDonald, C. and MacDonald, G., eds. (1995). *Connectionism*. Oxford: Blackwell.

MacLeod, C. (1996). Anxiety and cognitive processes. In I. G. Sarason, G. I. Pierce, and B. R. Sarason, eds. *Cognitive Interference*. Mahwah, NJ: Lawrence Erlbaum, pp. 47–76.

Marcel, A. J. (1993). Slippage in the unity of consciousness. In G. R. Bock and J. Marsh, eds. *Experimental and Theoretical Studies of Consciousness*. New York: Wiley, pp. 168–80.

Marcel, A. J. and Bisiach, E. eds. (1988). *Consciousness in Contemporary Science*. New York: Oxford University Press.

Markman, E. M. (1989). *Categorization and Naming in Children*. Cambridge: MIT Press.

Marr, D. (1982). *Vision*. San Fransico: Freeman.

Martin, C. D. (1993). The myth of the awesome thinking machine. *Communications of the Association of Computing Machinery*, 36(4), 120–33.

Maunsell, J. H. R. (1995). The brain's visual world: Representation of visual targets in cerebral cortex. *Science*, 270, 764–9.

McClelland, J. L. (1996). Integration of information: Reflection on the theme of attention and performance XVI. In Inui and McCelland (1996), pp. 633–56.

McConkie, G. W. and Currie, C. B. (1996). Visual stability across saccades while viewing complex pictures. *Journal of Experimental Psychology: Human Perception and Performance*, 22, 563–81.

McDermott, D. (1976). Artificial Intelligence meets Natural Stupidity. Reprinted in Haugeland (1981), pp. 143–60.

McDowell, J. (1991). Intentionality *De Re*. In E. Lepore and R. van Gulick, eds. *John Searle and His Critics*. Cambridge: Blackwell, pp. 216–24.

McDowell, J. (1992). Putnam on mind and meaning. Reprinted in Pessin and Goldberg (1996), pp. 305–18.

Mcewen, B. S. (1995). Stressful experience, brain, and emotions: Developmental, genetic, and hormonal influences. In Gazzaniga (1995), pp. 1117–35.

McGaugh, J. L. (1991). Neuromodulation and the storage of information. In R. G. Lister and H. J. Weingartner, eds. *Perspectives in Cognitive Neuroscience*. New York: Oxford University Press, pp. 279–99.

McGaugh, J. L. (1995). Emotional activation, neuromodulatory systems, and memory. In D. L. Schacter, ed. *Memory Distortion*. Cambridge: Harvard University Press, pp. 255–73.

McLeod, P. and Dienes, Z. (1996). Do fielders know where to go to catch the ball or only how to get there? *Journal of Experimental Psychology: Human Perception and Performance*, 22, 531–43.

Medin, D. L. (1989). Concepts and conceptual structure. *American Psychologist*, 44, 1469–81.

Meltzoff, A. N. and Moore, M. K. (1995). Infants' understanding of people and things. In Bermúdez et al. (1995), pp. 43–70.

Merleau-Ponty, M. (1945). *Phenomenology of Perception*. London: Routledge & Kegan Paul.

Meyer, D. E. and Kornblum, S., eds. (1993). *Attention and Performance XIV*. Cambridge: MIT Press.

Mill, J. S. (1843). *A System of Logic*. In E. Nagel, ed. *Philosophy of Scientific Method*. New York: Hafner Press.

Miller, A. I. (1984). *Imagery in Scientific Thought*. Boston: Birkhäuser.

Miller, J. M. and Bockisch, C. (1997). Where are the things we see? *Nature*, 386, 550–1.

Milner, A. D. and Rugg, M. D., eds. (1992). *The Neuropsychology of Consciousness*. London: Academic Press.

Minsky, M. L. (1985). *The Society of Mind*. New York: Touchstone Books.

Mitchell, D. C. (1994). Sentence parsing. In Gernsbacher (1994), pp. 375–410.

Mitchell, P. (1997). *Introduction to Theory of Mind*. London: Arnold.

Mlot, C. (1998). Probing the biology of emotion. *Science*, 280, 1005–7.

Morris, D. B. (1991). *The Culture of Pain*. Berkeley: University of California Press.

Morris, J. S., Öhman, A., and Dolan, R. J. (1998). Conscious and unconscious emotional learning in the human amgydala. *Nature*, 393, 467–70.

Moscovitch, M., Goshen-Gottstein, Y., and Vriezen, E. (1994). Memory without conscious recollection: A tutorial review from a neuropsychological perspective. In C. Umilta and M. Moscovitch, eds. *Attention and Performance XV*. Cambridge: MIT Press, pp. 619–60.

Nagel, T. (1986). *The View from Nowhere*. New York: Oxford University Press.

Nagel, T. (1997). *The Last Word*. New York: Oxford University Press.

Nagle, T., Schiffman, S. S., and Osuna, R. G. (1998). The how and why of electronic noses. *IEEE Spectrum*, September, 22–34.

Neisser, U. (1981). John Dean's memory: A case study. *Cognition*, 9, 1–22.

Neisser, U. (1993). The self perceived. In U. Neisser, ed. *The Perceived Self*. New York: Cambridge University Press, pp. 3–24.

Neisser, U. (1997). The future of cognitive science: An ecological analysis. In Johnson and Erneling (1997), pp. 247–60.

Newell, A. (1990). *Unified Theories of Cognition*. Cambridge: Harvard University Press.

Newell, A. and Simon, H. A. (1976). Computer science as empirical enquiry: Symbols and search. Reprinted in Haugeland (1997), pp. 81–110.

Newquist, H. (1994). *The Brain Makers*. Indianapolis: Sams Pub.

Nietzsche, F. (1874). *On the Use and Disadvantage of History for Life*. New York: Cambridge Universtiy Press.

Nietzsche, F. (1887). *On the Genaeology of Morals*. New York: Vintage Books.

Nietzsche, F. (1886). *Beyond Good and Evil*. New York: Vintage Books.

Nietzsche, F. (1901). *The Will to Power*. New York: Vintage Books.

Nijhawan, R. (1997). Visual decomposition of color through motion extrapolation. *Nature*, 386, 66–9.

O'Meara, D. J. (1993). *Plotinus, an Introduction to the Enneads*. New York: University of Oxford Press.

Oppenheim, P. and Putnam, H. (1958). Unity of science as a working hypothesis. Reprinted in Boyd et al. (1991), pp. 405–28.

Orr, H. A. (1996). Dennett's dangerous idea. *Evolution*, 50, 467–72.

Parasuraman, R., ed. (1998). *The Attentive Brain*. Cambridge: MIT Press.

Parker, S. T. and McKinney, M. L. (1999). *Origin of Intelligence*. Baltimore: Johns Hopkins University Press.

Parkin, A. J. (1996). The alien hand. In P. Halligan and J. C. Marshall, eds. *Cognitive Neuropsychiatry*. Hove, UK: Earlbaum.

Paul, D. Y. (1984). *Philosophy of Mind in Sixth-Century China*. Stanford: Stanford University Press.

Peacocke, C. (1992). *A Study of Concepts*. Cambridge: MIT Press.

Penfield, W. (1958). *The Excitable Cortex in Conscious Man*. Springfield, IL: Thomas.

Penrose, R. (1994). *Shadows of Mind: A Search for the Missing Science of Consciousness*. New York: Oxford University Press.

Pessin, A. and Goldberg, S., eds. (1996). *The Twin Earth Chronicles*. Armonk, NY: Sharpe.

Pessoa, L., Thompson, E., and Noë, A. (1998). Finding out and filling-in: A guide to perceptual completion for visual science and the philosophy of perception. *Behavioral and Brain Science*, 21, 723–802.

Petitot, J., Varela, F. J., Pachoud, B., and Roy, J. M., eds. (1999). *Naturalizing Phenomenology*. Stanford: Stanford University Press.

Piaget, J. (1954). *The Construction of Reality in the Child*. New York: Basic Books.

Piatelli-Palmarini, M., ed. (1980). *Language and Learning*. Cambridge: Harvard University Press.

Picard, R. W. (1997). *Affective Computing*. Cambridge: MIT Press.

Pickering, A. (1984). *Constructing Quarks*. Chicago: University of Chicago Press.

Pickering, J. (1999). The race may be on, but where's it going? *Journal of Consciousness Studies*, 6, 72–4.

Pillemer, D. B. (1998). *Momentous Events, Vivid Memories*. Cambridge: Harvard University Press.

Pinker, S. (1994). *The Language Instinct*. New York: Harper Perennial.

Pinker, S. (1997). Words and rules in the human brain. *Nature*, 387, 547–8.

Pinker, S. and Prince, A. (1988). On language and connectionism. *Cognition*, 28, 73–193.

Place U. T. (1956). Is consciousness a brain process? Repr. in Lycan (1990), pp. 29–36.

Poizner, H. (1987). *What the Hands Reveal About the Brain*. Cambridge: MIT Press.

Pols, E. (1998). *Mind Regained*. Ithaca, NY: Cornell University Press.

Port, R. F. and van Gelder, T., eds. (1995). *Mind as Motion*. Cambridge: MIT Press.

Posner, M. I., ed. (1989). *Foundations of Cognitive Science*. Cambridge: MIT Press.

Posner, M. I. and Dehaene, S. (1994). Attentional networks. *Trends in Neuroscience*, 17, 75–9.

Power, M. and Dalgleish, T. (1997). *Cognition and Emotion*. Hove, UK: Psychology Press.

Priestley, J. (1777). *Disquisitions Relating to Matter and Spirit*. New York: Garland Pun.

Price, D. D. (2000). Psychological and neural mechanisms of the affective dimension of pain. *Science*, 288, 1769–72.

Pullum, G. K. (1991). *The Great Eskimo Vocabulary Hoax*. Chicago: University of Chicago Press.

Putnam, H. (1975). *Mind, Language and Reality*. New York: Cambridge University Press.

Putnam, H. (1981). *Reason, Truth and History*. New York: Cambridge University Press.

Pylyshyn, Z. W. (1984). *Computation and Cognition*. Cambridge: MIT Press.

Quine, W. V. O. (1953). *From a Logical Point of View*. Cambridge: Harvard University Press.

Quine, W. V. O. (1960). *Word and Object*. Cambridge: MIT Press.

Quine, W. V. O. (1981). *Theories and Things*. Cambridge: Harvard University Press.

Radford, A. (1990). *Syntatic Theory and the Acquisition of English Syntax*. Oxford: Blackwell.

Radner, D. (1996). *Animal Consciousness*. Amherst, NY: Prometheus Books.

Rainville, P. (1997). Pain affect encoded in human anterior cingulate but not somatosensory cortex. *Science*, 227, 968–70.

Ramachandran, V. S. and Anstis, S. M. (1986). The perception of apparent motion. *Scientific American*, 254(6), 102–9.

Ramachandran, V. S. and Blakeslee, S. (1998). *Phantoms in the Brain*. New York: Morrow.

Rao, K. R. (1998). Two faces of consciousness. *Journal of Consciousness Studies*, 5, 309–27.

Rao, S. C., Rainer, G., and Miller, E. K. (1997). Integration of what and where in the primate prefrontal Cortex. *Science*, 276, 821–4.

Reed, E. S. (1988). *James J. Gibson and the Psychology of Perception*. New Haven: Yale University Press.

Reeke, G. N. Jr. (1996). Review of P. S. Churchland and T. J. Sejnowski, *The Computational Brain*. *Artificial Intelligence*, 82, 381–91.

Rees, M. (2000). *New Perspectives in Astrophysical Cosmology*, 2nd ed. New York: Cambridge University Press.

Rescher, N. (1968). *Topics in Philosophical Logic*. Dordrecht, Holland: Reidel.

Revonsuo, A. and Kamppinen, M., eds. (1994). *Consciousness in Philosophy and Cognitive Neuroscience*. Hillsdale, NJ: Lawrence Erlbaum.

Ristau, C. A. (1996). Animal language and cognition projects. In A. Lock and C. B. Peters, eds. *Handbook of Human Symbolic Evolution*. New York: Oxford University Press, pp. 644–85.

Robinson, J. A. (1996). Perspective, Meaning, and Remembering. In Rubin (1996), pp. 199–217.

Robinson, T. M. (1970). *Plato's Psychology*. Toranto, Canada: University of Toronto Press.

Rock, I. and Mack, A. (1994). Attention and perceptual organization. In S. Ballesteros, ed. *Cognitive Approaches to Human Perception*. Hillsdale, NJ: Lawrence Erlbaum, pp. 23–42.

Rogoff, I. B. and Lave, J., eds. (1984). *Everyday Cognition*. Cambridge: Harvard University Press.

Rorty, R. (1994). Does academic freedom have philosophical presuppositions? *Academe* (Nov.–Dec.), pp. 56–7.

Rosenthal, D. M. (1986). Two concepts of consciousness. *Philosophical Studies*, 49, 329–59.

Ross, A., ed. (1996). *Science Wars*. Durham: Duke University Press.

Rubin, D. C. (1995). *Memory in Oral Traditions*. New York: Oxford University Press.

Rubin, D. C., ed. (1996). *Remembering Our Past*. New York: Cambridge University Press.

Ruby, J. E. (1986). The origins of scientific "law." *Journal of the History of Ideas*, 47, 341–60.

Rumbaugh, D. M. and Savage-Rumbaugh, E. S. (1996). Behavioral roots of language: Words, apes, and a child. In B. M. Velichkovsky and D. M. Rumbaugh, eds. *Communicating Meaning*. Mahwah, NJ: Lawrence Erlbaum, pp. 257–75.

Rumelhart, D. E. and McClelland, J. L. (1986). *Parallel Distributed Processing*, 2 vols. Cambridge: MIT Press.

Sacks, O. (1985). *The Man Who Mistook His Wife for a Hat*. New York: Summit Books.

Sacks, O. (1995). *An Anthropologist on Mars*. New York: Alfred A. Knopf.

Saffran, J. R., Aslin, R. N., and Newport, E. L. (1996). Statistical learning by 8-month-old infants. *Science*, 274, 1926–8.

Sahraie, A. (1997). Pattern of neuronal activity associated with conscious and unconscious processing of visual signals. *Proceedings of the National Academy of Science, USA*, 94, 9406–11.

Sarason, I. G., Pierce, G. R., and Sarason, B. R., eds. (1996). *Cognitive Interference*. Mahwah, NJ: Lawrence Erlbaum.

Saussure, F. (1959). *Course in General Linguistics*. New York: McGraw Hill.

Savage, L. (1954). *The Foundations of Statistics*. New York: Dover.

Savage-Rumbaugh, E. S. (1986). Spontaneous symbol acquisition and communicative use by two pygmy chimpanzees. *Journal of Experimental Psychology: General*, 115, 211–35.

Schacter, D. L. (1990). Toward a cognitive neuropsychology of awareness. *Journal of Clinical and Experimental Neuropsychology*, 12, 155–78.

Schacter, D. L., ed. (1995). *Memory Distortion*. Cambridge: Harvard University Press.

Schacter, D. L. (1996). *Searching for Memory*. New York: Basic Books.

Schacter, D. L., Norman, K. A., and Kontstaal. (1998). The cognitive neuroscience of constructive memory. *Annual Review of Psychology*, 49, 289–318.

Schacter, D. L. and Tulving, E., eds. (1994). *Memory Systems 1994*. Cambridge: MIT Press.

Schrödinger, E. (1961). *My View of the World*. Woodbridge, CN: Ox Bow Press.

Searle, J. R. (1983). *Intentionality*. New York: Cambridge University Press.

Searle, J. R. (1992). *The Rediscovery of the Mind*. Cambridge: MIT Press.

Searle, J. R. (1997). *The Mystery of Consciousness*. New York: New York Review of Books.

Searle, J. R. and Freeman, W. (1998). Do we understand consciousness? *Journal of Consciousness Studies*, 5, 718–33.

Sejnowski, T. J. and Rosenberg, C. R. (1987). Parallel networks that learn to pronounce English text. *Complex System*, 1, 145–68.

Sekuler, R., Sekuler, A. D., and Lau, R. (1997). Sound alters visual motion perception. *Nature*, 385, 308.

Sen, A. (2000). East and west: the reach of reason. *New York Review of Books*, July 20, pp. 33–8.

Sereno, A. B. and Maunsell, J. H. R. (1998). Shape selectivity in primate lateral intraparietal cortex. *Nature*, 395, 500–3.

Shadmehr, R. and Holcomb, H. H. (1997). Neural correlates of motor memory consolidation. *Science*, 277, 821–5.

Shapiro, K., Driver, J., Ward, R., and Sorensen, R. E. (1997). Priming from the attentional blink: A failure to extract visual token but not visual type. *Psychological Science*, 8, 95–100.

Sharma, J., Angelucci, A., and Sur, M. (2000). Induction of visual orientation modules in auditory cortex. *Nature*, 404, 841–7.

Sheinberg, D. L. and Logothetis, N. K. (1997). The role of temporal cortical areas in perceptual organization. *Proceedings of the National Academy of Science USA*, 94, 3408–13.

Sheth, B. R., Sharma, J., Rao, S. C., and Sur, M. (1996). Orientation maps of subjective contours in visual cortex. *Science*, 274, 2110–15.

Simon, H. A. and Kaplan, A. (1989). Foundations of cognitive science. In Posner (1989), pp. 1–47.

Skinner, B. F. (1967). *Verbal Behavior*. New York: Appleton Century-Crofts.

Sloman, S. A. and Rips, L. J., eds. (1998). *Similarity and Symbols in Human Thinking*. Cambridge: MIT Press.

Smith, E. E. and Jonides, J. (1999). Storage and executive processes in the frontal lobes. *Science*, 283, 1657–61.

Smith, N. and Tsimpli, I. (1995). *The Mind of a Savant*. Cambridge: Blackwell.

Smolensky, P. (1991). Connectionism, constituency, and the language of thought. Reprinted in Macdonald and Macdonald (1995), pp. 164–98.

Sokal, A. (1996). Transgressing the boundaries: toward a transformative hermeneutics of quantum gravity. *Social Text*, 14, 217–52.

Spelke, E. S. and Newport, E. L. (1998). Nativism, empiricism, and the development of knowledge. In Damon (1998), Vol. I, pp. 275–340.

Sperry, R. W. (1966). Brain, bisection and consciousness. In J. Eccles, ed. *Brain and Conscious Experience*. New York: Springer-Verlag.

Sperry, R. W. (1969). A modified concept of consciousness. *Psychological Review* 76, 532–6.

Sperry, R. W. (1987). Structure and significance of the consciousness revolution. *Journal of Mind and Behavior*, 8, 37–66.

Springer, S. P. and Deutsch, G. (1989). *Left Brain, Right Brain*, 3rd ed. New York: Freeman.

Stein, N. L., Ornstein, P. A., Tversky, B., and Brainerd, C., eds. (1997a). *Memory for Everyday and Emotional Events*. Mahwah, NJ: Lawrence Erlbaum.

Stein, N. L., Wade, E., and Liwag, M. D. (1997b). A theoretical approach to understanding and remembering emotional events. In Stein et al. (1997a), pp. 17–35.

Sternberg, R. J. and Wagner, R. K., eds. (1994). *Mind in Context*. New York: Cambridge University Press.

Stiewert, C. P. (1998). *The Significance of Consciousness*. Princeton: Princeton University Press.

Stillings, N. A., Feinstein, M. H. and Garfield, J. L. (1995). *Cognitive Science*, 2nd ed. Cambridge: MIT Press.

Stipp, D. (1995). 2001 is just around the corner, where's HAL? *Fortune*, 132(10), 215–28.

Stoeckler, M. (1991). History of emergence and reductionism. In E. Agazzi, ed. *The Problem of Reductionism in Science*. New York: Kluwer Academic, pp. 71–90.

Stoerig, P. (1996). Varieties of vision: From blind responses to conscious recognition. *Trends in Neuroscience*, 19, 401–6.

Strawson, G. (1997). The self. *Journal of Consciousness Studies*, 4, 405–28.

Strawson, P. E. (1979). Perception and its objects. In J. Dancy, ed. *Perceptual Knowledge*. New York: Oxford University Press, pp. 92–112.

Streri, A., Spelke, E., and Rameix, E. (1993). Modality-specific and amodal aspects of object perception in infancy: The case of active touch. *Cognition*, 47, 251–79.

Tanenhaus, M. K., Spivey-Knowlton, M. J., Eberhard, K. M., and Sedivy, J. C. (1995). Integration of visual and linguistic information in spoken language comprehension. *Science*, 268, 1632–4.

Taubes, G. (2000). Biologists and engineers create a new generation of robots that imitate life. *Science*, 288, 80–3.

Taylor, C. (1985). *Human Agency and Language*. New York: Cambridge University Press.

Taylor, J. (1999). *The Race for Consciousness*. Cambridge: MIT Press.

Thelen, E. and Smith, L. (1994). *A Dynamic Systems Approach to the Development of Cognition and Action*. Cambridge: MIT Press.

Thompson, R. K. R. (1995). Natural and relational concepts in animals. In H. L. Roiblat and J. A. Meyer, eds. *Comparative Approaches to Cognitive Science*. Cambridge: MIT Press, pp. 175–224.

Tong, F., Nakayama, K., Vaughan, J. T., and Kanwisher, N. (1998). Binocular rivalry and visual awareness in human extrastriate cortex. *Neuron*, 21, 753–9.

Tootell, R. B. H. and Hadjikhani, N. (2000). Attention—brains at work. *Nature Neuroscience*, 3, 206–8.

Trefil, J. (1997). Scientific literacy. In Gross et al. (1997), pp. 543–50.

Tulving, E. (1995). Organization of memory: Quo vadis? In Gazzaniga (1995), pp. 839–47.

Tulving, E. and Markowitsch, H. J. (1997). Memory beyond the hippocampus. *Current Opinion in Neurobiology*, 7, 209–16.

Turvey, M. T. and Shaw, R. E. (1995). Toward and ecological physics and a physical psychology. In R. L. Solso and D. W. Massaro, eds. *The Science of Mind*. New York: Oxford University Press, pp. 144–72.

Tversky, B. (1997). Spatial constructions. In Stein et al. (1997a), pp. 165–80.

Tye, M. (1995). *Ten Problems of Consciousness*. Cambridge: MIT Press.

Ullman, S. (1980). Against direct perception. *Behavioral and Brain Science*, 3, 373–415.

Ullman, S. (1996). *High-Level Vision*. Cambridge: MIT Press.

Underwood, G. (1994). Subliminal perception on TV. *Nature* 370, 103.

Ungerleider, L. G. (1995). Functional brain imaging studies of cortical mechanisms for memory. *Science*, 270, 769–75.

Van Essen, D. C. and DeYoe, D. A. (1995). Concurrent processing in the primate visual cortex. In Gazzaniga (1995), pp. 383–400.

Van der Linden, M. and Coyette, F. (1995). Acquisition of word-processing in an amnesic patient: Implication for theory and rehabilitation. In Campbell and Conway (1995), pp. 54–76.

Vargha-Khadem, F., Gadian, D. G., and Watkins, K. E. (1997). Differential effects of early hippocampal pathology on episodic and semantic memory. *Science*, 277, 376–80.

Varela, F. J. and Shear, J. (1999). First-person methodology: What, why, how? *Journal of Consciousness Studies*, 6, 1–14.

Varela, F. J., Thompson, E., and Rosch, E. (1991). *The Embodied Mind*. Cambridge: MIT Press.

Velmans, M., ed. (1996). *The Science of Consciousness*. London: Routledge.

von Molchner, L., Pallas, S. L., and Sur, M. (2000). Visual behaviors mediated by retinal projections directed to the auditory pathway. *Nature*, 404, 871–6.

Verdú, S. (1998). Fifty years of Shannon Theory. *IEEE Transactions on Information Theory*, 44, 2057–78.

Wallenstein, G. V., Eichenbaum, H., and Hasselmo, M. E. (1998). The hippocampus as an associator of discontiguous events. *Trends in Neuroscience*, 21, 317–23.

Webb, B. (1996). A cricket Robert. *Scientific American*, 275(6), 94–9.

Webster, M. J. and Ungerleider, L. G. (1998). Neuroanatomy of visual attention. In Parasuraman (1998), pp. 2–16.

Weinberg, S. (1999). T. S. Kuhn's "non-revolution": an exchange. *New York Review of Books*, February 18, p. 50.

Weiskrantz, L. (1997). *Consciousness Lost and Found*. New York: Oxford University Press.

Weitz, M. (1988). *Theories of Concepts*. London: Routledge.

Weizenbaum, J. (1976). *Computer Power and Human Reason*. New York: Freeman.

Wellman, H. M. (1990). *The Child's Theory of Mind*. Cambridge: MIT Press.

Werker, J. (1989). Becoming a native listener. *American Scientist*, 77, 54–9.

Wilson, B. A. and Wearing, D. (1995). Prisoner of consciousness: A state of just awakening following herpes simplex encephalitis. In Campbell and Conway (1995), pp. 14–30.

Winograd, T. (1990). Thinking machines: Can there be? are we? In E. Partridge and Y. Wilks, eds. *The Foundations of Artificial Intelligence*. New York: Cambridge University Press, pp. 167–89.

Winograd, T. and Flores, F. (1986). *Understanding Computers and Cognition*. New York: Ablex Press.

Wittgenstein, L. (1921). *Tractatus Logico-Philosophicus*. London: Routledge & Kegan Paul.

Wolfe, J. M. (1997). In a blink of the mind's eye. *Nature*, 387, 756–7.

Wong, R. F. and Simons, D. J. (1999). Active and passive scene recognition across views. *Cognition*, 70, 191–210.

Woodward, A. L. and Markman, E. M. (1998). Social and pragmatic cues to word meaning. In Damon (1998), Vol II, pp. 371–420.

Wright, M. R. (1990). Presocratic minds. In C. Gill, ed. *The Person and the Human Mind*. New York: Oxford University Press, pp. 207–26.

Wuethrich, B. (2000). Learning the world's languages—Before they vanish. *Science*, 288, 1156–9.

Yaeger, L. S., Webb. B. J., and Lyon, R. F. (1998). Combining neural networks and context-driven search for online, printed handwriting recognition in the NEWTON. *AI Magazine*, 19(1), 73–89.

Yamada, J. E. (1990). *Laura: A Case for the Modularity of Language*. Cambridge: MIT Press.

Young, A. W. (1994). Neuropsychology of awareness. In Revensuo and Kamppinen (1994), pp. 173–203.

Index

Objectivism, 59, 409–410, 412–415, 482
Objectivity, 22, 367, 394. *See also* Mind
    open to the world
    of knowledge, 18, 348, 395
    not objectivism, 60, 409–410, 413–415
    primary meaning of, 391
Object-specific advantage, 278
Open mind, 8, 17–20, 22, 231. *See also*
    Mind open to the world
    emotion of, 325–327
    memory of, 302, 306–308, 311, 316
    language of, 470, 473
    perception of, 271–272, 274–278
    possibility in, 384
Open mind emerging from
    infrastructures, 4, 7, 8, 20–22, 95–96,
    343, 463. *See also* Emergence *and*
    Levels
Openness, 4, 17–18, 95, 100–101, 188,
    210, *see also* mind open to the world
Optic flow, 62–63, 266, 268, 272, 300
Other people, 428–431, 433
    empathy about, 428–430, 435
    theory about, 429–431, 435
Other mind
    problem of, 433
    simulation- and theory-theories of, 429
Orr, Allen, 78
Orwell, George, 351
Own-level explanation, 143, 145–146,
    200

Pain, 329–331
    affective aspect, 330–331
    as C fiber firing, 139–140, 144, 331
    neural substrates for, 330–331
Parmenides, 27
Particularity, 274, 275, 276
Part-whole relation, 150, 192
Peacock, Christopher, 236
Penfield, Wilder, 134, 286, 359
Perception, 10, 23, 101, 178, 223, 262,
    306, 343–344, 445–447
    and action, 423–425
    awareness in, 262–263
    characteristic time of, 114–115
    concept of objects in, 262, 263, 271,
    278, 281, 344, 423

and emotion, 334
    immediate, 392, 394, 445
    meaningful, 445–447
    sensual, 27, 30–31, 243
    of stable world, 268–279, 446
    subliminal, 111–112, 114, 127
    unconscious, 104, 105
    versus selective sensitivity, 115, 453
    of whole objects, 246, 259–260, 262,
    272, 275–276
Perception, theory of, 243
    active, 124, 244, 252, 344, 423,
    446–447
    causal, 35
    for closed mind, 263–264, 271–272, 445
    ecological, 265–268, 271–272
    evidence of active perception, 255–262,
    269–270, 275–278, 424
    mediated, 265
    for open mind, 271–272, 274–278
    purely receptive, 103–104, 124, 244,
    252, 424, 445
Performance
    and competence, 142, 217
    without awareness, 130–133
Person, 97, 343
Personal identity, 11, 298, 301, 349, 358,
    367, 435
Perspective, 18–20, 22, 392–396, 402. *See
    also* Mind open to the world
    field and observer, 315
    first-person, 23, 28, 61, 134, 315, 345,
    347, 361, 367, 397, 438
    multiplicity of, 314–315, 345, 367,
    372–373, 395–396, 402, 406
    not perspectivism, 395
    as part of mental frame, 348
    subjective, 19, 345, 348
    third-person, 23, 28, 315, 345, 361, 397
    transformations among, 19, 348
    variable of, 19, 348, 392–396, 402
Phenomenological reduction, 86
Phenomenology, 81, 84, 85, 360, 397
Philosophy of language, 213, 347, 365,
    461, 473
Philosophy of mind, 6, 42, 43, 64, 69,
    72, 74, 118, 141, 150, 177, 345, 352,
    361, 365, 395